THE PROBLEM OF GOD
IN MODERN THOUGHT

The Problem of God
in Modern Thought

PHILIP CLAYTON

WILLIAM B. EERDMANS PUBLISHING COMPANY
GRAND RAPIDS, MICHIGAN / CAMBRIDGE, U.K.

Wm. B. Eerdmans Publishing Co.
255 Jefferson Ave. S.E., Grand Rapids, Michigan 49503 /
P.O. Box 163, Cambridge CB3 9PU U.K.

Printed in the United States of America

05 04 03 02 01 00   7 6 5 4 3 2 1

Library of Congress Cataloging-in-Publication Data

Clayton, Philip, 1956-
The problem of God in modern thought / Philip Clayton.
p.   cm.
Includes bibliographical references and index.
ISBN 0-8028-3885-5 (hardcover: alk. paper)
1. God.   2. Philosophy, Modern.   I. Title.

BT102.C545 2000
212 — dc21
00-023129

www.eerdmans.com

In Memoriam

Robert Bovee Clayton

July 1, 1927–April 27, 1991

Dolores Virginia Richardson Clayton

February 18, 1931–April 9, 1993

Contents

PART III:
TOWARD A THEOLOGY OF THE INFINITE

Preface

The following pages reflect a commitment to two theses: that language about God represents a problem with a history that can be reconstructed and evaluated; and that careful analysis, combined with thorough historical scholarship, can provide reasons for preferring some metaphysical and theological views over others.

"Preferring some views over others" need not entail dogmatism, rationalism, or intolerance. This is especially true if one replaces "proofs of the existence of God" with the framework of inference to the best explanation.[1] Accepting competing explanatory accounts means a *pluralistic metaphysics:* multiple models of God instead of a single univocal theory. What remains, then, of the modern tradition? Certainly not deductive proofs and indubitable knowledge, but rather the more enduring features of the metaphysical quest: commitment to evaluation over relativistic arbitrariness; the search for systematicity and for comprehensive, coherent theories; and the realization that the early modern theories are in many respects as sophisticated and as worthy of attention as much of what is offered for consumption today.

The last few decades have seen a remarkable renaissance in philosophical theology. Many factors have contributed to this renaissance — more, certainly, than can be chronicled here: the disappearance of the last vestiges of positivism, which had dismissed God-language as meaningless; a robust discussion of theological themes within Anglo-American analytic philosophy; the new "multicultural" emphasis within American universities and within the Ameri-

---

1. For a persuasive argument in defense of this shift, see Robert Prevost, *Probability and Theistic Explanation* (Oxford: Clarendon, 1990).

can Academy of Religion, which has allowed theism (both "in general" and in its various particularities) to understand itself as a bona fide field of reflection freed from the overtones of hegemony or intolerance; and a new emphasis on theological models that breaks free from the need for metaphysical foundations in favor of a "postfoundational" framework.[2] Whatever the reasons, the last years have brought a resurgence of systematic theological reflection, both among professional theologians and within neighboring disciplines such as philosophy. At the same time, we are witnessing a new interest in "spiritual questions" on the part of many who would in no way consider themselves to be theologians and may not in fact label themselves theists.

In the excitement of this period of rebuilding and searching for new models, it becomes increasingly important that one not neglect the context for modern thought about God. One may criticize modern assumptions about the divine, but one ignores them at one's peril. Any theology that is to be credible in the modern (or postmodern) intellectual world must understand how and why the notion of God became a problem. Its roots have something to do with Descartes clearing out the theological storeroom of medieval lumber in order to begin again, with Leibniz's failure to construct a modern metaphysics of perfection, with Kant's reduction of God to a regulative concept, and with the increasing power of the Spinoza tradition as it met the challenge of German idealism and became incorporated into it. These developments provide the backdrop against which theology's prospects today can be assessed.

When I first encountered Ian Barbour's *Myths, Models and Paradigms*[3] in the 1970s and Sallie McFague's *Models of God*[4] in the 1980s, I thought that the history of modern philosophical theology could be rewritten as a series of models for present consumption. What I failed to realize was that this history tells a very distinct story of its own, which is in some sense our own story. It is not as malleable to the agendas of contemporary theologians (or to the agendas of their critics!) as many have claimed. At its heart, it is a story of how the two major strands of premodern thought about the divine — the divine as infinite, and the divine as perfect — became entwined, defined the agenda for modern thought in a form known as "ontotheology," and then separated again, perhaps permanently. In our age, the age of Newton and Einstein, the metaphysics of infinity and the metaphysics of levels of perfection are not equally viable, and it

2. See especially J. Wentzel van Huyssteen, *Essays in Postfoundationalist Theology* (Grand Rapids: Eerdmans, 1997).

3. Ian Barbour, *Myths, Models and Paradigms: A Comparative Study in Science and Religion* (New York: Harper and Row, 1974).

4. Sallie McFague, *Models of God: Theology for an Ecological, Nuclear Age* (Philadelphia: Fortress Press, 1987).

may be that one of these strands is no longer viable at all. There is no use writing systematic theologies that presuppose a conceptual world deeply at odds with what we have now learned about the natural world, the human person, and the plurality of religious options.

The following chapters are concerned not only with theoretical results, but also with the *standards* for an adequate treatment of "the problem of God." That I have here omitted other important discussions — interacting with modern and contemporary developments in science for one; responding to research in comparative religions for another — indicates not disinterest but an expression of the limits of what one book can hold (and what one scholar can master!).[5] The methodological goal was to provide a careful study of the literature on each major thinker, since specialists can best assess individual parts of the overall argument. Still, there is something in the philosopher that resists overspecialization. After all, are there not fascinating general questions that cannot even be posed, much less answered, within the thought-world of a single thinker or discipline? There is thus value in the risky hypothesis (a lesson from Karl Popper), in the ambitious attempt to say how things all fit together in the end. Certainly there are interesting questions that cut across the boundaries of existing specializations, and to rule them out from the start is a great pity. Indisputably, the question of God is one of these questions.

Various groups of experts dialogue in these pages: analytic philosophers of religion; Anglo-American historians of modern philosophy; scholars of the classical idealist tradition in German philosophy; representatives of the great tradition of French scholarship in modern philosophy up to and including Jean-Luc Marion; theologians of the Jewish and Christian traditions, especially where they have been concerned with the nature of the God of their tradition; and, throughout, metaphysicians in the systematic tradition: Platonists, Aristotelians, Plotinians, Thomists, process philosophers, and others. Of course, one could consult only one of these groups of experts, analyzing their intuitions about a perfect being, say, or reconstructing Hegel's reading of Spinoza and Leibniz, or exegeting their religious tradition's pronouncements on the divine Trinity. Typically, I fear, this is how the problem of God is "solved" in the literature. But to limit one's audience merely to one reference group is to fall beneath the standards required by the question of God. This book is published not (just) with the goal of winning support for one particular set of conclusions, but equally with the hope of bringing these various groups of experts back into dialogue with one another.

---

5. I have addressed the former in *God and Contemporary Science* (Edinburgh: Edinburgh University Press; Grand Rapids: Eerdmans, 1997).

Of course, I know that this hope may be utopian. One or another group may miss reference to its key commentators, or find too many pages devoted to "questionable" thinkers, or bemoan the absence of key arguments, concepts, distinctions, or styles of argument. Some have said that nonspecialists are no longer able to understand the true complexity of the concept of God in modern thought, and that "insiders" in this age of specialized arguments and disciplines will never be convinced by an argument that spans so many thinkers. Wouldn't it be a pity, however, to conclude in advance that neither specialists nor generalists can address the problem of God any longer? Clearly the problem is still with us. The nonspecialist will, I hope, not lose the forest for the trees; and to the specialist I plead for a willingness to move up the scale of detail to the point where the question of God can be raised — lest, in refusing to pose the question, one guarantees in advance that no answer *can* be found. Without a doubt, more detail in analytic philosophy would allow for a more rigorous formulation of arguments and counterarguments; more detail in the history of philosophy would reveal more extensive interconnections and insights into context; more metaphysical detail would yield deeper systematic cohesion; and more detail in theology would allow the theological traditions to inform and be informed by the arguments presented here. The result, however, would be five books instead of one . . . and the loss of the clear formulation of the question that a single volume alone can provide.

The focus of this inquiry rests primarily on the period between Descartes and Schelling, though the pre-Cartesian context receives a lengthy treatment (chapter 3) and the contemporary setting is continually in the wings (and sometimes occupies center stage) of the discussion. I hope later to be able to extend the narrative even further, including the continuing relevance of Hegel and the nineteenth-century debates through Nietzsche. Nonetheless, I have paused for a breath after Schelling because he represents the culmination of a line of thought that is particularly important for theology today. Also, a word should be said about the nonhistorical order of the treatment: starting with Descartes, then exploring the premodern roots of philosophical theology before moving through Leibniz to Kant and Schleiermacher, and then stepping back in time to trace the emergence of a metaphysics of infinity from Spinoza through the eighteenth century to the German idealists. No apologies: I have placed the goal of presenting (what I take to be) the most powerful reconstruction of modern thought about God *above* the task of retracing the historical path in chronological order. Readers will have to judge the book's success based on how compelling are the arguments for the failure of the one tradition and the philosophical and theological resources of the other.

Research for this project was begun during a Senior Fulbright Research

Fellowship at the Ludwig-Maximilians-Universität München, and completed with the support of the Alexander von Humboldt Foundation, which financed a second year of research at that same university. Without the generosity of these two great supporters of international academic exchange it would not have been possible to do the detailed historical and textual work required by this project, and I am indebted to them. The results of this research were first published in German;[6] although the arguments of the two works differ at numerous points (the one work is not merely a translation of the other), the conclusions are the same.

When a research project lasts close to a decade, one incurs more debts than can easily be listed. Several in particular are so pervasive that footnotes fail to do them justice. Wolfhart Pannenberg first proposed the topic and later supervised the research. Our two decades of conversations have left more marks than I can chronicle; I hope only that what follows begins to meet the high academic standards reflected in his life and work. Likewise, to the great phenomenologist of religion and historian of ideas Louis Dupré, my mentor at Yale, I owe my first exposure to the profound philosophers of the infinite, Meister Eckhart, Nicholas of Cusa, and Giordano Bruno. The excitement and authority with which Louis Dupré presented the Neoplatonic tradition as a living theological resource have made an indelible impression on this book's thesis, as has his own constructive approach to the problem of God.[7] Lorenz Bruno Puntel at the University of Munich has influenced my philosophical development since 1981, playing the multiple roles of teacher, discussion partner, analytic *and* Continental critic, and friend. Bernd Burkhardt not only read the entire manuscript with a fine-tooth comb and corrected many errors, but also held the *Hauptthesen* of German Idealism continually before my eyes. Finally, I am grateful to my research assistant Tim Zalunardo for the preparation of the Index.

I dedicate this study to the memory of my parents, both of whom died during the period of its composition. What I owe them can be summarized neither in a single sentence nor in an entire book, but only in the work of a lifetime.

---

6. Philip Clayton, *Das Gottesproblem*, vol. 1: *Gott und Unendlichkeit in der neuzeitlichen Philosophie* (Paderborn: Ferdinand Schöningh Verlag, 1996).

7. On the latter, see Dupré's groundbreaking work, *The Other Dimension: A Search for the Meaning of Religious Attitudes* (New York: Seabury Crossroad, 1972, 1979); on the former, see among many works his *Passage to Modernity: An Essay in the Hermeneutics of Nature and Culture* (New Haven: Yale Univ. Press, 1993).

PART I

THE CONTEXT FOR MODERN THOUGHT ABOUT GOD

CHAPTER ONE

Toward a Pluralistic Theology

INTRODUCTION:
SKEPTICISM AND METAPHYSICS

Not to put too fine a point on it: the context for treating the question of God today must be skepticism. Propositional language about God can no longer pass as unproblematic. The history of reflection in this area is littered with skeletons — or better: it is immensely difficult to discern which are the skeletons and which the living, progressing models. Past thinkers may appear overly bound by the philosophical fashions of their day and by the world as they constructed it; yet we have no reason to believe ourselves more free of such forces than they. Even theologians today have grown squeamish of the "God's-eye point of view," and many reasons have been advanced for worrying that the very idea of such a point of view is confused.[1]

The concept of God refers to a reality that is in some essential sense transcendent of, and thus not locatable within, experience. In our day, I shall argue, this concept presents itself more as a problem than as a solution.[2] God is not at

1. Hilary Putnam, *Reason, Truth, and History* (Cambridge: Harvard Univ. Press, 1981), 49ff.

2. Gordon Kaufman, *The Problem of God* (Cambridge: Harvard Univ. Press, 1972), e.g., 7. The literature on the changed context for the use of God-language, and on the contemporary problem of God, is immense. See, e.g., Langdon Gilkey, *Naming the Whirlwind: The Renewal of God-Language* (Indianapolis: Bobbs-Merrill, 1969); David Tracy, *Blessed Rage for Order* (New York: Seabury, 1975); John Macquarrie, *Thinking about God* (London: SCM, 1975); Hans Schwarz, *The Search for God* (Philadelphia: Augsburg, 1975); Anthony Flew, *God: A Critical Inquiry*, 2nd ed. (La Salle, Ill.: Open Court, 1984; first published in 1966 as

3

home in any of today's disciplines outside theology — and even there the professionals voice misgivings. Whatever its accessibility in the context of religious faith (and there are also reasons to wonder about this accessibility, especially among an academic public), the concept of God has inherited a variety of unresolved intellectual difficulties. Arguably, the status of God-language has never fully recovered since the collapse of the Scholastic doctrine of analogy. It is a concept that is construed in mutually exclusive fashions. As long as we do not know whether God-talk has a solid basis in human experience — and, if so, *where* in human experience — the relationship between theism and the various sciences, both in content and in method, remains problematic.

Since the theme of this book is the concept of God, the problems associated with this concept will thus serve as its backdrop. At the outset, atheism must be taken as a full and live possibility.[3] Perhaps naturalism is right; we may be the doomed inhabitants of a dying universe. As Nietzsche wrote,

> Once upon a time, in a distant corner of this universe with its countless flickering solar systems, there was a planet, and on this planet some intelligent animals discovered knowledge. It was the most noble and most mendacious minute in the history of the universe — but only a minute. After Nature had breathed a few times their star burned out, and the intelligent animals had to die.[4]

Such a naturalistic scenario, whether its tone is negative (as in the Nietzsche quotation) or more optimistic, must be treated as a live option by any contemporary theory of God. It is thus methodologically unacceptable to immediately assume the impossibility of atheism. For instance, Rahner assures us, humans "cannot — logically and existentially cannot — believe that the hopefulness, the scent of something more, that they experience is only a bold but insane delusion, or that, finally, everything has its basis in an empty nothingness."[5] But of course we *can* believe this. It is fully possible that there is no gen-

---

God and Philosophy); and most recently Karen Armstrong, *The History of God* (New York: Knopf/Random House, 1993).

3. For a vibrant example of contemporary intellectual atheism see the work of Kai Nielsen, e.g., his collection of essays *God, Scepticism and Modernity* (Ottawa and London: Univ. of Ottawa Press, 1989).

4. Friedrich Nietzsche, "Ueber Wahrheit und Lüge im aussermoralischen Sinne," in *Nietzsche Werke,* ed. Giorgio Colli and Mazzino Montinari (Berlin: de Gruyter, 1973), part 3, 2:369.

5. Karl Rahner, *Grundkurs des Glaubens. Einführung in den Begriff des Christentums* (Freiburg: Herder, 1976), 44.

eral meaning to be had, only the meanings that we create. Indeed, don't religious skeptics from Hume to Kai Nielsen offer ample evidence that it is possible to orient oneself toward the atheist conclusion? It is therefore overquick to assume that "in our explicitly religious turning toward God in prayer, and in metaphysical reflection, we merely bring to our conscious attention what we had always implicitly known about ourselves at the very base of our personal existence."[6]

A crucial way in which the philosophical tradition has expressed this general skepticism concerns the question whether language about God can be "constitutive," that is, can refer to an object and express actual positive content about it. The distinction between constitutive and nonconstitutive goes back to Kant, for whom concepts without empirical content — and thus especially the concept of God — could only be "empty" as knowledge claims (A 51; B 75).[7] But one need not be a Kantian to approach theistic language with a certain degree of doubt; the lines of argument leading toward skepticism about the rationality of God-talk are legion. As examples I trace only two here: the difficulties with "metaphysical explanations" in general, and the problems stemming from the historicity of knowledge.

Evidence and Rational Explanations

If language about God is to be constitutive, it must evidence some explanatory value vis-à-vis human experience. But, to put the issue in general terms, it is not clear how explanations that refer to God could be rational explanations. Many specific versions of this criticism have been formulated: theistic explanations are literally meaningless (A. J. Ayer); they are untestable and thus vacuous (Anthony Flew); they are unfalsifiable and therefore must be sharply bordered off from scientific language (Karl Popper); the series of causes in a theistic explanation cannot be reconstructed and hence natural explanations should be preferred over supernatural explanations (the presumption in favor of naturalism).

The difficulties with such efforts at sharply demarcating science from metaphysics have been widely discussed and need not be rehearsed here.[8] It seems, at least, that it is no longer possible to rule out reflection on first princi-

---

6. Ibid., 63.

7. References to Kant's *Critique of Pure Reason* are given in the text in this form, "A" referring to the first and "B" to the second edition.

8. Among many other examples see Philip Clayton, "Religious Truth and Scientific Truth," in *Phenomenology of the Truth Proper to Religion: An Anthology,* ed. Daniel Guerrière (Albany: SUNY Press, 1990), 43-59.

ples using dichotomies such as scientific vs. mythical, falsifiable vs. falsification-immune, or meaningful vs. meaningless. Science is just not as neat as we once thought.[9] Still, one does need to focus on the differences that still remain, especially where they help reveal the epistemological challenges — the challenges about its status as knowledge — that theology faces. One way to grasp these remaining difficulties is in terms of a distinction that Bernard Williams draws: scientists are required to provide a theory of error — a newer theory must be able to say why and where its predecessor went wrong — whereas philosophers working in ethics or metaphysics cannot and need not do so.[10] So the question becomes, Can metaphysics provide a theory of error? Does it possess procedures for testing its claims — or at least for separating out those areas that are rationally undecidable? Can one specify procedures for the critical treatment of theological truth claims?

The following chapters claim to make some progress in addressing these questions. Nonetheless, it does seem unlikely that the explanatory claims of theology could ever achieve the same rational status as the knowledge claims advanced within more concrete and precise disciplines.[11] And it will be hard to claim truth for selected theological theories if the community of scholars is unable to say of *any* theory in the field that it is false. Ironically, the oft-heralded eternality of metaphysical debates is at the same time their chief weakness. For example, it is often viewed as a strength if a contemporary thinker can trace her or his position back to Parmenides or Heraclitus, Plotinus or Thomas Aquinas. Unfortunately, though, such practices give the impression that in this field absolutely nothing has been resolved since the beginning of its history. If we are to rescue the possibility of progress on the question of God, we have to provide a clear notion of what constitutes progress and which criteria signal its presence.

I open this book with a chapter on method, written against the backdrop of pluralism and skepticism, out of deference to the difficulty of these worries. For those of us who do not want to abandon all explanations containing the term *God*, the task is clear: we must specify a way of treating theological questions that justifies their claim to be rational explanations — for instance, by showing how such explanations are necessary for specific dimensions of human experience. This means showing how metaphysical claims are to be evalu-

9. See, e.g., Larry Laudan, *Progress and Its Problems* (Berkeley: Univ. of California Press, 1977).

10. Bernard Williams, *Ethics and the Limits of Philosophy* (Cambridge: Harvard Univ. Press, 1985), chap. 8. Williams's immediate reference is to ethics; still, the epistemic worries he raises about moral theories apply directly to traditional metaphysics as well.

11. As argued in Philip Clayton, *Explanation from Physics to Theology: An Essay in Rationality and Religion* (New Haven: Yale Univ. Press, 1989).

ated critically. Should we fail at this effort, then we have to acknowledge that decision procedures are absent in metaphysics. This would presumably leave an irreducible pluralism of gods — or no god(s) at all.

Historicity

A second major challenge to the present project involves historical skepticism — limitations allegedly placed on one's knowledge (or on one's knowing that one knows) because of one's particular position within the history of thought.

The Hermeneutical Shift

The pervasiveness of interpretive issues in the study of history may not ultimately be a block to knowledge, for history could of course lead to a final unity of perspectives. Nonetheless, the plurality of perspectives or "conceptual schemes" does present problems for interpreting past metaphysical positions; it also raises questions about the possible time-boundness of our own reflection about the nature of God. Advocates of the hermeneutical shift have argued convincingly that there are disparities between our "horizon" and the horizons of those whose texts we study; criticism and appropriation always require that one achieve a fusion of disparate horizons.[12]

Now admittedly, exorbitant claims are sometimes made about how hermeneutics, the "science of interpretation," will change everything. One reads occasionally, for example, that one can no longer draw a distinction between theory and observation, between fact and value, between knowledge and interpretation, between interpreting and appropriating a text — even between reading and writing a text! I have argued elsewhere that hermeneutics does not force one into complete skepticism of this sort.[13] Nonetheless, the discussion of hermeneutics does suggest certain limits on any reconstruction of the theories of past thinkers. On the one hand, one must be constantly on the watch for the "otherness" of the historical texts and authors one interprets. Although it may sometimes be possible to criticize or appropriate an author's position and arguments directly, at other times a radically different set of assumptions may sepa-

12. Important works include Hans-Georg Gadamer, *Truth and Method,* ed. and trans. Garrett Barden and John Cumming (New York: Crossroad, 1975); and Paul Ricoeur, *The Conflict of Interpretations: Essays in Hermeneutics,* trans. Kathleen McGlaughlin et al., ed. Don Ihde (Evanston: Northwestern Univ. Press, 1974).
13. See Clayton, *Explanation,* chap. 3.

rate that world from ours. Only by carefully reconstructing the author's own intellectual and social context can we understand the meaning of her or his concepts, that is, what *the author* meant by them. As a by-product, such reconstructions often bring home the huge distance between the present and, say, the thought world of the sixteenth and seventeenth centuries, a distance that one does not automatically perceive merely by reading the texts of that time.

On the other hand, contemporary theologians need to be equally aware of the links between their metaphysical assertions and their own historical or cultural context. We are initially much less likely, for example, to give credence to theories of timeless being, or to definitive theories of the Absolute — in fact, to definitive theories of anything! Footprints of our zeitgeist rest on titles such as *Reason, Truth, and History* or *On the Plurality of Worlds* or *The History of God* or *God: A Biography*.[14] Are these prejudices justified? To the extent that we recognize the objects of our study to be time-bound, we must suspect our own conclusions to be so as well.

Philosophy in History

An important collection of essays on the historiography of philosophy, entitled *Philosophy in History*, edited by Richard Rorty and others, illustrates the insights and pitfalls of the hermeneutical shift. The common thesis of the book's sixteen authors is that we must expect to read historical lines on the faces and in the books of even the "greats" in philosophy. The demise of the time-transcendent view of philosophy affects the way one should approach these "greats," the way to treat their texts, and the claims one makes on behalf of one's own. Call it *perspectivalism*: our values and goals inhabit present-day beliefs and interpretations just as much as did the values of a Descartes or Leibniz. The movement from the rational — which now means: rational by our best lights, at this particular time — to the timelessly true becomes progressively more difficult to justify. For a pointed formulation one looks, as usual, to Richard Rorty:

> It is natural for [the philosopher] to write *Geistesgeschichte* by stringing a lot of [his] notes together, thus skipping between the same old peaks, passing over in silence the philosophical flatlands of, e.g., the third and fifteenth centuries. This sort of thing leads to such extreme cases as Heidegger's attempt

14. Putnam, *Reason, Truth, and History;* David Lewis, *On the Plurality of Worlds* (New York: Blackwell, 1986); Karen Armstrong, *A History of God: From Abraham to the Present* (London: Heinemann, 1993); Jack Miles, *God: A Biography* (New York: Alfred A. Knopf, 1995).

to write "the history of Being" by commenting upon texts mentioned in Ph.D. examinations in philosophy in German universities early in this century. In the aftermath of being enthralled by the drama Heidegger stages, one may begin to find it suspicious that Being stuck so closely to the syllabus.[15]

In short: "What we need is to see the history of philosophy as the story of the people who made splendid but largely unsuccessful attempts to ask the questions which we ought to be asking" (ibid., pp. 73-74).

Rorty notwithstanding, how far does the historicity of knowledge really drive us? Discontinuities of interest and compellingness need not lead to incommensurability.[16] Is it really impossible to know what Spinoza was saying unless one shares his same interests? Nevertheless, awareness of discontinuities does force a more careful look at context. It must affect our expectations as well, as Schneewind argues:

> Since the reason for exhuming the great philosophers of the past is to help us arrive at better answers to our own questions, we must be prepared as much as necessary to recast their thought in our own idiom, seeking to produce a rational reconstruction of their beliefs rather than a picture of full historical authenticity where these two projects begin to collide. (p. 200)

We can grant this last point, fortunately, without having to follow Rorty all the way: There is more in common in the philosophical conversation through history than Rorty grants (p. 51), which means that rational reconstructions can tell us more about the authors' interests *and our own* than Rorty thinks (p. 54). Still, he has correctly seen the connection of meaning and truth: "Just as determining meaning is a matter of placing an assertion in a context of actual and possible behavior, so determining truth is a matter of placing it in the context of assertions which we ourselves should be willing to make"; more briefly: "Truth and meaning are not to be ascertained independently of one another" (p. 55). It need not follow that philosophy is to be disbanded in favor of "*Geistesgeschichte* as canon-formation." Still, such cautions do help to control widely speculative rational reconstructions of past philosophers through a clearer sense of their otherness, and to supplement plodding historical recon-

---

15. Richard Rorty, J. B. Schneewind, and Quentin Skinner, eds., *Philosophy in History: Essays on the Historiography of Philosophy* (Cambridge: Cambridge Univ. Press, 1984), 71. The next several references in the text are also to this work. See also Jorge J. E. Gracia, *Philosophy and Its History: Issues in Philosophical Historiography* (Albany: SUNY Press, 1992).

16. As several of the contributors to *Philosophy in History* also insist; see, e.g., 193n2.

structions with more probing questions into past authors' assumptions and perspectives.

Perhaps Rorty's *Philosophy in History* boils down to the lukewarm exhortation, "Do not ignore the context, but do not be ruled by it either." Still, the book serves as a good up-front reminder of how various historical contexts affect the thinkers discussed below — and on the way one must evaluate them. Our reflection on theism may well be influenced by personal, social, cultural, and historical factors without, I suggest, having to be reduced to them.

First Implications for Metaphysics

General skeptical worries associated with the hermeneutical shift, and specific difficulties involved in knowing the sort of being that God would be, have transformed the manner in which one must approach theism today. We have already seen how the changes affect the study of the history of modern thought, how they demand a movement toward hermeneutically sensitive methods of study. Typically, they result in the call to recognize the ineliminable role of *context* in all intellectual inquiry.

Yet one discipline still claims to rise above the fray: theology's philosophical sibling, metaphysics. Throughout its history, metaphysics has been concerned with timeless truths. Perhaps the challenge of contextualization would be relatively unproblematic for historians, or even political theorists, for whom timeless truths are not the issue. But how can metaphysical reflection do justice to this changed epistemological climate and still remain metaphysics? Can there be a metaphysical reflection on God whose claims remain preliminary and hypothetical, whose method builds in a sensitivity to context? Is "pluralistic metaphysics" a viable shift within this discipline or a *contradictio in adjecto*?

I will argue that metaphysical reflection must ultimately remain by its nature dissatisfied with multiple outcomes; the driving force in this discipline is always to unify, to select the best theory from among competing alternatives. Still, there are cases where a clear rational decision cannot yet be made between the competitors. In such cases, claims for the finality and certainty of one's own position can only appear as absurd and unwarranted.[17]

17. Consider, e.g., the dismissive opening words of Thomas Morris's collection of essays, "it is hard to see how anyone whose personal faith is rooted in the Judeo-Christian religious tradition, and who is aware of the metaphilosophical facts of the matter, could be tempted in the slightest to buy into any such impoverished philosophical perspective [such as Hume, Kant, or positivism], vetoing as it would effective human reflection on ultimate

Our own epistemic position is characterized by the lack of ultimacy — no less when it is the Ultimate that is under discussion! This fact calls for a certain continuing attitude of humility toward one's own constructive theological proposals. But it also suggests handling the great texts of the past in a different manner. No longer can they appear as necessary, canonical moments in a perfectly unfolding story. This gives us a new task: not just to interpret authors' intentions but also rationally to reconstruct their work in light of the narrative as we now see it. As a positive example of interpretation qua rational reconstruction, take Jonathan Bennett's widely discussed book on Spinoza.[18] Compared to earlier treatments such as Wolfson's, Bennett's method is unabashedly reconstructive: coming to the text from contemporary developments in physics, psychology, and philosophy, he freely rejects or reinterprets large segments of Spinoza's *Ethics*. The line of argument at which he finally arrives is inspired, in some sense, by Spinoza, but it is certainly not Spinoza's own. Merely to restate Spinoza's position as he himself understood it, Bennett recognizes, is both uninteresting and unhelpful.

At the same time, Bennett does not fall into the postmodern treatment of historical authors that Rorty advocates. His analysis is clear, careful, and solidly philosophical — little sign here of a move from philosophy toward "*Geistesgeschichte* as canon-formation." Bennett assumes that there is clear progress in the history of thought, that the conceptual tools available today are markedly sharper than those of the past and better able to overcome the limitations affecting Spinoza's own presentation. However important the acknowledgment of contextual considerations, I suggest, there is no reason to give up the rigor of careful reconstructions such as Bennett's, or to forego the use of recently developed analytic tools such as set theory or modal logic. Hermeneutically aware treatments need not be as vague and rambling as Rorty's (post-Kehre) publications; they do not condemn us all to writing in the manner of French deconstructionists. It is possible to return to early modern metaphysics with the clarity of, for example, recent analytic work in philosophical theology.[19] Such, anyway, is my goal in what follows.

But given the skeptical worries already canvassed, how can one find a way still to claim that the goal of theistic metaphysics is true statements about the divine nature? Is there any reason to think that this activity achieves its goal, even in part?

---

matters" (Thomas V. Morris., ed., *Divine and Human Action: Essays in the Metaphysics of Theism* [Ithaca: Cornell Univ. Press, 1988], 4). Clearly, analytic philosophers are not immune from absolutist claims.

18. Jonathan Bennett, *A Study of Spinoza's Ethics* (Indianapolis: Hackett, 1984).

Nonconstitutive Approaches to Metaphysics

Since Kant a number of thinkers have responded to skeptical considerations such as the ones adduced above by denying that statements about God serve an explanatory or epistemic role at all; language, they say, is being used in other than a constitutive sense in this realm. Some of these critics interpret God-language in a noncognitive sense, so that it has cognitive force only when eliminated or translated (one can call these *eliminative views*), whereas others would continue to theorize in something like the traditional mode while interpreting its status differently *(revisionist views)*.

Eliminative Views of Metaphysics

Most eliminative views are explicitly reductionistic. This is certainly true of the reduction of talk of God to socioeconomic forces, to psychosexual developmental phases, or to the resentment of a powerless priestly caste. But the tendency toward metaphysical reductionism has a much broader intellectual clientele than the vigorous skepticism of a Marx, Freud, or Nietzsche. In our day it is perhaps most clearly the attitude (presupposition? working hypothesis?) of much natural and social science. Scientific reductionists are modern-day Comteans: the only way to clear the terrain for science, they seem to assume, is to attack metaphysics as a nonempirical form of reflection that stands outside, indeed opposed to, the scientific sphere of empirical research and theorizing. The assumptions underlying this thesis are more often unreflectively empiricist and naturalist than they are militantly positivistic or scientistic.

A large number of philosophical treatments of the God problem today are implicitly reductionistic — whatever the stated goal or premises of the work. One thinks, for example, of various noncognitivist construals of theistic metaphysics that presuppose emotivism, the view that theistic language merely expresses the emotional attitude and priorities of the asserter.[20] Those who hold this position need not argue that theistic language should therefore be abandoned or replaced by psychological descriptions. But clearly, when the cognitive and argumentative core that has characterized traditional metaphys-

---

19. See, e.g., the essays in Morris, ed., *Divine and Human Action;* Morris, ed., *The Concept of God* (New York: Oxford Univ. Press, 1987); or the authors cited in Edward R. Wierenga, *The Nature of God: An Inquiry into Divine Attributes* (Ithaca: Cornell Univ. Press, 1986).

20. Richard Braithwaite, *An Empiricist's View of the Nature of Religious Belief* (Cambridge: Cambridge Univ. Press, 1955). Similar remarks could be made about existentialist and functionalist approaches.

ics has been eliminated — such anyway is the impression they create — little reason is left not to reject theistic language as well. (At best it is a matter of taste.)[21]

These comments on metaphysics and rationality suggest a criterion for what counts as "the elimination of metaphysics." If a given interpretation of discourse about God does not allow for argumentation, for the formulation and criticism of positions in conceptual terms, then the result can only appear to be a set of assertions about, say, divine intentions or attributes. Whether the interpreter actually goes on to urge us to abandon all God-language is irrelevant; its status as rational discourse has already been implicitly rejected. Not to replace theological theories with a new operative discipline such as psychology or anthropology appears then merely as a failure of nerve (or as aesthetic preference).[22]

I have elsewhere urged the untenability of a priori or methodological reductionism, using as grounds the demise of positivism and the implications of the hermeneutical shift.[23] Nonetheless, we cannot close out the possibility of a final reduction-in-fact, namely the failure in practice of theistic metaphysics to maintain itself as a form of critical inquiry. If contemporary talk about God fails to satisfy the standards for a cognitive interpretation, then the consequences should be drawn: better to treat such language as poetry or as a source for rational hypotheses than to keep up the pretense of progressive debate. Our openness to this possible final outcome will have a crucial impact on determining the status of theistic conclusions in what follows.

Revisionist Views of Metaphysics

A number of views eschew reductionism yet find reason to deny metaphysical language about God a fully constitutive status. An uncontroversial example might be the Scholastic doctrine of analogy or various "apophatic" theories of theistic language. Here language about God is not literally or univocally true of its object, yet neither is it equivocal. Advocates have worked hard to spell out a precise mediating position (however unsuccessful they may have been in their attempts). Various contemporary views fall into this "cognitive but not literal"

---

21. One thinks in this regard of Peter Forrest's *God without the Supernatural: A Defense of Scientific Theism* (Ithaca: Cornell Univ. Press, 1996).

22. The same goes, I believe, for Wittgenstein's own view of religious language as expressing the attitude of believers, implicitly in the *Investigations* and more clearly in his *Lectures and Conversations on Aesthetics, Psychology and Religious Belief*, ed. Cyril Barrett (Oxford: Blackwell, 1966).

23. See Clayton, *Explanation from Physics to Theology*, chaps. 2–3.

category, even though few try to state the exact manner in which their language does and does not correspond to its referent.

Theistic Language as Limit Language: Ricoeur, Tracy

Paul Ricoeur is well known for his assertion that language about God is a particularly effective way of expressing aspects of the human experience of the world.[24] In a well-known work, David Tracy has taken Ricoeur's suggestions and developed them into a full-fledged theological position.[25] Other theologians who might be considered in this regard include John Macquarrie and Karl Rahner. The strength of theories like Ricoeur's is that they give meaning to theistic language within the context of human experience, without having to claim that such language is fully literal or constitutive.

Unfortunately, the disadvantages are equally clear: For Ricoeur or Tracy, whatever transcendent intentionality the term *God* has, it must finally express a disposition of the human subject rather than of an active divine agent.[26] Further, the Ricoeurian move does not leave place for critical discourse about such language. If, for instance, I find post-Holocaust literature to be more illuminating of human experience than Jesus' parables, there can be no remaining ground for dialogue between us. Ricoeur and Tracy are apparently willing to accept this consequence. But it removes what has been for theistic metaphysics its distinguishing feature: the competition between alternative conceptions to see which can provide the best arguments in its defense.

Metaphor

A number of recent works stress the role of metaphor in science and the importance of avoiding a literal construal of theological metaphors.[27] In general, these views hold that language about God is a tertium quid, being neither literally true of its object nor known to be false. They focus instead on the "disclosive" power of the language, its ability to create new experience or new insight based on the juxtaposition of concepts not normally associated in our language.

24. E.g., Andre Lacocque and Paul Ricoeur, *Thinking Biblically: Exegetical and Hermeneutical Studies,* trans. David Pellauer (Chicago: Univ. of Chicago Press, 1998).

25. See esp. Tracy, *The Analogical Imagination: Christian Theology and the Culture of Pluralism* (New York: Crossroad, 1981).

26. This is the conclusion of the excellent analysis in Kevin J. Vanhoozer, *The Philosophy of Paul Ricoeur: Philosophical Hermeneutics and Biblical Narrative* (Cambridge: Cambridge Univ. Press, 1990).

27. See esp. Janet Martin Soskice, *Metaphor and Religious Language* (Oxford: Clarendon, 1985). In the next section I discuss the similar work of Sallie McFague in *Metaphorical Theology* and related works.

There is much to be said for the openness to new ways of speaking about God fostered by metaphor-based theories. Still, the danger with the metaphor concept is that it can turn this openness into an insurmountable barrier, ruling out any subsequent theoretical confrontation between competing metaphors. So we read that metaphor is a call to openness, to the novel, to the revelation of God.[28] Indeed, Berggren warns in one article that any attempt to specify what it is that metaphorical language about God is asserting — "a reduction of the metaphor's cognitive import to non-tensional statements" — threatens the "vitality" of the metaphor and precipitates a fall into myth or "a believed absurdity."[29]

The irony of positions such as Berggren's or Soskice's is that they base their use of metaphor in part on the role of metaphors in science, and then argue that, because metaphors are crucial in theistic language, such language should be treated more like literature. But the difference in the use of literary and scientific metaphors is crucial. It is true that literary metaphors are not meant to be the basis for argumentation; they foster aesthetic appreciation and emotional involvement with the subject matter. By contrast, in science metaphors give rise to testable theories. Though the metaphor itself may not be testable, if it is to be retained it must form the core of a successful research program, as Lakatos has convincingly argued.[30]

In short: the parallels with scientific metaphors do not justify an end or limit to rational discussion of theological themes. Instead, they provide the opposite impetus: to find contexts in which the merit of various metaphors can be compared and contrasted. Such, anyway, is my task in these pages. Of course, the process may not prove the ultimate superiority of only one metaphor, any more than the physicist is compelled to choose between the wave and particle models of light. Still, as the wave/particle example shows, the resultant pluralism of metaphors is acceptable only to the extent that each has demonstrated its explanatory power in some specific context. God-language can of course be transformed into poetry, as can physics; but the inevitable presence of metaphors within theological discussions is not sufficient grounds for transforming them in this way.

28. Cf. Eberhard Jüngel, "Metaphorische Wahrheit," in Ricoeur and Jüngel, *Metapher: Zur Hermeneutik religiöser Sprache* (Munich: Chris Kaiser, 1974).

29. Douglas Berggren, "The Use and Abuse of Metaphor, I," *Review of Metaphysics* 16 (1962): 237-58, quotation 244.

30. Imre Lakatos, *The Methodology of Scientific Research Programmes, Philosophical Papers,* vol. 1, ed. John Worrall and Gregory Currie (Cambridge: Cambridge Univ. Press, 1978), esp. chap. 1. Cf. Peter Achinstein, "Theoretical Models," *British Journal for the Philosophy of Science* 16 (1965): 102-20; and Clayton, *Explanation,* 48-58.

Models of God: McFague

A recent school of thought reinterprets theistic language as presenting models for God. Of course, one finds a stress on multiple perspectives in earlier twentieth-century metaphysicians. A. N. Whitehead, for one, viewed pluralism within metaphysics as healthy: "When we survey the history of thought . . . we find that one idea after another is tried out, its limitations defined, and its core of truth elicited."[31] But in the more recent work of Sallie McFague and Janet Soskice, *all* metaphysical or theological language becomes metaphorical. No single theoretical framework is adequate for the concept of God: "A metaphorical theology will insist that *many* metaphors and models are necessary, that a piling up of images is essential, both to avoid idolatry and to attempt to express the richness and variety of the divine-human relationship."[32]

The strength of McFague's position lies in her insight that theistic language cannot remain purely metaphorical, that there is a drive, within religion as well as metaphysics, to bring metaphorical language to conceptual expression (ibid., pp. 22-23). In the reciprocal movement between these two poles, she argues, models arise. A model is "a dominant metaphor, a metaphor with staying power"; it gives us "a grid, screen, or filter which helps us to organize our thoughts about a less familiar subject" by seeing it in terms of a more familiar one (p. 23).

Stressing theological theories as models thus represents a mediating position between full metaphoricity and the univocity of a single established theory. In science, as Achinstein has argued, models express the assumptions about an object or system, and are "treated as approximation[s] useful for certain purposes."[33] This in-between status — not quite theory, not quite fiction — allows for pluralism in science: since models are used for different purposes, there may be alternative models in use at the same time. Still, theoretical models do claim to be approximations to the actual structure of the system in question (p. 118), and they can serve all the same functions as theories: They can be used "for purposes of explanation, prediction, calculation, systematisation, derivation of laws and so forth" (p. 106).

These considerations help to justify the rubric "models of God" as the starting point for the constructive systematic work in the following chapters. Models begin as a heuristic aid for thought in a complicated area; they simplify,

31. A. N. Whitehead, *Process and Reality,* ed. David Ray Griffin and Donald Sherburne (New York: Free Press, 1978), 14.

32. Sallie McFague, *Metaphorical Theology: Models of God in Religious Language* (Philadelphia: Fortress, 1982), 20. The next two references in the text are to this work.

33. Achinstein, "Theoretical Models," 104; the next two references in the text are to this essay. Cf. the works cited in n. 37 below.

organize, and guide our reflection. If successful, a given model (of the atom, of God) may become firmly embedded in our conception of the subject. And in their claim to approximate the truth, they give rise to theory, namely the attempt to say precisely where the model is correct and where its limitations lie. The model of God as an infinite or a perfect being may be accessible to theoretical examination in a way that the concept God alone is not.

The models that McFague proposes in *Metaphorical Theology* serve the goal of bringing God closer: God as friend, mother, lover. In a more recent book, she urges the acceptance of models that further feminist, antinuclear, and ecological concerns.[34] Likewise, Elisabeth Schüssler Fiorenza has worked to uncover nonbiblical models for divinity in the Hellenistic milieu with which women can more easily associate.[35] Of course, if models for God are chosen exclusively for their helpfulness in forwarding a particular social or political agenda, theologians open themselves to Feuerbach's criticism that their language is really about human relationships rather than about a divine agent;[36] and McFague's presentation is certainly open to this criticism. To avoid this danger, one must also — indeed, in the first place — look for models that successfully formulate a full, coherent notion of the God whose existence is being asserted. A particular advantage of the early modern period is the conceptual strength of the various models developed. By the time one has traced the strengths and corrected the weaknesses of the major positions through the time of Schelling, one has a clear sense of what an adequate model of God should include. Then (and I would like to say: only then) is one in the position to evaluate the adequacy of the contemporary models presented.

As we saw, the crucial role of models in science has long been acknowledged,[37] and the explicit appeal to models in theology is not new. In his quest for an originary principle (*archē* or *archai*), Plato employed multiple concepts

---

34. McFague, *Models of God: Theology for an Ecological, Nuclear Age* (Philadelphia: Fortress, 1987).

35. Fiorenza, *In Memory of Her* (New York: Crossroad, 1983).

36. Cf. Wolfhart Pannenberg, *Metaphysics and the Idea of God,* trans. Philip Clayton (Grand Rapids: Eerdmans, 1990), 62.

37. McFague, *Models of God,* chap. 3. The focus on scientific models in the philosophy of science became popular through the work of Max Black (*Models and Metaphors* [Ithaca: Cornell Univ. Press, 1962]), Mary Hesse (*Models and Analogies in Science* [Notre Dame: Univ. of Notre Dame Press, 1966]), and indirectly through Thomas S. Kuhn's *Structure of Scientific Revolutions* (Chicago: Univ. of Chicago Press, 1962); the area has become a growth industry in contemporary academics. Good secondary works include W. H. Leatherdale, *The Role of Analogy, Model and Metaphor in Science* (Amsterdam: North-Holland Pub. Co., 1974); and Ian Barbour, *Myths, Models, and Paradigms* (New York: Harper & Row, 1974).

in different contexts, including myths *(Timaeus)* and similes (*Republic* books 6 and 7). If anything, the impetus to focus more on models within science has come from traditional metaphysics, from its awareness of the (at best) analogical status of its language, rather than the reverse. Nonetheless, the recent emphasis on "models of God," inspired in part by developments in the philosophy of science, offers a particularly helpful framework for mediating two otherwise untenable sides of contemporary theological debate. There are good reasons to be hesitant about ascribing literal status to language about God; yet a theology of pure equivocation or indeterminate metaphorical reference might just as well be replaced by literature (with its greater evocative powers) or reduced to cultural anthropology. The idea of models well connotes the ideal, if not the reality, of full conceptual expression. It allows for a gradual movement from predominately nonconceptual language (mystical experience or poetic images of the divine) toward — if never in fact to — a completed metaphysical system.

THE REGULATIVE STARTING POINT
FOR METAPHYSICS, AND BEYOND

Beginning with Kant

In attempting to understand and to unify our experience, we formulate general ideas that serve to guide our reflection, to help us attain greater consistency and to extend our comprehension further. Kant calls these ideas *transcendental concepts*.[38] Such concepts do not express an existing but a "projected" unity (B 575). Still, this striving for unity is fundamental to human thought: "The law of reason which requires us to seek for this unity is a necessary law, since without it we should have no reason at all" (B 679).

The status of such principles is an extremely difficult question, and one on which (as chapter 5 will show) Kant has not said the last word.[39] I take it to be indisputable that various disciplines, including philosophy, make at least heuristic use of broader, unifying principles, of what Kant also calls heuristic principles (B 691). Concepts such as nature, power, pure earth, pure air, and frictionless plane

---

38. Kant, *Critique of Pure Reason,* trans. N. K. Smith (New York: St. Martin's, 1965), B 380.

39. See, e.g., the treatment of the transcendental/metaphysical contrast in the context of the third *Critique* in Paul de Man, "Phenomenality and Materiality in Kant," in Hugh J. Silverman and Gary Aylesworth, eds., *The Textual Sublime: Deconstruction and Its Differences* (Albany: SUNY Press, 1990), 87-108.

may be termed "hypothetical" (B 675), since they are not derived from or tested by anything in nature. Instead, "we interrogate nature in accordance with [them], and consider our knowledge defective so long as it is not adequate to them" (B 673-74). Such concepts — and the concept of truth seems to belong here as well — serve us ultimately as ideals; they are used for "directing the understanding towards a certain goal upon which the routes marked out by all its rules converge, as upon their point of intersection" (B 672). Since, according to Kant, they cannot ever be objects of knowledge, they remain merely regulative rather than constitutive concepts; they regulate the quest for knowledge rather than serving as actual items of knowledge themselves.

The concept of God, which by definition can never derive from experience, provides for Kant the archetypical example of such a concept. The ideal of a supreme being, despite the difficulties in giving it empirical meaning or content,

> is yet *an ideal without a flaw,* a concept which completes and crowns the whole of human knowledge. Its objective reality cannot indeed be proved, but also cannot be disproved, by merely speculative reason. . . . Necessity, infinity, unity, existence outside the world (and not as world-soul), eternity as free from conditions of time . . . are purely transcendental predicates. (B 669)

When we imagine or presuppose the unity of reason, according to Kant, we inevitably speak "as if" there were a God.

This analysis is certainly correct as far as it goes. The concept of God does work to express the goal that is inherent in rationality: to unify human intellectual striving (not to mention moral and spiritual striving). One can easily see how much the idea of God is bound up with what human reason views as flawless or perfect. Perhaps such language is indeed best viewed, initially, as serving a regulative function. The crucial question to debate, however, is whether God must remain, as Kant argues both here and in the *Prolegomena,* an "as if" concept, a useful fiction, or whether we can move beyond this point to a constructive theory of God as well. In light of the Kantian critique, how could one ever get from the former to the latter?

First Steps beyond Kant

Generalization

What Kant said of the concept of God is true of other concepts. Kant had to acknowledge multiple regulative principles, since a variety of notions can point toward intellectual unification. It is important to stress that there is no set hierarchy of such concepts; depending on one's starting point, the concept of nature, or mathematical simplicity, or human self-identity may receive greater emphasis. In the following chapters we will discover exactly why the concept of God is particularly apt as a unifying concept, while acknowledging that this is a controversial judgment that must be defended against competing options.

Nonetheless, it does seem that, among the regulative ideas, a particular group of metaphysical concepts stands apart and deserves particular attention because of its generality. In order to recognize what these concepts share in common with other philosophical concepts and what sets them apart, one might imagine the thought experiment of ordering various views of the human person along a continuum running from the most particular or disunified to the most unified.

1. Existentialist approaches are noted for their stress on particularity. Still, even philosophies that are relativized to individual human agents aspire to a certain unity. For instance, the early Heidegger placed a special emphasis on unifying function of death as the locus for the "possibility of being whole" (*Ganz-sein-können*) of an individually existing entity or *Dasein*. Among analytic philosophers, Bernard Williams is famous for his rejection of "eternal reasons" in ethics and his stress on the particular. He nonetheless continues to emphasize the need for unity within one's "subjective motivational set" (albeit a unity only of one's own dispositions, since the scope need extend no further than the individual self).[40] Even the existential starting point must employ unifying concepts.

2. Philosophical anthropology generally goes beyond this first approach by looking for a unified understanding of human nature in general, often in dialogue with the social sciences.[41] But even reductionist theories of the human person unify disparate data within an overarching materialist framework. On this view, particular natural sciences seek to make sense of their particular domains within nature, moving downward via bridge laws from, for example, the neurosciences to biology and biochemistry. Physics is often viewed as the limit case of this scientific progression toward a fully unified account, since (it is claimed) it offers explanatory accounts that extend in principle to all things in

40. Williams, *Ethics and the Limits of Philosophy*; idem, "Internal and External Reasons," in *Moral Luck: Philosophical Papers 1973-1980* (New York: Cambridge Univ. Press, 1981), 101-13.

41. See Leslie Foster Stevenson, *Seven Theories of Human Nature* (Oxford: Clarendon, 1974); J. F. Donceel, *Philosophical Anthropology*, 3d ed. (New York: Sheed and Ward, 1967); and Nicholas Rescher, *Human Interests: Reflections on Philosophical Anthropology* (Stanford: Stanford Univ. Press, 1990).

the natural world. Of course, the hegemony of physics comes at a certain price; it can only establish a connection with, say, psychology by means of reducing psychological phenomena to general physical laws. Still, if this program were successful (and I think there are good reasons at present to be skeptical of its chances), it would supply a unified physical theory of the scope of classical philosophical theories of the human person.[42]

3. Metaphysics appears to stand at the "unification" extreme of the continuum, since it looks for overarching connections between the disciplines that both transcend and unify them. Metaphysics has traditionally sought statements that are true not only as a contingent matter of physical law but necessarily, and true not just of physical being but of all being whatsoever. (Some doubts about whether this goal is still viable will occupy us below.) Of course, it may be that nothing said at such a level of generality will qualify as knowledge; maybe the search for broad ideas running through all the disciplines is doomed from the outset. Still, its interest in (attempting) such high-level connections is one reason why metaphysics is still worth pursuing today. Its final terms need not be "being in general" or "substance"; they need only suggest — and in the best-case scenario, establish — connections between the various more specific areas of human experience.

This brief thought experiment shows the sense in which all metaphysical reflection has the status that Kant ascribed to the notion of God. Metaphysics designates a multifaceted intellectual endeavor that is characterized by *the striving for unity*. Many of its nontheistic concepts (essence, identity, possibility, being itself) seek to establish such broader connections, and many of its theories specify the precise nature of the unity (e.g., monisms from materialism to pantheism). Indeed, we might even define metaphysics as the attempt to express connections that represent *the implied end points of rational reflection in other fields*. Like the idea of God, then, metaphysical proposals formulate the regulative ideals of unified human knowledge — at least this, and, as we will see, perhaps more.

Limit-Case Dualism

Talk of regulative ideals, Kantian or otherwise, stems from a certain skepticism — specifically, from the belief that the striving for unity tells more about the

42. See, e.g., the presentation in Ian Barbour's Gifford Lectures, *Religion in an Age of Science* (San Francisco: Harper & Row, 1990); Arthur Peacocke, *God and the New Biology* (San Francisco: Harper & Row, 1986); idem, *Theology for a Scientific Age: Being and Becoming Natural, Divine, and Human* (Minneapolis: Fortress Press, 1993); James B. Ashbrook and Carol Albright, *The Humanizing Brain: Where Religion and Neuroscience Meet* (Cleveland: Pilgrim, 1997).

tendencies of our own understanding than about what really is. Such skepticism is dualistic; it posits a basic gap between how our understanding works and the way the world really is. Unlike Hegel and those in his tradition, I think this possible gap represents a very serious challenge to both metaphysics and theology. Everything turns on how the possibility of a gap is expressed. Let me explain.

The particular epistemic dualism that Kant inherited from Hume — sense impressions versus ideas of reason — is untenable. Kant's tidy distinctions between intuitions, forms of intuition, percepts, schematized and unschematized concepts do in fact, as Hegel and others have argued, require one already to have bridged over the very gap that the dualism is asserting.[43] Intuitively, it seemed (and may still seem) attractive to demarcate sharply between the empirical input to the human knower and the universal categories of human reason. But the sharpness is artificial: when one gives up universal a priori categories of knowledge in favor of conceptual schemes (as in the hermeneutical shift described above), one loses the grounds for insisting on exclusively empirical input for knowledge. The selection of a particular conceptual scheme or paradigm, be it the theoretical structure of contemporary physics or the set of beliefs that define a social world for a given tribe or culture, is not purely a priori. "The mind and the world jointly make up the mind and the world."[44] Observations, believed facts, and contingent factors of history and society affect conceptual scheme selection. Yet the Kantian limitation to purely empirical intuitions presupposed the application of purely a priori (universal) categories of the understanding. To abandon the latter while insisting on the former is to knock the ground out from under oneself and then to insist on standing on it. Let's banish this Kantian myth of purely empirical inputs, then, along with the myth of a complete table of a priori mental categories, the theory-observation dichotomy, and other mistakes of the past.

This step has many consequences, as these pages will show. For example, one will now be suspicious of attempts to specify fully which propositions may and may not qualify as knowledge using detailed criteria that one "knows" a priori. Criteria for selection and the propositions they select walk hand in hand; we have no choice but to try to make sense of this hermeneutical codependence.

---

43. These Hegelian criticisms of Kant are clearly presented and defended in Bernd Burkhardt, *Hegels Kritik an Kants theoretischer Philosophie: Dargestellt und beurteilt an den Themen der metaphysica specialis* (Munich: Profil, 1989). See also the criticisms of Kant in chapter 5 below.

44. Putnam, *Reason, Truth, and History*, xi.

Nonetheless, banishing Kant's particular dualism does not dissolve the basic skeptical possibility: that our ideas might fail to mirror truly what is. Of course, if the failure is too extensive we would never have grounds for knowing it (if the Real is too distant, its absence may not be noted); but this fact does not make it any less of a possibility. I shall call the possibility that our ideas might fail to mirror the Real *limit-case dualism,* since it represents a possible break or limit of knowledge, and thus a duality, at the heart of the knowledge project. The question remains, So must our best candidate for knowledge be true, or could it still be mistaken? Kant's particular dualism, the alleged duality between empirical and nonempirical inputs for reflection, may be untenable, but limit-case dualism is both unavoidable and important.[45]

Transitions from Regulative to Constitutive?

It follows from the argument to this point that concepts which currently play a *regulative* role in our thought may later come to play a *constitutive* role within the context of a specific theory. Today's merely useful postulation may become tomorrow's testable hypothesis. Take the debate with Kant in the previous section: if we come to accept a broader concept of "experience," then notions that once provided only the framework for theories might come to qualify as actual testable theories. (What counts as theory depends in part on what one takes the data to be.) Likewise, when new empirical techniques are developed, or when a new theoretical apparatus becomes available, formerly regulative concepts may become objects of direct analysis and evaluation.

These are not considerations that Kant would have accepted. Still, there are aspects of Kant's presentation that hint at a much more slippery distinction between regulative and constitutive uses of concepts than he wishes to acknowledge. Think, for instance, of his discussion of the regulative concept of a unified power (B 676ff.). Our initial postulation of a unified power underlying the heterogeneous manifestations of power, he says, is (empirically) groundless; it is a pure postulation of reason. In employing it, however, we take it to be not only "subjectively and logically" but also "objectively" necessary (B 676); we assume "such a systematic unity . . . to be necessarily inherent *in the objects*" (B 678, emphasis mine). If no neat distinction can be made between what we assume methodologically (heuristically) and what we assume about the world, and if further (as I argued above) Kant's distinction between initial intuitions and what is later loaded onto them turns out to be more problematic than he thought, then the labeling of a given concept as

45. We return explicitly to these themes in chapter 6 below.

regulative or constitutive will also turn out to be a more fluid matter. Of course, the general distinction between the regulative and constitutive functions of concepts remains useful. Yet it may turn out that concepts that were introduced with a regulative function and justification will later be validly used and evaluated in a constitutive theoretical context. The importance of this consideration for post-Kantian theistic metaphysics and theology cannot be overestimated.

Transcendental Arguments as Less Than Necessary

This last revolutionary change suggests another: that transcendental arguments may occur with less than a priori necessity. One can of course list what, according to one's intuitions, are the necessary prerequisites for a given activity, linguistic practice, or type of experience. But one's sense of (and arguments for) what are "the conditions of the possibility" of some phenomenon is highly fallible. To begin with the trivial: imagine someone asserting that chess *requires* a board with alternating black and white squares until presented with a board of pink and purple squares, or with diamonds instead of squares, or with the latest computer software program, and then coming for the first time to agree that neither change altered the essence of the game. Another, less trivial example: in the past the subordination of woman to man was often asserted as a necessary condition for the happiness of both genders. And it once seemed unavoidable, as it did to Kant in the *Metaphysical Foundations of Natural Science,* that a successful physics requires the world to be Euclidean. Who could have intuited in advance that Reimannian geometries would play a crucial role in general relativity theory?

Moreover, the strength of the conclusions tends to decrease as the scope of the phenomenon under (transcendental) investigation increases. A specific activity like chess (or linguistic practice like ordering food in a restaurant) is easy, because for specific practices at least we have some clear intuitions about what is necessary and what is not. Activities that exist for a specific purpose wear their necessary conditions on their sleeves. Moreover, they are optional activities; we might agree on necessary conditions for a game to be chess; but not everyone needs to play the game. By contrast, when a Kantian enunciates necessary conditions for experience in general *(Erfahrung überhaupt),* no specific context whatsoever can provide criteria for evaluating his claims.

It looks, then, as though transcendental arguments will not lie at the center of metaphysical activity. They might continue to play a heuristic role, suggesting hypotheses that one might later submit to testing. But they cannot be granted the sort of a priori necessary that Kant wanted to claim for them.

Avoiding the "Fiction" Critique: Hans Vaihinger

The Kantian challenge to God-language represents the most serious threat to theology in the modern era. Before attempting to answer it, we must grasp why Kant's innocent-sounding comments on regulative concepts had such revolutionary implications. How did philosophers get from this point to the claim that theology is just a human projection?

Above I faulted Kant for his Humean brand of empiricism, his claim that knowledge is the combination of two sharply separated components: sensory input or appearances on the one hand, and the forms of intuition and categories on the other. It was this dichotomy that led Kant to construe all metaphysical language as no more than regulative — and occasionally, as in the *Prolegomena,* as fictitious. Of course, Kant sought to avoid the vacuousness of a completely fictive God by emphasizing the necessity of postulating God, freedom, and immortality in the context of practical reason, at one point urging that the *Critique of Practical Reason* formed the core of his thought and the base of his overall architectonic.[46] But this argument, based on the alleged a priori conditions for rational agency, is widely viewed as unsuccessful. Critics cite difficulties both with Kant's derivation of the Categorical Imperative and with his move to God as the guarantor of the highest good *(summum bonum).*[47] Actually, with reference to the problem of regulative language, note that even a successful second *Critique* would not change the status of the concept of God; it would only make it a more important or unavoidable fiction! Either way, under this position the *as if* threatens to take over: we speak *as if* there were a God, but we recognize that theistic language really just expresses features of human reasoning in the theoretical or practical sphere.

As early as 1843 Feuerbach argued for the elimination of the God-term if it could be given no positive content of its own.[48] If theistic language has fictitious status, then the projection of theistic predicates into the heavens must fulfill some human wishes. Once we recognize its basis in projection, we can uncover the qualities of the human species that were illicitly read onto the (nonexistent) Godhead. Yet, for all Feuerbach's influence in the nineteenth century (and beyond), it was Hans Vaihinger who more convincingly worked out the logic of the Kantian position. His *Philosophy of "As If"* does still plead for an

---

46. Immanuel Kant, *Critique of Practical Reason,* trans. Lewis White Beck (Indianapolis: Bobbs-Merrill, 1956), p. 1.

47. See Philip Clayton and Steve Knapp, "Ethics and Rationality," *American Philosophical Quarterly* 30 (1993): 151-60.

48. Ludwig Feuerbach, *The Essence of Christianity,* trans. Marian Evans (New York: C. Blanchard, 1855).

unambiguous acknowledgment that the concept of God is a pure fiction. Since it is a fiction that serves important (indispensable) functions, however, God-language should be preserved. Impressed with the continuing success of science, and with Kant's willingness to banish freedom out of the natural realm, Vaihinger proclaimed his system of "idealist positivism" or "positivist idealism"[49] as completed Kantianism.

Vaihinger is not a bad interpreter of Kant: There *are* difficulties in asserting the real existence of the *Ding-an-sich* (chap. 17), and more portions of Kant's transcendental philosophy deserve the label "fictive" than Kant actually concedes (chaps. 34, 37–40). Vaihinger is also right in generalizing the appendix of *The Critique of Pure Reason* to the Transcendental Dialectic: the status of the categories and the schematism are not ultimately different from the regulative principles. But he is also unambiguous about the necessity of breaking from Kant at major points (e.g., pp. 190-91, 284-85).

The trouble is that Vaihinger wanted to correct Kant in the direction of positivism, which generally meant a move from bad to worse. Of the numerous difficulties raised by a positivism of this sort, four illustrate broader challenges to theology and thus deserve mention here.

1. Vaihinger knew that certain concepts, such as God, were fictions because he knew that the natural world was all that existed and that science, rather than metaphysics, was the only source of reliable knowledge. But the demise of positivism in this century means at least that such assumptions stand in need of careful demonstration.

2. Once such positivist assumptions are questioned, the allegedly clear distinction between hypotheses and fictions collapses (chap. 21; part 2, sec. 28). We do not "verify" hypotheses and "justify fictions as useful" in two completely separate spheres; the two sorts of operations are indissolubly linked.[50]

3. Vaihinger's work stands in a much closer relationship to the reductionism of Feuerbach than he himself acknowledged. In his treatment of the concept of God — but also in the way he used concepts such as freedom, value, and teleology — metaphysics becomes de facto anthropology. And if a given set of theistic predicates is the product of human nature, then we might as well dispense with all language about the *subject* of these predicates. However weak and unsophisticated Feuerbach's view of the precise human motivations for projec-

---

49. Hans Vaihinger, *The Philosophy of "As If": A System of the Theoretical, Practical and Religious Fictions of Mankind* (New York: Harcourt, Brace and Company, 1925).

50. See Clayton, *Explanation*, 34-48, on the collapse of the "received view." As early as 1962 Hilary Putnam played a key role in the shift; for a recent version of his attack on the fact/value distinction, see his *Many Faces of Realism* (La Salle, Ill.: Open Court, 1987).

tion, he remains right that predicates which are purely the product of linguistic projections should be returned to their anthropological sources. (In our day, the growth and success of the psychology and anthropology of religion have only strengthened this basic point.) Vaihinger was not consistent enough in following out the logic of this argument; conversely, one who would resist Feuerbach's conclusions must resist Vaihinger's as well.

4. The preceding points, together with the critique of Kant above, suggest that the "philosophy of the *as if*" is better construed as the philosophy of the "whether really or only as if." It is not enough merely to assert that all theistic language involves a projection of human attributes; *argument* must establish whether a given claim is constitutive, heuristic, or pure fiction. And only a look at the metaphysical arguments themselves, pro and con, can decide this question.

An Aside on Transcendental Thomism

Transcendental Thomism bears some resemblance to the method sketched in these pages; we should pause to note the parallels. An (initially) regulative metaphysics, like the present one, will start "from below," in the sense that it derives its epistemology from the results of the sciences and its existential starting point from the experiences of everyday life. It then attempts to determine whether such "data" justify the introduction of metaphysical concepts, concepts that transcend the limits of naturalism and physicalism.

But the conclusions of a Marechal or Rahner are too strong. Philosophers have not (yet) been able to formulate a sound argument that justifies the move from the transcendental conditions of human existence to the existence of God. Whatever Kantian terminology Thomists may employ, one always detects that the choice for the transcendent has already been made at an earlier stage of their thought. If the Absolute is assumed from the outset to be built into human nature, it will be no surprise when anthropological or transcendental reflection "discovers" it there. Recall the quotations from Rahner above: surely in these texts the decision for a particular metaphysics (specifically, for Thomistic Christian theism) precedes rather than follows the debate about nihilism. Perhaps this fact helps to account for the somewhat awkward tone of the Kantian terminology, which sometimes appears to be tacked on to a deeper-level Thomism.[51]

The Kantian limitations on knowledge of God can of course be chal-

---

51. This point is argued in detail in F. Reiner, *Die Menschlichkeit der Offenbarung: Die transzendentale Grundlegung der Theologie bei Karl Rahner* (Munich: Kaiser, 1978). For an even greater integration see Louis Dupré, *The Other Dimension: A Search for the Meaning of Religious Attitudes* (New York: Seabury, 1979).

lenged, as in the present work. But if one accepts the Kantian limitations, one is committed to taking Kant's problem seriously, viz. that there are radical doubts about the very possibility of meaningful metaphysical discourse. It will turn out that the costs of overcoming Kant's critique of God-language (part II below) is an openness to a far greater variety of viable models than metaphysicians have allowed in the past — and thus to a genuine metaphysical pluralism. In order to see this, however, we must first consider the role of pragmatic considerations in language about God.

The Pragmatic Shift

I have argued that Kant's particular dualism — the appearances and what appears, the things of experience and the things-in-themselves — does not adequately determine in advance which sorts of propositions are knowable and which are not. Merely reflecting in the abstract on the nature of theoretical reason does not determine the "conditions of the possibility of experience *überhaupt*"; the only conditions we can obtain emerge in much more precise practical contexts. If, as I argued in the opening, theistic metaphysics should be viewed with some initial skepticism today (even by theists!), and if a transcendental critique of pure reason cannot provide a priori guidelines for determining the rational status of such reflection, what sort of approach can defend metaphysics as a rational endeavor?

Analyzing the procedural requirements for rational discourse provides a good starting point toward an answer — think of it as a fusion of Kant and C. S. Peirce. What does it mean procedurally for metaphysical claims to be put forward and defended? Can the goal of metaphysics be expressed procedurally? In light of the criticisms of Kant above, there can be no question of buying into an account of the pragmatically necessary conditions for meaningful discourse, as in the transcendental pragmatism of Karl-Otto Apel.[52] A more skeptically oriented response will not offer a priori necessary conditions but will focus instead on *the implied telos* of this activity. Put differently, it will ask about the sort of *procedures* that would lend credence to theistic claims and the epistemic *ideals* that theism guarantees or supports. This project is the red thread that runs through the more historical chapters that follow.

How might theism be linked to the guiding ideals of the knowledge quest? I

---

52. See, e.g., Karl-Otto Apel, ed., *Sprachpragmatik und Philosophie* (Frankfurt: Suhrkamp, 1976), translated into English as *Towards a Transformation of Philosophy*, trans. Glyn Adey and David Frisby, 2 vols. (London: Routledge and Kegan Paul, 1980).

maintain that the striving for a final unification of knowledge is an inherent part of the practice of rational debate, and that this striving is best expressed by the concept of God. If one cannot defend truth claims rationally — or even make sense of the search for truth — without utilizing the language of final unification as a limit case, then clearly such language has a regulative status; it regulates the activity of inquiry. Of course, the fact that specific concepts (such as truth, or possibly God) are implied by our reasoning practices does not alone prove that truth is knowable or that God exists; still, it does suggest that these notions are intrinsic to our quest for knowledge and to the possibility of its success.

The following sections flesh out this argument in two stages. First, the project of a "logic of theoretical discourse" may supply some pragmatic conditions for achieving rational consensus through argumentation. Second, this theory of rationality, understood in terms of the convergence of opinion, may be able to show how language of God (and other metaphysical terms) may be, or may never be, rational. Think of it as a brief excursus on theological methodology, or at least on the philosophical side of theism. Whether these procedures finally give God-talk merely a regulative or also a constitutive status is an issue that cannot be resolved in advance; the final answers must await the concrete treatment of the specific arguments in later chapters.

Procedural Rationality and Ideal Speech Situations

One way to understand the significance of the pragmatic shift for theology is to examine and critique the "logic of theoretical discourse" as explicated by the great German social theorist Jürgen Habermas. Habermas asks what are the *pragmatic* conditions that make it possible to achieve rational consensus through argumentation. What is it to justify truth claims discursively? Above all, he argues, it is to be motivated by the "force of the better argument."[53] The goal of this sort of speech situation may be consensus, but it must be a consensus that is "rationally motivated." One way to determine whether an agreement is rationally motivated is to examine the *content* of the discourse, to see precisely what positions are put forward and what reasons are given on their behalf.

I have argued elsewhere that Habermas underemphasizes the importance of content, the formal-semantic side of communicative action.[54] Among other

---

53. See Habermas, "Wahrheitstheorien," in *Wirklichkeit und Reflexion: Festschrift für Walter Schulz*, ed. Helmut Fahrenbach (Pfüllingen: Neske, 1973); Habermas, "Toward a Universal Pragmatics"; and Thomas McCarthy, *The Critical Theory of Jürgen Habermas* (London: Hutchinson, 1978).

54. Clayton, *Explanation*, 74-86.

problems I blame Habermas's decision to define truth as consensus rather than retaining the notion of correspondence with reality as a necessary component of truth.[55] But even if one lays adequate stress on the content side of debate, I suggest, it is still necessary to consider the process of rational discourse: How is the interaction organized? Are there external constraints on the participants? The result is a fuller sense of the standards for rational debate in any discipline, and a fortiori in theology.[56] McCarthy summarizes some of the criteria that Habermas develops:

> In addition to having the same chance to speak at all (to initiate and perpetu-ate communication), participants must have the same chance to employ constative speech acts, that is, to put forward or call into question, to ground or refute statements, explanations, and so on, so that in the long run no as-sertion is exempted from critical examination. But the conditions under which rational consensus is possible . . . must ensure not only unlimited dis-cussion but discussion that is free from distorting influences, whether their source be open domination, conscious strategic behavior, or the more subtle barriers to communication deriving from self-deception.[57]

The result is equal access to a dialogue that is driven by the intersubjective pur-suit of truth and that demands the subordination of individual goals and wishes when these come into conflict with that pursuit.

Admittedly, what results from the "theory of communicative action" is an ideal, and a clearly counterfactual one at that. Yet its fundamental role for theo-logical or metaphysical debate is not minimized by the fact that it represents an ideal located (at best) in the distant future. As Habermas correctly argues, "Even if [this supposition] is made counterfactually, it is a fiction that is opera-tively effective in the process of communication. There I prefer to speak of an anticipation of an ideal speech situation."[58] The notion of an ideal speech situa-tion is not merely a future fiction brought to current debates from the outside, since "with the first step toward agreement in language we must always in fact make this supposition." Put differently, it is not a transcendental illusion, since

---

55. Even the concept of coherence can suffice for this purpose; see Clayton, *Explana-tion*, chap. 4.

56. For an explanation of this distinction, see the typology in L. B. Puntel, *Wahrheits-theorien in der neueren Philosophie: Eine kritisch-systematische Darstellung* (Darmstadt: Wissenschaftliche Buchgesellschaft, 1978, 1983).

57. McCarthy, *Critical Theory*, 306.

58. Habermas, "Wahrheitstheorien," 258. The next reference in the text is also to this work.

the goal of the ideal speech situation is a constitutive condition of rational speech. I suggest that we might speak of it instead as a "practical hypothesis" (ibid., p. 259).

Peirce and the Telos of Rational Discourse

For all his strengths, Habermas remains too fully locked within the pragmatic side. His exclusive focus on speech acts, communicative action, and ideal speech situations tends to usurp the role played by the *content* of the discourse.[59] After a brief caveat regarding the pragmatic theory of truth, I turn to a thinker whose work serves as a corrective to Habermas's pragmatic epistemology.

Definition of the Telos

Most of the theorists examined in the following chapters had as one of their goals to develop a true theory of God. This represents perhaps the most difficult task that human reason has ever set for itself; understandably, the contemporary reader brings a healthy batch of skepticism to the very idea of a "true theory of God." Indeed, even the job of formulating the criteria for good and bad efforts in this direction raises serious, and perhaps insurmountable, difficulties. Nonetheless, I suggest that our contemporaries have inferred too quickly on the basis of these difficulties that a sharp and permanent line must be drawn between God and truth (or between God and reason).[60] Truth as the goal of theological reflection does not simply disappear because the theological project is difficult. (If one thinks that successful scientific theories are true, and that scientific results raise metaphysical questions, then one is confronted with at least one area in which the question of metaphysics' truth inevitably arises.) As long as the interest in truth remains central to metaphysical reflection, as I think, the predicate *true* will continue to belong to any adequate specification of the goal of this endeavor.[61]

At the same time, there is some (initial) reason for thinking that one

59. Incidentally, it was not necessary for Habermas to make this mistake. His own notion of redeeming validity claims should have suggested a closer look at the content (formal-semantic) side of the process; and the telos of agreement can be expressed without the liabilities of a consensus theory of truth. See Clayton, *Explanation*, chap. 3.

60. See Armstrong, *The History of God*; Miles, *God: A Biography*.

61. Clearly the goal here cannot be even to present the outline of a theory of truth. One important systematic presentation of the topic, which has influenced the treatment here, runs some 400 pages and nevertheless dares only to advance the title "Foundations for a Theory of Truth"; see Lorenz Puntel, *Grundlagen einer Theorie der Wahrheit* (Berlin: de Gruyter, 1990). The following comments indicate only a line of correction to Habermas and Peirce.

would not know with a high level of certainty which theories of God are true and which false. If one then continues to speak of the truth of such theories, one must therefore do so under the guise of a regulative ideal, or at best a working hypothesis.[62] If truth is indeed the goal, however elusive, of God-language, it behooves us to reflect for a moment what we mean by this term. Most begin with the intuition that truth means the *correspondence* of assertions with states of affairs: an assertion is true when it gets the world right, when it asserts that things are a certain way and they are in fact that way. But serious reservations have also been raised about correspondence definitions: What are these states of affairs? What is the correspondence relationship? How can words and world correspond in this way? How could one *know* that they do (if they do)? Wouldn't one have to step outside both in order to ascertain their relationship? The philosophical difficulties with correspondence are serious enough that a number of philosophers have turned to *coherence* as a more adequate umbrella concept for making sense of the multiple dimensions of truth.[63] Defined broadly, coherence can be understood to imply correspondence, which then gets parsed as the coherence of theory-terms with observation-terms. At the same time, other criteria that philosophers have held to be relevant to the truth question (broadly understood) can now be incorporated as well. Thus *consistency* is expressed as the (logical) coherence of statements with each other, *comprehensiveness* as the coherence of a theoretical proposal with experience as a whole (including perhaps future experience), and *usefulness* as the coherence between a theory and desired practical outcomes. Even Habermas's *consensus* notion can be specified as a pragmatic coherence between a set of opinions or viewpoints (thus obviating the need to shift to a consensus theory of truth).[64]

If coherence can in fact serve as an umbrella concept for the theory of truth in this way (and admittedly I have offered nothing more than a proposal here), it has very important consequences for the development and defense of a theistic metaphysics.[65] Correspondence theories tend to favor empirical inputs for true (or even meaningful) statements (cf. the logical positivism that grew out of Wittgenstein's early logical atomism), whereas consensus and exclusively use-based theories tend to relativize one's theory of God to one's particular context. I have argued that we must take the Kantian critique of metaphysics

62. So Puntel at a number of points in his argument, e.g., *Grundlagen*, 97, 267, 288, 293-94, 337.

63. This is also the tendency of Puntel's discussion, even though he seeks to avoid the term *coherence*. But don't his central tenets, the context principle and his theory of the proposition, present in effect a coherence theory of truth?

64. Clayton, *Explanation*, chap. 4; cf. 47-48.

65. See Pannenberg, *Metaphysics and the Idea of God*, esp. chap. 5.

extremely seriously, which means taking the regulative status of theistic language seriously. This discussion has shown (or at least suggested) that beginning with the regulative status of truth is fully compatible with the stress on propositional content entailed by the coherence theory.[66]

Criteria for the Telos

What then of the criteria for true theories within philosophical theology? Following Peirce, I suggest that *one is justified in calling a theory "true" in anticipation of the convergence of informed ("expert") opinion at the imagined end of the process.* As we saw, truth remains the goal of rational inquiry; and this goal involves a coherence among beliefs, toward things, and between persons. Because coherence covers the pragmatic component as well, the discursive ability to link one area of knowledge with another, to foster agreement, is a truth-relevant criterion. How precisely should this goal of successful inquiry be understood?

On this view, the goal of rational inquiry is that final point where a consensus of expert opinion emerges (or: would emerge) — for example, the point at which the claims in a particular discipline are no longer disputed. As Peirce argues, "Truth is that concordance of an abstract statement with the ideal limit towards which endless investigation *would* tend to bring scientific belief, which concordance the abstract statement may possess by virtue of the confession of its inaccuracy and one-sidedness, and this confession is an essential ingredient of truth."[67] I think this formulation tells us more about the criteria than about the definition of truth. Still, it nicely summarizes the insight that the outcome of rational debate concerning the nature of God plays an indispensable role in sorting out better and worse proposals in theistic metaphysics. As Peirce adds elsewhere:

> All the followers of science are animated by a cheerful hope that the processes of investigation, if only pushed far enough, will give one certain solution to each question to which they apply it. . . . Different minds may set out with the most antagonistic views, but the progress of investigation carries them by a force outside of themselves to one and the same conclusion. . . . The opinion which is fated to be ultimately agreed to by all who investigate, is what we

66. A discursive theory therefore does not imply internal realism à la Hilary Putnam. See Clayton, "Two Kinds of Conceptual-Scheme Realism," *Southern Journal of Philosophy* 29 (1991): 167-79.

67. C. S. Peirce, *Collected Papers,* ed. Charles Hartshorne and Paul Weiss, 8 vols. (repr. Cambridge: Harvard Univ. Press, 1960), 5:565, emphasis mine. For further documentation for this position see Peter Skagestad, *The Road of Inquiry: Charles Peirce's Pragmatic Realism* (New York: Columbia Univ. Press, 1981), esp. 75ff.

mean by the truth, and the object represented in this opinion is the real. (5:407)

Perhaps Peirce's view does not do justice to all the components that a complete theory of truth must include. But he does see clearly how well the telos of inquiry can serve as the unifying principle for rational inquiry. The opinion that would finally result from investigation expresses the limit case of ideal intersubjectivity, since it is no longer subject to change or to the vagaries of subjective prejudice or error (5:408).

It is of course possible that there will be no final convergence of inquiry, or that experts could finally converge "in the long run" and still be wrong. One might use the phrase *limit-case dualism* to express the same possibility: the best of human rationality could still be mistaken. As Peirce puts it, justified consensus might lie infinitely in the future. He thus speaks of it as the opinion investigators would ultimately come to, even if our race dies out without ever having reached it. But if even our final judgments should turn out to be false, we would have ex hypothesi no other access to the truth of the matter, and hence no means available to us to ascertain that they are false. Therefore, for all practical purposes — in the strongest sense: for all we could ever know — the convergence of opinion may be taken as the true. Hence Peirce's interest in transcendental realism: *to engage in rational reflection of the sort here outlined just is to presuppose the attainability of the goal of the process.* Note the parallels with the "as if" position discussed above in connection with Kant, which held that the ultimate convergence of inquirers remains a postulate of human reason, however indispensable. But (against the neo-Kantians) one can no more show that the convergence of opinion is a mere fiction than one can prove (on the opposite side) that the assertions on which inquiry finally converges will represent absolute truth. What I wish to stress here is that the ideal of rational convergence has a *present* value; it constitutes (in part) the practice of asserting and testing explanations. One makes implicit use of this ideal whenever one examines theories about the nature of God for their unifying potential, meaningfulness, or compatibility with the results of the empirical sciences.

The argument that I have just sketched amounts to a de facto rejection of the noumenal realm posited in Kantian epistemology. Or, more accurately, the argument subdivides Kant's noumenal realm into two conceptually distinct aspects. One aspect — that which expresses the difference between the most that humans could ever know and "what is indeed the case" — I have deemed inaccessible, even in principle, and therefore dismissed as irrelevant to the practice of epistemology. This first aspect serves only to remind us of an ineliminable possibility of error, of epistemic failure, that transcends our best efforts (though the ultimate failure to know can never be ruled out in principle). A second aspect of Kant's noumenal realm I have historicized, retrieving it under the guise of "that which we don't currently know but some day might." This aspect is expressed as the end of the process of rational inquiry, as the telos toward which we strive — whether or not humanity will ever attain it. If humans do not attain it, the search for truth will be transformed from a historical process with its end point in the future to a fictional one; it will become a process with an only imagined culmination. Which of the two possibilities is the case — for human theories in general, and for theories of God in particular — it is as yet too early to say.

God-Language as Regulative and as Constitutive

The Categories and Status of Metaphysical Discourse

Much ink has been spilt on the question of whether God-language is meaningful, rational, or testable. Critics argue variously that God-statements can only be emotive, that they can only express one's sense of the meaningfulness (or meaninglessness) of the universe as a whole, or that they have to do only with the presuppositions of human reason. If God-language serves only one of these functions, then it cannot refer; it cannot be about a being or dimension that really exists. Theistic language, it is argued, is regulative but not constitutive.

I suggest that the theory of knowledge sketched in this opening chapter makes a contribution to this debate. Four major categories have played a role in our discussions. Each of the four categories represents a crucial component in metaphysical discourse, and thus in any theories about the nature of God. Let's consider them in ascending order, starting from the most skeptical possibility and moving toward the most robust.

The Unknowable "Thing-in-Itself"

Can we know that the theory of God that is ideally justified (if there is one) is true? Or could our best theories still fail to capture the divine? If the latter is true, then the nature of God is analogous to a Kantian "thing-in-itself" — essentially unknowable, at least in part. To make explicit acknowledgment of this possibility is a crucial part of the prolegomenon to this book: in theistic metaphysics even the rationally perfect theory may fall short of its object (i.e., may be only partially true).

Following Kant, I take the concept of a "thing-in-itself" to mean "things as they really are but as we could never know them." There could be a difference between what we could ever know and what "really" is (cf. the section on limit-case dualism above). Kant was right to insist that this possible difference makes sense and is significant for assessing the status of human claims to knowledge.[68] What is true for all knowledge claims is true a fortiori for knowledge claims about God. Of course, there is an obvious critical response: How can this distinction make sense at all? If it involves a falling short that humans could never have access to, even in principle, then — on pragmatic criteria at least — it is by definition a distinction without a difference. Why retain it at all, and especially why give it a central role in one's theory of knowledge for theology?

But I believe the criticism is mistaken. Retaining the distinction serves as a continual reminder that ideal rationality need not yield true knowledge of the way things really are. In my view, the concept of a thing-in-itself, of "things as they really are but as we could never know them," helps specify the limits of what this — or any — human effort at knowledge can know about its success or failure. Applied to theistic language, it says that human theories of God could be mistaken even if the errors are undetectable to theologians and philosophers. Something in the concept of truth (and thus in the claimed truth of God-language) transcends any actual uses that one may make of these truth claims in actual practice.

What would be the status of the epistemically perfect metaphysics — say, a perfectly rational, necessary, universally accepted theory of God (if humans ever achieved such a thing)? It could indeed capture the real nature of the divine, that is, there might be no difference between such a theory and the divine reality. Or this imagined victorious theory might establish analogies to God's nature in some precise sense, say, via the analogy of proportion. Or (unfortunately) it is conceivable that even the epistemically perfect theory would not fully correspond to "things as they really are."[69] Which of these three possibilities is the case? This question can never be answered, even in principle, since by definition no one can know what lies beyond all possible knowledge. Thus the various claims to have resolved the ultimate truth question in one direction or another — and such claims are, sadly, legion in the history of metaphysics — deserve our deepest skepticism.

68. Perhaps, pace Kant (in some passages), no causality, etc., can be asserted of a thing in itself; things-in-themselves, apart from anything we could ever know about them, do not add an iota to what we know about the world. At any rate, my assertions here mean that I agree that neo-Kantians such as Hermann Cohen and Paul Natorp — and modern-day pragmatists and neo-pragmatists — were wrong to dismiss the *Ding an sich*. See, e.g., Paul Natorp, "Kant und die Marburg Schule," *Kant-Studien* 3 (1912): 193-221.

69. Note that this claim provides ground for retaining the concept of correspondence to "things as they really are": this concept expresses an epistemic possibility, the possibility of epistemic failure, which I maintain is a serious possibility in our quest for knowledge.

The Convergence of Informed Opinion

There may be no way of eliminating this one skeptical possibility. But there is nonetheless a way to speak of progress, and of rationality, in the ongoing debate over theories of God. The pragmatic theory of rationality outlined above offers the key. I argued there that the ultimately agreed-on outcome of rational discourse among the relevant experts would have strong credentials for being called true. Given category 1, we have to admit that such an outcome might not be ultimately true; but again, we would ex hypothesi never have any reason to assert its falsity. We then saw in the previous section that the convergence of rational discourse supplies the best criterion for the truth of assertions that humans possess. On this view, a given assertion is probable to the extent that stronger reasons can be formulated and agreed on through critical discourse for asserting it than for denying it. Now there is no inherent reason why this theory of rationality should not apply to metaphysics as much as any other discipline. Those who work in this field may come to agree that the concept of God and its various entailments do or do not succeed in providing justified explanations of particular areas of human experience. To the extent that they do so, they warrant the use of the predicate *true* with regard to theistic claims (though always under the limiting perspective of category 1).

Admittedly, explanatory claims in theology do not evidence the sort of strong falsifications or progressive agreement that disciplines like physics, or even psychology, have experienced over the last one hundred years. Metaphysics does not have clear cases of decisive refutation, like the cases of phlogiston or ether in natural science; there is no agreement that the existence of God has either been proved or disproved (though there is now widespread agreement that the question cannot be settled by proofs). Still, efforts at proving a difference in principle between theistic and nontheistic explanations have consistently failed, as have (even more dramatically) the efforts to show that metaphysical language is meaningless (A. J. Ayer, Anthony Flew, the early Kai Nielsen). As the following chapters make clear, it is possible to demonstrate specific strengths and weaknesses of theistic metaphysical positions. Comparative judgments between competing explanations remain possible even when few views are completely discarded, and I believe there are good reasons for ceasing to hold particular positions about the nature of God, at least in their traditional forms.

Consider three examples: Descartes inaugurated modern metaphysics with a view of the perfection of God inherited from the Middle Ages, a view that dominated the modern debate for some 150 years under the guise of "ontotheology." Part II below traces the growing difficulties with this view, which led eventually to its almost total rejection. To speak of a final refutation of Cartesian ontotheology is too strong. Yet there is widespread agreement about why it is not a viable program, and most would now agree that one cannot begin a treatment of the problem of God today based on the Cartesian metaphysics of perfection. To do so would be to fall beneath the level that the discussion has achieved over the last centuries. A similar point holds for the question of divine substance. It is not as though one can no longer use the term *substance* in a traditional (pre-Hegelian) sense. Still, advances were made in the German idealist theories of "substance-as-subject" that demand our attention; today one must either accept post-idealist uses of the substance notion or give good reasons for rejecting them. Finally, in part III we will struggle with the paradoxes of "an" infinite being, especially in connection with the famous "Atheism Dispute" surrounding Fichte. That thinkers still write naively of the Infinite as one being among others does not prove that "there is no progress in metaphysics"; it only shows that some writers are ignorant of the historical developments in this discipline. Even if it should eventually prove possible to speak without contradiction of "an" infinite being, one will be able to do so in a justified manner only by interacting with the criticisms of this idea and finding adequate answers to them.

Of course, discussions of metaphysical topics are not generally resolved as decisively as in, say, the natural sciences. In this field there is greater reason to think that the agreement lies infinitely in the future. Still, as these examples show, reasoned consensus is sometimes possible. When the questions are formulated with sufficient precision, alternatives that are clearly better and worse emerge. In the chapters that follow I thus talk of metaphysical hypotheses, metaphysical programs that are progressing and degenerating, better and worse theories of God. It is my goal to show that at least some metaphysical language is *constitutive:* it makes truth claims about what is actually the case.

The Regulative Status of Metaphysical Claims

Category 2 stressed the *outcome* of rational inquiry; category 3 focuses more on its *presuppositions*. It could turn out that certain metaphysical concepts are indispensable for there to be any rational discourse at all. Philosophers may be able to spell out these concepts in a detailed and rigorous manner; if they do, one will have good reason to grant them a crucial place in the human cognitive enterprise. If the idea of God is one of these concepts, as Kant thought, then it will play a crucial role in any adequate metaphysic — not perhaps as a theoretical term, but as the expression of something basic to the goals of human reason.

The theist would naturally like to find God-language deeply anchored in the bedrock of human reason.[70] Note, however, that presuppositional or "transcendental" arguments of this type do face some serious dilemmas. When they are based on experience as a whole, they are (notoriously) so broad that they are prone to error. It is difficult to get a purchase on "experience *überhaupt*," since hefty disagreements break out concerning what the "experience" is with which one is to begin. By contrast, arguments regarding the presuppositions for more limited realms of experience are at least in part empirical, because they seek to specify the prerequisites for a given type of inquiry or human activity. The conclusions are therefore not necessary, since it always remains possible that one could abandon the activity completely (e.g., numerology, astrology, chess). Moreover, the parameters for particular activities or types of experience need not be immutable. God-language may have been crucial to metaphysics as Kant knew it in 1781 but may be peripheral to the metaphysical work of analytic philosophers today. The Harvard philosopher Hilary Putnam, for example, proposes a treatment of "reason, truth, and history" that is based on dispensing with the "God's Eye point of view" altogether.[71]

Of course, even if the necessity claims usually made on behalf of transcendental arguments for God are suspect, this does not prove them false.[72] Hence it must remain an open question for us whether specific metaphysical concepts like the idea of God are merely useful fictions, suggested by the human quest for knowledge, or whether they can play a role in propositions that one might actually come to know. The openness of this question suggests a particularly interesting possibility: that a concept like the idea of God might first be justified as a regulative principle, functioning as a presupposition of human reason, and *later* become an object of direct rational inquiry in its own right.

This change in status would occur if a guiding principle later came to be thematized on its own as an explanation that is potentially true, not just as a basic assumption for some discourse or area of experience that is accepted only because it functions in a useful manner. For example, skeptics assert that there is no possibility of evaluating whether statements about God are true or false; they can at best tell us something about the aspirations of human reason to-

70. Alvin Plantinga has attempted an equally ambitious weaving of theism into the very fabric of human rationality; see "The Theistic Argument against Naturalism," in *Warranted Christian Belief* (Oxford: Oxford Univ. Press, 2000).

71. See Putnam, *Reason, Truth, and History,* chap. 3, e.g., p. 49.

72. To assume the falsity of regulative principles — they do not pick out any actual objects or beings — would be to commit the same error we discovered in Vaihinger's philosophy. Principles that pick out basic features of human reason may or may not also represent truths in their own right.

ward a final unity or overarching explanation. But in category 2 above I gave one way of conceiving the rationality of metaphysical explanations, and the book as a whole attempts to show that the God-question can also be an object of direct rational inquiry.[73] If these arguments are convincing, then we have an instance of a regulative principle that can also be evaluated as a constitutive theory.

Many claims about necessary presuppositions might in principle be subject to testing in this way. It is then no overstatement to assert that the failure of scientific positivism has again opened the question of God. Metaphysical concepts such as this one could be merely human posits (necessary or otherwise), fictions that thinkers employ in their search for comprehensive theories. But they could also emerge as explanatory hypotheses that arise out of specific fields of inquiry and the attempt to tie these fields together.[74] Thus the strategy of this book: I first attempt to show how specific concepts linked with the idea of God (the infinite, the absolute, the perfect) served as limit concepts in early modern philosophy, and to suggest that at least some of them could still serve a similar role today. But succeeding in this task is not finally sufficient for the theist, since "necessary conditions" can always be interpreted as merely useful fictions (and any theism worthy of our interest must surely mean something more than adherence to the God fiction!). I therefore also take on the second challenge of evaluating the claims of theism as theoretical hypotheses, with the ultimate goal of lifting them to constitutive status.

The Subjective Leftovers

At any given time, people advance specific truth claims about which agreement is not yet forthcoming. Nothing that we now know proves that there will someday be a final consensus on all contentious questions. Unfortunately, justified consensus may remain merely a regulative ideal in many fields, indicating a goal that scholars strive for but that will always elude them. For it is plausible that even a final consensus (if one were achieved) would leave certain knowledge questions unresolved — say, whether a brontosaurus drank from a particular African river on a specified date prior to the arrival of Homo sapiens, or whether John Cage wrote great music, or whether Heidegger was right about

---

73. In *Explanation* (e.g., chap. 4) I attempted to show that the changed view of science today (including recent acknowledgments of the role of models in science) no longer allows one to segregate nonempirical concepts from rational examination and testing as hypotheses.

74. Indeed, this book attempts to defend a stronger claim regarding regulative principles, namely that a number of these concepts play an important role within various particular disciplines, and that some are indispensable for rational thought as a whole.

the structure of *Dasein*.[75] Those questions that would remain undecided even at the imagined end of inquiry, the convergence of expert opinion, I shall call the *subjective leftovers* in the pursuit of knowledge.

Diversity — cultural, historical, psychological — may simply never disappear in some areas; pluralism may be permanent. Metaphysics is a good candidate for a pluralist discipline, a discipline where agreement is likely to remain incomplete. For despite their abstractness, metaphysical discussions are not immune from external influence; a broad variety of conceptual traditions have affected them in the past and presumably continue to do so in the present — including highly diverse religious traditions, intellectual frameworks, and types of experience. The entire debate over theistic truth claims may thus turn out to be intrinsically undecidable, reflecting matters of choice (or faith) rather than argumentation.[76] Agnosticism — global or local — may be the last word for some, or many, philosophical debates.

Nonetheless, one observes a tendency today to jump immediately from cultural or historical pluralism to the conclusion that "all is relative." That question is yet to be decided. Subject matters that in the present vary by culture or presupposition are not ipso facto irrelevant to the truth; they may later emerge as competing options in the context of a clear decision procedure. For any presently contested claim, arguments may later be provided that decisively resolve it. For example, the formalizations of modal logic (the logic of possibility and necessity) have provided a means for resolving debates that formerly depended largely on intuitions. One may *believe* that metaphysics will never overcome pluralism, that there will always remain vast tracks of unresolved differences, the subjective leftovers of rational debate. But to end rational discourse with one's Thomist or Hegelian (or Buddhist) colleagues based on this expectation is as unjustified as to pretend that one has already refuted their positions through arguments. Not all pluralists must be relativists.

What of the God-question? Clearly there is immense variation among the theories of God advanced within various historical epochs, schools of thought, and intellectual traditions.[77] Are the claims made within specific debates

---

75. Some of these may not be knowledge questions at all, of course. But to lay down by fiat what is and is not a matter of knowledge is to beg in advance some of the central questions of metaphysics.

76. Or perhaps there is a particular religious tradition, or some combination of them, that contains a revelation of God's nature to humanity (as many of them claim), rendering a priori metaphysical reflection otiose. We return to this possibility in chapter 9.

77. See the recent work by Armstrong, *History of God;* or the comparative work of scholars like Joseph Campbell, e.g., *The Hero with a Thousand Faces* (New York: Pantheon, 1949).

knowably true or false, or do they simply vary by culture, such that we have no access to the truth question beyond a given cultural context? For example, John Hick has argued that the cultural differences cannot be overcome, that the very notion of God is of a "Real *an sich*," a Real that lies beyond even the contrast between personalist and nonpersonalist views of the religious object.[78] Is one forced to choose between one or the other pole of an uncomfortable dilemma: either rampant (cultural, historical) pluralism, bordering on complete laissez-faire relativism, with cultural differences having the last word and no possibility of judging between them; or culturally blind absolutism, with no room for pluralism?

I suggest that this is only an apparent dilemma; the choices are more complicated, and more interesting, than the simple dichotomy implies. For example, in an important critique of Hick, Keith Ward distinguishes among Hick's "hard pluralism," an even more radical view ("extreme pluralism"), and more moderate positions ("soft" and "revisionist" pluralisms).[79] Although I side with the last alternatives, I will argue that there can be no a priori answer to skepticism about God-talk. There are important cases of mediation and rapprochement between metaphysical traditions, as I hope to show below. Such cases provide evidence that, for example, personal and impersonal theories of the divine do not form an ultimate and rationally insurmountable impasse for human reflection, as Hick thinks; nor is it possible to know in advance that the stalemates of today will be permanent.

Faced with competing and as yet unresolved differences among theories of the divine, one must wager for or against continued rational discourse about the nature of God. This book wagers for it, on the grounds that only actual debate between positions will reveal whether agreement is possible in the long run. (The debate is also important — I would even say essential — for the self-understanding of individual religious traditions, as I have argued elsewhere.)[80] If the reader finds no sign by the last chapter that progress has been made, that one is in the end in a somewhat better position to make a rational decision between at least some theological options, then (and only then) will one have reason to spurn further discussion and to proclaim that all such discussions fall into the category of the subjective leftovers of reason.

78. Hick, *An Interpretation of Religion* (New Haven: Yale Univ. Press, 1989), e.g., 236.

79. Keith Ward, "Truth and the Diversity of Religions," *Religious Studies* 26 (1990): 1-18.

80. See Clayton, *God and Contemporary Science* (Edinburgh: Univ. of Edinburgh Press; Grand Rapids: Eerdmans, 1997).

God-Language between the Regulative and the Constitutive

I have argued that many metaphysical questions waver between the regulative and constitutive. When scholars debate, they measure their success by the convergence of opinion based on argument and by whatever degree of theoretical coherence is necessary for achieving it. Still, one should be able to show that progress is possible on some specific topics. For example, one might cite cases of convergence and explanatory success as evidence that scholars can distinguish between progressive and degenerating research programs. Is this the case for theories about God?

A research program is an ongoing and definable program of inquiry that ties together the activities of a number of thinkers over an extended period of time.[81] The program might be extremely specialized, or it might be broad enough to include the activities of an entire subdiscipline or discipline. Though it is not particularly helpful to construe metaphysics as a whole as a single research program, one can identify particular programs of inquiry within the discipline (e.g., meta-reflection on the results and methods of science, programs for grounding ethical intuitions, efforts aimed at integrating the religious aspirations of humans with other areas of human experience and knowledge). Note that talk of competing research programs suggests a *pluralistic model of metaphysics,* just as speaking of conclusive falsifications suggests a clear and unambiguous decision procedure. The pluralistic model acknowledges that more than one program can exhibit theoretical strengths (relative to its particular goals) at a given time. We might have to grant, for example, that an Anselmian "perfect-being theology" (see chapter 3 below) is expanding in scope and surviving objections at the same time that trinitarian or process theories of God are making advances relative to the particular problems that *they* are addressing. It does not follow from such pluralism that competing and for now successful programs will never become commensurate (i.e., find themselves addressing the same set of problems with the same criteria). Still, for a time we may have to be satisfied with arguments and counterarguments that rely on assumptions that we cannot strictly universalize.

What then is metaphysical progress? Something like Thomas Morris's

---

81. The following comments represent an expansion of Imre Lakatos's theory of rationality; see his *Philosophical Papers,* ed. John Worrall and Gregory Currie (Cambridge: Cambridge Univ. Press, 1978) and the discussion in Clayton, *Explanation,* 48-58. On the applications of research programs to disciplines, see Clayton, "Disciplining Relativism and Truth," *Zygon* 24 (1989): 315-34. For another important application of Lakatos's work to this question, see Nancey Murphy, *Theology in the Age of Scientific Reasoning* (Ithaca: Cornell Univ. Press, 1990).

definition represents the minimal criterion: "In metaphysics, progress involves laying out clear options, charting interconnections among views, and discovering exactly where the problems and strengths of various alternatives lie."[82] Even given the skeptical worries that framed the opening of this chapter, there is evidence that metaphysical argumentation makes progress in this sense. We may not be able to make definitive judgments about which positions are finally true and which are false, but we can distinguish fruitful lines of inquiry from those which have fallen into more and more serious internal difficulties, have become increasingly counterintuitive, or have failed to provide viable explanations of certain phenomena.

Progress claims are of course always disputable (and disputed). Nonetheless, there remains a hierarchy of disputability, and hence of justification; some claims are more hotly, and more justly, disputed than others. One recognizes particular debates where no particular position seems able to gain a decisive upper hand. The competing parties continue to wrestle back and forth over substance-based and event-based theories of reality, over realism and idealism, over timeless and time-indexed theories of God's relation to the world. Worse are the questions that are so comprehensive that one cannot even imagine a decisive resolution: Why is there something rather than nothing? What is the meaning of Being?[83] Other debates, as we shall see in these pages, have admitted of significant clarification and development over the years. The point is not to bemoan areas of undecidability but to structure the remaining disputes so as to encourage the maximum possible progress.

Addressing the Question of God "from Below"

The aim of the following chapters is to approach the God-question "from below," without presupposing the absoluteness, final decidability, or adequacy to truth of "the metaphysical standpoint." The initial goal is merely to determine whether theistic language has at least a regulative function, whether it unifies human experience (in particular areas) in a significant sense. As one examines specific theistic concepts and defends their regulative role, however, one must ask whether they function (and can be evaluated) as explanatory hypotheses as well. To the extent that we find metaphysical concepts serving as adequate explanations, we have reason for construing them in a constitutive fashion — and thus reason, it may turn out, for calling them true.

82. Morris, ed., *Divine and Human Attributes*, 5.
83. We return to the problem of the extremely abstract and the extremely general areas of metaphysics in chapter 6.

The constant danger of theology "from below" is that God will become merely the name for an aspect of human experience, rather than a divine agent in its own right. It is often alleged that merely to consider this possibility — that language about God might involve a projection of human predicates — opens the door to a reduction of all theistic language to its "real" sources in human experience à la Feuerbach.[84] Two mistakes are to be avoided when considering the possibility of projection. On the one side, that one takes the possibility of projection seriously does not mean that one *knows* that all theistic language should be reduced to the human level — even though the critics of theism are all too eager to make this leap. On the other side, conservatives often show the opposite overreaction: "Well, then, the only way to avoid a reduction of theistic language is to avoid all theology from below. So we will start by assuming the autonomy of theological discourse. God-language is sui generis and needs no justification from outside; it is directly revealed, or authoritatively established, or immune to criticism." Even as skeptical a thinker as Gordon Kaufman tries to draw a sharp line between "religious" and "theistic" worldviews, arguing that Christianity's assertion of a personal God must be separated at the outset from any more general religious perspective.[85]

Unfortunately, the separation often cannot be made at the outset. At least for many today, language about God simply cannot be warranted apart from its grounding in other cultural, political, scientific, and philosophical concerns.[86] For such persons, theism, if it is to be credible at all, must lift itself from its starting point in human experience up toward a genuinely nonprojective discourse about a reality that transcends the finite realm. Perhaps, if the task is successful, one will later be able (as Wittgenstein puts it) to "throw away the ladder" and understand the grammar of theistic language primarily within the context of a particular religious tradition or "faith community."[87] But first, at least for many thinkers today, the connections to God-language must be established "from below." If it proves impossible to draw such connections, then — for these individuals at least — the Feuerbachian critique will be deemed to have had the last word.

---

84. See Ludwig Feuerbach, *The Essence of Christianity.*

85. Kaufman, *God the Problem,* chap. 9.

86. I have described such persons as "secular believers" and have explored the type of religious belief available to them in *Explanation,* chap. 5. More recently see Clayton and Steven Knapp, "Belief and the Logic of Religious Commitment," in *The Rationality of Theistic Belief,* ed. Godehart Bruntrup and Ronald K. Tacelli (Boston: Kluwer Academic Publishing, 1999).

87. That one should understand the grammar of religious language solely in this fashion has been the thesis in most of D. Z. Phillips's publications. See, e.g., D. Z. Phillips, *Faith after Foundationalism* (Boulder: Westview Press, 1995).

Herein lies the strength of Dieter Henrich's notion of an "ascent" *(Überstieg)*.[88] As self-conscious beings we begin to reflect on our selves and our environment, attempting to understand them as they are given to us. This effort at understanding leads gradually to broader and broader concepts that are less and less bound to our initial experiences. Ideally,

> [this] process of understanding is part of a reinterpretation of the natural world and yet takes the form of a metaphysical counter-proposal — one which, although only an interpretation, is able to grasp the unity of this world in a clearer and more refined fashion than would have been possible using only the conceptual resources that are a part of our basic relationship to the world. (ibid., 179)

In Henrich's view, the "ascent" culminates in a theory of the Absolute, though (he claims) without breaking out of the limitations imposed by a "from below" methodology. I am less sanguine about the prospects for a smooth, continuous movement from "theology from below" to a "from above" theory of the Absolute; and Henrich's own failure to produce such a theory does little to diminish this skepticism. In my terms, to arrive at a constitutive theory of the Absolute would be to have made a leap from the "from below" perspective to a "from above" perspective — and hence to have fallen back into traditional metaphysical claims to knowledge that are no longer credible.

I wish to suggest an epistemically more humble path: to enter into and explore metaphysical language not as the product of a gradual ascent but as a possible source for explanatory hypotheses about our experience of the universe taken as a whole. This more cautious path does not presuppose that an unbroken ascent is impossible; to do so would be as arbitrary as to allege at the outset that one is standing eye-to-eye with the Absolute. It does presuppose, however, that the prospects for classical metaphysics or natural theology are somewhat dim. In short, one does not need first to succeed at Henrich's ascent in order to be justified in using language about God; the justification can issue from comparisons of available positions and through the explanatory power of the results.

Conclusion: The Prospects for a "Theology from Below"

There is no guarantee that theology pursued in the manner I have been suggesting will finally converge on the results or the methods of traditional theology

---

88. Dieter Henrich, *Fluchtlinien: Philosophische Essays* (Frankfurt: Suhrkamp, 1982), 179. The next reference in the text is also to this work.

— or, for that matter, on traditional metaphysical language about God. Three options are logically possible: perhaps theology pursued "from below" will diverge further and further from the traditional language of a transcendent being; perhaps it will come to be subsumed by metaphysics in some sense; or perhaps new and interesting analogies between the theological and metaphysical projects will emerge.

Theology without Transcendence

Perhaps it will turn out that the boundaries of subjectivity cannot be broken. If one starts from below, from human experience, perhaps one will always remain within its sphere. On this view, whenever theistic language is employed, it will always refer exclusively to human, or at least this-worldly, realities.[89] It may be, for example, that the God-idea serves various positive functions — in ethics, in epistemology, or for religious persons. But note that the idea "God" might serve a variety of useful functions without picking out any being or state of affairs whatsoever. Indeed, its usefulness as an idea is compatible with the complete unknowability of God — and indeed with the nonexistence of God as well!

Nothing in this opening methodology chapter can prove in advance that transcendence will survive the critical objections raised against it. Perhaps the cleft between human thinkers and the concept of the Absolute is unbridgeable; perhaps our fate as would-be knowers is to grasp the infinite only as a projection out of the finite reality that we experience. If this is the case, philosophies of immanence will eventually have to be substituted for traditional theism, emphasizing even more its fictional status — as in Feuerbach's critique of religion or A. J. Ayer's critique of metaphysics. Could it be that in the end theology is fated to consist of nothing more than aesthetic preferences and bourgeois sensibilities?[90]

Theology qua Metaphysics

Perhaps, by contrast, exercises in philosophical theology like the present one will uncover a powerful version of philosophical theism, one that answers the

---

89. Those who advocate this view are fond of citing as an example the concept of "world" in Heidegger's *Being and Time,* insofar as it clearly remains (for the early Heidegger at least) an existential feature of *Dasein,* stemming out of (and in this sense relativized to) human experience.

90. Of course, transcendence and immanence are not exclusive options. Several of the more recent versions of theism suggest new ways to mediate between them. Perhaps the most important initiative in this regard is panentheism (e.g., chapters 7-9 below). For further references to the literature on panentheism see Clayton, *God and Contemporary Science;* idem, "The Case for Christian Panentheism," *Dialog* 37 (summer 1998): 201-8.

major objections as well as incorporating and explaining the major assertions of traditional theology. In this case the reduction of theology to the human dimension would be circumvented, but at the cost of making theology a special case of metaphysics.

I must admit to a certain degree of skepticism about this happening, though I suppose it remains possible in principle. Imagine the following scenario: a conceptual structure (a philosophical theory) is developed that provides the first principles of scientific rationality *and* persuasive interpretations of the major theories in the sciences and theology. Imagine, for example, that all of these things come to be understood as moments in the self-unfolding of the Absolute. In this case, the theory of the Absolute would subsume all the steps taken to reach it. One would then have to say that exploratory studies of the problem of God in modern thought — and theology in general, for that matter — were prolegomena on the way to a fully adequate theory of God. They would be merely "phenomenology" in Hegel's sense: arguments that only appear to climb their way upward from below but are really guided (unbeknownst to them) by the end that they anticipate. If this were to occur, no cleft would remain and all other items of knowledge would be sublated (*aufgehoben*) into the true philosophy, to which efforts like the present one would be mere propaedeutic. It could happen, I suppose, but in the meantime I recommend the attitude perfected by the fine people of Missouri: "Show me."

Theology and Metaphysics as Parts of a Common Project

There is a possibility between these first two options, however, which I hold as the most likely of the three. Examining concepts such as infinity or perfection or "the unity of all that is" may point toward (something like) traditional metaphysics as its ideal, without ever being able to demonstrate that these ideas are actually components of true theories. Put differently: metaphysical concepts may prove useful, even indispensable, in various disciplines; they may summarize important areas of experience; they may even act as vital components of theories in various areas (from cosmology to theories of human nature).

One of the disciplines in which they have proved most useful is theology. It is a basic premise of this book that theologians can make use of metaphysical concepts and theories (as metaphysicians can make use of contributions from theology) without the subsumption of the one discipline by the other. Those who know the histories of the two disciplines know that they have been closely associated from the beginning (often by those who are most eager to assert their total independence). If the analogies between them can be recognized and the common ground tilled together, apart from the foolish struggle for hierarchy and dominance, then the potential for cross-fertilization can be maximized. But I will only convince readers to turn their swords into plowshares if I can demonstrate the mutually beneficial nature of the dialogue in actual practice.

With this challenge it is time to turn from epistemology to the questions themselves. For eventually one must set aside the "what if . . ." and "what would be the status of . . ." questions and begin to look at the best constructive responses to the problem of God that have been made over the last several hundred years. Perhaps we will be able to make some progress, and perhaps we will bog down in hopelessly confused concepts and marshlands of implausible assumptions. Which of these will be the outcome is not something that can be settled a priori, and certainly not by the ruminations of methodologists! Only by wrestling with the major authors of the modern period and with the actual arguments they advance can we hope to reach some informed conclusions. It is time to start.

CHAPTER TWO

Beyond the Cogito: In Search of Descartes's Theology of the Infinite

INTRODUCTION

Recent Interpretations of Descartes

In recent years Descartes has been increasingly castigated as the founder of modernism and the metaphysics of subjectivity. One author defines the flawed project of modernism in terms of a set of "Cartesian coordinates." Another influential book blames the "dead end" of modern epistemology as a whole, and foundationalism in particular, on Descartes, who saddled us with the hopeless picture of the "mirror of nature." And poststructuralist treatments with titles such as *Subjectivity and Representation in Descartes: The Origins of Modernity* constitute a flourishing genre.[1]

Analytic philosophers are equally critical of Descartes (constituting possibly their only point of agreement with postmodernists and poststructuralists!). Most analytic commentators dismiss his metaphysics as hopelessly foundationalist. Authors usually focus on what Descartes did *not* achieve: The argument of the *Meditations* is circular; his arguments for the existence of God fail; the *cogito* can at any rate prove only "there is thinking" rather than "I am a

---

1. See, respectively, Nancey Murphy, *Theology in the Age of Scientific Reasoning* (Ithaca: Cornell Univ. Press, 1990), 201; Richard Rorty, *Philosophy and the Mirror of Nature* (Princeton: Princeton Univ. Press, 1979); and Dalia Judovitz, *Subjectivity and Representation in Descartes: The Origins of Modernity* (Cambridge: Cambridge Univ. Press, 1988).

thinking substance"; his mind/matter dualism is untenable; and his theory of the material world is a nonstarter. With the exception of major French commentators such as Gilson, Guéroult, and Gouhier, the secondary literature on Descartes is probably more critical of his basic theological position than is the case with any other major Western philosopher.

This dismissive attitude is reflected in the themes that are typically emphasized in treatments of Descartes — or, better, the themes that are generally absent from such treatments. Consider for a moment five major English and two French anthologies on Descartes published in recent decades.[2] Doney's 1968 collection focuses, as the introduction states, primarily on problems in the theory of knowledge; metaphysical themes, such as Bréhier's excellent piece on the creation of the eternal truths, are included only as they bear on epistemological issues. The book's primary themes are the *cogito,* Descartes's criteria for knowledge, and the theistic proofs. In his 1978 anthology, consisting of articles written in the 1970s, Hooker claims to have discovered an even greater convergence of themes over the preceding ten years. Now, he thinks, the central question for Descartes scholarship, alongside Cartesian dualism, is "whether Descartes was attempting to use reason to defend the use of reason, and if so whether that can be done and how" (p. vii). Two of the anthologies (Gaukroger and Rodis-Lewis) are dedicated specifically to Descartes's mathematical and scientific work, and Doney's 1987 collection is concerned solely with the circle problem and the question of the creation of the eternal truths. By contrast, Amélie Rorty's 1986 book is the most pluralistic, covering a wide variety of topics from a number of different philosophical standpoints. Apart from a few of the essays in Rorty[3] and the Rodis-Lewis metaphysics collection, however, the

2. Willis Doney, ed., *Descartes: A Collection of Critical Essays* (Notre Dame: Univ. of Notre Dame Press, 1968); Michael Hooker, ed., *Descartes: Critical and Interpretive Essays* (Baltimore: Johns Hopkins Univ. Press, 1978); Stephen Gaukroger, ed., *Descartes: Philosophy, Mathematics and Physics* (Sussex: Harvester, 1980); Amélie Oksenberg Rorty, ed., *Essays on Descartes' Meditations* (Berkeley: Univ. of California Press, 1986); and Willis Doney, ed., *Eternal Truths and the Cartesian Circle: A Collection of Studies* (New York: Garland, 1987). Geneviève Rodis-Lewis edited two collections of French essays: *La science chez Descartes: Etudes en Français* (New York: Garland, 1987), covering various specific mathematical and scientific themes in Descartes; and an excellent anthology on metaphysical issues in Descartes, *Méthode et métaphysique chez Descartes: Articles en Français* (New York: Garland, 1987). The bibliographies in Doney (1968) and Hooker give some sense of the topics covered in the massive secondary literature; see also the *Bulletins Cartésien* in the *Archives de philosophie,* beginning with vol. 35 (1972).

3. And these, by the way, are not overwhelmingly sympathetic. Jean-Luc Marion's essay "Essential Incoherence of Descartes' Definition of Divinity," 297-338, presents a significant (and pervasively critical) argument for the inconsistency of Descartes's definitions of

vast majority of the articles in these seven anthologies devote surprisingly little attention to the metaphysical core of Descartes's position. In general, one is left with the impression that, once the theistic arguments have been proved invalid, nothing else of interest is left to Descartes's reflections on God.

Unquestionably, there is value in the topics that permeate recent Cartesian scholarship; progress has been made. Cartesian foundationalism, to the extent that it was really present in the writings, deserved the sound thrashing it has received. Nonetheless, the relative silence regarding Descartes's overarching metaphysical and theological position is disturbing. How can one make sense of a systematic thinker when the basic tenets of his system remain unexplored? Is our task completed when we have cast individual arguments into question? Interpretation — but also, I suggest, evaluation and appropriation — requires reconstructing the systematic interconnections of an author's position, with special attention paid to unearthing and examining the concepts that lie at the very center of his or her thought.

One area where the danger of misinterpreting this particular thinker looms large is the proclamation of Descartes as the father of modernity. To the extent that one focuses exclusively on the *cogito* argument ("I think, therefore I am") or on epistemological issues, one creates a Descartes who aimed to ground all thought in the subject — a forerunner to Kant's "Copernican revolution," an anticipator of transcendental subjectivity. The present chapter challenges this interpretation by looking more closely at Descartes's understanding of God. The case could also have been made by examining the context and nature of philosophical reflection in the seventeenth century.[4] It was a period that was only gradually breaking with the conceptual framework that had been taken for granted during much of the Scholastic period. But French philosophy in 1620 was not yet ruled by the spirit of the eighteenth-century French En-

---

God. I have presented and criticized his argument in "Descartes and Infinite Perfection," *Journal of the American Catholic Philosophical Association* 6 (1992): 137-47. Annette Baier provides an idiosyncratic reading of the *Meditations* through the glasses of Feuerbachian reductionism in "The Idea of the True God in Descartes," 359-88 ("the idea of God" is "the self-conscious thinker," p. 385). Only Margaret Wilson's careful analysis of the infinite and the indefinite in Descartes ("Can I Be the Cause of My Idea of the World," 339-58) could be said to have a nonnegative conclusion ("positive" would be too strong).

4. See, e.g., Henri Gouhier, "Les philosophes du XVIIe Siècle devant l'histoire de la philosophie," *XVIIe Siècle* [Revue publiée par la Société d'Etude du XVIIe Siècle] 45 (1962): 5-16; G. Rodis-Lewis, "Les philosophies du XVIIe siècle devant Dieu," ibid., 17-28. Among English monographs, Marjorie Grene does perhaps the best job of presenting the seventeenth-century context in her *Descartes* (Minneapolis: Univ. of Minnesota Press, 1985), e.g., chap. 7.

lightenment, and it was certainly not on the verge of grounding all knowledge in the synthesizing activities of the human subject à la Kant (and even this stereotype about Kant comes in for criticism in chapter 5 below). Descartes may have unwittingly set the stage for "modernity" by means of his rejection of the remains of Aristotle, his recourse to clear and distinct ideas, or his separation between mind and body. And the weaknesses of the so-called ontotheological tradition that he founded may have led directly to Kant's influential criticisms of the ontological argument and, more generally, to the attack on God-language in the first *Critique*.[5] Still, none of these factors dictates a subjective interpretation of Descartes's writings or exhausts their significance.

Cartesianism beyond the *Cogito*

Contemporary commentators often approve of Descartes's epistemology because of the "turn to the subject," and then reject it because the *cogito* (with the incidental help of God) is allegedly made to play a foundational role as the source for knowledge of God and world. Such a position would indeed be absurd. But Descartes never meant his entire metaphysics to rest on the human subject as its foundation. Instead, he holds that God as *essentia infinita* is the ontological source for all finite subjects, who are in their very essence dependent on this infinite grounding. The theology of the infinite that Descartes advocates may affirm an ultimate principle as the source of its systematic unity. But — so the argument of this chapter — the final criterion for evaluating it lies not in the viability of the *cogito* as ultimate foundation but rather in the coherence and explanatory power of the overall proposal (or, should it fail, the lack of such coherence).

With this goal in mind, I suggest the strategy of reversing the starting point of most recent Descartes scholarship. Rather than looking only at how Descartes's theory of God functions in his theory of knowledge, let us examine his epistemological assumptions and theistic proofs to see what they tell us about his theology. I shall argue that (and show how) Descartes's thinking subject is subordinated to a very different concept: that of an infinite and perfect being. The *cogito* plays a specified role *within* this overall system rather than being the absolute foundation on which all else rests. Thus, interestingly, Cartesian doubt emerges as an ontological feature of finite being in contradistinction to the infinite being in which it is grounded; in revealing limitation and lack of

---

5. On the final point see Dieter Henrich, *Der ontologische Gottesbeweis: Sein Problem und seine Geschichte in der Neuzeit* (Tübingen: Mohr [Siebeck], 1960).

self-sufficiency, doubt reveals what we are as agents.[6] For Descartes, the finite and imperfect nature of the human thinker implies immediately the existence of an infinite and perfect being as its source.

To see this, we must pay special attention to how Descartes employs the concepts of perfection and infinity in his texts. The infinite, for example, is associated with the mathematical way of thinking that was central to the natural philosophy of seventeenth-century thinkers. The combination of mathematical and traditional metaphysical elements made the concept of the infinite especially attractive to Descartes. This concept connected with (and supported) his work in natural theology, was suggested by the subject's immediate awareness of itself as finite, and seemed to summarize a number of the traditional attributes of divinity. I will also argue that, suitably modified, the concept of the infinite could play a similar role in theological reflection today. In other words, a reconstructed Descartes may provide one model for doing philosophical theology today — with the help of other early modern concepts and distinctions that we will explore in subsequent chapters.

My suggested interpretation should also affect how we assess Descartes's place within the history of modern thought. On the one hand, Descartes does not deserve the lion's share of the praise, or the blame, for the modern philosophy of the subject, or for epistemology, or for the development of early modern science — there are claimants enough to these roles in the centuries that follow him. On the other hand, he is not a pure prisoner of the Middle Ages, as others wish to argue. One cannot help but suspect that these two mutually exclusive interpretations, while clearly having a moment of truth, ultimately cancel each other out; the truth must lie somewhere in between. Let's consider them individually.

Parts of Descartes's philosophy — like most metaphysics written in the seventeenth century — are "foundationalist," and where he espouses absolute foundations for knowledge his work should be rejected. The strengths of his position emerge more clearly when we read him not as the founder of a foundationalist philosophy of subjectivity but as the advocate of a theology of infinite difference. Only later, after his death, were his attack on the Schools and his arguments in the *Meditations* transformed into the attempt at making the human subject the central, or sole, metaphysical and epistemological category. (This was a development that occurred in interestingly different ways in the British empiricist and Continental traditions, and the differences reveal to what extent it was a post-Cartesian development.) Descartes became "the father of

6. Cf. Walter Schutz, *Der Gott der neuzeitlichen Metaphysik* (Pfüllingen: Neske, 1957), 38-39.

modern subjectivity" (or epistemology, or science) only anachronistically, that is, in light of what his sons and daughters, particularly those in the idealist tradition, went on to do. In his own thought, however, the *cogito* is of a piece with his theory of the infinite and not a foundation independent of that theory. Getting clear on this point entails rejecting the naive epistemic confidence that Descartes places in individual arguments; still, only in this way can Descartes's own insights emerge in their most credible form.

Of course, Descartes was not merely a prisoner of the Middle Ages, as other commentators have argued. In breaking methodologically from the Schools, Descartes contributed to a period of immensely creative reflection in early modern thought. His work allowed certain strands in philosophical theology, marginalized during several centuries of Scholastic dominance, to emerge again in a purer, simpler form. In particular, Descartes's theology of infinity turned from the predominant Aristotelian-Thomistic tradition back toward certain Neoplatonic themes that had repeatedly surfaced in medieval thought without ever becoming dominant. (Indeed, hints of these themes in the present chapter will send us back in the next to reconstruct two of the central concepts of Neoplatonism.) For some reason, however, the significance of Descartes's introduction of the infinity and perfection ideas into modern thought is often missed. It means that theological themes played an important role in setting the agenda for modern philosophy, an untold story that the following pages attempt to narrate. More particularly it means that modern thought, outside the circle of professional theologians, was quietly reconceiving the relationship between God and world. The second untold story involves the gradual realization — by Hartshorne and others earlier this century, and by theologians only in recent years — that the modern era had left classical philosophical theism behind and had turned to a more intimate construal of the God/world relation which many today are calling *panentheism.* The first decisive steps in this direction were Descartes's, even if he knew not where he led.

The ultimate goal, then, is to treat Descartes not just in the context of early modern epistemology and idealism — however much his thought may have contributed to these movements — but as a contributor to a viable philosophical theology for the present. Methodologically, I am sympathetic to Gassendi's critique: the Cartesian *method* of doubting and/or rejecting all previous opinions and then only accepting what one intuits as clear and distinct, as given by natural light or "common notions," is naive and unsuccessful. Nonetheless, Descartes's *metaphysics,* which posits an infinite subject as the ground of all finite subjects and as guarantor of the (possible) veracity of our thought, remains an attractive option.

The Task

In our search for the metaphysical Descartes we will move from Descartes's methodological and scientific writings to the *Meditations*. This approach would not have disturbed Descartes, who, in order to establish the unity of science against the Schools, planned to argue from a "continuous application of *a single and identical method* to all the various sciences, for the possibility and practicability of its application in common would imply that the sciences together are nothing else than the very unity of human reason."[7] The *Meditations* turn out to contain a more coherent position when approached from his other writings. In opposition to most contemporary treatments of Descartes, I suggest that the themes of perfection and infinity produce the most unified and most convincing interpretation of the Cartesian opus taken as a whole.

It is interesting to find that many of those whose chief interest is Cartesian method still grant the centrality and indispensability of an explicitly metaphysical decision concerning Descartes's views.[8] Cartesian method presupposes Cartesian metaphysics. One should decide to hold (or reject) Descartes's theory of God not because it is inescapable or its foundational premises indubitable but, as with all such positions, because of its systematic explanatory power.

(A note on manner of citation: The English-speaking student of Descartes is well served by new translations. All major published and unpublished works of Descartes have been recently translated, and an excellent selection out of his correspondence is available.[9] I thus cite only the Cartesian title and sec-

---

7. Cited in L. J. Beck, *The Method of Descartes: A Study of the Regulae* (Oxford: Clarendon, 1952; repr. New York: Garland, 1987), 307. That such a unitary thesis indeed exists is the central argument of Beck's book.

8. Take Beck, for example. After eleven chapters on Descartes's method, he notes: "these statements of position [sc. on the question of Descartes's method] remain fundamentally unsatisfactory since the explanation of Descartes' vital modification of the 'purely mathematical' method lies in a metaphysical theory, of which the truth itself lies outside any methodological discussion. There cannot therefore be any final decision until the metaphysical court of appeal has been reached" (*Method of Descartes*, 255).

9. *The Philosophical Writings of Descartes*, 2 vols., trans. John Cottingham, Robert Stoothoff, and Dugald Murdoch (Cambridge: Cambridge Univ. Press, 1985), now replaces the older two-volume translation by Haldane and Ross. For selections from the correspondence, see *Descartes: Philosophical Letters*, trans. Anthony Kenny (Oxford: Oxford Univ. Press, 1970; repr. Oxford: Blackwell, 1980); and *Descartes: His Moral Philosophy and Psychology*, trans. John J. Blom (New York: NYU Press, 1978). For complete translations of works abridged in Cottingham et al., see *René Descartes: The World*, trans. M. S. Mahoney (New York: Abaris, 1979); *Descartes: Discourse on Method, Optics, Geometry and Meteorology*, trans. P. J. Olscamp (Indianapolis: Bobbs-Merrill, 1965); and *Descartes, Principles of Philosophy*,

tion, or letter and date, along with the page references from the standard critical edition of Descartes's complete works.[10] Since these citations are sufficient for locating the passage in English translation, page references to specific English editions are not included.)

THE METHODOLOGICAL
AND SCIENTIFIC WRITINGS

I begin with these particular writings rather than with the *Meditations* for two reasons. First, the *Meditations* are a narrative account of discovery and, as such, are open to a broad variety of interpretations. They have also been the object of much recent attention.[11] Since the careful analyses of this work by contemporary philosophers make a strong case that there is little hope for establishing its soundness as an independent argument,[12] it seems clear that any positive appropriation of Descartes will have to rely on a different approach. Second, the problematic emphasis on the epistemological/foundationalist Descartes in the recent literature is rooted primarily in readings based (solely or primarily) on

---

trans. V. R. and R. P. Miller (Dordrecht: Reidel, 1983). Also important is *Descartes' Conversation with Burman,* trans. J. Cottingham (Oxford: Clarendon, 1976).

10. C. Adam and P. Tannery, eds., *Oeuvres de Descartes,* 12 vols., rev. ed. (Paris: Vrin/ CNRS, 1964-76). For the correspondence I have generally used *Descartes: Correspondance,* 8 vols., ed. and with accompanying French translations by Charles Adam and G. Milhaud (Paris: Félix Alcan, 1936). References to this work are preceded by "AM."

11. So, e.g., a rash of analytic monographs on Descartes in the late 1970s is focused either solely or mostly on the *Meditations:* E. M. Curley, *Descartes against the Skeptics* (Cambridge: Harvard Univ. Press, 1978); Felix Grayeff, *Descartes* (London: Goodall, 1977); Leon Pearl, *Descartes* (Boston: Twayne, 1977); Bernard Williams, *Descartes: The Project of Pure Inquiry* (Brighton, Sussex: Harvester, 1978); Wilson, *Descartes.*

12. Bernard Williams speaks of "these hopeless arguments for the existence of God" (*Descartes,* 210), and tells us that a historical analysis of Descartes will "yield an object essentially ambiguous, incomplete, imperfectly determined by the author's and his contemporaries' understanding" (10) (presumably in contrast to his own philosophy). Curley tends to view Descartes's theology as coterminous with the proofs (partly due to his stress on reading Descartes in the context of late Renaissance skepticism), so that the failure of the arguments leads him to ask "whether any of Descartes' other central claims in the *Meditations* can be saved from the wreckage of his system" (*Descartes against the Skeptics,* ix; cf. 125, 141). See also Wilson, *Descartes,* 100. Even Hiram Caton, who emphatically does not wish to be classed with the analytic interpreters of Descartes, suggests that the *Meditations* may be "an elaborately contrived logical chaos"; see his "Analytic History of Philosophy: The Case of Descartes," *Philosophical Forum* 12 (1981): 273-94, quotation 282.

the *Meditations*. As we saw, these authors have concentrated on Descartes's method, on the *cogito* argument, on the proofs for God's existence, and on the charge that the arguments are circular, whereas few studies include the context for and significance of Descartes's use of the concept of God. The core of Descartes's work, I shall argue, emerges rather differently if one proceeds from a systematic exposition of Descartes's work as a whole — or, say, from a treatment based on the *Principles* alone.

I therefore begin with Descartes's other major publications — the *Rules*, the *Discourse*, and the *Principles*, with some additional help from the correspondence and the *Conversation with Burman*. The goal is to unearth and to reconstruct the underlying tenets of the Cartesian project. I introduce the *cogito* argument and the theistic proofs as only part of this project — not with the goal of deciding whether the arguments are sound (they are not), but to see what they reveal about Cartesian metaphysics. We will discover that specific theological themes supply the framework for Descartes's discussions of method and gradually move to the foreground in the *Discourse* and the *Principles*. Only when we have nailed down the place of these themes in Cartesian thought will we be in an adequate position to evaluate this nonfoundationalist rereading of the *Meditations*.

Rules for the Direction of the Mind (the *Regulae*)

The *Rules*, probably written in 1628 but not published during Descartes's lifetime, contain little direct reference to Descartes's theory of God. Their importance lies instead in laying a methodological foundation for a new way of doing philosophy. Descartes here opposes what he calls the dictates of "common sense" to the Scholastic systems, which he viewed as a series of complicated definitions and overly abstract arguments.[13] The aim — of the *Rules* and of "our studies" in general — is "to direct the mind with a view to forming true and sound judgments about whatever comes before it" (Rule 1; X,359). Descartes's rules vary from very general ("we need a method if we are to investigate the truth of things," Rule 4) to very specific ("once we have found the equations, we must carry out the operations . . . never using multiplication when division is in order," Rule 20).

No metaphysical foundation for the rules is given in this early work. Hu-

---

13. Descartes also uses this term in "The Search for Truth" as a metamethodological description of his procedure: "all we need for discovering the truth on the most difficult issues, is, I think, common sense *(sensum communem)*, to give it its ordinary name" (X,518).

man cognitive functioning can only be read from how we actually proceed intellectually. In this work scientific and mathematical reflection supply the paradigm cases for the method. Descartes's success in applying them to various philosophical questions, he says, gives him sufficient reason to believe in their validity. But in another sense the rules do have an implicit metaphysical basis. For we are the animal who is so designed that we function best by following these rules. We know from other writings (esp. *The Passions of the Soul*) that the nature of mind is not to be separated from the nature of its functioning.[14] Likewise, the best theory of human nature is one that describes how humans actually function *(Treatise on Man)*, and the best theory of the emotions is one that describes how they arise, what their functions for the human person are, and what physiological correlates they have (the *Passions*). In this sense, a strictly methodological book like the *Rules* is not opposed to metaphysical arguments developed elsewhere but is intrinsically linked to them.[15]

The only mention of God in the *Rules* comes as an example of "things that are necessarily conjoined." Along with the example, "I understand, therefore I have a mind distinct from my body," Descartes lists "I am, therefore God exists" (Rule 12; X,421-22). It is interesting that he would emphasize this example as an instance of necessary conjunction. If Descartes does not actually accept the immediacy of the connection, as some have said in the context of the *Meditations,* why hang it out to dry in such a gratuitous context? There was no need for him to introduce an insincere appeal to immediate knowledge of God here as (some claim) there was in the *Meditations.* Yet when Descartes wishes to find, in passing, a good example of mutually implicating concepts, it is the ordered pair my existence/God's existence that comes to mind. We will have to wait for the *Discourse* to learn why these concepts should be so closely linked in his thought.

14. It is interesting to note that there are close parallels between this conception and Alvin Plantinga's recent appeal to "proper functioning" as the core of a philosophy of religion and the answer to skepticism about religious knowing. See his *Warrant and Proper Function* (New York: Oxford Univ. Press, 1993).

15. This is also the conclusion reached by Beck in his methodological study of the *Regulae (Method of Descartes;* see nn. 7-8 above). See esp. Beck's chap. 11, which argues that Descartes held that "the final explanation of physical phenomena must be based on metaphysical propositions" (p. 256).

The *Discourse on Method and Essays in This Method* (Discours de la Méthode)

The *Discourse,* Descartes's first published writing, appeared in 1637 along with three "essays in this method," the *Optics,* the *Geometry,* and the *Meterology.* As with the *Rules,* the goal here is to provide a commonsense method for arriving at adequate (clear and distinct) knowledge. The method advances in a specific order, first giving the reader justification for accepting as known what one thinks one knows, and then building outward from what one knows most surely to increase the overall scope of one's knowledge. The role of metaphysics is clearer here than in the *Rules.* As Descartes begins to move from method to content, the indissoluble link of his method and his philosophical theology emerges: doubt, and the pursuit of clear and distinct principles, give rise immediately to a specific theory of God.

The Centrality of Theology

After a series of autobiographical comments and a quick sketch of his moral code, Descartes comes to the core of his position in part 4. Only after these central doctrines are in place does he begin to suggest some first implications for the sciences of anatomy and physiology, sketching out his current projects and what he intends to explore in the future. The place of metaphysics in his scientific work is thus indisputable in the *Discourse;* such broader questions, he holds, need to be settled before one can proceed with the desired increase in knowledge.

Descartes tells us in his autobiographical sketch that "I revered our theology" (part 1; VI,8). Still, it is clear from the structure of the work and from the issues he selects for treatment that the methods of the theologians need revising. The theology with which Descartes was familiar was the theology of the Schools, and it is their convoluted method that he opposes most fundamentally. The theologians have been unsuccessful: "There is still no point in [their work] which is not disputed and hence doubtful" (ibid.). Further, once a metaphysical position has been established, Descartes is more concerned than most theologians to see what implications it will have for the natural philosophy (science) of his day. Nonetheless, the idea of God plays a no less central role in his suggested revisions: God is the source of the "light" that enables us "to distinguish truth from falsehood" (part 3; VI,27). Descartes may wish to emancipate his reader from the strictures of tradition, but he leaves the theological grounding for human knowledge untouched.

Part 4 (VI,31-40), then, forms the core of the *Discourse.* Before turning to its content, we should pause to note that Descartes's correspondence during this period supports the interpretation I have just given. In many of his letters Descartes is searching for a philosophical theology that will ground physical knowledge without inhibiting empirical progress.[16] A number reveal his overriding preoccupation with finalizing and publishing his theological position. In the letter to Mersenne of Nov. 25, 1630, he had proclaimed that his principal goals were "to prove the existence of God [and] of that of our souls, when they are separate from the body, whence follows their immortality" (I,181). Again in March 1636, he writes that in the *Discourse* "I reveal a part of my method, I seek to demonstrate the existence of God and of a soul separate from the body, and I add many other things which will not be, I believe, disagreeable to the reader" (to Mersenne; I,339, AM 1:301). The *Discourse,* he writes soon after its appearance, is about the metaphysical notions that are indispensable for physics, and concerns the existence of God, which "is the most important part *(la pièce la plus importante)*" (to P. Vatier, 2/22/1638; I,560, AM 2:134).

It appears from the letters between 1630 and 1638 that Descartes was growing increasingly convinced of his theology, but had some hesitation about publishing his speculations in natural philosophy — a hesitation of which, incidentally, there are signs right up to the end of his life. Given this background, the condemnation of Galileo in 1633 may even have been a welcome excuse for Descartes to cease work on his unfinished great work in cosmology, of which *The World (Le Monde ou le Traité de la Lumière)* was a part. But there is no question that he was eager to get the theological part of his philosophy into print. On July 13, 1638, he wrote to Morin,

> I believe that the particular truths, which I have treated in my *Essays* (assuming of course that they were true) give greater opportunity to judge that I must have some knowledge of the general causes on which they are dependent than I would have had without them. And because it was only the general causes which served as the subject of that other treatise, I don't think I made such an incredible advance when I wrote what I did.[17]

16. See Henri Gouhier's excellent treatment, *La pensée religieuse de Descartes* (Paris: Vrin, 1972), esp. 91-96. Gouhier's own conclusion is that Descartes is to be understood as a religious apologist and that this concern motivates his metaphysics and controls his natural scientific work.

17. Descartes, II,201, AM 2:313: "je crois que les vérités particulières, que j'ai traitées en mes *Essais* (au moins si ce sont des vérités), donnent plus d'occasion de juger que je dois avoir quelque connaissance des causes générales dont elles dépendent, que non pas que j'aie pu sans cela les découvrir. Et parce qu'il n'y a que les causes générales qui soient le sujet de cet autre Traité, je ne pense pas avoir rien avancé de fort incroyable, lorsque j'ai écrit que je j'avais fait."

He had written already in 1630 that even the eternal truths depend on God, "for the existence of God is the first and the most eternal of all the truths that can be, and the only truth from which all others proceed." The problem is that "most men consider God only as an infinite and incomprehensible being, who is the sole author on which all things depend"; because their view of God is "no higher" than it is, they "can easily become atheists."[18] Descartes attempts to respond to such persons out of his concern "to find an evident demonstration which will lead all the world to believe that God exists"; the remainder of the letter expresses his confidence that he now has the proof that he needs (to Mersenne, 11/25/1630; I,181-82, AM 1:172).

The Question of Perfection

Back to the *Discourse*. After a three-paragraph summary of the "I think, therefore I am" argument, Descartes comes to the proof of God. The overriding framework for the proof is the question of *perfection*. Looking back over the *cogito* argument just presented, Descartes sees that his nature as a doubting being is to be "not wholly perfect" (VI,33). How could he think something more perfect than himself, he continues? Its source could not be himself, and it could not come from nothing. Its source could only be "from some nature that was in fact more perfect." So God must exist. In briefest form, the argument amounts to *dubito, ergo Deus est:* I doubt, therefore God exists. Gilson comments: "Thus, finding in doubt itself, through which it knows its existence, the idea of the perfect, which then implies the existence of God, thought discovers two existences in a single intuition."[19]

From here Descartes then makes the transition directly to his version of the ontological argument, leading one to suspect a similarly close connection between the same two theistic proofs in the *Meditations*. Looking at the idea of a perfect being, "I found that this included existence in the same way as . . . the idea of a triangle includes the equality of its three angles to two right angles. . . .

18. Letter to Mersenne, 5/6/1630; I,150, AM 1:139: "car l'existence de Dieu est la première et la plus éternelle de toutes les vérités qui peuvent être, et la seule d'où procèdent toutes les autres." Yet "la plupart des hommes ne considèrent pas Dieu comme un être infini et incompréhensible, et qui est le seul auteur duquel toutes choses dépendent"; thus they "peuvent aisément devenir athées."

19. E. Gilson, *Descartes, Discours de la Méthode: Texte et commentaire* (Paris: Vrin, 1925), 314: "Ainsi, trouvant par le doute même, dans lequel elle saisit son existence, l'idée de parfait qui implique l'existence de Dieu, la pensée découvre cette double existence dans une seule intuition."

Thus I concluded that it is at least as certain as any geometrical proof that God, who is this perfect being, is or exists" (VI,36).

We will come back to the question of the cogency of these arguments when we discuss the *Meditations;* here, as noted above, we want to tap them at a few points for the theology they release. First, we discover one clear leap not justified by Descartes's argument. In the first argument he jumps from "a being more perfect than I was" (which is a valid inference from the argument's premises to that point) to a being "even possessing in itself *all* the perfections of which I could have any idea" (which is not valid). But why would an otherwise unbroken argument make this leap here? Descartes needs not just a more perfect being but an all-perfect being; only the latter allows him to add "that is, God." The text suggests that Descartes is striving to develop a theology of unlimited perfection, and is seeking the arguments that will compel his readers to the same conclusion. Second, the first proof — from the idea of God to the existence of God via the notion of perfection — is the only passage in the *Discourse,* and one of the few in Descartes's oeuvre as a whole, in which he acknowledges explicitly his reliance on the Scholastic discussion ("here, by your leave, I shall freely use some Scholastic terminology"). The perfection argument, Descartes says, allows him to know that he is not the only being who exists; there had to exist some other, more perfect being "on which I depended and from which I had acquired all that I possessed" (VI,34). Here we have the first signs that at least on the question of perfection his distance from the Scholastic tradition is much smaller than in matters of epistemology or other theistic attributes such as the Trinity.

These two points are linked, and they confirm what we have already seen in the correspondence from this period. As much as Descartes wants to offer a new way of getting to metaphysics (the *Meditations*), and as much as he wants this theological foundation not to interfere with scientific research, the core of his position is not as revisionary as has often been thought. Marjorie Grene's metaphor is apt, whether or not one agrees with her final judgment: "Descartes has cleaned out the lumber room of scholastic thought so thoroughly as to leave what seems a barely habitable shelter."[20] The contrasts are remarkable; one need only compare Descartes on perfection with Duns Scotus or Suarez on the same subject. However sparse the lodgings, the core of the position is remarkably similar.

Can we take a first stab at the underlying theology that peeps through in the *Discourse?* Descartes declares as basic the relation of dependence to independence, finitude to infinitude. He thus begins his reflection with an imper-

---

20. Marjorie Grene, *Descartes* (Minneapolis: Univ. of Minnesota Press, 1985), 104.

fect (finite) being and immediately thereafter with the perfect (infinite) being on which it depends, arguing for a relationship between them so close that everything else is "less certain" than my knowledge of God's existence (VI,37). The framework is, one might say, more Neoplatonic than Aristotelian. The perfect being possesses the transcendentals: One, goodness, truth. We "participate" in it *(je participois de l'être parfait);* he speaks of "what little of the perfect being I participated in" (VI,35). Even more clearly Neoplatonic (or directly Augustinian?), imperfection and nothingness are connected. Descartes notes that false ideas are confused and obscure, "for in that respect they participate in nothingness" *(elles participent du néant),* and then adds, "that is, they are in us in this confused state only because we are not wholly perfect" (VI,38). The converse holds, he continues: There can be no falsity in (or from) the creating and sustaining being, just as no truth or perfection can proceed from nothingness (VI,39). In this schema, there is a correlation between one's level of perfection and the percentage of one's ideas that are true.

From Theology to Science

The remainder of the *Discourse* is consistent with these conclusions. In summarizing his "treatise" (of which *The World* and the *Treatise on Man* are parts), Descartes contrasts his presentation with the multiple assumptions made by the Schools, claiming not to have based his arguments on any other principle than "the infinite perfections of God" (VI,43). Out of his anthropology he lists as most important the conclusion that the human soul, in contrast to animals, is immortal; yet an even more serious mistake, he notes, is to deny the existence of God (VI,59). (By contrast, he admits [p. 61] that his method of clear and distinct ideas might be wrong.) The method remains unambiguously rationalist. Descartes's goal is to discover the "principles or first causes" of everything that exists in the world: "To this end I considered nothing but God alone . . . [which allowed me to] derive those principles only from certain seeds of truth which are naturally in our souls" (VI,63-64). Interestingly, he omits the *cogito* argument from both summaries of his argument.

When one turns then to the three "essays in the method" that follow — the *Optics,* the *Geometry,* and the *Meterology* — it is interesting to note by contrast how *un*metaphysically Descartes proceeds. The essays do help us (as he claims) to understand the method described in the *Discourse* and the *Rules:* They are certainly clear and simple in their descriptions and theoretical foundations. But they do not claim to be giving the "real" foundation of things, as Descartes does claim for his metaphysics in both published writings and correspondence. Note for example the different status ascribed to the conclusions of

the *Optics:* since he is concerned only with the physical perception and rework-
ing of light by the body, "I need not attempt to say what is its true nature"
(VI,83). The fissure between the scientific and metaphysical work is evident
also in the *Geometry,* which he understands as finitistic.[21] However much Descartes believed in the truth of his scientific conclusions, he clearly assigned
them a lower epistemic status than the metaphysical core argument sketched in
part 4 of the *Discourse.* The famous freedom of Cartesian science from theological interference is bought with a price.

In conclusion, the stance of the *Discourse* is unambiguous: Cartesian
methodology and epistemology depend on Cartesian theology. Finite agents
have their knowledge, and their being, only to the extent that they participate in
God. This all-perfect being is closer to us than a highest category or first principle; in a Neoplatonic sense, we are said to participate in or receive being from
the one who is the source of all being. The order of ideas is specific: a few clear
first principles must be (Descartes says: have been!) found, and then all other
things that are knowable will clearly and distinctly follow by the natural light of
reason.

The *Principles of Philosophy* (Principia Philosophiae)

The *Principles,* first published in Latin in 1644, give a "synthetic" presentation of
Descartes's system. The position here is, he claims, the same as that of the *Meditations,* except for the difference that the latter follows the "order of discovery" and
the former the "order of exposition."[22] Since Descartes adopted the style of the
Schools in the *Principles,* hoping to produce a textbook that would replace the Aristotelian texts that they used, one finds a more explicit acknowledgment of parallels with Scholastic thought than in the *Meditations.* This text also offers a
clearer statement of Descartes's final views than the *Meditations,* which had presented his voyage of discovery without organizing its results in a systematic manner. The *Principles'* four books are made up of over five hundred articles, moving
in order through metaphysics, the basic principles of physics, a general theory of
the history and nature of the universe, and a brief theory of the origin of the earth
and selected physical phenomena. Part I, particularly the concepts of infinity, perfection, and God, forms the heart of the work and the framework — indeed, even
some of the specific content — for the scientific books that follow.

21. Jules Vuillemin, *Mathématique et métaphysique chez Descartes* (Paris: Presses
Universitaires de France, 1960), 140.
22. See *Conversation with Burman,* V,152-53.

In part 1 Descartes repeats the well-known arguments for the necessity of universal doubt and for the resultant certain knowledge that "I" exist. He then notes, consistent with my conclusions from the *Discourse*, that the *cogito* is not the foundation for knowledge: "Knowledge of all other things depends on the knowledge of God" (art. 13, VIIIA,9). God's existence can be proved in two ways: via an inquiry into the cause of the idea of God, and from the nature of the idea of God itself. In contrast to the *Meditations*, though, the ontological proof comes first here: we have the idea of a being, God, who has the attribute of necessary existence (art. 14). The causal argument — God must exist as the cause of the idea of God because we cannot be the cause of this idea — comes later as a "second reason" for asserting God's existence (art. 18). Descartes's higher priority here is to work out what is contained implicitly within the idea of God itself.

Note what binds these two central proofs: the idea of a being with "supreme perfections" *(summas perfectiones)*, that is, having all perfections and having each to a supreme degree (cf. art. 22). As a result, Descartes argues, we recognize that we are finite — that is, in comparison to divine infinity (art. 19), which leads immediately to the ontological conclusion that God is the source of our being (art. 20). The path to knowledge, and even the epistemic foundation for science, is thus unmistakably theological; one must "pass from knowledge of God to knowledge of his creatures" (art. 24). His fundamental method, we now see, is to clarify "the knowledge of God himself" and only then "to deduce an explanation of the things created by him" (ibid.). Since we cannot fully know infinite perfections (art. 19), our deductions will be incomplete, scientific knowledge will be limited, and we remain reliant on divine revelation in some areas (e.g., the Incarnation or Trinity, art. 25).

The Infinite and the Indefinite

The theological core of the *Principles* is, moreover, the ground for Descartes's controversial insistence that things in the world that appear to be without limits — the extension of the world, the division of matter, the number of stars — should be called "indefinite" *(indefinita)* rather than infinite (art. 26). One must speak of indefinites rather than infinites in the world because we do not know the physical limits of these things, whereas we do have a positive reason to assert that God is without limits (art. 27). Given the centrality of the concept of God in what has preceded, it is rather surprising to find commentators stumbling over the infinite/indefinite distinction, or even accusing him of bad faith at this point. For example, Alexandre Koyré calls Descartes's refusal to label the world infinite "a pseudo-distinction" and "by no means convincing":

"To assert the indefiniteness of the world, or of space, does not mean [as Descartes thought], negatively, that perhaps it has limits that we are unable to ascertain; it means, quite positively, that it has none because it would be contradictory to posit them."[23]

But Koyré abstracts, inexplicably, from the context in which art. 27 appears. In the structure of Descartes's thought, as we have seen, knowledge of the world is grounded in the ontological distinction between infinite and finite (imperfect and perfect, independent and dependent) beings; this insight is the first and most immediate insight of the Cartesian reflecting subject. It is no coincidence that Descartes introduces the indefinite/infinite distinction at this point, immediately following his statement of the theological source for all natural knowledge (art. 24). For it is crucial for the coherence of his system to answer the potential objection that there are infinites in the world and hence that God and world are not, as he claims, qualitatively distinct.

In stressing the finite/infinite distinction, Descartes establishes the basic framework for the remainder of the *Principles,* if not for his opus as a whole. In part 2, for example, while working out the implications of his theory of extension, he maintains that it is not possible that there be any intrinsically indivisible particles (*atomi, sive materiae partes ex naturâ suâ indivisibiles;* art. 20, VIIIA,51). In the same vein, he argues that the world should have no limits to its extension, since the idea of extension in a given space and the idea of corporeal substance are the same. Matter occupies "all imaginable space," and we can indefinitely extend our imagination (art. 21). Still, we cannot obtain any positive understanding of limitlessness in the case of matter; we discover only our own inability to establish limits. As Gouhier points out, the argument is a theological one, since it turns on the theological significance of the human ability to proceed indefinitely in extending extension: "In that the finite spirit becomes temporal, the power to advance indefinitely is like a reflection of the infinity of the One who is his being, and all his being, in act."[24] If the later books of the *Principles* usually avoid (with one exception) speaking of the world as infinite, it is because they depend crucially on *God's* being so.

Reflecting on the nature of the concept of the infinite (a task to be pursued further in the next chapter) supports Descartes's position. We are unable to think limits to space and time. Still, it does not therefore follow that there are

23. Alexandre Koyré, *From the Closed World to the Infinite Universe* (Baltimore: Johns Hopkins Univ. Press, 1957), 109, 116, 124, respectively. But if Descartes holds the latter position, Koyré complains, it is pointless for him not to go ahead and call the world infinite.

24. Henri Gouhier, *La pensée métaphysique de Descartes* (Paris: Vrin, 1962), 200-201: "dans le devenir temporel de l'esprit fini, le pouvoir d'avancer indéfiniment est comme le reflet de l'infinité de Celui qui est son être et tout son être en acte."

none. We can encounter massive power (say, in the case of energy, that of a supernova or the sum of the energy of all stars in the universe) without having any ground to speak of actually infinite power. We would have to negate the notion of *all limits* — which can only mean negating the finite as such — in order to think the truly (positively) infinite, the infinite in duration (eternity), the infinitely powerful (omnipotence), and so forth. But this would be an explicitly theological move — precisely the move that Descartes actually makes.

To anticipate a later development, it is interesting to find Georg Cantor, the founder of modern set theory, also granting the theological significance of the absolutely infinite. His work transforms Descartes's simple dichotomy into at least a trichotomy. Descartes's "indeterminate" became in the differential calculus (Leibniz, Newton) the "potential" infinite. A potential infinite is "a quantity that is variable and that has grown beyond all finite limits." Infinitesimals are "quantities that we think of as indefinitely small as a [mathematical] aid"; since infinitesimals no longer appear in the final results of computations in calculus, Cantor like Leibniz viewed them as fictions.[25] But with Cantor's theory of transfinite numbers, it finally became possible to view some infinite quantities as actual infinites and not as mere fictions. For Cantor, an actual infinite (in contrast to potential infinites such as the infinitesimals) is "a quantum that is in itself firm and constant, yet which lies beyond all finite quantities."[26]

We could say, pace Descartes, that there are two kinds of actual infinites — or, better, we should say that we now have the conceptual means to speak of Descartes's *in*definites as definite, though infinite, quantities. Cantor's infinite sets ("transfinites") are actually infinite and yet can still be increased *(ein noch Vermehrbares)*; hence some infinites are greater than others. However — and here is the other kind of infinite — transfinites must be distinguished from the absolutely infinite, which is "to be thought of as something that essentially cannot be increased and is therefore beyond all mathematical determination." Cantor defined V as the Absolute, or the class of all sets; more recent formalizations of set theory use the symbol Ω (capital omega) for Absolute In-

---

25. See Georg Cantor, *Zur Lehre vom Transfiniten: Gesammelte Abhandlungen aus der Zeitschrift für Philosophie und philosophische Kritik*, vol. 1 (Halle, 1890), quoted in H. Meschkowski, *Das Problem des Unendlichen: Mathematische und philosophische Texte von Bolzano, Gutberlet, Cantor, Dedekind* (Ausg. München: Deutscher Taschenbuch-Verlag, 1974).

26. Georg Cantor, "Über die verschiedenen Standpunkte in bezug auf das aktuelle Unendliche," in *Zur Lehre vom Transfiniten* (Halle, 1890), 1st section; repr. in *Das Problem des Unendlichen*, ed. Herbert Meschkowski (Munich: Deutscher Taschenbuch, 1974), 116-23, here 121: "ein in sich festes, konstantes, jedoch jenseits aller endlichen Größen liegendes Quantum."

finity. In both cases, the absolutely infinite cannot be conceptually specified. There are two reasons: "the class of all sets" cannot itself be conceived as a set without contradiction, and hence cannot be properly defined within set theory; and Ω cannot be defined, for any property predicated of it must also hold of ordinals other than Ω as well.[27]

This threefold distinction stemming from Cantor (finites, transfinites, the absolute infinite) solves the limit problem more neatly than Descartes's view was able to. It is not the Absolute but the transfinite quantities that form the ideal limit (*die ideale Grenze*) of the finite. This allows the Absolute to be thought not merely as a negative concept — as the limit or extension of the finite — but exclusively as that which is the maximum thinkable in every respect, that which cannot be increased in any conceivable way.

What bearing does this mathematical discussion have on Descartes's theological question concerning the nature of an infinite being? Such a being would be, strictly speaking, inconceivable. Still, one might begin to think it by way of negation, on analogy with the mathematical case. Cantor's absolute infinity is not the set of all sets; it cannot be expressed within set theory; but it would amount to, roughly, the *class* of all sets. Likewise, we cannot fully conceive the infinity of Descartes's God, though we might understand it as something like the lack of all limits that one encounters in certain phenomena of natural philosophy, only now taken in a positive rather than a negative sense. As we will discover, Descartes emphasizes this positive quality by speaking of divine perfections, or positive qualities. The nature of God is to be perfectly infinite, or to have infinite perfections.

The Correspondence with More

To stress Descartes's distinction between the indefinite and the infinite as I have done is not to say that he was free of all confusion on the matter. Descartes often calls the will infinite[28] — although, since the human will lacks the infinite knowledge available to the divine will, its power (and hence its action) must be more limited than God's. Further, later in the *Principles* he speaks of "an infi-

27. These questions form the central theme of Rudy Rucker, *Infinity and the Mind: The Science and Philosophy of the Infinite* (Boston: Birkhäuser, 1982), e.g., 78-87. Rucker asks how we could discourse rationally about an inconceivable object like Ω: "I would respond that Ω is a *given*, an object of our immediate pre-rational experience. . . . We have a primitive concept of infinity"; and he speculates: "This concept is inspired . . . by the same deep substrate of mind that conditions religious thought" (p. 81).

28. See, e.g., *Meditations* 4, *Principles*, part 1, art. 35 (though "in a certain sense" infinite), and the letter to Mersenne of Dec. 25, 1639 (II,628).

nite, or indefinite, division of the various particles of matter" (VIIIA,59), a confusion of the terms studiously avoided in part 1. In the French edition, light radiates "instantly," thus having infinite velocity (part 4, art. 187). At the beginning of the correspondence with More, Descartes is unambiguous about the distinction:

> For it is God alone whom I conceive to be positively infinite; for the rest, such as the extension of the world, the number of parts into which matter is divisible, and similar [things], I do not profess to know whether or not they are truly infinite *(an sint simpliciter infinita)*. I know only that I do not find in them any end, and thus I say that they are indefinite. (2/5/1649; V,267ff., AM 8:131)

But he then grants that we cannot actually imagine some place on the other side *(ne quis extra illam locus fingi queat)*, and that wherever one imagines space one must conceive matter. Consequently, saying that space is indefinitely extended amounts to saying that it is extended beyond everything that humans are able to conceive. "You are a very cautious man, and quite modest," More responds (*Nae tu hic cautus homo es, et eleganter modestus;* 3/5/1649; V,298ff., AM 8:168). "For doesn't your answer imply precisely that the world *is* infinitely extended?" Note that the problem is intensified when one includes Descartes's admission, in the conversation with Burman, that the world is indefinite from our point of view and *may be* in itself infinite (*et sic nostri respectu sunt indefinita, quin etiam forsan infinita;* V,167).

The theological bottom line in this whole debate is unmistakable when one reads Descartes's response to More. In the end he grants that it is "repugnant" to his ideas to assign any limit *(terminum)* to the world, and adds that he can perceive no limits to it. Still, though, he does not want to call the world infinite. Interestingly, the final reason comes from the theory of perfection rather than from the theory of the infinite: "Because I perceive that God is greater than the world, not by reason of his extension which, as I have frequently said, is not appropriate to God, but by reason of his perfection" (*non ratione extensionis . . . sed ratione perfectionis;* 4/15/1649; V,340ff., AM 8:210). It is as if Descartes is granting that infinity alone is not enough to preserve this central distinction of his system; it only works when combined with the notion of perfection. Once again, we note a conceptual link between infinity and perfection: both are indispensable, and reflecting on one leads inevitably to the other. (Yet we will find that this link becomes the Achilles' heal of Cartesian metaphysics if, as I argue in chapter 4, the philosophy of perfection fails at the hands of its greatest defender, G. W. Leibniz.)

Science and the Attributes of God

We have found that the distinction between finite world and infinite (perfect) God is central to Descartes's systemic statement of his position in the *Principles*. Note, though, that other attributes of the infinite being play important roles in this work as well. In the transition to part 2, while summarizing the rules for correct thought, Descartes adds after "there is a God" and "we depend on him" the strong claim that "a consideration of his attributes enables us to investigate the truth of other things, since he is their cause" (part 1, art. 75). It is clear from the context that this theological ground is a necessary condition for scientific investigation; at moments (not Descartes's greatest moments!) it even threatens to become a sufficient condition. Not infrequently in what follows, the immensity of God, or God's infinite power, is used to ground specific tenets within physics. For instance, in the reflections that begin part 3 on the visible universe, Descartes exhorts his reader once again to recall "the infinite power and goodness of God" as the context for what follows (VIIIA,80). Descartes's "hypothetical" reconstruction of the origin of the world, the framework within which he develops much of his physics, presupposes the infinite goodness of God as its necessary condition.

God "in his omnipotence" (French edition only) must have created matter, one reads in the section on God as the primary cause of motion (part 2, art. 36). The laws of nature, which are the "secondary" causes of motions in bodies, can be developed only after specifying God's role as primary cause. And humans can know these (what physicists would today call the primary laws of physics) only because of a divine attribute: immutability (art. 37). Descartes also concludes, based on God's immutability, that there must be a fixed quantity of motion (art. 36). The immensity of God (and, Descartes added in the French, also the perfection of the creator's power) forces us to grant that there may be further, unseen stars, even that they may be in motion (part 3, art. 29; VIIIA,92) — and hence that the earth moves too (though Descartes is cautious here, insisting that the earth is still stationary relative to the stars). Epistemologically, he later adds, we can conclude that the highly probable is true as long as God is not a deceiver (art. 43).

Finally, it is important to note that Descartes drew no distinction in principle between creation and conservation: God is as active at each moment, and in qualitatively the same way, as he was at the moment of the creation of matter.[29] One consequence of this view is that the understanding of power in Des-

---

29. See part 2, art. 36 (VIIIA,61-62); and Martial Gueroult, "Métaphysique et physique de la force chez Descartes et chez Malebranche," *Revue de Métaphysique et de Morale* 59

cartes is thoroughly theological; as he writes in his last letter to More, "Moving force is the force of God himself conserving as much displacement in matter as he put in it at the first moment of creation" (August 1649; V,403). God is the supreme craftsman (part 4, art. 204) and the condition for our ability to distinguish truth from falsehood at all (art. 206). All of these factors make it somewhat ironic that Descartes has been credited by history with supplying the major impulse toward deism.[30]

The Ontology of the *Principles*

A word should be said about the ontology of the *Principles*. One has the impression that Descartes, like Thomas Aquinas but in his own fashion, is seeking to incorporate both the substance-based ontology of Aristotle and the participation-based ontology of the Platonic traditions, yet without the detailed conceptual harmonization that typifies Thomas. Descartes presupposes substances, things that can exist on their own, along with modes, qualities, and attributes of substances (part 1, arts. 51-57). Each substance has a principal attribute, either thought or extension, which is its essence.[31] At the same time, alongside this substantival metaphysics Descartes employs another framework, which plays a no less important role in his work. We have already seen the kernel of it: the dichotomy between independent being (God) and all finite beings, who exist only through their participation in God. In the *Principles* Descartes insists repeatedly on the dependence of all knowledge on the existence of an all-powerful, nondeceiving God. Without the conserving work of God, matter would not continue to exist: "God imparted various motions to the parts of matter when he first created them, and he now preserves all this matter in the same way, and by the same process, by which he originally created it" (part 2, art. 36). The ontology of participation comes to clearest expression in the initial definition of substance: "There is only one substance which can be understood to depend on no other thing whatsoever, namely God. In the case of all other substances, we perceive that they can exist only with the help of God's concurrence" (part 1, art. 51).

(1954), translated by Stephen Gaukroger as "The Metaphysics and Physics of Force in Descartes," in Gaukroger, ed., *Descartes: Philosophy, Mathematics and Physics*, chap. 9.

30. But cf. *The World*, chap. 7: the constancy (immutability) of God's action in conservation means that all change will have to be accounted for on *nontheological* grounds. Physical explanations can therefore only be given in terms of the laws of nature (XI,37).

31. Part 1, art. 53; part 2, art. 42; see also Stephen Schiffer, "Descartes on His Essence," *Philosophical Review* 85 (1976): 21-43 (definition of essence, pp. 22-23). Schiffer's treatment emphasizes the inconsistencies in Descartes's doctrine of essence.

It is important to see, on the one hand, that this "strong" definition of substance follows unambiguously from the central tenet of Descartes's philosophy, viz. the distinction between finite and infinite. Since the *cogito* immediately and primordially recognizes itself as dependent, the ultimacy of the infinite is expressed by saying that it alone is truly substance. On the other hand, Descartes cannot allow the one substance completely to usurp the agency of dependent substances, since that would destroy the realm of clearly and distinctly perceived items of knowledge on which knowledge of the world is to rest. Unfortunately, he provides no detailed or adequate treatment of how these two perspectives are to be united. (We will find in chapters 7–9 that the Spinoza tradition faced precisely the same difficulties and found, ultimately, a better solution.)

Descartes's failure to unite these two ontological approaches (independent things vs. omnidependence on God) sets the stage for the developments in philosophical theology over the next several centuries. In Spinoza's hands, Descartes's halfhearted substantivalism was discarded and the criterion of absolute independence for substance given unlimited sway. Only one substance exists; all other so-called substances become modes of the One. Conversely, the tradition of British empiricism (excluding Berkeley) could be said to have abandoned the ontological unity grounded in the one God, granting instead unlimited primacy to the individual substances via the atomic givens of sense perception. Nonetheless, perhaps Descartes was right to attempt to hold onto both frameworks, despite the resultant tensions, rather than demanding that one or the other be eliminated, for both serve an indispensable role. There could be no knowledge of the world if we could not isolate parts of it, "objects," and predicate of them qualities, specify their interactions, and so on. The perspective of science, for example, requires one to insist on a relative independence. At the same time, an ontology of levels of reality, each one participating in a higher and more unified level and rising up toward a level of total unification, provides the greatest conceptual unity that a metaphysical system could attain (short of the *advaita* Vedanta claim that all distinctions are illusory). The consequences of this conceptual unity, however, include the doctrine of ontological dependence and the necessity of divine preservation for the world's continued existence. (Note that these consequences may be unavoidable for any position that espouses a creation ex nihilo.)

In practice Descartes, pragmatist or closet pluralist that he was, allowed his contemporary context to determine which facet of his ontology he would emphasize. When he was fighting for the independence of scientific inquiry — and this characterizes most of his epistemology — he had recourse to a pluralistic world of distinct items of knowledge: "I call a perception 'distinct' if . . . it is so sharply separated from all other perceptions that it contains within itself only what is clear" (part 1, art. 45). By contrast, when he was insisting on the theological foundation for the new physics, as in the responses to Hobbes and Gassendi (3rd and 5th Objections), he stressed the ontological dependence. The same holds also — even especially, as we will see below — for the frequent contexts in which Descartes argued from the concept of perfection. Whether the two perspectives can finally be reconciled will concern us further in chapter 3.

Conclusion

How is one to judge a work such as the *Principles?* Philosophers of science often emphasize the paradigm change brought about by seventeenth-century physics, quoting as an epigram Descartes's words in part 2: "The only principles which I accept, or require, in physics are those of geometry and pure mathematics; these principles explain all natural phenomena, and enable us to provide quite certain demonstrations regarding them" (art. 64). Descartes and the other progressive physicists of his time did undoubtedly institute a new program for natural philosophy. The philosophical housecleaning they instigated, which made mathematical physics possible, was far-reaching: the dismissal of final causes,[32] of occult qualities (part 4, art. 187), of substantial forms and real qualities (art. 198), and of complicated categories and taxonomies in general. But it did not include the elimination of the theological foundation for physics. There is no sign that Descartes viewed such a foundation as dispensable, as if his physics could get along quite well without it; neither in published works nor in the correspondence did he offer any other grounding for his physics or suggest that physics might not need one. Thus I find no justification for interpreters' frequent recourse to ad hominem (circumstantial) speculations about the motives for Descartes's theism (e.g., it was meant only to please church authorities, Jesuit professors, etc.). Like Newton, Descartes thought the theological foundation was indispensable to science — even if, like Newton, his work was to give rise to a tradition that would later say, "I have no need of that hypothesis."

In sum, I have argued that Descartes wanted to replace what he took to be a convoluted and constraining (medieval) theological foundation with one that was more accessible to the natural light of reason and more conducive to independent physical research,[33] but which was no less crucial as a foundation. Typ-

---

32. See part 1, art. 28; and, regarding Descartes's vehement attack on final causality, E. Gilson, "Les causes finales et l'idée de l'infini," chap. 3 of part I of Etienne Gilson, *La Liberté chez Descartes et la Théologie* (Paris: Félix Alcan, 1913), 76-127.

33. For more details on the development of that physics, see the essays in Gaukroger, ed., *Descartes: Philosophy, Mathematics and Physics,* esp. John Schuster, "Descartes' *Mathesis universalis,* 1619-28," and Stephen Gaukroger, "Descartes' Project for a Mathematic Physics."

ical for his new approach is the thought experiment that structures parts 3 and 4. Here natural philosophy no longer begins with the biblical account literally understood, which threatened to impose a static (nonevolutionary) creation and which advanced divine interventions in lieu of physical explanations. Instead, in the thought experiment Descartes uses reason to reconstruct the physical and biological laws that would have to hold if "a world" were created by an omnipotent and perfect being. For example, all particles must have been initially equal in size and motion, since "confusion seems less in accordance with the supreme perfection of God the creator of all things than proportion or order" (part 3, art. 47). The argument is still theological, but it turns on philosophically accessible attributes of God rather than on exegetical or doctrinal considerations. (The parallels with Leibniz are striking.)

This sort of philosophical theology of creation has fallen on hard times in twentieth-century philosophy, at least until recently.[34] But I suggest that its dismissal has been overhasty. It is not clear why thinkers should eschew the philosophical territory that lies between traditional systematic theology (a theology of creation in the doctrinal sense) and straight physical theory (in which appeals to God are of course irrelevant). Further, there is value in exploring this territory. It allows us to reflect philosophically on the first principles of physics in a way that supplements the work of contemporary mathematical physics; it also encourages a rational rethinking of (or thinking toward) theological conclusions. Ironically, physicists have been less reticent than philosophers to take on speculative, even theological questions in cosmology.[35] There is no reason to avoid similar reflection within philosophical cosmology; indeed, the results might even evidence some parallels with the sort of philosophical theology developed in Descartes's *Principles*.

---

34. The tide has changed in recent years. See, e.g., Paul Davies, *God and the New Physics* (New York: Simon & Schuster, 1983); Ernan McMullin, ed., *Evolution and Creation* (Notre Dame: Univ. of Notre Dame Press, 1985); and Ted Peters, ed., *Cosmos as Creation: Theology and Science in Consonance* (Nashville: Abingdon, 1989), among many others.

35. See Robert Jastrow, *God and the Astronomers* (New York: Norton, 1978); A. R. Peacocke, *Creation and the World of Science* (Oxford: Clarendon, 1979); James Trefit, *The Moment of Creation* (New York: Charles Scribner's, 1983); John Barrow and Joseph Silk, *The Left Hand of Creation* (New York: Basic Books, 1983); John Barrow and Frank Tipler, *The Anthropic Cosmological Principle* (Oxford: Clarendon, 1986). More extreme, perhaps, are attempts at an "astrophysikalischen Theologie," e.g., Gerhard Staguhn, *Das Lachen Gottes: Der mensch und sein Kosmos* (Munich: Carl Hanser, 1990); Robert J. Russell et al., eds., *Chaos and Complexity* (Vatican City State: Vatical Observatory Publication, 1995); Russell et al., eds., *Quantum Cosmology and the Laws of Nature* (Vatican City State: Vatican Observatory Publications, 1993).

THE FOUNDATIONS OF DESCARTES'S THEOLOGY
IN THE *MEDITATIONS*

It is clear that the concept of God is supposed to play some sort of important role in the *Meditations;* the reader bumps into it during even the quickest reading of the work. Without God, Descartes maintains, there is no answer to the doubt that drives the argument from start to finish. We have already learned from surveying Descartes's other works that the concept of God is tied up closely with his understanding of his philosophical project and, he believes, with the success of his work in natural philosophy.

Now there is no doubt that Descartes meant his theistic proofs to do more than assert a theological position about God; he meant them actually to compel assent from any reader with any starting point. In examining the proofs below, however, I will conclude, in agreement with most commentators, that his theistic proofs fail. The arguments as stated are not compelling, and they employ assumptions that even the sympathetic reader may have good reason to reject. Our idea of perfection could have other causes than God's existing, and from the idea of God we are not compelled to assert God's existence. In the Replies, rather than strengthening his case, Descartes tended to talk past his objectors. If one of them let himself into the Cartesian way of thinking (as Arnauld did), then Descartes showed himself ready to compromise on details, even to employ his readers' concepts (whether those of the Schools, the theologians of Port Royal, or the natural philosophers). But when they challenged basic premises (as did Hobbes and Gassendi), Descartes's arguments failed noticeably to compel assent. His frequent recourse to rhetoric and to the mere repetition of problematic points strikes one as a tacit admission of defeat.

I therefore suggest another orientation to reading the *Meditations* than the question, Were Descartes's proofs valid? Suppose we read the proofs with an eye not to probative force but to the *content* of Descartes's concept of God. His argument for the existence of a perfect being is not a terribly complex one: we recognize ourselves as imperfect (finite), therefore there exists a perfect (infinite) being, since imperfection presupposes perfection (cf. V,162). I propose as a goal not to pronounce the arguments sound or unsound but to tease out of them the underlying theological position — Descartes's theology of infinity and perfection — with all its sources, complexities, strengths, and weaknesses. Only when this position is on the table can we assess the value of his philosophy as a whole.

The task, then, will be to hunt for the systematic position that gave rise to Descartes's arguments for the infinite. Moreover, since this is not to be a purely historical study, we will also be guided by the question, What elements of the

Cartesian way of thinking still have some force today? When we have reconstructed the system and motivated the background intuitions that drove Descartes's thought, we will be in a good position to step back and evaluate the resulting proposal for relating the finite and the infinite.

The Role of the "I Think, Therefore I Am"

In surveying Descartes's other major writings, we repeatedly found ourselves pointed toward the thesis that the *cogito* was never meant to serve as the ultimate foundation of Cartesian reflection. A closer examination of the *Meditations* buttresses this conclusion. Indeed, one can only interpret the theistic proofs and the place of the *cogito* argument correctly when one has abandoned the foundationalism of the subject. In this section I offer three arguments for a relativization of the "I think" in Descartes's thought.

The Genre of the *Meditations*

Before one starts to analyze arguments, it is valuable to reflect on the nature of this work as a series of meditations. Recall that the method of the *Meditations* is the "order of discovery" *(ordo inveniendi)*, in contrast to the *Principles*, which follow the order of "exposition" *(ordo docendi)* or what Descartes calls the *synthetic* order (*Conversation with Burman*, V,153).

Indeed, there is some good evidence that Descartes was consciously imitating the classical form of meditations, of which Augustine's *Confessions* is perhaps the best known. In this genre, one attempts to free oneself from the world, in order to discover both God and one's self in their proper relation; only then can one reappropriate and reintegrate God, body, and world. The goal of this genre of religious meditative writing is to convey a vision of the perfect order of nature. As Aryeh Kosman puts it, "The ultimate end of the *Meditations* is not the certainty which the narrator sets out to accomplish, but rather his discovery of faith in God's trustworthiness, which releases him from an undue desire for certainty."[36] Meditations in this genre help the reader to recognize the limitations and fallibility of her or his nature — but also, through God, its fundamental reliability. The God who emerges in Meditation 3, for example,

---

36. Aryeh Kosman, "The Naive Narrator: Meditation in Descartes' *Meditations*," in A. Rorty, ed., *Essays on Descartes' Meditations*, 21-43, quotation 33. The next reference in text is also to this essay. See also Ashok Gangadean, *Meditative Reason: Towards Universal Grammar* (New York: P. Lang, 1993).

is an entity whose being is analogous to the "I" that emerges at end of Meditation 2; or, put differently, the idea of perfection arises as a condition of the possibility of my awareness of myself as imperfect. The discovery of subjectivity already means "to discover the respect in which the world is given to me," to discover that subjectivity cannot be the source of itself. Put theologically, "I am not God" is consciousness's first self-recognition. Perhaps, pace Descartes, knowledge of one's limitedness is not a sufficient condition for knowing God's existence. But it is "a central component in the belief in God" (p. 38).

The *Cogito* Argument in Theistic Context

To the extent that we find Descartes to be working under the influence of the medieval context, including his treatment of the human subject, it becomes less likely that he meant to base everything on an (ontologically or epistemologically) independent center of human subjectivity. Of course, the argument from context has its limits, for couldn't Descartes have instituted a completely new movement in philosophy, orienting his thought on the human subject despite his medieval debts? But it is important to observe the burden of proof here. Authors argue frequently that Descartes must have been the institutor of a new tradition because he based knowledge claims on the certainty of the individual subject: from "I doubt" comes "I exist," and from "I exist" he derives God, mind/body dualism, and knowledge of the eternal world. In the face of this argument, however, the conceptual background for the *cogito, ergo sum* becomes much more important. If the argument already played a traditional role in nonsubject-centered theologians, and especially if these thinkers had a demonstrable influence on Descartes,[37] then his stress on the *cogito* as an answer to skepticism supplies by itself little or no evidence of a discontinuity with his medieval predecessors. Since the *cogito* argument does in fact have solid medieval roots, and since the medievals knew no independent subject, the appeal to the *cogito* is therefore not by itself evidence that Descartes was founding a new philosophy of human subjectivity. In this case, his break with the past must then be found elsewhere.

At least since Antoine Arnauld's comments in the Fourth Objections, it has been manifest that Descartes's *cogito, ergo sum* evidences strong similarities with earlier versions of the same argument, especially in Augustine. The proof had continued to play an important role in the Augustinian tradition, had been used by Nicholas of Cusa and Campanella,[38] and had shown a resurgence in the

37. As Henri Gouhier has argued at length in *Cartésianisme et Augustinisme au XVIIe Siècle* (Paris: Vrin, 1978).

38. For a description of Campanella's position and arguments for its influence on Des-

early years of the seventeenth century, when it was used by the apologists as a proof of the spirituality of the soul. Given these parallels, it is not surprising that the burden of proof falls on those who would draw a sharp distinction between the Cartesian and the Augustinian versions. Thus in his classic study Gilson had to work to argue the *discontinuities* between Descartes and the late medieval thinkers.[39] Since these similarities are so significant for understanding the *Meditations*, we must pause for a moment to consider the *cogito* argument in Augustine.

Like Descartes's, Augustine's goal had also been to refute all the arguments of the skeptics with a single argument. In the *Contra Academicos*, for example, his argument turns on the indisputability of internal knowledge. For the academics cannot refute a man who says, "I know that this appears white to me, I know that my hearing is charmed, I know that my nose perceives an agreeable odor. . . . I know that I am cold."[40] Likewise, in *De libero arbitrio* Augustine is looking for a certain starting point. He challenges Euodius with the *cogito* argument: "So I ask you in the first place, in order to begin with what is the most manifest, whether you really exist, or whether you are perhaps afraid to make a mistake in this matter? For if you did not exist, it would not be possible for you to make any mistake in this matter."[41]

The proof is internal; it involves an immediate intuition, whose truth is guaranteed through its being clear and distinct.[42] The clearest parallel to Descartes occurs in *De civitate Dei*: "Let [the academics] say, What happens if you are deceiving yourself? If I am deceived, I exist. For whoever does not exist cannot be deceived; therefore I exist if I am deceived. Since according to this I exist when I am deceived, it cannot be a deception that I am; for it is certain that I exist when I am deceived. Since I would have to exist even if I were deceived, I am certainly not deceived when I know that I am."[43] Augustine, like Descartes, be-

---

cartes, see Léon Blanchet, *Les antécédents historiques du "Je pense, donc je suis"* (Paris: Félix Alcan, 1920), part II.

39. Gilson, *La liberté chez Descartes et la theologie* (Paris: J. Vrin, 1982); see esp. ch. 5.

40. Augustine, *Contra Academicos*, book 3, chap. 11, par. 26. Interestingly, par. 25 also raises the question of whether I can know that I am not asleep and dreaming — the same question that worries Descartes in the second meditation.

41. "Utrum tu epse sis . . . cum utique si non esses falli omnino non posses" (*De libero arbitrio*, book 2, chap. 3).

42. "Vera atque certa" (*De civitate Dei*, book 11, chap. 26). Cf. Augustine's talk of "the knowledge by a sort of presence which is not feigned but real, not external but internal" (*De Trin.*, book 10, chap. 10).

43. "Quid si falleris? Si enim fallor, sum. Nam qui non est, utique nec falli potest, ac per hoc sum, si fallor" (11, 26).

gins with doubt and is searching for certitude. The goal is to discover the most intimate (type or token of) knowledge. And the answer is the same: "When it is said to the soul: 'know yourself,' at that moment when it understands that what was said was 'yourself,' it knows itself *(eo ictu quo intellegit quod dictum est te ipsam cognoscit se ipsam);* and there is no other reason than this to know that it is present to itself" *(De Trin.* 10.9).

Introspection in Augustine is not a carte blanche for knowledge claims. At the opening of *Soliloquia* book 2, he grants that introspection will not tell us, for example, whether we move or whether we are simple or composite; and we do not know at the outset how we know. But Reason *(Ratio)* can show him immediately and beyond all deception that he exists and that he thinks: " — Do you know that you think? — Yes. — It is therefore true that you think. — Yes, this is true."[44] As in Descartes's case, Augustine then derives a variety of knowledge from the "I think":

> Doubt leads to life and memory and intelligence and willing and thought and knowledge and judgment. For if one doubts, one grasps that one doubts; if one doubts, one knows the reasons that one has to doubt; if one doubts, one understands that one doubts; if one doubts, one wants to be certain; if one doubts, one thinks; if one doubts, one knows that one does not know; if one doubts, one judges that it is not sufficient to consent randomly. *(De Trin.* 10.10)

Naturally, there are differences from Descartes. As we have seen, Augustine's *cogito* is sometimes formulated less as an argument — although it is clearly meant to be one — and more as an internal meditation on what is immediately evident. Further, Augustine moved from the *cogito* to meditate on the presence of God in an explicitly religious manner (e.g., he included prayers in the same texts in which the *cogito* appears), whereas Descartes wanted a notion of God that was available through the natural light, and equally to all.[45] As a result, Augustine's argument often appears in a rather more immediate and unstructured form, skipping the intermediate step of the consciousness of doubt or error.

Finally, especially in *De Trinitate* and in the *Confessions,* it is clear that Au-

44. "Cogitare te scis? Scio. Ergo verum est cogitare te" *(Soliloquia,* book 2, chap. 1). At the end of the chapter, Reason notes that Augustine has demanded to be, to live and to understand, and reminds him that he knows through introspection that "you know that you are, you know that you live, you know that you understand."

45. See Wolfgang Kersting, "'Noli foras ire, in te ipsum redi': Augustinus über die Seele," *Prima Philosophia* 3/3 (1990): 309-31.

gustine hopes to find in human nature an image of the Trinity, whereas Descartes's thought is in no significant sense trinitarian. For the former, the introspective move is tied to the question of needing to know "the one whom I love, the one who has saved me"; the soul's knowledge of itself is only a facet of the broader religious quest to know God (book 10, chaps. 3, 4). In knowing the self, one discovers the three fundamental characteristics of human being: being, knowledge, and willing; and the three faculties: knowledge, wisdom, and love. In the *Confessions* the only allusion to Augustine's *cogito* argument — "For I am, I know, and I will. I am one who knows and wills, I know that I am and will, and I will to be and to know" (book 13, chap. 11) — is employed to demonstrate the image of the Trinity in humanity. Finally, in the famous *De civitate Dei* passage cited above, knowing the self *just is* knowing the trinitarian Creator. For although, like the rest of creation, we are not of the same essence as God, our knowledge, wisdom, and love more accurately reflect his image than any other created things (cf. the opening of *De civ.* 11.26).

Indisputable for both thinkers, therefore, is the belief that the *cogito* provides a crucial source of indubitable knowledge and does so for a self that is ontologically dependent on God. The manner in which they handle their insight is different: Augustine moves in a theological and devotional direction, Descartes in the direction of a metaphysics of the infinite and the foundations for natural science. This difference in the nature of their systems accounts for the appearance of the Cartesian subject as more independent and autonomous. It does not, however, remove the fundamental similarity in their treatment of the *cogito*.

The *Cogito* Relativized

There is a third argument for the claim that the human subject has only a relative, dependent status in the *Meditations* rather than playing an absolute, foundational role. It is a negative argument: no coherent interpretation can be given of Meditation 3 unless one relativizes the *cogito;* Descartes's use of God is inexplicable if (as is often claimed) the human subject is primary. For example, introducing the notion of God within Meditation 3 is arbitrary if the subject is indeed the real foundation for knowledge. If it is, Descartes deserves the complete rejection demanded by his critics. For example, Anthony Kenny complains of the idea of God that "out of the hat of the *cogito* yet another rabbit is produced."[46] But just as Kenny criticizes Hintikka's interpretation for making Descartes "patently confused," he should be criticized for a reconstruction that

---

46. Anthony Kenny, *Descartes: A Study of His Philosophy* (New York: Random House, 1968; repr. New York: Garland, 1987), 129.

makes Descartes's argument into nonsense. Not only is the idea of God inexplicable under this interpretation; Descartes's entire argument would be viciously circular were the *cogito* ultimately foundational. The criticism goes back to the Fourth Objections by Arnauld: there is no way to get from the *cogito*, understood as primary, to God. We return to this issue in the following section.

Finally, stepping back from the *Meditations* for a moment, one notes that it is conceptually impossible to combine an independent human ego and an infinite being. If the thinking subject is taken as the ultimate and independent instance, no place is left for a being on whom all other beings depend for their creation as well as their conservation from moment to moment (VII,49) — which was Descartes's position in the *Principles*. If the *cogito* is given the self-sufficient status often attributed to it, then the concept of a self-sufficient divine being is ruled out by definition — little surprise that commentators have trouble making sense of such a Descartes! The word *infinite* may be a privative etymologically (Greek *apeiron*, Latin *infinitas*), but the *concept* of the infinite cannot be. Conceptually, the notion of the infinite claims for itself an irrevocable priority, as is seen perhaps most clearly in the modern philosophy of the Absolute.[47]

I conclude that the finite subject and the infinite being that Descartes calls God are discovered *together,* not through an argument that ascends from self as foundation to God as consequence. Either one can portray Meditation 3 as a meditation on my imperfection and the experience of my limits, on the fragility of my being, which can pass out of existence at any minute; or one can interpret it as a meditation on the infinity of the one who created me, whose self-sufficiency is complete, who contains in himself the reason for his existing. In either case, the stress on the subordination of the finite to the all-encompassing realm of the infinite is unavoidable. The independently thinking subject can only represent a preliminary stopping point. It is a sort of whole (or substance) with a certain integrity and indubitability of its own, but a whole that is preliminary because finite. The subject's certainty may ground justified belief — to this extent Descartes deserves his title as the father of modern epistemology — but not metaphysical ultimacy. Ultimately, "the awareness that I derive from my lack and the knowledge that I acquire of the grandeur of God are only one and the same reality, that of the 'I think.'"[48]

---

47. For the development of this notion from Descartes to the early Kant (and subsequently in German idealism), see Horst-Günter Redmann, *Gott und Welt: Die Schöpfungstheologie der vorkritischen Periode Kants* (Göttingen: Vandenhoeck & Ruprecht, 1962), e.g., 57.

48. Ferdinand Alquié, *Le découverte métaphysique de l'homme chez Descartes* (Paris: Presses Universitaires de France, 1950), 221: "la conscience que je prends de ma misère et la connaissance que j'acquiers de la grandeur de Dieu ne sont qu'une seule et même réalité, celle du je pense."

Metaphysically, then, the *cogito* is discovered as a *lack*; it is the being who doubts. Hence the certainty of the *sum* that flows from Cartesian doubt is also preliminary. The lack — "I am aware of myself as finite" — immediately gives rise to the idea of a ground that is not finite: "I have in me the idea of a perfect being." The subjective starting point is completed for Descartes by an objective framework that both accounts for the experience of certainty and solves the epistemic problems caused by the limits of subjectivity. The key questions of Cartesian epistemology — Can I be sure of ideas that I merely remember having been clear and distinct? Can I be mistaken in thinking that some idea is clear and distinct? And why should clear and distinct ideas be true? — can only be answered by placing the *cogito* within the context of the infinite. As Marion notes, "the spirit understands itself in the infinite; it discovers itself always already encompassed; it glimpses that being encompassed in this way is the only way to its proper identity."[49]

On Intuitions and Arguing in Circles

The Circle Objection

These claims regarding the status of the "I think, therefore I am" confront us directly with the famous circle objection. The circle criticism is the oldest and most often repeated objection to the *Meditations*. Arnauld complained already in the Fourth Objections,

> I have one further worry, namely how the author avoids reasoning in a circle when he says that we are sure that what we clearly and distinctly perceive is true only because God exists. But we can be sure that God exists only because we clearly and distinctly perceive this. Hence, before we can be sure that God exists, we ought to be able to be sure that whatever we perceive clearly and evidently is true. (VII,214)

Descartes apparently felt the criticism could be easily answered. We need only distinguish between "what we in fact perceive clearly and what we remember having perceived clearly on a previous occasion" (VII,245). What we are

---

49. Jean-Luc Marion, *Sur la théologie blanche de Descartes: Analogie, création des vértités éternelles et fondement* (Paris: Presses Universitaires de France, 1981), 404: "l'esprit se comprend dans l'infini; s'y découvrant toujours déjà englobé, il entrevoit que cet englobement seul l'ouvre à sa propre identité."

now perceiving clearly is indubitable, but we could not trust the contents of our memory "if we did not know that God exists and is not a deceiver."

Descartes's answer is, I fear, unsatisfactory; it talks past the actual objection. Indeed, it seems that Descartes is guilty of a stronger form of circularity, namely:

1. I can know (be certain) that (p) whatever I perceive clearly and distinctly is true only if I first know (am certain) that (q) God exists and is not a deceiver.
2. I can know (be certain) that (q) God exists and is not a deceiver only if I first know (am certain) that (p) whatever I perceive clearly and distinctly is true.[50]

I take the circle objection, in the form in which it is formulated here and as usually discussed in the analytic literature, to be insoluble. Descartes clearly held that both 1 and 2 are true; arguments employing both 1 and 2 are viciously circular; and Descartes employed both 1 and 2 in contexts that appear to be arguments.

Many attempts have been made to mitigate the effects of the circle by drawing distinctions on Descartes's behalf. Perhaps Cartesian doubt does consistently apply only to the reliability of memory and not to demonstrations on which I am currently meditating, so that I could validly prove God's existence at time t and then know that memory is generally reliable at all times subsequent to t (Doney and others). Or perhaps Cartesian doubt encompasses only radical or "metaphysical" doubt, leaving me free first to prove God's existence with practical ("psychological") certainty and then later to use this certainty to dismiss the danger of metaphysical doubt (Fred Feldman). Important criticisms have been raised regarding both proposals; neither appears to save Descartes's deductions from all circularity.[51] Indeed, even the most sophisticated defense of the *Meditations* as a single sound argument, Martial Gueroult's *Descartes's Philosophy Interpreted according to the Order of Reasons,* acknowledges the existence of a Cartesian circle. As Gueroult notes, one cannot move from the *cogito* to God — with or without the clear and distinct criterion — since the *cogito* as a dependent being is only definable (knowable) given God:

50. James Van Cleve, "Foundationalism, Epistemic Principles, and the Cartesian Circle," *Philosophical Review* 88 (1979): 55, now in Doney, ed., *Eternal Truths and the Cartesian Circle,* 245.

51. On Doney see Harry G. Frankfurt, "Meaning and the Cartesian Circle"; and on Feldman, Peter J. Markie, "Fred Feldman and the Cartesian Circle," in Doney, ed., *Eternal Truths and the Cartesian Circle,* 72-79 and 217-20, respectively. I argue below that certain immediate intuitions do remain immune from Cartesian doubt even in its strong form.

The demonstration of the true God must necessarily rest on principles actually established in him, but whose validity cannot be established before the conclusion (before the positing of God), although their validity is recognizable before that. . . . There is therefore no way to lead an atheist — or someone who holds an atheist position — to the certainty of God except by having him experience it, [namely] . . . that the idea of the perfect he has in his soul could not have been introduced there except by the action of God himself and that, consequently, God exists.[52]

One does not have to look hard to see that all pretense of a purely rational demonstration has been abandoned here; the Cartesian "order of reasons" is simply not linear! Gueroult himself grants at one point that there is a "break" in the "unilinear" linkage of reasons, concluding that the *Meditations* offers a "rational network" *(nexus rationum)* rather than a deductive case (pp. 166-67).

I therefore recommend that we abandon once and for all the attempt to reconstruct the *Meditations* as a foundationalist argument. One cannot argue merely from the *cogito* to God (or from God to the *cogito*); neither pole of the position can support the other by itself. This acknowledgment allows one to affirm rather than hide the reciprocal relationships between the *cogito*, the clear and distinct criterion, and God. *These three represent interlinked elements of a single theological proposal;* they receive whatever epistemic strength they have from the credibility of the resultant metaphysic as judged against its competitors and the particular goals one brings to the discussion (see chapter 3 below).

This insight provides the entrée for any adequate study of Cartesian philosophy. It will enable us in the next section to discover in Descartes, the arch-foundationalist, the outlines of a nonfoundational, coherentist approach to metaphysics, one based finally on the relation between the finite and the infinite. Such a reconstruction is possible, however, only after one acknowledges the circular relationship between human knowledge and divine existence. There is a sense in which the clear and distinct criterion is not required for knowledge of God, since this knowledge stems directly from a (preargumentative) intuition. Once we have clarified the role of intuition for Descartes, we can turn to a discussion of the concepts of infinity and perfection freed from foundationalist remnants.

52. M. Gueroult, *Descartes selon l'ordre des raisons,* trans. by Roger Ariew as *Descartes' Philosophy Interpreted according to the Order of Reasons* (Minneapolis: Univ. of Minnesota Press, 1984), vol. 1: *The Soul and God,* 172, 246. The next reference in the text is also to this work.

Reason and Intuition in Descartes

A circular argument is unavoidable, I have suggested, if Descartes uses a particular premise to prove that (God exists and therefore that) this premise is reliable. But what if the probative force of the *Meditations* lies not in a serially ordered series of premises but in a fundamental intuition, a basic theological perspective that is strengthened by the coherence and explanatory power of the system taken as a whole? "But," the critic might complain, "Descartes clearly took himself to be *arguing* when he wrote the *Meditations*. Now you begin to stress the role of intuition instead. What, for instance, is the intuitive faculty, and how is it related to reason and argumentation? What sort of justification can it supply?"

I am not the first to suggest that Descartes's position relies on some basic intuitions not touched by his methodological doubt. In an influential article Henry Frankfurt has argued that Descartes did not take on the task of showing that what we intuit is true. He was only trying to answer the skeptic, and thus to show that there can be no reasonable grounds for doubting the results of intuition. Cartesian doubt is bypassed whenever one has a clear intuition of some proposition in the present, as long as one does not later come to have grounds for doubting it.[53] Likewise, Kenny insists on a Cartesian distinction between first-order doubt, or doubt about a specific intuition, and second-order doubt, doubt about basic principles, such as doubting whether "what seems to me most obvious" or "what I clearly remember" is really true.[54] In terms of Kenny's distinction, we can say that Descartes never questions the truth of clear and distinct first-order intuitions but only that of general principles. Hence there is no contradiction in using the immediate intuition of God's existence to answer doubts about specific second-order principles. Kenny concludes,

> the simple intuition by itself provides both psychologically and logically the best grounds for accepting [its truth]. Thus, there is no circle. Deduction is called in question, and deduction is vindicated by intuition. The truth of particular intuitions is never called in question, only the universal trustworthiness of intuition, and in vindicating this universal trustworthiness only individual intuitions are utilized.[55]

53. See Harry G. Frankfurt, *Demons, Dreamers, and Madmen: The Defence of Reason in Descartes's Meditations* (New York: Garland, 1987).

54. Kenny, *Descartes*, chap. 8.

55. Ibid., 194. Even given this defense of intuition, we must nonetheless grant Kenny's point that it does not necessarily save Descartes's representationalist epistemology. We cannot demonstrate the direct contact of our ideas to reality, yet the ideas must be known accu-

Suppose we grant the viability in principle of appeals to philosophical intuitions. Can any defense be given of Descartes's central intuition in the *Meditations*, the intuition of the infinite? If we are to develop a positive account of it, we must first note what it is *not*. First, an intuition of the infinite need not imply full comprehension: "I do not grasp the infinite," Descartes insists, "for it is in the nature of the infinite not to be grasped by a finite being like myself. It is enough that I understand the infinite."[56] Thus things not comprehended can still be understood, not *comprehendi* but *intelligi*. Second, not all sorts of things can be intuited. "Intuition" appears to have an Aristotelian/Thomistic sense in the *Rules*, providing one with the axioms or first principles to which one applies the power of reason (Rule 3, X,366ff.). But *intueri*, which plays a significant role in the *Discourse*, no longer serves this function in the *Meditations*. In the latter work it is the "natural light" rather than intuition that he calls on to defend his major philosophical presuppositions, especially the causal principles he uses to establish the existence and veracity of God.[57] In the *Meditations* and the Replies, intuition surfaces only by implication, as in the activity of contemplation, which Descartes often discusses in the context of the knowledge of God.[58]

---

rately to represent this reality if the representationalist is to have knowledge (justified true belief). Descartes wants to appeal to the clear and distinct criterion as sufficient for ascertaining the correspondence of ideas with reality; but this would mean that clarity and distinctness must be internal properties of ideas, not properties relating them to extramental objects (p. 197). It is possible to be mistaken about whether an idea is clear and distinct, and we lack any clear and distinct criterion by which to judge if an idea is clear and distinct. (Even if we had one, this would start an infinite regress.)

56. VII,46; cf. VII,112. The translation by Cottingham et al. (n. 9 above) footnotes the interesting comparison, "just as we can touch a mountain but not put our arms around it. To grasp something is to embrace it in one's thought; to know something, it suffices to touch it with one's thought." But the reference (letter to Mersenne, 5/26/1630) is incorrect and I have not been able to locate the passage elsewhere in the correspondence.

57. This is the conclusion of the excellent analysis in John Morris, "Descartes' Natural Light," now in Doney, ed., *Eternal Truths and the Cartesian Circle*, 163-81. The only serious counterexample to sharply separating intuition from the natural light is Descartes's locution "the natural light or *intuitus mentis*" in the letter to Mersenne, 10/16/1639; II,597ff. Morris concludes — fairly, I think — that "the supposed revelations of the natural light are indistinguishable, to the outside observer, from the prejudices that [Descartes] once sought to abandon" and calls it "an elaborate set of foundations for a castle built in the air" (p. 181).

58. So, e.g., "Those who attempt to pay attention to [God's] perfections one at a time, and try not so much to capture them as to be captured by them and to use all their mental ability to contemplate them, will surely find in him a richer and easier source of clear and distinct knowledge than in any created things" (First Replies, VII,113-14, following Beck's translation in *Metaphysics of Descartes*, 180). Cf. the exhortation to contemplation at the close of Meditation 3.

Still, intuition does not disappear; it continues to indicate the immediate awareness of fundamental truths that are generally of a religious nature. In a late letter Descartes defines intuition as "an elucidation of the spirit *(une illustration de l'esprit)*, through which it sees in the light of God the things that it pleases him to disclose to it by means of a direct impression of divine clarity on our understanding." Because of this immediacy and the mind's passivity, intuition results in an understanding that is clearer and more certain than the results of active reasoning. Descartes cites the clarity of *je pense, donc je suis* as "a proof of the capacity of our souls to receive intuitive knowledge from God." Understanding by intuitive knowledge *(par la connaissance intuitive)* means "to know God through himself, that is to say, through an immediate elucidation by the divinity upon our spirit." As such it contrasts with reasoning from one attribute of God to another (letter to [Silhon?], March or April 1648; V,136ff., AM 8:21-22).

The importance of this faculty for interpreting Descartes cannot be overemphasized. It is indisputable that he is affirming an immediate awareness, a *connaissance intuitive*, of the existence of God. Perhaps more important, the faculty by which he intuits the existence of the infinite supplies the model for intellectual activity as a whole. As Brunschvicg notes, "in Cartesianism, the intuition is not itself a distinct faculty of the intelligence; it is the intelligence itself, it is the soul in its entirety, according to the saying of Plato."[59] Intuition provides the standards for clarity and certainty, as well as the criterion for accuracy: *la connaissance naturelle* must finally agree with *la connaissance intuitive* regarding the existence of God and attributes such as divine simplicity.

I suggest that this reliance on intuition and the natural light explodes the myth of autonomous reason in Descartes. Cartesian reflection begins with a basic intuition concerning the existence of an infinite being and the dependence of the self on it. Of course, Descartes also believed that "natural knowledge" could retrace the steps of intuition; he thought he had a proof on his hands. As we will see, he failed at this task: though the proofs may suggest a metaphysic, they do not compel assent to it. In reconstructing Descartes, the reader must instead use the proofs to point toward a systematic metaphysic and to evoke the corresponding intuitions. Comparison with competing systems may strengthen, weaken, or even alter one's intuitions on the matter. If one does not come to find these intuitions plausible, the Cartesian metaphysic will never

---

59. L. Brunschvicg, "Mathématique et métaphysique chez Descartes," *Revue de métaphysique et de morale* 34 (1927): 315-16: "dans le cartésianisme, l'intuition n'est même pas une faculté distincte de l'intelligence; c'est l'intelligence elle-même, c'est l'âme tout entière, selon le mot de Platon." See also Beck, *Method*, chaps. 4–5.

become compelling; conversely, if one does find Descartes's starting point intuitive, one may still discover difficulties in what he thinks it entails.

From Epistemology to Metaphysics

Descartes's reliance on intuition is sometimes taken as a stopping point or final appeal. The position runs something like this: Cartesian doubt is overcome because the self discovers in the knowledge of its existence an item of indubitable present knowledge. After all, Descartes writes in Meditation 2, "I am, I exist" is true "as often as it is put forward or conceived in my mind" (VII,25). Thus, for instance, John Cottingham concludes, "As long as I keep it in focus, I know it to be true."[60] The doubt of Meditation 1 had concerned only memory. If one can prove his existence, God will insure the verisimilitude of the dictates of memory, or at least allow one "to rely (with due caution) on all the props and aids which finite beings need in order to gather their fleeting intuitions together and weld them into a systematic whole" (ibid., p. 71). And if the weld fails, well, at least one still has one's intuitions.

There is admittedly something attractive about Descartes the epistemologist of subjective convictions — which may account for the volumes written on his epistemology in recent years. It may be that the truth value of our basic intuitions and rational inferences is, from a "God's-eye point of view," a little shaky. Still, perhaps one could defend some form of "internal realism" (Hilary Putnam), the view that one is justified in accepting a realist construal of one's language even though correspondence claims with Reality are meaningless. Thus Frankfurt argues that Descartes wants only to show the subjective structure of knowledge; it is enough if agents work from, and are satisfied with, beliefs that are subjectively fundamental to them and carry great subjective conviction.[61]

But Cottingham (pp. 68f.) is certainly right to insist that it was not Descartes's final intention to defend subjective certainty without truth. Descartes

---

60. John Cottingham, *Descartes* (Oxford: Blackwell, 1986), 69. The next two references in the text are also to this work. Cf. Descartes's comment in the *Conversation with Burman:* "I know I am not deceived with regard to [the axioms needed to prove God's existence], since I am actually paying attention to them *(scit se in iis non falli, quoniam ad ea attendit).* And as long as I do pay attention to them, I am certain that I am not being deceived and I am compelled to give my assent to them" (V,148).

61. Frankfurt, in Rorty, ed., *Demons, Dreamers, and Madmen,* 180ff. He can appeal to Cartesian passages such as, "What is it to us that someone may make out that the perception whose truth we are so firmly convinced of may appear false to God or an angel, so that it is, absolutely speaking, false? Why should this alleged 'absolute falsity' bother us" as long as we have "a conviction so firm that it is quite incapable of being destroyed" (VII,145).

was actually looking for something more. Indeed, I suggest that this Descartes supplies a needed corrective in the contemporary context — not the Descartes of absolute skepticism, whose ubiquitous doubt demands as antidote, and fails to find, absolute foundations; but rather Descartes the systematician, who sought to develop a system in which both metaphysical and epistemological questions work together. The goal, then, is to reconstruct a Cartesianism of viable intuitions in interaction with systematic considerations, avoiding on one side the historical error of "Kantianizing" Descartes into a philosopher of subjectivity, and rejecting on the other his flawed foundationalist epistemology. This corrected Descartes (to use the metaphors of Wittgenstein and Neurath) does not sink his piles down into bedrock, but rather ropes together enough metaphysical and epistemological planks to keep the whole thing floating.

The task of discovering and evaluating this analytic reconstruction of Descartes will occupy us in the rest of this chapter and most of the next. First we should pause long enough to note a few of the metaphysical tenets on which his epistemology crucially depends:

- The self has immediate knowledge of itself. Through this knowledge it knows itself to be finite and dependent; it knows both of these things because an infinite and creating being exists.
- Since God is not a deceiver, we can know that our clear and distinct ideas in fact represent the way the world is.
- Intuitions provide models of clearness and certainty for our discursive efforts. Intuitive knowledge is passive; the active (revealing) agent is God.
- We cannot but think the world according to certain a priori truths, such as those of mathematics. But even these "eternal truths" were created by God; they did not have to be necessary but are so only because of the free decision of God.[62]

I have argued that the circle objection ruins Descartes's project as foundationalist philosophy or apologetic theology. Still, one must distinguish

---

62. This Cartesian doctrine has been widely discussed. See esp. Emile Bréhier, "The Creation of the Eternal Truths in Descartes's System" (trans. W. Doney), in Doney, ed., *Descartes: A Collection of Critical Essays*, 192-208; the collection of G. Rodis-Lewis's essays, *Idées et vérités éternelles chez Descartes et ses successeurs* (Paris: Vrin, 1985), esp. "Création des vérités éternelles, doute suprême et limites de l'impossible chez Descartes," 119-38; and esp. the essays by Frankfurt, "Meaning and the Cartesian Circle," and E. M. Curley, "Descartes on the Creation of the Eternal Truths," in Doney, ed., *Eternal Truths and the Cartesian Circle*, 72-79 and 341-70, respectively. My formulation reflects Curley's position, which I find the most convincing.

between an epistemic grounding for clear and distinct ideas and a metaphysical or theological account of them.[63] If the two sides can be forged together into a convincing whole (a theological epistemology?), the failure of foundationalism need not destroy Descartes's value as a systematic thinker.

Attaining the Concept: Descartes's Theistic Proofs

Descartes employs what appear to be three different theistic proofs: two separate versions of a causal argument, based on our possession of the idea of an infinite (perfect) being, and an ontological argument, based on the very notion of a perfect being. Typically, treatments of Descartes begin by assessing the arguments' validity. The proofs are usually praised as innovative, and then inevitably found wanting: They either equivocate, bouncing back and forth between several different conceptions of God (Marion); or predicate human qualities of God in a way that falls to Feuerbach's projectionist critique of religion (Pannenberg); or prove, if anything, only the potentially endless power of human thought (Baier); or, more often, are dismissed as a hopeless attempt at persuasion that never gets off the ground (Williams, Caton).[64]

What is almost never done, at least in English, is to look beyond the validity question to the role of the arguments as conceptual explications of the being who is the telos of the proofs and, indeed, of the *Meditations* as a whole. What happens when we think *with* Descartes, to see where his work points? Why not admit at the outset that Descartes (along with the rest of the tradition) has not achieved a sound proof of God? What is the nature of his theology when reconstructed systematically? I do not attempt to argue that Descartes is successful in compelling us to acknowledge the existence of an infinite being. My interest lies instead in what he understands this concept to imply. What I find is an intriguing appropriation and adaptation of Scholastic and late medieval themes that was to become basic for reflection on the nature of God throughout the early modern period, at least until the *Critique of Pure Reason* — and, if the criticisms of Kant in the following chapters are sound, perhaps beyond it as well. At

---

63. Or, as Koyré puts it, we must distinguish between their epistemic value and their ontological significance; see *From the Closed World to the Infinite Universe* (Baltimore: Johns Hopkins Univ. Press, 1997), chap. 4.

64. See, respectively, Marion, *Sur la théologie blanche,* and the parallel argument in his "Essential Incoherence," in Rorty, ed., *Essays on Descartes' Meditations,* 297-338; Wolfhart Pannenberg, *Systematic Theology,* vol. 1 (Grand Rapids: Eerdmans, 1988), e.g., 88ff.; Annette Baier, "The Idea of the True God in Descartes," in Rorty, ed., *Essays on Descartes' Meditations,* 359-87. On Williams and Caton, see above, n. 12.

minimum, we gain through this analysis a better understanding of Descartes's legacy to the seventeenth and eighteenth centuries. More optimistically, I hope to show that some of the Cartesian core principles remain viable options for contemporary theological reflection as well.

The Causal Proofs

The general idea behind Descartes's causal proofs is the same: (1) We recognize ourselves (our ideas, our existence) as finite and imperfect; (2) such recognition implies the existence of something infinite; (3) therefore God exists, who is an infinite and perfect being on whom we depend for our creation and preservation. Seen this way, the proof is a particular instance of traditional proofs *a contingentia mundi*. Descartes wants to make his case using a causal argument; as he says, "a consideration of efficient causes is the primary and principal way, if not the only way, that we have of proving the existence of God" (4th Replies, VII,238).

The Proof from My Idea of God

The particular form of the first causal argument has the structure just outlined:

> I must consider whether there is anything in the idea [of God] that could not have originated in myself. By the word *God* I understand a substance that is infinite, independent, supremely intelligent, supremely powerful *(infinitam, independentem, summe intelligentem, summe potentem)*, and that created both myself and everything else . . . that exists. All these attributes are such that, the more carefully I concentrate on them, the less possible it seems that they [sc. the ideas of these attributes] could have originated from me alone. So from what has been said it must be concluded that God necessarily exists. (VII,45)

The argument depends on a number of crucial (including some problematic) epistemological assumptions. It begins by bracketing the question of whether these attributes really exist in some object (i.e., have "formal reality"), concentrating instead on the content and reality that they have as ideas (their "objective reality").[65] The argument next assumes that there are levels of reality

65. This is the one part of the argument that may find broad concurrence in contemporary philosophy. Edmund Husserl gave it convincing expression in his notion of the "bracketing" *(epoché)* that makes possible the phenomenological analysis of ideas as intentional objects, apart from the question of their correspondence to some extramental reality. His *Cartesian Meditations: An Introduction to Phenomenology*, trans. Dorion Cairns (The Hague: Nijhoff, 1960), makes clear his debt to Descartes on this point.

in the formal *and* the objective realm: just as things can be ranked in terms of the amount of reality they have, so also ideas can be ranked depending on what they are ideas *about* (whether or not their *ideatum* really exists).[66] It then presupposes a correspondence between these two realms, as well as a causal condition governing the correspondence: Each idea, whether or not its *ideatum* really exists, must stem from a source that *really* (Descartes says "formally") has at least the same level of reality that the idea has *as idea* (or, he says, "objectively"). Finally, it assumes that we are finite and that we have the idea of an infinite being. If one accepts all these assumptions, then (and only then) will one judge the proof to be sound.

I do not find all these assumptions compelling; and one is hard-pressed to find a (non-French) commentator today who does.[67] As I have suggested, however, it is possible to distinguish between the argument's epistemic claims and the metaphysic that is contained in it (e.g., the metaphysic of infinity). How might the causal argument look when read, so to speak, from the top down rather than from the bottom up?[68] I will concentrate on three features:

1. *The principle of levels of reality.* All ideas or things come in levels; the degree of reality or perfection of some ideas (or things) is greater than that of others. Descartes uses this premise in arguing to God. The trouble is, the principle seems already to presuppose the existence of such a being; for what would serve as the principle of determining and ordering levels of reality apart from the idea of a perfect being? One might possess an intuition pointing toward such a being, but the actual scale of reality could be worked out only after the nature of this being had been elucidated. Even Martial Gueroult, perhaps the greatest (and probably the most sympathetic) of Descartes's commentators, seems to admit this at one point. He writes that the idea of God enables me (and, it seems, *only* that idea could enable me) to recognize the differences in perfection of the contents of my various ideas, along with the imperfection of my self and the imperfection of philosophical knowledge of the *cogito,* when that knowledge is posited separately, indepen-

---

66. Beck, *Metaphysics of Descartes,* 180-81.

67. For details on the difficulties with the arguments see, e.g., Wolfgang Röd, *Descartes: Die Genese des Cartesianischen Rationalismus,* 2nd ed. (Munich: C. H. Beck, 1982), e.g., chap. 4; and, in more detail and occasionally with more sympathy, Kenny's treatment in his *Descartes.*

68. These need not consist in proofs that such a being exists. In the next chapter I defend a coherence epistemology, according to which one does not first need to ground an idea within a foundationalist structure in order to introduce it validly into philosophical discourse. The strength of metaphysical ideas shows itself only in the process of their systematic development and in comparison with competing ideas.

dent of the knowledge of the perfect that alone can lift the *cogito* to a perfectly clear and distinct knowledge.[69]

Nevertheless, speaking of levels of reality in this way seems eminently justified after one has introduced the model of a most perfect being. One need not have recourse to an intricate system of levels — unless one had other reasons to prefer complicated hierarchies (as the Scholastics did when they appropriated Aristotle's categories). Still, in working out the implications of his metaphysic the contemporary Cartesian would by all means insist on two fundamental levels: the amount of reality (perfection) possessed by an infinite being, and the (relatively) lesser amount of being possessed by noninfinite beings. It is Descartes's intuitive sense of the power of this basic contrast that convinces him of the indispensability of levels of reality.

2. *The explanation of ideas in terms of correspondence.* For Descartes, explaining an idea involves specifying the ontological relationship between any idea and what caused it. The reality that any given idea has qua idea (what he calls its "objective" reality) must ultimately be accounted for by something that is not an idea, by some actual ("formal") reality to which it corresponds. The causal sequence cannot just remain within the realm of ideas; it must finally be anchored in the way things really are. Moreover, this ontological relation must also anchor the actual content of the idea; it is not enough just to specify the status of the subject, who can then have whatever ideas she or he pleases.[70] Descartes thus presupposes a correspondence theory of truth[71] and, implicitly, the epistemic thesis that the correspondence relation is knowable (since it can be employed in assessing the status of individual ideas).

I see no reason to accept this epistemic thesis ab initio; it must itself be justified. If it is not, and if one posits only individuals and their ideas, Descartes's theory of ideas will turn out to be a sure recipe for skepticism. How is one to be assured of a movement outward from the contents of one's thought to a world at all, much less to an infinite being? Even Descartes grants that (apart

---

69. Gueroult, *Descartes' Philosophy,* 1:166 (translation modified).

70. In Gueroult's terms (ibid., 138), ideas are in their basic character representational. The object of an idea is the reality to which it refers; ideas can only be adequately explained if the world actually contains what they represent — or at least objects on an ontological level high enough to match or beat the ontological level of the idea.

71. "Ce mot *vérité,* en sa propre signification, dénote la conformité de la pensée avec l'objet" (to Mersenne, 10/16/1639; II,587ff., AM 3:254); see also Curley, *Descartes against the Skeptics,* 108-12. Although Frankfurt at one point maintained that Descartes held a coherence theory of truth ("Descartes on the Creation of the Eternal Truths," *Philosophical Review* 86 [1977]: 36-57, e.g., 52), he later ascribed to him a correspondence theory ("Descartes on the Consistency of Reason," in Hooker, ed., *Descartes: Critical and Interpretive Essays,* 37).

from theological considerations) the belief that "things beyond" really "resemble the ideas" is precarious; our belief in the existence of things "outside" may be due only to "blind impulse," or, as Descartes puts it in Meditation 6, to the "teaching of nature." The problems are familiar to students of empiricism; as Hume argued, we believe in external objects not because of the senses or reason but due to "the natural propensity of the imagination," to "a kind of instinct or natural impulse."[72]

Once again, however, matters look somewhat different if one begins not with the *cogito* and empiricism, but with rationalism and the concept of an infinite creator. Descartes presupposes causal rationalism, a tenet he shares with Spinoza and Leibniz. Causal rationalism is the position that refuses to separate between cause and ground or reason. We think that it is logically possible for a given causal interaction to have happened otherwise. But causal rationalists deny this; cause and effect, they hold, are as closely linked, and in the same way, as a set of premises and the conclusion that follows from it.[73] This means that it is not enough to provide an efficient cause for the occurrence of the idea; there must also be a ground or reason for its being this particular idea. Descartes obviously felt that causal rationalism could in turn be grounded in the existence of a creator God. On this point, however, I cannot follow him. It does not seem that causal rationalism is a consequence of theism (unless all theisms are deterministic), and it is hard to conceive a nontheistic case on its behalf. Element 2 of his argument, then, remains problematic with or without taking Descartes's theism into account.

3. *The principle of causality applied to the objective reality of ideas.* Descartes then applies 1 to 2: the level of reality or perfection of whatever real thing gives rise to an idea must be greater than or equal to the reality of the idea itself (to its "objective reality"). Since most of my ideas are about finite things, I could have given rise to almost all of them; thus most of them are compatible with solipsism. But there is one major exception: the idea of God "has an infinite amplitude and

---

72. David Hume, *A Treatise of Human Nature*, ed. L. A. Selby-Bigge (Oxford: Clarendon Press, 1978), I.iv.2, 210, 214. On the parallel between Hume and Descartes here, see Gerd Buchdahl, *Metaphysics and the Philosophy of Science: The Classical Origins, Descartes to Kant* (Oxford: Blackwell, 1969), 167-68.

73. Causal rationalism is nicely presented in Jonathan Bennett, *A Study of Spinoza's Ethics* (Indianapolis: Hackett, 1984), 29ff.; cf. chap. 7 below. Dolch shows convincingly that Descartes likewise makes the equation *causa sive ratio:* "*causa* wird nicht als verursachendes Sein, sondern als begründender Sinn verstanden"; see Heimo Dolch, *Kausalität im Verständnis des Theologen [Thomas] und der Begründer neuzeitlicher Physik: Besinnung auf die historischen Grundlegungen zum Zwecke einer sachgemässen Besprechung modernen Kausalitätsprobleme* (Freiburg: Herder, 1954), 106.

surpasses infinitely the formal finite reality of my soul."[74] Thus something must exist outside me that has as much reality or perfection as the idea of an infinite and perfect being. Hence an infinite and perfect being exists.

But is the actual existence of God necessary for explaining the idea of God? One scarcely needs to go back to Feuerbach, Durkheim, or Freud to be convinced that the idea of God could have other sources, such as empirical input, augmentation of existing ideas, religious training, psychological or social wish fulfillment. As long as the idea could be otherwise accounted for, Descartes's case is not compelling. But we are asking the question of coherence, not of proof. There is nothing strange about using God's existence to help account for the idea of God within a theistic conceptual system. For in this case an existing infinite being represents a natural explanation for the idea that we possess of such a being. Here a causal principle like the one Descartes posits would hold: the actual existence of this being would have to play a causal role in accounting for the ideas (explicit or implicit) that we possess of it. Reconstrued from the top down (and with the exception of 2), Descartes's premises thus constitute a credible account of how metaphysical and epistemological factors might be linked within a particular philosophical theology; only in this sense — and not as an allegedly freestanding proof — do they begin to constitute a coherent position.

The Proof from My Existence

The end of Meditation 3 offers a separate argument from the idea of God to God's existence.[75] In responding to Caterus, the author of the First Objections, Descartes called it "a further inquiry, *whether I could exist if God did not exist*," introduced not as an entirely new proof but to give "a more radical explanation" of the first argument (VII,105-6). With some justification, Caterus took this new causal proof to be a version of Thomas's second way (VII,94). In Descartes's words:

> I should therefore like to go further and inquire whether I myself, who have this idea [of a perfect being], could exist if no such being existed. From whom, in that case, would I derive my existence? From myself presumably, or from my parents, or from some other beings less perfect than God. . . . Yet if I derived my existence from myself, then I should neither doubt nor want, nor lack anything at all; for I should have given myself all the perfections of which I have any idea, and thus I should myself be God. (VII,48)

74. Gueroult, *Descartes' Philosophy*, 1:129.
75. The distinctiveness of the second way is argued in ibid., chap. 6; and in Curley, *Descartes against the Skeptics*, 138ff.

Moreover, he continues, even if the cause of my existence were discovered, I would still need to find some real power outside myself capable of preserving me in existence. What is the nature of this cause? To account for me, it has to be a thinking thing not dependent on anything else for its existence, that is, with enough power "to exist through its own might." But if it has this degree of power, and if it possesses the idea of all the perfections that we ascribe to God, then it has enough power for "actually possessing all the perfections of which it has an idea" (VII,49). Such a being, it seems clear, must actually be God; hence God exists.

The proof is not compelling; the difficulties with which it is saddled include the ones faced by Thomas's argument for a first uncaused cause as well as the problems with the first causal argument discussed above. Thus, once again, I suggest we concentrate on what sort of philosophical theology the argument implies rather than on poking further holes in it as a demonstration. In the first place, this metaphysic assumes that all entities require a preserving cause to maintain them in existence:

> The same power and action are needed to preserve anything at each individual moment of its duration as would be required to create that thing anew if it were not yet in existence. . . . I must therefore now ask myself whether I possess some power enabling me to bring it about that I who now exist will still exist a little while from now. . . . If there were such a power in me, I should undoubtedly be aware of it. But I experience no such power, and this very fact makes me recognize most clearly that I depend on some being distinct from myself. (VII,49)

As soon as one begins to experiment with the notion of an infinite (all-powerful) being, the sense of such an assumption becomes clear. Whatever things this being wills will exist for as long as it wills them; should it cease to will them, they would cease to be.[76] So understood, the quotation expresses a further consequence of the fundamental ontological distinction between necessary being and contingent being discussed above.

This point might be paraphrased by saying that preservation and creation are only temporally distinct; in terms of causal influence they come to the same thing. Now the contemporary reader might complain that only outmoded theological presuppositions — Descartes's own or those of his age —

---

76. The immediacy of this being's causal efficacy has been nicely worked out in Richard Francks, "Omniscience, Omnipotence and Pantheism," *Philosophy* 54 (1979): 395-99: everything that it willed would occur immediately and apparently without effort.

could warrant this claim. Few today find it obvious from common sense that the same force is needed to cause something to exist and to keep it in existence, for we tend to hold that, once made (or moved), a thing will continue to be (or to move) until some other force stops it — that is, we assume that the law of inertia in physics will apply to the ontological question of the very existence of things. But there is good theological reason to question this extension of the law of inertia: a created world would presumably be radically contingent and would continue in existence only with the continued willingness of its creator. Moreover, to say that its existence depends on two different decisions (or powers) of God would be inconsistent with the divine simplicity that Descartes wished to maintain: there can be only one type of divine act. Thus theism is better conceptualized by refusing to multiply types of divine causality; one achieves a greater theological simplicity (explanatory parsimony) if one does not.

Descartes's proof from his existence can ultimately be generalized into a two-term relation and a basic intuition. In this form it expresses an important insight even if it does not force assent. The first term expresses the starting point: the recognition that my mind has an individual and finite existence. The argument then appeals to the intuition that (as Beck puts it) "this existence of the finite is essentially contingent, dependent, and, *qua* merely finite and *qua* separate, illusory."[77] The intuition that human existence is contingent and transitory has not lost a lot of ground since 1600; one quickly thinks of examples of senseless massacres that have occurred just in the last year or so. The first term and the intuition then lead to the second term: the concept of noncontingency, necessary existence, enduring existence, or a ground of existence.

Now, since Feuerbach and Freud, it is harder to argue that, merely because we have the idea of noncontingency, a being must therefore exist who in fact has this nature. Nevertheless, the sense of finiteness and the corresponding intuition of a nonfinite ground are the sorts of intuitions one would expect were it the case that such a ground really existed. To infer to its necessary existence would amount to affirming the consequent. Still, in line with Peirce's method of abduction, one can note that the hypothesis of God's existence provides one rather natural explanation of the existence of such intuitions; one can then compare and contrast its explanatory strength with that of its nontheistic competitors. In short: philosophical theology may assert the world's contingency not as a ground but as an implication; the theistic hypothesis may be more or less convincing as an explanation of the sense of contingency than its

---

77. Beck, *Metaphysics of Descartes*, 184.

rivals. And to be judged convincing in this manner does constitute some evidence on behalf of the theory.

The Ontological Proof

The ontological proof takes two forms in Descartes, one focusing on the idea of a most perfect being *(ens perfectissimum)*, the other on the idea of a necessary being *(ens necessarium*, hence for Descartes *causa sui)*.

On Perfect Being and Necessary Existence

The argument from the concept of a perfect being has its sources in the Platonic-Augustinian tradition. It depends on the philosophical intuition that there are levels of perfection chaining up to a highest instance that is the source of all else. Put in these terms, the proof recalls Anselm's proof in the *Proslogion*. According to the argument, one begins with the idea of a supremely perfect being *(entis summe perfecti)* (VII,65) or a being who has all perfections (VII,67). I find an idea of this being within me,

> and my understanding that it belongs to his nature that he always exists is no less clear and distinct than is the case when I prove of any shape or number that some property belongs to its nature. Hence, even if it turned out that not everything on which I have meditated in these past days is true, I ought still to regard the existence of God as having at least the same level of certainty as I have hitherto attributed to the truths of mathematics. (VII,65-66)

In brief, it is a contradiction to think of a God (i.e., a most perfect being) who lacks existence (i.e., one of the perfections). I am therefore no more free to think of God without existence than to think of the most perfect being without all the perfections.

The ontological proof in this mode is thus based on the internal necessity of the concept of perfection.[78] The concept emerges in the *Meditations* (*summe perfecti*, VII,65), in the *Discourse* (*un Etre parfait*, VI,36) and — linked with the notion of power — in *Principles* I, art. 14 ("a being all-knowing, all-powerful and supremely perfect," or simply "an all-perfect being" [VIII,10]) and in the First Replies ("our mind . . . thinks of these perfections . . . [which] belong to an all-powerful being," VII,119). One can thus conclude, following Beyssade, that in this proof "*parfait* replaces *infini*." The logic of the ontological argument lies

---

78. Jean-Marie Beyssade, *La philosophie première de Descartes: Le temps et la cohérence de la métaphysique* (Paris: Flammarion, 1979), 311.

in the observation that, since God is infinite in *all* respects, only God is *perfectly* infinite: "Infinity is therefore the property of the one who is sovereignly perfect, and sovereign perfection is the nature or reason of the infinite."[79]

The driving force behind this argument is the premise that existence is a perfection. "He has all perfections," Descartes tells us, "and existence is one of them" (VII,67). Against Gassendi (VII,323), he maintains that existence is a valid property just as much as omnipotence is — as long as "property" stands for "any attribute, or for whatever can be predicated of a thing" (VII,382). Indeed, it is a "contradiction" if we try "to think of God (that is, a being supremely perfect) who lacks existence (that is, some perfection)" (VII,66). Finally, existence is called the supreme perfection (*absque summa perfectione,* "without a supreme perfection," VII,67).

It is not hard to name the operative presupposition of this argument. For Descartes (and for perfect-being theologians at least through Leibniz, if not up to the present day), existence is a good; it is better to exist than not to exist. Call it the premise of the value of Being. If one accepts this premise, one may be able to reformulate Descartes's argument so that it does not make existence into just another one of the predicates ascribed to a thing, which is the move that Kant so successfully criticized. One might argue: it is good to exist (the premise of the value of Being). What can be given existence can be given all the other perfections. Hence existence is the supreme perfection, insofar as it is the good that is the presupposition for having any of the other goods. The idea of a triangle, Descartes argues, is "superior" to the idea of a chimera (VII,383), since triangles can exist; they can have that unique perfection, existence, which is the prerequisite for having any actual perfections at all. And God is the supremely perfect being, since God not only can but *must* have the first perfection, existence, upon which all other goods depend. Now this argument does not compel assent, I think, since it presupposes the premise of the value of Being, a premise for which it is difficult to find independent grounds. Nevertheless, if one already takes everything that exists to be the creation of a good God (as Descartes did), then one would be inclined to hold that existence is a good in the sense required by the proof.

What of necessary existence? Dieter Henrich notes that the proof from the *ens necessarium* stems from the Aristotelian-Thomistic tradition: from the contrast between the finite world (in which all beings are contingent and cannot account for themselves by themselves) and their source or first cause (which depends on nothing else, i.e., has its cause within itself).[80] In contrast

---

79. Ibid., 313: "L'infini est donc le propre du souverainement parfait, et le souverainement parfait la nature ou raison de l'infini."

80. Henrich, *Der ontologische Gottesbeweis,* 4. Henrich claims to find a significant de-

to the Thomistic arguments *a contingentia mundi*, however, Descartes's argument can also be made without appealing to contingent (merely possible) beings. One sees from the very concept of this being that it is self-caused; since its existence stems already from its concept, it is a necessary being. Caterus complains that although one has the *idea* of a perfect being, hence an existing being, "it still does not follow that the existence in question is anything actual in the real world" (VII,99). To remove the difficulty, Descartes counters, "we must distinguish between possible and necessary existence" (VII,116); we perceive that only God has the latter. Later he adds: "We notice that necessary existence is contained in our concept of God (however inadequate that concept may be)" (VII,152). According to the axiomatized version following the Second Replies, "To say that something is contained in the nature or concept of a thing is the same as saying that it is true of that thing. But necessary existence is contained in the concept of God. Therefore it may be truly affirmed of God that necessary existence belongs to him, or that he exists" (VII,166-67; cf. *Principles* I, art. 15).

Ultimately, I conclude, Descartes did not intend to separate the arguments from perfection and from necessity. When we look more closely at the notion of the most perfect being, we recognize that necessary existence is one of its characteristics: a perfect being is necessary; a necessary being is perfect. We are now far enough to begin to spell out the logic of this position more fully.

The Intuition of the Ontological Proof

In this section — reflecting the reciprocal (hermeneutical) relationship that exists between philosophy and history — we anticipate a conclusion that will emerge in later chapters, in order to formulate a preunderstanding that will structure the historical treatment later in the book. The tradition of necessary-being theology or "ontotheology" that extends (roughly) from Descartes to the early Kant can be boiled down to the claim that we can form a clear and distinct idea of a necessary being; and the core of Kant's later critique lies in the oppos-

---

velopment in Descartes's thought between the perfection argument in Meditation 5 and the arguments from necessity in the Replies. But the textual evidence does not support his case, nor does he need it for his broader argument. That God's existence necessarily follows from his essence is clearly maintained in Meditation 5 (VII,68-69); conversely, perfection continues to be the guiding framework for the discussions of the ontological argument in the Replies (e.g., VII,118-19). More difficult still is to justify Henrich's choice of the First Replies as "der einzigen authentischen Stelle" for the Cartesian ontological proof (p. 21). Why would the true version of the proof appear here and yet not be repeated in the Second Replies or the *Principles* (so Henrich, 19), whereas the idea of perfection continues to play a key role in both later writings?

ing claim that no clear (nonconfused) idea can be formed of such a being. Already in the writings of More and Cudworth, however, it began to become clear that a being is really necessary only when the concept of its essence already includes its existence. Leibniz's insight was to realize "that the possibility of denying an ontological proof of God's existence amounts to the same thing as disputing the possibility of a particular conception of God."[81]

The evaluation of the ontological proof therefore has less to do with the validity of the argumentative moves themselves than with the truth of the single premise: "we have a clear notion (intuition) of a necessary being." This same tendency comes to light, I believe, when one examines the debate surrounding the ontological proof in recent analytic philosophy. Here too the argument appears to boil down to one's evaluation of the central premise. One thinks of Alvin Plantinga's claim that we can form the idea of a maximally excellent being, a being that exists in all possible worlds. If this being is possible, then it exists in all possible worlds and therefore necessarily exists in our world. Plantinga argues that there is nothing unreasonable about positing the existence of such a being.[82] But critical treatments have questioned whether we can in fact form a clear (consistent) idea of such a being. Is affirming the possible existence of such a (necessary) being a more or a less reasonable move to make? Unfortunately, it appears to be an intuition that, generally, theists have and nontheists do not have — which rather limits the value of any arguments based on this intuition!

The conclusion of this section therefore matches the result of the previous treatment of the causal proofs. The premises of the ontological proof are coherent outworkings of Descartes's theological position; they make the nature and implications of that position more perspicuous. But if one does not already view the metaphysic as a live option, one is unlikely to find the argument's central premise (and hence the argument itself) compelling.

Interestingly, Descartes seems already to have seen this. At several points he presents the ontological proof as resting on a single intuition. For instance, in the French translation of the Second Replies he observes, "For there are some things that are as well known without being proved by something else, as other

---

81. Henrich, *Der ontologische Gottesbeweis,* 171. The preceding three sentences summarize perhaps the central thesis of Henrich's classic treatment — esp. if one adds, "And Kant was right." For a more recent exhaustive history of the ontological argument, which is in several respects critical of Henrich's conclusions, see Jan Rohls, *Theologie und Metaphysik: Der ontologische Gottesbeweis und seine Kritiker* (Gütersloh: Gütersloher Verlagshaus Gerd Mohn, 1987).

82. Alvin Plantinga, *The Nature of Necessity* (Oxford: Clarendon, 1974), chap. 10, esp. pp. 219-20.

things are understood only through a long process of discourse and reasoning."[83] Brunschvicg comments, "Of all the faculties, therefore, it is intuition to which the ontological argument reduces; it reduces not to a partial intuition, of which the argument is a step-by-step expression, but to a total intuition that covers the whole field of the metaphysical analysis following the *cogito*."[84] The same stance underlies Descartes's statement that the ontological proof perhaps should not be viewed as a proof at all; its conclusion "can be grasped as self-evident *(per se nota)* by those who are free from prejudices" (VII,167). A major point of the *Geometrical Summary* after the Second Replies is that the argument "is reduced to a single proposition that constitutes an axiom."[85] This also explains Descartes's confidence that reflection on the idea of a supremely perfect being will reveal it to contain "wholly necessary existence." For "this alone, without a formal argument, will make them realize that God exists; and this will eventually be just as self-evident to them as the fact that the number two is even or that three is odd, and so on. For there are certain truths which some people find self-evident, while others come to understand them only by means of a formal argument" (VII,163-64).

We might say that, in the case of the ontological proof, a syllogism can be constructed, although the real function of such a proof is simply to make more obvious the logic of its central premise. For Descartes, it is a logic that the mind will conceive intuitively and without need of syllogisms as soon as one has clearly understood the proposition: God is a necessary being.

Conclusion

How then are we to evaluate the Cartesian ontological proof if in fact the decision rests solely on whether a clear and distinct idea can be formed of a necessary being? How is one to answer the criticism (to which we shall return) that the various concepts of God in Descartes are incompatible, even contradictory? Certainly not, as Descartes did in the Replies, merely by repeating his assertion that the proof *just is* clear or by complaining that his critics are simply missing the point. Instead, the solution is actually to present a clear and distinct theory of such a being, focusing initially on only the most fundamental attributes and

---

83. "Car il y a des choses qui sont ainsi connues sans preuvres par quelques-uns, que d'autres n'entendent que par un long discours et raisonnement" (IX/1,127).

84. Brunschvicg, "Mathématique et métaphysique chez Descartes," 315: "De toutes façons donc, c'est à l'intuition que ramène l'argument ontologique et non pas à une intuition partielle dont l'argument, pris à part, serait l'expression, mais à une intuition totale qui couvre tout le champ de l'analyse métaphysique depuis le *Cogito*."

85. Gueroult, *Descartes' Philosophy*, 1:251.

their interconnections. God's existence cannot be directly (foundationally) grounded in a single argument; only the coherence of the overall conception could supply sufficient evidence of its clear and distinct conceivability and — in proportion to its clarity or confusedness — the requisite evidence for or against the likelihood of its existence. To specify a coherent philosophical theology and to assess the conceptual difficulties it faces are the central goals of the present book.

Of course, to reduce the ontological proof to a debate about theological coherence represents a negative conclusion vis-à-vis the soundness of the proof taken as an autonomous argument. Perhaps Kant's criticisms will in the future be circumvented by a more sophisticated modal logic; perhaps philosophers will someday generally agree that "God" is a concept that contains its own existence and hence that this being exists. I remain skeptical; there is little evidence to date of such a convergence. Still, what fails as proof may still succeed as conceptual explication. In the case of the ontological proof, even more clearly than in the proofs from causality, we are led to focus on the logic of a certain concept: the concept of a necessary being who, if it exists, exists with necessity, possesses all conceivable perfections, and possesses them in the highest conceivable degree, viz. infinitely.

From Many Proofs to One Theory of God

It is crucial for the Cartesian project (and for ours) to think the theistic proofs together. The contemplation of God, according to the end of Meditation 3, "enables us to know the greatest joy of which we are capable in this life" (VII,52). If this is so, argues Alquié, the distinction between the proofs cannot be essential: "leur nature se découvrira mieux à qui considérera, au contraire, leur unité."[86] In a letter to Mesland Descartes is explicit: "It doesn't matter whether my second demonstration, founded on our own existence, is considered as different from the first or only as an explication of the first," for "there isn't any effect coming from God, from which one would not be able to demonstrate his existence."[87] The question gains further importance in light of Marion's detailed argument that Descartes's various conceptions of God — specifically, the con-

---

86. Alquié, *Le découverte métaphysique*, 219.

87. Descartes to Mesland, 5/2/1644; IV,112, AM 6:141: "Il importe peu que ma seconde démonstration, fondée sur notre propre existence, soit considérée comme différente de la première, ou seulement comme une explication de cette première," for "il n'y a aucun effet venant de lui, par lequel on ne puisse démontrer son existence."

cepts of God as infinite, as perfect, as all-powerful, as self-caused, and as necessary being — are incompatible.[88] How can we move from Descartes's multiple ways to a single, consistent theory of God?

The Complementarity of the Proofs

Much turns on the relationship between the theistic proofs in Meditations 3 and 5, a topic that Descartes scholars have hotly debated. In a now classic interchange, Gouhier argued that the two meditations contain independent arguments, to which Gueroult responded that the arguments are really one.[89] According to Gueroult, the ontological argument, taken alone, has only the status of any other mathematical demonstration. Unfortunately, Descartes's skepticism about the accuracy of his memory makes it problematic to affirm that one still knows things that one once demonstrated (e.g., VII,69-70). For this reason, Descartes intentionally delayed the argument from the essence of God until Meditation 5, the meditation whose topic is the problem of essence. As a result, the ontological proof can depend on the Meditation 3 proof, which guarantees that "God is not a deceiver," hence that our clear and distinct ideas, such as clear memories and the ideas of mathematics, are true:

> Detached from the argument through effects [in Meditation 3], the ontological argument cannot escape falling under the spell of the metaphysical doubt that is concerned with the validity of intuitions of evidence. It is metaphysically insufficient, as insufficient as the certitude of a mathematician who has not inquired into the reasons for resting content with [her or his certainty].[90]

88. See Marion, "Essential Incoherence," 297-338; see also, more recently, his *Sur le prisme métaphysique de Descartes: Constitution et limites de l'onto-théo-logie dans la pensée cartésienne* (Paris: Presses Universitaires de France, 1986), chap. 4. At a number of points, however, Marion seems deliberately to ignore available attempts at conceptual reconciliation in the interest of convincing us that Descartes's view is a mass of contradiction. Doesn't he all but grant this in the end when he acknowledges that the notion of God as infinite is the most fundamental of the attributes and meets all three of his criteria ("Essential Incoherence," 329-30)? I have criticized Marion in "Descartes and Infinite Perfection," *American Catholic Philosophy Association Proceedings* 66 (1992): 137-47.

89. H. Gouhier, "La preuve ontologique de Descartes," *Revue internationale de philosophie* 8 (1954): 295-303; Gueroult, *Descartes' Philosophy*, chap. 8; idem, *Nouvelles réflexions sur la preuve ontologique de Descartes* (Paris: Vrin, 1955). Some of the important passages from the debate have been translated in Donald Cress, "Does Descartes' 'Ontological Argument' Really Stand on Its Own?" *Studi internazionali di Filosofia* 5 (1973): 127-40.

90. Gueroult, *Nouvelles réflexions*, 71.

In short, "the a priori proof draws all its rightful validity from the a posteriori argument," since only the latter insures the truth of clear ideas; properly speaking, there is only one proof for the existence of God: "The proof by effects [the a posteriori argument] must be considered as the principle and even sole proof of the existence of God."[91]

I suggest, however, that Gouhier's criticisms of this position should be taken as decisive. Descartes suggests elsewhere that the proofs in the *Meditations* are given in the order in which he discovered them, not in their "synthetic" order. He himself places the ontological argument first in the *Geometrical Summary* (after the Second Replies) and in the *Principles* (I, arts. 5, 13-14). Moreover, under Gueroult's view it is hard to see how Descartes would have called the ontological argument a "proof" at all, if there is really only one proof, the a posteriori. How should we conceive a proof of the existence of God "which would be of value only in the case where another proof had already demonstrated the existence of God?"[92] The proofs cannot be conceptually unrelated, of course — at least that much follows from our analysis of Descartes's position to this point. Still, each on its own is meant to be a sound argument for the existence of God.

In the reconstruction of the *Meditations* that follows, I show that the two arguments can and should be understood as complementary. The "persuasion" in Meditation 3, as Rodis-Lewis notes, "has a tentative validity before the grounding of science in God."[93] Even if the ontological proof does not depend conceptually on the causal proofs, it evidences perhaps a genetic or psychological dependence. Initial doubt had cast into question even the conclusions of mathematics. The *cogito* establishes knowledge of myself; then I discover gradually that more and more items of knowledge are free from doubt until I arrive at the transcendent God. One of the first areas of knowledge to reemerge from doubt is that of the mathematical truths (cf. *Principles* I, art. 13). "*Psychologically*," Rodis-Lewis argues, "the ontological argument only appears when spontaneous confidence in its evidence has been strengthened" (p. 285). First one must be convinced that everything one clearly and distinctly perceives in a thing actually belongs to it (VII,54).

---

91. Gueroult, *Descartes' Philosophy*, 1:243. See also idem, "La vérité de la science et la vérité de la chose dans les preuves de l'existence de Dieu," in *Descartes* [Second Royaumont Conference] (Paris: de Minuit, 1957), 108, 112.

92. Gouhier, "La preuve ontologique," 296.

93. See Geneviève Rodis-Lewis, "On the Complementarity of Meditations III and V: From the 'General Rule' of Evidence to 'Certain Science,'" in Rorty, ed., *Essays on Descartes' Meditations*, 270. The next reference in the text is also to this essay.

Toward a Unity of the Cartesian Concepts of God

The First Replies offer, I believe, a consistent way of connecting the various components of Descartes's theory of God.[94] First, he argues, we form the idea of the essence of perfection. Then we doubt whether it is a "true idea," and look for a way to show that it is not an arbitrary construction of our minds. The discussion leads to the notion of the highest degree of one particular perfection, power: infinite power or omnipotence. We discover that the greatest conceivable power must also have power over its own existence; but this is to say that this being must exist. Moreover, from the idea of this power one can derive the other perfections, since a being that has power over its own existence could and would give itself the other perfections. Consistent with this reconstruction, Descartes's important notion of God as self-caused *(causa sui)* can (and must) be interpreted in the sense of necessary existence. It connotes having power over one's own existence such that no outside cause is needed for one to exist.

It is absurd, by contrast, to interpret "self-caused" in a temporal sense (a being *S* brings itself into existence at time *t*). Arnauld's Fourth Objections argue decisively against the ambiguities in Meditation 3 that imply such a temporal causal relation. An infinite being, Arnauld complains, cannot derive its existence from itself "in the positive sense," but only "in the negative sense of not deriving it from anything else" (VII,210). A supremely powerful being must always have existed; it is self-caused only in the sense that it is a being "whose existence is its essence" (VII,213). In a 1641 letter to Mersenne, Descartes grants that Arnauld is correct and changes his manuscripts accordingly (3/4/1641; III,318ff., AM 4:308). He substitutes the word "understand" for "acquire" *(adipisci)* in Meditation 3 ("acquire all the other perfections of God," VII,47), in order to avoid the impression of a temporal process. And he alters the First Replies, changing his construal of what it means for God to be able to exist by his own power *(propriā suā vi posse existere)*. For the temporally loaded phrase, "a power can be given by means of which he exists" *(aliquam dari posse potentiam cujus opere existat)*, Descartes now speaks more vaguely of the necessity of considering God's immense power *(ad immensam ejus potentiam attendentes)*. I conclude that the cause in "self-caused" has been correctly transformed into an assertion of ontological status. This allows the notion of immense power to serve as the key conceptual link between the causal proof, which depends on the notion of a perfect being, and the ontological proof, which turns on the notion of a necessary being.

94. The basis for this reconstruction is First Replies, VII,118ff. See also Henrich, *Der ontologische Gottesbeweis*, 15-16.

Relating the Infinite and the Finite

Combining the foregoing with our discussion of Descartes's causal proofs above, we obtain something like the following as a general description of the conceptual movement from the finite to the infinite. (1) Descartes begins with a version of the Scholastic proofs *a contingentia mundi,* closest perhaps to the *via causalitatis.* He notes that we have an idea of the infinite; he inquires into the causal chain leading back from that idea, remarking that there must be some ultimate source, that it cannot be endless, and so on; and he concludes that a being must really exist who has these qualities "to the limit" and who is the cause of our idea of perfection. (2) He then makes a negative move (reminiscent of the *via negativa*), and this in a twofold manner. (a) He asserts that such a negative being could not be fully knowable: Although we see with necessity where the argument must lead, we do not thereby possess its final term (more on this below). (b) The move backward is not just in the order of causes, as in Thomas's second way; it involves an essential ontological negation. We recognize that the very order that we are examining — the order of ideas stemming from a finite thinker — itself needs to be negated, and only from the negation of the finite do we arrive at the infinite. (3) In reflecting on this fact, we make a move reminiscent of the *via eminentiae:* we posit something qualitatively different from ourselves, and in understanding this qualitative difference we understand God.

What is interesting about this reconstruction is that it implies both quantitative and qualitative components in the movement from the finite to the infinite. According to the purely quantitative approach, God has the particular attributes that finite beings have but to a higher degree. To arrive at a theory of God, we simply increase each of our own qualities. By contrast, qualitative approaches maintain that God is the opposite of whatever characterizes our nature; God is the negation of the negation, the being who is what we are not and in whom whatever we lack is not lacking. To reconstruct Descartes, as we will see, we must give a place to both approaches; in some way we will have to think of them together.

Quantitative versus Qualitative Approaches

The *quantitative way* of conceiving God is the method of taking qualities that we know "to the limit." It most often surfaces when Descartes draws comparisons and analogies between his procedure and mathematics. We have already examined the Cartesian distinction between the infinite and the indefinite (pp. 67-71 above). When Burman raises, as a counterexample to *Principles* I, art. 26 ("that only God is infinite"), the example of things that seem to have no limits, such as the world, numbers, and greatness, Descartes grants that the world might be infinite in itself, though we can know only its indefiniteness. He adds, "for the indefinite, *multiplied without ceasing,* as is here the case, is the infinite itself *(nam indefinitum semper et semper multiplicatum, ut hic fit, est ipsum infinitum).* Thus perhaps we can say of the world that it is infinite, and also of numbers, etc." (V,167, emphasis mine). Likewise, in the Second Replies he also compares the relation between the divine and the human intellect to the relation between "the idea of an infinite number" and "the idea of a number raised to the second or fourth power" (VII,137).

In general, Descartes seems to have recourse to quantitative arguments when critics argue that infinity is not thinkable, or that a particular segment of his argument no longer works when applied to infinity. For instance, when Arnauld protests that the concept of efficient cause could not be applied to an infinite being (VII,213), Descartes seeks to justify our applying concepts appropriate to finite things also the infinite. He has extrapolated to the limit, to infinity, he says; in doing so he has merely used the same argument form as Archimedes' demonstration of the properties of a sphere (VII,245). Archimedes had demonstrated the properties of a solid rectangle inscribed in a sphere and then applied these to the sphere itself conceived as a solid having an infinite number of sides.[95] Like Archimedes, then, Descartes wants to rely on an analogy between the finite infinitely extended (a rectilinear figure with an infinite number of sides) and the infinite.

Still, beyond the theological reasons introduced above, there are other difficulties in the way of Descartes's use of a truly quantitative argument. Moving through ever smaller or ever larger numbers (e.g., number of sides) to the *infinitely* small or large presupposes the principle of continuity, a form of argumentation that would later be central to Leibniz's understanding of the infinite.[96] Now there is no problem with arguing in this way if one is willing to apply the principles of infinitesimal calculus to pure ideas. But it seems that Descartes cannot employ such a Leibnizian principle, since in the *Geometry* he is committed to using the pure theory of proportions. Indeed, the method of proportion is central in Cartesian metaphysics as well as in geometry; the arguments frequently employ three terms and fill in the fourth. How then can he justify the appeal to the infinite as continuous with the finite?[97] It seems that,

95. The example is analyzed in Jules Vuillemin, *Mathématique et métaphysique chez Descartes* (Paris: Presses Universitaires de France, 1960), note III, p. 145.

96. The principle was first formulated by Leibniz in 1687 in *Nouvelles de la République des Lettres,* 744. See chap. 4 below.

97. It is possible that Descartes could consistently employ a principle of contingent relations to justify his method, as Vuillemin has suggested (*Mathématique et métaphysique,*

whatever quantitative techniques Descartes employs, finally they will have to be supplemented by an insistence on the qualitative difference.

The *qualitative way*, in contrast to the quantitative, negates the finite as a whole to get to the infinite, which is qualitatively different from the finite. Descartes correctly stresses the structure of difference in the movement from finite toward infinite, despite the quantitative metaphors used to justify the introduction of the latter notion. It may appear, prima facie, as though Descartes in Meditation 3 constructs a notion of God by taking all the perfections that the human mind can conceive, stretching them to the limit, reconciling them, and then attributing them to God.[98] For I add together "all [the perfections] which I conceive to be in God," controlled by the perfection of the "unity, the simplicity, or the inseparability of all the attributes" (VII,50). It is manifest, however, that the process of adding up the perfections can never be completed. The allegedly quantitative process could never be carried out by the human mind, for whoever says "God" says something such that absolutely all perfections are comprised in it (*Deus tale quid dicat quod omnes omnino perfectiones in se comprehendit; Conversation with Burman*, V,161). Moreover, the being that I conceive as God is "the possessor of all the perfections *which I cannot grasp*," though I can "somehow reach [them] in my thought" (*omnes illas perfectiones, quas ego non comprehendere, sed quocunque modo attingere cogitatione possum*; VII,52, emphasis mine).

The Method of Augmentation

What is finally involved in attaining the notion of God, I suggest, is a sort of combination of the quantitative and qualitative ways, namely the process of amplification or augmentation. How is this accomplished? Any perfections I wish to ascribe to God must first be qualified as *infinite* perfections. When the authors of the Second Objections demand that Descartes "add something further which lifts us up to an incorporeal or spiritual plane" (VII,124), he replies

---

145-46). This geometrical method works only with a property of the most general construction and transports it to another figure of no less general construction, which differs from the first only in secondary and accidental circumstances. The property in question cannot be used, directly or implicitly, in explaining the property that it is concerned to demonstrate. As long as the principle of causality is a contingent relation in the connection being made between the finite and the infinite, it would meet this condition and could be used. But the generality required threatens to make the comparison vacuous.

98. For a presentation and critique of this view, see Marion, "Essential Incoherence," esp. 315-16; and my critique in "Descartes and Infinite Perfection," 137-47. I am grateful to Michael Degnan for helpful criticisms of this argument.

pointedly that the Second Meditation "was designed with this sole aim in mind" (VII,137). In the Fifth Replies, he argues that we have "a faculty for amplifying all created perfections (*facultas omnes perfectiones creatas ampliandi*), that is, for conceiving of something greater or more ample than they" (VII,365). Finally, note Descartes's response to Regius, who had claimed that we already have in us ideas of wisdom, power, goodness, quantity, and so on, which we then apply (project?) as God's perfections. He responds that this is exactly how we form the idea of God, but that we would not be able to extend these qualities to infinity "if we did not have our origin from the being in whom [these qualities] exist in actual infinity" (*in quo actu reperiantur infinitae;* letter of 5/24/1640; III,64). Clearly, for Descartes there is finally a qualitative break. Our own capacity to conceive perfect attributes even in limited form can be explained only by the actual existence of a being who first possesses them in augmented — namely in superlative — form.

Descartes's method thus implies a fusion of quantitative and qualitative elements. The quantitative method provides an initial framework for introducing the concept of the infinite, giving cognitive content to an attribute such as omnipotence by placing it on a continuum with finite quantities of power. It therefore helps to explain the presence of such infinite ideas in us. Nonetheless, an infinite perfection remains always qualitatively different from the human conception of it. The notion of augmentation nicely expresses the connection: We are dealing with perfections that we can conceive *and* with their cognitive distance from the finite. A break remains: They are possessed by God in a manner that finite minds cannot fully grasp.

We have been able to show the proofs to be compatible, even part of a single, unified strategy. But a unified Descartes is not ipso facto a convincing Descartes. Doesn't an augmentation argument for God open itself up directly to a Feuerbachian projection critique? According to Feuerbach, the God of unlimited perfection is postulated as an (improved) extension of qualities that we already find present in human nature. After all, all that we actually know is the mode of being proper to the human species, which Feuerbach called *human species-being.* More generally, empiricists might respond that it is simply a given of our mental life that we can augment or amplify our finite ideas to the point of the idea of God. Even Descartes admits in Meditation 3 that he can conceive God as actually infinite to such a degree that it is not possible to add to the sovereign perfection that God possesses. As soon as we grant the faculty of augmenting human qualities a necessary role in attaining the idea of God, can we not dismiss the idea of an infinite being as a product of human projection or wish fulfillment, returning the perfections thus ascribed to their proper owner, the human species?

Descartes acknowledges that his theology relies on this power to amplify ideas indefinitely; "but this passage to the limit, to the absolute, cannot itself be derived from experience, which is what lends the argument its force."[99] I do think there is some justice in the demand for an explanation of this faculty, possessed by finite beings, which is able to take finite ideas and augment them to the level of infinity. But empiricists might declare themselves still dissatisfied. The source of faculties is, after all, no longer an empirical question; all that needs to be explained are the actual processes by which we transform ideas. Can we prove that we have an idea that could not have been augmented in this fashion? How would such a thing be proved? By coming up with a human idea that, say, developmental psychologists and anthropologists agree is inexplicable, that is, for whose presence in our minds no social scientific explanation can be given? One does not have to have read much social science to recognize how unlikely such a result would be.

I suggest that a final refutation of projectionist accounts remains unlikely and therefore that proofs based on augmentation cannot be judged as sound. Nevertheless, only an idea of God that is comprehensible and at the same time developed "from above," out of its own logic, can establish its credibility over against the projection critiques. Judged by this criterion, then, the theory of augmentation represents an intriguing specification of the finite/infinite relation. On the one hand, it provides conceptual guidelines that give some content to the notion of the infinite, thus avoiding equivocation; as Descartes says, we can understand what the infinite means without "grasping" it. Further, we would expect the infinite to be related to the finite in *some* way; the concepts imply some sort of connection to which the notion of augmentation does justice. On the other hand, it still (rightly) maintains the qualitative difference between them: The infinite is the nonfinite; the finite is the not-unlimited. We return to these questions in the following chapter.

CONCLUSION

In this chapter we have watched as the *cogito* was stripped of its alleged foundational role and subordinated to *essentia infinita*, which I defended by means of its coherence rather than by foundational proofs. This reinterpretation led in turn to a rereading of the theistic proofs. Although it could appear, for example,

---

99. Geneviève Rodis-Lewis, *Descartes et le rationalisme* (Paris: Presses Universitaires de France, 1970), 33.

that the ontological argument grounds all else as an a priori starting point, standing outside all systems, we have instead found it to function as a conceptual tool for conceiving that infinite ground that is (and must be) always already presupposed by the *cogito*. This switch in status for Descartes's notion of God might even have the tendency to transform his theology into a meditation from within the infinite on the being "in whom we live and move and have our being," a sort of *fides quaerens intellectum*, rather than an ontotheology that successfully consummates the inference to God from independent human experience.

I have espoused the goal of systematicity. Yet the attentive reader will have noted how much of the treatment was developed in the context of *achieving* the concept of God, either through arguments or intuition. This is no coincidence: Descartes paid much more attention to getting *to* the concept than he did to giving it a detailed systematic outworking. However, if I am skeptical about Descartes's achievements in this regard, doesn't this leave him in a rather weak position? Descartes never became a systematic metaphysician, and what he put his time into — the proofs — cannot be judged sound.

I suggest, however, that this fact is just what makes Descartes a model for discussions of the idea of God in early modern philosophy (and today). The concept of God *is* a problematic concept in modern thought. Its exposition can never escape the controversial nature of the concept itself. One way to express this fact is to develop a doctrine of God exclusively in the context of deductive proofs or natural theology, as in Descartes's case. But we have come to the conclusion that the foundationalist quest of natural theology was unsuccessful. Another way to convey that the concept of God is a matter of dispute is to embed it in a metaphysic the status of which is held always to be hypothetical, preliminary, open to revision. My attempt to develop such a Cartesian metaphysic, working from the context of the Cartesian proofs, represents one means of conveying this hypothetical status — as the insistence in chapter 1 that theology may have to remain pluralistic or regulative was another. Given Descartes's similar sense of the burden of proof borne by the concept of God, it is fair to conclude that, in one important sense, the attempt of this book to develop models of God in a pluralistic context is, at heart, a continuation of the Cartesian project. How extensively Descartes's own concept of God will have to be revised will become clearer and clearer as we move into the criticisms of the perfection idea in part II.

PART II

ON THE FATE OF
PERFECT-BEING THEOLOGY

CHAPTER THREE

On the Very Idea
of an Infinite and Perfect God

We have discovered that the concept of the infinite, like that of perfection, plays a — perhaps *the* — central role in Descartes's philosophy. It is "so important," urges Koyré, "that Cartesianism may be considered as being wholly based upon that idea."[1] These two ideas became if anything more central in the philosophy of Leibniz, to whom we turn next. Before doing so, however, I propose stepping back from the early modern tradition and exploring the logic of these two concepts on their own. How are they connected to major features of the traditional doctrine of God? Are they presuppositions or entailments? Did they always play this role? Are infinity and perfection conceptually compatible?

This last question is particularly important since, as we will see, traditional philosophical theology required that both be predicated of God *and* that they be linked, such that divine infinity implied divine perfection (i.e., moral perfection or absolute goodness). Together, it was thought, they would point toward the highest concept of metaphysics, the idea of the Absolute. The study in this chapter and the next will show, however, that the two concepts evidence radically different logics and that one is saddled with difficulties not borne by

---

1. A. Koyré, *From the Closed World to the Infinite Universe*, 106. Geneviève Rodis-Lewis concludes that "l'originalité de Descartes est de faire de l'infini positif la condition même de la pensée du négatif, trait qui va marquer profondément le 'grand rationalisme' du XVIIe siècle" (*Descartes et le rationalisme*, 32); and F. Alquié argues, "L'être est ce à partir de quoi toute existence est pensée, l'infini est ce à partir de quoi toute chose finie est comprise, l'Être infini est donc toujours déjà présent, et si la science fut le domaine de l'Être perdu, la métaphysique est celui de l'Être retrouvé" (*La découverte métaphysique*, 219).

the other. If in the end, as I think, we are driven to a doctrine of God that employs the one and distances itself from the other, this will direct us toward a whole new series of theological models, including some that diverge from traditional theism in important respects.

But first the concepts of infinity and perfection demand some philosophical and historical attention of their own. This analysis contributes to an understanding not only of the metaphysical core of early modern philosophy but also of some key contemporary debates. That it serves both functions is no accident: Descartes's philosophy, and that of many of his followers, sought to make maximal use of their strengths and to avoid their pitfalls. Descartes had freed himself from enough of Scholastic Aristotelianism to grant the real existence of the infinite; indeed, it is fair to say that Cartesianism stands or falls on whether one can construct a compelling and convincing theory of infinite perfection.

I propose that we begin by examining the intuition of infinitude, watching how the intuition gets developed into a philosophical and theological theory and what pitfalls it is subjected to along the way. After an aside on the analytic program of "perfect-being theology," we will need to go back and review the historical development of the concepts of infinite being and perfect being. By combining historical and conceptual analysis in this fashion, one allows the connections between the two concepts, and their tensions, to emerge. Only then, with the conceptual terrain laid out before us, will we be in a position to advance in our understanding of the modern problem of God.

INTUITING THE FINITE, INTUITING THE INFINITE

We have seen something of the richness of the notions of infinity and perfection in Descartes's own work. In this section I develop a constructive line of thought that attempts to mediate between some concerns in contemporary analytic philosophy and the older tradition of immediate knowledge of and participation in the divine. Building on the discoveries from the last chapter, I suggest we trace the movement from the intuitive to the conceptual — specifically, the movement from the initial intuition of human finitude, through its first intuitive implications, and on toward a systematic theory of God that seeks to account for these initial intuitions as well as to explain the broader data of science and human experience.

Such an approach presupposes an at least initial distinction between the infinite as *intuitive idea* and the infinite as *concept*. Specifically, it seeks to avoid the (all too frequent) move from the intuition of infinitude to the concept of an infinite being. Against Descartes, I shall argue that the intuition of infinitude is not sufficient to determine the corresponding concept, much less the existence of such a being! With the move to concepts, pluralism arises: intuitions of finitude and infinity can be diversely conceptualized. They can lead us, for example, to analytic philosophical theology, to trinitarian doctrinal theology, to a real but in principle ungraspable furthest horizon (as in Cantor's absolute infinite), to a regulative limit notion as in Kant's philosophy — or the whole thing can be dismissed as a philosophically uninteresting feature of the human psyche. There are numerous ways to conceive the infinite; each demands separate evaluation as one moves from one's starting intuitions to constructing metaphysical systems based on them.

First, then, the more general question: What happens when one begins to reflect by paying attention to intuitions? Are there any shared intuitions that point in the direction of the infinite? What implications do they have and of what use are they for constructive metaphysics or theology? To gain some clarity on these issues I offer the following meditation in the spirit of Descartes.

The Original Intuition

"When I turn my mind's eye upon myself," writes Descartes in Meditation 3, "I understand that I am a thing which is incomplete and dependent on another and which aspires without limit to ever greater and better things" (VII,51). This is the Cartesian original intuition: I am finite.

There is much to recommend the intuition of finitude as a starting point for metaphysical reflection. We know immediately that we are finite in the sense of being dependent on others and things outside ourselves. The sense of dependency begins already when one reflects on perception, with its passive element of dependence on the world that is perceived. Likewise, ontogenetically young children know their dependence on their parents. To live they require food, drink, affection from outside themselves. Studies also show a broader sense of dependence as children age;[2] their fears now expand to include the fear of bodily injury, social rejection, later the fear of death, destruction of the environment, or nuclear catastrophe. Although types of dependencies change, the phenomenon of dependency itself hardly lessens: beyond the continuing physical needs, adults know the needs for affection, friendship, success or acknowledgment, challenge, relaxation — and ultimately for a sense of the meaningful-

---

2. See Erik H. Erikson, *The Challenge of Youth* (New York: Anchor, 1963); idem, *Childhood and Society* (New York: Norton, 1950).

ness of one's lifework. Analogously, everything we see around us evidences a similar dependence or limitation; it is a pervasive feature of the biological realm as a whole.

We intuit ourselves as finite. The original intuition can be expressed in a myriad of ways, of course; how it is expressed is a function of how one reconstructs it conceptually and therefore belongs to a later point in our inquiry. Maybe my original intuition of finitude has its roots in the sense that my power is limited. Or perhaps, following Descartes, it lies in the *dubito:* I know I am finite because no amount of skepticism can cast into question that I doubt. Or perhaps the awareness of finitude even forms the core of the *cogito,* of my existence as thinking subject.

What is the status of this immediate intuition of finitude? It has been called a logical truth — but also conceptual, analytic, a priori, or a basic given of human experience. I suggest that it deserves the name, if anything does, of a fundamental intuition. Whichever status one ascribes to it, it is the sort of intuition for which no additional evidence needs to be (or perhaps can be) adduced. "Analytic" is probably a bad label, since, even if the intuition is not preconceptual, it has not (yet) risen to the level of distinct concepts. Something similar holds for the label "a priori," although many have been tempted here, as with the Cartesian *cogito,* to speak of a synthetic a priori item of knowledge. At any rate, as fundamental the intuition of finitude is an early and a central component of metaphysical reflection. I will speak of it as an intuition and also as an idea, since it is, after all, an intuition with content; but (at least initially) it should not be treated as a philosophical concept. What it "really" means and what existence statements it implies are matters for subsequent conceptual explication and argumentation.

From the Finite to the Infinite

I am finite; I am not infinite. Insofar as it arises without argument and almost by negation alone, the transition from intuiting finitude to an intuition of the infinite has good claim to immediacy. The original intuition — I am finite — gives rise immediately to the idea of something without limits. To be aware of finitude is to have, however implicitly, the idea of the infinite. The two are equiprimordial — if indeed the idea of the unlimited is not actually the more primitive of the two. Since when I intuit limits I can only do so against the backdrop of an unlimited whole, perhaps my sense of dependence already implies the idea of a prior independence. But this is a matter for later reflection. For now, we have only the Cartesian insight: the idea of the infinite is that intuitive awareness we as finite beings have of that which is without limits..

Like the original intuition, this idea also has an immediate link with human being in the world; one could deepen it by developing a philosophical anthropology.[3] Since the idea of the unlimited arises directly out of our immediate intuition that we are finite, it suggests a religious side to human existence — as long as "religious" is taken in the broadest possible sense and as neutral (at this point) on all questions about the existence or nature of the divine. The point is important: whatever theoretical positions may later emerge, this reciprocal relationship between human finitude and the *idea* of the infinite is a key defining feature of human existence. "Finite being," with its implicit contrast to infinity, thus becomes a general term for designating our ontological status as beings with limits. (Something analogous could be shown for the idea of perfection with its intrinsic contrast to that which is fully perfect.)

It is easier to grant the intuition of the infinite when one acknowledges what it does *not* prove. If I am right that the ontological proof is not compelling, the idea of the infinite (or of perfection) does not entail the existence of an infinite or perfect being. Moreover, it does not entail an actual comprehension of this infinite. At times, but only at times, Descartes was clear on this fact: "My point is that, on the contrary, if I can grasp something, it would be a total contradiction for that which I grasp to be infinite. For the idea of the infinite, if it is to be a true idea, cannot be grasped at all, since the impossibility of being grasped is contained in the formal definition of the infinite" (5th Replies, VII,368).

In his zeal to defend the *Meditations* just as it stood, Gueroult demanded more of the original intuition than it could ever supply. He alleged that Descartes's argument would work only if the idea of God were "effectively the picture of [the] object outside of it" — something that could not be discovered "unless we can know that an object exists outside its idea *and corresponds to it.*"[4] Gueroult later insisted that Descartes's proof, "if it succeeds, must not [only] end up proving that God exists, but establishing that we really know this existing God, that our idea is the exact tracing of his essence, that it is the exact copy of his nature" (p. 134). Yet such standards, however necessary they might be for a causal proof from the idea of God, are not justified by the Cartesian intuitive starting point. If we focus instead on the original emergence of the idea of the infinite, as I have done in this meditation, we find reason only to assert an onto-

---

3. Arguably, this is the central project or goal of Wolfhart Pannenberg, *Anthropology in Theological Perspective,* trans. Matthew J. O'Connell (Philadelphia: Westminster Press, 1985).

4. Gueroult, *Descartes' Philosophy,* 110, emphasis mine. The next reference in the text is also to this work.

logical link between finitude and infinitude, even though no clear content for the idea of an infinite God can yet be formed.[5]

The intuition of the infinite therefore plays a crucial role even before the beginning of formal reflection. Indeed, why should this claim be controversial? Who denies the existence of intuition? It is only its use as a weapon to resolve philosophical disputes or to stab one's theological opponents that needs correcting. For example, analytic thinkers have long ascribed a central place to human intuitions. Philosophers of science, even those as epistemically conservative as Karl Popper, grant them a standard role — at least in the heuristic process of formulating hypotheses to be tested — which is analogous to the position developed here. Empiricists in the Lockean tradition need not rule out a similar use of intuitions (except in certain forms of positivism), and their role in rationalism is indisputable. (Of course, the rationalists were wrong to take intuitions to be sufficient for knowledge, but we are engaged in the project of rethinking Descartes without such rationalistic or foundationalist claims.)

What then is the ground for the dismissal of intuition? Its sources are, I suggest, Kantian. Of course Kant allows intuitions; they are the basis to which he applies the categories. Nonetheless, he disallows intuition of the infinite; instead, all intuitions must be empirical intuitions, since it is the input of the world that sets the categories in motion, and categories can be applied only to experience. But why should we follow Kant on this point? Acknowledging that humans always operate within conceptual schemes, or that it makes sense to postulate a reality itself apart from anything we know or can know, or even that language about God has a kind of limit function — none of these requires us to accept Kant's limitation to empirical intuitions. In chapter 1 I challenged the positivistic side of Kantianism in the form developed by Hans Vaihinger. Later we will find grounds to reject Kant's precritical decision to eschew the concept of the infinite in favor of that of all-sufficiency or *ens a se*. I thus find no compelling reason to reject intuition of the infinite as impossible.

One other objection to this meditation might run as follows: Perhaps we have an intuition of ourselves as finite. But it is wrong to think that we thereby have any specific idea of infinitude. Instead, from the intuition of ourselves as limited a number of different conceptual moves are possible. We can postulate an indefinite mental ascent, with the infinite as its imagined end point; or we

---

5. Here Jean-Luc Marion is right: "Si l'infini doit se percevoir par idée, ce sera non par l'impossible représentation d'un objet, mais par la présence de l'infini même, manifeste par le jeu contrasté de l'ego avec Dieu" (Marion, *Sur la théologie blanche de Descartes*, 404). Marion adds elsewhere that "noncomprehension does not signify nonawareness": "one can (and must) know God as infinite without the clarity of a methodical object" ("Essential Incoherence," in Rorty, ed., *Essays on Descartes' Meditations*, 335n.56).

can seek to establish a "contradiction" in the notion of finitude that leads to the infinite (Hegel); or we can invert the pyramid with Feuerbach and look for explanations of all such lofty ideas within psychology or sociology. Since a rational case must be made for various of these options, the critic objects, it is false to lay claim to any sort of basic intuition in this area.

But isn't it enough to respond to such worries by emphasizing the preliminary nature of all intuitions? The intuitions we are exploring are still conceptually vague; they do not beg the existence question one way or the other. All one can say is that we intuit the finite; we thereby form the idea of an infinite; and we intuit that, if there is an infinite dimension, it must be equiprimordial with (or prior to) the finite. The nature of the move to the infinite is not given by the move itself — and much less full conceptual understanding. Nor can we tell at this stage what needs are met by this idea, or where it comes from (or what it might be hiding). Discovering the answers to any of these questions might explain away the idea in finitistic terms. But only later conceptual reconstruction will tell.

So perhaps we have not yet achieved very much: the intuitive ideas are rich, but many conceptual questions remain open. Still, if the intuition of the infinite is admissible in the sense presented, the history of this idea will deserve careful attention and testing as we reflect on the *concept* of infinity in this and the following chapters. Further, although the intuition is not a proof of theism, it does help to foster one's understanding of theistic belief, and it may even point our reflection in the direction of theism in particular contexts.

The Two Implications

Once the ideas of the finite and infinite are given, certain implications follow with greater or lesser immediacy. Of course, perfect immediacy is a chimera; little or nothing we do is not conceptually mediated. For instance, it takes at least some reflection to realize that, in that I intuit myself as finite, I have already intuited an infinite dimension. Likewise, the following two implications are also reflective implications; however close their connection to the originary intuition, it still requires reflection in order to "see" that they are consequences. Nonetheless, I suggest that they lie only a short remove from the points we have already reached.

Priority of the Infinite

I see manifestly that there is more reality in infinite substance than in finite substance, and yet that I have in some way in me a notion of the infinite that is prior to my notion of the finite — that is, the notion of God is prior to the

123

notion of myself. For how would it be possible that I can know that I doubt and that I desire — that is, that I lack something and that I am not perfect — unless I had in me an idea of a being more perfect than me, by comparison to which I might know the defects of my own nature. (Meditation 3, French ed., IX,36)

If the idea of an infinite is granted, then by its nature, I suggest, it will be prior to the idea of the finite. This first implication thus turns my initial presentation of the ideas upside down: the infinite is prior to the finite in everything except the order of discovery. One does not understand the infinite by negating a boundary or limit, Descartes argues; instead, all limitation implies a negation of an infinite dimension that precedes it (5th Replies, VII,365). The infinite cannot be subordinated to the ego, nor can the ego and an infinite be placed on the same level.[6]

Incidentally, the same argument works for the idea of the perfect. "Strictly speaking," Descartes writes, "a limitation is merely a negation or denial of any further perfection" (1st Replies, VII,111). And in conversation with Burman he insists on separating the order of discovery from the real priority of the ideas, which he takes to reflect an ontological priority:

Explicitly, we can know our imperfection before knowing the perfection of God, because we can attend to ourselves before we attend to God, and we can conclude that our being is finite before arriving at divine infinity. However, implicitly, knowledge of God and his perfections must always precede knowledge of ourselves and our imperfections. For, in reality, God's perfection is prior to our imperfection, the latter being a defect and a negation of divine perfection, and every defect and every negation presupposes the thing of which it is a defect, a negation. (V,153)

This insight completely reverses the subjectivism that one might have suspected when I began with individual intuitions above. The ego may play a unique role in revealing the idea of infinity, yet it is only qua dependent on the infinite that it does so. If we replaced "the infinite" with "God," as in classical theism, we would say that the self discovers within itself an intimate link between self and God. The link is not necessarily between two independent substances, nor (to jump to the other extreme) is it automatically a sign of unlim-

---

6. The former claim is made by Annette Baier, "The Idea of the True God in Descartes," in Rorty, ed., *Essays on Descartes' Meditations*, 359-87; the latter by Marion in *Sur la théologie blanche*.

ited human self-affirmation. The closer analogy is to the reciprocity of the Augustinian soul, which finds its rest, and its self-understanding, in God alone. To put it in more conceptual terms (and this will need a fuller defense later): the connection between the infinite and the finite amounts to a double dependence, a dependence not only for knowledge but also for its very being.[7]

"The infinite has logical priority over the finite": this thesis of Hegel seeks to turn this first implication into a matter of conceptual necessity. The finite is "something with its immanent limit, posited as the contradiction of itself, through which it is directed and forced out of itself" to the infinite.[8] But what happens if we grant Hegel's argument only intuitive strength rather than conceptual finality? Being limited or bounded *(begrenzt)* intuitively implies the idea of something that is *un*bounded or infinite. To think a something is to think at the same time the border that makes it this something rather than another. Beginning with finite things, our mind stretches toward the indefinite, whether it is indefinite in number, size, or quality. But to (try to) think the *totality* of things that are bordered leads to the idea of something that is beyond all borders, which Hegel calls the "truly infinite." We thus arrive at the idea of something that is not dependent on anything outside itself. Nondependence, all-sufficiency, might then be taken as the content of the infinite. Suppose we let the word *God* stand for these characteristics of nondependence, all-sufficiency, or *ens a se.*[9] In this sense we could say, with Descartes, that we discover God within us, in the same immediate fashion that we discover our own self-knowledge. As Koyré notes, "The starting point for Cartesian philosophy is the unmediated (but also indistinct) intuition of the *cogito*, the I — a viewpoint in which God and the I are 'given' in one and the same act."[10] Put differently,

---

7. Koyré points out the parallels with Duns Scotus: Descartes "leugnet, daß sich irgend etwas seiner schöpferischen Tätigkeit in irgend einer Weise widersetzen könnte; daß etwas — sei es ein reelles, sei es ein idelles Sein, in seinem ideelen oder wirklichen Sein, in seinem Sein wie in seinem Möglichsein, unabhängig von Gott, von seiner freischöpferischen Macht bestehen könne. Die Unendlichkeit Gottes ist sein eigentliches Wesen, darum müssen wir alle Aufstellungen vermeiden, durch die die Idee einer Einschränkung seines Wesens nahegelegt werden könnte" *(Descartes und die Scholastik,* 85). The exception is the law of perfection: Descartes is ready to deny that God would do anything that can be construed as imperfect, and to predicate of him what belongs to a perfect being. He finally grants to More that God could not wish the impossible, which comes closer to Scotus than the total voluntarism he advocates at other points.

8. *Hegel's Science of Logic,* trans. A. V. Miller (New York: Humanities Press, 1969), 129.

9. The assumption is false, and we will return to the difficulties it raises. But introducing the term *God* in this minimal sense allows us to recognize the kernel of truth in the Cartesian argument before dismissing it as a theistic proof.

10. "Der Ausgangspunkt der cartesianischen Philosophie ist die unmittelbare, aber

Cartesianism begins with an intuition without thereby centering itself on absolute human subjectivity, since it is an intuition of that which (if it exists) transcends the human subject.

Condition of the Possibility

"It is this idea [of a supremely perfect being] which provides me with the opportunity of inquiring whether I derive my existence from myself, or from another, and of recognizing my defects" (1st Replies, VII,108). This second implication follows directly from the first. In the inquiry into subjectivity — an inquiry in which both Descartes and Kant were in different ways involved — one presupposes the centrality of the knowing subject: its perceptions set the parameters for knowledge, and what is unknowable to it is declared meaningless (or at least inadmissible). Insofar as the first piece of solid knowledge for Descartes was the *cogito*, it functions as the initial condition on which the possibility of everything else is based. At this stage the subject is the center of activity and thought, the condition or ground for all reflection. Kant would later call it a transcendental condition: there is knowledge of the world only if there is a thinking subject.

What fewer notice is that Cartesian meditation leads to a further type of inquiry, after the idea of the infinite has been introduced and its priority to the finite has been defended (cf. the first implication above). In this later stage, one begins to reflect on what it means to say that the infinite is prior to the finite. It must mean a reversal of the initial possibility conditions that were based on the thinking subject. The idea (intuition) of this dimension thus becomes a new condition for the possibility of understanding finite beings. If the idea of the infinite is presupposed in thinking any thing as finite, the infinite becomes the condition for all knowledge of the finite.

Gueroult presents an analogous argument from the idea of the perfect:

> In fact, *I cannot think of myself without the idea of the perfect,* for originally I have no consciousness of myself except as an imperfect being; and this consciousness is impossible without the prior knowledge of the idea of the perfect. . . . The idea of the perfect is a condition of the *cogito,* and the perfect being is the absolute reason of my thinking self, a relative nature. . . . [Hence] the idea of the perfect, originally present at the core of my self, must also be originally present at the core of the inquiry.[11]

---

undeutliche Intuition des Cogito, des Ich — eine Anschauung, in der Gott und Ich in einem und demselben Akt gegeben sind (Koyré, *Descartes und die Scholastik,* 104).

11. Gueroult, *Descartes' Philosophy,* 158.

There is a certain intuitive force to this suggestion in the case of infinity: The idea of the infinite is prior to the finite because I can only understand the phenomenon of doubting — I can only know that I lack something or am not wholly perfect — if I presuppose the idea of something that is wholly unlimited. But as we will see below, the primacy of the perfect is somewhat more difficult to establish, because the latter notion depends on the conception of an objective scale of value (as in Thomas's fourth way). Still, if the implications do hold for the perfection idea as well, then the argument will be structurally similar in both cases.

This second implication involves an interesting reversal of transcendental argumentation in Kant. We think of transcendental arguments as grounded in the subject; yet there is nothing about "condition of the possibility" language that need be limited to the subject. Why couldn't the infinite play a similar role in determining parameters and making human reflection possible? Note that the argument is still in the subjunctive. One can ask, "If such a being or dimension existed, what would be its status vis-à-vis a finite being such as myself?" The answer must be, "It would be prior, and the ground of my being." In theological terms, God must be a principle that is self-attesting. As Spinoza later wrote, *veritas signum sui ipsius est et falsi,* "If God is truth, then he is the ground of himself; he is his own 'sign' or criterion."[12] The same would be true of the Absolute (if this turns out to be a meaningful notion): it must have its grounds in itself and ground all else.

But now it is time to end this brief meditation, since by this point we are pushing against the limits of what can be gleaned from intuitive ideas. Though conditions of the possibility have a certain intuitive force, as I have tried to show, they also cry out for conceptual development and defense. We have now covered a long stretch of abstraction from the original intuition of dependency, even if the line was an unbroken one. With greater abstraction comes decreased certainty.[13] At the one end of the scale, it does seem that all finite experience, as finite, presupposes something nonfinite. Otherwise it would be pointless to introduce the distinction in the first place, since a distinction without an other (or a name without a distinction) is meaningless. At the other end of the scale, it is somewhat less clear what it means to *intuit* that the infinite is the condition of the possibility for all finite experience. One can certainly have experiences as

---

12. "Ist Gott die Wahrheit, so ist er Rechtsgrund seiner selbst, sein eignes 'signum' oder Kriterium" (Koyré, *Descartes und die Scholastik,* 97).

13. Cf. Thomas Morris's distinction between immediate epistemic intuitions and our intuitions concerning metaphysical matters, such as metamodal intuitions (*Anselmian Explorations: Essays in Philosophical Theology* [Notre Dame: Univ. of Notre Dame Press, 1987], 63).

a human subject without having that intuition. Further, what is the scope of this intuition: is the infinite the condition of the possibility for all knowledge whatsoever, or only for knowing that what I know will be finite? Does the awareness of this necessary condition accompany *all* items of knowledge in the way that Kant argued the unity of apperception does? It seems obvious — both for specifying the nature of this intuition and for justifying it — that the move from meditating on intuitive ideas to attempting a rigorous conceptual account of these ideas is now required.

From Intuitions to Concepts

So much for immediacy. One must eventually make the transition to systematic concepts developed in the context of rational argumentation, for which the givens of intuition supply only the starting points for reflection. For instance, I am tempted to add panentheism as a third implication: "the infinite cannot be 'other' than the finite; it cannot be 'outside' it or separate from it. The finite is always contained within the infinite, although the infinite remains in its essence *more than* the finite." But this is much more a conceptual implication of the idea of the infinite than it is a basic intuition that most people have. If I cannot present a full theory of rational discourse and explanation here,[14] I can at least note a few features of this inevitable transition.

Intuitions are defeasible; hence in defending a philosophical position we cannot remain with them. A position is stronger if it can "make sense of" the particular intuitions we have, explaining why we have them, why the intuitions of our opponents are mistaken (by providing a theory of error), and how particular sets of intuitions can be tied together into a coherent system of beliefs. Intuitionists apparently differ as to the relative importance of this task of explaining and defending compared to merely explicating one's own intuitions. Anselm, for example, remained unapologetically with the task of intuition explication, the task of proclaiming his faith and seeking to understand it. In a more pluralistic context such as the present, I suggest that it is equally as important, if not more important, to show why a given set of intuitions should be credible. For example, the strengths of process philosophy have caused even nonprocess theists to question certain traditional intuitions about divine simplicity and about the desirability of God's being unrelated to the world.[15]

---

14. I have attempted such a theory in Clayton, *Explanation from Physics to Theology.*

15. Charles Hartshorne presents and defends such process intuitions in "The Logic of Perfection," chap. 2 of *The Logic of Perfection and Other Essays* (La Salle, Ill.: Open Court,

Of course, the transition from the intuitive to the conceptual is not black and white, nor is it made once and for all. Yet there are clear differences between the two. We will consider first the manner in which intuitions give rise to arguments, and then how argumentation appeals back to intuitions.

The previous section showed how intuitions do not remain at the intuitive level; they frequently suggest inferences from some ideas to others that in turn rely on (more or less explicit) conceptual assumptions. As long as the later inferences do not cast the first intuitions into question, whole conceptual systems can be constructed on this basis. One can take a given set of intuitions about an infinitely perfect being and develop out of it an entire systematic theology, complete with complex argumentative interconnections. The foundationalist option is to allow moves in only one direction, arguing that the system is only as strong as its grounding intuitions are. But the better option is to grant that, with the move to the conceptual level, a hermeneutical reciprocity between intuitions and conceptual systems is introduced.[16] This (coherentist) view considers systems of intuitions and their implications as groups or webs, comparing them to closely related and to distant webs. The same criteria for conceptual evaluation still apply here, but with the caveat that conceptual difficulties can cast the initial intuitions into question.

Argumentation appeals back to intuitions too. In the course of developing an argument we inevitably rely on intuitions to justify premises and to decide (for instance) whether it is preferable to accept a consequent or to deny an antecedent. One's opponent may challenge whether certain intuitive ideas (such as the ideas of finitude and the infinite!) are really as universal as one claims, constructing other arguments to show the inconsistency of one's intuitions or to "explain them away." Further, the presentation of new arguments can give rise to a whole new set of intuitions. For many readers, the intuition that we are "locked into a conceptual scheme" becomes stronger after they read Kant and weaker after reading Davidson.

Still, the line between intuitions and concepts does not disappear in this process. If the ontological proof or Descartes's argument from the idea of God were sound, the matter would be more ambiguous, for then some intuitive ideas would lead directly to the existence of their objects. But they fail as conceptual arguments. By comparison, by the time one gets to cosmological or te-

---

1962). Theistic opponents who acknowledge their debt to process philosophies include Morris, *Anselmian Explorations*, chap. 7; and Wolfhart Pannenberg, "Atomism, Duration, Form: Difficulties with Process Philosophy," chap. 6 of *Metaphysics and the Idea of God.*

16. See J. Wentzel van Huyssteen, *Essays in Postfoundationalist Theology* (Grand Rapids: Eerdmans, 1997).

leological arguments for the existence of God, a fair amount of mediating reflection is already called for — despite the frequent appeal to intuitions such as "an infinite chain of causes is impossible" or "I sense order in the world." And if (as I think) these proofs, like the ontological, also fail as direct arguments, such that the credibility of theism can be shown only over the evidential long haul, then truly it will be such a long detour, with so many places for negative decisions about the idea of God, that no one can accuse one of dodging argumentative responsibilities when one insists on the (relative) immediacy of the original intuition.

Incidentally, these examples show that the movement from intuitions to concepts can also be conceived in a second way: as the movement from *ideas* to the debate over the *existence* of their objects. Under this view, there is no reason that one cannot say, "I have the idea of an infinite being (or realm or dimension) as the implied 'other pole' of knowing myself as finite." But exactly what the idea of an infinite being entails and whether such a thing really exists are questions that cannot be decided in any intuitive fashion; they require systematic attention. Such a view correctly leaves it open to the finitist to say, "Fine, I will grant you your intuitions and their immediate implications as well. But if it were shown that the existence of an infinite being would follow directly from having these intuitive ideas, then I reserve the right to rescind my provisional acceptance and to reject the intuitions after all." Of course, the only way to move directly from the idea of an infinite being to its existence is the ontological proof, and I have already argued that it is not successful.

To summarize this second view of the transition, then: I have proposed that "I am a finite being" is an idea suggested immediately by certain features of my existence, for example, that I doubt, that I recognize my power as limited, that I am the passive recipient of data from outside myself. This idea then gives rise immediately to the *idea* of an infinite other — one need only ask, "In contrast to what does one insist that one is finite?" in order to evoke this response. By contrast, the statement "An infinite being exists," like any other existential statement, can be judged true or false only on the basis of the evidence subsequently brought for or against it. Intuitions do not decide existence statements.

ON THINKING AN INFINITELY PERFECT BEING

We have taken an initial look at the intuitions of infinity and perfection, and have outlined an epistemology for the movement into explicit argumentation. Now for an explicit look at conceptual content: Can one argue from infinity to perfection? from perfection to infinity? What then of the idea of an infinite and perfect being? Is the idea coherent, what are its sources, and what are the implications of positing its existence? Before considering the two ideas separately, let us briefly note some of the conceptual connections between them. In the process we must evaluate an important school of contemporary analytic philosophy that bases its work on the intuition of an infinitely perfect being.

Connecting the Concepts

The two concepts evidence a close conceptual connection. *Infinity* is often defined in terms of the perfections, for example as "the absence of any imperfections and the possession of all perfections."[17] Infinity allows for augmentation from finite quantities. It includes the difference of God from the world, as well as points of contact (e.g., though finite, I could perhaps have an immediate intuition of an infinite other). One can use infinity as an umbrella concept to derive (or at least explain) some of the other traditional attributes such as omnipotence, omniscience, or omnipresence. *Perfection* has an analogous structure to infinity, allowing both for an augmentation of human qualities and for the qualitative difference of God from creation. Arguably, if one thinks through the notion of perfection in itself, without thinking of it as either finite or infinite, one is led to the concept of infinity, at least in the sense of "good without limit." For perfection expresses the evaluative dimension in its connotation of supreme goodness. It also helps establish the human relation with the divine, since the theology of perfection normally assumes that all good things somehow participate in a supreme perfection as their source.

The two attributes are mutually correcting when combined. The attribute of *perfect infinity* connotes a qualitative difference between the finite and the infinite, a maximum (for any given attribute) that cannot be further extended. By contrast, *infinite perfection* suggests the highest degree of good: holding "great-making properties" to the highest possible extent. It can be applied to a number of the traditional divine attributes, including more directly religious ones such as justice, love, or impeccability. Taken together, these two concepts may represent the first steps toward a theory of the Absolute (if such a theory is possible).

In Cartesian philosophy, as we saw, the two concepts are also integrally linked. The framework of infinity seems to be the first chronologically, since

17. Bill Alston, "Functionalism and Theological Language," in Morris, ed., *Concept of God*, 32.

the argument from infinity was already clearly formulated in Descartes's 1630 correspondence with Mersenne. In discussing the *Principles*, we noted several points at which arguments from perfection were added by Descartes to the French translation of 1647; similar glosses in the direction of perfection were added to the French translation of the *Meditations*, published the same year. At least one commentator holds that Descartes took arguments from infinity to be more certain than those from perfection.[18] It could be that Descartes realized that arguments from perfection are in greater danger of projecting human values onto the divine than are arguments from infinity — though I doubt that he was aware of these dangers. At any rate, by the *Meditations* he viewed the two concepts as most intimately connected. In a commentary on Meditation 3 he defines an infinite substance as "a substance having all real and true perfections that are actually infinite and immense,"[19] and by the time of the conversation with Burman God is defined simply as *infinita perfectio* (V,153).

Perfect-Being Theology in Contemporary Philosophy

A major school of contemporary analytic philosophical theology — which calls itself "Anselmian," though it could just as well have used the label "Cartesian" — also bases its theistic reflection on God as infinitely perfect. A major spokesperson for "perfect-being theology," Thomas Morris, has claimed that this "single unifying conception" underlies much of reflection on God over "the past 20 years," such that there is a "prevalence of perfect being theology in contemporary philosophical theology."[20]

According to the school, starting with the intuition of perfection gives rise to an exact and detailed analytic discussion of God's attributes, and therefore to a progressive program of research in philosophical theology. Ever more qualities can be deduced, and in a progressively more refined fashion, by reflecting on God as perfect, as "that than which none greater can be conceived." So William Alston is able to conclude, "Thus among the modes of divine infinity will be omnipo-

18. Marion, "Essential Incoherence," in Rorty, ed., *Essays on Descartes' Meditations*, 324-25. I do not think Descartes believed this: the differences in his presentation of the two concepts can be explained by his tendency to react differently to different correspondents and by a certain tendency toward hyperbole.

19. Descartes to Clerselier, 4/23/1649; V,356, AM 8:224: "Per infinitam substantiam, intelligo substantiam perfectiones veras et reales actu infinitas et immensas habentem."

20. See Morris, "Perfect Being Theology," *Nous* 21 (1987): 19-30, quotations 20, 22; idem, ed., *Concept of God*, 8. See also idem, *Anselmian Explorations*.

tence, omniscience, and perfect goodness."[21] The major philosophical attributes, Alston argues, follow immediately from the definition of God as perfectly infinite. Any quality that we associate as a good, a perfection, can be predicated of God in its highest form — as long as it is interpreted in a manner consistent with other attributes that God must necessarily have, such that, for example, God's simplicity (or timelessness, or benevolence) is preserved. In one reconstruction of the core position of the school, Morris represents in a "simple, idealized manner" the line of argument that "accords with the intuitions of most perfect being theologians." The result is a list of the central attributes of an infinitely perfect being: "God is conceived of as . . . a thoroughly benevolent, necessarily existent conscious agent with unlimited knowledge and power who is the ontologically independent creative source of all else."[22]

Much important work has been done on this subject in recent years. It is now widely accepted that a strict view of divine simplicity must be rejected, since it rules out even contingent relatedness of God to world. Omnipotence has been analyzed not only in terms of logical limits but under the constraints of what features are *com*possible for a perfect being. In particular, this allows one to think God's power in a manner compatible with his moral goodness and with human freedom. Omniscience (particularly God's foreknowledge) can be understood in a manner that is reconcilable with human freedom of choice and with God's timelessness, and the latter attribute has been (perhaps surprisingly) reconciled with divine actions in history such as an incarnation and resurrection.

The movement has thus made a number of significant advances in the area of the divine attributes, many of which one can indeed derive once one grants the existence of an infinitely perfect being. Beginning with the criterion of infinite perfection, it is possible to compare traditional attributes with one another, to note their inconsistencies, and to make appropriate alterations, producing a tighter doctrine of God along traditional lines. There are, however, also unresolved difficulties within modern-day Anselmianism. I consider five:

1. The reasons for, and difficulties with, construing God as a perfect being are scarcely discussed. Morris suspects that "for everyone who endorses the idea of divine perfection, it is an intuitively obvious conception of deity" (p. 23). But he also admits at one point that the understanding of God as perfect emerged rather late in the history of religions. How did it emerge, and what are the problems inherent in the idea of moral perfection? Is the notion of a perfect being coherent, or does it (like Thomas's fourth way) depend on as-

---

21. Alston, "Functionalism and Theological Language," 32.
22. Morris, "Perfect-Being Theology," 26. The next several references in the text are also to this essay.

sumptions we can no longer make? Detailed historical work (below, and chapter 4), as well as adequate responses to the difficulties raised, will be required to establish this position.

2. Perfect-being theology looks rather different if one is not convinced of the soundness of the ontological argument as a proof. To the extent that one has doubts about the argument, perfect-being theology begins to look much more similar to the position in the first section of this chapter: If an infinite being exists who is in some way prior to and the condition of the possibility for finite existence, how shall we understand it? Without an ontological proof, one can only begin with a hypothetical being; the discussion gets underway as a conceptual exercise and is resolved *probabilistically* by the explanatory power of this particular hypothesis. Interestingly, even Morris, who defends the ontological proof, sometimes argues hypothetically: "*If* anything like a thoroughgoing theism is true . . . [then] the divine being exemplifies maximal perfection" (pp. 28-29, emphasis mine). If we are not persuaded by the ontological proof, perfect-being theology may become a set of "internal" conceptual analyses significant perhaps only to Christian theists.

3. What Morris does not acknowledge is that any probability that accrues to the antecedent ("if anything like a thoroughgoing theism is true . . .") must come not only from the internal consistency but also from its adequacy as an explanation, using precisely the "empirically based methods"[23] of the "empirically minded theologians" (p. 22) that he rejects. For the opening part of the exercise, the discussion may begin in the subjunctive — what qualities would a perfect being have? — since the idea begins only as a hypothesis. Yet whatever probability finally accrues to this theory must stem from its internal coherence over against its competitors *and* from its explanatory value. Morris is wrong to dismiss the explanatory project on the grounds that its concept of God is too "minimal and unsatisfying" (ibid.). The nature of the hypothesized God can be as rich and fully developed as one wishes (Popperians would say: the more detailed the better), and it can draw on rational theology as well as on the appropriate religious traditions. Finally, though, the question becomes, Does this being actually exist? To answer this query, one must struggle with difficult comparative questions in the study of religions, as well as with historical evidence, scientific developments, and assessments of its contemporary meaningfulness.

4. Even as a thought experiment perfect-being theology is not conclusive. The debate about divine attributes contains widely divergent voices, and it would be incorrect to claim that the appeal to perfection has led to widespread consensus. Inconsistencies have been alleged between almost all the "perfect-making

23. Morris, *Concept of God*, 9.

properties," even by perfect-being theologians: between immutability and omniscience, between omniscience and omnipresence, between omnipotence and impeccability, between omniscience and immutability, between omnipotence and freedom. For example, William Mann derives the doctrine of divine simplicity (DDS) directly from perfection: "The DDS in turn is motivated by the consideration that God is a perfect being, and that *qua* perfect, he must be independent from all other things for his being the being he is, and he must be sovereign over all other things,"[24] whereas Morris insists that his intuitions do not demand that God be simple. Some intuit that a perfect God must be omnipotent; others construe omnipotence in a much more attenuated sense, or feel that the perfection of the Christian God is not compromised if we deny omnipotence of him.[25] Is it not a sign of incoherence, or at least unclarity, in one's starting notion if contradictory conclusions can validly be derived from it?

5. These disagreements lead to a more general point. Morris deserves credit for making clear the pervasive role of intuitions in Anselmianism: intuitions are responsible for choosing perfection in the first place, for deciding what attributes are perfect and in what sense, and for deciding which attributes are compossible. He also makes no pretension that intuitions are clear, infallible, or sufficient for these tasks. Intuitions are context dependent and require "proper circumstances" to emerge, including, it seems, adequate exposure to the "Judeo-Christian revelatory tradition" (pp. 23-24). There is an "underdetermination" in the apriorist tradition[26] that cannot be fully resolved by our battery of "value intuitions," "logical intuitions," "semantic intuitions," "metamodal intuitions," and "religious intuitions" (pp. 50ff., 63-64). Intuitions are also defeasible, though Morris thinks he has reasons to trust at least "a few intuitions about metaphysical matters," including those "relevant to the existence and basic nature of God" (p. 67).

I conclude that Morris is right to dismiss extreme positions that deny to intuition any role whatsoever in metaphysics and theology. But his position also begs for a closer examination of the ideas, intuitive or otherwise, upon which perfect-being theology is constructed. From what sources do they stem, and what problems are raised by understanding God in terms of them? Do in-

24. William Mann, "Simplicity and Immutability in God," in Morris, ed., *Concept of God*, 253-67, quotation 255.

25. Morris, *Anselmian Explorations*, 24. The next two references in the text are also to this work.

26. For an opposed position, see Lewis Ford, "The Infinite God of Process Theism," in Daniel Dahlstrom, David Ozar, and Leo Sweeney, eds., *Infinity*, Proceedings of the American Catholic Philosophical Association 55 (1981): 84-90; cf. idem, "In What Sense Is God Infinite: A Process Perspective," *The Thomist* 42 (1978): 1-13.

finity and perfection inevitably imply one another? Aren't there significant tensions between them? Do they in fact lead to a full knowledge of God's attributes, or do they instead entail a certain unknowability in the divine being? And if they are likely features of a supreme being, what sort of being or Being do they suggest? Both Anselmianism and the position developed in this chapter assume the defeasibility of intuitions as a method, and both acknowledge that we must move from intuitions to conceptual explication and defense. Given the defeasibility of intuitions, it is clear that they cannot alone play the grounding role for intersubjective argumentation in metaphysics or theology. Conceptual and historical analysis must supplement Anselmian intuitions, either substantiating or radically altering them.

THE CONCEPT OF AN INFINITE BEING

We began the chapter with the intuitions of finitude and the infinite, defending an exploration of the latter even if we are unable to prove the existence of some being possessing it. In the previous section we took note of an important contemporary research program into the nature of an infinitely perfect being, though I again expressed skepticism about a priori arguments to show that this being exists. Any such arguments must instead be (largely) a posteriori, probabilistic, and based on explanatory power and religious meaningfulness. It is not the goal of this work to settle the question of God's existence, even if (like perfect-being theology) conceptual inquiries such as this affect judgments about the coherence of the idea of God and thus, indirectly, about the probability of God's existence.

Instead, let us see now what can be made conceptually out of the intuition of an infinitely perfect being. In this section I explore the options that are open to those who find themselves with the intuition of infinity, as in the meditation above; in the following I turn to the notion of perfection. We will find that the inquiry produces conclusions that are of both philosophical and religious interest. It seems important, however, not to begin only with the intuitions of traditional philosophical theology, since reflecting on the notion of infinity may well lead in some surprising new directions. The examination must therefore also note the points of divergence; only in this way can theologians recognize areas where certain traditional assumptions may require rethinking. In the process, we will need to observe the distinction between philosophical theology and systematic theology. Both attempt to give conceptual expression to the scriptures and tradition, but systematic theology is more explicit about its roots in these two sources, whereas philosophical theology stands a step further from its biblical sources and a step closer to metaphysics. Failing to distinguish their different tasks might lead one to equate the concept of infinite perfection with the God of Abraham, Isaac, and Jacob, or to set up, say, panentheism in opposition to Christian theism.

One important note: I have concentrated here on the metaphysical infinite rather than on the mathematical infinite. This focus must not be allowed to give the impression that the two approaches to the infinite had no influence on one another; there has been, appropriately enough, a continual cross-fertilization between them. Indeed, the mathematical and physical paradoxes of infinity set important parameters for the pre-Cartesian theological discussion. Some philosophers took the paradoxes to show the impossibility of a real infinite. For instance, the world could not be of infinite age if (as was thought) all infinites are equal, since the infinite length of time up until today would be longer than the infinite time up until yesterday. Others avoided the paradoxes by positing the incommensurability of infinites; equality and inequality simply do not apply to them. Only later (by Descartes's time) was it granted that there could be actual infinites that are not equal, though this fact appeared to surpass the human ability to conceptualize (at least until Cantor).

Likewise, Descartes's theology actually depended on cross-fertilization between the mathematics and the theology of the infinite. The late medieval period had stressed the quantitative mathematical side of the concept, focusing on theories of infinite series, the problem of the infinitely small (e.g., curvilinear angles), and the paradox of infinites that are parts of and yet at the same time equal to other infinites.[27] Descartes made a not insignificant contri-

---

27. See John Murdoch, "Mathematics and Infinity in the Later Middle Ages," in Dahlstrom et al., eds., *Infinity*, 40-58; and Murdoch, "William of Ockham and the Logic of Infinity and Continuity," in Norman Kretzmann, ed., *Infinity and Continuity in Ancient and Medieval Thought* (Ithaca: Cornell Univ. Press, 1982), 168ff. The late medieval philosophers had begun to treat the mathematical problems as issues on their own: are there indivisibles within continua; could continua be composed out of indivisibles; how can limits be ascribed to a continuous sequence or series (the problem of first and last instants, beginnings and endings to continuous changes or processes); can there be unequal infinites? These questions contrast sharply with the Scholastic discussions of infinity, which raised the mathematical problems in connection with directly theological issues such as angelic motion and being, God's omnipotence (could God create actual infinites, or are they contradictory and thus beyond even the power of omnipotence?), and the *latitudo entium*, the hierarchy of the perfections of the various species (is God's perfection an infinite or finite distance from other species' perfection?). The convoluted nature and Aristotelian assumptions of these debates probably lie behind Descartes's dismissive comments concerning speculation on the infinity

bution to this mathematical discussion: by discovering the continuity of the numbers, he was able to bring discrete numbers into conformity with lines and quantities, as well as to introduce infinite distinctions into the realm of the finite numbers. Further, he was quick to see the implications of these mathematical developments for theology: the mathematics provided a key for connecting a mechanistic and anti-Aristotelian physics with the traditional understanding of God as infinite source of the world.

Nonetheless, the ultimate goal of the present inquiry is the explicitly metaphysical tradition with its affirmations (and denials) that God is infinite. The following treatment of premodern philosophy and theology can provide little more than an excursus, albeit an indispensable one. For to understand early modern philosophy, one must understand Cartesianism; Cartesianism depends on the concepts of infinity and perfection; and they, in turn, arise out of their use in the *loci classici* of the Western tradition.

The Actually Infinite in Greek Philosophy

The acceptance of an actual infinite was not a matter of course in Western history, nor is it a matter of course today. If the ontological argument fails to compel assent, there is, I believe, no proof that something actually infinite really exists. We may have intuitions in this direction, strengthened by the positive role that the infinite appears to play in science or mathematics or as a limit concept or as a solution to certain paradoxes. But before one can assert the existence of an actual infinite, one has to address the arguments, already familiar to Greek thinkers, regarding the impossibility of actual infinites and the equation of the infinite with imperfection.

The general Greek tendency was to associate infinity *(apeiria)* with imperfection, and limit or border *(peras)* with perfection. For Plato and Aristotle, the concept of infinity arises in the context of the realm of the "more-or-less," which in turn is associated with indefiniteness and thus with imperfection. By contrast, what is limited has thereby real parameters and a definite form. Such things, insofar as they participate in a form (Plato) or are "hylomorphic" or enformed (Aristotle), are more perfect. Even if there were an actual infinite, it would be the last thing one would call perfect.

But of course, most Greek philosophers continued, there are no actual infinites, only potential ones; a finite line is potentially infinitely divisible but never really infinitely divided. Aristotle provides a number of specific argu-

---

in *Principles,* I, art. 26. The best work on the transition to modernity remains Louis Dupré, *Passage to Modernity* (New Haven: Yale Univ. Press, 1993).

ments against the possibility of infinites, based mostly on paradoxes raised by the notion.[28] For instance, the parts of an infinitely large substance could not be finite in size, since then they would not add up to an infinite object; nor could they be infinitely large, since then each part would be as large as the whole (all infinite quantities being equal). But any object must as such be extended and therefore must have parts; hence there are no infinite objects. The core of Aristotle's resistance boils down to this: an infinite that actually existed would have to exist in the world, and then it would have to be physically comprehensible; but a worldly infinite would lead to insoluble paradoxes in the context of his physics; therefore no actual infinite can exist. Appealing to mathematics does not help, for mathematical entities have to be "of a specific quantity" or "countable," and infinites are neither. Aristotle is willing to make use of the concept of the infinite for solving certain paradoxes such as Zeno's paradoxes of motion, and he grants that this concept is suggested by certain metaphysical lines of argument. For example, the claim that the infinite is already implied by the concept of the finite (mentioned above in connection with Hegel) was already traditional by Aristotle's time. But one can grant the intuitive force of this argument without granting infinites physical actuality.

As long as we do not accept Aristotle's exclusion of infinites from mathematics, or his assumption that an infinite being would have to be a physical object (Aristotelian or otherwise), we need not take his arguments against actual infinites as decisive. Further — and fortunately for the philosophy of infinite perfection — Greek philosophers were not unanimous in tying infinity to imperfection. Already Anaximander took as the *archē* or first principle the *apeiron,* the boundless, which "is neither water nor any other of the so-called elements but some different boundless nature, from which come into being all the heavens and atmospheric orders within them."[29] The *apeiron* is "ungenerated and imperishable, as a starting point. . . . [It] seems rather to be the starting point for the rest, and to encompass all things and to guide them all . . . and to be the divine, for it is immortal and uncorruptible."[30]

What subsequently occurred in this strand of the Greek tradition, I suggest, is that philosophers were able to transform the notion of the infinite from a negative concept — that which fails to have limits or specificity and is therefore imperfect — to a positive one. The infinite could then be construed as

---

28. Aristotle treats the infinite in *De caelo* 1, and in *Physics* 3 (on extension), 6, and 8 (on the infinite divisibility of continua). On the following, see esp. *Physics* 3, 4.

29. Simplicius, *In Physicorum* 24.13, quoted in Charles H. Kahn, *Anaximander and the Origins of Greek Cosmology* (New York: Columbia Univ. Press, 1960), 166.

30. So Aristotle, *Physics* 203b4-15. See also Theo Gerard Sinnige, *Matter and Infinity in the Presocratic Schools and Plato* (Assen: Van Gorcum, Prakke and Prakke, 1968).

source and (in a partial sense) creator, since all emerges from it; it is comprehensive and directive. Qualities such as immortality and incorruptibility set it apart from and made it superior to what is limited, viz. the realm of becoming and perishing. According to Sweeney, *to apeiron* was also linked in this way with perfection in the thought of Anaximenes, Melissus, Anaxagoras, Leucippus and Democritus, Epicurus, and Plotinus.[31] I take this fundamental separation from the finite realm to be a crucial step toward attaining a full concept of infinity. By setting the infinite apart in this manner, philosophers gradually acknowledged its transcendental significance, and consequently also its role as creative, as prior, and as the standard for whatever else exists.

The Transcendent Infinite

Metaphysical speculation regarding the nature of an actual infinite took a major step forward in the patristic period. According to Plotinus, the One is infinite at least by implication, because it is above all distinctions. Gregory of Nyssa then asserts, with remarkable clarity, that God is the being who has no beginning or end and hence is fully and essentially infinite. Gregory holds himself to a Christian doctrine of creation and to a trinitarian God; yet — perhaps because he is concerned to do justice to Christian doctrines — he asserts God's actual infinity and God's possession of positive perfections much more clearly than Plotinus. By contrast, Plotinus's approach, stressing more strongly the One beyond Being, becomes the paradigmatic theory in Western philosophical theology of a single transcendent source, a One above all distinctions.

The Unlimited One

The concept of the infinite plays an important, though often implicit, role in Plotinus's thought. The One is above all predicates and distinctions; it is indeterminate *(aoriston)*. Because it is not limited by anything, it is infinite *(apeiron)* and the source *(archē)* of everything (*Enneads* 5.1.7). It is the source even of Being and of Form:

> The One therefore must be without form and hence is not an entity, for an entity must always be a "this" and hence determined. . . . But if all things are in that which is generated from the One [i.e., in the Nous], which of the

31. See Leo Sweeney, *Infinity in the Presocratics: A Bibliographical and Philosophical Study* (The Hague: Nijhoff, 1972); see also his "Surprises in the History of Infinity from Anaximander to George Cantor," in Dahlstrom et al., eds., *Infinity*, 3-23.

things in it will one say that the One is? Since It is none of them, It can only be said to be beyond them. Now since such realities are beings and Being *(ta onta kai to ōn),* the One is beyond Being. This phrase, "beyond Being," does not mean that the One is some "this" (for it makes no positive statement about It) and is not its name, but only implies that the One is not a "this" or "that." That expression does not at all encompass the One, for to seek to encompass its immense nature is ridiculous.[32]

In explaining what this implies, Plotinus says variously that the One is self-sufficient, perfect, omnipotent, complete, and pure unity utterly beyond our finite experience.[33]

Plotinus's position is one of great richness; it has a fundamental place in Western reflection on the infinite, and we return to his doctrine of participation in the penultimate section of this chapter. His reflection on the One serves as a constant reminder of the untamed aspect of this notion: what is truly without any limits or distinctions must be utterly transcendent and ineffable. Still, with all due reverence and panegyric, I would like to indicate some areas in which a theory of the infinite should try to move beyond his limitations. First, although Plotinus sometimes speaks of infinity in relation to the One/Good, he denies at the same time that the One is infinite in its very nature: "The One can neither be spoken nor written of. If we nevertheless speak and write about It, we do so only to give direction, to arouse ourselves to pass from mere words to its vision, as one might point out the road to somebody who desired to see some object" *(Enneads* 6.9.4). Ultimately, he eschews any positive theory of infinity. As Armstrong notes,

> Though in the thought of Plotinus only the One or Good is infinite in the absolute sense in which we speak of the infinity of God, he is reluctant to speak of him as *apeiros* or *aoristos.* . . . He will say that the power of the One is unbounded or that the One is the source of infinity; but he prefers to express the infinity of the One in terms of the "negative theology," by denying that any of our names or concepts (including "One" and "Good"), which necessarily involve the thought of some kind of limitation, can strictly be applied

32. *Enneads* 5.5.6, following the translation given by Leo Sweeney in "Infinity in Plotinus," *Gregorianum* 38 (1957): 515-35, 713-32.

33. A. W. Moore, *Infinity* (London: Routledge & Kegan Paul, 1990), 46. The positive role of infinity in Plotinus is stressed also by E. Gilson, *La Liberté chez Descartes et la théologie* (Paris: Félix Alcan, 1913), 205. See Ekkehard Mühlenberg, *Die Unendlichkeit Gottes bei Gregor von Nyssa: Gregors Kritik am Gottesbegriff der klassischen Metaphysik* (Göttingen: Vandenhoeck & Ruprecht, 1966), 86, e.g., n.7, for a more negative view.

to him, and in particular by refusing to apply to him the predicate of existence.[34]

But it is not so obvious that we must eschew *any* positive use of the predicate *infinity*. At least positive theorizing should be attempted before one proclaims its impossibility. I seek to show in this chapter that the competing demands are best served through a dialectic that arises between the concrete efforts to think the infinite and the ultimate insufficiency of all such attempts over against their object.

Next, Plotinus does not reserve the predicate *infinite* for the One alone. Nous, and elsewhere the individual soul, are also called infinite.[35] In fact, everything that lacks form is infinite, including evil and matter: "One can conceive of evil as measurelessness opposed to measure, as the infinite opposed to limit, as formlessness opposed to a forming principle" (*Enneads* 1.8.3). To my knowledge, Plotinus nowhere addresses the problems raised by this proliferation of infinites.

Finally, I believe that infinity and perfection are not as closely linked in Plotinus as they deserve to be from the nature of the concepts. Of course, there is no question about the One's value-ladenness in the *Enneads*: the One *is* the Good. As such, it is the source of all good and the object of all striving for perfection. Still, Plotinus seems hesitant to assert that the One is perfect in any positive sense. The absence of form in the Nous would certainly be a lack and an imperfection. But Plotinus insists that this is not the case at this higher level: "[The One] is without form, not that it lacks one but that all intelligible forms

---

34. A. H. Armstrong, *Christian Faith and Greek Philosophy* (London: Darton, Longman and Todd, 1960), 12-13. The same position is taken by Leo Sweeney, "Infinity in Plotinus," *Gregorianum* 38 (1957): 515-35, 713-32. However, Sweeney later reversed the position taken in his two *Gregorianum* articles, arguing that infinity is an attribute of the One itself; see, e.g., idem, "Another Interpretation of *Enneads*, VI,7,32," *The Modern Schoolman* 38 (1961): 289-303, which argues that the love for the Good can be, as Plotinus says, "measureless" because the object loved characterizes the love and the One is infinite. This brings Sweeney into agreement with W. N. Clarke ("Infinity in Plotinus: A Reply," *Gregorianum* [1959]: 75-98), who argues that Plotinus is "the first great philosopher in the West to have identified the supremely perfect principle in the universe as positively infinite in its very nature, because, as the ultimate source of all forms, it is itself above and beyond all form and life" (p. 76). This is probably the majority position on Plotinus; nonetheless, I believe the interpretation is mistaken and that Plotinus's position remains in the end a negative theology.

35. See *Enneads* 5.8.4, line 33; and Plato Mamo, "Is Plotinian Mysticism Monistic?" in *The Significance of Neoplatonism*, ed. R. Blaine Harris (Norfolk: International Society for Neoplatonic Studies, 1976), 199-215.

come from It" (*Enneads* 6.7.32). Plotinus had apparently not yet begun to explore the conceptual connections between infinity and absolute perfection in the way the later tradition would.

We may conclude that the notion of the infinite is not yet a transcendent principle and the basis for a theory of the infinite in the *Enneads*. The side of the notion of infinity that points — I think inevitably — toward a *via negativa*, a theology of denial, receives in Plotinus perhaps its classic expression. But the other side, the understanding of infinity that leads to a constructive theory of the highest principle as we know it in Descartes, in Hegel, and in the work of many theologians, does not emerge in these writings. I suggest that one can make a few further steps, however trembling, in reflecting on this subject without being forced into negation and silence.

The Infinite Creator

Gregory of Nyssa was the first to stress and elaborate in detail on the infinite as an appellation for God. As an important study argues, "The negative theology that Plato inaugurated had never appropriated one of the attributes of God: the infinite. This particular attribute of God is found in Gregory of Nyssa for the first time in the history of philosophical and Christian reflection."[36] Gregory realized that God must be understood as infinitely extended in time, as having infinite qualities or names, and as transcendent to the world, thus as its creator ex nihilo. But these features are possible only if he is not limited by anything. Hence God is infinite.

Gregory does more, however, than give clear expression for the first time to the necessity of understanding God as infinite. He makes infinity into the central attribute of God and then begins systematically to derive other attributes from it, such as God as creator, or at least to interpret the others in terms of it, as in his treatment of the Trinity. He corrects Aristotle's epistemology where it conflicts with the idea of an unending increase in knowledge. For in-

---

36. See Mühlenberg, *Die Unendlichkeit Gottes*. Mühlenberg's attribution of complete historical priority to Gregory is highly controversial and has been frequently attacked. Although the question cannot be decided here, it does appear that he underemphasized the importance of the notion in earlier thinkers. For example, J. E. Hennessy has argued that Mühlenberg systematically underestimated the role of the concept of infinity in theists before Gregory such as Philo ("The Background, Sources and Meaning of Divine Infinity in St. Gregory of Nyssa" (diss., Fordham University, 1963, cited in David L. Balas, "A Thomist View on Divine Infinity," in Dahlstrom et al., eds., *Infinity*, 91-98). For example, Guyot's case for the infinite in Philo continues to recommend itself despite Mühlenberg's excursus on the subject; see Henri Guyot, *L'Infinité divine depuis Philon le Juif jusqu'à Plotin* (Paris: Alcan, 1906).

stance, he separates the infinite from the realm of more and less. Only things that are good in a limited fashion, by participating in something good, admit of more and less: "Nothing which possesses the good not as something acquired but in virtue of its own nature can be defective in wisdom or power or in any other good. . . . Now, the infinite *(to aoriston)* is not such by its relation to another, but, considered in itself, escapes limit. It is, then, difficult to see how a reflecting mind can conceive one infinite as greater or less than another infinite" (*Contra Eunomium* 1.234, 235-36).

Finally, in agreement with the Neoplatonic tradition, Gregory presents a Christian account of the mystical ascent toward the infinite Christian God. Nothing can be known of the divine *hypokeimenon*. We call him "Being" since he transcends all designation by names; and when the apostle says that his name is above every name, this is because "'the real Being' is above every name" (*Contra Eunomium* 3.9.41). But Being *(ōn)* is not merely the key to a negative theology; it also implies that God exists, that he is self-sufficient, and that he is infinite in the sense of everlasting and immutable.[37] As such, knowing God as infinite is the condition of the possibility for all knowledge of the finite. Thus Mühlenberg concludes, "The existence of God is known by reason and is the presupposition of all thought."[38]

After Gregory the infinity of God played no crucial role over the next several centuries; for example, it appears in Augustine's entire corpus only eight times.[39] Still, after Gregory a number of theologians began to connect infinity and perfection as attributes of God, including Bonaventure, Albert the Great, and Henry of Ghent (on whom more below). Speculation concerning infinity reemerged especially in the mid-thirteenth century under the influence of Aristotle's writings, albeit less frequently in relation to the concept of God.[40] For example, Thomas Aquinas did clearly maintain God's infinity: "The notion of

37. Here I follow David Balas, *Metousia Theou: Man's Participation in God's Perfections according to St. Gregory of Nyssa* (Rome: Herder, 1966), e.g., 112ff. (who in turn appeals to F. Diekamp, *Die Gotteslehre des hl. Gregor von Nyssa*, vol. 1 [Münster, 1896]), against the stress on the primacy of infinity in Mühlenberg's interpretation. Balas also cites passages showing that Gregory placed "real Being" and "Goodness Itself" on the same level as primordial attributes of God.

38. Mühlenberg, *Die Unendlichkeit Gottes*, 196.

39. Sweeney, "Surprises," 8. An important exception is Henry of Ghent, to whom I return in the section on perfection.

40. Leo Sweeney, S.J., "Lombard, Augustine and Infinity," *Manuscripta* 2 (1958): 24-32; idem, "Bonaventure and Aquinas on the Divine Being as Infinite," in Robert W. Shahan and Francis J. Kovach, eds., *Bonaventure and Aquinas: Enduring Philosophers* (Norman: Univ. of Oklahoma Press, 1976), 133-54.

form is most fully realized in existence itself. And in God existence is not acquired by anything, but God is existence itself subsistent. It is clear, then, that God himself is both limitless and perfect."[41] However, although Thomas insisted that God's infinity was not tinged by any imperfection, the attribute did not form the center of his doctrine of God.

Infinity as the Central Attribute of God

What happens when one moves the concept of the infinite into the center of philosophical theology, as Gregory of Nyssa had begun to do, subordinating all other features to or deriving them from this attribute? In the next pages we consider three responses to this question (Scotus, Cusa, Bruno). To anticipate the study's conclusion: if infinity is kept under the control of (or "limited" by) a specific concept of perfection, for instance one informed by the Christian tradition, and especially if the infinite is held to mediate order to the finite realm through a causal relationship (say, as creation or providence),[42] then a distinction between nature and God can be maintained and (paradoxically?) some knowledge of God is preserved. Let's call this the *infinite perfection* school. When, however, the concept of infinity is not "limited" in any way by other conceptual considerations (say, by perfection or consciousness or a theological tradition), when the gap between finite and infinite is widened until they become incommensurable, then the infinite tends to become the absolutely unknowable (let's call it the *absolute infinity* school). As we will see, the latter school also tends toward the *hen kai pan* of absolute monism, leaving no place for a genuine creation or a separately existing world.

Duns Scotus was the first after Gregory of Nyssa to move the concept of God as infinitely perfect to the center of his theology.[43] Infinity is an intrinsic mode of God. We have, says Scotus, "a concept of what is essentially one,

---

41. Thomas Aquinas, *ST* Ia, q.7 a.1. See also *I Sent.* d. 43 q.1; *Summa contra Gentiles* I, chap. 43; *Compendium theologiae*, chaps. 18, 20.

42. The role of the concept of order in medieval theology cannot be overestimated. Its centrality is argued in Wolfhart Pannenberg, "Die Gottesidee des hohen Mittelalters," in Albert Schaefer, ed., *Der Gottesgedanke im Abendland* (Stuttgart: Kohlhammer, 1964), e.g., 32: "Der Gottesgedanke des Mittelalters aber hat gerade darin sein Charakteristikum, daß er auf die Ordnung der Schöpfung und die Heilsordnung der Kirche bezogen ist."

43. See Etienne Gilson, *Jean Duns Scot: Introduction à ses positions fondamentales* (Paris: Vrin, 1952), esp. chap. 2, "L'existence de l'être infini," 116-215. See also Martin Tweedale, "Scotus and Ockham: On the Infinity of the Most Eminent Being," *Franciscan Studies* 23 (1963): 257-67.

namely of a subject with a certain grade of perfection — infinity."[44] An infinite being "is that which exceeds any finite being whatsoever not in some limited degree but in a measure beyond what is either defined or can be defined."[45] He later adds, "This notion of God as an infinite being is the most perfect absolute concept we can have of him."[46]

The first thing that emerges in this position is a qualitative difference between the finite and the infinite. An infinite being has unity, simplicity, and uniqueness, for there cannot be multiple infinites. In understanding Scotus's advance over Thomas Aquinas, we might say that *esse* in Thomas and *infinitas* in Scotus play analogous roles in their respective systems:[47] what Thomas does with Being as the essence of God and the link between God and creation, Scotus does with infinity. In Scotus, God is thought as it were outward from the concept of infinity alone.[48] God's absolute singularity *just is* his infinity; God is singular and one because he is infinite. Scotus even evidences Neoplatonic leanings, as when he quotes John Damascene, "for like some infinite and limitless sea of substance, he contains all being in himself."[49]

Nevertheless, despite this stress on unity, Scotus believes he can argue from the concept of infinity to its actual existence, and hence (!) to the existence of God:

> I proceed as follows: first I show that the first efficient cause is endowed with will and possesses such intelligence that this cause understands an infinity of

---

44. *Duns Scotus: Philosophical Writings,* ed. and trans. Allan Wolter (London: Thomas Nelson, 1962), 27: "non habeo conceptum quasi per accidens ex subjecto et passione, sed conceptum per se subjecti in certo gradu perfectionis, scilicet infinitatis, sicut albedo intensa non dicit conceptum per accidens sicut albedo visibilis; immo intensio dicit gradum intrinsecum albedinis in se et ita patet simplicitas hujus conceptus ens infinitum."

45. *Quodlib.* 5, par. 9; see Scotus, *God and Creatures: The Quodlibetal Questions,* trans. F. Alluntis and A. B. Wolter (Princeton: Princeton Univ. Press, 1975), 110.

46. Wolter, ed., *Duns Scotus: Philosophical Writings,* 76. "ergo aliquod infinitum ens existit in actu, et istud est perfectissimum conceptibile et conceptus perfectissimus absolutus quem possumus habere de Deo naturaliter quod sit infinitus, sicut dicitur distinctione tertia."

47. So Gilson, *La liberté,* 209. Scotus moves from showing the infinity of the divine will and intellect to the conclusion that God's essence is infinite. Contrast this with Thomas, who argues from the infinity of the divine being to the other perfections that an actually infinite being must have.

48. Cf. Gilson, *Jean Duns Scot,* 210: : "Car à prendre les choses en toute rigueur, une essence qui serait l'infinité même, c'est-à-dire une infinité d'être, devrait nécessairement trouver en soi toutes ses autres modalités. Parce qu'*infinitum,* ces être il serait Celui Qu'il Est, et c'est par là qu'il serait aussi Celui Qui Est."

49. John Damascene, *De fide orthodoxa* I, chap. 9, quoted in *Quodlib.* 1, par. 7.

distinct things and that its essence, which indeed is its intelligence, represents an infinity; secondly, I go on from this to infer the infinity of this Being. This approach, coupled with the triple primacy which we have established [efficiency, finality, and eminence], provides four ways of showing the infinity of this Being.[50]

In the pages following this passage, Scotus argues that God is infinite, inter alia, because he is first efficient cause, because as first cause and agent he knows all that can be made, because he is the final telos of everything that has been made, and because he is the most excellent being.

Scotus also links infinity to necessary existence in a fashion reminiscent of Descartes. One can conceive infinity as an attribute of that entity whose essence is prior to its existence as a singular being. But existence follows from this attribute: if existence does not enter into the concept of this being, it would not be the infinite being nor have its essence in itself; it would not possess in itself all perfection.[51] Now if a being exists essentially, possessing in itself all perfection, then it exists in the fullest sense of the term. Finite beings, which exist in virtue of an *esse* distinct from their essence, do not exist in the fullest sense of the term, although they "grasp hold of a certain measure of perfection of being" when they receive it from the infinite being. Infinity is thus an "intrinsic mode" for Scotus; it constitutes the essence of God. In this one attribute, he claims, are revealed God's existence *(esse)* and necessity and aseity, along with all the other perfections, just as the finitude of human creatures is the source of all their various *im*perfections.

The Infinite and the Ontological Union of God and World

Prima facie, it seems that one could assert an infinite source for the world without ascribing infinity to the world itself, even when one also holds that finite things participate in some way in their infinite source. Nonetheless, there is his-

---

50. See Scotus, *Ordinatio* (also referred to as the *Opus Oxoniense*), Qu. 3, in Wolter, ed., *Duns Scotus: Philosophical Writings*, 52. Cf. also Duns Scotus, *A Treatise on God as First Principle*, ed. and trans. A. Wolter (Chicago: Franciscan Herald, 1966), e.g., 133ff. "procedo sic: Primo ostendo quod primum efficiens est intelligens et volens, ita quod sua intelligentia est infinitorum distincte, et quod sua essentia est repraesentativa infinitorum, quae quidem essentia est sua intelligentia. Et ex hoc secundo concludetur sua infinitas."

51. The following summary of Scotus's position in drawn from Hieronymus de Montefortino, *Ven. Joannis Duns Scoti . . . Summa theologica*, P. I, q.3 a.4, as quoted in Gilson, *Jean Duns Scot*, 210ff.

torical evidence that the stress on an infinite ground of the world creates a certain presumption toward an ontological union of God and world, and therefore toward a view of the world as contained within the all-encompassing infinite. A short look at one important expression of this view, the philosophy of Nicholas of Cusa, helps to illustrate this important dynamic of modern thought about God.

Nicholas and Meister Eckhart rejected the ascent from an independent, finite realm of nature to absolutely perfect divine Being. The finite and the infinite have nothing in common and there is no proportionality between them: *infiniti ad finitum proportio non est.* This view reflects the transcendence of the infinite that I defended against Aristotle: it becomes absolutely separate from the realm of more and less. In theological terms this means that we have to open ourselves to an instruction or illumination from above if we are to have any knowledge of God whatsoever.[52] In other words, the concept of the infinite leads in Nicholas's thought to a strong theocentrism: one must proceed from God, in order "to see in the creature, and paradigmatically in the human spirit or soul, the mirroring, the picture, the formative influence of the Creator."[53] The finite has its ground in God; the world is *explicatio Dei.* Nicholas rejects the analogy of being from below, only to reintroduce it from above: There is no understanding God from creation, since creation can be comprehended only by thinking downward (outward?) from God. The full transcendental significance of this claim must not be overlooked: "Whoever does not know God, knows nothing of the world. Thus [for Nicholas] the knowledge of God is the first precondition for all knowing."[54]

But how is one to conceive God's relationship to the world if one starts from the absolute One but does not wish to embrace the whole metaphysic of a necessary emanation outward from the One and an ascent back up the "ladder of participation" to the One? (Similar questions could be raised of Eckhart's *esse est deus.*) Nicholas tries to think of God's infinity as a positive trait instead of appealing to emanation from and participation in the One as the Neoplatonists did.[55] But stressing the primacy of the infinite in this way tends to lead to

52. Cf. Rudolf Haubst, "Nikolaus von Kues als theologischer Denker," *Trierer theologische Zeitschrift* 68 (1959): 129-45.

53. "Im Geschöpf, vornehmlich in der menschlichen Geistseele die Spiegelung, das Bild, die Prägung des Schöpfers zu sehen" (Friedrich Dessauer, *Auf den Spuren der Unendlichkeit* [Frankfurt: Josef Knecht, 1954], 41-42).

54. Siegfried Lorenz, "Das Unendliche bei Nicolaus von Cues," *Philosophisches Jahrbuch* 40 (1927): 57-84: "Wer Gott nicht kennt, der weiß nichts von der Welt. Also ist [for Cusa] die Erkenntnis Gottes die erste Vorbedingung für jedes Wissen" (60).

55. See Josef Koch's comments on Eckhart in his excellent historical study,

the co-infinity of the world — unless one postulates some sort of eternal matter that limits individuals and makes them finite. Think, for example, of the metaphors employed by the two schools. Pseudo-Dionysius conceived unity as the middle of a circle and numbers (i.e., plurality) as the radii; the radii become more separate and distant from one another as one moves outward from the center.[56] By contrast, in Nicholas's famous picture God is the circle whose center is everywhere and whose circumference (limit) is nowhere. Here there appears to be no room for a real separation of the Many from the One through emanation or "dégradation" (Jules Guitton).

According to Nicholas the many finite things, being encompassed and pervaded by the one infinite, are indeed ontologically closer to the infinite than in Plotinus's view. For this reason Nicholas may be taken as an early precursor of the theology of *panentheism,* which understands the world as within God at the same time that God also transcends the world (see chapters 7–9 below). As if to confirm this impression, Nicholas writes that the individual is a microcosmos; in each part is the whole, and only through the whole does each part exist.[57] In God all opposites coincide (the *coincidentia oppositorum*); conversely, the world is the unfolding of the "divine complication." God as infinite is not a finite thing, yet he is also every thing.[58] The world is the finite God; God is the world in the potency of the infinite (ibid., II, 2). Man is God — not in an absolute sense, since we are still human, but as a human God; humans stand "on the horizon between time and eternity."[59]

Nicholas's theology is fascinating, and I find much to recommend it as an outworking of the logic of infinity. Here there is no ultimate confusion of God and world, for God remains the absolute maximum and minimum to which the world never attains, the self-sufficient source and ground on which the world depends. Consequently, the world has only a "privative infinity." Insofar

---

"Augustinischer und Dionysischer Neuplatonismus und das Mittelalter," *Kant-Studien* 48 (1956): 117-33, 132.

56. Pseudo-Dionysius, *De decem dubitationibus* chap. 1; cf. *Enneads* 6.8.18. Koch stresses the impact of this thinker on the early Middle Ages: no one could attack Dionysius, the pupil of the apostle, yet whoever made use of his thought — John Scotus, Eckhart, or Cusa — "geriet in den Verdacht häretischen Pantheismus, weil die Trennung von Gott und Geschöpf nicht gewahrt schien" (p. 133).

57. *De docta ignorantia* 2.4; on microcosm see *De ludo globi* I. Admittedly, however, in other passages Cusa seems to stand much closer to Plotinus, as when he asserts that God is the absolute unity and the world a unity that has been split into plurality and contradiction, e.g., *De conjecturis* 1.11.

58. *De docta ignorantia* 1.4.21. The next reference in the text is also to this work.

59. See *De conjecturis* 2.14 and *De venatione sapientiae* 32.

as God has no center and is everywhere, he encompasses the world; he is its infinite border, a border that, as infinite, does not limit. Still, the world remains less than absolute since it derives from God; it is the image of God, a limited way of seeing or representing the infinite.[60] As Alvarez-Gómez summarizes, the world "is not absolute or perfect in itself, but rather not yet complete or perfected; it is not the *infinitum* in its primary sense, but the *indefinitum*; it is not eternal, but only of unending duration."[61]

It is possible now to combine the notion of the infinite as I have specified it up to this point with the notion of a creation from nothing. The two notions may even be, as Nicholas argues, mutually implicating. If God has created all finite things, he is infinitely Other from them in eternality and power (but also ontologically close to them as their only source). If a being is absolutely infinite, then it can be limited by nothing; everything must be derivative from it (but in this sense also one with it). God's infinity implies that there can be no difference between creating and being created. God is the creating self-creator, hence *causa sui* in the Cartesian sense; he creates in that he sees (and therefore, again, what he creates is not other than he). As a result we are led again to the coincidence of opposites: "Your creating is your Being, and creating and simultaneously being-created is nothing else than that you impart your Being to all, so that you are all in all and remain separate from all. That you call into Being what is not means that you impart Being to the nothing" (*De visione Dei* 12).

Like Thomas Aquinas, Nicholas stresses that finite things depend for their very being (as well as for their essence) on God. Creation implies continuous dependence on the Creator in order to be — a notion later incorporated in Descartes's equation of creation and preservation. Yet in contrast to Thomas, Nicholas refuses to interpret this as a causal relationship, in order to preserve the absolute disproportionality of infinite and finite. The infinite is all that is. Hence "things can come into existence because they are contained within God and are thus one and the same with him. . . . Thus insofar as things are created by God, they are not only dependent on him but are also in him."[62] Since there

---

60. Walter Schulz, *Der Gott der neuzeitlichen Metaphysik* (Pfullingen: Günther Neske, 1957), esp. chap. 1, "Cusanus und die Geschichte der neuzeitlichen Metaphysik."

61. "[Die Welt] ist nicht absolut in sich vollkommen, sondern das Unvollendete, nicht das infinitum in eigentlichem Sinne, sondern das indefinitum; sie ist nicht ewig, sondern nur von unendlicher Dauer" (Mariano Alvarez-Gómez, *Die verborgene Gegenwart des Unendlichen bei Nikolaus von Kues* [Munich: A. Pustet, 1968], 40), citing *De docta ignorantia* 2.1.65. Cusa's doctrine of creation is the central topic of part 2 of Alvarez-Gómez's excellent book.

62. "Die Dinge können entstehen, weil sie in Gott enthalten sind und dabei ein und dasselbe mit ihm sind. . . . [Darum] sind die Dinge, insofern sie von Gott geschaffen sind,

is no "place" outside God, creation can only take place *within* God. Of course God and creation are not equivalent, Nicholas insisted, for God is in his essence more than Creator, more than his relatedness to the world; still, the "distance" between God and world has been greatly decreased. Because he located the world within God, and because of the cogency of his arguments for this move, Nicholas represents one of the most important precursors of panentheistic theologies today.

The Monist/Pantheistic Infinite

We have found a clear tendency of theologies of the infinite God to deny any dualism between Creator and creation — whether under the influence of emanation and participation or, as with Nicholas of Cusa, even in the context of creation ex nihilo. In the modern period, as we shall see later, this movement culminated in Spinoza's thought and in the dialectical philosophers of immanence influenced by him. As Josef Koch has shown (n. 55 above), the antidualist tendency in theologies of the infinite led repeatedly to charges of heresy against these theologians, and especially against the Neoplatonists, since (it was claimed) they failed to conceive creation as both freely created and as separate enough from God. In fact, multiple means exist for avoiding the dangers of pantheism. One can rely on appeals to an orthodox doctrine of creation, on evidence that we are separately existing finite beings, and on the panentheist stress on the moment of transcendence in God. Before assessing the adequacy of such responses, let us look at one last premodern thinker, Giordano Bruno. The guiding question is: To what extent is Bruno's thought the consistent and inevitable outworking of a philosophy that starts and ends with the infinite?

Infinity implies monism — this is perhaps the basic teaching of Bruno's philosophy: "This world, this being, this truth, this universe, this infinite, this immensity, is wholly in all its parts, and consequently is the (ubiquitous) everywhere itself."[63] Since there can only be One, all parts are modes of the One. Their appearance of separateness, like the appearance of motion and change, is merely illusory. In the mystical ascent to perfect cognition we "simplify the manifold" until, like the first intelligence, we see the universe as infinite and

---

nicht nur von ihm abhängig, sondern sind auch in ihm" (Alvarez-Gómez, *Die verborgene Gegenwart*, 81).

63. Bruno, *De la Causa*, Fifth Dialogue, translated as "Concerning the Cause, Principle, and One," in Sidney Thomas Greenburg, *The Infinite in Giordano Bruno* (New York: Kings Crown Press, 1950; repr. New York: Octagon, 1978), 164. The next reference in the text is also to this work. See also Dupré, *Passage to Modernity*, 59-66, 182-86.

unified: "The first intelligence comprehends everything in one perfect idea; the divine mind and the absolute unity . . . is itself, at one and the same [time], that which understands and that which is understood" (p. 168).

The universe is "not other" to God; hence it too must be infinite. But where Nicholas spoke of its privative infinity (it is the "explication" of the infinite God), Bruno distinguishes extensive and intensive infinity. The universe is infinitely extended; it has an infinite number of parts — even infinite worlds — though its parts, unlike God's attributes, are finite. By contrast, "I call God all-infinite, because he excludes from himself every term, and every one of his attributes is one and infinite; I call God totally infinite, because all of him is in all the world, and in each part infinitely and totally."[64]

In Bruno we find the clearest proponent of the "absolute infinity" school, at least prior to Spinoza. Novalis's famous description of Spinoza applies to Bruno as well: he is the "God-intoxicated philosopher." In dialogues such as "De l'infinito" and "De la causa" Bruno is utterly preoccupied with the theme of the absolute One. Conceptually, we can say that he held unwaveringly to the implications of this single concept and allowed nothing else to mitigate its consequences; intuitively, one senses a spiritual commonality with Plotinus, Eckhart, Nicholas of Cusa, and Spinoza. These advocates of the absolute infinity school — and none more clearly than Bruno — take the first implication from the first section above (that the infinite must be prior to the finite) to its final conclusion, absolute monism, based on an uncompromising application of the logic of the concept of infinity. When all other factors are left behind in this fashion — nature, perfection, even God — absolute monism becomes the inevitable final step in the gradual ascent initiated by the concept of infinity.

Conclusion: Positive and Negative Infinities

The preceding comments have often presupposed but have not yet clearly drawn the distinction between positive and negative infinity. A *positive infinity* is one that is characterized by one or more positive attributes. A *negative infinity* is one that results from removing all limits or determinations from something that is otherwise determined (a space, a span of time, a quantity of power). Descartes expresses the distinction by separating the infinite from the indeterminate; Hegel drew a similar distinction between "the bad infinite" and "the true infinite." I shall argue that the positive infinite is the proper object of a

---

64. Bruno, *Opere italiane*, I:291, cited in Greenburg, 17.

theology of the infinite, even though the nature of the Highest, the truly unlimited, may make achieving any adequate theory of it difficult or impossible.

In chapter 2 we traced Descartes's realization that the indefinite (e.g., an indefinitely large universe) falls short of the infinite.[65] Descartes granted that the distinction is a difficult one, since there is nothing in the apparently unlimited expansion of the universe that proves that it is *not* infinite (to More, 2/5/1649; V,274-75). Still, he saw correctly that apparently unlimited quantities or stretches of space are not equivalent to the positively infinite, and he held onto the true infinite as something different from anything to which we can extrapolate merely by extending the finite.

As usual, Descartes's paring down of Scholastic distinctions brings with it certain dangers. For instance, he did not bother with the distinction between intensive infinity (the preeminence of God's very essence) and extensive infinity (the fact that, as infinite, God must encompass everything that is). This leaves him unable to specify the God-world relation in the precise manner that Nicholas of Cusa did. Still, as a result the formal structure of the Cartesian argument is easier to reconstruct. One makes an inference (better, perhaps: an intuitive leap) from indefiniteness (e.g., the extension of the world) to a being who is truly infinite. The two are related, since both are without limits; yet the indefinite, which is still an extrapolation from the finite, must in some way be negated in order to attain positive infinity. This process of negation to reach a positive goal is reminiscent of the Scholastic *via eminentiae*, the way of eminence. On this method one begins with predicates that have some human content, such as "X is wise." One then negates the predicate: God is *not* wise, since the divine nature is absolutely simple whereas being wise is attributed as a single distinct property. Finally, one reintroduces the predicate in the way of eminence: God is wisdom itself, and we are wise only by participating in this quality in its pure form.

As a formal structure, this Cartesian method for conceiving the infinite has much to recommend it; in the next section we explore in particular the contribution of the concept of participation. But it also has its limits. First, as we have seen, it does not work as a proof of the infinite, as Descartes had hoped. Second, supplying positive content to the resultant eminent qualities (divine wisdom, divine volition) turns out to be problematic. Finally, there are unique problems when we apply the *via eminentiae* to Being itself. One can say that everything that is shares in God's Being, but then one needs a further ground to

---

65. Descartes writes, e.g., "Je n'oserais dire qu'il [le monde] est infini, parce que je concois *(percipio)*, que Dieu est plus grand *(majorem)* que le monde" (to More, 4/15/1649; V,344).

explain exactly how things are different from the Being they participate in. Here Descartes did not adequately protect himself from the monistic or pantheistic tendencies inherent in his own line of argument.[66]

At any rate, the importance of distinguishing between negative and positive notions of infinity has become clear. After one has taken seriously enough the contrast with the indefinite, the infinite emerges as a positive conception. In all fields where the notion of infinity is used, it comes as a specifiable concept: "Wherever the researcher encounters 'the infinite,' he does not meet the unordered, formless, undetermined *apeiron* from which the Greeks drew back with horror, but instead he encounters [this concept] in specific contexts; he meets it in structured form."[67] To dispense with all structure whatsoever, to posit an infinite with no other attributes, is to move quickly to the One beyond Being and beyond all language. In this case, the philosopher has nothing to provide. If such an absolute infinite is the final truth, it is one before which its advocate can only stand in silence.

Within theology, the concept of *perfection* has traditionally provided a key structure for specifying and speaking of God's infinity. God must be fully infinite, "since infinity in him is both the absence of all imperfection arising from any potentiality and the presence of total perfection issuing from his subsistent actuality."[68] Perfection had within Western theology a prophylactic function: one tended to forbid any argument from infinity that reduces God's perfection. But it also functioned as a positive criterion, insofar as one ascribed to God only those levels or types of infinity that explicitly increased his perfection. Infinite infinity is not a perfection; perfect infinity is. But with the introduction of this criterion we have already made the transition to the following section.

---

66. For instance, he might have distinguished (as Proclus did) between *unum superexaltatum* and *unum coadunatum:* the latter is what everything has as existing, while the former is above all distinctions and, although it can only be spoken of through negation, is also the absolutely perfect. Cf. the opening of Proclus, *The Elements of Theology*, ed. E. R. Dodds (Oxford: Clarendon Press, 1933).

67. "Wo immer der Forscher dem 'Unendlichen' begegnet, trifft er nicht das ungeordnete, formlose unbestimmte Apeiron an, vor dem die Griechen schaudernd zurückwichen, sondern er begegnet ihm in 'Zuordnungen,' er trifft es strukturiert" (Dessauer, *Auf den Spuren*, 96).

68. Sweeney, "Surprises," in Dahlstrom et al., eds., *Infinity*, 18. As process thinkers have urged (nn. 15 and 26 above), however, the identification of perfection with the absence of all potentiality (such as the ability to respond) raises problems of its own.

THE CONCEPT OF A PERFECT BEING

In this section we approach the problem of God in modern thought from the other main pillar of premodern philosophical theology, the concept of perfection. I first draw out of the preceding discussion some of the reasons why metaphysical reflection might find itself compelled to employ this concept. The remainder of the chapter explores particular characteristics of the philosophy of perfect being, beginning with the details of its historical emergence.

On Limiting Infinity through Perfection

What does it mean to call God infinite, to say that God's essence is unlimited in all respects? As we found, it may imply a degree to which any given attribute can be taken ("God's infinite power," omnipotence), or it can be used as a selector for which qualities to ascribe to God: God has the qualities a being would have to have to be infinite. But how should we understand this latter criterion? Does God as comprehensive being have all conceivable attributes, or only those that admit of infinite degrees, or just the perfect-making properties?

Let's look for a moment at the question of infinite power. Recall that Descartes took the strongest conceivable position on God's power, ascribing to God absolute omnipotence. Everything that can meaningfully be asserted, God could do, whether or not doing so involves a contradiction. This is the point of the doctrine of God's creation of the eternal truths: even the laws of logic are only contingently necessary; it is possible that God could have made the Law of Noncontradiction false. Even for Descartes, of course, there is one exception: God could not do something that would make him no longer God; "it is possible that God should not exist" is necessarily false in all worlds. Thus God's nonexistence is necessarily impossible — but aside from that, God's omnipotence is as complete as we can possibly think it.

What exactly would propel someone to such a view? Suppose we assume God is a being who is infinite and who acts. It then follows deductively that God acts with infinite power. And how great should infinite power be? As great as such power could be, that is, without all limit. But if God were confined to the logically possible, his power would know a limit; hence he must be able to do even the logically impossible.

I believe that the logic of this argument is unconvincing. Multiplying powers without a principle is theologically pointless; there must be some other or more specific control over the degree of power predicated, one that stems from the nature of the being who acts using this power. Judged from the standpoint of a theory of God, the multiplication process, left unguided, leads quickly to results that conflict with other God-making attributes. We have already seen one example of this: Descartes (rightly) did not want to ascribe to God the power to cease to be God. When he introduces this limitation, he implicitly follows a more general principle, namely that the infinity argument should not induce one to ascribe to God anything incompatible with divine perfection. Here again Descartes and his followers read the concepts of infinity and perfection together. It is less perfect to ascribe to God the power to do evil, or to do things that conflict with his power to reveal himself. Still, we will have to ask whether one needs to pay all the costs of a perfection-based metaphysics to block such problems. Asserting *any* inconsistent predicates of God is enough to move God into the realm of the wholly unknowable. As Geach observes, just as we cannot say how a nonlogical world would look, "we cannot say how a supra-logical God would act or how he could communicate anything to us by way of revelation."[69]

The Creation of Eternal Truths

What, more precisely, does it mean for perfection to "limit" infinity? Let's start with Descartes's own position, which, although it clearly accepts perfection as a criterion, supposes only the most minimal of limitations. When Burman asks whence come the ideas of possible things that precede the will, Descartes replies that they, like everything else, come from God,[70] for God's will is the cause also of possible things and of simple natures. The key is that we cannot and may not find anything that we do not say depends on God.

The argument has a theological core:

> As for the eternal truths [what we call necessary truths], I say again that they are true or possible because God knows them to be true or possible, but not that they are known by God to be true as if they were true independently of him. . . . One must not say, then, that if God did not exist, nevertheless those truths would still be true, for the existence of God is the first and most eternal of all the truths which can be, and the only one from which all the others proceed. But what makes it easy to be mistaken in this is that most men do not

---

69. P. T. Geach, "Omnipotence," *Philosophy* 48 (1973): 7-20, quotation 11; repr. in Doney, ed., *Eternal Truths and the Cartesian Circle,* 183-96.

70. "Et illa et omnia alia pendent a Deo," V,160, quoted from *L'entretien avec Burman,* ed. and trans. Jean-Marie Beyssade (Paris: Presses Universitaires de France, 1981), marginal 160. The following references to the dialogue with Burman are from the same source.

consider God as an infinite and incomprehensible being, who is the only author on whom all things depend.[71]

How powerful is God? Powerful enough to create the eternal truths and to be the source of all possibility. Yet there must be a limit, lest we have the absurdity that God could have made it the case that he did not exist. What is this limit? Whatever is compatible with "God is omnipotent," says Descartes at one point.[72] Thus we clearly need a doctrine of omnipotence that is consistent enough to serve as a criterion. But, Descartes maintains, omnipotence alone is insufficient; the criterion must ultimately be *whatever is compatible with God's perfection.* This is the sense of the claim to Burman that God necessarily willed the best.[73] The mind, which clearly and distinctly perceives God's essence, can rule out what would be inconsistent with the divine essence. As a result of this criterion, Descartes boasts, he can escape the whole host of Scholastic debates — his own example is whether God could have brought it about "that there is a mountain without a valley" — by noting where "such things involve a contradiction in my conception" of God (V,223-24).

The value of the Cartesian doctrine of the creation of eternal truths is that it helps show the contingency of the whole created order. Even necessary truths are necessary only contingently, because of God's creative choice; the very order within which they are necessary could have been decided otherwise. Margaret Wilson calls it a conflict that is "resolved 'upward'": "The intuition of God's infinite power is accorded priority over our seeming intuitions of ineluctable mathematical necessity."[74] Why then can't we even conceive what Descartes is affirming God can do, which is to make "necessary" truths false? Because we are created as part of the order in which they hold. In this specific sense, God exceeds what we can think, since he could have grounded another

---

71. Descartes to Mersenne, 5/6/1630; I,147ff., AM 1:139. Descartes also stresses that all truth depends on God in the 4/15/1630 letter to Mersenne and in the 6th Replies (VII,432-33, 435-36). As Rodis-Lewis notes, "L'Etre fonde la vérité parce qu'il en est la source; cette expression augustinienne prend chez Descartes un sens neuf" (*Descartes et le rationalisme* [Paris: Presses Universitaires de France, 1970], 36). This is the only way that God's existence could be the solution to hyperbolical doubt: God grounds an enduring order, even though he could have grounded another one.

72. Letter to Hyperaspistes, August 1641, III,429.

73. "Necessario tamen ita decrevit, quia necessario optimum voluit" (V,166).

74. Margaret Wilson, *Descartes,* 127. Wilson notes correctly, referring to the history of mathematics since Descartes, that the concept of necessity has at any rate been found to depend much more on "the structure and workings of our own minds" than Descartes's opponents, notably Leibniz, were willing to acknowledge (pp. 125-26).

order that is unthinkable to us. Here, of course, is where the evil demon hypothesis gains its foothold, since a being who exceeds one's comprehension could as easily be infinitely evil as infinitely good. It is also a major reason why Descartes must turn to the assumption that God is *ens perfectissimum,* the most perfect being, and thus not a deceiver. (Note that theologies that are not haunted by the ghost of an evil demon may not need to inhabit the thought world of perfect and imperfect beings.) Descartes's epistemology requires that he show that God is "the very being the idea of whom is within me, that is, the possessor of all the perfections that I cannot grasp, but can somehow reach in my thought, who is subject to no defects whatsoever."[75]

The Logic of Perfection

The preceding paragraphs began to develop the implicit connections between the theory of infinity and the theme of perfection. From the perspective of the knower, the initial connection is epistemic: to think infinity in any way we must somehow limit it, and the least limiting limit we can conceive is that of total perfection. For example, unlimited space (the *indefinitum*) lacks a positive limit or character. But to know space (or time, or power) as unlimited would be to ascribe to it a positive attribute rather than only the lack of limits. One must not be thrown off by the privative *in-* here. The question is: If infinity is to be thought in the positive sense, what must this imply? Of what sort of concept or being is it possible to turn a negative (limitlessness) into a positive, and what quality of infinite being could specify the essence of this being? In this manner perfection is introduced into the doctrine of God.

To qualify infinity in this manner turns us back from Bruno toward Anselm, from the Absolute One to the perfectly good being, from the philosophy of absolute monism to the theology of an entity with the characteristic of unsurpassable perfection. Infinite perfection would mean having each perfect-making quality to the point where it could no longer be increased. As we saw, Descartes followed this movement for omnipotence; perfect-being theologians argue that the grounds that lead one to ascribe one perfection to God also justify ascribing many others to him. For instance, an entity that was essentially infinite and possessed infinite power would be the creator of whatever else exists. Now, they argue, if one follows out the implications of "infinite creator," one arrives at a hierarchy of more and less limited creators. For example, one might begin first with the (Greek) concept of a demiurge or a former of matter, who works (more or less successfully) to impose order on preexisting stuff. Second,

75. Meditation 3, VII,52.

it would be more perfect if this being were the creator of matter too, hence a creator ex nihilo, since otherwise the creator's power would be limited by the resistant properties of matter as a given. Descartes then argued, third, that the highest grade on the scale pertains to a being who would be the creator of possibility and necessity as well. Of course, as one ascribes other perfections to this being, one may encounter new limitations that arise out of the need for the perfections to be *com*possible. Greatest possible power will be limited by omnibenevolence or perfect love, for example (on the assumption that it is better for a creator to respond to what it has made), since responsiveness implies a type of passivity. If creating the best world implies having creatures who can freely acknowledge the creator, a further limitation of power will be implied so as to allow free beings alongside God. Still, ignoring the limitations for a moment and looking just at the concept, Descartes's God would be the more perfect being.

It should be obvious that adding the predicate "perfect" to the theory of infinity means doing theology in a fairly explicit fashion. Is it more or less perfect to be absolutely simple? to be above change? to remain unaffected by the world? to suffer on behalf of creatures? As theological intuitions have changed, so too have the answers to these questions. This fact reveals the crucial difference between perfection and infinity. To assert that God is infinite is an extremely minimal specification, lying close to "God is One" or "God is the absolutely unknowable." Recall for example Gregory of Nyssa's inferences from "God can be limited in no way" to "God has infinite names" to "God is infinite." If ineffability were to rule out all the other divine predicates, infinity would be the last to go. It connotes a nature that humans could never fully grasp, even while it may express this nature in a positive way that goes beyond bare incomprehensibility. One hardly needs to add that it is a difficult matter for finite knowers to attain a positive conception of what is forever beyond (all limits). Yet this is what is required in both cases, since the idea of a perfect being cannot be reduced to the negation of the imperfect any more than the infinite is merely the negation of the finite.[76]

It does remain open to the opponent to deny that there is any nonnegative sense to the term *infinity,* a strategy that (if successful) would turn us back again to a purely negative conception of the infinite. Unfortunately, such a turning back is not open to the perfectionist since, as far as I can see,

76. See Emmanuel Levinas, *Totality and Infinity: An Essay on Exteriority,* trans. Alphonso Lingus (Pittsburgh: Duquesne Univ. Press, 1969), e.g., the section "Transcendence is not negativity," 40ff. Levinas here (p. 41) takes the relation imperfect/perfect to characterize the relation of the finite to the transcendent, building it into a basic theme of his book.

there is no "purely negative" concept of perfection (e.g., the lack of all imperfection). Thus "perfection" implies that much more can be known than "infinite." It implies, for example, a scale of good, an "objectivity of value structures" (Thomas Morris), that goes far beyond what the predicate *infinite* accomplishes. This greater content supplies it with its particular strength, at least from the standpoint of the quest for a rational theology. But we will also find that the increased content leads to some serious weaknesses and a possibly insurmountable set of epistemic difficulties.

On Predicating Perfection of God

Thinkers today too often take it as obvious that God would be perfect. After all, if God is both good and unlimited, then he must be unlimitedly good, that is, perfect. But there is nothing automatic about predicating perfection of an infinite being, and for many centuries the tradition resisted doing so. For in Aristotle's doctrine of the categories — and some of these have been preserved in philosophical "commonsense intuitions" today — to say that something has perfect virtue presupposes both form and content, and hence limits; the predicate "perfect" simply could not be applied to an unlimited thing. We will find that the connection between these attributes was only gradually made in Western thought; it came both from the side of infinity and from the side of perfection.

Adding "Perfect" to Infinity

Major impulses away from the Aristotelian position, which held that the infinite could never be perfect, came from the Neoplatonic tradition. Schematically, one could say that the opposition to Aristotle was already present in Plato's (and later in Plotinus's) view of the highest as both the One and the Good. As we have seen, further tendencies come from Gregory of Nyssa and Pseudo-Dionysius. The former, for example, challenged Aristotle's understanding of virtue in his *Vita Moyses*.[77] Basing his argument on the Bible, he held that the only border or limit *(horon)* for virtue is that it has none. Our striving for good must be endless. God is the good in itself; any conception of a limit already presupposes the unlimited beyond it. Since the divine can never be grasped by finite beings, "the divine is grasped *(katalambanetai)* as infinite and unlimited" (4.9-10).

77. 3.4–5.4; see Mühlenberg, *Die Unendlichkeit Gottes*, 159-60.

Pseudo-Dionysius was the first to use the infinite as "the connoting perfection of the supreme principle."[78] In *De divinis nominibus* he considers the divine names, moving from "the Good" to a climax in chapter 12, "On the perfect and the One."[79] On the other hand, the influence of Plotinus kept the notion of perfection from coming fully into its own: Pseudo-Dionysius still stresses the attribute of the One more strongly than perfection, as his negation of even the son-ness and father-ness of God elsewhere shows.[80] In Henry of Ghent, by contrast, the connection is emphasized rather more strongly. In his *Summa quaestionum ordinariarum*, the discussion of God's infinity follows discussions of God's unicity, nature, life, simplicity, immutability, eternity, truth, power, goodness, perfection, and totality. Only after the article on whether God is infinite does he move on to questions of the relations between the divine attributes.[81]

Adding "Infinite" to Perfection

Thomas Aquinas offers a good example of the movement in the opposite direction, since the concept of perfection plays a more significant role in his thought than that of infinity. The fourth *via*, as is well known, begins from the degrees of all things that admit of more or less (*ST* q.2 a.3). But degrees — of truth, good, nobility, being, and all other perfections (*et cujuslibet perfectionis*) — presuppose a maximum, a most perfect, which is the cause for everything in their genre. Hence there must be something that is for all essences the cause of their being. Schematically, we could say that Thomas begins with the perfections and increases them in degree until they become infinite perfections. Thus he argues elsewhere:

> [God] possesses all the perfections of every kind of thing . . . in a more excellent way than other things, because in him they are one, whereas in other things they are diversified . . . because all these perfections belong to him in virtue of simply being. In the same way, if someone could produce the operations of all the qualities through one quality alone, in that one quality he

---

78. David L. Balas, "A Thomist View on Divine Infinity," in Dahlstrom et al., eds., *Infinity*, 91.

79. Pseudo-Dionysius the Areopagite, *De divinis nominibus*, Bibliothek der Kirchenvater, Series 2, German trans. by Joseph Stiglmayr (Nendeleln, Liechtenstein: Kraus Reprint, 1968), 2:152; cf. p. 47.

80. See the final chapter of *Die mystische Theologie*, V, PG 3:1045-46.

81. Henricus Gandavensis, *Summae Quaestionum Ordinariarum* (St. Bonaventure, N.Y.: Franciscan Institute, 1953). The treatment of infinity is in book II, art. 44.

would possess every quality. Similarly, God possesses all perfections in his being itself.[82]

It is clear that this argument is a recipe for deriving attributes from perfection, with infinity appearing only to designate the degree of perfection implied. Actually, it is not a pure instance of the argument from perfection, since perfection is still subordinated to being. Thomas stresses that something has to *be* in order to be good; perfection is only the highest degree of being.[83]

Duns Scotus supplies perhaps the clearest instance of the perfection argument prior to Descartes. In his theology the good, perfection, is the basis and ontological ground for everything that exists. Goodness and perfection are the essence of the highest essence itself, God. Why can't God will the impossible, if he cannot be limited in any way by external essences or laws? Because to will the bad or the contradictory would be an imperfection. The unlimited divine power can only realize itself in the form of perfection, in the creation of a divine order.[84]

With this last position we reach the full equation of infinity and perfection — and thus the true starting point for posing the modern question contained in this book's title. As an intrinsically infinite being, God is *perfectio simpliciter,* pure or unqualified (unlimited!) perfection. He is also *extensively* infinite, which entails that there is no pure perfection of any sort lacking in him.[85] Scotus thus ascribes to God all names that designate perfections in creatures — all qualities that it is better to have than not to have and that imply no imperfection as such. Each is to be predicated of God in its essential form. Creatures have them, as they have their very being, only by participation; they "capture a part of that entity present [in God] perfectly and totally" (*Quod.* 5, par. 57). All finite things are parts; but since being a part means being exceeded in reality by something else (viz. the whole), it is inferior, less perfect, to be a part. The infinite whole must therefore be thought as prior to the parts (as in the first implication of the meditation that opened this chapter).

In his understanding of God as infinitely perfect, Descartes merely fol-

---

82. Thomas Aquinas, *On Being and Essence,* trans. Armand Maurer (Toronto: Pontifical Institute of Medieval Studies, 1968), chap. iv, #7, pp. 56-57.

83. See Koyré, *Descartes und die Scholastik,* 87.

84. Duns Scotus, *Opus Oxoniese* I d.44 qu. un. n.3 and 1; cf. Koyré, *Descartes und die Scholastik,* 92.

85. "Probatur perfectio istius conceptus, tum quia iste conceptus inter omnes nobis conceptibiles conceptus virtualiter plura includit, sicut enim ens includit virtualiter verum et bonum in se ita ens infinitum includit verum infinitum et bonum infinitum et omnem perfectionem simpliciter sub ratione infiniti" (Wolter's ed., 27).

lows the major thrust of Scotus's doctrine. Of particular importance, he takes over from Scotus, as the latter had from Thomas, the doctrine of levels of perfection. If there is an infinitely perfect being, other beings must be ranked by the level of perfection that they share or fail to share with this being. Wolter notes, "In his analysis of a given entity, Scotus often arranges the various perfections or *rationes* the mind distinguishes therein according to an ontological priority, accordingly as one *ratio* presupposes the other for its existence but not vice versa."[86] Once again, it seems that the attribution of perfection leads with a certain inevitability to a hierarchical ontology, as in the theory of levels of being.

Perfection and Participation

Finally, perfection and participation belong indissolubly together. If the highest being (or being itself) is viewed as perfect, all other beings will have their being, and whatever other positive qualities they have, only through their participation in the highest instance. As Balas argues, "all limited perfection is participated perfection (and this implies an intrinsic composition between the perfection participated and the recipient), whereas unparticipated perfection must be infinite and simple."[87] Let us briefly examine this sister concept to perfection which, I will argue, has traditionally provided an important bulwark for the notion of a perfect being — so much so that, should it cease to be philosophically credible, all of perfect-being theology will find itself in crisis.

Participation characterizes the relation between the most perfect and the less perfect. It is a two-place predicate; hence the German *Teilhabe* distinguishes between *Teilgeben* and *Teilnehmen*.[88] Further, it is unidirectional: the more perfect bestows and the less perfect receives a perfection. Consequently, there is always an ontological priority of the more perfect in participation, even if the order of knowledge moves in the other direction. Plato's philosophy provides the normative example of a metaphysics of participation:[89] things in this world are

---

86. Wolter in Dahlstrom et al., eds., *Infinity*, 180n.43. He adds, "To conceive the entity under some prior *ratio* in order to discover what additional attributes are implied in virtue thereof is to conceive it according to a *prior instance of nature*."

87. Balas, in Dahlstrom et al., eds., *Infinity*, 92; cf. Balas, *Metousia Theou*, 121-40.

88. H. R. Schlette, "Teilhabe," *Handbuch theologischer Grundbegriffe*, ed. Heinrich Fries (Munich: Kösel, 1963), 2:634-41.

89. Plato, *Tim.* 27d5-30c1 and 51e4-6; *Parm.* 132c12-133a10, 134bc. Variants of *metechein* and *methexis* appear also in *Phaid.* 65a-68b; *Symp.* 202a-204b; *Pol.* 508bc.

merely a reflection of their archetype in the forms, yet they also participate in and hence have an ontological unity with that world.

There is a certain tendency in Plato — and perhaps in the doctrine as a whole? — for the participator to disappear into unity with the form in which it participates, since Plato does not provide a separate principle to distinguish them. One might think that matter can play this role, but in Plato's thought pure matter is, ontologically speaking, nothingness, and nothingness cannot distinguish one specific thing from another. The problem of differentiation emerges more sharply in Neoplatonism, the clearest example being Plotinus. The procession from the One, and particularly the connection of the soul with matter, is said to create a separation from the One. The concept of participation is called on to maintain the connection of each individual with the One and to motivate its striving for reunification with the One; but it is also used in the context of explaining the independent existence of each thing, to the extent that it really exists (*Enneads* 5.5.4; 5.9.13; 6.7.38). But whereas its usefulness for the first two tasks is beyond dispute, participation obviously does not answer the question of what it is that participates and how it is different from its source; hence it is useless for the third.

Early Christian theologians were not slow to appropriate the participation idea for theological purposes. On their view, it allowed them to specify the relation of creation to creator. It specified the ethical model that God the Father or Son could supply for humans, as well as the mode in which the redeeming actions of Christ could be possessed by humans ("the partnership [*koinōnian*] in his sufferings," wrote Paul in Phil. 3:10). Pseudo-Dionysius, whose influence on the early Scholastic period was immense, made participation the central category for regulating the divine/human relationship, though he still did not use it for the communication of being from level to level. He and those working in his tradition (e.g., John Scotus Erigena, Hugo of St. Victor, Albertus Magnus, Meister Eckhart) sought in different ways to avoid the tendency toward pantheism that is inherent in the concept. Their work also shows that if one does not include *being* in what is participated — and especially if participation is understood in opposition to the chain of causality — the result can easily be a *theologia negativa* that denies the possibility of adequate knowledge of the participated source.[90]

Even these brief historical comments should be sufficient to show why the concept of participation is intrinsic to perfect-being theologies and played

90. In contrast to this tendency, Thomas understood the notion in terms of a participation *more causalis,* separating himself from the idea of an objective participation of essences; hence his stress on an essential difference in *ST* I,84,4-5.

such a large role in early modern thought about God. All of Descartes's arguments for the existence of an infinitely perfect being presuppose human participation in its perfections, as well as a scale of degrees of reality (and dependence) leading up to a highest instance. Consider the analogy to the relationship between the categories in classical metaphysics. For Aristotle, modes are dependent on accidents and accidents on substances; also some substances are dependent on others. At several points[91] Descartes extends the dependence relation into an ordering of created substances as well: as a hand is an incomplete substance, depending on the body as a whole, so also substances that are less than fully perfect depend on the perfect being. Obviously, this set of assumptions lies at the very heart of the causal argument for God in Meditation 3, and we shall see that it plays a no less significant role in Leibniz's thought as well.

What are we to make of participation and its implications? Bernard Williams berates it as hopelessly Scholastic, calling it "this unintuitive and barely comprehensible principle."[92] Hobbes attacked it in the Third Objections (VII,185) — to which Descartes responded that the principle is "quite self-evident." I noted in the previous chapter that as an argument it is (today) hardly compelling. The reason should by now be clear: only when one is already prepared to posit not merely an infinite but an infinitely perfect being does the required notion of *participated* perfections find the conceptual foundation it requires. The order of credibility is therefore the inverse of what would be needed for a deductive proof. Only if one already finds a perfect being plausible will one have reason to speak of levels of reality; without the intuition of such levels one may find perfect-being theology "unintuitive." By contrast, if one is already working within the framework of perfect-being theology, participation in the more real becomes a basic concept. But there are still further consequences of this view of God that require careful consideration before a decision can be reached about perfect-being theology.

Consequences of an Ontology of Perfection

What are the characteristics of a philosophical theology that is based on the notion of a perfect being? Even a quick historical survey reveals the diversity of options; narrowing the selection down far enough to allow for an organized

---

91. See Descartes's response to Hobbes, as well as a key passage in the 4th Replies (VII,222).

92. Williams, *Descartes*, 135.

discussion requires some arbitrariness. This section defends what I take to be the most promising alternative, without attempting to justify all its assumptions or to trace their historical antecedents. Still, even a selective summary can fairly represent the major tradition of thought on the subject; it should help to count the costs of espousing a metaphysics of perfection.

According to this proposal, the name "God" refers to the infinitely perfect being, a being who is essentially perfect and who possesses all perfect-making attributes. All less perfect things strive by nature for greater perfection and, ultimately, for the being who is perfect by essence. Perfections are in one sense relativized to the individual thing, or at least to each type of thing, since there is an appropriate perfection for each type. At the same time, these individual perfections each have a place in an overarching hierarchy; each stands at a greater or lesser distance from God. One might picture it by analogy with Thomas's two orders: each thing has its own essence, as well as its level of perfection. The latter scale, the scale of perfections, works by participation. In the following I briefly consider three implications of this ontology: levels of reality, monism, and identity in difference.

Levels of Reality

The scale of perfection underlies and necessitates degrees of reality: What is more perfect "contains in itself more reality," as Descartes argues in Meditation 3. God's supreme perfection implies that he has the fullest being on this scale, and distance from God entails lesser reality. This conceptual framework commits one to a conceptual framework something like Descartes's notion of the "formal reality" of a thing, as in his causal proof of God: "Since knowledge and power admit of degrees, we should, presumably, say that a being with a greater degree of knowledge has, other things equal, more formal reality than one with less knowledge."[93] Likewise, if eternity is limitless duration, then a being has less perfection if its duration is more limited, and hence less formal reality. A similar perfection presumably pertains to immutability as the capacity to resist change. Although the various perfections can be understood as multiple properties, they can also be summarized as differences in degree of only one property, the capacity for independent existence.

It is important to note that an ontology of perfection does not automatically compel one to accept all the details of the "great chain of being" with its

---

93. Curley, *Descartes against the Skeptics*, 129. In the French revision of Meditation 3, Descartes adds to (the Latin) "contains more objective reality" (VII,40) the phrase "i.e., participates by representation in a higher degree of being or perfection."

infinite levels.[94] Nor does accepting the levels notion require one to posit a myriad of actually existing beings who occupy each of the various levels in between.[95] In its most minimalist version, the scale might imply only two fundamental levels of perfection, a more and a less perfect. Especially when one adds the qualifier "infinite" to the one side, a clear bifurcation emerges between a most perfect being and those things that are less perfect (say, the created order). Note that even on the minimalist account the difference between the divine and human levels is both qualitative and quantitative. It is qualitative because one level is infinitely beyond the other. But it is quantitative because they both lie on one scale, and because the lower has its existence from the upper (whether through creation or emanation), has some knowledge of it (if only the knowledge that it is infinite), and should strive to understand and to emulate it.

There are difficulties even with the minimalist framework, however. For example, it seems to imply that the created order is *as such* imperfect, which clashes with the teaching of the basic goodness of creation in the Christian tradition. Still, it does seem that the monotheism of Jews, Christians, and Muslims requires that God be perfect, the highest moral instance, and the cause of goodness in the world — however perfection is to be understood. It could well be that the two-category account of divine perfection will survive the serious difficulties that we shall soon encounter with more lofty forms of perfect-being theology.

Monism

We have just seen that talk of degrees of reality implies a quantitative connection between less and more perfect beings.[96] Unless some other conceptual means is introduced, I have suggested, this framework does push in the direction of monism, the doctrine that, ultimately, only one thing really exists. If the participator has its being and its positive qualities only from (or relative to)

---

94. See Arthur O. Lovejoy, *The Great Chain of Being: A Study of the History of an Idea* (Cambridge: Harvard Univ. Press, 1970); Louis Dupré, *The Other Dimension* (New York: Seabury, 1979).

95. It is interesting to note that already in the twelfth century theologians in both branches of Neoplatonism rejected the plethora of intermediate beings between God and humans. See the treatment of this period by M.-D. Chenu, *Théologie au douzième siècle* (Paris: Vrin, 1957), 108-41. The independent existence of matter was also widely challenged in this century.

96. See also H. G. Redmann, "Von der Unendlichkeit Gottes und der Welt," chap. 5 of his *Gott und Welt: Die Schöpfungstheologie der vorkritischen Periode Kants* (Göttingen: Vandenhoeck & Ruprecht, 1962), esp. 51-53.

some perfect source, by what principle is it to be distinguished from its source? Perhaps by something essentially imperfect that characterizes the participator, say, matter? That response, too, leads to a dilemma. On the one hand, if the perfect is also the most real, the least perfect must be as such the least real, and to lack all perfection is to be unreal. But what is unreal cannot be the cause or ground of ontological separation. Then what is it that participates? On the other hand, if matter is a separate metaphysical principle with a separate reality of its own, then the perfect is neither the source of all that is, nor is its power unlimited. In cases where the individuating principle is antithetical to the perfect, as in the inherently evil matter postulated by Gnosticism, a dualism results that also rules out participation. Consequently, one is left with the troubling conclusion that there cannot be any real separation between the participator and the participated.

Theologians since Augustine have responded to this dilemma by appealing to the doctrine of creation: God created, from nothing, a realm separate from himself. If God can indeed create a world apart from himself, without relying on any materials outside himself, then participation becomes, it was thought, a happy way of expressing the ontological analogy between creation and creator. The goods or perfections of created beings are then similar to their source because they have these perfections through participation.

But could an infinite and perfect being create a world that would then exist outside himself? The answer is not obvious. Nicholas of Cusa and Bruno were right, I think, to insist that a truly infinite (unlimited) being would have no place outside itself; the creation would have to be in some sense within it. Both thinkers — not to mention non-Christian philosophers of infinity such as Plotinus and Spinoza — accepted at least this monistic implication of total infinity: *there is no "outside God."* Similarly, much of early Scholastic thought struggled to avoid monistic conclusions. One thinks, for instance, of Erigena's famous statement, for which he was often accused of pantheism: Created things, "to the extent that they are, are nothing other than participation in him"; and he concludes, "Can you then deny that God and creation are one?"[97] I argue later that divine transcendence can be preserved by considering God's eternality and essential nature and, further, that this is sufficient for avoiding pantheism and remaining within theism. Still, we have found that powerful forces pull against traditional attempts to separate the world and its infinite divine source; it is they that motivate the panentheistic turn that the following chapters trace.

---

97. John Scotus Erigena, *De divisione naturae* II, chap. 2, 528 A-B. Instead of a causal relationship to the world, he sees a manifestation of God, a theophany.

Unity in Difference

How can the world be identified with God without implying that the world *is* God? One must think of creation as manifesting a unity in difference. The Jewish Kabbalah expressed it with the picture of God's self-limitation: God creates a space within himself where something can exist that is different from him. Nicholas of Cusa's remains perhaps the most helpful philosophical model in this regard, since he offers a rich variety of options for expressing the place for the finite within the infinite: the picture that reflects its source, the "explication" in plural forms of the absolute and infinite One, the coincidence of opposites.[98] The nature of the problem of God and creation, I suggest, compels one either to a dialectical framework in the attempt to do justice both to the quantitative sameness and the qualitative difference of infinite and finite — or to the admission of defeat. Of course, the suggestion that participation must be understood dialectically is not new. It goes back as far as Plato, who appealed to participation in order to solve the analogous dilemma of continuity and change, which is the temporal equivalent of the "place" question just discussed. In Plato's account, the world of being is different from our world of becoming; but whatever *really is* in the world of becoming *is* through its participation in, even unity with, the realm of the forms.

The exact nature of the unity-in-difference is not specified by an appeal to participation alone, however. Of course, many have tried to find a broader conceptual framework that can mediate between the infinite source and the finite recipient. For instance, some have argued that the doctrine of analogy justifies the appeal to sameness-through-difference — though I see little evidence that the problems with the Scholastic doctrine of analogy have been solved. Or one might follow Hegel in constructing an entire metaphysics, epistemology, and logic to explain how something can be (indeed, must be) both itself and the other of itself. Without being able to prove here that Hegel was unsuccessful in his attempt, I suggest that his may be a case of demonstrating the unclear through the less clear. If one is at all convinced of the qualitative difference between the infinite and the finite, one may doubt that their interactions can be governed by means of an overarching logic.

It therefore appears that the chances of "proving" a participation theology are about on a par with proving God. One can, of course, take a metaphysics of participation as a primitive. It does, after all, attempt to explain why the world's being and goodness would require a transcendent source; it claims to specify their similarity and difference; and it fits hand-in-glove within the framework of a the-

---

98. See the detailed discussion in part 2, "Die Schöpfung," of Alvarez-Gómez, *Die verborgene Gegenwart*. See also Dupré, *Passage to Modernity*, 50-62, 182-89.

ology of infinity and perfection. The exact balance between participator and participated will depend on whether and how one develops a doctrine of creation. If one holds that matter is eternal and is merely informed by a (more or less) perfect being, then the position remains fundamentally dualistic: the most perfect is confronted by (and our relationship with it limited by) something imperfect. Conversely, if one posits a creation out of the infinite ex nihilo, the inclination toward monism will be much stronger. It is on this precarious middle ground between the monism of absolute infinity and the plurality of really independent substances that the traditional doctrine of creation ex nihilo stands — attempting to do justice to our sense of ontological separateness and to the priority of the infinite One, yet tempering both separateness and Oneness through a delicate dialectic of independence-within-dependence.

Perfection and the Transcendentals

We have painstakingly begun to work out the conceptual interconnections between infinity or the One and perfection. In this context there is time only to gesture toward a further task, the connection with the other so-called transcendentals, in particular being and truth. The infinitely perfect must be the source of being; must it also be "being itself," or even beyond being? Is it likewise the source of truth, or "truth itself" (and what would this mean?), or even beyond truth?

Clearly Descartes thought these issues were interconnected, however (typically) undeveloped his comments were. Note how infinity, being, and truth are linked in his late letter to Clerselier: "Truth consists in being, and the false in non-being only, because the idea of infinity, comprehending all being, includes everything there is of truth in things; and it cannot have in itself anything of falseness, lest one wishes to suppose that it is not true that this infinite being exists."[99] Indeed, the same connections are present in Meditation 3. "This idea of a supremely perfect and infinite being is," Descartes writes, "true in the highest degree"; infinity and truth, at least in the realm of ideas, are correlated (VII,46). Likewise, even if we can suppose that a perfect being does not exist, we cannot suppose that its idea "represents something unreal" — presumably because, at least in the realm of ideas, perfection is the highest reality. In infinite

---

99. "Le vérité consiste en l'être, et la fausseté au non-être seulement, en sorte que l'idée de l'infini, comprenant tout l'être, comprend tout ce qu'il y a de vrai dans les choses, et ne peut avoir en soi rien de faux, encore que d'ailleurs on veuille supposer qu'il n'est pas vrai que cet être infini existe" (4/23/1649; V,352ff., AM 8:224-25).

perfection is "wholly contained . . . whatever I clearly and distinctly perceive as *being real and true*" (ibid., emphasis mine).

We have already looked at Descartes's case as an argument "from below" and found it wanting: the idea of infinite perfection, however precocious, does not require a real infinite to explain it. But I am here advocating another way to approach philosophical theology: not as proof or natural theology but rather as the search for relationships of coherence. Important connections between infinity and goodness can be drawn, for example, if one understands the infinite (as much of the tradition has) as infinite being and hence as the source of being. (Difficulties with this assumption will concern us in later chapters.) Something's degree of perfection would then correspond to its degree of being; the most perfect would be the most real, and the infinite being the most perfect. Again, note that it need not be a scale with infinite steps; it is simplest to posit merely two, finite being and infinite being.

The language of a "participation in truth" is more difficult to preserve. It is, admittedly, parsimonious: everything, even truth, would then be unified within a single conceptual framework. This fact helps to explain the attractiveness of the transcendentals tradition for metaphysicians. But the point of truths is to state particular correspondences, to identify particular propositions that are true of states of affairs. Whatever unity metaphysicians require could be established by locating these truths together at the level of mind (Nous), just short of the One, or in the mind of God as in the Augustinian tradition. Hence I judge the Cartesian attempt to unify all the transcendentals finally to be unjustified.

Perfection and Projection

I have construed the notion of infinite perfection as involving a quantitative connection with as well as a qualitative break from the finite. But asserting a quantitative connection raises epistemic difficulties that cannot be bypassed. For whence do we derive these notions of perfection that we attribute to God? Is it not, as Ludwig Feuerbach argued, merely a matter of taking what one most values and projecting it onto the universe itself? Even theistic arguments appear to use projection arguments unapologetically; so C. A. Campbell: "Theism in general proclaims that God is wholly perfect; and, as is entirely natural, it interprets this Divine perfection in terms of 'the highest we know' in human experience; applying to God accordingly such concepts as those of goodness, wisdom and power in their highest manifestations."[100]

---

100. Campbell, *On Selfhood and Godhood* (London: George Allen and Unwin, 1957), 307, quoted in Morris, "Perfect Being Theology," 21.

Doesn't this method beg for a Feuerbachian critique? Yet any notion of perfection — and hence any perfection-based metaphysic — cannot do otherwise than argue from what we take to be good. This fact rather curtains its apologetic usefulness, since one can always account, one way or another, for human ideas of good without a most perfect being. But when used nonfoundationally, a theory of an infinitely perfect being can still play a part in a broader metaphysical position, without relying on a certain anthropocentric style of arguing for which theism has been rightly faulted.

If one is not already convinced of the risks inherent in the argument from perfection, a quick look at Descartes's method of arguing will provide sufficient incriminating evidence. Descartes bases all three of his theistic arguments in the *Meditations* on attributing to God all conceivable perfections, in order to reach the being "who possesses all those perfections which I can . . . in some manner attain in thought."[101] Notwithstanding his comments about the difference between humans and God, Descartes grants in the Second Replies that the idea we have of the divine intellect "does not differ from that which we have of our own intellect," except that the former is taken to be infinite (VII,137). We need only to think the idea of "a supremely perfect being" in order to form a correct conception of the idea of God (VII,138). Finally, in the Fifth Replies he describes the human capability as "the faculty for amplifying all created perfections (i.e. conceiving of something greater or more ample than they are)" or as "this very power of amplifying all human perfections up to the point where they are recognized as more than human."[102]

The projection criticism is not new. Since the responses of Descartes's contemporaries to the *Meditations,* his method has raised the charge of projection: doesn't Descartes explicitly project human predicates onto an imagined Absolute? As Gassendi charges in the Fifth Objections, "Such perfections [as you want to attribute to God] are all taken from things which we commonly admire in ourselves, such as longevity, power, knowledge, goodness, blessedness and so on. By amplifying these things as much as we can, we assert that God is eternal, omnipotent, omniscient, supremely good, supremely blessed and so on" (VII,287). Now the *possibility* of projection does not alone invalidate all use of the predicate *perfection.* As long as moral realism is not a conceptual contradiction, it is conceivable that a being might be good, better than another being, or unsurpassably good. Surely the mere mention of the term *projection* is not enough to bring all

101. "Omnes illas perfectiones quas ego . . . quocunque modo attingere cogitatione possum" (VII,52).
102. "Vis perfectiones omnes humanas eousque ampliandi ut plusquam humanae esse cognoscantur" (VII,371).

talk of perfection to a stop. Obviously, though, projection arguments do handicap proofs of a perfect being. For such proofs require one already to possess criteria for establishing what is objectively good. Without such criteria one cannot establish the sort of scale of increasing perfections that (the argument alleges) will finally require one to posit a highest instance, a most perfect being. Unless there were agreement on goods and a consensus on their status as objective, the best one could achieve would be a hierarchy of things that the person, or group of persons, values. To label the top of this scale "God" is to be guilty of projection in the most blatant possible manner. For these reasons, the notion of a perfect being faces serious difficulties not raised by the notion of the infinite.

Are there any resources, then, for addressing the projection critique? I can think of two possible responses to Feuerbach, one from the infinity side of infinite perfection and one from the power to augment. Although neither may be finally successful, they do work against more naive forms of the projection objection.

First, the idea of perfection may beg for a projection critique, but the same does not apply to the idea of absolute infinity. Mathematics and set theory after Cantor have been able to conceive infinites without difficulty. As a thought experiment, imagine the set of all cardinal numbers; since the series of cardinal numbers by definition continues without limit, one has an infinite set. One then quickly encounters infinite numbers of infinites. For instance, one cannot count the points on a line segment using the members of the first infinite set, since between any two points is another, and between them another. Hence this new number, the number of points on a line, is uncountable; it is "nondenumerably infinite," or infinite to the second degree. In chapter 2 we examined Cantor's argument that there is finally an absolute infinite, the class of all sets, which is presupposed by all smaller infinite sets but can itself never be named mathematically (i.e., contained within a set). This real highest entity in set theory is clearly analogous to the absolutely infinite being or God. If there is no fear of projection in the one case, why should there be in the other?[103]

As neat as the analogy may sound, however, there are difficulties in moving from the mathematical to the metaphysical infinite. For example, Cantor's argument rests on the assumption of Platonic realism in mathematics. Challenging that assumption, one could construe mathematical concepts instead as

---

103. In fact, at one point Descartes employed an argument similar to the one Cantor used for the absolute infinite: "Je ne me sers jamais du mot d'*infini* pour signifier seulement n'avoir point de fin, ce qui est négatif et à quoi j'ai appliqué le mot d'*indéfini*, mais pour signifier une chose réelle, qui est incomparablement plus grande que toute celles qui ont quelque fin" (Descartes to Clerselier, 4/23/1649; V,352ff., AM 8:224).

constructions of the human intellect, and the absolute infinite as a regulative idea that serves merely as the posited end point of human reason. Thus in a famous article David Hilbert grants that Cantor's theory of the infinite has "a well-justified place" in our thought; it is "a paradise out of which no one will be able to drive us." Nonetheless, the infinite is a construction of our own minds:

> the infinite is never found realized; it is neither present in nature nor reliable as a foundation in any kind of thinking we can understand. . . . The infinite divisibility of a continuum is only an operation that is present in thought; it is only an idea, and indeed one that is falsified through our observations of nature and the experience of physics and chemistry. . . . From the fact that outside the limits of a particular space another space is always present follows only the unlimited nature of space, in no way however its infinity.[104]

One need not finally be convinced by Hilbert's Kantianism. But the answer to it is a long metaphysical story — and one that cannot be bypassed by a single deductive argument for the real infinite based on our idea of infinity.

Second, as rational agents, we have the powers of compounding and augmenting, even as far as infinity. We have seen how Descartes relied on the augmenting argument in formulating his theistic proofs. Could one not then defend a nonprojective metaphysics of infinity based on the power of augmenting itself? Even if we cannot form a full idea of the infinite, we are beings who have the capability to advance in thought to (or at least in the direction of) infinity. Consequently, either we must ourselves be infinite, or we must be the products of a being who is.

But this argument, too, is not finally satisfying. First, there are other ways to account for our power to amplify (e.g., as an evolutionarily conditioned mental survival mechanism). Second, one can always dispute that we really grasp the infinite. By amplifying, we can create a set {1,2,3,4 . . . 1,000,001, 1,000,002 . . .} ; but does the ". . ." here really prove that we can amplify *to* the infinite rather than merely in its direction? Finally, even if we can amplify to the point of thinking the infinite, what would this prove? We have already noted

104. David Hilbert, "Über das Unendliche," *Mathematische Annalen* 95 (1926): 161-90: "das Unendliche findet sich nirgends realisiert; es ist weder in der Natur vorhanden, noch als Grundlage in unserem verstandesmäßigen Denken zulässig. . . . Die unendliche Teilbarkeit eines Kontinuums ist nur eine in Gedanken vorhandene Operation, nur eine Idee, die durch unsere Beobachtungen der Natur und die Erfahrungen der Physik und Chemie widerlegt wird. . . . Aus der Tatsache, daß außerhalb eines Raumstückes immer wieder noch Raum vorhanden ist, folgt nur die Unbegrenztheit des Raumes, keineswegs aber seine Unendlichkeit" (pp. 190, 164, 165).

the problems with the argument from the idea of an infinite to its existence (and with the idea of a necessarily existing being). Consequently, it does not appear that either the first or the second response is sufficient to prove the existence of an infinite over against the projection critics.

Nonetheless, the dilemma "Descartes or Feuerbach" — "God is provable or God is nothing more than a projection" — is a false one. Both sides rest on the false assumption that it is possible to provide a metaphysical demonstration for or against the existence of God. Instead, I suggest that one encounters here a basic epistemic ambiguity: our power to amplify and to think infinity or perfection can be accounted for theistically *or* naturalistically. Only a complex argument, spanning anthropology, natural science, and metaphysics, can finally determine the better answer. There is no easy answer to the fear that theistic language in general, and perfect-being theology in particular, involve a projection of human attributes. Or rather, the fear raises its own dilemma, which I shall call Feuerbach's Dilemma: either God is unknowable through attributes accessible to humans, which is another way of saying that God is simply unknowable to humans; or God is knowable in this way, but at the cost of our never knowing for sure whether we have come to know a being separate from ourselves or whether we have projected our own ideas of perfection onto the universe. The horns of Feuerbach's Dilemma, then, are complete ineffability on the one side and the possibility that God-talk involves a projection on the other.[105]

We need not quite end all discussion with Feuerbach's Dilemma, however. The pill will be softened if we can find reason to think that a metaphysical position about theism will inevitably evidence this same ambiguity. The reason is provided, once again, by the concept of infinity, which is able to correct for the anthropocentric tendencies of attributions of perfection. Consider the following three-step argument.

1. The infinite could not be fully knowable and still be infinite. Gassendi had complained, for example, that Descartes could not have a true idea of the infinite, that he could at best know a part of it (VII,296-97). Descartes's response is intriguing: "My point is that, on the contrary, if I can grasp something, it would be a total contradiction for that which I grasp to be infinite. For the idea of the infinite, if it is to be a true idea, cannot be grasped at all, since the impossibility of being grasped is contained in the formal definition of the infinite" (VII,367-68). Spinoza would later specify the same insight in terms of his well-known theory of definition, *omnia definitio determinatio est*: to define

---

105. The dilemma presupposes that we lack an adequate doctrine of analogy, which I assume to be well enough established not to require defense here; at any rate, it was Descartes's assumption in the *Meditations*.

something is to distinguish it from other things, and hence there can be no positive grasping of the infinite in itself.[106]

2. Now this sounds at first as if we have fallen back onto the first horn of the dilemma, viz. the unknowability of God through any predications whatsoever. To avoid such an impalement, one would have to show how there can be enough knowledge of the infinite to make a theology of infinite perfection possible. Again, Descartes's response is helpful: we can form a correct idea of the infinite without fully grasping it when we understand that "it is a thing that is bounded by no limits" (VII,368). This definition connects with the medieval tradition that makes infinity the first positive attribute of the transcendent One. It does not supply a theology, but it does open up the space for one. It is the first positive attribution, the most minimal one that can be made, and it may be sufficient to keep us from stumbling speechlessly down some sort of *via negativa*. If it can be combined with reflection on God as perfect, over which it functions as a kind of control, it will provide a credible program for metaphysical reflection.

(3) Finally, we must return in conclusion to the framework with which this chapter began: the intuitive antecedents to reflection on the infinite. Prior to reflection, and therefore not justified by it, lies a certain intuitive leap from things that are very large or (apparently) unlimited to that which is truly infinite. Descartes, not one for caution, interpreted this phenomenon as the discovery of God within himself, in a more immediate fashion than his own self-knowledge; at its core the Third Meditation seeks to evoke what (Descartes assures his reader) each person already implicitly knows but perhaps has not paused long enough yet to realize. God is closer than an idea; as Alquié notes, "Humanity does not have the idea of God; humanity *is* the idea of God, the sign of God, and in this world the *signal* that the [finite] object is not being itself" (emphasis mine).[107]

Some might say that this intuitive element gives theology a leg up over its competitors. But a prereflective intuitive leap is not yet a reason, at least to others than oneself, and an intuition of the infinite is not yet an intuition of an infinitely perfect being. Indeed, in one respect the intuitive moment also heightens the epistemic ambiguity, since at this level it is impossible to exclude the possibility of anthropomorphic projections or wish fulfillment. If the knowledge of God is as close as the intuition argument suggests, it becomes extremely difficult to know whether one is really intuiting the existence of another dimension within myself, or whether one is merely extrapolating from human quali-

---

106. See Dessauer, *Auf den Spuren*, 17-18.

107. Alquié, *La découverte métaphysique*, 236-37: "L'homme n'a pas l'idée de Dieu, il est l'idée de Dieu, le signe de Dieu et, en ce monde, le témoignage que l'objet n'est pas l'Etre."

ties and longings (for greater power, greater understanding, etc.) to the idea of a being who has what we lack. Only the explanatory power of the resultant theory can finally answer the charge of projection.

CONCLUSION

In this chapter I have argued that the concept of the infinite can be understood in a determinate and an indeterminate sense. In the latter case it becomes merely the indefinite extension of number, space, or time; in the former, it refers to a particular reality that is qualitatively distinct from the finite. This determinate sense can in turn be taken negatively — as the negation of the finite — or positively, as that which precedes and grounds all finite things. Finally, the positive view can be construed monistically (the One excludes any independent existences) or dualistically (a world of finite objects can exist apart from the infinite) or as some combination of the two (the world is within God, though God is also more than the world). I have argued that the concept of infinity provides the initial context for a philosophical doctrine of God, though it must be supplemented by other sources in order to fill it with positive content. Still, it is not without its impact on subsequent theologizing; for example, it inclines one toward a world-within-God (panentheism) rather than the separation of world and God.

The concept of perfection offers a similar set of possibilities. By applying to it an analogous set of arguments, and by attempting to establish a close conceptual reciprocity between it and infinity, perfect-being theologians have attempted to defend the notion of an infinitely perfect being. If their arguments are successful, they will be able to draw direct lines outward from that notion toward an analysis of the various divine attributes (as we saw in the case of the "Anselmians" above). This in turn will connect their project closely with the philosophy of Descartes as presented in the previous chapter.

Nonetheless, more clearly than in the case of the theory of infinity, the concept of perfection faces some weighty difficulties. These include not only the charges of anthropomorphism and projection, but also, for example, an inadequate response to the problem of evil (how could a perfect being be the source of so much imperfection in the world?). Given the serious (though perhaps not insurmountable) difficulties with moral realism, it would be premature to suggest that the perfection or goodness of such a being could be established by extrapolating from human experience. In light of these further difficulties, it begins to appear that the concept of perfection will have to play (at best) a secondary role in a philosophical doctrine of God. We are thus forced to conclude that it is significantly less difficult to defend a notion of the quantitative or even qualitative infinite than of the *evaluative infinite,* infinite perfection. Perhaps the problems are not insurmountable, but they remain unanswered at present.

The discussion in this chapter has not been without its share of negative conclusions. (1) The existence of an infinitely perfect being cannot be derived from its mere idea (unless one could prove that a necessary being possibly exists). (2) The infinite cannot be thought as the cause of the finite; Thomas's arguments from the existence of something moved and something caused to an infinite source are not successful. Rather, the absolute disproportionality of infinite and finite, stressed by Nicholas of Cusa and Bruno, turns out to be basic to this concept. (3) The infinite, taken alone, manifested a certain pull toward monism; it tends to imply an overarching ontological unity, which mitigates against a final separateness of the creation. If there is an infinite, one must ask, how can there be finites as well? (4) These last two points entail that one can move neither from the world to the infinite as its cause, nor from the infinite to give a causal account of the world. (5) We have only touched in passing on the so-called paradoxes of the infinite. Thinkers from before Aristotle to after Kant have taken the idea of an actual infinite to raise insoluble paradoxes or antinomies. Even if the mathematical and physical paradoxes of the infinite were all solved (a strongly counterfactual assumption!), a positive metaphysical account of the infinite would still have to be provided. The latter task has been the dominant one in these pages.

Nevertheless, the discussion has provided some grounds for optimism. The "Cartesian" intuitions regarding the finite and the infinite with which the chapter opened have stood up well in light of the historical exploration and conceptual analysis that followed. The "ascent" from acknowledging oneself as finite to the idea of an infinite ground or dimension has not run into insuperable difficulties. The two initial implications — that the infinite be taken as primary, and that it form the condition of the possibility for all finites — have found a solid place in our conceptual reconstruction. In these last few pages it remains only to note the connections between the conclusions reached so far and three additional projects: transcendental philosophy, the theory of the Absolute, and the term *God* in its religious sense.

The Transcendental Infinite

In the first implication, I suggested that whatever is infinite must be prior to the finite. Should we take this as a causal priority, as a logical-conceptual priority, or in some other way? I have already argued that the causal arguments fail. For example, Descartes gives two arguments in the First Responses against the

178

Thomistic argument to God as first cause. The first is that the causal argument bypasses the subject's intuition of God: "I regarded the existence of God as much more evident than the existence of anything that can be perceived by the senses" (VII,106). More crucially, one's failure to imagine an infinite series of causes does not prove that such is impossible:

> An infinite chain of such successive causes from eternity without any first cause is beyond my grasp. And my inability to grasp it certainly does not entail that there must be a first cause, any more than my inability to grasp the infinite number of divisions in a finite quantity entails that there is an ultimate division beyond which any further division is impossible. (ibid.)

Yet the very failure of causal arguments points to a more adequate approach. All that follows from their failure, Descartes notes, "is that my intellect, which is finite, does not encompass the infinite." Similarly, my inability to grasp the infinite leads to "a recognition of the imperfection of my intellect." With these two qualities we reach the most fundamental (philosophical) designation of God in relation to the world: God is the infinite that grounds the finite; God is the perfect that provides the context within which alone the imperfect can be thought. Knowledge of God is not mediated through a causal chain; it is as immediate as the opposition between necessity and contingency, ground and grounded . . . infinite and finite.

It is in this sense that one can best speak of the "transcendental" infinite: the infinite is prior to finite things in that it is the condition of the possibility for conceiving them as what they are.[108] This is the insight that modern thought owes to Descartes. Famously, he argued that the primary and immediate knowledge of the *cogito* is its awareness of doubt; yet "how could I understand that I doubted or desired — that is, lacked something — and that I was not wholly perfect, unless there were in me some idea of a more perfect being which enabled me to recognize my own defects by comparison?" (VII,45-46). The intuition of the infinite is thus the condition of the possibility for the knowledge of all finite things, including the knowledge that I think. As such, it is parallel to the status of the *cogito* itself: if the "I think" implicitly accompanies my mental acts whenever I think or doubt, then so also does the immediate intuition "I am finite, and hence different from that which is infinite." Both the human subject and the infinite dimension (for similar reasons) are presuppositions for all further knowledge.

---

108. The argument in the following paragraphs stems in part from conversations with Wolfhart Pannenberg on this subject. See Pannenberg, *Metaphysics,* chap. 3, esp. 26ff.

It is crucial to separate this type of transcendental argument from the subject-centered transcendental arguments of Kant's first *Critique*. In the context of Descartes's philosophy, the transcendental condition pertains to the subject in a different sense than in Kant; it refers to the human subject without being grounded in it. For, as we saw, Descartes's subject knows itself immediately as finite and imperfect, and therefore as dependent on its infinite ground. There is therefore no question of equating this Cartesian transcendental condition with Kant's grounding of all thought in the nature of the human subject as independent (absolute?) foundation.

Infinite Perfection, the Absolute, and God

Even if the attribute of infinity by itself tends toward negative conclusions, we have found that its positive content is preserved when it is combined with the concept of perfection, as in Scotus, Descartes, and Leibniz. What does this fact have to say about the possibility of a philosophy of the Absolute? I suggest that if the two concepts could be fully and successfully woven together into a single metaphysical system,[109] they would indeed represent (and require) something like the traditional philosophical theory of the Absolute. This was clearly the position taken by Hegel, who spoke of the infinite as the "definition of the Absolute."[110] Pannenberg notes correctly: "For [the Absolute] connotes not only self-sufficiency, in the sense of independence from all else, but also that everything else (if there is anything else) be thought as proceeding from the Absolute — and not only as proceeding from it according to a law foreign to the Absolute, but as produced through the Absolute itself, as the expression of itself."[111]

The Absolute is the highest concept of metaphysics, that idea or entity on which all else depends for its existence. It is philosophy's unifying concept, the self-sufficient ground of all else. But, I suggest, it is also philosophy's limit concept. There is something about the absolutely infinite, when taken in the strongest sense of the word, that is inherently unknowable to finite knowers. The turning point toward this insight may have come with Nicholas of Cusa, who saw that the disproportionality between finite and infinite forces one beyond the Aristotelian causal arguments, and thus beyond the realm of what can be

109. I use "metaphysical" broadly here to include the synthesis of classical metaphysics with the insights of German idealism, including, e.g., Hegel's appropriation of the metaphysics of Spinoza within the context of Absolute Idealism.

110. *Hegel's Science of Logic*, trans. A. V. Miller (New York: Humanities Press, 1969), 137; *Wissenschaft der Logik,* ed. Lasson (Hamburg: Meiner, 1967), 1:125.

111. Pannenberg, *Metaphysics,* 38.

known. If causal arguments fail, so too does analogical knowledge of God. Admittedly, the notion of perfection at first seems to lead in the opposite direction, insofar as it establishes a connection with what one takes to be good and thus retains (if successful) some specific content. In the end, however, the notion of infinite (absolute) perfection forms more of a final goal for reflection than a present possession. One must be extremely careful about knowledge claims regarding superlative concepts of this type. The Absolute could only be given content if it were established as the central concept of a completed philosophy or metaphysics — if the idea of completion is even a coherent one given our epistemic nature as historical subjects.

Infinite perfection points us toward the Absolute. But is the Absolute God? What is the connection between infinite, perfect being and the personal agent of the Western theistic religions? At best, the Absolute is the framework in which God would have to be thought if an integration of theology and metaphysics were to be possible. What the idea of the Absolute requires is qualities that one would have to ascribe to God as well. This holds even more clearly if one discovers additional reasons to understand the Absolute as Spirit — as thought, as self-conscious, as thinking, as a volitional being. We return to this theme in part III below.

These connections notwithstanding, there are strong reasons to think that the designation of a being as infinitely perfect, though necessary, is not yet sufficient to describe God. If one is already working with a concept of God, then it is natural to say that God must have (at least) the qualities that we have predicated here of an infinitely perfect being. But the content of such a being is not yet the full content of the idea of God. There is a specificity, and a religious intentionality, to the term *God* in the Western religious traditions that is not fully matched by speculations on infinite perfection. Moreover, there is a historical dimension to "the God of Abraham, Isaac, and Jacob" or to "the God and Father of Jesus Christ" that is wholly missing from the metaphysical project. Of course religious believers can still respond that, where one's original intuitions exceed philosophical reason, there is room left for the specifically religious dimension of the term *God*. And the concepts of infinity and perfection can certainly serve as "criteria for presenting the understanding of God within a religious tradition."[112] Still, nothing so far has justified the wholesale identifi-

---

112. Ibid., 42. Of course, as Pannenberg notes, "if we have arrived at the idea of God (especially in its monotheistic version) on other grounds, and if we then form the conception of a being with maximal perfection — and if, in addition, we raise the question of to whom we should affirm this highest perfection — then in such a case it must be clear that this attribute can be affirmed only of the one God" (pp. 28-29).

cation of the God of infinite perfection with (for instance) the trinitarian God of Christian systematic theology.

No treatment of the theme of perfection is complete without Leibniz, who developed a theology of perfection, on something like this model, in greater detail than any other figure in Western history. If it turns out that he was largely successful, we will have established a natural genealogy for the contemporary "perfect-being theologians" in analytic philosophy. But if Leibniz's philosophy raises insuperable problems, then a more radical break with the tradition of perfection theology is called for. Pursuing the nature and consequences of that radical break will occupy us until the closing chapters of this book.

CHAPTER FOUR

Leibniz: Reaching the Limits of a Metaphysics of Perfection

INTRODUCTION

We began our study of modern theories of God with the question, How could Descartes have argued in such an obviously circular manner in the *Meditations*, presupposing the very God whose existence he was apparently trying to prove? In contrast to many recent readings of Descartes we discovered that his philosophy in fact works outward from the intuition of an infinitely perfect being that is prior to and the source of all finite beings; all the other aspects of his metaphysics, epistemology, and natural science flow from this starting point. Surprised at the silence of commentators on this theme, we turned in chapter 3 to the historical antecedents for the idea of God as infinite and perfect, trying to determine whether the Cartesian position was an anomaly. We found that Descartes was in fact part of a long tradition. In reducing its complex terminology to its bare — albeit still crucial — minimum, he gave perhaps clearer expression than any his predecessors to the central tenets of a theology based on an infinitely perfect being.

With Leibniz we jump directly to the apex of this tradition in early modern philosophy. Here is a thinker who, working with largely Cartesian assumptions, became the last major modern philosopher to build a distinctive system around the *ens perfectissimum* as its core. By contrast, the infinity of God now plays a slightly less important role as a complement to the perfection of God — this despite a mathematics (and metaphysics!) that conceives the infinity of the world and God in a much more sophisticated manner than Descartes. There is some irony in the fact that Leibniz, with his more thoroughly developed theory of the infinite, fell short of some key Cartesian insights into the strengths and weaknesses of theologies of the infinite, and we will have to sort out why this occurred. Later, after we have sorted out the damaging and mistaken elements in Kant's critique of metaphysics (chapter 5), we will return to examine the Spinoza tradition as a counterbalancing (though also not fully adequate) approach to the problem of God.

In the following pages I argue that Leibniz's philosophical theology requires the corrective that the notion of infinity offered to Descartes — this despite his claim to be a good Cartesian on this point. To be convincing, this criticism must be demonstrated internally to the Leibnizian system, by pointing out specific weaknesses and implications of positions that Leibniz himself held. We explore in particular the difficulties with Leibniz's atomistic theory of the perfections, noting the tendency of the position on the one hand to devolve into monism and the denial of freedom and on the other hand to move toward an absolute pluralism in which God's role as *monas monadum* becomes impossible to maintain. These internal problems, when contrasted with the resources offered by the theory of the infinite, help us to formulate a final evaluation of the theology of infinite perfection.

A note on Leibniz scholarship: The interpreter of Leibniz faces at least three separate sets of hurdles. First, there is no single work, parallel to Descartes's *Principles* or Spinoza's *Ethics*, that gives an adequate systematic overview of Leibniz's position. Instead, one must cite from a variety of original-language editions and (where they are available at all) from a larger number of translations.[1] Second, as in the case of Descartes, the theological side of

---

1. I use the following abbreviations for Leibniz editions:

   AG for Roger Ariew and Daniel Garber, trans., *G. W. Leibniz: Philosophical Essays* (Indianapolis: Hackett, 1989).

   Discours for *Discours de Métaphysique*, ed. and trans. Herbert Herring, PhB 260 (Hamburg: Felix Meiner, 1985); based on the critical edition by H. Lestienne, *Discours de Métaphysique* (Paris, 1907, repr. 1952).

   G for C. I. Gerhardt, *Die philosophischen Schriften von G. W. Leibniz*, 7 vols. (Berlin: Weidmann, 1875-90).

   Grua for Gaston Grua, *G. W. Leibniz: Textes inédits d'après les manuscrits de la bibliothéque provinciale de Hanovre*, 2 vols. (Paris: Presses Universitaires de France, 1948).

   Guhrauer for G. E. Guhrauer, ed., *Leibniz: Deutsche Schriften*, 2 vols. (Berlin, 1838-40; repr. Hildesheim: Olms, 1966).

   L for Leroy E. Loemker, ed. and trans. of G. W. Leibniz, *Philosophical Papers and Letters*, 2nd ed., 2 vols. (Dordrecht: D. Reidel, 1969).

   M for C. I. Gerhardt, *Die mathematischen Schriften von G. W. Leibniz*, 3 vols. (Berlin, 1849-55).

Leibniz's thought has been somewhat neglected in recent decades. While this tendency may reflect a certain antipathy toward theology, it also reflects the major influence of one work: Bertrand Russell's *Critical Exposition of the Philosophy of Leibniz*. For Russell, of course, theological arguments — and hence most of the arguments involving perfection — are not arguments at all; a thesis "only due to theological reasons" he takes as completely ungrounded.[2] Recall Russell's opening to his treatment of the proofs:

> I come now to the weakest part in Leibniz's philosophy, the part most full of inconsistencies. Whatever, in the doctrine we have examined [so far], seemed arbitrary, or in need of further explanation, was easily explained by the lazy device of reference to an Omnipotent Creator. And not only unavoidable difficulties, but others which might have been avoided, were left, because they reinforced the arguments upon which Leibniz's orthodoxy loved to dwell. (p. 172)

A surprising number of commentators have followed Russell's lead, in attitude if not in depth of passion. This is unfortunate, as I hope to show. If the present chapter accomplishes anything, it should move the theological dimensions of perfection and divine infinity back into the center of Leibniz interpretation, serving thereby as a corrective to the one-sided heritage of the Russellian reading.

Finally, the secondary literature (again as with Descartes) is deeply divided in style and approach, leaving in particular an urgent need to integrate the results of French and Anglo-American scholarship.[3] The in-depth analysis of arguments and positions in the Anglo-American literature is without equal.[4]

Mollat for Georg Mollat, *Mittheilungen aus Leibnizens ungedruckten Schriften*, 2nd ed. (Leipzig: H. Haessel, 1893).

NE for *Nouveaux essais sur l'entendement humain,* ed. André Robinet and Heinrich Schepers (Berlin: Akademie-Verlag, 1962); marginal page references to this text in *New Essays on Human Understanding*, trans. Peter Remnant and Jonathan Bennett (Cambridge: Cambridge Univ. Press, 1981).

2. The latter phrase occurs in Russell, *A Critical Exposition of the Philosophy of Leibniz* (Cambridge: Cambridge Univ. Press, 1900; 2nd ed. 1935), 143n.3. See Russell's reaction to Leibniz's arguments concerning the vacuum, 92-93.

3. No slight of German interpreters is intended. One work that came to hand too late to be utilized here is Klaus Erich Kaehler, *Der methodische Zwiespalt der Metaphysik der Substanz* (Hamburg: Meiner, 1979).

4. One thinks, e.g., of Robert Adam's analysis of the notion of contingency or Robert Sleigh's treatment of truth and sufficient reason in Leibniz. See Robert M. Adams, "Leibniz's Theories of Contingency," *Rice University Studies* 63 (1977): 1-41; Robert C. Sleigh Jr., "Truth and Sufficient Reason in the Philosophy of Leibniz," in *Leibniz: Critical and Interpretive Es-*

At the same time, there is a depth of insight in the French commentators — especially with regard to the nature of Leibniz's thought as a systematic whole — that contemporary Leibniz scholarship can ill afford to neglect. Since it would be tendentious, a sign of dogmatic adherence to a particular school or method, to rely exclusively on the one literature at the expense of the other, an adequate reading of Leibniz must incorporate the strengths of both interpretive traditions while (if possible) avoiding their weaknesses.

ESTABLISHING THE CONTEXT

Connections with Descartes and the Cartesians

Leibniz stood squarely within the Cartesian context. The similarities not only include Leibniz's view of God but also extend to the goals and methods of philosophy, the importance of natural science, and the complex of problems related to the mind/body problem that Leibniz inherited from Descartes.[5] In evaluating Leibniz's philosophical theology one needs to grasp both its sophistication and the ways in which it unfortunately falls below some of Descartes's insights. To set the stage for this analysis, I first consider the central areas in which Leibniz made progress over his French predecessor before exploring the theological significance of the principle of sufficient reason and the role of intuition in Leibniz.

Leibniz's Advances over the Tradition

Descartes never quite overcame his fence-sitting between absolute monism — the direction Spinoza would later push Cartesianism (chapter 7 below) — and

---

says, ed. Michael Hooker (Minneapolis: Univ. of Minnesota Press, 1982), 209-42. Also see Sleigh's *Leibniz and Arnauld: A Commentary on Their Correspondence* (New Haven: Yale Univ. Press, 1990); and the essays contained in Nicholas Jolley, ed., *The Cambridge Companion to Leibniz* (Cambridge: Cambridge Univ. Press, 1995).

5. Richard Watson provides an excellent brief statement of this complex of issues in *The Breakdown of Cartesian Metaphysics* (Atlantic Highlands, N.J.: Humanities Press, 1987), 47-53. Since his criterion of selection seems to be "the view that Foucher successfully criticized," the mind/body issues are presented from the start as inherently unresolvable. Louis Loeb's summary of "continental metaphysics," although less precise, gives a rather broader and hence less one-sided construal of the Cartesian heritage; see Loeb, *From Descartes to Hume: Continental Metaphysics and the Development of Modern Philosophy* (Ithaca: Cornell Univ. Press, 1981), e.g., 25ff.

the plurality of substances needed for the development of an adequate physics and for a "commonsense" account of the world. Recall that Descartes's approach pulled him in both directions: the requirements of the category of substance suggested to him that there should ultimately be only one substance, one independently existing (infinite) being; yet to make any contributions to physics he had to acknowledge many separate bodies interacting according to the laws of motion. Leibniz thought he had finally overcome the monistic implications of Descartes's concept of substance — although we will have reason below to question how successfully — and that he could therefore proceed to give physics the metaphysical foundation that it required.

As is well known, Leibniz's solution involved the switch to *monads,* or units of mental substance, as the ultimate building blocks of reality. This solution obviously re-spiritualizes the physical universe, amounting to an intentional correction to the materialist atomism of Hobbes and Gassendi. Developmental studies of his thought show that Leibniz waffled on whether to reduce material substance to mental centers of organization and force, or to eliminate it altogether. The general direction of his thought was certainly in the latter direction.[6] If there is no material substance, then clearly Descartes's untenable dichotomy between mind and body is left behind, along with a whole series of unsuccessful rejoinders to it that had preoccupied philosophers in the second half of the seventeenth century.[7] Of course, Leibniz's solution had a cost associated with it: the loss of the physical reality of the universe — a rather expensive price to pay up front! We will have occasion to see whether he was able to avoid paying the bills for his ontological renovation.

Lastly, Leibniz addresses a major lack in Descartes's treatment of the ontological argument: in marked contrast to his predecessor, he attempted to show that a perfect (hence necessary) being is in fact possible. I will address this claim in some detail, showing how his solution involves linking the ontological

---

6. Leibniz did not always begin with the PSR. In the correspondences with Arnauld, Bernoulli, and De Volder (which were not contemporaneous), despite very different starting points his idealism gradually emerges under the pressure of criticism, only to be suppressed at the beginning of the following correspondence. Catherine Wilson nicely surveys Leibniz's ambivalence in her *Leibniz's Metaphysics: A Historical and Comparative Study* (Princeton: Princeton Univ. Press, 1989). See also L. J. Russell, "The Correspondence between Leibniz and de Volder," in *Leibniz: Metaphysics and Philosophy of Science,* ed. R. S. Woolhouse (Oxford: Oxford Univ. Press, 1981), 104-18. Russell argues that Leibniz never really became an idealist because doing so raised insuperable problems for him. I grant the latter but am less sanguine about the former.

7. Again, see Watson, *Breakdown of Cartesian Metaphysics,* for a listing of the major responses to dualism and the argument that none of them was or could be successful.

and cosmological arguments together into a single structure. As it turns out, it was this combination that paved the way for Kant's refutation of all three arguments by showing that all presuppose the ontological argument and that it is invalid — if Kant's criticisms are effective against Leibniz's reformulation of the ontological proof.

The Principle of Sufficient Reason

An indispensable part of Leibniz's system is the principle of sufficient reason (PSR); there is scarcely a part of his thought that does not presuppose it. When Leibniz shifts to metaphysics in the late (1714) introduction to his thought, *The Principles of Nature and of Grace,* he begins with: "that great principle, normally little used, that nothing *takes place without sufficient reason,* that is, that nothing happens without it being possible for someone who knows enough things to give a reason which suffices to determine why it is so and not otherwise."[8] Therefore, for everything that is the case, there is a reason why it is so rather than otherwise. We might say that the PSR amounts to the claim that there is a metaphysical reason for all truths and falsehoods. This fact gives it a bidirectional status: for everything that is (exists), there is a reason, and all reasons must (and can) be grounded in the world, the way things are. The parallels with Hegel's maxim, "The real is the rational and the rational is the real," are unmistakable.

The PSR has immediate metaphysical and theological consequences. For example, if accepted it may even be sufficient to guarantee the soundness of (at least a limited form of) the cosmological argument. As Leibniz rightly notes, it immediately allows us to pose (and expect an answer to) the question, Why is there something rather than nothing (G 6:602)? With regard to everything whose existence is contingent, the PSR requires us to answer in terms of its cause or ground. It thus allows Leibniz — anticipating Bertrand Russell's criticism in the famous debate with Father Copleston — to insist that there must also be a reason for a series of contingent things as a whole, even if the series is endless (G 7:302; L 486). Given the PSR, the only adequate answer can be an explanans that has its final or sufficient reason within itself; and "this last reason for things is called *God*."[9] Thus Holtze calls the PSR thoroughly theological: "The path from rational determination to the ratio-

---

8. G 6:602; AG 209-10: "rien ne se fait sans raison suffisante," i.e., "que rien n'arrive, sans qu'il soit possible à celuy qui connoitroit assés les choses, de rendre une Raison qui suffise pour determiner, pourquoy il en est ainsi, et non pas autrement."

9. "Cette derniere raison des choses est appellée *Dieu*" (G 6:602; AG 210).

nal sufficiency of this determination makes the principle of sufficient reason into 'the principle of God.'"[10]

The PSR is, and should be, a hard pill for philosophers to swallow, especially if it has such immediate theological consequences. What reason could one have to maintain that everything must have a "sufficient" reason both for its existing at all and for its being this particular thing? I see only two possibilities, a theological or a regulative ground. If one knew, or were willing to presuppose, that everything that exists owes its existence and its nature to a Creator who created nothing without a reason, one would have reason to ascribe to the PSR. There are good reasons to think that Leibniz's own thought processes worked in this way: theism was in his system the major bulwark for his firm adherence to the PSR. But of course, one could not then proceed to argue for theism without vicious circularity — a mistake that Leibniz did not always manage to avoid.

Barring such a theological ground, and *eo ipso* any "higher" proof of the PSR, one might nonetheless still posit it as a basic principle of human reflection. That is, it does appear contradictory (or at least rather pointless) to engage in metaphysics — understood as the quest for the broadest explanation (reason) for what is — if one does not presuppose that there *is* some reason to be had. It is thus fair to say that the PSR makes a good strategy for, and perhaps a basic regulating assumption of, the discipline. If the metaphysical quest fails to produce the sufficient explanations required by the PSR (or a theological justification of the principle itself), then it is possible that there simply are no reasons of a "higher" sort for what is. Yet we will only know that this is the case by making the effort to construct an argument in its defense and failing. The PSR therefore represents a sound, if defeasible, methodological postulation for metaphysics.

The Shift from Intuition to Logic

Leibniz does not accept the Cartesian argument that we have the concept of a most perfect being because we know ourselves as imperfect and we know that there are beings more perfect than we. He does not deny that we are immediately aware of imperfection, but instead challenges Descartes's contention that from imperfection one immediately knows the most perfect. To make his case, Leibniz makes use of a mathematical analogy. I know that the number two is not an infinitely perfect number, because "I have, or can perceive in my mind,

10. Erhard Holze, *Gott als Grund der Welt im Denken des Gottfried Wilhelm Leibniz,* Studia leibnitiana Sonderhelft 20 (Stuttgart: Franz Steiner, 1991), 186-87.

the idea of another number more perfect than it, and still another more perfect than this. Yet after all, I still do not get from this any idea of an infinite number, though I see very well that I can always find a number greater than any given number whatever."[11] Likewise, he adds, how can I conclude from the idea of something immense that I have thought the truly infinite? Leibniz therefore rejects the idea of an immediate intuition of the infinite. As a result, he must attain by purely theoretical means what Descartes was willing to accept as an immediate given of intuition: that we know ourselves as imperfect and thereby have already presupposed a most perfect being.

Indeed, the role of intuition is diminished in all parts of the Leibnizian system. What Descartes introduced into his philosophical system via clear and distinct intuitions, Leibniz sought to achieve by means of clear and distinct *definitions* (and his follower Wolff obtained through syllogistic reasoning).[12] For if one can give a full definition of some name, Leibniz thought, exhaustively listing its attributes, then one fully knows and understands the thing that the word names. Disagreement regarding the attributes of a thing, or whether two names are synonymous, can then be resolved by appeal to these definitions. As a result, Leibniz had a sophisticated notion of proof where Descartes scarcely had one at all. For the latter, the *cogito* argument, for example, is successful because it "displays a truth one cannot doubt."[13] A related contrast emerges in their models of God. For both, God is omniscient. Whereas for Descartes this means precisely that God *intuits* all truths, for Leibniz it means that God *knows* all proofs and can prove all that he knows through the method of exhaustive definitions.

Leibniz is right, of course, when the question concerns the standards for argumentation: a proof is verifiable in a way that an appeal to intuition cannot be. Yet Leibniz's own proof method was, it seems, a miserable failure. Exhaustive definitions of natural-language terms are as impossible to provide as is a unique formalization of a natural language. It follows that his dream of an "art of combinations" *(ars combinatoria)* was a mere chimera. Even God cannot ac-

---

11. Letter to Malebranche, 6/22/1679, G 1:331-32; L 211: "parce que j'ay ou puis appercevoir dans mon esprit l'idée d'un autre nombre plus parfait que luy et encor d'un autre plus parfait que celuycy." But regardless of how often I repeat this procedure or how large the numbers get, "je n'ay pas pour cela aucune idee du nombre infini," because I can always find a larger number than the last. Leibniz adds in a marginal note, "perfectionem summam tamen absolute concipio" (G 1:332n; L 212n6).

12. See, e.g., Charles A. Corr, "Christian Wolff and Leibniz," *Journal of the History of Ideas* 36 (1975): 241-62.

13. So Ian Hacking, "Proof and Eternal Truths: Descartes and Leibniz," in Stephen Goubroger, ed., *Descartes: Philosophy, Mathematics and Physics* (Sussex: Harvester, 1980), 172.

tually carry out an infinite demonstration, Leibniz must admit, though he could know its conclusion immediately (intuitively?).[14] Moreover, in tension with his official anti-intuition stance, Leibniz evidences an ongoing fascination with the intuitive and the mystical, whether he is writing on the true *theologia mystica,* on Pascal's *Pensées* (e.g., the passage on the two infinities), or on Henry More and the mystical side of Neoplatonism.[15] The intuitive origins and underpinnings of the Leibnizian system continue to play around its edges, in an all-but-unacknowledged echo of Descartes. I suggest that Leibniz is as much to be blamed for not providing a place for the intuitive dimensions of his metaphysics (esp. the finite/infinite relationship) as Descartes is for not adding a theory of proof to his appeal to intuition.

The Proofs

For Leibniz there was no question but that God's existence could be proved: "Now we have no need of revealed religion, in order to know that there exists such a unique principle of all things, perfectly good and wise."[16] As in chapter 2, our task again is not so much to inquire whether the proofs are valid, but to use them for unearthing the model of God that lies beneath and is revealed by them.

The same methodological assumption that structured chapter 2 also guides the presentation here. Leibniz thought he could prove decisively that an infinitely perfect being exists. I suggest that he was wrong. For one, those (few) contemporary philosophers who argue that one or another of his proofs is formally valid inevitably challenge the credibility of one or more premises; even the most Leibniz-friendly among them stop short of agreeing with Leibniz that

14. Margaret Wilson does not resolve this problem in her book (originally her dissertation), *Leibniz's Doctrine of Necessary Truth* (New York: Garland, 1990), and indeed draws attention to it at the conclusion of her work (pp. 132-34).

15. See, respectively, "Von der wahren Theologia mystica" (Grua, 146ff.); Leibniz's "Infinité," in Hans Heinz Holz, ed., *Kleine Schriften zur Metaphysik* (Frankfurt: Insel, 1965), 372ff.; Walter Feilchenfeld, "Leibniz und Henry More: Ein Beitrag zur Entwicklungsgeschichte der Monadologie," *Kant-Studien* 28 (1923): 323-34, e.g., 329: "In der Tat darf die ganze Metaphysik von Leibniz als ein großartiger Versuch aufgefaßt werden, die Begriffswelt des neuplatonisch-mystischen Systems der geistigen Struktur eines theoretisch-mathematisch denkenden Menschen kommensurabel zu machen."

16. *Theod.* pars. 41-44, 61; quotation par. 44 (G 6:75): "Or nous n'avons point besoin de la foy revelée, pour savoir qu'il y a un tel principe unique de toutes choses, parfaitement bon et sage."

the premises are obvious. More importantly (again analogously to chapter 2 above on Descartes), it is no longer possible to deny the coherentist structure of his (or any) metaphysical system. Everything is so interconnected — Leibniz's politico-ethical ideal, the Being who embodies all the perfections presupposed by this ideal, the nature of the minds who strive to be like this perfect being, the logical and mathematical notions that link the physical and metaphysical components of the system — that it strikes the modern reader as absurd when one reads that the proofs are supposed to provide a privileged and compelling point of entry. Instead, one must today speak of a "family" of "tightly interconnected" doctrines, so interlaced that "what is really metaphysically primary is the circular design itself."[17] Whatever strength we ascribe to Leibniz's views will stem from their overall explanatory power as a comprehensive system in competition with other equally comprehensive positions. It is in this light — and hence within a coherentist rather than foundationalist framework — that one must examine the Leibnizian proofs and evaluate the model of God that they express.

The Ontological

The question whether Leibniz, like Descartes, takes existence to be a perfection — and hence whether his version of the ontological argument also falls immediately to Kant's critique — is a matter of ongoing debate. In some passages he explicitly labels existence a perfection,[18] insisting in yet others, as Kant might, that the existence or nonexistence of an essence is not a component of the essence itself. But I suggest that this popular topic of debate does not yet get at the heart of the Leibnizian argument. Leibniz did not think his proof turned on the existence/perfection connection as Descartes's did, and he raises the question of their connection only in other contexts (e.g., in his discussions of the God/world relation and in the doctrine of creation).

The core of Leibniz's position on the ontological proof is that the concept of perfection is not in itself *sufficient* to prove the existence of God. The existence/perfection link does its real work only when Leibniz moves outward to develop the intuitions of the ontological proof into a systematic philosophy — and, in particular, when he adds the key contention that *existence adds to the*

17. These phrases are drawn from Fabrizio Mondadori's balanced and detailed treatment of "The Leibnizian 'Circle,'" *Rice University Studies* 63 (1977): 69-96. When Mondadori argues that none of the concepts "has a right to be regarded as metaphysically primary" (p. 91), however, he confuses the order of justification or derivation and the relative orders of priority within the system itself. From an internal perspective, the concept of God receives the clear priority.

18. E.g., in perhaps his fullest presentation of the ontological proof in *NE* 437-38.

perfection of something. The ontological arguer, by contrast, faces a rather different challenge: she or he must show not only the "logical" but also the *real* possibility of this necessary being.[19] Leibniz thus explicitly criticizes Descartes for espousing a circular version of the ontological argument using perfection (note the Kantian overtones): Descartes "asserts that God is perfect only because he thinks that this proposition contains the proposition that God exists. But he has not yet proved that God is perfect in the sense that he already exists; this in turn rests on the question *whether* he exists."[20] There is no question for Leibniz that a perfect being must be necessary. He therefore transforms the traditional logical detail of the ontological argument — including earlier attempts to show that existence must be a perfection — into the simple but apparently modally unimpeachable claim: if a necessary being is possible, then it exists. In his terms, "This is in fact an excellent privilege of the divine nature, to have need only of his possibility or essence in order to actually exist, and it is precisely this which one calls *ens a se*."[21]

Leibniz's switch very much changes the terms of theistic argumentation over against Descartes. Working out the details of an ontological argument simply does not concern him. Hence I must disagree with Dieter Henrich, who attempts to interpret Leibniz by distinguishing (as Descartes had) between ontological arguments from necessity and from perfection.[22] The Leibnizian texts, although employing the argument in both forms, simply do not rest on the sort of distinction implied by Henrich's influential thesis. Instead, necessity and perfection are typically interrelated, as in Leibniz's notes for the discussion with Spinoza: "But it is asked whether it is in our power to set up such a [most per-

---

19. These are Leibniz's terms. In "Leibniz and the Modal Argument for God's Existence," *Monist* 54 (1970): 250-69, L. E. Lomasky has helpfully reconstructed Leibniz's arguments in terms of four different possibilities: (1) metalinguistic possibility, (2) causal or physical possibility, (3) possibility as absence of contradiction, and (4) possibility as compossibility. To transform his ontological argument into a version of the contemporary modal argument for the existence of a necessary being, Leibniz would have to demonstrate that necessary existence (rather than mere existence itself) is a perfection. He also has to show that the proposition "A necessary being is possible" is true not only (as he thinks) in sense (3) but also in sense (1); that is, he must show that (and how) this proposition is cognitively meaningful, how it "obeys the syntactical and semantical rules of [a particular] language" (p. 252).

20. (1671); L 144, translating from W. Kabitz, *Die Philosophie des jungen Leibniz* (Heidelberg, 1909), 141-42, emphasis mine.

21. "Ce qui est en effect un excellent privilege de la nature divine, de n'avoir besoin que de sa possibilité ou essence, pour exister actuellement, et c'est justement ce qu'on appelle *Ens a se*" (*Discours*, par. 23).

22. Henrich, *Der ontologische Gottesbeweis*, 45ff.

fect] being, or whether such a concept has reality. . . . For opponents will say that such a concept of a most perfect being, *or a being which exists through its essence,* is a chimera."[23] As the text that I have italicized shows, Leibniz uses the two phrases (*notionem Entis perfectissimi* and *Entis per Essentiam*) interchangeably. The argument, here as elsewhere, does not turn on the perfection/necessity distinction. For Leibniz, the task is instead to show whether — and how to demonstrate that — God is possible.

Moreover, if Leibniz speaks so often of a necessary being, it is not because he had (or sensed in his readers) any qualms about the potency of the concept of perfection. He had inherited from Malebranche an extremely high view of perfection arguments,[24] and he showed no sympathy to attacks on perfectionistic teleology, whether in the form of Gassendi's atomism or Spinoza's attack on final causes. Leibniz still understood his task to be to show the existence and metaphysical resources of the most perfect being. Within this task, necessary being (*ens necessarium*) played such an important role only because Descartes had failed to demonstrate the possibility of the perfect being.[25] Rectifying this lacuna in perfect-being theology was by its very nature a modal task; as such, it called for emphasizing the inference from *ens perfectissimum* to *ens necessarium*. It was not until decades later that a major thinker began to recognize the dangers and limitations inherent in both concepts (Baumgarten being apparently the first).

Indeed, Leibniz's treatment of the theistic proofs is so strikingly different from Descartes's that I doubt whether the traditional typology of theistic proofs (retained as headings in this chapter) really describes the task as he saw it. The Leibnizian procedure for theistic argumentation might instead be reconstructed as follows: (1) The logical or definitional task: to give a full definition of God, the most perfect being. This entails reflecting on all the various implications of the *ens perfectissimum*. One of these attributes is that it be a necessary being, from which it obviously follows that if the concept is possible (noncontradictory), God exists. (2) The modal task: to show that a most

---

23. "Quaeritur autem an sit in nostra potestate tale Ens fingere. . . . Dicent enim adversarii talem notionem Entis perfectissimi sive Entis per Essentiam existentis esse chimaeram" (G 7:262; L 168).

24. Details of the Malebranche/Leibniz connection are given in Catherine Wilson's *Leibniz's Metaphysics;* in idem, "Leibnizian Optimism," *Journal of Philosophy* 80 (1983): 765-83; and in Robinet's collection of the correspondence with Malebranche. More recently, see Steven Nadler, *Malebranche and Ideas* (New York: Oxford Univ. Press, 1992).

25. This against G. H. R. Parkinson in his introduction to Gottfried Wilhelm Leibniz, *De Summa Rerum: Metaphysical Papers,* trans. G. H. R. Parkinson (New Haven: Yale Univ. Press, 1992), xix.

perfect being is indeed possible. Leibniz provided several arguments directly from the definition of perfection, but he (correctly) saw that the task involved more than merely definitional analysis. If a priori possibility arguments are not decisive, some progress might be made, for example, by showing that a most perfect being is indispensable for explaining anything metaphysically (transcendental argument), or that a theology in which a most perfect being has the most reality is superior to all other ultimate explanations (the argument from the best explanation). (3) The systematic task: to show, once an adequate metaphysical system is in place, at how many points it implies the existence of such a being.

Although I will now treat task (2) under the heading of cosmological arguments, it is obvious that it extends beyond the traditional understanding of this category. And (3) explains why traditional arguments such as the teleological argument appear in Leibniz's writings in such an apparently haphazard fashion: on his view, all instances of order point one toward (without proving) a perfect orderer. Indeed, Leibniz's systematic interests led him to be less interested in proving God's existence than in noting the various theological implications of his system as he worked it out.

The Cosmological

How then can one show that a necessary being is in fact possible?[26] There are in Leibniz's writings at least four different ways, including:

1. An a priori argument for the possibility of God's essence. God is defined as a being that is "without limits, without negation, and consequently without contradiction."[27] (We return later to the contribution of the theory of infinity to this argument.) Therefore, by definition, nothing could hinder the possibility of this being existing. It is perfect in an absolute sense, since something that is not limited in any way cannot entail any internal absurdity or contradiction.[28]

2. An a priori argument from the nature of perfection as simple. If perfections are absolute simples, logical building blocks that are not further analyzable, then "it is not difficult to show that all perfections are

26. As Loemker notes (L 120n17), already Duns Scotus saw the need to supplement the ontological proof with a demonstration of the possibility of God's existence.

27. "Aucunes bornes, aucune negation et par consequent aucune contradiction" (*Monadology* par. 45).

28. See William E. May, "The God of Leibniz," *New Scholasticism* 36 (1962): 506-28, esp. 515-16.

compatible with each other or can be in the same subject."[29] Consequently there can be nothing inconsistent in the notion of a being possessing all perfections in the highest degree. Hence, given the ontological argument, this being must exist.

3. The traditional cosmological argument from contingent beings. There exists at least one contingent being, C. C must have a reason why it exists rather than not existing. But, as contingent, C cannot have that reason in itself, for it might just as well not have existed (since ex hypothesi its existence is not necessary). Since this fact is true of every contingent being (and every aggregate of them), there must be a *necessary* being that is the reason for C's existence.

4. An argument (in two formulations) from the reality of the possibles or essences or what he calls necessary or "eternal" truths (*les verités éternelles, Monad.* pars. 43-44). Actuality has priority over possibility; that is, any reality that possible beings (or possible essences) have must be "grounded in something existent and actual." But there are possible beings, that is, essences of beings that exist but might not (or do not exist but could). Hence a necessary being exists.

One could not single out any one of these four arguments and compel a contemporary philosopher to assent to the existence of a most perfect being on the basis of it. I defend a version of (3), assuming the rational viability of something like traditional metaphysical argumentation, in this and the following chapter; yet defending the assumption of "something like traditional metaphysical argumentation" is not something that a single theistic proof can accomplish. Even if (2) were successful — and we explore an important criticism of it at the end of this chapter — we will find that Leibniz's "atomism of perfections" raises serious problems of its own for perfect-being theology. (1) is an intriguing argument, to which I return in discussing the infinity of God. But it alone does not yield a most perfect being as its product, and there is some reason to wonder what it could possibly mean to call a being "most perfect" when it is beyond all possible distinctions (cf. chapter 3). Finally, each of these arguments launches us into a whole slough of underlying assumptions about reality whose explanatory value (and hence possible truth) can be evaluated only in light of a fully worked out theological or metaphysical system.

Take (4), for example. Leibniz intentionally develops a subject-predicate logic consonant with these independent essences, a theory of individuals based

---

29. "Omnes perfectiones esse compatibiles inter se, sive in eodem esse posse subjecto" (G 7:261; L 167).

on it (including implications for psychology, ethics, and freedom), and a related ontology in which the most perfect (= necessary) essence is the most real and all less perfect (merely possible) essences strive for more perfection or reality. Are we to say that the role of God is subsequently superimposed on this structure (hence proved by it) or, conversely, that the structure itself is derived from sustained reflection on the nature of God? Clearly, neither; the two constitute an interdependent system of ideas in which it is difficult to separate neatly between grounds and what they ground.

What then is the link between postulating eternal natures (or possibilities) and positing God? Relying on Plato, Leibniz suggests that the world originated in "Understanding united to Necessity."[30] Necessity he determines by inquiring into the essential natures of things. One might also derive ontological consequences from an analysis of understanding: everyone who understands (e.g., this sentence) admits that there is something understood and something or someone that understands. God (if he exists) would then be the being with the highest possible understanding, and necessity (including the knowledge of all merely possible essences) would be the object of his understanding. Now this line of argument makes it look as though things are necessary apart from any decision of God. How then could Leibniz maintain the dependence of the necessary and the possible on the highest actuality, God? All necessities, he responds (following Augustine), are located within the divine understanding, rather than in some mind-independent realm of forms. He then draws what I take to be the inevitable (Neoplatonic) conclusion: "without [God] there would be nothing real in possibles, and not only would nothing exist, but also nothing would be possible."[31] The result is a dependence on God as strong as in the Cartesian system, though without Descartes's dependence on the *will* of God. Yet, as this paragraph shows, the result is clearly not an analytically distinct theistic proof of God.

Leibniz is not brilliant at formulating detailed individual arguments for the existence of God; the logical tightness in contemporary modal or possible-worlds arguments for God goes far beyond his analytic achievements. In his writings, even more than in Descartes's, numerous theistic arguments are in circulation, leaving the answer to the question of what is meant to ground what less than completely perspicuous. Judged by the standards of a demonstration of the existence of God, Leibniz's attempt must be judged a failure. Yet, I suggest, Leibniz has masterfully fused the various arguments into a single, over-

---

30. *Theod.* par. 20.

31. "Et que sans [Dieu] il n'y auroit rien de réel dans les possibilités, et non seulement rien d'existent, mais encore rien de possible" (*Monad.* par. 43).

arching system. Indeed, perhaps only Hegel rivals him in the comprehensiveness of the metaphysical vision within which the so-called proofs play a part. Nevertheless, we have found that one can adequately evaluate the strengths and weaknesses of this system only if it is taken as a whole, not by viewing each argument in isolation.

The Teleological

Leibniz also offers, en passant, a teleological argument:

> Anyone who sees the admirable structure of animals will find himself forced to recognize the wisdom of the author of things.[32]

> The final analysis of the laws of nature leads us to the most sublime principles of order and perfection, which indicate that the universe is the effect of a universal intelligent power. . . . The principles of mechanics themselves cannot be explained geometrically, since they depend on more sublime principles, which show the wisdom of the Author in the order and perfection of his work.[33]

Unfortunately, none of Leibniz's teleological arguments really succeeds as an internal critique of a mechanist worldview. They all either presuppose the PSR, using it as a reason to conclude that broader (nonmechanistic) explanations must be given for the mechanism itself, or they presuppose a hierarchy of perfections, complaining that mechanism cannot account for the reality of moral differences. Argumentatively, what is really occurring is that Leibniz is recommending a view of the universe that is teleological as well as mechanical, theological as well as physical. But if one insists on supplementing naturalistic with teleological explanations, then one has already decided to acknowledge the operation of two levels of explanation or causality:

---

32. "Tous ceux qui voyent l'admirable structure des animaux se trouvent portés a reconnoistre la sagesse de l'auteur des choses" (*Discours,* par. 19).

33. *Tentamen anagogicum: Essay Anagogique dans la recherche des causes* (1696); G 7:270, 272; L 477-78: "la dernière resolution des Loix de la Nature nous mene à des principes plus sublimes de l'ordre et de la perfection, qui marquent que l'universe est l'effect d'une puissance intelligente universelle. . . . Les principes mêmes de la Mécanique ne sçauroient estre expliqués Géométriquement, puis qu'ils dependent des principes plus sublimes, qui marquent la sagesse de l'auteur dans l'ordre et dans la perfection de l'ouvrage." The following quotation is from the same passage.

There are, so to speak, two kingdoms even in corporeal nature, which inter-penetrate without confusing or interfering with each other — the realm of power, according to which everything can be explained *mechanically* by effi-cient causes when we have sufficiently penetrated into its interior, and the realm of wisdom, according to which everything can be explained *architec-tonically,* so to speak, or by final causes when we understand its ways suffi-ciently.[34]

From here it is but a short distance to acknowledging some sort of cosmic orderer. One need only rule out the operation of immanent (teleological) cau-sality, the view that things develop on their own accord toward this ultimate goal or telos; and Leibniz thought that the PSR could accomplish this in a single step. Once again, then, the probative force of Leibniz's case lies not in the theis-tic "argument" itself but only in the broader system that can (or, perhaps, can-not!) provide a convincing account of how the two kingdoms hold together.

There is another reason why Leibniz must rely on some version of the te-leological argument. If monads are in fact cut off from one another and yet so perfectly mirror their surrounding world and the universe as a whole, this is a very great miracle; only a divine orchestrator could have brought about such a universal harmony. Obviously, "there is none but God [who could be] the cause of this correspondence of their phenomena."[35] The only surprising thing is that Leibniz would think of this as a proof: "So this mutual relationship of different substances (which . . . harmonize as if they did act upon one another), is one of the strongest proofs of God's existence or of a common cause."[36] Once again we have an instance of what I have called "the systematic task," Leibniz's attempt to show at how many points his overall metaphysical system can imply the exis-tence of a most perfect being.

The root form of Leibniz's teleological argument is reminiscent of Thomas's fourth way. Our moral, aesthetic, and axiological experience show us, he believes, that there is a scale of perfection. Now a scale of perfections, unlike

---

34. "Il y a, pour parler ainsi, deux Regnes dans la nature corporelle même qui se penetrent sans se confondre et sans s'empecher: le regne de la puissance, suivant lequel tout se peut expliquer *mecaniquement* par les causes efficientes, lorsque nous en penetrons assez l'interieur; et aussi le Regne de la sagesse, suivant lequel tout se peut expliquer *architecto-niquement,* pour ainsi dire, par les causes finales, lorsque nous en connoissons assez les us-ages" (ibid., G 6:273).

35. "Or il n'y a que Dieu qui soit cause de cette correspondance de leur phenomenes" (*Discours,* par. 14).

36. To Arnauld in Gottfried Wilhelm Leibniz, *The Leibniz-Arnauld Correspondence,* ed. and trans. H. T. Mason (Manchester: Manchester Univ. Press, 1967), 147-48; cf. L 458.

the series of natural numbers, presupposes a highest instance in terms of which the rest of the scale must be defined. So there must be a highest member. Unfortunately, in practice Leibniz usually argues from humankind's *quest* for greater perfection. This of course exposes him rather strongly to the objection that human reason merely posits that final goal (perhaps as a useful fiction) rather than knowing its existence. For instance, Leibniz often begins from the striving for the most perfect political system, postulating God as the monarch over all beings in the universal republic.[37] This whole direction of argumentation — from human standards of perfection to God — begs for a reductionist explanation in terms of human projections (cf. chapter 2). So Stuart Brown:

> It is not surprising that Leibniz's doctrine that spirits are made in the image of God can be turned on its head. God becomes the absolutely rational philosopher-king who perfectly conforms to the eternal laws of justice and goodness. He is an *homme honnête* [man of honor] writ large and perfected, Whose actions are totally free of any willfulness and Whose creation of the world exhibits perfect wisdom and goodness.[38]

Although a view of God that was in tension with our evaluative standards would be hard to swallow, the argument from our standards to God is not by itself sufficient.

Finally, note that the teleological argument also required an explanation for evil (apparent evil) in the world, and thus led directly to the project of the *Theodicy*. Leibniz's theodicy, and hence his teleological argument, is particularly unconvincing to the contemporary reader, for at least two reasons. First, much of it is a probabilistic argument that the existence of God is compatible with this amount of evil in the world. (The logical point, that the existence of God is in principle compatible with some evil, can be more easily accepted.) Leibniz grants at one point that probabilistic reasoning was in his day at a particularly primitive stage and hence not overly reliable. Since the *Theodicy* was, whether he wanted to admit it or not, a compilation of probabilistic reasoning, one is perhaps not unjustified in applying this slighting comment to his own ef-

37. See Albert Görland, *Der Gottesbegriff bei Leibniz: Ein Vorwort zu seinem System*, Philosophische Arbeiten 1 (Giessen: Töpelmann, 1907), e.g., 168-69, on the postulation of God in order to make a better future. But surely Görland's neo-Kantianism is foreign to Leibniz's thought, e.g., "Die Leibnizsche Gottesidee bedeutet ein Postulat des Sittlichen, die Idee des Garanten eines messianischen Reiches von dieser Welt" (p. 178). From the fact that God, or the PSR, is only a postulate hardly follows that the whole Leibnizian system belongs in the realm of practical reason!

38. See Stuart Brown, *Leibniz* (Minneapolis: Univ. of Minnesota Press, 1984), 191.

forts. Second, Leibniz's position does not include a radical enough conception of evil, especially for the late twentieth-century reader. As Loemker notes, "Evil, being merely the religious term for the finiteness implied in existence, time, and plurality, thus becomes virtually a datum in the teleological argument" (L 51). But after Hume it would be strange not to take evil as at least prima facie opposed to perfect-being theology. I conclude that Leibniz's teleological arguments are neither successful proofs nor even particularly interesting failures. If Leibniz's system has an enduring significance, it does not lie in this area.

AN ANALYTIC RECONSTRUCTION OF LEIBNIZIAN THEOLOGY

We are now in the position to attempt a reconstruction of the systematic perspective that is repeatedly presupposed by Leibniz's theistic arguments. Contemporary treatments of his thought criticize individual arguments, often in great analytic detail; but one almost never finds a statement of just what his theology looks like when taken as a whole. The task is even more urgent insofar as Leibniz himself never wrote out the system behind his systematic intuitions. Leibnizian philosophical theology, we will find, stands in the tradition of Descartes's reflections on infinity and perfection; even more strongly than the Cartesians it moves perfection to the absolute heart of the system; and in doing so it allows us finally to detect the inherent limits of the appeal to perfection in this field.

Perfection

The project of stating the central principle of Leibniz's system is a precarious one. The history of Leibniz interpretation contains numerous presentations of his system that try to express its coherence from a single perspective[39] — logic, biology, panpsychism — but that tend to cancel one another out by their very

39. Such as Otto Saame's appeal to the PSR in *Der Satz vom Grund bei Leibniz: Ein konstitutives Element seiner Philosophie und ihrer Einheit* (Mainz: Hans Krach, 1961). Holtze also claims to have shown that "Leibniz's theologisches Denken in Gestalt seines Gottesgedankens das Fundament ist, auf dem sein weitgespanntes Gedankengebäude aufruht, daß sein Gottesbegriff der Schlüsselbegriff seiner umfassenden Begriffswelt ist" (Erhard Holze, *Gott als Grund der Welt im Denken des Gottfried Wilhelm Leibniz*, Studia leibnitiana Sonderhelft 20 [Stuttgart: Franz Steiner, 1991], 186).

disagreement. One must therefore state the case somewhat cautiously: the principle of perfection provides one of the central organizing pillars, and arguably the most central one, for Leibniz's system. The perfection idea runs through his natural philosophy, his practical reflection, and of course his theology; it is also central to any knowledge of God, since "God is known to us through knowledge of the perfections."[40] Surveys of Leibniz often pay lip service to the role of perfection, though its systematic function as an organizing principle is, I think, usually underappreciated. Perhaps more important, the systematic consequences of the weaknesses of this idea in Leibniz have rarely been treated. If I can establish its absolute centrality in Leibniz's thought, and if it turns out to be untenable, then this will have far-reaching implications for the whole tradition of perfection-based philosophical theology.

In chapter 2 we traced Descartes's extensive use of the perfection idea, ranging from his response to skepticism right into natural science; and in chapter 3 we researched the origins of the tradition on which Cartesianism is based. As the following sections show, perfection is at least as central to Leibniz — although his conceptual analysis of the notion goes much deeper, thanks to a more extended use of logical and mathematical considerations. At the same time, Leibniz greatly reduces the role of intuition in metaphysics. One is therefore tempted to combine the two thinkers according to the schema introduced at the beginning of chapter 3: Descartes provides an intuitive explication of the concept of perfection, while Leibniz concentrates on conceptual definition and analysis. Intuition and concept — the two notions suggest a certain complementarity, a unity within diversity, without denying serious areas of disagreement (and they are not hard to find).

There is a certain tendency for the perfection notion, thanks in part to the notions of emanation and participation on which it relies, to push in the direction of an ultimate oneness of all things with, or within, the Ground of Perfection. Or, to put it more carefully, the perfection notion implies *degrees of being*, such that finite (less than fully perfect) beings have only subordinate existence; they can be substances only in a derivative or subordinate sense of the term, if at all. Thus there is some tension between Leibniz's use of this notion and his pluralism of monads. But this tension, I will argue, is endemic to theologies of perfection. Leibniz has thus brought the theology of perfection to completion in a twofold sense: revealing its conceptual implications more fully than his predecessors, and thereby demonstrating its limitations. If I am right about the limitations, Leibniz thus represents the culmination (and perhaps also the

---

40. Opening of "Von der wahren Theologia mystica" (Grua, 146): "Gott wird von uns erkand durch erkantnis der Vollkommenheiten."

end?) of one particular chapter in theistic metaphysics, one in which perfection was taken as the guiding feature of the doctrine of God and as the solution to its central problems. One thinks of Hegel, who also represents the culmination of a particular tradition within philosophical theology. Just as, after Hegel, one had either to write commentaries on him or to alter the nature of the project in a fundamental way, after Leibniz one must either do something like Leibnizian perfect-being theology or reject the project itself.

We will find that there is no unitary definition of perfection in Leibniz's opus; he appears ready to introduce the term in different senses as suits his context or discussion partner. In what follows we look explicitly at a number of specifications — perfection as clear perception and activity, as simplicity, as harmony, as reality, as connected to the PSR, and as linked to moral perfection — before turning explicitly to the infinitely perfect being. Each of these specifications will turn out to be inadequate, either because it is one-sided or because of conflict with the others. Admittedly, Leibniz made advances on the largely intuitive view of perfection espoused by Descartes, thereby helping to stave off the projectionist critique of Descartes's opponents much longer than one might have expected; and he was right to strive for a sophisticated theory of perfection, which (had he been successful) would have defused the charge of anthropocentrism. Leibniz's failure at this task is of more than antiquarian interest, however, since no other modern thinker developed a metaphysics of perfection that matches his in scope. If Leibniz has failed, it will strongly suggest that the notion of perfection, taken as the mainstay of a philosophical theology, is not able to withstand the onslaughts of modernity, the objections brought to it by modern philosophy, science, religious pluralism, and culture.

Perfection as Clear Perception and Activity

As a perfect-being theologian Leibniz takes as fundamental the notion of *a being who possesses all positive qualities that can have a maximum and possesses them to the highest degree.* A number of divine qualities follow immediately — either intuitively or as suggested by the history of the tradition — from this definition: omnipotence, omniscience, perfect goodness. In Leibniz's post-Cartesian context, omniscience, for example, would involve a God who possesses all knowledge immediately and with maximal clarity and distinctness, and who can immediately grasp every infinite definition by fully analyzing every term or subject.

It is interesting to observe how much more mileage Leibniz gets out of the perfect-being approach than earlier thinkers had. For instance, he argues that it entails a hierarchy of substances, arranged depending on the clarity with which they mirror the universe.[41] Based on this important passage, Rescher suggests that one define the amount of perfection for some possible substance in some particular state as the degree of clarity with which it mirrors its universe.[42] Now for Leibniz the theory of perception is the same as the theory of action: "The creature is said to act externally insofar as it is perfect, and to be acted upon *(patir)* by another, insofar as it is imperfect. Thus we attribute action to a monad insofar as it has distinct perceptions, and passion, insofar as it has confused perceptions."[43] The result is a perfection scale that encompasses all beings (actual and possible) within a single hierarchy, depending on their activeness, that is, the distinctness of their perceptions.

Perfection from the Simple to the Optimal

In 1676, in the preparatory notes for his meeting with Spinoza, Leibniz defined perfection purely in terms of simplicity: "By a *perfection* I mean every simple quality that is positive and absolute or that expresses whatever it expresses without any limits."[44] Leibniz is here concerned to use the resources of the perfection idea to address what I call Descartes's Problem, viz. that *we seem unable to show that a necessary being is possible.* As we saw, talk of a most perfect being is practically worthless if one cannot solve Descartes's Problem. Yet, Leibniz reasoned, if each perfection is absolutely simple then there can be no contradiction, and hence no impossibility, in combining them. Clearly, his goal was to apply his early logical atomism to the theory of perfection as well, allowing him to move beyond Descartes's more intuitive approach. The *ars combinatoria* and logical calculus would then allow him to construct a clear doctrine of God as the sum of all perfections.

But perfection as simplicity turned out to be too simple. When Leibniz came to apply it to worlds of objects God might create, he found that the perfec-

---

41. "Mais comme chaque perception distincte de l'Ame comprend une infinité de perceptions confuses, qui enveloppent tout l'univers, l'Ame même ne connoit les choses dont elle a perception, qu'autant qu'elle en a des perceptions distinctes et revelées; et elle a de la perfection, à mesure de ses perceptions distinctes" (*Principes de la Nature et de la Grace,* par. 43, G 6:604).

42. Rescher, *The Philosophy of Leibniz* (Englewood Cliffs, N.J.: Prentice-Hall, 1967), 27.

43. "La Creature est dite agir au dehors en tant qu'elle a de la perfection, et patir d'une autre en tant qu'elle est imparfaite. Ainsi l'on attribue l'Action à la Monade en tant qu'elle a des perceptions distinctes, et la Passion en tant qu'elle a de confuses" (*Monad.* par. 49).

44. "Perfectionem voco omnem qualitatem simplicem quae positiva est et absoluta, seu quae quicquid exprimit, sine ullis limitibus exprimit" (G 7:261; L 167).

tion requirement must include not only the simplicity of the means but also the quality of the effect. The 1686 *Discours de Métaphysique,* the first synthesis of his mature metaphysics, thus augmented his earlier view in a way that became decisive for his later thought. Here the perfection of divine action implies also "that the simplicity of the means is in balance with the richness of the effects" (par. 5). The criterion for perfect is maximal richness with minimally complex means, or, elsewhere, "that a maximal effect should be achieved with a minimum outlay."[45] Rescher entitles this the *minimax principle.* Note that the "means" here include natural laws as well as direct miraculous interventions in history; the principle would thus exclude Ptolemaic epicycles as well as miracles in the sense of divine corrections to the world God had already set in motion. The best possible world, the most perfect one, will be the one with the greatest richness of phenomena that can be obtained from a relatively parsimonious set of natural laws; and God will have to create precisely this world. It is startling to note how much of Leibnizian metaphysics falls into place once one has opted for the minimax principle.

In light of this definition of perfection, it becomes possible to read other (apparently conflicting) Leibnizian passages on perfection as elliptical or, less charitably, as simply mistaken. For example, the best world is not merely that with the most beings. Some formulations in *De rerum originatione radicali* (1697) give rise to this impression, as when Leibniz valorizes the world "in which the greatest number of possibles is produced" or in which there would be "as much as there possibly can be, given the capacity of time and space."[46] Given the minimax principle, we must read these formulations as elliptical, the denominator of the equation having simply been omitted. In sum, as Gale notes correctly, the best possible world is not just maximal ("entirely filled no matter what") but *optimal* ("maximized with respect to some parameter").[47]

It would seem, then, that the divine goal must be more than just to obtain the most essence possible. But doesn't this make it false that, as Leibniz once alleged, "perfection is nothing but the quantity of essence"?[48] Apparently. Note in Leibniz's defense, however, that he does give an interesting twist to this doctrine: he seems to hold that degree of essence means degree of harmony:

> Perfection is the harmony of things, or the observability of universals, or concord *(consensus)* or identity in variety; then too you can say that it is de-

45. "A Maximo Minimove petendum est, ut nempe maximus praestetur effectus, minimo ut sic dicam sumtu" *(De rerum,* G 7:303; L 487).

46. "Existere quantum plurimum potest pro temporis locique" (G 7:304; AG 151).

47. George Gale, "On What God Chose: Perfection and God's Freedom," *Studia Leibnitiana* 8 (1976): 69-87, quotation 78.

48. "Perfectio [est] nihil aliud quam essentiae quantitas" (G 7:303).

gree of thinkability *(considerabilitatis)*. Of course order, regularity, and harmony come to the same thing. You can also say that [*perfection*] *is degree of essence,* if essence is estimated from harmonious properties, which give, so to speak, weight and momentum to essence.[49]

Brown concludes, "if so, then these two notions of perfection, viz., simplicity of laws in conjunction with richness of phenomena, on the one hand, and quantity or degree of essence, on the other, are not in conflict, but come indeed to the same thing" (ibid.).

Note that a theory of perfection that was supposed to be atomistic, built up out of simple perfects, has now found itself forced to accept a systematic element, a reference to the whole, at the heart of the theory — hardly the atomistic view of essences as unrelated parts that one thinks of as typically Leibnizian. We will find that Leibniz's pluralism of substances (and much else in his thought!) depends crucially on there being uncountably infinite numbers of possible individuals, each of which is ontologically distinct, has its own "degree of essence," and is eternally possible independent of any thought or volition on God's part. But what happens if "degree of essence" involves the question of a monad's "harmonious properties"? This would make the monad not an essentially individual entity but essentially dependent on others. Put differently: it would reverse the priority of part and whole, of atom and world, in the Leibnizian system. If the essential nature of an individual involves the factor of its interconnection (harmony) with others, then this theory of perfection is not genuinely atomistic.

Perfection as Harmony

We have already anticipated the theory of perfection as harmony in the last section. The most famous manifestation of this definition is the doctrine of preestablished harmony that Leibniz required to make his mental atomism work. It may not at first be obvious that the doctrine of preestablished harmony is linked to perfection. According to Russell and Couturat, Leibniz's whole metaphysics arises out of his logic. For example, his subject-predicate logic gives rise to the PSR — which, according to Russell, makes the notion of a preestablished harmony just an add-on to keep the whole rather unlikely system from collaps-

---

49. *Briefwechsel zwischen Leibniz und Christian Wolf,* ed. C. I. Gerhardt (Halle, 1860), 172, emphasis mine; cited in Gregory Brown, "Compossibility, Harmony, and Perfection in Leibniz," *Philosophical Review* 96 (1987): 173-203, quotation 200. The next reference in the text is also to this page in Brown.

ing. Likewise, Louis Loeb raises the "horrifying possibility" that preestablished harmony emerged early as an answer to the problems of dualism and that it remains in Leibniz's mature philosophy "as nothing but an artifact" of the earlier, dualistic metaphysics.[50]

But these criticisms miss the mark; preestablished harmony is not just an ungrounded or anachronistic portion of Leibniz's thought. Whether he came to it for independent reasons and then applied it to the mind/body problem, or first introduced it because of its fruitfulness for that problem, preestablished harmony is intimately linked to his systematic theology of perfection. In Leibniz's dualistic writings, in which he posited a mental substance associated with every group of matter, he needed the doctrine to explain both this happy distribution of spiritual substances through matter and their fortuitous ability to represent the matter with which they happened to be associated. In the later, idealistic philosophy, the preestablished harmony, the "hypothesis of agreement," became even more crucial, for the perfect coordination between the perceptions of the various windowless monads could not possibly arise by chance. "As soon as one sees the possibility of this hypothesis of agreement," Leibniz writes with enthusiasm, "one sees also that it is the most reasonable one and that it gives a wonderful idea of the harmony of the universe and of the perfection of the works of God."[51] Loeb concludes, as this passage also suggests, "Apart from its aesthetic appeal, [Leibniz's] motivations for the preestablished harmony and for the denial of interaction were entirely religious" (p. 316).

Once the outlines of Leibniz's position are clear, we can ask what would recommend its acceptance. It may not be difficult to conceive harmony as in general *a* good, but what grounds are there for a general theory of perfection *as* harmony? To sort things out, one must distinguish among epistemic, ethical, and aesthetic goods (perfections) more clearly than Leibniz did. Influenced as he was by the doctrine of the unity of the transcendentals — in this case, the True, the Good, the Beautiful — he seems to have assumed that what characterizes perfection in one area would be equally applicable to others, and hence that the arguments in the previous paragraph support a global theory of perfection as harmony.

But on this point serious reservations are in order. Ethical judgments do not work according to the rules of aesthetics, though it may have taken Kant's

50. Loeb, *From Descartes to Hume,* 312. Loeb goes on to reject this possibility. The next reference in the text is also to this work.

51. "Systeme nouveau de la nature et de la communication des substances" (1695), G 4:485; L 458: "Ainsi dès qu'on voit la possibilité de cette Hypothese des accords, on voit aussi qu'elle est la plus raisonnable, et qu'elle donne une merveilleuse idée de l'harmonie de l'univers et de la perfection des ouvrages de Dieu."

third *Critique* to drive the point home to modern philosophy. In the *Theodicy* and elsewhere, Leibniz justifies evil in terms of the balance or harmony of the whole. His examples are dissonance in music and the "trivial dangers" that make us aware of our own power. I suggest that it is not by accident that the taste example also plays a role here:

> By the same principle, it is insipid always to eat sweets; sharp, sour, and even bitter things should be mixed with them to excite the taste. He who has not tasted the bitter does not deserve the sweet; indeed, he will not appreciate it. This is the very law of enjoyment, that pleasure does not run an even course, for this produces aversion and makes us dull, not joyful.[52]

What grounds are there, however, for thinking that this "very law of enjoyment" should determine God's selection among possible worlds? Why should a world that mixes good with the evils of the Holocaust (or even the Lisbon earthquake) be more perfect, ethically as well as aesthetically, than one that lacks such evils? It may be, on the one hand, that there is some ultimate explanation for suffering, human and otherwise. For instance, it may be that "though afflictions are temporary evils, they are good in effect, for they are short cuts to greater perfection."[53] But on the other hand such afflictions may also be instances of pointless suffering, as in Voltaire's *Candide* or Camus's *The Plague*. Likewise, there may be no possible world that contains the amount of good our world does (opportunity for virtue, charity, free choice, etc.) and yet less suffering than in this world. But how could one demonstrate that no such better world is possible? I find no concrete evidence for this claim; indeed, a good case could be made that the evidence lines up against it. Why wouldn't a world be possible in which the school building collapsed five minutes later, after the students had departed? It is hard even to imagine a non-question-begging argument that precisely the amount of suffering that we in fact find is necessary for the best of all possible worlds.

I therefore challenge the perfection as harmony equation, both on the level of its conceptual support and in the (ethical) form it takes in the actual outworking of Leibniz's thought. Leibniz's theory of perfection requires that he show that this *is* the best of all possible worlds. He has been unsuccessful in do-

---

52. "Eodem ex principio insipidum est perpetuo dulcibus vesci; acria, acida, imo amara sunt admiscenda, quibus gustus excitetur. Qui non gustavit amara, dulcia non meruit, imo nec aestimabit. Haec ipsa est laetitiae lex, ut aequabili tenore voluptas non procedat, fastidium enim haec parit et stupentes facit, non gaudentes" (G 7:307).

53. "Afflictiones pro tempore malas, effectu bonas esse, cum sint viae compendiariae ad majorem perfectionem" (ibid.).

ing this. Thus perfection as harmony — where the evils of the world are justified by the need to balance with the good — must be said to be a dismal failure.

Perfection and the Principle of Sufficient Reason

Many (e.g., Russell and Rescher) maintain that the PSR has a source separate from the principle of perfection. It is not necessary to dispute this, for Leibniz does sometimes present the PSR as independent, without making reference to perfection. But the close proximity between the two is often overlooked. Indeed, it is a small conceptual step from the principle of perfection to the PSR. At least two lines of argument lead from the one to the other.

1. Recall that the amount of perfection for a possible substance is "the degree of clarity with which at a given state [it] mirrors its universe,"[54] since each monad expresses the entire universe according to its manner.[55] Clearer perception, which Leibniz defines as a greater perfection, means grasping or expressing more clearly than another "the cause or reason" of change. If there is a most perfect being, then it must comprehend the causes or reasons for everything that exists; but it could only do so if there is a reason for all that is. In short: the definition of perfection as clear perception of reasons, combined with the existence of an *ens perfectissimum,* entails the acceptance of the PSR.

2. Clearly, the principle that there is a sufficient explanation for everything that exists is the cornerstone of rationalism. Yet note that a perfection argument can be given for this as well: the perfect universe would have to be fully know*able,* even if not fully known. For recall the connection of perfection and harmony: a world with a "fit" between the epistemic capabilities of its creatures on the one hand and the objects to be known on the other would be more harmonious (perfect) than one whose things-in-themselves were unknowable in principle.[56] The PSR thus merely expresses the epistemic side of the principle of perfection.[57]

Let us grant for a moment that the principle of perfection does entail the

---

54. Rescher, *Philosophy of Leibniz,* 27.

55. "Mais comme toutes les substances sont une production continuelle du souverain Estre, et expriment le même univers ou les même phenomenes, elles s'entraceordent exactement, et cela nous fait dire que l'une agit sur l'autre, parce que l'une exprime plus distinctement que l'autre la cause ou raison des changement" (to Foucher, G 1:382-83).

56. Does this mean that we must say that Kant's world, with its unresolvable dualism, could not be the product of an *ens perfectissimum,* but would have to be the work of something like Descartes's evil demon?

57. Loemker argues similarly, "The law of sufficient reason itself rests on the perfection of the universe and the possibility of the analysis which is implied in identity" (L 45).

PSR. This entailment relation, like the previous two senses of perfection, may, however, raise problems for perfect-being theology. For now the notion of perfection may be in conflict with Christian theism. Is "divine mathematics"[58] — creation according to the timeless requirements of the perfection idea — consistent with a religious doctrine of a creation? Theologians have traditionally held that creation cannot be necessary but must be the result of a free divine decision — a claim with which certain modern philosophers (notably Hegel) have struggled. Like Hegel, Leibniz finds himself in conflict with the idea of a free creation as he attempts to conceive a creation consistent with the PSR. For instance, he sometimes speaks of the emanation of the world from God, and at other times of things automatically actualizing themselves on their own in proportion to the perfection inherent in their (eternal) essences. Of course, Leibniz is careful to deny the allegation that this world is metaphysically necessary; it is merely "physically" or "morally" necessary, since its contrary would be less (physically or morally) perfect. Nonetheless, there is reason to conclude that the principle of perfection itself stands in tension with the theism that it hopes to assist.

Perfection as Degree of Reality

This fifth specification is a particularly important one, especially if it turns out (as I hinted in the preceding point) that the others will entail it in the long run. Certainly, the claim that perfection involves the degree of reality of a thing has a central place in the Leibnizian system as a whole. The claim emerges in its clearest form in the famous essay *De rerum originatione radicali:* "perfection is nothing but quantity of essence," and later, "perfection or degree of essence is the principle of existence."[59] In another comparison, Leibniz defines force as the degree of action, intensity as the degree of quality, and perfection as "the degree of reality or essence."[60] A similar view emerges in the late letter to Wolff, where he defines perfection as "the degree of positive reality, or what comes to the same thing, the degree of affirmative intelligibility."[61] The root of the problem

58. *Mathesis Divina;* see G 7:304; English L 488.

59. "On the Radical Origination of Things" (*De rerum,* G 7:303, 304; L 487): "est enim perfectio nihil aliud quam essentiae quantitas" and "Et ut possibilitas est principium Essentiae, ita perfectio seu Essentiae gradus . . . principium existentiae."

60. Letter to Arnold Eckhard, summer 1677 (G 1:266): "perfectionem esse gradum seu quantitatem realitatis seu essentiae."

61. To Wolff, winter 1714-15, in *Briefwechsel zwischen Leibniz und Christian Wolf,* ed. Gerhardt, 161 (AG 230). Hence he can say that existence is itself a perfection ("l'existence est elle-même une perfection," *NE* IV, 10, par. 7).

lies in the entailment that possibles contain their own impetus to exist in proportion to their degree of perfection: that "there is a certain urgency *(exigentia)* toward existence in possible things or in possibility or essence itself — a pretension to exist, so to speak — and in a word, that essence in itself tends to exist."[62]

With this conceptual move, perfection takes on an ontological weight, a direct link to reality. We found something similar already in Descartes, in his doctrine of levels of reality and in his principle that the cause of an idea must have at least as much reality as the idea itself. And chapter 3 showed that the connection extended back through much of the Neoplatonic tradition, which usually provided the central conceptual resources for the perfection idea. Leibniz summarizes the basic idea as the assumption that "being involves more perfection than nonbeing."[63] I suggest that the close connection between being and perfection also carried much of the probative weight for Leibniz's ontological argument: if we can think a most perfect being, surely we cannot think it without the quality of maximal reality, which means thinking it as existing.

But this specification, like the previous three, faces serious problems. If one is convinced by Kant (as I am) that the maxim "existence is a perfection" is untenable, its failure is a serious blow not only to the ontological argument but also to Leibniz's very definition of perfection. Even if one can still make use of the perfection concept in philosophy, one can no longer automatically correlate perfection and existence. Leibniz's notion of possibles striving for existence, for example, then becomes nonsensical. On the one hand, rejecting the perfection/existence link leaves a larger role for God in creation than would otherwise be the case, since now nothing would come into existence, or even tend to do so, without an explicit divine decision and act of creation. On the other hand, without the perfection/existence link God would have no compelling grounds for choosing this particular world over other possible worlds, for now no possible world can make any particular claim on God and the criteria for the divine decision become unclear. The question is a difficult one. If God's grounds for deciding are weakened, God's volition will play a more central role, moving Leibniz closer again to Descartes. Yet if the connection between perfection and existence slips far enough (as I will argue it does), then God will lack any grounds for deciding, spelling the end both of rationalism and of an inherent rationality of divine actions. (In chapter 9 we will find ourselves forced to conclusions such as these.)

62. "(Quod) aliquid potius existit quam nihil, aliquam in rebus possibilibus seu in ipsa possibilitate vel essentia esse exigentiam existentiae, vel (ut sic dicam) praetensionem ad existendum et, ut verbo complectar, essentiam per se tendere ad existentiam" (G 7:303).
63. L 487.

Moral Perfection

Leibniz's theology gives rise directly to his ethics; any problems with the former will directly influence the latter. His motto is *theoria cum praxi:* "We must recognize that the true morality is related to metaphysics as practice is to theory, because the knowledge of spirits in general, and particularly of God and the soul, depends on the nature of substances, and this knowledge provides a proper understanding of justice and virtue."[64] If I am right about the centrality of divine perfection in Leibniz, this notion should then be equally determinative for his ethics. And this is precisely what one finds: his ethics "is grounded, not on hope or fear, but solely and alone on the beauty and perfection of God."[65]

Parallels between Leibniz's metaphysics of perfection and his ethics abound: complete perfection entails clarity of perception, making one active rather than passive, in ethics not less than in epistemology. To the extent that one acts one has perfection, and suffering at the hands of another expresses imperfection (*Monad.* pars. 49-50). At its root, "the impulse to action" arises from a striving toward perfection, although in the psychological context it takes the form of pleasure.[66] Thus Leibniz ascribes to a doctrine of hedonistic perfectionism in ethics and aesthetics (L 486). He chooses the pleasure principle with the goal of providing what at first glance looks like a fully naturalized and deterministic ethics: the sufficient causes of all moral action reside within each person, since "moral perfection is in reality physical perfection with respect to minds."[67]

The concept of striving or *conatus* is therefore as central to Leibniz's phys-

---

64. "La vraye Morale est à la Metaphysique, ce que la practique est à la Theorie, parce que de la doctrine des substances en commun depend la connoissance des Esprits et particulierement de Dieu et de l'Ame, qui donne une juste etendue à la justice et à la vertu" (G 5:413).

65. See Onno Klopp, *Correspondance de Leibniz avec l'electrice Sophie de Brunswick-Lunebourg* (Hannover: Klindworth, 1874), 2:65, quoted in Leroy Loemker, "The Ethical Import of the Leibnizian System," in Ivor Leclerc, ed., *The Philosophy of Leibniz and the Modern World* (Nashville: Vanderbilt Univ. Press, 1973), 209.

66. See the preface to the *Mantissa codicis juris gentium* (1700); L 424. More simply elsewhere, "Pleasure is the experience *(Empfindung)* of a perfection or an excellence," or even "I call any elevation of being *(alle Erhöhung des Wesens)* a perfection" (Guhrauer, 1:420, 422; L 425-26). In the correspondence with Wolff (5/18/1715), Leibniz repeats that "perfection is the harmony of things, or . . . the state of agreement *(consensus)* or identity"; and pleasure is merely "the sensation of perfection" (*Briefwechsel zwischen Leibniz und Christian Wolf,* ed. Gerhardt, 172; AG 233-34).

67. "Moralis perfectio ipsis mentibus physica est" (G 7:306; AG 153).

ics, anthropology, and ethics as it is to Spinoza's. The difference is that Leibniz attempts to be naturalistic and teleological at the same time. Right action always involves a striving for perfection: "Thus our happiness will never consist, and must never consist, in complete joy, in which nothing is left to desire, and which would dull our mind, but must consist in a perpetual progress to new pleasures and new perfections."[68] Virtue and vice, though explained naturalistically, are still called "the perfection or imperfection of the will."[69] The tensions that Leibniz encounters in this unlikely juxtaposition are precisely those of his (unsuccessful) compatibilist doctrine of freedom, in which one is free as long as the prediction of a given (determined) action involves an infinite number of steps. I return below to these tensions in his position.

Leibniz's theory of moral perfection represents an interesting (though ill-fated) attempt to mediate between Descartes and Spinoza. Cartesian dualism had separated moral and metaphysical perfection, while Spinoza had discarded all talk of teleological perfection with its anthropocentric dangers and tendency to separate humans out from the natural order. Leibniz fought against an ontological dualism, yet wished somehow to retain a dualism of moral and physical perfection. What he desired is clear: "The world is not only the most admirable machine, but insofar as it is made up of minds, it is also the best republic, the republic through which minds derive the greatest possible happiness and joy."[70] One can only conclude that their reconciliation remained an unpaid promissory note. Again: these problems are not unique to Leibniz; it has become fundamentally difficult in modern thought to advance a unity of fact (or existence) and goodness.

Leibniz's philosophy clearly subordinates the moral to the theological. One notes this tendency, for example, when he develops the absolute perfection argument (the ontological proof) not in terms of goodness but primarily in terms of contingency and necessity. Still, something is thereby lost, namely the unity of the theological and moral dimensions. The reconciliation of philosophy with theology needs both dimensions, yet Leibniz fails finally to bring them together. One way to see this is to note again the contrasts with Spinoza. Whereas Leibniz develops an ethics of striving meant as an ideal for all moral

68. "Ainsi notre bonheur ne consistera jamais, et ne doit point consister dans une pleine jouissance, où il n'y auroit plus rien à desirer, et qui rendroit notre esprit stupide, mais dans un progrès perpetuel à de nouveaux plaisirs et de nouvelles perfections" (G 6:606; AG 213).

69. "Reflections on the Common Concept of Justice" (1702); Mollat 61, L 569.

70. "Unde Mundus non tantum est Machina maxime admirabilis, sed etiam quatenus constat ex Mentibus, est optima Respublica, per quam Mentibus confertur quam plurimum felicitatis seu laetitiae, in qua physica earum perfectio consistit" (G 7:306; AG 153).

agents, Spinoza's ethics are designed only for the elite and the few. Whereas Leibniz tries to conceptualize God in Christian and morally acceptable terms, Spinoza acknowledges no such criteria. The result is a greater consistency within Spinoza's view and a continuing tension within Leibniz's. Finally, one must conclude with Georges Friedmann, "the drama of Leibniz sometimes seems to be that of a meditation that is driven where it does not want to go, or where at least an important part of it refuses to go."[71]

Perfection and Natural Science

We have challenged Leibniz's claim that his principle of perfection is able to ground a theistic philosophy compatible with Christian theology. Is it any more successful in wedding theology and science or "natural philosophy"? The answer here must also be no. Leibniz's overarching goal was to provide a general account that allows for both mathematical and mechanistic explanations of natural events, while at the same time leaving room for an explanation of the universe in terms of final causes (viz. the goals of God and other monads). Since metaphysics must supply the overarching framework, this means ideally that physics could derive from the notion of a perfect being. Leibniz explicitly acknowledges the importance of this task. As Stuart Brown notes correctly, however, the *Discours* is "rather vague about just what could be inferred for physics from the assumption that the world was created by a perfect being."[72]

Since "God has chosen the most perfect world," it must be the one that is "at the same time the simplest in hypotheses and the richest in phenomena."[73] But Leibniz did not succeed in linking natural science closely to his philosophical theology in the manner he hoped for. God's existence may be a sufficient condition for concluding, for example, that simpler hypotheses are preferable (the parsimony principle), but it is not really necessary to call on the authority of theology for defending the use of such principles in science. Many of his principles — for instance, "natural science should seek to optimize explanations, covering the most data by means of the least complex hypotheses possible" — can just as well be justified on pragmatic grounds, or as regulative max-

71. Georges Friedmann, *Leibniz et Spinoza*, 2nd ed. (Paris: Gallimard, 1962), 256.

72. Brown, *Leibniz*, 177. A major thesis of Brown's book is that in the Leibnizian system physics should derive from the divine perfections, but that in fact Leibniz drew the content for his perfections from natural philosophers and from the things that they were discovering empirically.

73. "Dieu a choisi celuy qui est le plus parfait"; hence "celuy qui est en même temps le plus simple en hypotheses et le plus riche en phenomenes" (*Discours*, par. 6).

ims for the practice of science.[74] There are exceptions, of course: postulating God does explain why maxims such as the law of parsimony or the PSR should be true of the world and not merely crutches that scientists cannot otherwise dispense with. But before taking such explanatory proposals seriously, one would first have to convince philosophers of science that their methodologies require not only pragmatic or instrumental but also metaphysical justification — no easy task.[75] Even if one could make this case, the resultant explanations would not really guide science in the manner that Descartes attempted to do in the *Principles* with his appeals to the omnipotence and omniscience of God (see chapter 2 above).

Philosophical theology could make a stronger case for its indispensability to science if it were able to provide concrete parameters or if it entailed specific scientific positions. But — even were it possible — this is a role theology should not play. As even a cursory examination of the history of science shows, it is deadly to shackle empirical research in advance to a priori principles. Leibniz's failure to base natural science in a theology of perfection thus rightly ended a phase in Western philosophy that had dominated, and harmed, science since its origins in the pre-Socratics. This is not to say that theology no longer has anything to offer the scientist. But after Leibniz the division of labor has become increasingly sharp. Metaphysics has now come (rightly) to serve other functions for science, representing a source of scientific models and metaphors, helping to justify the regulative principles that scientific practice presupposes, and expressing the goal (rather than the reality) of a comprehensive or global explanation for our experience of the world.

Perfection and Neoplatonism

There should be no surprise about the source of the concepts of perfection that we have been examining. The overall picture of perfection that has emerged, and the general use to which Leibniz puts it, is in close continuity with the tradition of reflection on perfection that we examined in chapter 3. In that chapter I showed that an unbroken line leads from at least Plotinus via Pseudo-Dionysius to early medieval thinkers such as John Erigena, through the Renais-

74. See Leroy E. Loemker, "The Metaphysical Status of Regulative Maxims in Leibniz and Kant," *Southern Journal of Philosophy* 11 (1973): 141-47.

75. Interestingly, however, there has been some movement in this direction. Think, for example, of the "top down" approach to scientific explanation in Philip Kitcher, "Explanatory Unification and the Causal Structure of the World," in Kitcher and Wesley C. Salmon, eds., *Scientific Explanation*, Minnesota Studies in the Philosophy of Science 13 (Minneapolis: Univ. of Minnesota Press, 1989), 410-505.

sance rediscovery of the Neoplatonic thinkers (and of the Hermetic tradition)[76] to Nicholas of Cusa and Bruno, and on into the early modern period in the work of Descartes, the Cambridge Platonists, and now Leibniz.

What is most noteworthy about Leibniz is the degree to which he followed out the implications of the perfection tradition in Western thought to their logical conclusion. As Lovejoy has shown in his well-known *Great Chain of Being,* Leibniz inherited the basic outline of the Principle of Plenitude and the PSR.[77] He then brought it to its fullest formulation: "Everything is a plenum in nature; . . . everything is connected *(lié)* because of the plenitude of the world."[78] The divine perfections require an infinite degree of continuity in the world. The scale of perfection, derived and leading downward from God, must be unbroken:

> All the different classes of beings which taken together make up the universe are, in the idea of God who knows distinctly their essential gradations, only so many ordinates of a single curve, [and they are] so closely united that it would be impossible to place others between any two of them, *since that would imply disorder and imperfection.* . . . And, since the law of continuity requires that when the essential attributes of one being approximate those of another all the properties of the one must likewise gradually approximate those of the other, it is necessary that all the orders of natural beings form but a single chain, in which the various classes, like so many rings, are so closely linked one to another that it is impossible for the senses or the imagination to determine precisely the point at which one ends and the next begins.[79]

76. The later influence, and its nature, has been conclusively demonstrated by Frances Yates, *Giordano Bruno and the Hermetic Tradition* (London: Routledge and Kegan Paul, 1964). Yates stresses particularly the role of Ficino as a predecessor to Bruno (chaps. 2, 4).

77. Arthur O. Lovejoy, *The Great Chain of Being: A Study of the History of an Idea* (Cambridge: Harvard Univ. Press, 1957), esp. chap. 5. The Renaissance background of the principle of plenitude is masterfully traced in chap. 4.

78. "Principes de la Nature et de la Grace" (1714), par. 3 (G 6:598-99): "Tout est plein dans la nature; . . . à cause de la plénitude du Monde tout est lié."

79. Letter of Leibniz to Varignon on the principle of continuity; published in Ernst Cassirer, ed., *Leibniz: Hauptschriften zur Grundlegung der Philosophie* (Hamburg: Felix Meiner, 1966), vol. 2 (PhB 108), 558; German trans., 77-78: "toutes les différentes classes des Etres, dont l'assemblage forme l'Universe, ne sont dans les idées de Dieu, qui connoit distinctement leurs gradations essentielles, que comme autant d'Ordonnées d'une même Courbe, dont l'union ne souffre pas qu'on en place d'autres entre deux, *à cause que cela marqueroit du desordre et de l'imperfection.* . . . Or puisque la loi de la Continuité exige, que, quand les déterminations essentielles d'un Etre se rapprochent de celles d'un autre, qu'aussi en conséquence toutes les propriétés du premier doivent s'approcher graduellement de celles

As the italicized words show, the principle of perfection necessitates the hierarchy or scale of being, its source in a perfect being, and its infinite complexity and unbroken continuity.

The Perfect God

Now I will summarize the theistic side of the Leibnizian system from the perspective of the theory of perfection as it has emerged in the analysis up to this point. The primary definition of God in Leibniz's work is *l'Etre parfait*. God's being is in the first place defined through its perfection. If there is such a thing as a perfect being (or a perfect source of being), it must be conceptually first: "the ultimate reason for the reality of essences as well as existences [is] in one being, which must necessarily be greater, higher, and *prior* to the world itself."[80] We can come to know the content of this perfection, according to Leibniz, through a process similar to continuous variation in arithmetic: perfection is the optimalization or high point of a continuous variation, at least in those cases where the variation allows for a highest possible term (e.g., greatest power but not greatest number). Since individual perfections are simple they cannot conflict (i.e., they must be compossible); hence one being could possess them all. As the optimalization of all possible perfections, the *ens perfectissimum* would be the source for all, the standard for all, and would encompass all. The perfect in this sense is the absolute, and the imperfect is the relative.

The God of the monotheistic traditions, then, is ultimately to be understood as the Absolute. There can be only one God, for it is not possible to admit two fully perfect beings. Hence all other beings must be dependent on him. He is the necessary being; hence the others must be contingent beings, that is, ontologically derivative, receiving their being from God.

On the one hand, the notion of perfection that Leibniz drew on for his perfect-being theology was a rich and conceptually well-developed one. As we have seen, he could appeal to considerations of necessity and contingency, of simplicity, of optimality, of harmony, of ultimate rationality, of reality, as well as to moral, aesthetic, and natural scientific considerations. Through the pre-

---

du dernier, il est nécessaire, que tous les ordres des Etres naturels ne forment qu'une seule chaîne, dans laquelle les différentes classes, comme autant d'anneaux, tiennent si étroitement les unes aux autres, qu'il est impossible aux sense et à l'imagination de fixer précisement le point, où quelqu'une commence, ou finit."

80. "Ita ergo habemus ultimam rationem realitatis tam essentiarum quam existentiarum in uno, quod utique Mundo ipso majus, superius anteriusque esse necesse est" (G 7:305).

cept that "where there are no limits, that is, in God, perfection is absolutely infinite,"[81] the theoretical strengths of infinity theory could be used to supply what perfection lacks. On the other hand, linking the nature of God completely to the fate of the perfection idea opens the philosophical theologian up to dangers as well. I have questioned the adequacy of the theistic proof from perfection, for example, as well as many of the major formulations of this notion in Leibniz's thought. At this point, at least, we have reason to be suspicious about whether the concept of perfection — even in Leibniz, where its conceptual resources have been more fully explored than in any other modern thinker — is able to accomplish the tasks in philosophical theology for which it has been employed.

Infinity

At the end of the seventeenth century the infinite was in the air. In chapter 3 we traced its role in the history of philosophical theology, especially in the tradition running through Cusa, Bruno, and Descartes. With the advent of the infinitesimal calculus by Leibniz and Newton, the infinite took on an expanded role in geometry and natural philosophy. After the introduction of the telescope and microscope, the sheer size of the universe, and its apparently infinite detail, struck home in a new way. The gradual abandonment of the geocentric picture of the universe in favor of a heliocentric (or even noncentered) view — in which the earth was only one of many planets, our sun perhaps only one of many suns, and (for Bruno) the Christian savior perhaps only one of many saviors — brought home the immensity of the universe and the smallness of humanity's place within it.[82] Leibniz realized that if a unitary worldview were to be defended, with a coherent place for God, humans, and world, it would have to be based on a convincing, and adequately comprehensive, theory of the infinite (hence, e.g., his claim that his metaphysics is completely mathematical, or could become so).[83]

It should therefore come as little surprise that Leibniz gives the infinite so large a place in his philosophy.[84] More unexpected are the limitations that he

81. "Et là, où n'y a point de bornes, c'est à dire en Dieu, la perfection est absolument infinie" (*Monad.* par. 41)

82. This transition is effectively presented in Hans Blumenberg, *The Genesis of the Copernican World,* trans. Robert M. Wallace (Cambridge: MIT Press, 1987).

83. Letter to de l'Hospital, 27.12.1694; M 2:258: "Ma metaphysique est toute mathematique pour dire ainsi ou la pourroit devenir."

84. E.g., the claim to Sophie in 1696 letter to her: "Mes méditations fondamentales

places on the concept; because these are surprising, they must play an important role in interpreting Leibniz. He holds, for instance, that the idea of an infinite number is absurd, a completed infinite demonstration is unthinkable (even for God), and infinitesimals are mere fictions. I suggest that epistemic limitations such as these are best explained by the hypothesis that Leibniz's is a basically theological notion of infinity, drawn at least initially from God's nature. The true infinite is the Absolute. As such it is the first principle and the source for all else: "it is precisely by modifying it that one limits oneself and forms a finite" (*NE* 158). The reason for this last conclusion is that the Absolute qua true infinite "precedes all composition and is not formed by the addition of parts" (*NE* 157).[85]

All other quantities or states — finite, immense but not infinite, the infinitesimal as the limit case of smallness — are then defined in contrast to the true infinite. In classical terms, the order of derivation corresponds to the *ordo essendi*. In the order of knowledge, Leibniz asserts, we can conceive the infinite through a progressive approximation (in a sense that the mathematical calculus states with complete precision), without ever knowing it in itself. This yields an interesting balance between the traditional *via eminentia*, which provides some knowledge of God, and the final unknowability of the divine. As Cohn rightly notes, "Leibniz's system is perhaps the most brilliant attempt to build a consistent philosophical line of thought upon the uncompromising assertion of the infinite, without denying the incomprehensibility of a completed infinite."[86]

I suggest that there are, implicitly, three levels to Leibniz's theory of infinity. The lowest is Descartes's *indefinitum*, the quantity that is greater than any that we can name; Leibniz preferred the term *immensum*. This notion derives from "the thought of likeness" or sameness (*NE* 158). The second is the idea of "largest in its species." For instance, the greatest extension is space as a whole; the greatest in series (*successorum*) is eternity. Even this level takes on an explicitly theological meaning, as Leibniz interprets each of the attributes of God as largest in its species. For instance, "the idea of the absolute, applied to space, is

---

roulent sur deux choses, sçavoir sur l'unité et sur l'infini" (see Onno Klopp, *Correspondance de Leibniz avec l'electrice Sophie de Brunswick-Lunebourg*, q.v.).

85. Note that these are comments that one might well have found in Nicholas of Cusa or Bruno, and that are fully consistent with Descartes's views on the infinite as we saw them in the last chapter. Hermann Brunnhofer (*Giordano Brunos Lehre vom Kleinsten als die Quelle der Prästabilirten Harmonie von Leibntz* [Rauert & Rocco, 1890]) shows that Leibniz drew directly from Bruno at the crucial points of his argument.

86. Jonas Cohn, *Geschichte des Unendlichkeitsproblems im abendländischen Denken bis Kant* (Leipzig: W. Engelmann, 1896), 190. Loemker speaks more broadly of "the mathematical basis of [Leibniz's] concept of God and creation"; see his "Leibniz in Our Time," *Philosophische Rundschau* 13 (1965): 106.

just the idea of the immensity of God, and thus of other things" (ibid.). The third or highest level is the "itself All" *(ipsum omnia),* the one who as One is at the same time everything.[87] Interestingly, in taking over this threefold distinction, apparently from Spinoza's 29th letter, Leibniz pointedly omits Spinoza's references to infinite numbers or quantities. It is clear that, with the exception of God, he still wishes to deny actually infinite quantities in the world. This highest infinite, given its unitary quality, cannot be understood in itself; the closest we can get is grasping the infinite quality of its attributes.

In a different though better-known trichotomy, Leibniz distinguishes between the three senses in which parts can be (or not be) present in an infinite. The basic categories are the (merely) potential infinite, God as the actual infinite, and the impossible infinite. Respectively,

> there is a *syncategorematic* infinite or a passive power having parts — namely the possibility of further progression in dividing, multiplying, subtracting, and adding. There is also a *hypercategorematic* or potestative *(potestativum)* infinite, an active power having parts eminently, as it were, not formally or actually. This infinite is God himself. But there is no *categorematic* infinite, or one actually having infinite parts.[88]

The first is the indefinite, the (potential) possibility of endless division. In denying the third, Leibniz insures that God would have to be absolutely simple, because any distinctions within his being could not be actually infinite (and of course he cannot have finite parts). According to the second, God can only have parts eminently, which should imply that we can have knowledge of his being through the *via eminentia* alone. This turns any nonsimple analyses of the divine being into fictions, much as in the infinitesimal calculus. In himself, then, God must be undivided, absolute simplicity. As we will find, the epistemic limitation expressed by the third point will raise serious problems for Leibniz's view of God as he works to integrate the infinite and the perfect.

87. Fragment published by Gerhardt in *Sitzberichte der Berliner Akademie* (1889), 1077; trans. in Jonas Cohn, *Geschichte des Unendlichkeitsproblems,* 173. The reference is clearly to God as infinite, "denn er ist als Einer Alles; denn in ihm ist Alles enthalten, was zur Existenz aller Dinge nötig ist."

88. Leibniz's note to the letter to Des Bosses of 1/9/1706; G 2:314n: "Datur infinitum syncategorematicum seu potentia passiva partes habens, possibilitas scilicet ulterioris in dividendo, multiplicando, subtrahendo, addendo progressus. Datur et infinitum hypercategorematicum seu potestativum, potentia activa habens quasi partes, eminenter, non formaliter aut actu. Id infinitum est ipse Deus. Sed non datur infinitum categorematicum seu habens actu partes infinitas formaliter."

Infinity in Descartes and Leibniz

These two thinkers represent two of the major approaches to interpreting infinity: intuitionism and formalism, respectively.[89] The distinction between *ratio essendi* and *ratio cognoscendi,* between a descent of being and an intuitive ascent, which we found so important in Descartes, does not reappear in the same form in Leibniz. For the scale of being leading down from the infinite to the finite is no longer matched by an intuitive ascent back up to the infinite. Leibnizian formalism may not be purely mechanical (as some critics have said), but it certainly does not work by direct seeing or intuition. For Leibniz what is certain need not be what is evident; rather, certainty is provided by analytic definitions that *stand for* sensible signs or empirical sense data. Using this method, he replaces Descartes's immediate evidence with evidence derived from the formal analysis of statements. Because he converts empirical causal explanations into rational chains of interlinked signs, Leibniz (like Spinoza) can ascribe to the rationalist equation *causa siva ratio* (cause, that is, reason).

Much in Leibniz's position is thus incompatible with the Cartesian reliance on intuitions. The differences stem ultimately, I suggest, from their different approaches to the infinite. For instance, Leibniz's defense of the continuity of duration — a given "slice" of time has priority over the "parts" that compose it — contrasts sharply with Descartes's view of intuitions as punctiliar. Recall that in the *Meditations* each intuition is certain only in the present tense and as a distinct intuition. Even more important, as we will see, is Leibniz's acceptance of infinitesimals, which move in the opposite direction from Descartes's reflection on the greatest number and on the procession ad infinitum. The resources of the calculus allow Leibniz to develop a detailed analysis of what it is to be a whole with a (potentially) infinite number of parts, where Descartes could speak only of the indefinite and the limits of human knowledge.

In particular, the calculus allowed Leibniz to specify what it means to pass "to the limit." Passing to the limit (of the infinitely small or large) can be taken as either a fiction or a fact. For Leibniz it is in one sense a fiction, since the infinite is always one step beyond us; we never actually possess an infinite number or an infinite set of real parts. Hence God as the actually infinite remains always qualitatively different, always beyond finite comprehension. But in another sense one can pass to the infinite, insofar as the calculus provides a precise conceptual means for expressing the movement all the way down to the infinitely small. If one has a continuous series, Leibniz might say, consisting mostly of fi-

---

89. The authoritative comparison between them on this question remains Yvon Belaval, *Leibniz critique de Descartes* (Paris: Gallimard, 1960).

nite, rational numbers, and one has an equation that "contains" the series at least implicitly, why deny that one thinks the whole series in its equation, including its end point, zero or infinity? When Leibniz argues in this fashion regarding passing to the limit, he has in effect challenged the qualitative distinction between the finite and the infinite.

Leibniz also went far beyond Descartes in the analysis of contingency. For Descartes, contingency depends only on a choice made by God. In the Leibnizian system, however, it depends first on the nature of the analysis involved: something is contingent if its analysis is interminable. Thus only the divine understanding can determine compossibility, and even God cannot do so deductively but only through an immediate awareness of compossibility and in light of the principle of the greatest possible good. This gives rise, second, to Leibniz's compatibilist theory of freedom. As a result, he interprets the relation between the divine will and understanding differently: God may *choose* which world is the best, but this choice is *determined* by his (freely) being who he is; it is a "moral necessity." In short, though divine choice produces contingency for both thinkers, for Descartes God has to will in order to judge, whereas for Leibniz God has to judge first in order to will.[90]

The Infinitely Small

Infinitesimals are closely linked with the analysis of the concept of infinity, since they represent the infinitely small, just as an infinite integer would represent the infinitely large. Studying the one casts light on the nature of the other. Of course, the conceptual connection of the two had already been suggested by the tradition; recall the dual movement to the minimum and the maximum in Cusa's *De docta ignorantia*. That Leibniz was impressed by this two-sided limit of the finite is clear, for example, from his agreement with Pascal's 72nd *Pensée*, in which the latter paints human existence as "sustained between those two abysses of the Infinite and the Nothing [by which he means the infinitely small] . . . , a Nothing in comparison with the Infinite, an All in comparison with the Nothing, a mean between nothing and everything."[91] Leibniz's response is unambiguous: "What he [Pascal] says about the double infinity is only an entrée into my system."[92] The paragraphs that follow, some of the most

90. Ibid., 388-91.

91. Blaise Pascal, *Pensées: Thoughts on Religion and Other Subjects,* trans. William F. Trotter, ed. H. S. and Elizabeth B. Thayer (New York: Washington Square Press, 1965), 20-21.

92. Holz, ed., *Kleine Schriften,* 373ff.: "Ce qu'il vient de dire de la double infinité n'est qu'une entrée dans mon systeme."

poetic in the Leibnizian opus, develop his theory of humankind directly out of the dual limits of the endlessly large and the endlessly small.

In some contexts Leibniz treats the infinitely small as an actual reality, and in others it remains merely a "well-founded phenomenon," that is, as in the case of the infinitesimals, a useful fiction. For instance, he tries to escape from "the labyrinth of the continuum" by positing the primacy of the continuum (the primacy of the whole): compared to a whole continuum, its parts have an only secondary status. Thus even though we clearly perceive slices of time (or portions of space), the whole of time is not built up out of its parts; rather, they are posited within it. Only as *phenomenal* realities can we speak of the infinitely small components of a given continuum. It follows that there can only be an infinitesimal (disappearingly small) difference between any two contiguous parts. Leibniz seems to make a direct transition from these mathematical observations to metaphysics: infinite numbers of monads exist, with infinitesimal differences between them; each monad has infinite perceptions, varying infinitesimally; each monad is itself composed of an infinite number of parts. Not only must there be no vacuums, but each portion of space must be as full as it can (com)possibly be. For only such an infinitely rich world would reflect the infinite power of its creator, as Bruno, Descartes, and Spinoza had also argued.

The Leibnizian system therefore advocates actual infinites with a vengeance, even while it maintains that no number or demonstration can comprehend them. Why this defense of actual infinites on Leibniz's part, when so much of the tradition had followed Aristotle in rejecting their existence? Reasons include seventeenth-century developments in astronomy and microscopy, the newly found mathematical resources for thinking disappearingly small quantities, and Leibniz's intellectual adherence to the Platonic/Neoplatonic tradition with its greater openness to actual infinites. I suggest, however, that it is ultimately a position he was compelled to by the principle of sufficient reason. Recall that the PSR requires not only a reason for everything that exists, but also some ontological basis for everything that we think or perceive. Now we find that thought can divide without limit; between any two geometrical points we can imagine a third; and we can divide with the mind beyond all countability. It follows that the world must be at least as rich as our thought; each identifiable unit must in turn be composed of innumerable smaller units (monads). Hence there must be actual infinities.

Somewhat inconsistently, Leibniz has more reservations about infinite size than about infinitesimals. It is clear that the extension of the world should be infinite under his theory: if it were finite, we would have to think of it as bordered (limited) within a larger space, which would mean already to have thought beyond these limits. Moreover, Leibniz cannot view everything that exists as floating around within a larger receptacle, since (against Newton) he has insisted on the ultimate phenomenality of space. Still, he insists, we cannot think infinite space; all we can think is indefinite extension beyond the highest we can count: the Cartesians "have some reason for replacing the term 'infinite' by 'indefinite', for there is never an infinite whole in the world, though there are always wholes greater than others *ad infinitum*" (*NE* 150-51).

The picture of the infinite just sketched amounts, I believe, to an at least credible metaphysical position. Still, Leibniz faced certain difficulties with the realist interpretation of infinitesimals and generally chose (wisely, I think) to support the view that they were mathematical fictions. (Given the newness of the concept, and the Aristotelian proclivities of his age, he would otherwise probably not have won acknowledgment of their mathematical usefulness.) If infinitesimals are defined in terms of the operation of passing to the limit, they seem to represent an "entity" that thought could never grasp. As one contemporary of Leibniz quipped, infinitesimals are what one supposedly obtains when one tries to stop the act of disappearing at the very moment when something is passing out of existence.[93] The difficulties in conceiving something that (as Berkeley complained) never changes the size of anything when it is added to or subtracted from it are certainly considerable. In fact, it was not until Weierstrass's introduction of the concept of constancy (*Stetigkeitsbegriff*) that the resources became available to make sense of these entities that were not determinate things at all.

These reservations notwithstanding, in his metaphysics Leibniz sided boldly with actual infinites. He may have equivocated a bit on the ontological status of the infinitesimals, but the push of his system (and his explicit statements on the infinite composition of monads) certainly should have led him to interpret them realistically as well. With this conceptual development the theory of infinity reached a new stage in contrast to Descartes: mathematics began to admit quantities that one can think (and symbolize) but can no longer grasp by means of spatial intuitions. Leibniz recognized the need to leave intuition behind; only purely intellectual apprehension would be adequate, for it alone "envelopes the consideration of the infinite and is thereby stretched to the limits of what the imagination can attain."[94] Of course, once one grants the meta-intuitive nature of the theory of the mathematical infinite, one must ask what this will mean for the theory of the metaphysical infinite, where formal consis-

93. Contemporary difficulties are nicely summarized by Belaval, *Leibniz critique de Descartes*, 329-68.

94. M 5:307: It "enveloppe la considération de l'infini et s'éloigne par conséquent de ce que l'imagination peut atteindre."

tency alone is not sufficient. Clearly metaphysics cannot remain satisfied with symbol systems whose ontological claims remain uninterpreted; but does it have the resources to interpret these claims?

Infinity and Contingency

As is well known, Leibniz held that universal determinism is consistent with contingency in the world; since humans are contingent, they are free and hence morally responsible. Leibniz was thus a *compatibilist*, because he held moral responsibility to be compatible with the fact that everything is in the end determined. The key to his compatibilism is, once again, the concept of infinity.[95] We should briefly consider three of his arguments for this position for the light they shed on his philosophical theology.[96]

The first argument holds that what a contingent being will do is not demonstrable, even by God. Only necessary truths can be demonstrated by analyzing them into their logically basic terms so that equivalencies can be constructed.

> In contingent truths, however, though the predicate inheres in the subject, we can never demonstrate this, nor can the proposition ever be reduced to an equation or an identity. Instead, the analysis proceeds to infinity, only God being able to see, not the end of the analysis indeed, since there is no end, but the nexus of terms or the inclusion of the predicate in the subject, since he sees everything which is in the series. (ibid., L 265)

As Catherine Wilson points out, it is by this means that Leibniz hoped to reconcile divine omniscience with human freedom. God can immediately see the whole series, for example, the infinite number of components contained in the complete concept of Socrates. He sees it "by an infallible vision" — one could only say, by an intuition of essences. Yet even though God knows what I will do

---

95. Leibniz acknowledges this explicitly: "a new and unexpected light arose at last, however, where I least expected it, namely, from mathematical considerations of the nature of the infinite" (L 264). This and the following quotations come from the important essay "On Freedom," in Foucher de Careil, ed., *Nouvelles lettres et opuscules inédites de Leibniz* (Paris, 1857), 178-85, translated in L and AG. Cf. "On Freedom and Possibility" (Grua 287-91; AG 19-23).

96. A fourth argument — that humans are free because their existence is contingent, that is, God might not have created them — will occupy us in another context. I omit it here because it equivocates between the contingency of a person as a whole and the contingency of a given action given the person's existence.

225

tomorrow, he cannot demonstrate it, "for this would involve a contradiction." It would take an infinite amount of time actually to complete an infinitely long demonstration; God can therefore not predict any action that I will commit before I actually carry it out. But if an omniscient being cannot know any of my actions in advance (and much less a normal knower!), then, Leibniz thought, my actions must be free. The underlying principle here seems to be that an action is free (sufficient condition) if it cannot possibly be predicted, and that this condition is fulfilled for most, if not all, of the actions of contingent beings.

The second argument holds that we are free because our actions are not determined by any cause outside us. No one chooses Judas's essence — who he will be, and hence what he will do — not even God. Each individual is an eternal possibility, God not having created the eternal essences but only having selected the best compossible group of them. It follows that God is not responsible for whatever imperfections or sins the creatures reveal. In fact, only the creature can be responsible, for "his original limitation or imperfection is the source of his wickedness [and] his evil will is the soul cause of his misery."[97] I grant that such an eternal and essential determinism might be sufficient to relieve God of responsibility for human sin. It does not, however, suffice to show that each human whose essence is eternally determined in this way is therefore responsible.

The third argument, frequently repeated by Leibniz, turns on our lack of knowledge of the future. We do not (and cannot) know what we will do in the future, and therefore cannot be influenced by this knowledge. So when faced with a decision, we are free to respond according to our nature or volition. But this last argument, even more clearly than the first two, reveals the limitations in the Leibnizian argument from infinity to contingency (and on to freedom and moral responsibility). Put critically, Leibniz considers humans to be free as subjects because they lack certain items of information, namely, knowledge of the outcome of future "free" choices. But is a subjective lack of knowledge really sufficient? In every case the outcome is fully determined and fully known by an infallible knower, God. Here infinity theory seems to be of little help: why should it be relevant to the freedom question whether God can demonstrate a future "free" decision in advance? Whether by demonstration or not, he infallibly knows the outcome of the "decision," and knows that it follows in a determinate fashion from each person's essence. The third argument, then, could provide at best only a subjective sense of freedom rather than ground a doctrine of real freedom.

97. "Sa limitation ou imperfection originale est la source de sa malice, [et] sa mauvaise volonté est la seule cause de sa misere" (*Theod.*, par. 167).

Infinity and Neoplatonism

There are significant parallels between infinity in Leibniz and in the Neoplatonic tradition.[98] In both it characterizes the pinnacle of the hierarchy of beings, the absolutely unlimited telos of the philosophical ascent. In both the infinite is known not qua infinite but only through those of its positive qualities of which we are aware. And what we know are those aspects of the highest One that are already part of our being as emanations from it.

It is where Leibniz wants to bring together the infinity and the perfection of God that he most needs Neoplatonic categories; his atomistic theory of perfection is of little help here. Thus when he turns to explain God's absolute perfection in the *Monadology* Leibniz switches to the definition of perfection as "the magnitude [*grandeur*] of positive reality."[99] How can we think this *grandeur* with sufficient greatness? Only by "setting aside the limits or boundaries of those things that have them." The image in the French *(en mettant à part les limites ou bornes)* is that of designating within something its various parts so that the core of the matter can emerge more clearly (in this case, the absolutely unlimited). But once we have begun to move beyond all limits or determinations, there can be only one outcome: "here, where there are no limits, that is, in God, *perfection is absolutely infinite*" (emphasis mine).[100] The move to the highest being, the One beyond all distinctions, is of course a central thesis in Plotinus's *Enneads*.[101]

Sometimes the parallels are remarkably close.[102] If Leibniz begins with something like the fully infinite One of Neoplatonism, then one would expect to find all finite things possessing, by participation, portions of the essence of the One. And so it is. He argues, for example, that "each substance has something of the infinite insofar as it involves its cause, God, that is, it has some trace *(vestigium)* of omniscience and omnipotence."[103] In a famous passage in the

---

98. See the excellent article by George MacDonald Ross, "Leibniz and Renaissance Neoplatonism," *Studia Leibnitiana Supplementa* 23 (1983): 125-34.

99. "La grandeur de la réalité positive" (*Monad.*, par. 41).

100. "Et là, où il n'y a point de bornes, c'est à dire en Dieu, la perfection est absolument infinie."

101. E.g., "The totality of things must come after the One, because the One itself has no determinate form. It simply is one, while Nous is what in the realm of Being constitutes the totality of things. Thus, the One is not any of the things that Nous contains. It is only the source from which all of them are derived" (Plotinus, *Enneads* 5.1.7).

102. May, "God of Leibniz," 506-28 (esp. 521ff.), provides a long and persuasive list of parallels, including Leibniz's views on monads, on creation, and on causality. He appeals to the medieval Neoplatonic writing, *Liber de causis,* as a likely source for many of the commonalities.

103. "Unaquaeque substantia habet aliquid infiniti, quatenus causam suam, DEUM, involvit, nempe aliquod omniscientiae et omnipotentiae vestigium" (G 7:311).

Systeme nouveau de la nature he speaks of the much greater perfection of minds over other souls, calling them "little gods."[104] The "rays of divine light" emanating from the infinite constitute the monads as themselves (at least partly) divine. Being finite, they are different from God; yet because they exist through participation in God, they are divine.

One might object that the fact of parallels with Neoplatonism — which we also explored in the section on perfection — is a mere historical curiosity. However, when one turns to disputed questions such as the part/whole relation, and especially when one attempts a final judgment on whether Leibniz succeeds in his pluralism of substances or falls back into inconsistency, one discovers that the Neoplatonic influences play a decisive role. But first I should summarize.

The Infinite God

In his theory of the infinite God, Leibniz attempts to do what the tradition had sought after: to balance the quantitative (comparative) aspects of infinity with the negation implied in the prefix *in-*. He manages to think infinity much more thoroughly than Descartes, yet (in general) without denying the difference of degree between the divine being and created being:

> His intention is not at all to underestimate the distance of the finite from the infinite, for the divine infinity is not a quantitative infinite; it is the infinity of perfection, the absolute. . . . Thus the difference in degree becomes a difference in nature. This is precisely the role of participation: to make the two of them at once resemble one another while remaining completely different.[105]

Recall that Descartes's God, because infinite, could never be fully known as such, even if we can attain some idea of who he is through our own powers of reason. By contrast, we will find in chapter 7 that for Spinoza the infinity of God/nature will actually become the ground for his knowability. Leibniz occupies an interesting — and according to his opponents, untenable — middle position between the two. He is willing to call some infinites thinkable, as in thinking an infinite series by means of its function.[106] Yet God remains infi-

---

104. "Estant comme des petits Dieux au prix d'elles, faits à l'image de Dieu, et ayant en eux quelque rayon des lumieres de la Divinité" (G 4:479).

105. Jacques Jalabert, *Le Dieu de Leibniz* (Paris: Presses Universitaires de France, 1960), 222.

106. See Leibniz's reading notes on Spinoza's theory of the infinite at G 1:135.

nitely far beyond anything we could know. He is not the highest element in a series of increasing quantity, but stands qualitatively apart from any series that we can identify. Is Leibniz able to preserve the strengths of both his major modern predecessors in the theology of infinity?

Leibniz's notes on Spinoza's theory of the infinite introduce a division within the theory of infinity that is indeed crucial for thinking the infinite God: that between quantity and quality. Quality is not essentially a comparative or relational concept, Leibniz argues, but has to do with what is one or absolute, whereas quantity involves the repeated adding together of similars in the case of things that are specifiable or limited.[107] Quantity is known through co-presence, quality through itself alone. The key to Leibniz's theological appropriation of infinity, I suggest, was *to conceive quantity always within the context of quality,* thereby showing its limitations and relativizing it as a category. Infinite quantity, then, is only a matter of speaking, a sort of analogy.[108] This allowed him to say that there are no actually infinite quantities whereas there are actually infinite qualities (and an *ens perfectissimum* that possesses them). The same theory helped, moreover, to specify the status of infinitesimals as fictions, and to locate an autonomous but limited mechanism (viz. Leibniz's physics) within the context of the overarching teleology of the universe. In short, the quantity/quality distinction provided the means for Leibniz to appropriate and systematically develop the notion of an infinite God as encompassing (yet different from) the finite world.

The result is thoroughly theological. There are admittedly multiple reasons why Leibniz does not want to admit a *totum infinitum,* or actual infinites in the world. Some of his reasons are Aristotelian, for example, because a finite length (of space or of time) could not be composed of an infinite number of extended parts. But others are explicitly theological: "the actual infinite is perhaps the Absolute itself, which is not composed of parts, but which comprehends *(comprehendit)* in itself the things that have parts within a huge relation and in certain respects according to the level of perfection."[109] In its first designation, the term *infinite* must be reserved for that which is One and Whole;

---

107. "Est autem Entis affectio (seu Modus) alia absoluta, quae dicitur Qualitas, alia respectiva, eaque vel rei ad partem suam, si habet, Quantitas, vel rei ad aliam rem, Relatio" ("Cum Deo," *Dissertatio de Arte Combinatoria,* G 4:35). Cf. M 7:19: "Qualitas autem est, quod in rebus cognosci potest cum singulatim observantur."

108. "Cum scilicet plura adsunt, quam ullo numero comprehendi possunt, numerum tamen illis rebus attribuemus analogice, quem infinitum appellamus" (M 5:389).

109. Letter to Bernoulli, 7/6/1698 (M 3/2:499): "Reale infinitum fortasse est ipsum absolutum, quod non ex partibus conflatur, sed partes habentia, eminenti ratione et velut gradu perfectionis comprehendit." Cf. Cohn, *Geschichte des Unendlichkeitsproblems,* 189.

once this metaphysical cornerstone is in its conceptual place, we can introduce another term (Descartes's *indéfini*, Leibniz's *immense*) to represent quantities that are uncountable or can be increased endlessly.

All of this represents an increased analytic rigor over Descartes's attempt to mediate by means of the indefinite. The Cartesian notion was epistemically agnostic: the extension of the world is indefinite because I can conceive no limits to it; still, it may actually be either infinite or limited in some way unknown to me. The indefiniteness idea thus left open the possibility that the world was in fact infinite (which would have made Descartes a proto-Spinozist!). Leibniz, by contrast, insisted that we have a positive notion (not just an intuition) of the infinite and showed why it is necessary for thinking the finite, indeed for thinking quantity in general.[110]

By moving from the theory of proportions to the concept of a true continuum, Leibniz was able to develop new resources for thinking the transition from finite to infinite quantities. We could thus say that Descartes comprehended infinity primarily through negation, that is, as an indefinite object capable of receiving determinations but incapable of being the source of determinations. By contrast, Leibniz conceived the infinite positively and (at least in his theology) as itself an activity of spirit rather than merely as an object of thought. Yet he did so at the cost of making the notion of the infinite completely dependent on an adequate theory of perfection in the world.

With this perfection-based method for thinking the infinite God Leibniz moved much closer to a theory of the Absolute, that is, a theory of something absolutely unconditioned that is at the same time the source (and explanation) for all else that exists. This explains why, in contrast to Descartes, he tried to develop the logic of his absolute into a doctrine of creation, in which the absolutely perfect being must actualize the fullest (most infinite) and most perfect possible world. One needs the theory of the infinite in mathematics and physics because the author of nature is himself infinite.[111] Once in the world, the infi-

---

110. So also Belaval, *Leibniz critique de Descartes*, 361: "Descartes ne pouvait comprendre l'infini que *per limitationis negationem*, donc comme un *objet indéfini* capable de *recevoir* des déterminations, mais incapable d'en être la source. En contraste, Leibniz conçoit positivement l'infini tout autant comme activité de l'esprit que comme objet de la pensée, encore cet objet exprime-t-il à sa manière le dynamisme de l'intelligible: dés lors, en sa limitation, notre entendement embrasse l'infini. . . . A l'intuition cartésienne se substitue la *cogitatio caeca*." Compare the letter to Varignon of 2/2/1702: "il m'a paru, que l'infini pris à la rigueur doit avoir sa source dans l'interminé, sans quoy je ne voy pas moyen de trouver un fondement propre à le discerner du fini" (M 4:91).

111. "Parce que le caractère de l'Auteur infini entre ordinairement dans les opérations de la nature" (M 5:308).

nite establishes the connection (via the PSR) between the infinite numbers of monads and the infinite perceptions of each. We will come back in a moment to the difficulties inherent in this project. For now it is clear at least that Leibniz has attained what Kant calls the true transcendental concept of infinity — and thereby brought the theory of the infinite face-to-face, perhaps for the first time, with the obstacle of the first antinomy.[112]

LEIBNIZ BETWEEN ATOMISM AND MONISM

We have considered Leibniz's extended theory of the infinite and perfect God; it is time now to turn to an explicit evaluation of the resultant system. Although a number of areas in this philosophical theology could be singled out as unsatisfactory, careful analysis points unambiguously to one particular area of recurrent problems and ambiguities: the tensions between Leibniz's atomism and his theory of perfection.

The Creator God and Other Monads

We begin with the question of the relationship of God to the world. Bertrand Russell was not the first to maintain that Leibniz was unsuccessful in preserving the theistic side of his metaphysics, though he has perhaps given the criticism its most succinct expression: "A monism is necessarily pantheistic, and a monadism, when it is logical, is as necessarily atheistic."[113] Russell takes it to be obvious that Leibniz's theism is a complete failure; the only question is why he would have tried to preserve theism in the first place when it is so utterly at odds with his monadism as a whole. I thus divide the evaluation into a section on God and other monads and a section devoted to the explicit examination of the monism objection.

Under this first heading two thematic areas in particular will occupy our attention: the manner in which Leibniz hopes to individuate the monads from one another and from God, and, in the context of their relation to God as the highest monad, the question of the nature and significance of Leibniz's doctrine of creation.

---

112. Belaval, *Leibniz critique de Descartes,* 275.
113. Russell, *Critical Exposition,* 172.

Creation versus Emanation

In light of Leibniz's apparent concern to avoid monism by remaining thoroughly theistic, one would expect to find an unambiguous doctrine of creation in which God freely creates a world of independent substances. If Leibniz holds, by contrast, that the world is an emanation of God, it is harder to see how he could advocate a classic doctrine of creation outside the divine.

Yet in at least four areas one finds signs that Leibniz did not hold to the traditional Christian doctrine of creation. (1) He speaks explicitly of the "emanation" of the world from God. A famous passage in the *Discours* argues that "created substances depend on God, who preserves them and who even produces them continually by a kind of emanation, *just as we produce our thoughts*" (emphasis mine).[114] In the *Monadology* he maintains that the monads "are generated, so to speak, by continual fulgurations of the divinity."[115] In the *Theodicy* Leibniz speaks of God preventing suffering "insofar as the perfection of the universe, which is an emanation *(ecoulement)* from him, permits it."[116] (2) Leibniz plays with the eternality of the world in a series of letters to Bourguet late in his life. At least once during the correspondence he paints the world as beginning without any need for God: "The concourse of all the tendencies toward good has produced the best, but because some goods are not compatible with others, the concourse and the result may entail the destruction of some good, and as a result some evil."[117] (3) At numerous points in Leibniz's opus the world's creation seems to be necessary.[118] (4) The question, finally, is whether the world is *in* God or takes on an existence separate from him. Because Leibniz has thought through the implications of God's infinite perfection more fully than most previous thinkers, he pushes at the limits of orthodoxy:

---

114. "Les substances creées dependent de Dieu qui les conserve et même qui les produit continuellement par une maniere d'emanation, comme nous produisons nos pensées" (*Discours*, par. 14).

115. They are "naissent . . . par des Fulgurations continuelles de la Divinité" (par. 47).

116. "Autant que la perfection de l'univese, qui est un ecoulement de la sienne, le peut permettre" (par. 167).

117. G 3:558: "Le concours de toutes les tendences au bien a produit le meilleur: mais comme il y a des biens qui sont incompatibles ensemble, ce concours et ce resultat peut emporter la destruction de quelque bien, et par consequent quelque mal." In the same volume cf. 572, 582, 591, 595; e.g., "Autrement il faudroit avouer que Dieu auroit fait quelque chose sans raison, ce qui étant une absurdité, il faudroit recourir à l'eternité du Monde" (2/7/1716; 595).

118. See the following section. Also see, e.g., R. C. Sleigh, *Leibniz and Arnauld: A Commentary on Their Correspondence* (New Haven: Yale Univ. Press, 1990).

this supreme substance which is unique, universal, and necessary must be incapable of limits and must contain as much reality as is possible, insofar as there is nothing outside it which is independent of it. . . . God is absolutely perfect — *perfection* being nothing but the magnitude of positive reality considered as such, setting aside the limits of bounds in the things which have it. And here, where there are no limits, that is, in God, perfection is absolutely infinite. (*Monad.* pars. 40-41, AG 218)

When one adds all this together — the Leibnizian doctrines of perfection through participation, the hierarchy of essences according to perfection, the inherent striving of essences toward existence, and the claim that all essences are "contained" in the divine understanding — it is difficult to avoid the conclusion that the resultant view of the world lies somewhere between classical theism and monism.

One can only conclude that there is some vacillation in Leibniz's position here. He vehemently insists that he does not confuse God and creatures, and that God has freely created a world with infinite numbers of mental substances. But frequently repeating a desired consequence does not make it so; as we have just seen, traces of an emanation doctrine are also clearly present. Some critics have even argued that Leibniz uses his protestations of orthodoxy to cover a tendency in his thought that he does not want to be publicly recognized. That this is possible in principle is undeniable: we find ample evidence of other cases where he shielded his more controversial theses from his correspondents and the public. One can trace, for example, how he hid his doubts about extended substances from correspondents, allowing them only to emerge under pressure, as in 1687 with Arnauld and in 1704 with De Volder.[119] Such protective maneuvers led Bertrand Russell to distinguish an esoteric and an exoteric doctrine within Leibniz's writings. Could a similar dynamic be at work on the monism question? On the issue of creation versus emanation, where Leibniz's acknowledged fascination with monism (whether emanationist or Spinozistic) represented a clear and serious heresy in his day, one would most expect to find him taking care to disguise or deny any tendencies in this direction. Indeed, Catherine Wilson has been able to trace Leibniz's curious dialectic of emanationist leanings and cover-up, confirming his sincere desire to reject monism while revealing at the same time his fascination with this position.

Beyond the historical question, however, one must show why the monist

---

119. The case has often been made. One clear and concise presentation can be found in Loeb, *From Descartes to Hume,* 299ff.

position would be attractive according to Leibniz's own criteria. For one, if the world emanated from a highest being it would be easier to demonstrate that it is perfect: no choice would have led to its creation, but its own "objective perfection" would bring it into existence according to necessary laws. By contrast, to the extent that the theist emphasizes the element of choice, à la Descartes, arbitrariness (and hence imperfection) threaten to enter. The same sort of dynamic is at work in the issue of God's immanence. If God is immanent in the world, then the world's perfection is insured, as is its connection with God. The only cost is the loss of the ontological separateness of the world from God.

I conclude that the (Neoplatonic) doctrine of emanation represented a serious philosophical temptation for Leibniz, one that he did not always manage to resist. His philosophical intentions are, as they say, honorable; by and large he adheres to a classical doctrine of creation and to the choice of God to create. Yet Leibniz wishes to preserve in his new system all the advantages of monism (e.g., Spinozism) without falling into its impious errors.[120] He wishes to give God choice, which requires (a) that there are multiple possibles-but-not-actuals to choose from and (b) that God can make a choice in some real sense. He opposes Spinoza's claim in the *Oeuvres posthumes*[121] with his own stress on the voluntariness of God's choice.[122] Broader intentions notwithstanding, what Leibniz actually does is to rely on both creation and emanation. Creation cannot go if his thought is to remain theistic (and I have argued, pace Russell, that it is fundamentally theistic); emanation cannot go because it is linked with the striving of the possibles, with participation in God's perfection, with Being as Good, and with God's having a sufficient reason for "choosing" this world. In light of these factors, Stephen Erickson has even argued that "the view of creation most basic to Leibniz's thought is that of emanation accomplished by means of an act of divine self-limitation."[123]

120. This is one of Friedmann's central theses; see *Leibniz et Spinoza,* 170. Friedmann bases his case on Leibniz's response to the *Elucidarius* by Wachter, who had in turn been strongly influenced by Spinoza (published as the *Réfutation inédite de Spinoza par Leibniz,* ed. Foucher de Careil [Paris, 1854]). According to Friedmann, Leibniz was first confronted with the impious (pantheistic, kabbalistic) implications of Spinoza's thought through the work of Wachter. Leibniz then recognized the closeness of his own views to Spinoza's, and began to define his own position in conscious opposition to the author of the *Ethics.*

121. "Deum ea necessitate mundum producere qua se intelligit," letter 49.

122. See the comments on Spinoza's letter to Oldenburg: "Exemplum de operatione Dei qua se ipsum intelligit, non videtur appositum, quia id fit citra interventum volontatis" (1676; G 1:124n.1).

123. See Stephen A. Erickson, "Leibniz on Essence, Existence and Creation," *Review of Metaphysics* 18 (1965): 476-87, quotation 476. Erickson goes on to demonstrate the "panthe-

Unfortunately, reconciling these two concepts within one framework is no easy matter, and the evidence suggests that Leibniz failed to accomplish it. A solution would require that one think God as in the world he has created, as partially identical with it, yet at the same time as transcending it as its infinite creator — precisely the claim made by panentheism. This makes creation unavoidably dialectical, since it must preserve separateness in identity. An adequate theory would need to preserve strengths from the approaches of both Hegel and Cusa, perhaps the two most important philosophical models.[124] Hegel is without equal in rigorously thinking through the rational dialectic of unity-in-difference, but (perhaps as a result) fails to preserve the contingency and the mystery of the decision to create. Cusa, whose "dialectic" amounts to little more than the juxtaposition of God's immanence and transcendence (of pantheism and theism?), does manage to preserve that mystical both/and of creation and emanation. He therefore provides a good corrective to the "bad faith" of Leibniz's approach, in which emanation appears as a philosophical desideratum without being openly acknowledged and integrated. Leibniz's theory of the origination of things, corrected in the direction of Cusa, could do fuller justice to the God who both creates "within" himself and yet, qua infinite, re-

---

istic consequences" of this side of Leibniz's thought. Although Erickson's approach to reading Leibniz is questionable in the extreme — he randomly draws together sentences out of widely disparate phases and contexts of Leibniz's thought and draws "analytic" consequences that Leibniz would never countenance — he has still managed to put his finger on a vital dimension of the Leibnizian theory of creation.

There is another problem with Leibniz's idea of God. Recall that he allows no exceptions to his metaphysical principles, even for God. No monad can act on (have an effect on) another monad. God is the highest monad, the *monas monadum*. Hence, it should follow, God cannot have an effect on another monad; he cannot create one by an action. So creation cannot be a transitive act. The only consistent view for Leibniz, I think, is to subordinate creation to the doctrine of preestablished harmony. The "act" of creation would thus never be externalized, but would remain an immanent act of the divine will. (This is one of the main arguments of Jaques Jalabert's article, "Création et harmonie préétablie selon Leibniz," *Studia leibnitiana* 3 [1971]: 190-98, esp. 195-96.) God is such that it is part of his nature to be related to this particular world, and each existing monad has as part of its nature to be created by God. Of course, Leibniz would add, the monad's existence is only derivatively necessary; it involves not a metaphysical necessity but a divine choice and is thus in some sense contingent. Once again, it seems, the classical Christian doctrine of creation is not available to Leibniz. Of course he wants to say that God produces real things in creating. But again here it fits better with the logic of Leibniz's own position to say that the "things" never have been external to God at all.

124. I attempt such a theory in *God and Contemporary Science* (Edinburgh: Univ. of Edinburgh Press; Grand Rapids: Eerdmans, 1997).

mains infinitely beyond all the finite things that arise out of himself. But this is a task that we will not complete until chapter 9 below.

Creation as Choice or as Necessity?

In defending the orthodoxy of Leibniz's philosophy, Jalabert insists on the *freedom* of God's decision to create, and to create this particular world: "There is a moral determinism, the influence of a personal God — not a blind necessity, not a power realizing all its potentialities without choice."[125] Yet there is another side to Leibniz's position, paralleling (but not identical with) the emanationist leanings just considered, to which Jalabert's optimism does not do justice. This is the side of the striving possibles that "demand existence according to their degree of perfection." Existence seems here to be an automatic result of essence: "For all these possibles trying for existence within the understanding of God in proportion to their perfections, the result of all these strivings is the actual world, the most perfect that is possible."[126] The problem is that Leibniz describes the mechanisms of world production as in themselves sufficient to produce a world:

> It being once posited that being is better than not being, or that there is a reason why something rather than nothing should be, or that we must pass from the possible to the actual, it follows that, *even if nothing further is determined,* the quantity of existence must be as great as possible. . . . Although the world be not metaphysically necessary, or determined in such a way that its contrary implies a contradiction or a logical absurdity, it is nevertheless physically necessary, or determined in such a way that its contrary implies imperfection or moral absurdity. And as possibility is the principle of essence, so perfection or *the degree of essence* (through which the greatest number of things are compossible) *is the principle of existence.*[127]

125. Jalabert, *Le Dieu de Leibniz,* 220.

126. "Car tous les Possibles pretendant à l'existence dans l'endendement de Dieu, à proportion de leur perfections, le resultat de toutes ces pretensions doit d'être le Monde Actuel le plus parfait qui soit possible" (G 6:603, L 639).

127. "Ita posito semel ens praevalere non-enti, seu rationem esse cur aliquid potius extiterit quam nihil, sive a possibilitate transeundum esse ad actum, hinc, etsi nihil ultra determinetur, consequens est, existere quantum plurimum potest pro temporis locique . . . etsi enim Mundus non sit metaphysice necessarius, ita ut contrarium implicet contradictionem seu absurditatem logicam, est tamen necessarius physice vel determinatus ita ut contrarium implicet imperfectionem seu absurditatem moralem. Et ut possibilitas est principium Essentiae, ita perfectio seu Essentiae gradus (per quem plurima sunt

This doctrine suggests that Jalabert is wrong: the necessity may not be blind but it is no less necessary. No choice is required on God's part, only adequate powers of concentration — and perhaps not even that.

Leibniz appears to equivocate between these two positions on the origination of the world, which again raises both an interpretive problem and a philosophical task. Shall we take the two positions to represent an esoteric/exoteric distinction, with the true pantheism (or atheism) being carefully hidden from the public (B. Russell), or do they reflect competing tendencies within his own thought (C. Wilson, Erickson)? If we side with the latter interpretation (as I do), what philosophical lessons can we derive from the tension? I suggest, first, that attempts to provide a sufficient explanation for creation within philosophical theology lead inexorably to a necessitarian doctrine of creation. For if I can exhaustively list the principles that explain creation, that is, that answer the question why there is this world rather than another or none, then I have to that extent reduced the need for appeals to divine volition. Even when such explanations are given in terms of God's nature, they still entail that, given this perfect being, the world will follow. The only way that the role of God's choice would be maximized is for the philosophical explanatory effort to fail — or for it to place an inherent limitation on itself by postulating unexplainables (as in God's creation of the eternal truths in Cartesianism). If I am right about this dynamic, the PSR stands in an inherent tension with a doctrine of free creation.

Second, and more surprisingly, it appears that the principle of perfection is in tension with free creation as well. We saw in chapter 3 that the perfection tradition has often inclined toward the Neoplatonic theses of the world's participation in God and thus God's immanence in the world. In the Leibnizian system — where perfection plays a more central and determining role than in perhaps any other — the perfection of the world likewise works against allowing a gap between God and the world. To the extent that the world is not God, it is imperfect; only a theology of divine immanence, or at least a necessitarian doctrine of creation, can provide a perfect enough world for the requirements of an *ens perfectissimum*. That is, given God's nature as infinitely perfect, and given the consequent definitions of existence and essence in terms of degrees of perfection, it was better for God to create than not to create, and it was best for him to create the most perfect world. But what it is better for God to do he *must* do, at the risk of not being the best possible being. Calling this "moral necessity" does not make it any less compelling. Hence God must create the best possible world. Note, moreover, that the same notions of perfection that give con-

---

compossibilia) principium existentiae" (*De rerum originatione radicali* [L 7:304; AG 151], emphasis mine; translation modified, following Wiener).

tent to the idea of God and his actions also provide detailed criteria for the best possible world: it must exhibit a hierarchy of being; it must be full (principle of plenitude); there must be no gaps (principle of continuity). In short, *God must create this particular world.*

Suppose we find these consequences unacceptable, whether because internally inconsistent or because they conflict with other nonnegotiable premises. What must we change? Combining the two previous paragraphs, the answer can only be: reject the assumption that there is a sufficient reason, knowable by us, for all divine actions, and limit the role of perfection in theology. The latter requirement could be met, for example, by denying that perfection is the primary category for a metaphysics of divine being. Once the possibility is raised, one has no difficulty adding additional grounds for being skeptical about centering a contemporary philosophical theology on the perfection idea. For one, divine infinity encourages a level of agnosticism that is hard to reconcile with the exhaustive criteria listed in the previous paragraph. For another, perfection arguments raise (justified) fears that we will illicitly project culturally conditioned values onto what we are positing as infinite. Where later philosophers still speak of God's perfection at all, they generally prefer (and with warrant) to treat it as an entailment of other qualities held to be determinative of such a being, such as the structure of self-consciousness or (with Whitehead) the ability to respond.

Of course, when one begins to step away from perfection in this manner, one moves beyond Leibniz; in so doing, one begins to move beyond perfect-being theology. The move is justified: Leibniz, by bringing the perfection tradition within philosophical theology to its culmination, also revealed the inherent limitations in the concept. From this point on, philosophical theology must either pursue options other than the metaphysics of perfection, or conceive God primarily in terms of other concepts that bear closer scrutiny. In particular, I will argue in the remaining chapters that the notion of infinity reveals itself as an increasingly important resource for modern theology.

Divine Agency

Leaving aside Leibniz's theory of creation — where we have found that God has rather less to do than one might have thought — what other causal roles does his God play in the world? Leibniz does advocate a role for God in conserving the world, and he follows Descartes and the tradition in taking this to involve a sort of continuous creation moment by moment. Note that it is again only in Neoplatonic terms that Leibniz can speak of conservation as participation in being or in perfection, since individual essences themselves are eternal and independent from God. Individual things only need divine assistance in each moment because their being is not contained already in their concepts but is superadded to them by God — and even this is not necessary where Leibniz portrays essences as striving on their own toward (and into) existence.

Could Leibniz have recourse to direct divine agency, conceiving God as directing the world or intervening in a miraculous fashion? Although he grants such intervention in principle, his broader position (as he acknowledges) really rules it out. The *Discours* admits miracles, but only such as conform to the general order anyway (par. 7). Once again, it is precisely God's perfection that prevents him from action. For a really perfect creator would orchestrate things so well at the beginning that additional interventions would be unnecessary. According to Leibniz, we can call God's action providential or good only with reference to a single action: his (morally necessary) choice of this world, this set of compossible substances, over all other possibilities.

I can only conclude that once again the perfection idea has diverted Leibniz's metaphysics away from the traditional theism to which it at least pays lip service. The parallels with deism cannot be ignored, although in Leibniz's case the reason for God's noninvolvement is not a theory of natural law but factors internal to the tradition of perfect-being theology itself: a perfect being should not have to be constantly tinkering with his machine! The line between God's doing everything and doing nothing is extremely thin, as Leibniz himself realized: "It is rather difficult to distinguish the actions of God from those of creatures; for some believe that God does everything, while others imagine that he merely conserves the force he has given to creatures."[128] This means that the line between pantheism and deism may be equally thin. On the one hand, if all actions are God's actions (as in certain versions of occasionalism), we are inclined to say that God qua sole agent is the only being. Certainly in this case the world would seem to function as a sort of machine for carrying out the resolves of the divine will. On the other hand, if God's only role for Leibniz is to set the universe in motion — or, worse, to allow the possibles to actualize themselves according to their own perfection as they are "striving" to do anyway[129] — then deism's "God outside the machine" in fact replaces traditional theism as the operative model. One finds little evidence of a resolution of these tensions in Leibniz's thought.

128. "Il est assez difficile de distinguer les actions de Dieu de celles des creatures; car il y en a qui croyent que Dieu fait tout, d'autres s'imaginent qu'il ne fait que conserver la force qu'il a donnée aux creatures" (*Discours*, par. 8); cf. Brown, *Leibniz*, 89.

129. See David Blumenfeld, "Leibniz's Theory of the Striving Possibles," in R. S. Woolhouse, ed., *Leibniz: Metaphysics and Philosophy of Science* (Oxford: Oxford Univ. Press, 1981).

Leibniz as Pluralist or Monist?

What happens when we push Leibniz for an answer to some of these difficulties? I can now present and defend the hypothesis that has implicitly guided the chapter to this point: *the difficulties with Leibniz's doctrine of God either propel his thought in the direction of a Spinozistic pantheism or force him to abandon the all-perfect God who supposedly gives rise to the pluralism of substances or monads.* The tension that we found implicit in Descartes's account of substance comes here to its (apparently inevitable) conclusion. Either there is one single substance, with all the masses of individuals in the world being merely modes or aspects of this one thing or being; or there are infinities of substances, with even the smallest objects themselves composed of an infinite number of smaller substances. But in the latter case, their relation to God as the absolute One becomes unclear; it can no longer be characterized as one of ontological dependence. And as long as the God/world relationship cannot be adequately resolved, we will have to accept Bertrand Russell's contention that monadism is incompatible with theism.

If I am right about this tension, and assuming that Leibniz's system cannot be resolved into absolute pluralism while still retaining the highest being who is supposed to hold it all together, then what of the other possibility, Spinozistic monism? I suggest in this section that the stronger tendency of Leibniz's own philosophical theology is indeed in the monistic direction. (By contrast, his hylomorphism and his doctrine of individual essences are fundamentally pluralistic.) Admittedly, this seems a shocking conclusion to draw regarding a thinker who is committed to infinite pluralism; and of course Leibniz's verbal opposition to Spinozism was vehement, long-lived, even bitter. Nonetheless, one has to recall that the term *Spinozism* represented to the late seventeenth century — and especially to a thinker who was by nature a mediator and who thus worried about the orthodox appearance of his thought — a dangerous and pernicious heresy. Like the term *murder,* its use implied immediately that one had done something wrong. Yet like other heresies in the history of thought, it also exercised a seductive attraction on metaphysicians of the period (and not just then!). One must finally agree with Catherine Wilson: "Spinoza was, in a sense, Leibniz's ghost. He was what Leibniz was afraid of being and saw himself as dangerously capable of becoming; the doctrine that God was in some way related to creatures as a whole to its parts, not as an extra item, was one which obsessed him. 'If there had been no monads,' he wrote to Bourguet once, 'Spinoza would have been right.'"[130]

130. Wilson, *Leibniz's Metaphysics,* 86, citing G 3:575.

It is clear that Leibniz himself would not give up the plurality of substances and thought he could justify their real existence. I think my treatment up to this point has provided some serious grounds for thinking that he was not successful. It remains for me now to make explicit the case against the success of Leibniz's theistic pluralism and to draw the consequences for philosophical theology. The result is crucial for this book's argument as a whole, since it both points us back to certain portions of Descartes's position and forward to the Spinoza tradition.

Before proceeding, let me note one inadequate reason that has been given for construing Leibniz as a monist. Bertrand Russell maintained that Leibniz's (Aristotelian) logic by itself had monistic implications:

> the traditional logic holds that every proposition ascribes a predicate to a subject, and from this it easily follows that there can be only one subject, the Absolute, for if there were two, the proposition that there were two would not ascribe a predicate to either. . . . We now know that the traditional doctrine is wrong, but respect for Aristotle prevented Leibniz from realizing that this was possible.[131]

But this is just wrong. As Fred Feldman has shown, Leibniz's logic commits him not to one substance only, but to the thesis that all propositions could be expressed by sentences of the (Aristotelian) forms A, E, I, and O.[132] As long as all properties can be properly (and essentially) related to some particular substance, there is no logical compulsion to reduce independent finite substances to their infinite source.

Each of the following few sections underscores from a different perspective what we have found to be a basic tension in Leibniz's theistic atomism. None is by itself sufficient to make the entire case (especially in the abbreviated form in which I must present them here). Nevertheless, as a group and in connection with the results already obtained, they suggest some fundamental difficulties with perfect-being theology of the Leibnizian sort.

---

131. Russell, *Our Knowledge of the External World*, 48; cf. idem, *Critical Exposition*, 12. Louis Couturat also speaks of the "purely logical reasons" that led Leibniz to deny all interaction between substances; see "On Leibniz's Metaphysics," in Harry Frankfurt, ed., *Leibniz: A Collection of Critical Essays* (Garden City, N.Y.: Doubleday, 1972), 45.

132. Fred Feldman, "Leibniz's Commitment to Monism," *Idealistic Studies* 3 (1973): 18-31. Feldman cites in this context G. H. R. Parkinson, *Logic and Reality in Leibniz's Metaphysics* (Oxford: Clarendon, 1965), 37. In *Philosophy of Leibniz* Rescher also criticizes Russell on this point (not surprisingly, since he criticizes Russell every time he refers to him); see p. 76.

Leibniz and Spinoza

Many authors have argued that certain basic features of Leibniz's philosophy stand much closer to Spinoza's than he ever acknowledged. If so, these might serve as further indicators of monistic tendencies in Leibniz's thought. Again, the claim is not (except perhaps rhetorically) that Leibniz was a Spinozist, but rather that he retained certain monistic tendencies stemming from Spinoza that are not fully reconcilable with his own atomism.

The literature comparing these two figures is massive and cannot be fully reviewed here.[133] The parallels that it reveals are significant: both philosophers are rationalists rather than empiricists.[134] Both are committed to treating as superstition whatever reason cannot validate — even if these should be classical theistic doctrines. Equally important, both are animists, panvitalists, and panpsychists — although in highly specific (and sometimes incompatible) senses that need to be carefully sorted out. My suspicions are that the problem of individuating individuals is more difficult for a panpsychist (see below) than for a materialist, especially one who is also a realist about space and time; but I cannot make the case here.[135]

The problem of individuation is compounded for Leibniz because he appropriated Spinoza's link of the infinite and absolute: "the true infinite, strictly speaking, is only in the *absolute,* which precedes all composition and is not

---

133. See esp. "Spinoza and Leibniz," the central theme of *Studia spinozana* 6 (1990), ed. E. Curley et al. (Würzburg: Köningshausen & Neumann), 11-228. Classic works are Foucher de Careil, *Leibniz, Descartes et Spinoza* (Paris, 1863); L. Stein, *Leibniz und Spinoza* (G. Reimer, 1890); G. Friedmann, *Leibniz et Spinoza* (Paris: Gallimard, 1946). More recently, see G. H. R. Parkinson, "Leibniz's Paris Writings in Relation to Spinoza," *Studia leibnitiana Suppl.* 18 (Wiesbaden, 1978), esp. 77-78; and Yvon Belaval, "Leibniz lecteur de Spinoza," *Archives de Philosophie* 46 (1983): 531-52. More recent are Renée Bouveresse, *Spinoza et Leibniz: L'idée d'animisme universel* (Paris: Vrin, 1992), including its extensive bibliography; and R. S. Woolhouse, *Descartes, Spinoza, Leibniz: The Concept of Substance in Seventeenth-Century Metaphysics* (London: Routledge, 1993).

134. For details on the commonalities in their rationalism see Franco Biasutti, "Reason and Experience in Leibniz and Spinoza," *Studia spinozana* 6 (1990), esp. 67ff.

135. To be specific, I do not think the task of individuating is impossible but only more difficult than is often alleged. I believe Dietrich Manke is ultimately right: "Bei Leibniz ist die Welt nicht wie bei Spinoza eine einzige Substanz, sondern eine Vielheit von Substanzen, aber trotzdem ein Universum, d.h. wörtlich ein zur Einheit Strebendes. Das Wesen der Welt ist bei Leibniz weder die bloße Vielheit wie in der Atomistik, noch die reine Einheit wie im Spinozismus, sondern die Einheit in der Vielheit. In der unübersehbaren Mannigfaltigkeit wechselnder Erscheinung von individuell verschiedenartigen Einzelwesen manifestiert sich doch ein universeller geistig-ideeler Wesenszusammenhang" (Manke, *Leibniz und Goethe: Die Harmonie ihrer Weltansichten* [Erfurt, 1924], 20).

formed by the addition of parts" (*NE* 157). All *modificatio* or *determinatio*, then, is *limitatio:* "It is precisely by modifying [the genuine infinite or absolute] that one limits oneself and forms a finite."[136] This position is clearly similar to Spinoza's dictum that all determination is negation.[137] But if *A* is separated from *B* only by negation rather than by anything positive in *A* or *B*, must not one conclude that what is real about *A* and *B* is, finally, the positive principle ("Being" or whatever one calls it) that they share?[138]

Given the infinite/absolute link, Leibniz had two major paths open for thinking together perfection and reality, the Platonic and the Spinozistic. Either he could say (1) that perfection is a form in which things (as only partly real) participate; or (2) that God, or the content of the divine ideas, is the principle of perfection, such that things that have reality or perfection *just are* God or the contents of his thought. Clearly (2) is the Spinozistic option. Despite himself, Del Boca argues, Leibniz remained closer to (2), since he holds that all that exists is the content of God's intellect rather than the product of his choice.[139] I find the matter rather more complicated; Leibniz is ambivalent and inconsistent. Still, when one reads the emanation passages (e.g., *Discours* par. 14), where (given the desubstantializing of space) the notion of proximity and distance between monads turns out to be derivative, one can only conceive them as immanent within (interior to) the divine *immensum*.[140]

136. *NE* 158: "dès qu'on modifie, on se borne ou forme un fini." Cf. Leibniz's letter to Bayle (1702): "la modification, bien loin d'adjouter quelque perfection, ne pouvant estre qu'une restriction ou limitation variable" (G 3:67). Along the same lines, Albert Heinekamp, *Das Problem des Guten bei Leibniz* (Bonn: H. Bouvier, 1969), 155, cites an April, 1676, manuscript: "Ad quodlibet attributum dum aluia referuntur omnia; resultent in eo modificationes, unde fit, ut eadem Essentia DEi in quolibet Mundi genere expressa sit tota; adeoque DEus infinitis se manifestet modis." Cf. G 1:214-15: "Eccardus: infinitum esse prius finito: finitum enim ab infinito quodammodo abscindi, atque negationem ulterioris processus significare."

137. Or, as Spinoza wrote to a correspondent, "determinatio ad rem iuxta suum esse non pertinet; set e contra est eius non-esse" (*Opera,* 2:299).

138. Malebranche perhaps saw the difficulty of the issue more clearly than many twentieth-century commentators: Spinoza was "not . . . able to understand . . . how God by his will alone could create the universe," and so he "took the universe for his God" (*Oeuvres complètes,* ed. A. Robinet [Paris: Vrin, 1958-72], 17/1:622).

139. Susanna Del Boca, *Finalismo e necessità in Leibniz* (Florence: Sansoni, 1936), esp. 74-80, cited in Heinekamp, *Das Problem des Guten,* 142-43. Belaval ("Leibniz lecteur de Spinoza," 542) points out that Spinoza uses the term "emanation" only once (in the letter to Oldenburg of 1675-76); the secondary literature is divided regarding the extent to which Spinoza relied on the concept of emanation and whether it is incompatible with his position.

140. So Belaval, "Leibniz lecteur de Spinoza," 542: in the context of the *Discours* "ce qui, dans le contexte alors établi de la désubstantialisation de l'espace où . . . les notions de

Unfortunately, Leibniz could not allow either the Platonic or the Spino-zistic tendencies to come into their own. The theory of emanation appeared to be inconsistent with the Christian doctrine of creation. Even greater is the ten-sion between the personal God of the monotheistic traditions — the providen-tial creator, sustainer, and guider — and Spinoza's God-as-Nature (deus siva natura). Orthodoxy, or at least its appearances, had to be preserved. Thus Leibniz attacked monism at every chance, and increasingly avoided the emana-tion idea in his later writings.[141] Whether these moves were philosophically ac-ceptable depends on one's view of the philosophical credentials of classical philosophical theism. I, for one, find them lacking — at least in their seven-teenth-century form. Therefore I conclude that the stronger philosophical move for Leibniz, the move that would have made for the more consistent metaphysic, would have been to stay closer to the Spinoza who obviously at-tracted his fascination during and just after the Paris stay in the 1670s. His later atomism is less successful as a philosophical theology than the view with which he flirted during those early years.

The Materialist/Idealist Debate

If Leibniz is a materialist, then he is an atomist. As long as he preserves matter as real, then he can maintain that there are many points and their unions are only aggregates; for if matter is real, substances are (for Leibniz) pointlike ma-terial entities that are grouped into aggregates or real beings by the mental enti-ties or entelechies that indwell them. Throughout his long correspondences with Bernoulli and De Volder on the subject, Leibniz defends various (often in-compatible) responses to this problem. Most likely he holds either an elimina-tivist or a reductionist theory of matter, that is, either that matter should be eliminated as a category or that it should be reduced to metaphysically more basic building blocks, such as monads, in terms of which it could be explained.

proximité et de distance entre monades n'ont aucun sense, suggère une immanence dans l'intériorité de l'*immensum* divin et, par là, fait rêver d'un rapprochement avec Spinoza." Belaval is not, however, finally satisfied with this line of thought.

141. E.g., *Theod.* par. 372. Note that Leibniz's caution was not enough: shortly after his death, in 1723, he was accused by Joachim Lange of Spinozism, who spoke of his preestab-lished harmony as "pseudophilosophiae spinozianae foetus" (cited in Max Wundt, *Die deut-sche Schulphilosophie im Zeitalter der Aufklärung* [Hildesheim: Olms, 1964], 236). Even Christian Wolff abandoned the preestablished harmony and was careful to avoid attributing *perceptio* to the brute monads because of its Spinozistic implications. Catherine Wilson (*Leibniz's Metaphysics*, 4) also emphasizes Leibniz's failure to meet the standards of ortho-doxy — despite his best intentions.

Jolley[142] thinks that it is obvious that Leibniz is a reductionist, citing a passage from a letter to de Volder: "I do not really eliminate body, but I reduce it to what it is. For I show that corporeal mass, which is thought to have something over and above simple substance, is not a substance, but a phenomenon resulting from simple substances, which alone have unity and absolute reality."[143] I think it more likely that he is finally an eliminativist about matter, viz. it has only phenomenal existence but is not ultimately real. Instead of debating this question, however, I propose addressing a different one: Are there tensions between Leibniz's theistic atomism and his claim that bodies are just "sets of harmonized perceptions" (G 2:275, AG 181), tensions that would be better handled within a nonatomistic metaphysics?

Some evidence suggests that Leibniz never found a position on matter that satisfied him, and as the two correspondences progress he continually weakens the concept of matter presupposed there.[144] He seems most concerned to show that the laws of nature can be preserved even under a phenomenalist theory of matter. Sometimes Leibniz pushes his system to its logical conclusion and ends up with idealism. But more often he is working "to *escape* the extreme interpretation of the doctrine of substance to which his metaphysical and logical speculations of 1686 had led."[145] He does well to do so, I think, since thoroughgoing idealism would make it more difficult (to put it mildly) to individuate the mental substances that he wants to use as the building blocks of his metaphysics.

But if Leibniz is truly an idealist, must he be a monist? This is the conclusion of Friedmann's masterful comparison between Leibniz and Spinoza: "The philosophy of Leibniz is, at core, a monism of the spirit"; or at least it is a philosophy "where, despite the efforts of the author, the reality of matter and its borders with spirit are evasive and fragile."[146] Throughout the correspondences

---

142. See Nicholas Jolley, "Leibniz: Truth, Knowledge and Metaphysics," in G. H. R. Parkinson, ed., *The Renaissance and Seventeenth-century Rationalism,* Routledge History of Philosophy 4 (London: Routledge, 1993), 384-423, esp. 399.

143. "Ego vero non tollo corpus, sed ad id quod est revoco, massam enim corpoream quae aliquid praeter substantias simplices habere creditur, non substantiam esse ostendo, sed phaenomenon resultans ex substantiis simplicibus quae solae unitatem et absolutam realitatem habent" (G 2:275, AG 181).

144. The process of development is nicely summarized in L. J. Russell, "The Correspondence between Leibniz and De Volder," in *Leibniz,* ed. Woolhouse, 104-18. Bernoulli's best reconstruction is that Leibniz makes *materia secunda* out of points endowed with forms; a material substance is a *punctum cum forma* (M 3/2:546-47).

145. Following Russell, "Correspondence," 118.

146. Friedmann, *Leibniz et Spinoza,* 242-43.

in which Leibniz works out the necessary details of his theories of perception, of motion, and of the relation of physics to metaphysics, he presents arguments for a plurality of substances that presuppose the existence of matter in at least some form. Take away this crutch, and the case for pluralism becomes, at least, rather more difficult to establish. We return to this theme below.

Leibniz and Composing the Continuum

As we saw, Leibniz insists that there cannot be an actual whole composed out of an actually infinite number of parts. Hence the parts of a real continuum must be merely potential divisions, as with the parts of a line in geometry. Conversely, where one starts with real parts (e.g., with the monads that constitute the physical world) and adds them together, one comes up with an aggregate of real individuals, not with a real whole. In considering the tensions in this area of Leibniz's thought, I suggest we find a recapitulation of the previous section, which turned on whether he is more materialist or idealist. When Leibniz writes as if there are real particles of matter, then he cannot argue that they compose real (second-order) individuals. Let's assume, by contrast, following Leibniz's major metaphysical writings, that idealism wins. How then would he be able to think an absolute being who is the source of all other beings and through whom they subsist?

If Leibniz wants to maintain real spiritual points, then they will have to be granted real, independent existence. This means that all aggregates of monads are ontologically derivative constructions, fictions or at least not ultimately real. He actually says this about communities of persons: societies, states, even the kingdom of heaven, all have a sort of derivative existence. (Leibniz's greatest twentieth-century follower, A. N. Whitehead, draws the same conclusion even more decisively.) How then can Leibniz think an absolute or all-encompassing being? If one starts with God as *ipsum esse*, Being or Perfection itself, as the theological tradition did, then God can be the source of all other beings, the One through whom they subsist; but then they are, to this extent, not truly separate from him. If, by contrast, as pinnacle of the pyramid of ever more general composed aggregates, God is somehow constituted by all the moments beneath him, then it will follow that, as the most abstract, God will be the most fictional of all!

Of course, many later philosophers have drawn exactly the latter conclusion; indeed, it may have become the dominant move since the death of Hegel. Certainly Ludwig Feuerbach presented God as a purely fictional construction out of human "species-being"; and Hans Vaihinger construed God as a fictitious regulative ideal suggested by our practices of reasoning. Moreover, the standard theological criticism of Leibniz argues that he, along with "the other rationalists," reduced God from an independent entity to a mere function within the system.[147] But, as I hope this chapter has shown, Leibniz would never have been willing to reduce God to the status of the highest (fictional) aggregate of spirits. If a potential solution to the problem of the continuum had entailed atomism without the *ens perfectissimum,* he would certainly have rejected it. Even in his "private" writings Leibniz never eschewed full personalist theism.

So the spiritual unity, even the primordiality, of God as an individual must be given priority in any adequate philosophical theology. For Leibniz there must be a highest monad, the king of the kingdom of ends. Yet now the problems with composing the continuum click in from the other side. If everything that exists, exists insofar as it is good, and Goodness involves a participation in the One who is Goodness itself, then the One is indeed the unity of and source for all that exists, as the Neoplatonic tradition held. But in this case, the "parts" could not also have real existence; they would become (to that extent) moments of the whole. This would give the multitude of monads, from human entelechies down to the smallest known particles and beyond, a derivative type of existence as over against the divine substance — a conclusion that Descartes was willing to countenance (and Spinoza to espouse) yet that Leibniz resisted. How derivative would the parts be? On Leibniz's theory of the continuum, the parts of a continuum can have only phenomenal existence when the whole is taken as real. The conclusion would therefore be even stronger than Descartes's conclusion: The parts of the spiritual whole would have not just derivative but imaginary existence (like Leibniz's view of the infinitesimals), being merely potential divisions of the whole. They would be modes of the one existing unlimited substance, distinctions that we can draw in thinking the One but that cannot be granted actual ontological status as individuals.

There are several escapes from this conclusion, but they are costly to Leibniz. One could make perfections independent of the most perfect being, making their perfectness into a primitive rather than being derived from the *ens perfectissimum.* (But wouldn't this cause problems for the PSR?) One would then have to dissociate perfection and existence, which would mean rejecting the entire framework sketched above that links perfection of essence to existence; the striving possibles would thus have to go. Simpler, I think, would be to grant the real existence of wholes that have actually infinite numbers of

---

147. This is the standard criticism in histories of philosophy such as those by F. Copleston or W. T. Jones. For a more careful (but no less one-sided) presentation, see James Collins, *God in Modern Philosophy* (Chicago: Henry Regnery, 1959), 79-85.

parts.[148] Of course, this would amount to admitting the existence of unknowables and that would mean, in turn, the rejection of the PSR and of rationalism in general. It is a move Leibniz would not have accepted, but I think it is one that philosophical theologians today must make. Granting wholes with actually infinite numbers of parts, and abandoning the PSR, means that the concept of substance can be used without facing Russell's Dilemma: atheistic monadism or pantheism. The cost involves populating the universe with unknowables (or not-fully-knowables) such as really existing infinitesimals and real infinite quantities. Perhaps a sort of "regulative ontology" could be developed for speaking of such entities that are never (fully) knowable and yet are built solidly into one's ontology. The important point for the present book is that another option is open to modern thought besides the monism that continually dogs Leibniz's efforts. That Leibniz himself would presumably have embraced monism before abandoning the PSR does not detract from the fact that another option was available to him.

Space and Time

There is not space (or time) to re-present this detailed debate here. As is well known, in the Clarke correspondence Leibniz denied the existence of an independent *sensorium* of space and time. As Stuart Brown notes, "the tendency of [Leibniz's] thought is in what can be called a 'phenomenalistic' direction, i.e. to explain matter, space and time in terms of the perceptions of monads. Material substances are reduced to well-founded phenomena as also are space and time."[149] On Leibniz's view, space and time are products of subjects' perceptions. Further, that each monad can occupy a separate "space" from which to "view" the universe is a result of the absolutely infinite monad who "sees" from all perspectives at all times.

As the literature shows, it is extremely difficult to determine exactly what are the consequences of this dependence relation for the reality of space; there are no easy answers here. Cautiously put: there is at least a tendency for the po-

---

148. So Jonas Cohn, *Geschichte des Unendlichkeitsproblems im abendländischen Denken bis Kant* (Leipzig: W. Engelmann, 1896), 191, after an extended discussion of this topic.

149. Stuart Brown, *Leibniz*, 147; see also Nicholas Rescher, *Leibniz: An Introduction to His Philosophy* (Totowa, N.J.: Rowman and Littlefield, 1979), 84, cf. 65. Benson Mates (*The Philosophy of Leibniz: Metaphysics and Language* [New York: Oxford Univ. Press, 1986], 230n13) calls it "far and away the best available account of this entire subject." Against this standard interpretation of Leibniz see Glenn A. Hartz, "Space and Time in the Leibnizian Metaphysic," *Nous* 22 (1988): 493-519.

sition to imply that what is really real are the thoughts of space in the mind of the absolute monad, and hence that there is not really any space outside this One. Recall the Leibnizian precept: "Where there are no limits, that is, in God, perfection is absolutely infinite" (*Monad.* par. 41). What is it to be "absolutely infinite"? Could there be a separate space outside the absolutely infinite, or would not all things have to be in some sense within it (as panentheists hold)? Leibniz's infinity passages point in the latter direction. He writes, for example, that "the highest level of the infinite is that it is itself everything; and thus is the infinite in God, who is namely, as one, everything."[150]

These worries are reminiscent of the well-known problem of whether an absolute being could create anything outside itself. Philosophers have often expressed the suspicion that there is something intrinsic to the notion of the absolute that leaves no place outside it for other things to exist.[151] If things are external to God, *where* are they? I suggest that such theological suspicions should be brought to the oft-discussed space-time problem in Leibniz. Recall, for example, the degrees of reality doctrine that we examined above in connection with the perfection idea. Just as, ultimately speaking, there is only one reality,[152] so also it may be that, for the theorist of the absolute, there can be only one space: the space of God's thought. Leibniz might not have been content with such a conclusion. Yet, I have argued, there were at least some serious grounds for him to conclude that things are internal to God, since they represent — and are constituted by — different perspectives on the one space/time continuum as it is internally experienced by the highest monad.

Leibniz's Mysticism

Commentators have often remarked on Leibniz's inclination toward a mystical view of religion. It may seem ironic that Leibniz, the hyper-rationalist, should also show an interest in the mystical tradition. But the fact should not be surprising. Rationalism disinclines toward dogmatic truth claims based on faith,

---

150. "Infiniti . . . summus gradus est ipsum *Omnia*, quale infinitum est in DEO, id enim est unus omnia" (Couturat, *La Logique de Leibniz d'après des documents inédits* [Hildesheim: Olms, 1961], 523; cf. 513). Klaus Reich Kaehler has attempted to do justice to these passages in *Leibniz — der methodische Zwiespalt der Metaphysik der Substanz* (Hamburg: Meiner, 1979), e.g., 63-64.

151. I make no pretense, however, that these are problems unique to Leibniz; to this extent mine is in fact an argument directed more generally against the God of infinite perfection as this concept is used in early modern philosophy from Descartes to Baumgarten.

152. "En général la perfection est positive, c'est une réalité absolue; le defaut est privatif, il vient de la limitation et tend à des privations nouvelles" (*Theod.* par. 33, G 6:122).

but it does not disincline toward a single principle of truth that might be known immediately through nonrational means — or might even exceed all rational knowledge. Indeed, the connection in the case of Leibniz is even stronger: The Platonism that inspired and characterized his metaphysics already contained mystical elements, which had become a constitutive part of the Neoplatonic tradition. The link with mysticism is even stronger for rationalists who are idealists: if the body is ultimately phenomenal or unreal, the relation to God can be expected to be closer than in the context of bodily separation.

In his essay on the true *theologia mystica*, Leibniz stresses the immediacy of the divine light, speaking of the means "to awaken the inner light."[153] Everything is created from God and from nothingness *(Nichts)*, and a trace of the *Nichts* remains in all creatures. Sin is an expression of this nothingness. But there is also a trace of the infinite: "Within our self-being there lies an infinity, a footprint or reflection of the omniscience and omnipresence of God."[154]

Once again, in "mystical" passages such as these, we find an inclination in Leibniz toward monism. For this ontology leads, as in many of the mystical traditions, to the view of the "self" as ultimately unreal and to a focus on the infinity or "light" within. Such passages should not be taken, of course, as expressions of the official Leibnizian philosophical doctrine. But they represent yet one more dimension of Leibniz's thought that inclines away from pluralism and toward monism.

The *Principium Individuationis?*

With this last heading we reach the crux of the matter. Leibniz's simple substances or monads are units of mental energy and identity that have their source of movement within themselves; they are entelechies or (to use the descriptive Latin term) *perfectihabies* (*Monad.* par. 48). At one point he speaks of them as "total-parts" *(partes totales)* (G 7:307; L 490). By design, each mirrors the rest of the world, though it is not in fact affected by any other object (except, in principle, by God). The nature of their perception, volition, and freedom has already been discussed.

There are no serious difficulties of interpretation here: Leibniz clearly intends to be a metaphysical pluralist, since he defends multiple finite substances, each dependent on an infinite and perfect being. If he were convinced that the tensions traced here are unresolvable, he would probably have abandoned the

---

153. "Das innerliche Licht [zu] erwecken" (Guhrauer 1:410; L 367).

154. "In unserem Selbstwesen stecket eine Unendlichkeit, ein Fußtapf, ein Ebenbild der Allwissenheit und Allmacht Gottes" (Guhrauer 1:411).

other tenets on which my charge of inconsistency rests in order to maintain atomism over monism. We might reconstruct his base argument as follows:

1. Finite individuals — the individuals studied by scientists, the individuals of which we predicate qualities — possess attributes.
2. Attributes inhere in substances (the Aristotelian *forma substantialis*, e.g., *Discours* par. 10).
3. Hence finite individuals are substances.
4. Clearly there exist multiple finite individuals.
5. Hence there are multiple independent substances.
6. Hence it is not the case that all things are merely modes of the one substance.[155]

Premise (3) expresses Leibniz's theory of entelechy. Basic to his thinking was the belief in independent, self-directing substances, centers of power or action, which he defines, in contradistinction to God, as independent mental units.[156] Such, let us grant at right at the outset, is the "official position"; this is the view for which Leibniz wished to be remembered.

Nonetheless, I have argued throughout this book that a thesis of strong ontological dependence pushes one's thought in the direction of monism. Prima facie, Leibniz's system presents an apparent counterexample to my contention. For he repeatedly insisted that he did not need to follow the path taken by Spinoza. In place of a single substance with infinite modes, he defended each permanent spiritual substance as basic — each is the principle of its own action; each has its own *conatus* or striving. The actions of each are explained in terms of its own essence, even if its essence is not a sufficient explanation for its existence or actions. Why then, Leibniz might respond, must one immediately make allegations of monism when the doctrine of ontological dependence is argued? If I have gone astray here, he might retort, then so has most of the Christian theological tradition, including such bastions of orthodoxy as Augustine and Thomas Aquinas.[157]

---

155. For a more detailed argument see Alan Hart, "Leibniz on Spinoza's Concept of Substance," *Studia leibnitiana* 14 (1982): 73-86.

156. A classic presentation of Leibniz's theory of entelechies can be found in Wolfgang Janke, *Leibniz: Die Emendation der Metaphysik* (Frankfurt: Vittorio Klostermann, 1963). See also Jacques Jalabert, *La théorie leibnizienne de la substance* (Paris: Presses Universitaires de France, 1960).

157. To accuse Leibniz of Spinozistic pantheism or emanationism is, according to Jalabert, "revient à dire que l'on refuse d'admettre la possibilité de *l'être relatif*, dont l'essence consiste à *dépendre*, tout in étant malgré tout *un être*. La seule métaphysique est alors le

But note that the failure of Leibniz's theistic atomism would not entail a reduction of *all possible* theistic positions to monism. One can acknowledge a tendency toward monism within philosophical theology without immediately declaring all nonmonistic alternatives to be failures. Recall that in chapter 3 we found an unmistakable tendency toward an ontological sameness of creator and creation — and at this point we cannot call it anything stronger than a tendency — within the tradition that speaks of the infinite and perfect God. In this chapter we have strengthened the case against perfect-being theology, taking as our lead this time the criteria for individuation.[158] Here, in order to draw together the strands of the ongoing debate between pluralism and monism, we have looked explicitly at the question, Is Leibniz in possession of an adequate principle of individuation? And is the means by which he wishes to individuate consistent with the more theological parts of his thought?

Matter cannot serve as the principle of individuation, since Leibniz has declared it to be ultimately unreal, ascribing it a phenomenal status;[159] and he claims explicitly that it cannot be the cause of evil (*Theod.* par. 380). Nor can he appeal to a separate source of being, or to a positive principle of evil, since all being is derived from God, and evil is a privation rather than a positive principle of its own.[160] Recall that the characteristics of a true substance are to have full autonomy and to have the power to cause changes. But (as Descartes already emphasized) these attributes belong without qualification only to God.

Spinozisme, et le reproche d'inconséquence ne s'adresse plus à Leibniz, mais à toutes les nuances du spiritualisme traditionnel" (Jalabert, *Le Dieu de Leibniz*, 218).

158. The difficulties that perfect-being theology raises for an adequate theory of individuating finite beings are visible in both Platonic and Aristotelian schools of thought. The Aristotelian Scholastics had to ask, In cases where there is no matter, how are individuals to be individuated? For instance, each astral intelligence (or angel), not being composed of matter, must be individuated by a form that is unique to it. Yet for Leibniz there is precisely no matter to constitute the "thisness" (say, Socrates-ness) of some shared form (say, personhood). This view moves him immediately much closer to the Platonic tradition. For such a position, where matter is not ultimately real, must not what really exists be the forms? No problem, the theistic Platonist responds; the forms may be organized into some sort of hierarchy, for example by placing the entire hierarchy into the mind or understanding of God. It seems clear that this move will make the nature of the other forms dependent on God, either as the highest form or as the reality within which they are located.

159. On matter as phenomenal, see Janke, *Leibniz*, 127-37; C. Wilson, *Leibniz's Metaphysics*, 180-99; and Stuart Brown, *Leibniz*, chap. 10, esp. 149ff. In a similar vein, Leibniz also denies that it can be the cause of evil (*Theod.* par. 380).

160. *Theod.* par. 29. Cf. "Dialogue" (Grua, 1:364): "le mal est un defaut, c'est à dire une privation ou negation, et par consequent vient du neant ou non estre."

Thus it is at least questionable whether the monads can fulfill the requirements for separate substances[161] — especially when we recall that monads are "active" only symbolically, by virtue of the clarity of their perceptions.

Leibniz initially seeks to individuate by appealing to position rather than to matter. Each monad perceives the universe from an angle or perspective unique to it, just as "the plan of a city, looked down upon from the top of a great tower placed upright in its midst, differs from the almost infinite horizontal perspectives with which it delights the eyes of travelers who approach it from one direction or another."[162] But can Leibniz really avail himself of this metaphor? It requires a set of objects arranged in space — or at least requires some objective notion of space, independent of there being any objects, which could account for *A*'s being in a different place than *B*. But, as we saw above, Leibniz's view of space provides neither of these prerequisites: space is itself phenomenal for him and does not have independent existence apart from the thoughts of monads. As Catherine Wilson argues, "Unable to decide whether being is something other than being perceived, he lays the groundwork of a theory of perception which remains permanently ambiguous on the question of the independent existence of 'external' things."[163] To use "differing perspectives" as the principle of individuation is a move that we should at least view with some suspicion in the context of his thought.

However, there is an alternative solution, due to Duns Scotus, as well as some good textual evidence to think that Leibniz wished to appeal to it. Perhaps there are not, as the Aristotelian tradition thought, general forms, with individuals being differentiated by the particular portion of matter allotted to them. Perhaps each individual has its own essence or thisness, or — like each angel in the ontology of Thomas Aquinas — is its own species.[164] Scotus called this the individual's *haecceity (haecceitas)*. Note that Scotist tenor of Leibniz's notion of an individual substance:

> God, seeing [for example] Alexander's individual notion or haecceity, sees in it at the same time the basis and reason for all the predicates that can be said truly of him, for example, that he vanquished Darius and Porus. He even knows a priori (and not by experience) whether he died a natural death or whether he was poisoned. . . . [Thus] we can say that from all time in Alexan-

161. That they cannot is argued by Stuart Brown, *Leibniz*, 113-14.
162. (1671), in W. Kabitz, *Die Philosophie des jungen Leibniz* (Heidelberg, 1909), 141 (L 142).
163. Catherine Wilson, *Leibniz's Metaphysics*, 67.
164. "Omne individuum est species infima." See Janke, *Leibniz*, 79-80.

der's soul there are vestiges of everything that has happened to him and marks of everything that will happen to him.[165]

Finally, Leibniz wants to say, creatures are distinguished from God due to "their own nature" (de leur nature propre) or essence (Monad. par. 42). The unique nature of each creature accounts for its limits (imperfections), such that — if this notion is acceptable — individuals are already differentiated essentially in themselves, without depending on anything material. Moreover, all of their properties are essential properties. This view, he would claim, is sufficient to distinguish individuals from God. Hence there is no danger of their being conflated together into the One of monism.[166]

But there are at least two lines of criticism against this response that, taken together, are strong enough to keep the monism worries burning. The first involves noting the rather high costs to such a theory of individuation. It clashes directly with one's intuitive sense of the difference between essential and contingent properties (e.g., "that Jane is a human being" versus "that Jane is wearing white today"). But there seems to be no way to preserve this intuition under Leibniz's view. Similarly, we believe that people develop, that they become different things during their lives. Yet for Leibniz they can only come to express various essential properties that have always been part of who they (eternally) are. Finally, at least for incompatibilists, free choice requires that one could choose one option or the other. But if all properties are essential, then one can only come to express the course of action that has always been part of one's essence. (We have already tried Leibniz's claim that he could avoid the deterministic consequences by means of his theory of contingency, and found it wanting.)

The other line of response points out that the multiple essences in Leibniz are not really all that independent. Of course, with many of the Scholastics, Leibniz holds that being must be added to their purely essential or possible existence, and that this being must come either through participation in God as the highest being, or at least with God's blessing (depending on which theory of creation one interprets him as finally espousing). Over and above this depen-

---

165. "Au lieu que Dieu voyant la notion individuelle ou heccëité d'Alexandre, y voit en même temps le fondement et la raison de tous les predicats qui se peuvent dire de luy veritablement, comme par exemple qu'il vaincroit Darius et Porus; jusqu'à connoistre a priori (et non par experience) s'il est mort d'une mort naturelle ou par poison. . . . [Aussi] on peut dire qu'il y a de tout temps dans l'ame d'Alexandre des restes de tout ce qui luy est arrivé, et les marques de tout ce qui luy arrivera" (Discours, par. 8).

166. See G 3:519; cf. Parkinson, Logic and Reality, 77: God has the attributes in their perfect or unlimited form.

dence-of-being, Leibniz also locates the eternal essences in the mind of God. So even here one does not really encounter separate essences, independently existing Platonic forms, but rather portions of God's being, items of his understanding (albeit items that he did not "create").

Let's imagine that one is willing to pay the costs of such an appeal to individual *haecceities*. It would follow that each nature must already have been determinate prior to the thing's actual existence. Hence Leibniz must (and does on occasion) affirm that God did not create the realm of possibilities; things are possible or impossible of themselves and not because of any divine decision (in contrast to Descartes's doctrine of the creation of the eternal truths). What Leibniz means is clear: it was always possible that Arnauld would someday exist as a real individual substance; and should Arnauld exist he would be a finite and imperfect being (esp. when criticizing Leibniz!). God chose to create the best set of compossible substances; our possible Arnauld had the good luck to be a member of this set; hence Arnauld really existed.

Imagine that the critic responds as I have argued here: these not-yet-existing essences are nonetheless located within God, subsisting eternally in his mind (*Monad.* par. 20). Moreover, when they do exist, they are still not truly independent, since nothing exists without the conservation of God (*Theod.* par. 27). Fine, retorts Leibniz, but what God chooses to keep in existence is something different from himself. How can this be, the critic continues, if its "being" *just is* the being of God? Ah, concludes Leibniz, the *being* of things may come from God (in the fashion of Thomistic transcendentals), but their *essences* are nonetheless eternal possibilities that God did not create. Moreover, God could not create individuals who were fully perfect, lest he create a series of equals to himself (and thereby cease to be God). So what he created had to be essentially imperfect. And it is better to have a rich harmony of such things than not to have them at all (ibid., par. 31).

The critic should not be satisfied. Evil is a mere privation; it does not really exist (*Theod.* par. 30). But in the same way imperfection, and hence finitude itself, is also a privation. So does it not follow that these finite things do not really exist? The objection is a weighty one: given the Neoplatonic assumptions in Leibniz's thought, he must treat the three concepts similarly. Everything that *is* in humans comes from God, who in his divine *concours* "giv[es] us continually all that is real in us and in our actions."[167] Yet again, Leibniz insists, only part of what each individual is comes through participation in God. The same passage adds the qualification, "insofar as it involves perfection" (*autant qu'il enveloppe*

---

167. "À nous donner continuellement ce qu'il y a de réel en nous et en nos actions" (*Theod.* par. 377).

de la perfection). His position must be that things do exist as limited substances, and their limitations have an origin independent of the will of God (though not of his thought). Finally, Leibniz's defense of beings that are separate (albeit dependent) and ontologically distinct is Platonic: there are many things because there are many "forms or ideas of the possibles," and these are eternal (*Theod.* par. 380).

Everything turns, finally, on whether there is "something real in possibility."[168] I am inclined to deny it. Possibles do not have their own independent reality; there is no "region of eternal truths"; possible-but-not-actual essences do not strive (because they do not exist at all); there are no such things as possible worlds and no possible person who is you with three legs (nor a "counterpart" of you, as David Lewis has argued). The credibility of a surprising amount of Leibnizianism pales once one has taken leave of real possibles. First (and refreshingly) they cease striving to exist, or demanding that God create them, or doing anything else for that matter. There is no independent given to which God's will must submit, and hence presumably the PSR is invalid.

Along with essences, however, Leibniz's independent principle for guaranteeing the ontological uniqueness of individuals also disappears, and the monism problem now returns with a vengeance. As Leibniz admits at one point, "without [God] there would be no reality in possibilities — not only nothing existent but also nothing possible."[169] If one wants to defend a philosophical theology, one must now say (with Descartes) that what exists, exists because of the concurrence of God's will. These are high costs to pay. In the long run, however, the result may be a more unified and coherent system of thought, in the same sense that Plotinus and Augustine offer more unified accounts of reality than Plato. We return to this argument in the following chapters.

CONCLUSIONS: THE PERFECTION
ARGUMENT AGAINST ATOMISM

In my effort at reconstructing the model of God at the center of the Leibnizian system, I have focused on the constellations of ideas clustered around the concepts of infinity and perfection. I found that these two central concepts were closely related; in particular, infinity was conceived from the very beginning in

---

168. "Ce qu'il y a de réel dans la possibilité" (*Monad.* par. 43).
169. "Sans luy il n'y auroit rien de réel dans les possibilités, et non seulement rien d'existant, mais encor rien de possible" (*Monad.* par. 43).

the context of the notion of perfection: "Infinity is nothing other than perfection."[170] Thus God has power, knowledge, and will, in analogy with human qualities, although in him these attributes are "absolutely infinite or perfect."[171] But the relationship between the two attributes raised serious problems, for example, regarding his theory of creation and the monism question. In particular, I found that Leibniz inadvertently removed the pillars that had allowed philosophical theology to maintain its extremely delicate balance between (on the one hand) an absolutely perfect God who is Being and Goodness itself and (on the other) an independently existing world. Leibniz of course still believed in a separate world outside God; yet his own modifications of the tradition — the denial of matter, of an independent *sensorium* of space and time, of essences independent of God, of real evil — left him finally without the conceptual means to make good on these classical claims. Despite himself, he left us with a philosophy many aspects of which fit more naturally within a monistic than within an atomistic framework. We are now in a position to see what went wrong.

Infinity

My thesis has been that Leibniz utilized the resources of the concept of the infinite in a more thoroughgoing manner than Descartes had done. Without eliminating the finite/infinite distinction (or so it appears), he was able to determine the qualities of infinite being in a way that Descartes could not have done. Recall that Descartes began with the infinite and came to posit its relative perfection through the greater reality *(plus realitatis)* that it has over the finite. Leibniz tacitly appropriated this argument but fit it into the context of a more fully developed theory of the infinite as well. What Descartes could only intuit, Leibniz tried to conceive.

Unfortunately — perhaps because he neglected the role of intuition? — in the process Leibniz comes to focus too exclusively on the theory of perfection. Although he continues to pay lip service to the finite/infinite distinction, the absolute primacy and otherness of the infinite becomes obscured in the undergrowth of details growing out of his philosophy of perfection and his mathematics of infinitesimals. Ironically, Leibniz loses sight of Descartes's central intuition by becoming too enamored of infinities. Infinitesimals give him infinities in miniature, and with all the exactitude of a formal struc-

---

170. "Infinitum nihil aliud est quam perfectum" (from Leibniz's reading notes on Cudworth [1689]; Grua 1:328).
171. "Absolument infinis ou parfaits" (*Monad.* par. 48).

ture.[172] Nature blossoms forth with infinities at every juncture: "I am so much in favor of the actual infinite, that rather than admit that nature abhors it, as one says vulgarly, I hold that nature exemplifies it everywhere, in order to display better the perfections of her author."[173] Leibniz continues to assert that God is ontologically distinct. But the ontological uniqueness of the absolutely infinite remains, despite his best efforts, unthought.

Perfection

I have argued that Leibniz was fundamentally concerned to establish a theology of the *ens perfectissimum;* he was in this sense a true follower of Descartes. His additional project — to show that a perfect being is possible — did not in itself amount to a major paradigm shift from Descartes. That is, it did not mean acknowledging any irremediable weakness in the perfect being tradition. Instead, Leibniz merely brought the resources of that tradition to bear on a new problem, exploring the tradition's resources in the areas of contingency, necessity, and freedom in more detail than Descartes had.

Nonetheless, Leibniz's system as a whole was in several ways less successful than Descartes's had been. Most damagingly, Leibniz's effort to show the possibility of a most perfect being, and his inclination toward atomism in general, led him astray into an atomistic theory of the perfections that raises insurmountable problems for perfect-being theology. For instance, what criteria will now decide which simple qualities should be added to the list of simple perfections and thus become attributes of God? Traditionally (cf. chapter 3), the perfections were constructed theologically from a unitary notion of God, which served in large measure as the standard for knowing what to admit or not to admit as perfections.

The Perfection Argument against Atomism

If we put together all that we have achieved so far, we get something like a perfection argument against atomism. Leibniz holds that evil is a mere privation; it

---

172. Though, again, the infinitesimals were a mixed blessing. Belaval charges that Leibniz lost his nerve: arguing on the basis of his infinitesimal theory, he should never have been a realist about infinities (*Leibniz critique de Descartes*, 355).

173. "Je suis tellement pour l'infini actuel, qu'au lieu d'admettre que la nature l'abhorre, comme l'on dit vulgairement, je tiens qu'elle l'affecte partout, pour mieux marquer les perfections de son auteur" (G 1:416, trans. Rescher).

does not really exist (*Theod.* par. 30). But in the same way imperfection, and hence finitude itself, is also a privation. Thus it should follow that these finite things do not really exist. Given the Neoplatonic assumptions in Leibniz's thought that we have explored, it appears that he should treat the three concepts (evil, imperfection, finitude) similarly. Everything that *is* in humans comes from God, who "giv[es] us continually all that is real in us and in our actions" (*Theod.* par. 377).

The argument can be put differently: The perfection of each individual will finally be measured according to what extent it reaches the goal of divine perfection. But this is a thoroughly ontological claim, as Heinekamp comments:

> To the degree that substances have realized the telos, Leibniz calls them real; insofar as they fall short of this task, they can be called *nonreal*. Because there are no specific perfections that a particular species of things is supposed to have, it follows that every respect in which a thing fails to attain perfection — that is, every *non-ens*, every *negatio* — is not only an imperfection but also a *privatio*, an evil.[174]

At the end of the day, Leibniz's defense of beings that are separate (albeit dependent) and ontologically distinct is Platonic: There are many things because there are many "forms or ideas of the possibles," and these are eternal (*Theod.* par. 380). But it remains unclear whether this conclusion is sufficient for things really to exist as limited substances whose limitations have an origin independent of the will of God (though not of his thought).

The Monism Question

Looking back over these various criticisms, one cannot help but note a number of areas in which true atomism has been modified de facto in the direction of

---

174. Heinekamp, *Das Problem des Guten*, 152: "In dem Maße, wie die Substanzen das Telos verwirklicht haben, nennt Leibniz sie real; insofern als sie hinter dieser Aufgabe zurückstehen, können sie nicht-real genannt werden. Weil es keine spezifischen Vollkommenheiten gibt, die eine bestimmte Gattung von Dingen haben sollte, ist all das, was einem Dinge an Vollkommenheit abgeht, also jedes non-ens, jede negatio, nicht nur eine Unvollkommenheit, sondern eine privatio, ein Übel." See his accompanying notes for numerous references to Leibnizian texts, e.g., Brua 1:364: things "sont bornées ou imparfaites par le principe de la Negation ou du Neant qu'elles referment, par le defaut d'une infinité de perfections qui ne sont pas en elles et ne sont qu'un Neant à leur égard."

greater ontological interconnection and dependence. (1) Not only existences but also the essences of finite things remain ontologically dependent on God.[175] (2) It is in the understanding of God that they aspire *(prétendent)* toward existence (to Bourguet, December 1714, G 3:572). (3) In some passages Leibniz tries to construct a view of reality with only the principles of *realitas* and *nihil*.[176] (4) The realization of each individual entelechy's telos, as Aristotle understood this process, is eternally deferred.[177] Still, he remained an atomist.

What happens when we push Leibniz for an answer to some of these difficulties? I have not argued that to be a theist is automatically to face the specter of monism. Instead, the argument is that the additional moves that are distinctive of Leibniz's particular metaphysical position have forced him into inconsistencies. Most damagingly, Leibniz's effort to show the possibility of a most perfect being, and his inclination toward atomism in general, led him astray into an atomistic theory of perfection that raises insurmountable problems for perfect-being theology.

Could it be that the real problem here is perfection-based theology itself? Isn't this what Leibniz's difficulties teach us? The problems with any such philosophical theology in the late modern context are substantial. For instance, what criteria will now decide which simple qualities should be added to the list of simple perfections and thus become attributes of God? Traditionally, the perfections were derived theologically out of a unitary notion of God, which served in large measure as the standard for knowing what to admit or not to admit as perfections. Lacking any general prior notion of this being — or even a general framework, such as the Cartesian *infinitas* as *plus realitatis* — we are thrown back on our random intuitions about what should and should not be taken as relevant perfections. In the absence of a *theo*logical starting point, the projection critique again rears its ugly head: Leibniz's God is merely a human monad writ large, a

---

175. He writes, "si l'Estre necessaire estoit impossible, tous les Estres contingens le seroient aussi, et qu'ainsi il n'y auroit rien de possible" (to Jaquelot, November 1702, G 3:444). Cf. *Monad.* par. 43, "It is true that God is not only the source of existences, but also of essences." Jalabert comments, "C'est la possibilité logique de l'essence divine, qui fait la possibilité logique des êtres finis" ("Création et harmonie").

176. E.g., M 3:661; Guhrauer 1:401ff. (with mathematical details); further references in Mahnke, 253n.89; Parkinson, *Logic and Reality*, 83ff.; and Heinekamp, *Das Problem des Guten*, 154.

177. *Principles of Nature and Grace*, par. 18 end). Thus Dietrich Mahnke writes, "Entelechie bedeutet für die Griechen 'das Fertige, Vollendete,' . . . während sie für den Deutschen eine *unendliche Sehnsucht* nach der Höherentwicklung aller individuellen Anlagen und einen nie ermattenden Tätigkeitsdrang bedeutet" (*Leibnizens Synthese von Universalmathematik und Individualmetaphysik* [Stuttgart: Frommann, 1964], 86-87).

random compilation of the qualities that humans value. Does one not, finally, lose all chance of conceptualizing the unity of the perfections in this single divine being? There appears to be no way to conceive the unity of God as long as the starting point remains a set of otherwise unrelated properties. We have observed Leibniz's dance of approach and avoidance in the face of Spinozistic monism. Because he is determined to eschew any system that sounds monistic, however, Leibniz ultimately loses his only opportunity to think the unity of the One who possesses the sum total of all simple perfections.

BEYOND PERFECTION?

The doctrine of the infinitely perfect being remained the central category for thinking about God and continued to play a key role in the rationalist tradition well into the eighteenth century. Leibniz, more clearly than Descartes, begins to speak of it as the Absolute, preparing the way for the renewal of philosophical theology in German idealism. I conclude, however, that Leibniz neither derives God's perfection from his infinity nor adequately uses the divine infinity as a control or limiting case for the divine perfections. Both of these are serious weaknesses. The infinite is reduced to a synonym for the *ens perfectissimum* (as in the opening quotation in the previous section) or to a qualifier for "perfection," as in "full," "complete," or "absolute" perfection.

In both respects his position falls behind that of Descartes. Leibniz may have moved us a step closer to the theory of the Absolute, yet at the same time he has obscured the self-limiting character of talk of the infinitely perfect God, the stress on the *Jenseits* (the beyond or more than) that we found in Descartes and Cusa. In his rush to think the fully perfect, Leibniz lost track of Hegel's insight (to put it anachronistically) that the infinite is determined only through its initial otherness over against the finite.

What are we to make of Leibniz's failure? The theory of perfection might still be part of an adequate model of God, but it now seems unlikely that it will be able to play the organizing role in such a theory. For one, we find in perfection too little place for the agency of God. This is ironic, of course, because Leibniz believed the opposite: God has pre-orchestrated absolutely everything, down through infinite infinities of monads; none of them interacts, each having been placed and preprogrammed by the divine; the only actual agent is God. Still, we have found God's role to be limited to an initial choice — a choice, moreover, that was rationally unavoidable and followed as a necessary consequence of the divine nature.

I conclude that these unsolved problems in Leibniz point us toward a more adequate approach to philosophical theology: the abandonment of a theology of atomic perfections — along with the entire moral, volitional, and teleological context from which it emerges — in Spinoza's thought (and subsequently). Arguably, Leibniz was never able to accomplish the task that Wolff realized was indispensable, namely how to show "that the unlimited is more perfect than the limited."[178]

Facing these apparently unavoidable consequences of a perfection-based model of God, it behooves us to look elsewhere. After a two-chapter examination of Kant's critique of metaphysics and the responses to it, we will turn back to the thought of Spinoza and those who reflected in his wake. There we will find the attempt to think what Leibniz only asserted: an infinite dimension, infinitely distinct from the finite at the same time that it encompasses the finite within itself. Although we will not find Spinoza's conception to be without problems of its own, it will offer a corrective to Leibniz at precisely the points of his greatest difficulty.

178. Quoted from Wolff's letter to Leibniz of 5/4/1715 in *Briefwechsel zwischen Leibniz und Christian Wolff*, ed. Gerhardt, loc. cit.

CHAPTER FIVE

Kant's Critique of
Theology and Beyond

KANT'S CRITIQUE OF METAPHYSICS

Kant's *Critique of Pure Reason* confronts language about God with the greatest single challenge of its history — not because that book demonstrates the impossibility of a constitutive metaphysics once and for all (it did not), but because it brought to an end a certain innocence about the language/reality relationship. Never before had a philosopher so forcefully stated the possibility that there might be an unbridgeable cleft between the manner in which humans (necessarily) structure their world(s) and the way that the World Itself — if that phrase even makes sense any longer after Kant — really is. No thinker since Kant has been about to find counterarguments that would return us to the (relative) state of innocence thinkers enjoyed before Kant's first *Critique*.

There is an interesting analogy between the deflowering role played by Kant and the function of the theistic proofs in the history of Western thought — an analogy made ironic by the fact that Kant stands as one of the most effective critics of these proofs. During the "classical" period of theistic proofs, starting with Anselm and Thomas Aquinas but running as late as Leibniz and his followers, readers and writers alike took it as (more or less) a matter of course that God exists. The function of the proofs was merely to lift this obvious truth to the status of a rational, even necessary, inference. Later, however, when the secularization of society and the methodological atheism of the natural sciences had rendered the existence of God questionable, the proofs proved unable to reopen the path back to Eden, to reestablish the reasonableness of theistic belief. In other words, only after the immediacy of the intuition that God exists had become questionable did the arguments' inability to produce such intuitions become obvious.

Something similar, I suggest, holds for the cleft between human experience and things in themselves. During the Scholastic period the idea of a direct *correspondentia res et intellectus* appeared incontestable, and this idea of a correspondence between mind and reality continued to dominate early modern philosophy, from rationalists such as Descartes to empiricists like Locke. As soon as one seriously entertains the possibility that the categories of our understanding do not correspond to a mind-independent reality, however, one discovers how difficult is the return to the paradise of direct realism, and philosophical arguments appear impotent to open the gates again. Traditional or "precritical" epistemologies and theories of God strike one as *uncritical*. One simply has no idea whether, and if so how, one can reestablish one's former belief in the reference of fundamental categories.[1]

Insofar as I affirm the worrisomeness of this possible cleft, and the centrality of the question, my position would appear to stand under the aegis of Kant. Nevertheless, the present chapter has a primarily *critical* goal: to show that a different Kantian dualism — or perhaps: a major argument for the dualism between our experienced world and things in themselves — should be rejected. Kant held that only those knowledge claims that are based on sense data (*sinnliche Anschauungen*) are valid:

> The pure concepts of understanding . . . extend to objects of intuition . . . if only it be sensible and not intellectual. But this extension of concepts beyond

1. Of course, Kant was not the first to argue for a cleft between language and reality. The Scholastic doctrine of analogy, for example, began with the fundamental inadequacy of human language, arguing that God-talk could never be understood as univocal. One can further show that the nominalism of the fourteenth and fifteenth centuries played a role similar to Kant's first *Critique*. See the brilliant study by Louis Dupré, *Passage to Modernity: An Essay in the Hermeneutics of Nature and Culture* (New Haven: Yale Univ. Press, 1993); and Hans Blumenberg, *The Legitimacy of the Modern Age*, trans. Robert M. Wallace (Cambridge: MIT Press, 1983). Even if Kant stands in a certain continuity with these earlier developments, his thesis (and its effects) were much more extreme.

In this chapter I use the following abbreviations: AA = Akademieausgabe (Berlin: 1909ff.); KrV = *Kritik der reinen Vernunft*, cited according to Raymund Schmidt, ed., Philosophische Bibliothek 37a (Hamburg, 1976); and according to the pagination of the 1st ed. of 1781 ("A") and/or that of the 2nd ed. of 1787 ("B"); KpV = *Kritik der praktischen Vernunft*, cited according to AA, vol. V. *Opus postumum* is cited according to AA, vols. XXI-XXII. Where the similarities or differences between A and B are not essential to my argument, I cite from B.

our sensible intuition is of no advantage to us. For as concepts of objects they are then empty. . . . They are mere forms of thought, without objective reality, since we have no intuition at hand. . . . Only our sensible and empirical intuition can give to them body and meaning. (B148-49)

Whatever cannot be the object of an empirical intuition can have, at best, a "regulative" or practical/moral function. This dichotomy affects the concept of God with a particular vengeance, insofar as it concerns a being who essentially transcends the realm of empirical perception. Should thought attempt "to grasp the infinity of God by means of an objectified (object-like) representation," Kant asserts, it will fall into a "transcendental illusion." The problem of illusion can be traced back to the reflecting *Ich*, "which in asking the question of God . . . actually oversteps the limits of its finitude."[2]

I shall argue that the Kantian limitation of knowledge to objects of the senses is both unnecessary and unacceptable. First I must show that his limitation can be defended only by means of de facto metaphysical arguments, since a refutation of metaphysics by means of metaphysical arguments is obviously a self-contradictory refutation. This means showing that Kant's limitation to sensible intuitions represents a form of the metaphysical doctrine of empiricism, which he defended by appeal to the subject or "unity of apperception" as a foundational ontological instance. It is also my task to trace certain inconsistencies in Kant: in his notions of experience, in the ontological presuppositions of his transcendental philosophy, and in the relationship between parts and wholes. If these counterarguments are sound, then the strict separation of constitutive and regulative uses of reason will collapse. Overall, then, my goal is to unearth the metaphysical bulwarks of Kant's critical philosophy. To do this, I will stress the continuities that run from the pre-critical period to Kant's *Opus posthumum*, since they indicate to what extent Kant's critical output remains indebted to metaphysical questions and arguments. This "Kantian metaphysic" — if I may be allowed to use this paradoxical-sounding expression — determines his choice of the categories, the schematism, and his construction of the antinomies; it makes its presence felt yet more strongly as one moves through the *Critique of Judgment* to his very latest writings. In the course of defending this interpretation I shall also refer to "conceptual scheme" philosophies and other developments in contemporary philosophy, since they serve as additional indicators and tests of credibility and relevance. Taken together, these argumentative strategies should help to defend the possibility and even to trace the

2. Christian Link, *Subjektivität und Wahrheit: Die Grundlegung der neuzeitlichen Metaphysik durch Descartes* (Stuttgart, 1978), 264.

contours of a post-Kantian metaphysics — not by ignoring Kant but by looking even more closely at his own project.

Kant once defined metaphysics as "the science of proceeding from knowledge of the sensible to that of the trans-sensible by means of reason."[3] We will find that even the critical Kant continued to tinker with the possibility of such a progression, albeit in a limited and specific sense, and that certain popular arguments against this "ascent" are unconvincing. Of course, the epistemic status of any resulting claims about God will have to be severely weakened in comparison to modern thinkers such as Leibniz or Wolff; we must constantly reckon with the possibility that we are being misled by our own categories into a transcendental illusion. Nevertheless, the possibility of an ascent to language about God — whether it sets out from empirical research, from the quest for a synthesis of our existing items of knowledge, or from classical metaphysical questions — cannot be ruled out in advance. The final result could no longer be a deductive theology that, having once established incontestable grounds and necessary inferences, would move on to demonstrate its superiority over all other options. Nonetheless, we can find grounds, even in post-Kantian philosophy, for designating some ways of speaking about God as stronger or weaker. How we are to do so once we have left Kant behind, and what a "theology of limit notions" might look like, forms the theme of the next chapter.

Kant's claim that he criticized knowledge of God only in order to make room for faith is well known. The plan was to overcome the limitations on the theoretical concept of God in the context of *practical* reason by means of the three postulates God, freedom, and immortality[4] — indeed, even to the point of speaking of a moral proof of God's existence. Why then have I not placed greater emphasis on the second *Critique* and on Kant's moral argument? In brief, I share the widespread view that many of the assumptions in Kant's practical argument for the (necessity of the) postulate of God, rather than being necessary, are questionable in the extreme; the proof itself is a dismal failure.[5] Now several of these well-known difficulties — Kant's claims for

3. Kant, *Preisschrift über die Fortschritten der Metaphysik,* AA XX, 260: "die Wissenschaft, von der Erkenntnis des Sinnlichen zu der des Übersinnlichen durch die Vernunft fortzuschreiten."

4. "Der Begriff der Freiheit . . . macht nun den Schlußstein von dem ganzen Gebäude eines Systems der reinen, selbst der speculativen Vernunft aus, und alle andere Begriffe . . . bekommen mit ihm und durch ihn Bestand und objective Realität" (*KpV,* V, 4). At one point Kant urged that the *KpV* formed the core of his thought and the base of his overall architectonic.

5. A classic argument for the failure of the moral argument to ground metaphysics is W. H. Walsh, "Kant and Metaphysics," *Kant-Studien* 67 (1976): 372-84.

the moral will, his stress on disinterestedness and the "rational agent," and the competing formulations of the categorical imperative — are inextricably tied up with his root argument for the a priori conditions of practical reason. Consequently, the resulting skepticism threatens, in my view, not only the introduction of God as the guarantor of the summum bonum but also the very derivation of the categorical imperative itself.[6] I do not devote more space to critiquing the second *Critique* because I take it that its weaknesses are widely acknowledged.

Even apart from these serious problems in the moral argument for God, it remains questionable whether — even if Kant were successful — we could really ascribe existence to a God who is conceived only as a fundamental postulate of moral action. Wouldn't it be more appropriate, especially in light of the danger of an unjustified projection of human predicates (Feuerbach), to view the practical God as at best an indispensable fiction for ethical behavior? Any attempt to draw an inference from this ethical postulate to reality itself would appear rather arbitrary. Clearly, these difficulties with Kant's moral philosophy have weighty implications for his own philosophy of religion and doctrine of God since, in his words, "Religion is nothing other than the application of theology to morality."[7] It will be my contention that Kant never overcame these difficulties. Of course, even if his moral-theistic argument is not sound, it could still express a *subjective* certainty, a conviction of the existence of a God.[8] Philosophers, however, are interested in *intersubjective* arguments, in warrants that reach beyond subjective conviction. Hence, until more credible moral arguments for God are advanced, the hopes of theistic metaphysics will have to be pinned on other portions of Kantian philosophy.

The importance of this point warrants a brief follow-up argument. Kant's *Critique of Practical Reason* makes a plea for the "objective reality" of God (e.g., V, 135), at least in the context of practical reason, and perhaps beyond it as well. Indeed, the doctrine of God in the second *Critique* includes a number of components that are theoretical in nature and hence not reducible to the purely

---

6. Some of the reasons for breaking with Kant's practical philosophy are listed in Philip Clayton and Steve Knapp, "Ethics and Rationality," *American Philosophical Quarterly* 30 (1993): 51-60.

7. *Vorlesungen über die philosophische Religionslehre* (Wintersemester 1783/84), AA, XXVIII.2,2, 997: "Religion ist nichts anders, als Anwendung der Theologie auf Moralität."

8. This is the thesis of Norbert Fischer's important book, *Die Transzendenz in der Transzendentalphilosophie: Untersuchungen zur speziellen Metaphysik an Kants "Kritik der einen Vernunft"* (Bonn, 1979); see esp. chap. 5 ("Die subjektive Gewißheit über die Gegenstände der speziellen Metaphysik im theoretisch-doktrinalen Glauben"), for example, on the subject of Kant's wager ("Wette," B 852-53).

practical realm.[9] In what sort of discursive context should they be examined? That of the purely practical employment of reason will clearly not suffice. The familiar answer — that the theoretical and practical realms in some way overlap in the case of the three postulates, even though nothing can be known about their theoretical content — only appears to open up a dialogue between theory and practice, since it silences one of the discussion partners from the outset. Could a new discursive framework be constructed that would someday overcome the differences between practical and theoretical reason, allowing for a synthesis of the two? In principle, yes. Kant himself never developed such a theory, however — especially not in the second *Critique,* which if anything sharpens the line of demarcation between theory and practice, and the prospects for overcoming the fact/value distinction have clearly grown dimmer during the twentieth century.[10] Therefore I suggest that the failure of the moral theistic proof and its subsequent defenses should direct our attention back toward the theoretical realm. If the following criticisms of the Kantian distinction between regulative and constitutive are sound, we will possess yet further grounds for looking again at constitutive theories about the divine. This, at any rate, is the overall strategy of the present chapter.

First Suspicions

Only the chapter as a whole can make the case for a more-than-regulative use of theistic language. Still, it will help to orient the discussion if we briefly review some of the well-known reservations about Kant's limitation of the constitutive use of reason to objects of the senses. The following points can only outline the objections that have been exhaustively developed in the literature; still, presenting them now in précis form will help focus the subsequent, more detailed discussion below.

9. The postulate of the "Existenz und Persönlichkeit desselben vernünftigen Wesens (welche man die Unsterblichkeit der Seele nennt)" is according to Kant "einen theoretischen, als solchen aber nicht erweislichen Satz" (V, 122). Later he calls the three concepts "theoretische Begriffe" and speaks of the "Erweiterung der theoretischen Vernunft" (V, 134).

10. Jürgen Habermas would presumably claim that he has already achieved such a synthesis; cf., e.g., *The Philosophical Discourse of Modernity: Twelve Lectures,* trans. Frederick Lawrence (Cambridge: MIT Press, 1987). In my view, however, some crucial problems remain to be solved. See Gerhard Schurz, "Grenzen rationaler Ethikbegründung: Das Sein-Sollen-Problem aus moderner Sicht," in *Ethik und Sozialwissenschaft* (1995).

The Acceptance of Humean Empiricism

Several good summaries exist of the criticisms raised by Kant scholars against Kant's use of the empirical criterion.[11] It is not difficult to reconstruct how he may have come to hold the position he did. Kant detected in Hume's derivation of all knowledge from sense impressions the possibility of introducing a more stringent control over metaphysical reflection, one that would avoid the epistemological misjudgments that (in his view) underlay the unjustified optimism of Wolffian metaphysics. For a philosopher such as Kant, who was interested in applying the results of nascent natural science to all theoretical reason, the equation of empirical knowledge with knowledge in general *(Erkenntnis überhaupt)* must have been extremely attractive.

That Kant's form of empiricism was attractive for numerous philosophers in the following two centuries is too obvious to need recounting. Indeed, it has primarily been empiricists working in the Humean tradition who have carried the banner for Kantian empiricism. Anglo-American philosophers such as Peter Strawson have found in the empiricist Kant an important ally. One could even say, more strongly, that a significant part of analytic philosophy has *defined itself* through its appropriation of (a particular interpretation of) Kant and its rejection of all later attempts in German philosophy to move beyond Kant, whether constructively (Hegel) or critically (Schopenhauer to Nietzsche). The analysts' selection of Kant the empiricist gave rise, for example, to that particular collection of theses which became the breeding ground for logical positivism and the assertion of the meaninglessness of nonempirical discourse. Likewise, these thinkers invariably either criticized or ignored Kant's own interest in non- or transempirical questions[12] — a lack that motivates the present treatment. It is no exaggeration to say that, were it not for its dependence on the Humean tradition, the empirical interpretation of Kant would not have seemed as plausible or have had the influence that it has.[13]

11. Cf. D. Henrich, "Ding an sich," in G. Wenz und J. Rohls, eds., *Vernunft des Glaubens,* Festschrift for Wolfhart Pannenberg (Göttingen: Vandenhoeck & Ruprecht, 1988), 42-92.

12. Above all, the interpretations of Kant by Jonathan Bennett and Peter Strawson have determined the understanding of Kant within analytic philosophy since 1965 or so. Bennett views the Transcendental Analytic as the heart of the first *Critique* and pays scant attention to the Deduction (in *Kant's Analytic* [Cambridge: Cambridge Univ. Press, 1966]). Strawson attempts to strengthen the role of empirical considerations in comparison to Kant by means of his "principle of significance" (in *The Bounds of Sense: An Essay on Kant's 'Critique of Pure Reason'* [London: Methuen, 1966], e.g., 192). As a result, he admits that the idea of God could function as an ideal of reason. Nevertheless, he dismisses it without further argument, telling us only that it is "hard to feel any sympathy with the suggestion" (p. 222).

13. Dieter Henrich ("Ding an sich," 69 note) also notes that Kant never took on the

Kant's Concept of Experience

It is perhaps ironic that, despite the empirical limits on knowledge just described, Kant held a rather unempirical understanding of experience.[14] For this reason Paton has called his theoretical system a "metaphysic of experience." Notwithstanding the important influence of Hume,[15] Kant's metaphysics of experience stands at some distance from Hume's own philosophy. The distance appears nowhere more clearly than in Kant's concept of experience, which, I hope to show, is marred by a deep ambivalence. Even such a decided opponent of the "metaphysical Kant" as W. H. Walsh must admit at the end of a long treatment of the Kantian concept of experience that "there seems to be an enormous gulf in outlook between Kant and the great Empiricists." He rightfully concludes, "If we have to choose between calling Kant a Rationalist and calling him an Empiricist, the first is to be preferred."[16]

The "pure" empiricist has no difficulty in establishing the limits of experience; all she or he needs to do is to discover the absolutely simple perceptual data on which all knowledge is built. Had Kant developed a clear theory of "sense impressions," as Hume did, it would have been easier for him to say exactly what can pass as "experience." But such a project was foreign to him. Hence, at the same time that we have to side with Kant in his criticisms of the sense-impression model of experience, we must acknowledge that his very success in overcoming it raises new problems of its own. For without such a theory it is difficult for him to avoid the objection that there may well be many more types of experience than the strictly sensible; experience may encompass much

---

problem of reference to individual things: "Sobald dies aber geschiet, erweist es sich als notwendig, auch Kants These über das, was unsere Erkenntnis von Dingen als Erkenntnis nur ihrer 'Erscheinungen' ausmacht, in anderer Weise zu entwickeln. Es ist dann nämlich nicht mehr möglich, das, was es positiv heißt, daß wir nur Erscheinungen erkennen, allein damit zu erklären, daß unsere Erkenntnis auf Gegebenes in der Form unserer Sinnlichkeit eingeschränkt ist." I see no way to overcome this inconsistency — unless Kant had cast the limitation to sensible intuitions itself into question.

14. For a nice overview of Kant's use of the term "experience," which has the goal of cleaning up ambiguities and showing the plain meaning, see Stephen Palmquist, "Knowledge and Experience: An Examination of the Four Reflective 'Perspectives' in Kant's Critical Philosophy," *Kant-Studien* 78 (1987): 170-200. Despite Palmquist's optimism, however, I fear that his "plain" treatment raises as many questions as it solves.

15. Cf. K. Fischer, *Immanuel Kant und seine Lehre*, vol. 1 (Heidelberg: C. Winter, 1928), 232ff.

16. W. H. Walsh, "Kant and Empiricism," in Joachim Kopper und Wolfgang Marx, eds., *200 Jahre Kritik der reinen Vernunft* (Hildesheim: Gerstenberg, 1981), 385-420, quotations 407 and 417.

more than he was ready to acknowledge. Only an implicit dependence on the British empirical tradition — a dependence inconsistent with Kant's own movement beyond Hume — could justify the claim to know that there cannot be any "intellectual experience" or intellectual intuition.

The sharp distinction between form and content, between categories and raw sense data, is unacceptable. I have already suggested that Kant's concept of experience is not as unambiguous as he maintains; in particular, his identification of the "given" with the input of the five senses becomes an arbitrary move unless one relies at least implicitly on an empiricist epistemology. The distinction between sensible input and categories is further challenged by contemporary developments in epistemology and the philosophy of science, especially by the collapse of the theory/observation dichotomy and by recent insights into the ubiquitous role of conceptual schemes.[17] Kant's assertion of a single group of necessary and unchanging categories has shown itself to be particularly problematic. Nicholai Hartmann formulates the objection forcefully:

> Knowledge does not stand still. It "moves" — not only in the sense that it undergoes increases in content, widening and deepening our picture of the world, but also in the sense that our activities aimed at knowledge change. We learn to work with different epistemic tools, even creating new ones, discovering, improving and sharpening them. The tools are the categories of knowledge. . . . There are also changes, even in a certain sense *exchanges,* of categories. . . . The basic motif of this change is the "pushing forward" of new categories (or categorial moments) into our consciousness. . . . Categories that have once pushed their way into awareness do not remain static but continue to change — a change that is driven by the tendency toward a progressive approximation to the object.[18]

It is my thesis that rejecting the notion of universal and immutable categories entails abandoning the idea that there was a sharp division in the first place between categories and intuitions. Instead, intuitions may suggest their own categories, and shifting categories may affect even our allegedly "basic" intuitions of the world, so that the very distinction between the two becomes difficult to

17. See Philip Clayton, *Explanation from Physics to Theology: An Essay in Rationality and Religion* (New Haven: Yale Univ. Press, 1989), chap. 2, for references to the literature.

18. Nicolai Hartmann, *Die Erkenntnis im Lichte der Ontologie*, PhB 347 (Hamburg: Meiner, 1982), 39, 43. Hartmann's criticisms of Kant — and indeed his broader attack on epistemology without ontology — help to bolster the case being made in this chapter.

hold steady. Should these distinctions become more fluid (as I believe they have), other Kantian dualisms may be swept away as well: sensible intuitions versus intellectual intuitions, constitutive ideas versus regulative ideas, theoretical reason versus practical reason. Of course, each separate challenge to Kant's various dualisms must be substantiated in detail; the goal here is only to suggest that (and why) the strict divisions in Kant's critical philosophy appear unacceptable today — and to trace what may result once they are abandoned.

The Subject as Ground

Kant presupposes that the subject (the transcendental unity of apperception) is primordial; it constitutes the world of our knowledge. Where it comes from or how it came to be hardwired with precisely these twelve categories are not answerable questions. The foundational role of the subject for Kant means, I suggest, that he attributes to it, de facto, a metaphysical status. The reflecting subject takes on the function that was earlier ascribed to the *arché* principle or to God. Because of this, one is justified in speaking of a Kantian "metaphysics of the subject." Of course, Kant leaves his metaphysics largely implicit; if he developed it as a metaphysical position, he would infringe on the self-imposed limits of transcendental philosophy.

Indeed, there are other fundamental components of transcendental philosophy also that Kant is not able to defend without moving beyond the limits of his own position. Consider the examples of space and time. As Heimsoeth's detailed study shows, "The entire pathos of the infinite in Kant's early period is retained in . . . its complete inner meaning in the practical-dogmatic metaphysics of Kantian Idealism. The accent has now been shifted, however, from the infinity of the cosmic developments to the infinity of mental occurrences."[19] However, "this form 'time' presupposes temporal reality, the quality of temporality."[20] In place of the traditional view of the divine understanding as an omnipresent *intuitus originarius,* in which the whole of space-time (or at least their forms) is present, Kant now limits himself to the human intuition of space and time: "Infinite space and time do not exist as the 'sensorien' of God, but rather as the 'intuitive a priori basic function of human reason.' In this sense the Aesthetic as a whole is based upon the separation between the pure intu-

19. Heinz Heimsoeth, "Metaphysische Motive in der Ausbildung des kritischen Idealismus," as found in his collected works, *Gesammelte Abhandlungen,* vol. 1: *Metaphysische Ursprünge und ontologische Grundlagen,* Kantstudien Ergänzungsheft 71 (Cologne: Kölne Universitäts-Verlag, 1956), 189-225, quotation 225.

20. Cramer, *Gottesbeweise,* 121.

ition of finite reason and the intellectual intuition of God."[21] Delekat is therefore exactly right on the question of space-time: we can "determine the meaning of Kant's 'Copernican revolution' quite precisely. It did not change anything in the content of the Newtonian concept of space and time; instead, it anchored them no longer in the *sensorium Dei* but rather in the understanding of man."[22] It will thus be our task to show that Kant never fully grasped the implications of his own appropriation and transformation of traditional metaphysics.

The *Ding an Sich*

The role of the thing-in-itself in transcendental philosophy is another case of an uneasy truce between the requirements of Kant's position and what is actually admissible within it.[23] Kant introduces the thing-in-itself as a given for transcendental reflection. But in order to do so, "he must presuppose within the understanding a fundamental noncategorial 'thinking,' that is, a grasping, an understanding of objects, or a givenness in sensory intuition,"[24] which can never be justified in light of his own analysis of knowledge. The same thing applies to the move by which the subject comes to serve the function previously fulfilled by the notion of being. Being, like the thing-in-itself, is by definition not something that can be reduced to a mere postulation of humans. Yet at times Kant is inclined to reduce it in precisely this manner, as when he asserts that "being is obviously not a real predicate," but rather "merely the position of a thing" (B 626).

To drive this criticism home requires a two-step argument. First I must show that Kantianism does not stand above all metaphysics but is itself dependent on an (often implicit) dualistic metaphysics of the subject and the *Ding an sich* as its other.[25] Then I will argue that this metaphysical position is inconsis-

21. Karl Heinrich Manzke, *Ewigkeit und Zeitlichkeit: Aspekte für eine theologische Deutung der Zeit* (Göttingen: Vandenhoeck & Ruprecht, 1992), 115; the quotation is taken from Heimsoeth. Manzke gives a masterful presentation of the theological motifs that continue to play an important role in the first Critique.

22. Friedrich Delekat, *Immanuel Kant: Historisch-kritische Interpretation der Hauptschriften* (Heidelberg: Quelle & Meyer, 1963), 62; for other difficulties that this raises for his theory of space and time, see 64ff.

23. An especially clear presentation of this argument can be found in Bernd Burkhardt, *Hegels Kritik an Kants theoretische Philosophie: Dargestellt und beurteilt an den Themen der metaphysica specialis* (Munich: Profil Verlag, 1989).

24. Horst Seidl, "Bemerkungen zu Ding an sich und transzendentalem Gegenstand in Kants Kritik der reinen Vernunft," *Kant-Studien* 63 (1972): 305-14, quotation 313.

25. "If the agnosticism of Kant's transcendental idealism is abandoned in principle [sc. as it ought to be], we need a metaphysics of the subject which can integrate the Kantian 'I

tent, incomplete, or inferior to other metaphysical options. As soon as Kant's position reveals itself to be only one option among others, we can contrast it (in the following chapters) with its competitors, siding with them if and where they can demonstrate their superiority.

The Confusion between Projection and Hypothetical Metaphysics

In one interesting sense Kant anticipated Feuerbach's critique of religion. He recognized in the tendency of speculative reason to infer to the existence of a highest being the constant danger that human thinkers will project their own conditions of knowing beyond the human realm — and possibly into a pure vacuum. In one sense Kant is right: it does indeed belong to speculative reason to presuppose a highest ideal — a ground, a Creator, or merely the ontological unity of everything that exists. Consequently, it always remains a serious temptation to humans "to be persuaded that a mere creature of its own thought is a real being" (B 612). Still, however right Kant was to warn of this false step, it remains unwarranted to conclude that all talk of a highest instance automatically involves an illicit projection of human ideals.[26] Just as we were able to grant the possibility of projection in previous chapters without justifying an immediate reduction of God-talk to statements about the human species, so also we will find it necessary in discussing Kant's philosophy to distinguish between the possibility and the actuality of such a reduction — and certainly to do so more clearly than Kant himself did.

Metaphysics after Kant?

Is it true, then, that theological truth claims about God are mistaken, that metaphysics has become impossible after Kant? Merely posing the question reveals the perplexing challenge this thinker has raised for thinkers today who wish to do something more than merely "descriptive" metaphysics. Ironically, even the fact that we are compelled to worry about the status of language about God and

---

think' into a positive account of the mode of being of the subject" (Joseph Claude Evans Jr., *The Metaphysics of Transcendental Subjectivity: Descartes, Kant and W. Sellars* [Amsterdam: B. R. Grüner, 1984], 84). For "thinking through Kantian issues forces us to go beyond Kant" (83; the complete argument is given in his chap. 4).

26. Such claims appear in particular in the *Opus postumum:* God is "das Produkt unserer eigenen Vernunft" and "das Ideal einer substanz, welches wir uns selbst schaffen" (quoted from Erich Adickes, *Kants Opus postumum*, Kant-Studien Ergänzungsheft 50 (Berlin: Reuther & Reichard, 1920), 793.

must argue in its defense — whether or not Kant wins in the end — already indicates the way in which Kant has transformed theological discussion.

I suggest that the question must be answered with both a yes and a no. On the one hand, no: even if metaphysical language can no longer be used in the same manner after Kant — no more pure deductions from first principles, no direct inferences to a thought-independent world, no substance metaphysics without a central place for the human subject — it does not follow that Kant's limitation of knowledge to the realm of the sensible must be accepted. In what follows I present the argument against Kant's epistemic limitation in three forms: by criticizing Kant's theory of knowledge, focusing on the concept of regulative language; by spelling out and attacking the implicit metaphysics that underlies Kant's critical philosophy, with an emphasis on his theories of God and the infinite; and by offering an alternative approach to theological language that avoids the epistemic sins of Kant's predecessors.

On the other hand, yes: after Kant, the epistemic status of metaphysics, and even the methods that it uses, can no longer be the same as before. The Kantian arguments surveyed below demonstrate what could only be asserted in chapter 1: that a theology adequate to the epistemic standards of today will be balanced delicately between the regulative and the constitutive. It will include more than God as a useful fiction for human agents (e.g., as a condition of the possibility of human knowledge), yet less than the absoluteness claims of pre-Kantian theories of God. In the post-Kantian context we must acknowledge the regulation functions of theistic language — its role, for example, in grounding knowledge claims and creating meaning. Yet God-language can also be part of constitutive theories, theories that make claims to truth and can be examined accordingly. Let us turn first, then, to the problem of regulative ideas.

REGULATIVE IDEAS AFTER KANT

We began by raising questions about Kant's theory of experience, and thus about the validity of his sharp separation between the knowable and the unknowable. At the same time, I had to grant the possibility of one epistemic dualism that might turn out to be unbridgeable: that of a final division between what we know and what is. No later philosopher or critique of Kant has been able to abolish this possibility. This fact alone requires a reorientation in the manner in which any theory of God might be interpreted. Specifically, talk of God is now seen as expressing at least the regulative ideas of human reason, and possibly also — if Kant is wrong in the ways I have suggested — as involving independent (constitutive) truth claims that can be examined and tested in at least some respects.[27]

This change of paradigms is so fundamental that it demands our attention already at this point in the book — after the failure of the perfection tradition and before the exploration of the Spinoza tradition (which explains the nonhistorical order of these chapters). It involves a transformation that is basic for contemporary treatments of the question of God: *doing theology after Kant can no longer be (fully) separated from the epistemological questions raised by the notion of God.* God-talk is also about the ideals and the limits of human reason. This means that problems of knowledge — such as the transition to a pluralistic metaphysics or the function of metaphors and models in theology — are intrinsic to language about God.

Let us then follow Kant's theory of regulative ideas (RIs) as the red thread for introducing his theories of God and infinity. RIs are connected with the search for a highest unity.[28] Kant also speaks of transcendental concepts, pure concepts of reason (B 379), and transcendental ideas or ideas of reason. In each case he is concerned with "concepts through which an object is known, namely highest unity or the unconditioned."[29] Especially important in this context is his notion of the *transcendental ideal*.[30] The transcendental ideal, the high point of metaphysics and the limit case of human reason in general, is the idea of the unconditioned. This ideal, which is the condition for all appearances, cannot itself be anything limited; only something unlimited can fulfill this function. Note that, for Kant, even the notion of a highest unity, which is itself a regulative idea, must still be conceived as an object. For example, as Cramer has shown, in the antinomies Kant moves directly from transcendental ideas to concepts, which presupposes that the object of such ideas must be thought as existing.

27. Cf. D. Henrich, "Grund und Gang spekulativen Denkens," in Henrich and R.-P. Horstmann, eds., *Metaphysik nach Kant?* (Stuttgart: Klett-Cotta, 1988), 83-120. Henrich's article, with its argument that reflection must move beyond the merely regulative, has become a sort of classic in recent German philosophy.

28. "Die Vernunft [sucht] im Schließen die große Mannigfaltigkeit der Erkenntnis des Verstandes auf die kleinste Zahl der Prinzipien (allgemeiner Bedingungen) zu bringen und dadurch die höchste Einheit derselben zu bewirken" (B 361).

29. Wolfgang Cramer, *Gottesbeweise und ihre Kritik: Prüfung ihrer Beweiskraft* (Frankfurt: M. Klostermann, 1967), 114.

30. It is not possible to provide a systematic account of this notion here. In the secondary literature see in particular Svend Andersen, *Ideal und Singularität: Über die Funktion des Gottesbegriffs in Kants theoretischer Philosophie*, Kantstudien Ergänzungsheft 116 (Berlin: de Gruyter, 1983), esp. chap. 5, 185-254.

Kant was the first to see clearly the problems raised by the existence of RIs of reason, although, because of a certain confusion that runs through the three *Critiques,* I do not believe he was able to solve them. The weakness in his theory of RIs affects his distinction between the regulative and the constitutive uses of reason and thus his attempt to transform the ideas of God, world, and soul. Later I try to show that they also affect his distinction between apodictic and hypothetical propositions, and thus the alleged necessity of the categories. If the categories that organize sensory input are not necessary, this will affect the status of most of Kant's major theories: the "unity of reason," the doctrine of freedom, the concept of purposefulness (and thus his theory of science), and of course the architectonic itself. But let us test these implications one at a time.

There is no scandal in raising fundamental doubts about Kant's argumentation: many of the central Kantian theories have long since become suspect, and philosophers would in many respects be better off to abandon some of them completely. The irony of the failure of Kant's theory of RIs, however, is that he was so nearly right. For it is true that particular ideas regulate the use of reason, and that such ideas earn a special status insofar as they waver between directly theoretical-constitutive and more fictive uses of language. Think of the status today of our assumption of the unity of truth or the belief in the regularity of nature. Equally important are Kant's insights into the ways in which the human understanding anticipates a final "unity of reason." Also ironically, the correct view of RIs depends on a recent development in philosophy — the recognition of the pervasive nature of conceptual schemes (CSs) — whose source, ultimately, is Kant. We shall see how the CS insight contributes to an adequate theory of the RIs of reason.

Kant thought that a transcendental critique could establish certain synthetic a priori truths. Among the benefits of his project, he thought, would be providing the conditions of the possibility of all knowledge whatsoever *(Erkenntnis überhaupt)* and an exhaustive table of the categories of the understanding adapted from Aristotle, available both in regular and in schematized forms. In this chapter I assume that Kant's attempts at a complete and necessary transcendental philosophy failed.[31] The German critiques are legion; in the English-speaking tradition, critics from Barry Stroud and Jonathan Bennett to Richard Rorty have chronicled in particular the failure of his attempt to specify a uniquely "transcendental" argument form.[32] Assuming they are right, one

31. D. K. Seung, for example, has subjected Kant's definitions of the categories and his various derivations to a scalding critique; see his "Kant's Conception of the Categories," *Review of Metaphysics* 43 (1989): 107-32.

32. The analytic case against Kant goes back at least to Patricia Crawford, "Kant's The-

must give Kant's deduction of the categories some other status than transcendental. (The schematism faces even worse troubles.)[33]

Instead of merely repeating well-known criticisms, I would like to concentrate on what happens to the RIs if Kant's categories of the understanding turn out to be less than necessary. Many commentators treat Kant's RIs as having only secondary status; they accord primary importance to the categories because of their transcendental necessity. But if the necessity of precisely these twelve categories is a chimera, then the second-class status of the RIs needs to be rethought as well. Or, more constructively: Kant would have done better had he interpreted categories such as substance and causality as *themselves* RIs, basic regulating assumptions that appear indispensable to the pursuit of knowledge. This modification is also suggested by more recent arguments against the purely transcendental character of synthetic a priori judgments, for example, those that question the transcendental status of the principle of causality.[34] The result is a new emphasis

---

ory of Philosophical Proof," *Kant-Studien* 53 (1962): 257-68. Strong criticisms (and attempts at reconstruction) include Barry Stroud, "Transcendental Arguments," *Journal of Philosophy* 65 (1968): 241-56; William Stine, "Transcendental Arguments," *Metaphilosophy* 3 (1972): 43-52; Peter Hacker, "Are Transcendental Arguments a Version of Verificationism?" *American Philosophical Quarterly* 9 (1972): 78-85; Jonathan Bennett, "Analytic Transcendental Arguments," in Peter Bieri et al., eds., *Transcendental Arguments and Science* (Dordrecht: D. Reidel, 1979); Anthony L. Brueckner's articles on "Transcendental Arguments" in *Nous* 17 (1983): 551-75 and 18 (1984): 197-225; Richard Rorty, "Transcendental Arguments, Self-Reference, and Pragmatism," in Bieri et al., eds., *Transcendental Arguments;* and the articles by Stephan Körner, M. P. Gram, and L. B. Puntel in *Zur Zukunft der Transzendentalphilosophie,* Neue Hefte für Philosophie 14 (Göttingen: Vandenhoeck & Ruprecht, 1978). For further references see Karl Ameriks, "Recent Work on Kant's Theoretical Philosophy," *American Philosophical Quarterly* 19 (1982): 1-24.

33. Daniel Dahlstrom notes: "According to the overwhelming majority of contemporary Kant critics, the whole theory of the schematism rests upon an artificial and unacceptable distinction between concept-possession and concept-applicability." See his "Transzendentale Schemata, Kategorien und Erkenntnisarten," *Kant-Studien* 75 (1984): 38-54, quotation 39. Dahlstrom himself does not share this judgment.

One can show that Kant's notion of substance is either compatible with the use of substance in Hume, Hegel, and Whitehead (to name just three) and therefore connotes (virtually) no content at all, or is incompatible with one or more of them, in which case it is unclear why his construal should be preferred to theirs. This is not to mention the equivocations in Kant's own use of these terms. For example, in the Deductions in A and B he uses *substance* in two different senses, once as *relatively enduring* and once as *permanence* (see Bennett, *Kant's Analytic,* 167-68).

34. See esp. Konrad Cramer, *Nicht-reine synthetische Urteile a priori: Ein Problem der Transzendentalphilosophie Immanuel Kants* (Heidelberg: C. Winter Universitatsverlag, 1985), e.g., chap. 5; and Hartmann, *Die Erkenntnis im Lichte der Ontologie.*

on the manner in which such concepts regulate research and theory construction. For example, one cannot imagine a theory of the world that omitted the questions, What is it that exists? What causes the specific changes that occur in physical systems over time? Under a regulative interpretation, substance becomes not a category that we know with transcendental necessity (as a condition of the possibility of any knowledge whatsoever) but rather a general framework to be filled in with specific content by specific disciplines according to their particular CSs.[35] This result is consistent with a spate of recent arguments against the purely transcendental character of synthetic a priori judgments.

My suggestion, then, is to reinterpret the categories of the understanding along the lines of Kant's appendix on the regulative employment of ideas — ideas that can be used for "directing the understanding towards a certain goal upon which the routes marked out by all its rules converge, as upon their point of intersection" (B 672). Clearly, a full reinterpretation of the categories in this direction exceeds the limits of this work. Still, enough grounds have been given to justify it as a working hypothesis to be considered in the following sections as we rethink the notion of RIs. If the hypothesis is correct, it has some startling implications for evaluating Kant's critical philosophy as a whole — and for his treatment of the problem of God in particular.

Kant's Regulative Ideas Are Systematically Ambiguous

Many have noted that Kant held ambivalent views concerning RIs. Consider the following arguments, which suggest that his RIs are systematically ambiguous and that he failed in the end to provide a consistent theory of RIs.

First, of course, is the problem of exactly what Kant meant by RIs and what he meant them to include. On the one hand, the appendix to the Dialectic labels as RIs certain hypotheses formulated by reason: the principles of the homogeneity of the manifold under higher genera, of the variety of the homogeneous under lower species, and of the continuity of the forms, that is, the gradual increase of diversity (B 685-86).[36] Yet the basic idea of the appen-

---

35. This suggested revision of Kant is, of course, not new here; it goes back at least as far as H. W. Cassirer's *Commentary on Kant's Critique of Judgment* (London: Methuen, 1938). See, e.g., 347: "If therefore by a constitutive principle we understand a principle that gives us absolute knowledge, a principle that determines the things as they really are and does not merely give us rules for the synthesis of our sensuous intuitions, then all the principles of the understanding may be called regulative principles."

36. See the helpful discussion in Iris Fry, "Kant's Principle of the Formal Finality of Nature and Its Role in Experience," *International Philosophical Quarterly* 29 (1989): 67-76, e.g., 68.

dix is that of "the systematic unity of nature as objectively valid and necessary" (B 679). Should we then take this as the highest RI of reason? On the other hand, the Dialectic as a whole had been concerned with the three great ideas of Wolff's *metaphysica specialis:* the soul, the world, and God. Since the whole point of the Dialectic is that these "ideas of reason" cannot be constitutive ideas, they too must be regulative. Finally, the overarching idea of the metaphysical use of reason is the idea of the unconditioned, an idea whose unique status Kant emphasizes by calling it "the transcendental ideal." Is this then Kant's ultimate RI?

The relations between the three RIs soul, world, and God are likewise somewhat obscure. As Dister has shown, only the last of the three is unambiguously an RI of reason. The soul is an RI for psychology but not for the unification of knowledge as a whole, and "world" actually refers to "nature in general" and thus "really serves the same function as God."[37] Worse, the idea of God itself turns out to be just a special case of the more general presupposition that the world is intelligible, viz. of the ideal of pure reason, "the highest and complete material condition of the possibility, to which must be traced back all thought of objects in general, so far as their content is concerned."[38] Could it perhaps be because of this problematic reduction of the concept of God that Kant finally concludes, "This ideal of the *ens realissimum,* although it is indeed a mere representation, is first *realised,* that is, made into an object, then *hypostatised,* and finally, by the natural progress of reason towards the completion of unity, is, as we shall presently show, *personified*" (B 611 note)?

Second, Kant seems to underestimate the essential role of the appendix on RIs for the entire Dialectic. Just as the brief chapter on the schematism in the second book of the Analytic determines a large section of the argument in the Analytic, the appendix determines the status of the Dialectic as a whole. Indeed, moving beyond the confines of the Dialectic, ideas of reason (esp. the notion of the completion of reason) are clearly relevant to reason in its transcendental function as well; thus their domain should extend to the entire

---

37. Cf. John E. Dister, "Kant's Regulative Ideas and the 'Objectivity of Reason,'" in Lewis White Beck, ed., *Proceedings of the Third International Kant Congress* (Dordrecht: Reidel, 1972), 262-69. Similarly, Peter Baumann has shown in detail how the regulative ideas God and World constitute one another in a reciprocal manner; see his "Kants vierte Antinomie und das Ideal der reinen Vernunft," *Kant-Studien* 79 (1988): 183-200, esp. 190-91.

38. B 604. Dister comes to the conclusion that the ideal of intelligibility is itself preconceptual and thus "should be considered the precise source of the regulative function of reason in its scientific endeavors" ("Kant's Regulative Ideas," 269).

first *Critique*.[39] (This follows automatically if I am right to suggest a reduction of the categories to RIs.)

Third, the problems are compounded when one attempts to think through what it would mean to expand the field in which RIs are valid. I have already argued that Kant calls the categories constitutive at points where he should speak of them only as regulative. Now it turns out that he dubs some principles "regulative" when, according to his argument, they should be constitutive. For example, in the second analogy Kant distinguishes the principle that everything has a cause from that of the uniformity of nature ("like causes have like effects"), labeling the former synthetic a priori and the latter only a regulative principle of reflective judgment. Yet recognizing the causal relation in the second analogy presupposes the latter principle; and once one recognizes their interdependence in the argument, it becomes clear that Kant is actually providing a transcendental deduction of both principles. Hence the principle of the uniformity of nature should be acknowledged as just as transcendentally necessary as the causal principle itself; if Kant were consistent, both would be taken as constitutive principles.[40]

Similarly, the principle that the world as a whole is ultimately purposive is supposed to be merely regulative; but on what grounds does Kant decide that this admittedly possible explanation could never be proved? It is clear in the *Critique of Judgment* that he was at least tempted to believe that the world is in fact purposive in the final analysis; and Van De Pitte has provided convincing arguments to show that a number of problems in Kant's philosophy would be solved if purposiveness is declared a constitutive principle.[41]

39. Ralph Walker argues, for example, that the regulative function for Kant provides "assertibility conditions" for assertions about empirical laws. Without utilizing such principles, categories such as that of causality could not even be applied to the world. See Walker, "Kant's Conception of Empirical Law — II," *Proceedings of the Aristotelian Society Supplement* 64 (1990): 243-58. If Walker's thesis is right, its repercussions would echo throughout the first *Critique*. For example, it would guarantee the relevance of the idea of the unconditioned or God for the theory of space and time in the Aesthetic.

40. For the complete argument see Jeffery Dodge, "Uniformity in Empirical Cause-Effect Relations in the Second Analogy," *Kant-Studien* 73 (1982): 47-54. Dodge's doctoral advisor, Lewis White Beck, published his version of his student's argument even before the latter's dissertation was published; see Beck, "Über die Regelmässigkeit der Natur bei Kant," *Dialectica* 35 (1981): 43-56, esp. 48-49. Jonathan Bennett has also given a convincing account of the ambiguities in the regulative/constitutive distinction within the Second Analogy in "The Status of Determinism," *British Journal for the Philosophy of Science* 14 (1963): 106-19.

41. Cf. Frederick P. Van De Pitte, "The Role of Teleology in Kant's Work," in W. H. Werkmeister, ed., *Reflections on Kant's Philosophy* (Gainesville: University Presses of Florida, 1975), 135-47. On Kant's temptations in this direction see J. D. McFarland, *Kant's Concept of Teleology* (Edinburgh: Univ. of Edinburgh Press, 1970), e.g., 42.

Fourth, the tensions are compounded when one compares the treatment of RIs among the three *Critiques*. The different treatment of the idea of freedom in the first and second *Critiques* has often been noted. But Kant also fails to reconcile the first *Critique* treatment of the RI of systematicity (as part of the faculty of pure theoretical reason, B 674-75) with the treatment in the *Critique of Judgment*, which depends on the newly introduced (and inadequately spelled out) faculty of reflective judgment. Indeed, the latter treatment does not even mention the revisions it has made over against the earlier view![42]

Fifth, Kant fails to resolve his vacillation between a methodical-subjective and a transcendental-objective interpretation of the RIs.[43] For instance, when the third *Critique* assumes a hypothetical "as if" existence of an intelligent designer as cause of the empirical system, it conflates an (allegedly) fictional postulation with the necessity of the categories; yet, like the categories, this postulation supposedly supplies a necessary condition for any knowledge whatsoever! Or (to take another example) to complete the synthesis of the manifold Kant requires two things: the temporally schematized categories and the RI of the finality of nature, which he calls the a priori subjective presupposition of empirical regularity and unformity.[44] It appears that objective experience and "subjective" ideas are more organically interconnected than the structure of Kant's own argument would imply.[45]

Finally, this confusion of subjective and objective leads to some confusion about whether there is to be knowledge in the case of RIs or only in the case of constitutive ones. I have already argued that the categories, which Kant takes as constitutive of experience, also serve a regulative role. How is one to draw a clear line between the knowable and the unknowable when (as we have just seen) regulative and constitutive principles work together reciprocally in providing the knowledge that we do have? Although Kant thinks that the need for

42. Paul Guyer, "Reason and Reflective Judgment: Kant on the Significance of Systematicity," *Nous* 24 (1990): 17-43, quotation 17.

43. Cf. Fry, "Kant's Principle," 69n.14; and Margaret Morrison, "Methodological Rules in Kant's Philosophy of Science," *Kant-Studien* 80 (1989): 155-72. Morrison shows how Kant ascribes a subjective status to the methodological laws: they do not share the objectivity of the categories (B 695), even though Kant insists that they are both objective and necessary (B 691).

44. Fry, "Kant's Principle," 75.

45. Connected with this notion is Kant's concept of the imagination, which he defines as "das Vermögen, einen Gegenstand auch *ohne dessen Gegenwart* in der Anschauung vorzustellen" (B 151). As J. Michael Young has shown, Kant interprets the imagination as "taking or treating or construing what is sensibly present as something other, or something more, than what immediately appears" (Young, "Kant's View of Imagination," *Kant-Studien* 79 [1988]: 140-64, quotation 141). Cf. B 103; A 115.

empirical intuitions clearly separates human knowledge from its regulative principles, the criterion of purely empirical input has proved to be more problematic than he imagined. The ideas Kant uses as his prime examples of regulative notions are sometimes treated as if they could be items of knowledge as well, which would mean that there would be at least some knowledge of the transempirical (we return to this point below).[46]

This result must apply to the concept of God as the third transcendental idea as well. In this case more than any other, the understanding seems to have to speak of the existence of its object:[47] the idea of God cannot be dismissed as a pure fiction, even for Kant; yet neither can he allow that there could be metaphysical knowledge of God. Nowhere in the Kantian opus do we discover a solution to this dilemma.

The Conceptual Scheme Insight

In order to make any progress on this question, we must step outside Kant's own structures for a moment. The basic mistake running through the six points just covered is, I suggest, that Kant leaves too little room for the essentially pluralistic (and sometimes divergent) nature of RIs. This error is symptomatic of the entire first *Critique*, filled as it is with necessity claims. Think, for example, of the antinomies. Kant shows that the concept of the unconditioned can be conceived in different — indeed, mutually contradictory — ways depending on one's perspective. Thus, as Schäfer notes, he lets the regulative role be "taken over by the questionable concept of the unconditioned," which furthers "the monotheoretical systematization of his treatment." Instead, the antinomies should be taken as "a set of alternative *types* or models for the construction of cosmological theories none of which can be eliminated without stagnation of empirical research."[48]

---

46. Many of these texts are discussed — and ultimately dismissed — in W. H. Walsh, *Kant's Criticism of Metaphysics* (Edinburgh: Univ. of Edinburgh Press, 1979).

47. So Burkhardt, *Hegels Kritik,* 99: "Ist die Vernunft genötigt, [dieser] Idee einen wirklichen Gegenstand zu setzen, um ihrer Funktion der Vollendung der systematischen Einheit aller Erfahrung entsprechen zu können, wie ist dann zu vermeiden, daß die Vernunft *bereits in regulativer Funktion konstitutiv* ist, d.h. die Idee zu einem überweltlichen Wesen hypostasiert?" Burkhardt formulates the problem as a dilemma on 100; but cf. 82-99 for a particularly helpful presentation of the problem in its full complexity. In chap. 3 (103ff.) Burkhardt appeals to Hegel's critique of Kant in order to show the insolubility of Kant's view on the status of God; cf. esp. 193-211 on the problem of God.

48. Cf. Lothar Schäfer, "The Restrictive and Proliferative Function of Kant's Regulative

The relationship between the categories and the ideas of reason lies at the heart of the argument in the first *Critique*. By beginning with necessary categories, Kant presupposes as his goal a single systematization of reason — a goal that he means to express by appropriately formulating the ideas of reason. By contrast, if we begin by casting the necessity of the categories into question — either by challenging Kant's necessity claims or by substituting a pluralistic model of philosophy — we eschew the expectation that the various RIs can be woven together seamlessly into a single system of thought. A pluralistic metaphysics allows tensions to surface that draw attention to the need to choose between contrasting RIs. The higher one estimates the degree of subjectivity (or even arbitrariness) of the ideas that guide human reflection, the more pluralistic will be one's approach to any proposed system of categories.

I therefore suggest a modification of Kant's RIs, according to which some would be raised to objective-hypothetical status and others transformed into optional models of thought by contrasting them with alternative models. This transformation corresponds to the continuum that we discovered in chapter 1 (pp. 35-42), the one that led from (apparently) necessary conclusions to the happenstances of particular cultural and intellectual contexts. For example, presumably the (or: some) idea of freedom will be maintained as necessary for any practical reasoning.[49] By contrast, the status of God as an RI of practical reason has to be somewhat less final; even theists are reticent today to buy into the cosmic lawgiver and rewarder who is suggested by Kant's moral argument for the existence of God. In place of Kant's moral argument we might postulate merely that there must be some sort of highest moral ideal presupposed by practical reason. The personal God who guarantees the final success of the ethical life (by giving awards in the afterlife for morally good actions here) then becomes merely one way to spell out the moral ideal. The problem, in short, is not that Kant postulates RIs that regulate our moral striving; it is that he acknowledges only one way to think the highest instance, raising it thereby to a necessary condition of any practical reason *überhaupt*.

This is the point at which we should supplement Kant with the theory of CSs. Humans do not have direct access to reality. Everything we say and think is

---

Ideas," in Beck, ed., *Proceedings*, 480-85, quotation 483-84. Schäfer argues correctly that the antithesis in the second antinomy should lead to progress in the empirical sciences, since it points beyond philosophical atomism and requires the postulation of smaller and smaller particles.

49. Of course, this presupposes that freedom is essential for moral responsibility and that such responsibility is given within (or follows from) practical discourse. If one were to reject one or the other of these presuppositions, one would also cast the necessity of freedom into question.

filtered through some CS, some perspective or interpreted system.[50] In many cases, basic CSs are not universally shared but are idiosyncratic to an individual, culture, or epoch. Nevertheless, a number of our linguistic predicates, such as *truth* and *knowledge*, presuppose the picture of breaking through the CS wall and establishing correspondences with something beyond — or at least they presuppose that the world of our perceptions reflects the influence of a noumenal reality. This feature of human reason is not so easily discarded as postmodern philosophers such as Rorty and Derrida wish us to believe.[51] We rightly ask about the truth of our particular conceptual schemes — even if every actual verification of epistemic claims is carried out within one or more of them.

There is no knowledge without language, and there is no language without a CS. Obviously Kant thought he could bring about his irreversible "Copernican revolution" and still write books detailing a "metaphysic of morals" or "the metaphysical first principles of natural science." Yet this merely proves that he misunderstood the radicality of his own insight into human world construction. For among the most important consequences of his philosophy is the fact that philosophical attention has turned increasingly away from the World and toward the many "ways of worldmaking."[52] Of course, many of our linguistic (and ethical) practices do presuppose an ultimate convergence of human epistemic efforts or a notion of correctness that goes beyond the pleasures of the current conversation. Still, present justification can only be assessed from within a framework that is created and not found.

It is a difficult task to do justice to the CS insight without giving up the striving for knowledge altogether or redefining knowledge as that which we happen to believe (however vehemently). Finding the right balance between these two insights may be the single greatest challenge facing philosophy today.

---

50. This approach has received widespread support in analytic philosophy, e.g., from Jonathan Bennett and Hilary Putnam. One typical example is that of K. Bagchi: "Kant's system of Transcendental Idealism may be regarded, in the contemporary philosophical perspective, as concerned with the problem whether *any* linguistic or conceptual system can be regarded as adequately explained in terms of the facts which the system organises"; see his "Kant's Transcendental Problem as a Linguistic Problem," *Philosophy* 46 (1971): 341-45, quotation 341.

51. The complete argument cannot be presented here; see Philip Clayton, "Two Kinds of Conceptual-Scheme Realism," *Southern Journal of Philosophy* 29 (1991): 167-79.

52. Robert E. Butts comes to a similar conclusion in his "Teleology and Scientific Method in Kant's Critique of Judgment," *Nous* 24 (1990): 1-16, esp. 15-16. The manifesto of conceptual-scheme philosophy remains Nelson Goodman, *Ways of Worldmaking* (Indianapolis: Hackett, 1978).

The task starts, I suggest, with the effort to understand, correct, and then appropriate Kantian philosophy. A purely Kant-internal treatment cannot respond to the urgency of the present-day debate with pluralism; yet a total disregard for Kant's formulations of the questions threatens to lose sight of insights already reached, falling back into an irretrievable relativism. (Perhaps the former tendency more characterizes German philosophy today, the latter Anglo-American philosophy.) In order to make progress on the questions it will be necessary to develop an approach that incorporates both methods; precisely this is the task of a modified Kantianism in contemporary philosophy.

Reason and Its Regulative Ideas

Toward a Definition

As we venture beyond Kant, the first and knottiest problem is to define RIs and to clarify their epistemic status. Certain minimal conditions for RIs can be specified without difficulty:[53] RIs are principles that cannot be conclusively proved or disproved at present. Still, experience can increase (or decrease) our confidence in the validity of a particular RI.[54] Different RIs underlie different research programs or are presupposed by particular theoretical endeavors and practical activities. They express assumptions that influence inquiry and action, determining what are the goals of the inquiry, what count as good reasons, or what argumentative moves are admissible.

The reciprocal relationship between RIs and experience confirms their partially constitutive status. For instance, when well-confirmed causal explanations fully explain human behaviors, this provides some evidence for determinism as an RI for the study of human behavior; when all explanatory attempts fail, it suggests determinism's falsity. Consequently, it makes sense to *believe* an RI or to *assent* to it. An RI is not only something like a piece of advice for the formation of beliefs; it can also represent a program for research or inquiry. Hence, pace Jonathan Bennett, an RI such as determinism is not "good advice with no risks attached"; some research programs are progressive and others "degenerating," even if none is conclusively falsifiable.[55]

---

53. In what follows I draw from Bennett, "Status of Determinism," 106-7.

54. I am grateful to my colleague in California, Ed Mooney, for discussions over several years that have influenced the theory and even some of the formulations that follow.

55. On research programs, see Imre Lakatos, "The Methodology of Scientific Research Programmes," in John Worrall and Gregory Currie, eds., *Lakatos' Philosophical Papers*, vol. 1

Beyond these minimal conditions, it is important to specify how and (in the next section) what RIs regulate. As a start, I propose construing RIs as *the framework assumptions that are alleged to be intrinsic to a specific activity or even to the activity of reasoning as a whole.* If correct, they express the conditions of a particularly activity, the underlying goals without which we would no longer be prepared to take it as that activity any longer. When they serve as background assumptions, RIs are not among the conclusions of a particular form of reasoning; for example, in the case of ethical deliberation, they are not individual ought-statements or maxims for action. Rather, they belong on a different level, having to do with the framework for carrying out any ethical action at all.

RIs vary greatly in scope. Some function at the broadest level of language, stating the intended ideal limit of an entire (theoretical or practical) activity (e.g., "the postulation of some sort of convergence between our language and reality remains fundamental to the quest for knowledge of the world"). But if some state extremely broad principles, such as assumption of the regularity of nature, others are much more concrete principles guiding a specific scientific subdiscipline (e.g., "explanations in evolutionary biology must include the physiological structures selected for or against and their specific functions"). Specific RIs in practical reasoning may also range from fundamental assumptions (the innate value of moral agents) to more specific maxims for behavior ("all other things being equal, it is better to tell the truth"). Indeed, in the limit case RIs may be indistinguishable from hypotheses that are not presently verifiable but may be at some later date or when more research has been done.

What this account does not retain are Kant's hard-core necessity claims. It is not required that RIs be basic and indispensable presuppositions for "experience as a whole" — or even necessary conditions for some specific area of experience. The reason is that, given the CS insight, it is impossible to remove a certain agent or community relativity. Jones takes belief in God (or capitalism, or human free will) as foundational for all her more specific cognitive efforts; she is able to explain how it regulates her efforts as a scientist and a moral agent. Smith strives equally as a scientist and moral agent, but explains his striving as motivated by a belief in the perfectibility of humankind. Jones points to some evidence of God's existence, and Smith to some evidence of human improvement; both take their present beliefs to represent the more justified inference (and both are ready to debate the matter); still, both must grant that their be-

---

(Cambridge: Cambridge Univ. Press, 1978); and, under its influence, Clayton, *Explanation from Physics to Theology.*

liefs go well beyond the evidence. In short, the pluralization of RIs in the present is a necessary consequence of their present undecidability, though this need not entail epistemic arbitrariness or the impossibility of some future convergence of belief on the matter.[56]

Between Knowledge and Fiction

The various options for the epistemic status of RIs suggest a continuum, the end points of which represent limiting cases (if an RI reaches them, it ceases to be an RI). From strongest to weakest, the continuum runs roughly as follows: (1) One end point is reached when a (former) RI becomes a constitutive theoretical statement, not merely guiding research or activity but becoming a part of it. In this case it might be separated from other theoretical statements by its extreme generality but not by the fact that it fails to play an actual role in theoretical discourse. (2) RIs can be put forward as transcendental in the strongest sense. Here they are identical with Kant's conditions of the possibility of knowledge (or some domain thereof); they express what is necessarily and objectively presupposed in the exercise of reason (in this domain) and are as such synthetic a priori. Given the problems encountered above with establishing transcendental necessities, I take it that convincing arguments for the synthetic a priori status of RIs are currently lacking. (3) In a less ambitious sense, RIs can be interpreted as hypotheticals, that is, as long-range posits about how things will turn out, which we would expect "in the final analysis" to be corroborated by the results of inquiry. (4) RIs can play a merely heuristic role, for example, by orienting and motivating our intellectual efforts to understand or act in various fields (science, ethics, aesthetics), or by operating historically to inspire cultural and political change or the increase in knowledge. In this last sense they have to do primarily with the psychology or sociology of inquiry, since heuristic principles do not have theoretical content and are not themselves parts of theories.[57]

---

56. Recall John Hick's response to the challenge that religious beliefs are not falsifiable and are thus cognitively meaningless: the believer can meaningfully predict an "eschatological verification" at the end of the road when one's beliefs will either be established or corrected; see *Faith and Knowledge* (1957; 2nd ed. Ithaca: Cornell Univ. Press, 1966).

57. Theodore A. Gracyk defends this view in "Kant's Doctrine of Heuristics: An Interpretation of the Ideas of Reason," *Modern Schoolman* 68 (1991): 191-210. Note that in their heuristic function RIs establish a sort of connection among Kant's three *Critiques*. If it were not such a formal and abstract commonality, one might be tempted to make it the basis for a new architectonic based on RIs alone.

A much fuller analysis of heuristics could be supplied. A heuristic is something like a scientific methodology, a standard for judging between truth candidates. Some heuristics are

Finally, (5) at the far end of the continuum RIs are limited by the notion of the merely fictional. Fictional statements are invoked when one grants that an actual answer is lacking (or is insufficient); they express the way we wish things were but know they are not.[58] Thus the limit includes quasi-fictive RIs such as hopes and anticipations. One wishes for a particular result (say, that knowledge efforts converge on a particular outcome) precisely because one knows that this outcome is presently lacking. But it is as unjustified to conclude from the beginning that all RIs are "pure fictions" as it is simply to assume that they represent metaphysical truths.

Kant is right that the status of RIs is "problematic"; nonetheless, he is unjustified in resolving their problematic status in one direction or the other.[59] That RIs remain "problematic" is no surprise, given that they point in the direction of the limits of reason. But their problematic nature does not exclude them from the realm of possible knowledge. They can continue to play at least a heuristic role, that is, as principles that model and motivate (e.g., inspiring or directing inquiry or action), and in some cases they may make the transition to actual items of knowledge. Critics of RIs often allege a dichotomy: "What are RIs anyway? If they are justified beliefs — beliefs we have some reason to think are probably true — then one does not need the regulative framework to defend them. And if they lack this justification, then how does calling them regulative overcome their epistemic failure? An unjustified belief remains unjusti-

more successful than others, since they identify assertions whose probability is higher than the assertions they reject. Even if a heuristic is not "true" in the same sense as an empirical assertion, it may nonetheless still be exact, helpful, productive, etc. (or the opposite). In this sense we might describe them as second-order beliefs.

58. The classic "fictional" interpretation of Kant's RIs is Hans Vaihinger, *The Philosophy of "As If,"* trans. C. K. Ogden (New York: Harcourt, Brace, 1924). "As if" status is fictional status: caught in the enchantment of a movie or play, it may seem *as if* a Batman or Hamlet exists; simultaneously, as adults, and in the strongest sense of what we know to exist and not to exist, we know that they do not exist. But RIs are not fictional in this sense for the decisive reason that they fall outside the bounds of strict knowledge. They cannot be known to exist or not to exist since we cannot at present make metaphysically dogmatic statements about their status. In contrast, we know in a perfectly straightforward, nonmetaphysical sense that Batman and Hamlet are fictional.

59. Note also that it is equally difficult to dismiss RIs as fictions as it is to establish them as constitutive truths (and for the same reasons). The belief in human free will remains a possible truth rather than a fictional hope *until* the truth of determinism is established. I thus fault Kant for (sometimes) making nature's pervasive causal structure into a dogmatic certainty — not just a required condition of any knowledge of nature but a freedom-excluding feature of nature. Kant's enduring insight is that attributing causality to nature is a *presupposition* of theoretical inquiry into nature only; universal causality (like free will) functions as an ideal rather than an item of knowledge.

fied, whatever one calls it!" But the examples we have looked at show that the critic, like Kant, has turned a continuum into a dichotomy. A particular RI may someday become a viable ("constitutive") hypothesis, or it may finally be generally dismissed as a mere fiction or wishful thinking.

Practical Regulative Ideas

The overarching RI for *theoretical* reason is knowledge attained through research and reflection; this is the final goal of this activity. The overarching RI for *practical* reason is to act correctly or "rightly." What has to be presupposed for right action to serve as the RI for practical reason? The question points in the direction of conditions for practical action that are interestingly analogous to Kant's own conditions. First, there must be an *ought* that pertains to the agent in question: when one pursues right action (through reflection or activity) one takes it to be the case that there are better and worse alternatives for action, and that one ought (in at least a weak sense of *ought*) to choose the better option. But, second, the existence of an ought, an ethical obligation of some sort, presupposes either ethical realism (there really are obligations faced by human agents, built into the fabric of the universe, perhaps, or in the mind of God) or ethical constructivism (agents or group of agents make it the case that there are things that they ought to do).[60] Third, if one accepts an ought in either of these two guises, one also presupposes a *can,* namely that the agent is capable of fulfilling (to some degree) the obligation in question. Or, if one wishes: the agent is *free* to perform it. Freedom thus becomes the basic presupposition or the fundamental RI within the practical realm.

What we do not have to presuppose is the rest of Kant's doctrine of freedom, the two kingdoms, and all that goes with them — much less the entire landscape of Kant's *Metaphysic of Morals* and (to a lesser extent) the second *Critique*. Notions such as that of a cosmic lawgiver or an omniscient judge who awards and punishes with complete justice (V, 455) may still be suggested by the process of morality, but they fall far below more basic notions such as freedom. Let's speak of them as *archetypes,* broad or foundational pictures expressing one's view of what the full activity would look like if its regulating ideas were perfectly realized. Archetypes, like models or paradigms, go beyond the level of minimally necessary conditions, in the way that More's and Marx's accounts of their particular utopias go beyond the mere assertion that a normative political theory must presuppose some ideal outcome of the political pro-

---

60. Philip Clayton and Steven Knapp ("Ethics and Rationality," *American Philosophical Quarterly* 30 [1993]: 151-61) attempt to mediate between these two options.

cess. The cost of opting for "richer" accounts of practical goals such as these, however, is justificatory pluralism. Abandoning necessity claims, one expresses one's preference for a picture, while acknowledging the existence (and even the desirability) of other pictures. Analogous to the treatment of theoretical RIs above, practical archetypes fall along a continuum from apparently necessary conditions to the highly specific assumptions and practical goals of concrete forms of life.

Aesthetic or Telic Reason

I have affirmed the general structure of Kant's treatment of the practical ideas and confirmed his basic principles without being able to follow all the details of his *Metaphysics of Morals*. Could one do something similar in the case of the *Critique of Judgment*? Consider, for example, Kant's discussion of viewing objects of nature from a teleological perspective. Kant's theory includes a regulative component, insofar as the connection between the empirical and the teleological perspectives could only be established within a transempirical framework. Moreover, he notes, the various contexts in the study of nature in which we speak of purposes would need to be thought together as a whole. Yet this would require the postulation of a final purpose *(Endzweck)*. A final purpose is that "which requires no other as a condition of its possibility" (V, 434). The ultimate purpose would therefore be unconditioned, since only something unconditioned could constitute the unity of the system of nature as a teleological system.[61] Kant notes that humanity — "yet considered as a noumenon," that is, as immortal soul — could also serve in this fashion as a final purpose. Another "fact" that he thinks requires the transition from the sensible world to the supersensible is freedom (V, 468). Finally, the idea of God consists of predicates that "are possible only on the basis of a supersensible ground, even though they must demonstrate their reality within experience."[62]

We need not reconstruct the details of the three Kantian ideas of reason within teleology. More important is to note that the teleological perspective, because of its contrast with the purely practical perspective, has an effect on the epistemic status of the practical ideas. The most important change involves the

---

61. "Ein Ding aber, was nothwendig seiner objectiven Beschaffenheit wegen als Endzweck einer verständigen Ursache existiren soll, muß von der Art sein, daß es in der Ordnung der Zwecke von keiner anderweitigen Bedingung, als bloß seiner Idee abhängig ist" (V, 435; cf. 427). The following quotation is also taken from this passage.

62. V, 473. See 442-50 for a version of the moral proof of the existence of God and Kant's "Ethikotheologie," that is, the derivation of the central divine attributes from the function of the idea of God as one of the three "reinen Vernunftideen" (474).

relation to the world, a relation that did not come to full expression in the *Critique of Practical Reason* because of its sharp separation between nature and freedom. The matter is quite different with the concept of a final purpose:

> It is thus required for the objective theoretical reality of the notion of a final purpose of reasonable beings in the world that it is not just we who have a final purpose given to us a priori. Equally necessary is that the creation, i.e. the world itself, also have a final purpose of its existence. This purpose, if it could be proven a priori, would add to the subjective reality of the final purpose an objective reality as well. (V, 453)

In this context Kant is clearly casting into question the very boundary between regulative and constitutive. Pure reason, he asserts, contains "a regulative principle of our action not only in the moral law, but at the same time gives thereby a subjective-constitutive [principle]" (V, 453). "Hence such a regulative principle . . . that we should act according to purposes [is] at the same time constitutive, i.e. determinative in the practical context" (V, 457). Of course, Kant is quick to close the door on the possibility that there could be any speculative knowledge of these principles. Still, two changes from his earlier position should be noted. First, his treatment of teleology has introduced a new perspective over against the earlier *Critiques*, significantly altering the status and function of the concept of God (we return to this below). Second, Kant himself now acknowledges the haziness of the boundary between regulative and constitutive. These two developments — in combination with my criticisms above of Kant's limitation of input to sense impressions — point in the direction of a new scope and stronger status for the notion of God, the significance of which will soon become clear.

The leading characteristic of teleology for Kant is *holism,* that is, the insistence that there is some final perspective, one that we can only anticipate in the present, by means of which we unify the various components of our experience into a whole. Again, one's anticipatory (telic) beliefs will be epistemically weaker than the results of "constitutive" arguments — certainly too weak for any necessity claims! Nonetheless, it does not follow that they are all on an epistemic par. I have good grounds for my anticipation that Swingin' Single will be one of the winners in the Daily Triple (among racing fans it passes as virtually certain), somewhat weaker grounds for my belief that supply-side economics is not the best U.S. economic policy for the 2000s, and virtually no grounds for my belief that humanity will achieve a fully egalitarian society at some point in the future (however much I may hope it). By speaking of RIs as *archetypes,* I have attempted to preserve their motivational importance while granting their weaker status epistemically. In the post-Kantian context a large number of RI candidates are available to the consumer: religious limit notions, sacred stories, narratives and metanarratives of various sorts, artistic images and symbols. There are, for example, religious archetypes, just as there are literary tropes or types and artistic images or themes that have been massively influential. Still, it would be false to conclude that all such visions or archetypes are therefore only "weakly" regulating principles. In fact, artistic, religious, or utopian visions, however warranted their hopes or predictions, are in practice frequently the strongest motivators of action. Such archetypes formulate our aspirations and mirror our anticipations of the desired outcomes of our actions. As in the earlier cases, the admixture of hope, religious yearning, and projection in these cases is so great that a full reduction to constitutive theories appears exceedingly unlikely. Nonetheless, some progress in evaluating their truth content by embedding them within an appropriate theoretical framework cannot be excluded a priori.

Conclusion

RIs thus fulfill a variety of epistemic roles. In some cases one is justified to treat an RI as a component of a research program and in this way to assess its theoretical adequacy. In other cases RIs function only as controlling assumptions that one presupposes when one engages in a particular activity or practice. Yet other RIs reflect one's anticipation of certain outcomes from one's activities, formulate one's aspirations, express one's wishes. The result, I have argued, is an epistemic continuum of RIs, running from those that appear to be necessary for the (even possible) success of some action, through the standard examples of RIs, down to subjective preferences and imaginary ideas (hopes, dreams). The continuum of RIs is constituted by two possibilities that themselves stand outside it: on the one side, the promotion to constitutive theories; on the other, the epistemic demotion to explicitly acknowledged fictions. Between the two lies this crucial realm of the various RIs with their diverse degrees of epistemic probability, which serve as conditions for particular activities or areas of activity. As we have found, no RI is an RI for life; what regulates inquiry as its ideal at one time could turn out to be among the results (or abandoned assumptions!) at a later point of inquiry. Whether the physical universe is infinite and eternal, for example, has become an empirically debatable question.

In these sections I have frequently moved outside the boundaries of Kant's own philosophical conception — even if the resulting view remained recognizably Kantian at least in spirit. It was my goal to cast Kant's necessity and uniqueness claims into question, along with his allegedly sharp boundaries between the "merely regulative" and the clearly constitutive. Yet the view defended here still preserves an important epistemic function for ideas such as truth, freedom, and final purposes (teleology), even when they cannot pass (at least at a particular time) as "grounded" in a constitutive sense. For later research or theoretical developments may either raise particular ideas to the status of well-founded beliefs or debunk them as mere fictions. In his attempt to provide a critique of pure and practical reason that would be universally valid, Kant was compelled to deny the ambiguity and revisability of the RIs. In light of Kant's shortfalls, however, philosophers today should be less tempted to commit the same mistake, treating only empirically rooted assertions as philosophically significant and consigning metaphysical propositions to the category of fiction.

THEISTIC METAPHYSICS AFTER KANT?

"What is transcendental philosophy within metaphysics? What is metaphysics within transcendental philosophy?" (XXII, 75). Kant's take on metaphysics is at least highly ambivalent, if not actually inconsistent. The first edition of the *Critique of Pure Reason* speaks of metaphysics as the "battle ground of endless disputes" and warns metaphysicians, "our age is the real age of criticism to which everything else must be subordinated" (A viii, xi Note). In the second edition, by contrast, Kant apparently wished to reformulate metaphysics according to the model of the natural sciences (B xiv); the unconditioned may not be able to pass as knowledge based on experience, yet it can still be given some determinate content as "practical knowledge" (B xx-xxi).[63] Here Kant appears to treat the supersensible as real — indeed, even to the extent that some justified statements can be made about some of its attributes from the perspective of ethical experience. As W. H. Walsh notes with reference to the pre-critical writings: "Kant was unlike other critics of metaphysics in having suffered from the disease seriously himself."[64]

Any realistic language about God — any statements about the divine that

63. Henry Allison argues that the unconditioned is "an analytic principle, depicting what is contained in our concept of a thing in general"; see Allison, "Kant's Refutation of Idealism," *Dialectica* 30 (1976): 223-53, quotation 237-38. Obviously, though, Kant uses the term in other manners as well.

64. W. H. Walsh, "Kant and Metaphysics," *Kant-Studien* 67 (1976): 372-84, quotation 376.

are meant to be true of God — are metaphysical statements. There are two general approaches to defending metaphysics of this sort after Kant. On the one hand, one can work within the assumptions of one or another part of Kant's opus. Although some have sided with the Kant of the pre-critical reflections or the moral philosophy, the vast majority who have followed this route have accepted the strictures of the first *Critique* as their guiding structure.[65] (A few have argued that Kant's writings are consistent throughout his career, so that one can accept them all together; but so many are the foes of this view that I shall not pause to criticize it.) Of course, one must then show why the one stage of Kant's thought is correct and the others misguided. On the other hand, one can come to conclusions that may not have been Kant's own, however deeply inspired they are by his themes, questions, and arguments. The present treatment follows this latter route. In particular, the following pages wrestle with the major stages of Kant's own philosophical development, tracing common themes and seeing how later emphases retain or alter earlier ones.

Such an approach places particular stress on how Kant later came to interpret and evaluate earlier stages of his career. How did Kant finally come to understand his own program? Max Wundt has given what I take to be compelling arguments for the conclusion that "the 'system of the *Critique of Pure Reason*' no longer represents a preparation for metaphysics; rather, it is meant to convey this metaphysic itself."[66] Kant came finally to hold the view that his *Critiques* served not only as propaedeutics to metaphysics but were themselves important contributions to that very discipline. In what sense? We find important hints of an answer in the *Opus postumum*, especially in Kant's emphasis on the transition *(Übergang)* from metaphysics to natural science in the book he planned to write, *Übergang von den Metaphysischen Anfangsgründen der Naturwissenschaft zur Physik.* Recent textual work, on which I rely in what fol-

65. This is true of Kant's first interpreters, of many neo-Kantians, and of some interpreters in the present day. For an excellent overview of the various versions of Kantianism and neo-Kantianism, see Gerhard Funke, "Die Diskussion um die metaphysische Kant-interpretation," *Kant-Studien* 67 (1976): 409-24; cf. in the same volume the articles by I. Heidemann and W. H. Walsh. Cf. also G. Funke, *Von der Aktualität Kants* (Bonn: Bouvier, 1979), esp. part IV.1, "Die Wendung zur Metaphysik im Neukantianismus des 20. Jahrhunderts."

66. Wundt, *Kant als Metaphysiker: Ein Beitrag zur Geschichte der deutschen Philosophie im 18. Jahrhundert* (Stuttgart: F. Enke, 1924), 398. Wundt's highly influential monograph incorporates all the phases of Kant's development, from the pre-critical influences up to his impact on his followers. I find most convincing his treatment of the *Kritik der Urteilskraft* (esp. of the first introduction) and of the later Kantian writings. It will come as no surprise that the metaphysics that underlies transcendental philosophy is not identical with that of pre-critical philosophers but rather points in the direction of German idealism.

lows,[67] has led to a new (at least partial) consensus on at least two points. The first point has to do with Kant's famous description of his plan in the *Opus postumum:* "How can we present a system of empirical knowledge a priori, which itself is neither empirical nor can be so?" (XXII, 342). The proposed "transition" book was supposed to achieve this goal by working out the principles "that specify the necessary attributes of any physical object without interpreting these constitutive conditions of the possibility of experiencing an object *überhaupt.*"[68] These principles were supposed to have a unique status, representing neither completely empirical components of a natural science such as physics nor purely transcendental conditions for knowledge. Kant's new proposal represents clear progress over against the *Critique of Pure Reason,* a work that should rule out principles with an in-between status of this sort. In this and the following chapter I hope to explain and defend the significance of such principles for a post-Kantian theology.

The second point of consensus is that there are multiple views of metaphysics in Kant's writings. In his later years, Kant tended more and more to view his critical philosophy not as a propaedeutics but rather as *itself* metaphysics. As a result of this change, he began more frequently to appeal to a category of judgment that is characterized by the fact "that [such judgments] are put forward independently of the knowledge of experience *(Erfahrungswissen),* while remaining valid for experience."[69] Such judgments are, I suggest, a model for theology after Kant. Because a discipline based on them would lay great stress on the touchstone of experience, it would not return to the rationalism — the natural theology and self-justifying intuitions — of pre-Kantian thought. At the same time, it goes beyond the view of the *Critique of Pure Reason,* since it allows for a constitutive employment of concepts in the realm of the supersensible. The resulting discipline would in fact not be far removed

---

67. See esp. *Übergang: Untersuchungen zum Spätwerk Immanuel Kants,* published by the Forum für Philosophie Bad Homburg (Frankfurt: V. Klostermann, 1991); Vittorio Mathieu, *Kants Opus postumum,* ed. Gerd Held (Frankfurt: V. Klostermann, 1989); and the excellent recent study by Stefan Schulze, *Kants Verteidigung der Metaphysik: Eine Untersuchung zur Problemgeschichte des Opus Postumum* (Marburg: 1994). Eckart Förster also acknowledges a transformation at this point, although he does not interpret it as a return to a more metaphysical perspective. See his "Kants Metaphysikbegriff: vor-kritisch, kritisch, nach-kritisch," in Dieter Henrich and Rolf-Peter Horstmann, eds., *Metaphysik nach Kant?* Stuttgart Hegel Congress 1987 (Stuttgart: Klett-Cotta, 1988), 123-36; idem, "Die Idee des Übergangs: Überlegungen zum Elementarsystem der bewegenden Kräfte," in *Übergang,* 28-48.

68. Schulze, 183.

69. Ibid., 177. In the following pages Schulze describes four different views of metaphysics that occur (more or less implicitly) in the Kantian texts.

from what Kant calls the "transcendental portion of the metaphysics of nature."[70] It is our task to see what can be said about God and infinity under these conditions (part III below).

Nonetheless, theological truth claims will be possible after Kant only if we can overcome the demotion of all assertions with transempirical content to the "merely regulative." In order to refute such a view, I have to show that an exclusively transcendental philosophy is impossible, that is, that it is impossible to develop a philosophy of regulative ideas according to the Kantian model without also presenting a theory of that which exists outside the subject. If I am right, the synthesizing subject and the synthesized content — the two main legs on which Kantian philosophy stands — require some broader theoretical framework within which they can be incorporated and explained. Consider in what sense four of the fundamental components of Kant's transcendental philosophy beg for a metaphysical interpretation of this sort:

The Subject

Transcendental philosophy presupposes a subject able to constitute the unity of apperception. Only as something that actually exists can it serve as a condition of the possibility of knowledge. Förster puts the point as follows:

> As a result we can conclude that experience is only possible if I myself actually exist in space as a corporeal subject. This means that I must constitute myself *(mich selbst setzen)* through a complete determination of appearances. With this insight the distinction between transcendental and metaphysical is finally overcome, inasmuch as the transcendental conditions of possible experience include an object of external sense: "The self-intuition . . . belongs to transcendental philosophy; it is synthetic and at the same time analytic." "For without this no self-consciousness would be a substance."[71]

Does Kant presuppose the subject as a foundational ontological moment? Some texts in the first *Critique* seem to demand this interpretation: "The synthetic unity of apperception is therefore that highest point, to which we must

---

70. Kant, *Metaphysische Anfangsgründe der Naturwissenschaft* (IV, 469-70): "Eigentlich so zu nennende Naturwissenschaft setzt zuerste Metaphysik der Natur voraus." Even more strongly, he allows that "eine reine Philosophie der Natur überhaupt, d.i. diegenige, die nur das, was den Begriff einer Natur im Allgemeinen ausmacht, untersucht, auch ohne Mathematik möglich sein [mag]" (IV, 470).

71. Förster, "Kants Metaphysikbegriff," 133. Förster quotes from AA xxii, 442, and 443.

ascribe all employment of the understanding, even the whole of logic, and conformably therewith transcendental philosophy" (B 134 note). Kant's implicit metaphysic of the subject receives even fuller expression in the *Opus postumum*: "The first *intellectuelle* is the consciousness of itself — an act of thinking a priori that is foundational, just as the subject is an object to itself."[72]

If the concept of the subject in fact forms the centerpiece of an implicit Kantian metaphysics, then the question of its origin is unavoidable. Only two possibilities, it seems, are open to Kant: Either he develops a doctrine of the self-postulating subject in the sense of Fichte, or he attempts — perhaps by means of the program of "transition" *(Übergang)* sketched above — to offer a broader metaphysical account of some sort. Which way he finally chose (or: would have chosen) is a matter of heated debate; my own view is that the second alternative is the more likely.[73]

Space

Kant asserts frequently that space is a form of representation; as a condition of sensibility in general, it tells us only about the human thinker and not about things-in-themselves.[74] Could objects then be spatial in themselves? Kant presupposes that space and time are attributes either of our representations or of the objects in themselves.[75] Because space is for him a "mere" form of intuition,

72. AA, XXII, 477-78. Kant adds, "Die Principien die das Subject vermittelst seines Verstandes bey sich führt Erfahrung anzustellen sind von denen unterschieden welche die Bedingungen der Möglichkeit deserlben betreffen."

73. The synthetic program that Kant begins to present in his latest writings also points in the same direction. Förster summarizes it insightfully: "*Selbstsetzungslehre*, ether theory, and the elementary system of the moving forces of matter thus hang together inextricably. The determination of my own existence, the transition from pure self-consciousness to knowledge of myself as an empirical being, takes place for Kant within the context of the ideal of a single, all-embracing experience, itself depending on the collective unity of moving forces of matter, which the subject investigates, guided by the table of categories, progressing to a thorough determination of all phenomena" (Förster, "Kant's *Selbstsetzungslehre*," in Förster, ed., *Kant's Transcendental Deductions: The Three Critiques and the Opus postumum* [Stanford: Stanford Univ. Press, 1989], 217-38, quotation 235).

74. See in B 59-61, 67, and 122, e.g.: "Der Raum stellt gar keine Eigenschaft irgend einiger Dinge an sich oder sie in ihrem Verhältnis auf einander vor, d.i. keine Bestimmung derselben, die an Gegenständen selbst haftete" (B 42); "Jener Raum selber aber . . . [und] alle Erscheinungen, sind doch an sich selbst keine Dinge, sondern nichts als Vorstellungen, und können gar nicht außer unserem Gemüt existieren" (B 520).

75. "Kant assumes that space and time must be features *either* of our representations

it at least appears that it should "pertain to objects [only] in virtue of our pecu-
liar mode or manner of representing them."[76] Could humans ever abstract
from our "particular manner of representing," we would realize that space itself
would disappear, that is, that things in themselves could not be spatial.

But the argument is not valid. It could be that space is both a mode of our
representation and an attribute of the world in itself. Put differently, the assumption that space can only be grounded in the subject is false. Kant asks,
"How, then, can there exist in the mind an outer intuition which precedes the
objects themselves, and in which the concept of the objects can be determined a
priori? Manifestly, not otherwise, then, insofar as the intuition has its seat in the
subject *only . . . ;* and only insofar, therefore, as it is merely the form of outer
sense in general" (B 41, my emphasis). But this inference is by no means obvious, for one can imagine the opposite just as easily. Guyer expresses the same
point by means of a question: "Why doesn't the indispensable role of space and
time in our experience prove the transcendental realism rather than idealism of
space and time themselves?"[77]

God

It has been maintained again and again that the moral proof of God's existence
"only brings to expression a subjective experience of the transcendent God in
the Categorical Imperative, that is, a purely personal belief," so that, even if it is
successful, only "the necessity of the *idea* of God has been shown and not the
existence of a corresponding object."[78] Yet surely Kant meant something more
by it. We know that one goal of his work on the concept of God was to allow for
a reasonable faith. Hence the moral proof must still be interpreted as a proof —
even if its status cannot be equated with that of the traditional proofs.[79]

Undoubtedly, the question of status remains the central issue in discuss-

---

or of objects but not both, rather than that space and time may be either properties of objects
or *both* necessary constraints on our perception of objects *and* genuine features of the objects
we do succeed in perceiving" (Paul Guyer, *Kant and the Claims of Knowledge* [Cambridge:
Cambridge Univ. Press, 1987], 363).

76. Henry Allison, *Kant's Transcendental Idealism* (New Haven: Yale Univ. Press, 1983),
114.

77. Guyer, *Kant and the Claims of Knowledge,* 349. In this context Guyer presents a detailed list of the relevant texts and a helpful analysis of them.

78. Adickes, *Kants Opus postumum,* 846, emphasis mine.

79. Bernard Reardon comes to similar conclusions in his *Kant as Philosophical Theologian* (Totowa, N.J.: Barnes & Noble, 1988), esp. chap. 10, e.g., 164-65.

ing Kant's treatment of the question of God. Belief in God is, according to the *Critique of Pure Reason*, less than objective. Yet if the *Opus postumum* is any indication, such belief cannot be interpreted as purely subjective — not even in the sense of a subjective penchant felt by every rational agent. Of course, one finds passages in which God's existence is treated as purely transcendental.[80] Other passages, however, those speaking of God as power or even as an actual person, demand an ontologically much stronger interpretation. The idea of God is "problematic" not because no true statements can be made about it that go beyond the level of conditions for knowledge, but because our use of this term continually (and perhaps essentially!) vacillates between the transcendental and the metaphysical. Adickes comes to a similar conclusion toward the end of his famous study:

> Even if transcendental philosophy acknowledges no proofs for God or treats him as a theoretical hypothesis, still it is in no way justified in denying his existence. It must rather treat this concept as problematic, labeling his transsubjective existence as possible and thus eschewing any final decision regarding the matter. In this sense Kant writes (C 372): "Transcendental philosophy is the principle of a system of ideas which in themselves [sc. with regard to their object and their reality] remain problematic (not assertoric), while at the same time remaining possible concepts that lie within the power of reason."[81]

The quotation suggests a program of interpretation for us to pursue in what follows. Its working hypothesis can now be formulated: Kant's own philosophy demands a construal of the existence of God stronger than that of the regulative ideas in the *Critique of Pure Reason*. For Kant, there will always be severe limitations on the knowability of this being. But if Kant is indeed able to speak of God's (transsubjective) existence, then it cannot be that, in the strictest sense, *no knowledge* of God is possible. For the Kantian will be committed to a variety of claims: this being exists (or: may exist); it can be distinguished from specific objects in the world based on particular attributes that it possesses; as a power it exercises specific causal effects on finite objects. Of course, Kant will immediately add that the problems raised by knowledge claims about God are much more serious than was previously acknowledged, for instance in the classical

---

80. See XXI, 27, where Kant speaks of God as a "Gedankending" or "ens rationis." Cf. XXII, 104-5: "Freiheit unter Gesetzen Pflichten als göttliche Gebote. Es ist ein Gott. . . . Es ist ein Gott: denn es ist in der moralisch practischen Vernunft ein categ. Imperativ."

81. Adickes, *Kants Opus postumum*, 792.

debate about the analogical status of God-language.[82] These difficulties notwithstanding, if the hypothesis is correct, Kantians are compelled to treat the concept of God as more than a mere idea of reason.

The Thing-in-Itself

The introduction of this concept into transcendental philosophy appears unavoidable, inasmuch as talk of "appearances" implies "that something that is not in itself appearance must correspond to it" (A 251-52). These "other possible things, which are not in any way objects of our senses," Kant calls "intelligible entities (noumena)" (B 306). As such, he argues, they must be (for us) completely undetermined and unknowable because we are unable to make any use of our categories to think things that lie behind all appearances (B 307-8). The *Ding an sich* is an "X," a transcendental object (A 250).

The contrast arises most plainly in comparison to the empirical world, which Kant defines as the "essence of all appearances" (A 506). The empirical world is not a *totum,* not an unconditioned whole, and this for three reasons: because the appearances are "nothing outside our representations — which is just what is meant by their transcendental ideality"; because every appearance is as such conditioned; and because we can never progress by means of individual appearances to a whole that is constituted by them (cf. A 507-9). Hence, he concludes, we can never reach "the absolutely unconditioned" (A 509). Consequently, ideas such as the thing-in-itself, absolute being, and the idea of an *ens realissimus* must be interpreted as transcendental ideas (A 576).

The status of the thing-in-itself remains nevertheless fundamentally ambiguous.[83] Sometimes Kant describes it as "real per se" (*für sich wirklich,* B xx), insisting "that though we cannot know these objects as things-in-themselves, we must yet be in a position at least to *think* them as things-in-themselves; otherwise we should be landed in the absurd conclusion that there can be appearance without anything that appears" (B xxvi). In other texts, he is more skeptical: "For we have then [without the unity of time] no means of determining whether things [in themselves] in harmony with the categories are even possible" (B 308).

---

82. So at any rate the rather surprising thesis defended by Andreas Inauen, "Kants Gottesbegriff," *Philosophisches Jahrbuch der Görres-Gesellschaft* 33 (1922): 209-32.

83. In his now classic monograph, *Kant und das Ding an sich* (Berlin: R. Heise, 1924), E. Adickes provides a detailed comparison of the passages that stand in conflict with one another. The next reference in the text to Adickes is also to this work.

Adickes (p. 52) claims that we can overcome these tensions by distinguishing between knowable sensible objects and the thing-in-itself, which, though not knowable, is still thinkable. There is much that speaks for this interpretation. Most frequently Kant writes of the thing-in-itself as a being of the understanding *(Verstandeswesen)*, that is, as "a something in general outside our sensibility" (B 307). In an important article, Horst Seidl has drawn together the evidence for a real or "ontological" interpretation of this notion, concluding that "the thing-in-itself is thought at least as an indeterminate 'something in general' when and insofar as we attribute to it an existence outside the subject, even if it is otherwise categorially unknowable."[84] Not only in Kant's late writings, but also in the Transcendental Deduction in the first edition of the *Critique of Pure Reason,* the thing-in-itself emerges as a necessary ontological, and not merely transcendental, foundation. Appearances are "only representations, which in turn have their object — an object which cannot itself be intuited by us, and which may, therefore, be named the non-empirical, that is, transcendental object = x."[85] This text expresses Kant's interest in objects that can be thought (in a limited sense) without meeting the other transcendental conditions. I shall argue that he is exactly right about their ontological status (even if wrong about their necessary unknowability) and that this result has important implications for the idea of God. In the next chapter we explore how it is that more can be said about limit notions of this sort.

Many have criticized Kant for reifying the thing-in-itself, insofar as he (sometimes) treats it as a substance and ascribes to it predicates that according to his own position should pertain only to empirical objects. For example, many argue that Kant is inconsistent to claim either that there are many things-in-themselves, or (conversely) only one, or that they (it?) exercise a causal influence on human experience. The critics are in one sense right; it does appear that Kant left himself without a consistent way out of these difficulties. For example, in his philosophy the thing-in-itself possesses the attributes of "being an object, being given, and of existing 'behind' what is given in intuition itself."[86]

---

84. Horst Seidl, "Bemerkungen zu Ding an sich und transzendentalem Gegenstand in Kants Kritik der reinen Vernunft," *Kant-Studien* 63 (1972): 305-14, quotation 311. Cf. Henry Allison, "Kant's Concept of the Transcendental Object," *Kant-Studien* 59 (1968): 184: "Kant wants at one and the same time *both* to affirm the existence of transcendental objects or things in themselves corresponding to appearances; and, since these objects are unknowable, to hold that by our concept of an object corresponding to appearances we cannot mean such entities, but merely the necessary synthetic unity of the appearances themselves."

85. A 109: This object "ist das, was in allen unseren empirischen Begriffen überhaupt Beziehung auf einen Gegenstand, d.i. objektive Realität verschaffen kann."

86. Seidl, "Bemerkungen zu Ding an sich," 313. In this sense it functions in a manner

Yet if Kant had abandoned the externality of the thing-in-itself as the source of sensory input, he would have had to interpret the world as the product of the ego's own self-postulation alone, thus in effect falling into the position of the early Fichte — a position that he vehemently rejected in his later years. In contrast to Fichte's *Science of Knowledge*, it is an essential part of Kantian philosophy to presuppose that there is something to which the categories are applied, something that itself is identical neither with the subject nor with its categories. The only choices open to Kant are to maintain that this something is thinkable or to deny that it is. The latter move reduces it to an ontological remnant about which nothing can be said; total silence becomes the only consistent reaction. In the former case — that is, in every attempt to speak of *what is* in a transsubjective sense — we necessarily presuppose that there can be, at least in principle, some knowledge of that which is not (directly) empirically given.

For this reason, I conclude that Kant's treatment of such notions — the thing-in-itself no less than the concept of God — demands a type of speculation that he at the same time tries to avoid. On the one hand, this plight reveals the inconsistency of Kant's approach; on the other, it points us in the direction of a fundamental modification. I suggest, namely, that it is philosophically necessary not only to reflect critically on the synthesizing activity of subjects but also to include the nonsubjective, that which precedes the subject and is cognized by it.

Now the critic might worry: As soon as philosophical reflection on the transempirical is readmitted, isn't the door thrown open to precisely the sort of fruitless metaphysical speculation that allegedly characterized much of pre-Kantian philosophy? No, only if one commits a metaphysical "slippery slope" fallacy, moving at once to claim full knowledge of various metaphysical entities. Correcting Kant need not imply that one claims infallible or uncontestable knowledge for oneself, say with respect to the truth of a particular theory. That such claims are mistaken in light of the abstract and controversial nature of metaphysical questions should be clear enough by this point in the book. Kant's enduring legacy is an awareness of the epistemic distance of the supersensible. Some latter-day Hegelians, for example, have turned Kant's thing-in-itself into the Other of the subject, claiming that all differences can eventually be overcome dialectically ("sublated") in a philosophy of Absolute Spirit; and some have made very strong epistemic claims on behalf of their conclusions. Even without taking on their claims in detail, one should be clear that overcoming

---

similar to the ontological argument: Out of the mere (transcendental) concept of the *Ding an sich* follows its existence. Cf. Edmund Husserl, *Cartesian Meditations: An Introduction to Phenomenology*, trans. D. Cairns (Netherlands: The Hague, 1964), 5th Meditation.

Kant's limitation to the empirical in no way leads inevitably to a theory of the Absolute. The "other" may always remain an absolutely other, as in the infinite other of Levinas's philosophy, which can never be grasped from a finite perspective.

At the end of our epistemological reflections we thus find reason to return to the theological question: How should the Other — whether understood as the thing-in-itself, the infinite, or God — be conceived? Are there theoretical advantages in conceiving it as a very large (infinite?) number of entities, perhaps as the world of things-in-themselves, which serves as the cause for the plurality of our perceptions? Or is it more productive to claim that this Other is a single infinite being, a ground or thing-in-itself, which as unitary source is better able to explain the "fit" and coherence of our experience? If there is to be any hope of making progress on such questions, we will have to consider them in light of the conceptual resources of pre-Kantian metaphysics, drawing in particular on the theories of God and infinity discussed there (see part III below). At any rate, the critique of Kant justifies us in now shifting the focus of attention from epistemological questions to matters of content and to specific theories about ultimate principles.

KANT ON GOD AND INFINITY

It is surely significant that Kant continued to give traditional metaphysical concepts a central place in his thought throughout all the stages of his development. In the *Critique of Pure Reason,* just as in his *Critique of Judgment* and his *Metaphysics of Morals,* he continues to ascribe just as much importance to the notion of God as did the early modern philosophers. Exactly how extensive is this continuity with the tradition? And where Kant distances himself from the tradition, do the resulting theories represent philosophical progress or a step backward?

The foundations of Kant's philosophy lie in his pre-critical phase. During that period he developed the guiding concepts that, as we will see, continued to influence the content of his later work. Of course, in later years — at first under the influence of Hume, and later while working out his own critical approach in the first *Critique* — he came increasingly to emphasize the unknowability of most of his own basic metaphysical concepts. Nonetheless, they never became meaningless or peripheral in his thought. For example, a central motif of the *Critique of Pure Reason* is to save the main metaphysical concepts of *metaphysica specialis* from empiricism. Kant's solution — to reinterpret them as regulative — was mistaken, but the importance of these ideas to him remains beyond question.

Indeed, after the first *Critique* and then continually up through his final writings in the *Opus postumum*, Kant actually strengthened the epistemic status of several key metaphysical concepts. At first it looked as though the concept of God, which (as Hume had driven home) cannot have an empirical source, could refer only to our ideals in reasoning and morality and not to an existing entity. Later, however, other aspects of the concept came more and more to the fore. Now Kant never quite allowed the idea of God to return across the line and become a theoretical-constitutive concept again; and in this, I shall argue, he was mistaken. Nonetheless, Kant's gradual movement toward recovering a constitutive concept of God[87] indicates the direction that theology must go as it moves through, and beyond, the challenge posed by the *Critique of Pure Reason*.

God and Infinity in the Pre-Critical Kant

The metaphysical principles of Kant's pre-critical work provide the foundation for his critical philosophy. The structure of a number of "critical" ideas — ideas such as the transcendental ideal, the regulative principles, and even some of the categories themselves[88] — can be traced back to metaphysical decisions made in the pre-critical period. Likewise, the roots of Kant's later critique of the theistic proofs and of the "critical" theories of soul, world, and God lie in decisions reached in those early years.[89] These decisions, some of them mistaken, as I

87. The most important sources for this recovery are found in the *Opus postumum*, the *Lectures on Metaphysics*, and the *Reflections*.

88. Heimsoeth gives a detailed defense of this claim in "Metaphysische Motive," cited above (n. 19).

89. This fact is often interpreted as a mere coincidence of Kant's philosophical development and hence as unimportant for understanding that philosophy itself. For example, Josef Schmucker has argued (in *Das Weltproblem in Kants Kritik der reinen Vernunft* [Bonn: Bouvier, 1990]), that Kant's critique of the theistic proofs is independent of his critical turn. Especially in his detailed discussion of the antinomies he tries to show that the critical elements in the antinomies are "Inkonsequenzen" and "Verstellungen seiner eigentlichen Konzeption" (p. xvi). He claims that Kant's criticisms of the theistic proofs as well as the antinomies "den transzendentalen Idealismus nicht voraussetzen" (p. 376), indeed, that they are incompatible with it! Instead, they are valid (if at all!) only under the presupposition of a transcendental *realism*. This would mean that the Dialectic presupposes a different conceptual framework than the Aesthetic and Analytic, and further that the criticisms of the theistic proofs should be evaluated apart from the tenets of Kant's critical philosophy. If Schmucker were right, we would possess a strong argument that there is a fundamental inconsistency in the project of the first *Critique*,

shall argue, extend even to the idea of a "critique of pure reason" and the claim that metaphysical ideas possess only regulative status.[90]

It would be particularly significant if one could show that Kant's critical philosophy is actually the result, at least in part, of a metaphysical dispute, since this would further challenge the assumption that he had left metaphysics behind. A number of scholars have come to precisely this conclusion, arguing that Kant's decisive turn in the years 1769-70 stems from what he took to be an irreconcilable opposition between his "pluralistic notion of the world and the henistic structure of the continuum of space."[91] The former suggests an ontological pluralism, while the unitary or unbroken nature of the latter pushes toward monism. For example, in the famous first sentence of the Dissertation of 1770 Kant distinguishes between composites (the *compositum substantiale*) and the world or continuum. In the former, introduced as the result of analysis, individual subjects appear as fundamental substances. Yet he says of the latter, which he connects with the faculty of synthesis, that it "as a whole is the ground of possibility of the parts, though it is not itself constituted by anything more simple" (Heimsoeth, p. 214). Kant cannot give up the primacy of the whole; and yet, as Heimsoeth correctly observes, "that there are in reality finite substances, finite centers of activity, is for Kant a basic certainty" (p. 221). Clearly both of these claims cannot be true at the same time — at least if both are taken as actual ("constitutive") metaphysical assertions.

Like Leibniz, who found himself confronted with the necessity of granting existence either to the parts or to the whole of the continuum, Kant had to

---

and thus further support for my thesis that the pre-critical philosophy continues to play a determining role throughout Kant's later work. And Schmucker has undeniably raised some serious questions about the consistency of Kant's critical philosophy that deserve careful attention from Anglo-American scholars. Nonetheless, the arguments for his basic thesis are not fully convincing. Along with the majority of contemporary German Kant scholars — and in line with Kant's own self-interpretation — I find a close conceptual connection between the results of the antinomies and the antimetaphysical arguments in the *Critique of Pure Reason*. On this subject, see Burkhardt, *Hegels Kritik,* 97-98.

90. There is no doubt about Kant's readiness to employ the concept of perfection: "Die Vollkommenheit im respectiven Verstande ist die Zusammenstimmung des Mannigfaltigen zu einer gewissen Regel. . . . Allein im absoluten Verstande ist etwas nur vollkommen, in so fern das Mannigfaltige in demselben den Grund einer Realität in sich enthält. . . . Und weil Gott die höchste Realität ist, so würde dieser Begriff mit demjenigen übereintreffen, da man sagte, est ist etwas vollkommen, in so fern es mit den göttlichen Eigenschaften zusammenstimmt" (II, 30n.).

91. Heinz Heimsoeth, "Der Kampf um den Raum in der Metaphysik der Neuzeit," quoted from his *Metaphysische Ursprünge und ontologische Grundlagen,* 213. The following three references are to the same work.

find his own answer to this problem of the one and the many. His solution was to change the status of the claims involved. In order not to deny the existence of the subject (and how could he, given Descartes's *cogito* argument?), he had to demote the simple whole to an unknown "x," a thing-in-itself, necessarily presupposed if there is to be any knowledge. Similarly, since space and time also presuppose a priority of the whole over the parts, as Kant showed in the Transcendental Aesthetic, he was compelled also to reduce the "spatial sensible world *(mundus sensibilis)* to that which merely appears" (Heimsoeth, 221).

Let us retrace the steps that led to this momentous decision. The process begins with Kant's strong dependence on the concept of infinity in the *Allgemeine Naturgeschichte* of 1755. Here he treats infinity as a fundamental attribute of God and attempts to work out the logic of this concept in a rigorous manner. In order to conceive the world "in a relationship with the power of the infinite being," the world, he thought, must have "no limits whatsoever." Similarly, he writes, "the field of the revelation of divine attributes is exactly as infinite as these themselves are."[92] In 1763 Kant was still defending the reality of the infinite, and in particular the infinitely small.[93] The Dissertation of 1770 represents a particularly interesting transitional phase in this development. On the one hand, although infinity cannot be grasped intuitively, it must also not be rejected. Only that which actually transcends the limits of the understanding is impossible, and not necessarily everything that surpasses the laws of intuition. Only an incautious philosopher would commit the mistake "of treating the limits, which circumscribe human thought, as by themselves determining the actual essence of things" (II, 389).

On the other hand, Kant now has critical words for those who defend the mathematical infinite as actual (II, 388 note), insisting that only "an intellect which is not human" will be able to grasp the infinite. His reason for this conclusion introduces, without explicit acknowledgment, a major shift into his theory of the infinite: from this point on *infinitum* comes to mean "the multitude of all large numbers." The particular concept of such an aggregate can only be formed, however, through the "successive addition of one to one." Note that this description is comparable with the concept *indefinitum* in Descartes's

---

92. Kant, *Allgemeinen Naturgeschichte*, I, 309; cf. 306 and Sebastian Wolf, *Das potentiell Unendliche: Die aristotelische Konzeption und ihre modernen Derivate* (Frankfurt: 1981), 163-64. The underlying reasons for Kant's intellectual development are worked out most convincingly by Horst-Günter Redmann, *Gott und Welt: Die Schöpfungstheologie der vorkritischen Periode Kants* (Göttingen: Vandenhoeck & Ruprecht, 1962), chap. 5.

93. "Versuch den Begriff der nativen Größen in die Weltweisheit einzuführen," II, 168. Kant's ontological claims at this point are noticeably stronger than Leibniz's own interpretation of the infinitesimals.

work: Kant's *infinitum* means something that is not countable and yet is reachable in principle through composition. The positive concept of the infinite, along with the whole logic of the infinite that we have worked out in the previous chapters, is thereby excised with a single stroke. That such a step will have immediate consequences for a theory of God — which for the pre-critical Kant depended above all on the concepts of necessity, unicity, and infinity — is obvious. What then was the doctrine of God in Kant's pre-critical writings?

I will not attempt to present Kant's critique of the traditional theistic proofs, which I take to be justified on many points. In the *Einzig mögliche Beweisgrund* of 1763 Kant still claimed to have proved, once and for all, the existence of God as the highest of all possible beings, along with the central divine attributes of uniqueness, infinitude, and all-sufficiency.[94] Yet one also notes at various points his growing distance from the tradition, particularly in the manner of his treatment of the proofs. He criticizes the cosmological argument, for example, because of its inability to ground the necessity of God and to rule out polytheism (II, 157-61). Similarly, his famous rejection of the ontological proof, central to the position on God in the first *Critique,* appears right at the beginning of the *Beweisgrund;* here Kant already insists that "existence is not a predicate for the determination of any thing."[95] In general, one has the impression (esp. in part 2) that Kant has begun to place much more weight on preserving a place for natural law within metaphysics and on doing justice to the demands and standards of mathematics. This, at any rate, seems to be the message he wishes to get across to his contemporaries.

These changes notwithstanding, the pre-critical writings portray an author whose thought is steeped in the metaphysics of his day and who continues to live within its categories. For example, Kant's arguments often use as their starting point a creation that reflects the infinite power and perfection of its Creator. Further, he praises the physico-theological proof of God because of the

---

94. Kant's criticisms of the theistic proofs are examined in exhaustive detail in (to mention only a few) Giovanni Sala, *Kant und die Frage nach Gott: Gottesbeweise und Gottesbeweiskritik in den Schriften Kants* (Berlin: de Gruyter, 1990); Josef Schmucker, *Die Ontotheologie des vorkritischen Kant* (Berlin: de Gruyter, 1980); and idem, *Kants vorkritische Kritik der Gottesbeweise: Ein Schlüssel zur Interpretation des theologischen Hauptstücks der transzendentalen Dialektik der Kritik der reinen Vernunft* (Mainz: Akademie der Wissenschaften und der Literatur, 1983). I will not take time to re-present them here.

95. II, 72-74; cf. Refl. 5783. Incidentally, since this critique can already be found in the *Dilucidatio,* there is no textual reason to assume "daß Kant zu irgendeinem Zeitpunkt ein Anhänger des ontol. Beweises gewesen ist"; on this question see Niels Otto Schroll-Fleischer, *Der Gottesgedanke in der Philosophie Kants* (Odense: 1981), chap. 1 ("Der Gottesbegriff in der vorkritischen Philosophie"), quotation 45.

obviousness of its conclusion and its tendency to support moral striving. I therefore follow Redmann in his observation "that Kant does not begin with the world but rather with God, insofar as he raises the question of the 'Why' of the infinity of creation, *grounding its infinitude theologically* rather than discussing the immeasurability of God cosmologically."[96] In view of this gradual transition to the first *Critique* — it owes many of its theses to the pre-critical writings, and they, in turn, anticipate it in numerous respects — it is incorrect to speak of Kant's leaving the metaphysical tradition behind. Whatever break occurred was limited and involved highly specific divergences.

In view of the continuing dependence on theological concepts, it is ironic that one of the few places where Kant sought to revise the tradition actually represents a weakness in his argumentation. Kant's "sole possible proof" of God leads, he claims, to a knowledge of the infinitude or (to use Kant's favored concept) the all-sufficiency of God. The argument begins with the distinction between logical and material possibility. There could not be possibility if there were not something actual (II, 78-79). But possibilities exist; hence there must be something actual (and necessary?). Unfortunately, the argument appears to make the invalid inference from "Necessarily, something exists (given that there is possibility)" to "Something actually exists with necessity" or "There exists an absolutely necessary being."[97] Kant tries to use this modal argument to infer that the necessary being is unique, simple, unchangeable, and eternal, hence God.[98] Above all the other options Kant prefers the term *ens realissimum* or "all-sufficient being."[99] This being is "unique," because God is not only the principle of all actually existing worlds, "but even of all possible worlds."[100] Kant believes that this state of affairs can be adequately described only by means of the concept of all-sufficiency or *ens a se;* and for this reason he breaks with the concept of infinity. In his view, only all-sufficiency can express the actual necessity of existence that pertains to the highest cause, and a theology of infinite perfection fails to achieve this goal.

---

96. Redmann, *Gott und Welt,* 62, emphasis mine. Note, however, that other passages conflict with Redmann's "überhaupt" claim. Redmann's treatment remains today the classical expression of a theological interpretation of the early Kant.

97. Cf. Schroll-Fleischer, *Das Gottesgedanke,* 48ff., for further details.

98. II, 83ff.; cf. 89: "Es existirt etwas schlechterdings nothwendig. Dieses ist einig in seinem Wesen, einfach in seiner Substanz, ein Geist nach seiner Natur, ewig in seiner Dauer, unveränderlich in seiner Beschaffenheit, allgenugsam in Ansehung alles Möglichen und Wirklichen. Es ist ein Gott."

99. Cf. Refl. 3889: "Die höchste Realität besteht nicht darin, daß alles *in* ihr sei, sondern *durch* ihr [*sic*] als einem Grund"; see also Refl. 4242-61, esp. 4245, from the years 1769-70.

100. Schmucker, *Das Weltproblem in Kants Kritik der reinen Vernunft,* 49.

This argument represents a step backward, however.[101] For it presupposes that the only viable concept of the infinite is the mathematical infinite and loses sight of the rich resources that we have traced in early modern thought. Moreover, in contrast to Leibniz, Kant interprets the mathematical infinite exclusively in the sense of a constructivist theory of mathematics. As Wolfgang Röd has shown, "When Kant explains that the distinct concept of the infinite is dependent on the intuition of time, he means that it results from the construction of a series. Infinity can thus only be attributed to something that has the character of a series." As a result, the infinite is treated as synonymous with the idea of something that is "extendable without limit."[102] Unfortunately, this step excludes by presupposition the possibility of conceiving the infinite as a *maximum*. Kant defines the infinite as a set that is larger than any number; a largest set, however, a *maxima multitudo,* he asserts, is just as impossible as a largest number.[103]

In view of this early decision, it is no surprise that Kant believes he has discovered an opposition between infinity and perfection, coming to the (to us surprising) conclusion that only the latter admits of a valid and physical application. According to his theory of the mathematical infinite, "the finite is connected to the infinite by means of a continually expanded (and always further expandable) increase according to the laws of continuity." It follows that "no greatest number is possible. A greatest degree of reality is, however, possible, and this one finds in God." Perfections are qualities such as independence, self-sufficiency, and omnipresence. Only in the case of the perfections "is the gap between infinite reality and finite reality preserved by means of a particular entity, who guarantees their difference."[104] And only in light of this exclusion of the possibility of a truly infinite can the argument in the *Beweisgrund* be understood: "The concept of divine all-sufficiency is a much more accurate expression than that of the infinite for characterizing the greatest perfection of this being" (II, 154).

Kant thus came to hold the view that metaphysics needed to decide between perfection and infinity. Given the assumptions just reviewed, it was easy for him to exclude infinity. For either it would have to be understood as that which can be extended without limit, in which case it would have no maximum

101. The impetus for the following line of argumentation is drawn in part from Wolfhart Pannenberg, *Metaphysics and the Idea of God,* trans. Philip Clayton (Grand Rapids: Eerdmans, 1990).

102. Röd, "Das Problem des Unendlichen bei Kant," *Deutsche Zeitschrift für Philosophie* 38 (1990): 497-505, quotation 499.

103. This anticipates Cantor's transfinite set theory; see chap. 2 above.

104. Kant, "Versuch einiger Betrachtungen über den Optimismus," II, 32-33.

and therefore be inappropriate as an attribute of God; or it would be completely unknowable given his assumptions and thus unable to rise above the status of a mere idea of reason. Under this set of assumptions, Kant had no other recourse but to lift the concept of perfection (in the sense of the "highest reality") to the place of honor within his philosophical theology. Yet this is precisely the point at which Kant falls beneath the level already reached by Descartes and Leibniz. These thinkers had understood infinity as the absolute difference from the finite or limited, thereby raising the notion to a qualitative rather than a merely quantitative one.[105] Kant's mathematical infinite, as that which can be extended without limit, corresponds only to the Cartesian *indefinitum* (and to Hegel's "bad infinite"); no trace remains of Descartes's positive infinity.

In view of this one-sided treatment and appropriation of the tradition, one must ask, What could have led Kant to pass wordlessly over the entire positive branch of the theory of the infinite? The best-argued hypothesis in the literature is that Kant was concerned to avoid any danger of pantheism.[106] Heimsoeth has worked out the logic of the Kantian decision with particular clarity:

> The *Critique of Pure Reason* expresses it clearly and unambiguously: If one does not accept the ideality of space, then some form of Spinozism will result, according to which all finite beings become mere "accidents" of God. At least one passage from the Lectures exactly fits this construal: "If I accept space as a being *an sich,* then Spinozism becomes unavoidable, that is, the parts of the world become parts of the divine. Space is [in that case] divinity; it is unitary, omnipresent; nothing can be thought outside it; everything is within it."[107]

The infinite as that which is absolutely unlimited would have to incorporate everything. Since in that case, Kant thought, there would be no room for finite subjects, or for finite natural science, he abandoned this attribute of God. As we saw, he accepted the Leibnizian presupposition of independently existing

---

105. See above, pp. 109-11; cf. also Wolfhart Pannenberg, "Religion und Metaphysik," in Henrich und Horstmann, eds., *Metaphysik nach Kant?* 728-41.

106. So Manzke, *Ewigkeit,* 82, 115; and Heimsoeth, *Kantstudien* I, 118.

107. Heinz Heimsoeth, "Der Kampf um den Raum in der Metaphysik der Neuzeit," quoted from his *Metaphysische Ursprünge und ontologische Grundlagen,* 93-124, quotation 118. Compare this with *KpV* (V, 101-2): "Wenn man jene Idealität der Zeit und des Raums nicht annimmt, nur allein der Spinozismus übrig bleibt, in welchem Raum und Zeit wesentliche Bestimmungen des Urwesens selbst sind, die von ihm abhängige [*sic*] Dinge aber . . . nicht Substanzen, sondern blos ihm inhärirende Accidenzen sind."

subjects. More clearly than Leibniz, he realized that attributing infinity to the *monas monadum* would stand in tension with any atomism of the subject — precisely the tension that gradually emerged in my treatment of Leibniz in the previous chapter. I suggest that a more effective solution involves preserving the transcendent moment inherent in the idea of the infinite and attempting to develop a consistent theology in harmony with it. This problem — how we are to do justice to the monistic side of the infinite without allowing the otherness of the world to disappear — becomes a major theme of the third part of this work, as I trace the Spinozistic tradition through to its culmination in the idealist thinkers who followed Kant.

Despite his normally astute awareness of philosophical issues, then, Kant lost sight of the reciprocity between the concepts of infinitude and perfection that had characterized the entire ontotheological tradition from Descartes to Leibniz and Wolff. Infinity had always received additional content from perfection; and the latter had been interpreted, with the help of the former, both as expressing some continuity with the world and as qualitatively different from it. We saw in the last chapter that this reciprocity had become problematic in Leibniz's philosophy, partially because the traditional supports for a theory of perfection had begun to crumble during the seventeenth century. This collapse seemed to leave only two alternatives open. On the one hand, philosophy could try to satisfy itself with a reduced or truncated notion of perfection. This move would later become Kant's solution.[108] In the *Lectures on Metaphysics,* for example, he could still use this notion without reservations: "Metaphysical perfection thus rests in the degree of reality."[109] Yet as soon as one divorces perfection in this fashion from the traditional metaphysics of participation and the

---

108. This can be seen, inter alia, in the *Vorlesungen über die Metaphysik* (Erfurt: In der Keyserschen Buchhandlung, 1821; repr. Darmstadt: Wissenschaftliche Buchgesellschaft, 1988). In the section on perfection Kant develops, with no obvious reservations, a transcendental reinterpretation of the notion of perfection: "Vollkommenheit, transcendental betrachtet, ist die Totalität oder die Vollständigkeit der vielen Bestimmungen. Ein jedes Ding ist transcendental vollkommen" (p. 43). Conversely, he chooses not to offer any transcendental translation of the *infinitum reale.* Only the mathematical infinite, which we have found to be conceptually similar to the Cartesian *indefinitum,* receives mention: "Das Infinitum ist eine Größe, von der kein bestimmtes Maß angegeben werden kann. Jede Größe ist unendlich, wenn es unmöglich wird, sie zu messen und zu schätzen; die Unmöglichkeit liegt aber im Subjekt, d.h. in uns" (p. 64).

109. P. 108. For this reason he can conclude that "die Welt ist ein Ganzes von Substanzen"; these substances are "zufällig," "indem sie sich wechselseitig determiniren, daß also eine die andere limitirt." "Demnach ist die allervollkommenste Welt doch nur ein Ganzes von zufälligen Substanzen; — die vollkommenste Welt ist also nur ein Ganzes, was mehr Vollkommenheit hat, als jedes andere Ding haben kann" (p. 109).

hierarchy of being (see chapter 3 above), a rather extreme dualism between the perfect and the imperfect emerges. Indeed, without a common ontological foundation it becomes completely impossible to comprehend the *ens perfectissimum*. Kant's own "solution" — the *ens realissimum* should be treated as the transcendental ideal, an ideal without constitutive content — then emerges as the almost inevitable result. Other post-Kantian alternatives, such as construing God as a human projection or relativizing the term *God* to its meaning in a particular culture or time period, lead to no less skeptical conclusions, since they abandon the claim that the term conveys any particular content. On the other hand, the notion of the infinite could continue to be employed without its traditional connection with perfection, hence without obscuring its otherness in contrast to the finite. It is this possibility that provides the red thread for my treatment of the Spinoza tradition in the remaining chapters.

To summarize this section: as Kant turned from his pre-critical work and began the long process of composing the *Critique of Pure Reason*, he called a whole series of his earlier beliefs into question, especially those involving the unification of all reality in a single *maximum realitatis*. He began to doubt whether the *maximum realitatis* was in fact a "real possibility of being," or whether instead concepts such as *maximum realitatis*, *ens realissimum*, and *omnitudo realitatis* — in short, the idea of a highest level of reality — "is only really possible in a *serie successiva*, that is, in a world."[110] Such concepts can never be shown to be actually self-contradictory (II, 86); nevertheless, Kant's earlier commitment to their epistemic accessibility and usefulness began to weaken.[111] Indeed, it was precisely his sense of their connection (or lack of connection) with other types of human reasoning that effected the transition to the *Critique of Pure Reason*. Kant finally came to view the highest perfection (and related ideas) as "a constructed concept, concerning whose real meaning nothing concrete can be said."[112] Many of the same conceptual structures still influenced Kant's philosophy after 1770; in the "critical" phase, however, they became merely subjectively valid but objectively problematic. It is fascinating to observe how the later Kant remains true to the content of his early metaphysical ideas while repeatedly modifying their epistemic status in the direction of transcendental philosophy. In the end he is ready to say: "Because each *ens*

---

110. Schmucker, *Das Weltproblem*, 57. Schmucker follows this development in much greater detail.

111. Cf. "Quo autem pacto eveniat, ut cogitationi laterum, spatii comprehendendi . . ." (I, 395). In *Der einzige möglich Beweisgrund* one of the two interpretations of possibilities that Kant offers is that they are "merely conceptual" *(nur denklich)* and not ontological (II, 79).

112. Schmucker, *Das Weltproblem*, 58.

limitatum is only possible through the presupposition of a *realis,* everything presupposes a *realissimum;* this however [involves] the necessary subordination of the concepts according to the law of human understanding. The absolute necessity of a *thing* is a limit notion" (Refl. 4253). Sala comments correctly, "According to Kant the finite levels of reality are thinkable only as limitations of a highest level of reality" — that is, the priority of the whole before the parts is preserved — "but this condition of our possible understanding of finite things need not be a *constitutive* condition of their possibility."[113] In later years Kant strengthened the "need not be" even more, of course. Still, in the Dissertation of 1770 he already distinguishes sharply between the two "goals" of the intellectual principles of knowledge, the dogmatic and the critical.[114]

It has become clear from this short overview of the pre-critical writings that Kant's critical period retains more of the ontotheological tradition than the standard (esp. the analytic) interpretations normally acknowledge. Pace Schmucker, this correction does not justify the conclusion that Kant left the possibility "of a knowledge of God through natural reason untouched."[115] Yet in connection with the difficulties with Kant's critique of metaphysics and with his limitation of knowledge to the objects of the senses (sketched at the outset of this chapter), it does raise some serious questions about the extent to which Kant was really a post-metaphysician. It must therefore be our goal to assess whether "Kant's inference in the Transcendental Aesthetic to the fundamental spacelessness and timelessness of reality in itself, and . . . [his] fundamental limitation of the employment of basic ontological concepts (i.e., the 'categories') to a merely phenomenal world, is . . . compelling or convincing" (p. 106). At any rate, it is clear that more remains of the metaphysical Kant within critical philosophy than at first meets the eye.

God and the Infinite in the *Critique of Pure Reason*

The *Critique of Pure Reason* is itself an extended essay on finitude. After the classical notion of infinity had been excluded from human reflection, it now appeared to be reason's task to reflect on its own limits from a *finite* perspective. Was it Kant's goal, then, to overcome every sort of metaphysical concept? Or was he merely concerned to overcome dogmatism (B 767), that is, illicit claims

---

113. Sala, *Kant,* 208.

114. The two terms are *elencticus* and *dogmaticus.*

115. Schmucker, *Das Weltproblem,* 106. The next reference in the text is also to this work.

to knowledge on the part of metaphysicians? It is my task now to show how overcoming dogmatism does not require leaving behind metaphysical concepts altogether in the way Kant attempted — but never quite succeeded — to do it.

The Concept of God

In the *Critique of Pure Reason*, Kant understands God as the highest being, the *ens realissimum*, or the All of Reality *(omnitudo realitatis)*. As is well known, Kant claims not to use the notion of God metaphysically (except as a negative example); instead, it is supposed to function only as a pure idea of reason, representing the ideal of the completion of reason or, in other cases, its highest instance. As a transcendental ideal, the concept of God does not refer to an object given to us in experience, but rather "[raises] the use of reason in its own right to an actual object."[116] By relativizing this concept and its function to the subject, Kant completes the long line of development in theistic metaphysics that began with Descartes's use of God as the guarantor of the veracity of human reason. God becomes "the condition of the possibility of *the very being a subject* of the subject . . . , the foundation that bears the weight of the system of reason."[117] Practically speaking, God is understood as the "ideal of the highest good" and of "moral perfection" (B 832).

In Kant's emphasis on the uniqueness and centrality of the notion of God we see signs, once again, of the influence of his early writings. The idea of God becomes "the idea of something which is the ground of the highest and necessary unity of all empirical reality" (B 703). It stems from the need of reason to view the world in such a way "*as if* all such connection had its source in one single all-embracing being, as the supreme and all-sufficient cause" (B 714). Whether, and if so in what manner, there exists "a supreme intelligence which, in originating the world, acts in accordance with wise purposes" (B 725), is not knowable; nonetheless, the idea of this being is no less thinkable and no less philosophically necessary than in the pre-critical writings.

The problematic status of the Kantian idea of God has already been argued above. Notwithstanding the impression sometimes raised by the *Critique of Pure Reason*, Kant does not argue against the possibility of God's existence outside the subject: "Thus, while for the merely speculative employment of rea-

---

116. Costantino Esposito, "Kants philosophische Religionslehre zwischen reiner und praktischer Vernunft," in G. Funke, ed., *Aktes des 7. Internationalen Kant-Kongresses* (Bonn: Bouvier, 1991), II/2, 244.

117. Christian Link, *Subjektivität und Wahrheit*, 193; cf. V, 125 (= *KpV*, A 226), *KrV* B 595ff. Link finds in Kant's view a complete "Trennung von Existenz und Wesen," which he calls "eine unerträgliche *Aporie* des Denkens selber" (p. 194).

son the supreme being remains a mere *ideal*, it is yet *an ideal without a flaw*, a concept which completes and crowns the whole of human knowledge. Its objective reality cannot indeed be proved, but also cannot be disproved, by merely speculative reason" (B 669). Only the assertion that one has actual knowledge of the *ens realissimum* leads (allegedly) to insurmountable antinomies of reason; such antinomies are not raised by the mere assertion of (the possibility of) its existence. We return to these problems below.

What is for Kant the content of this idea, which is so closely bound up with the notion of a completion of human reason? Whenever we attribute to a finite object positive characteristics (or deny them of it), we presuppose the idea of an "All of Reality" (*omnitudo realitatis*, B 604). This being "is therefore entitled the *primordial being (ens originarium)*. As it has nothing above it, it is also entitled the *highest being (ens summum)*; and as everything that is conditioned is subject to it, the *being of all beings (ens entium)*" (B 606-7). Moreover, there have to be an actually infinite number of "realities," because God is infinite in his very reality (B 612). The final result — if one were "able to determine the primordial being through the mere concept of the highest reality . . . to determine it, in its unconditioned completeness, through all predicaments" — would be a "transcendental theology," whose object would be "one, simple, all-sufficient, eternal, etc." (B 608).

From this short summary it becomes clear that the largest part of the Kantian notion of God is drawn directly from the ontotheological tradition and remains closely connected with it. Even the assertion that the highest being has both a theoretical and a practical function — as ideal, archetype, and exemplar — Kant borrowed from the precritical tradition of modern metaphysics.[118] Interestingly, even in Kant's appropriation of the traditional idea of God the same implication emerges that we have repeatedly encountered: an All of Reality would have to include all existing things within it. Kant expresses the apparent implication with particular clarity in his late Reflection 6404: "Because the reality, which is encountered in part in all things, must be thought together (*zusammen gedacht*) in God, thus Spinozism results: that all things inhere in God, because their essence is only possible *as a part* of his essence." If Kant had in fact merely been interested in the regulative and practical consequences of the idea of God, as some maintain, one would expect that he would pay little attention to the ontological implications of his concept of God. Yet he strives mightily to find a way of avoiding this implication, arguing vehemently

---

118. Cf. the Dissertation of 1770, §9: "Haec autem [sc. perfectio noumenon] est vel in sensu theoretico, vel practico talis. In priori est ens summum, DEUS, in posteriori sensu PERFECTIO MORALIS."

that the emergence of the world is not due to a "narrowing of the highest reality [of the highest being]" or a dividing up of himself. Instead, Kant insists that the highest reality is the ground and all multiplicity is "his perfect or complete consequence."[119]

I will not attempt to present a complete interpretation and critique of Kant's treatment of the theistic proofs here.[120] Because he reduces all the other proofs to the ontological proof, the challenge — the one that Leibniz called the most important task of the theistic proofs — is raised even more clearly: to decide whether the idea of God represents an acceptable theoretical concept. For, as Kant notes in Reflection 4588, "If a determinate concept of the absolute necessity of a being is *possible*, we will at the same time have proven the *existence* of such a being."[121] At least by the time of this Reflection, Kant appears to have returned to this central theme of modern metaphysics; he no longer takes the famous criticism from the first *Critique*, "existence is not a predicate," to be a sufficient refutation. Still, the defenders of the ontological proof face a daunting task: they must first overcome Kant's arguments for excluding metaphysical concepts in general, and then combat Kant's specific separation of existence and essence. The chances for rehabilitating the ontological proof in this way, however, seem rather slim.

Except for the transcendental ideal, discussed above, Kant's comments on the theistic proofs are mostly critical. His chief interest in the physico-theological and the cosmological proofs is to show their dependence on the ontological. Further, his presentation of the ontological argument is corrupted somewhat by his interest in the moral proof and in the moral use of the concept of God — the same shift in emphasis that later led nineteenth- and twentieth-century philosophical theologians to the serious problems of a purely moral theology.

119. B 607. This assertion stands in tension with the claim of Paulsen that Kant is the founder of a worldview of "poetisch-naturalistischen Pantheismus"; see B. F. Paulsen, *Immanuel Kant*, 6th ed. (Stuttgart: F. Frommanns Verlag, 1920). Schelling, by contrast, did develop such a view; see chapter 9 below.

120. Many excellent treatments of the subject are already available. See in particular the above-referenced works by Burkhardt, *Hegels Kritik*; Sala, *Kant*; Dieter Henrich, *Der ontologische Gottesbeweis: Sein Problem und seine Geschichte in der Neuzeit* (Tübingen: Mohr [Siebeck], 1960) (esp. 137-87), as well as W. Weischedel, *Der Gott der Philosophen: Grundlegung einer philosophischen Theologie im Zeitalter des Nihilismus* (Darmstadt: Wissenschaftliche Buchgesellschaft, 1977), 1:191ff.

121. My emphasis. From this it follows that the central problem does not lie with the transition from concept to existence: "Nur die Möglichkeit eines nothwendigen Wesens darf dargethan werden, so ist sein Daseyn auch bewiesen. Denn ein nothwendiges Wesen ist (nothwendig) da, das ist die definition desselben. Man braucht dazu nicht die realitaet" (Refl. 4661, XVII, 628-29).

Kant's negative treatment of the God concept, when combined with the otherwise traditional form of his theology, justifies us in seeking a different starting point for a successfully post-Kantian doctrine of God.

The Concept of Infinity

By contrast, Kant's treatment of the concept of infinity is mostly free from the confusions surrounding the moral argument. In what follows I use it as the red thread for revealing the inconsistencies in Kant's philosophy and for pointing beyond them. Insofar as this concept not only influences his doctrine of space and time but also plays a central role in the antinomies — which Kant claims are the decisive ground for the transition to critical philosophy[122] — it may offer the key for rethinking the critique of metaphysics in the *Critique of Pure Reason.*

It is not difficult to formulate Kant's basic stance: the concept of an infinite can only be formed through the continuous repetition of a mental process, of which the classical example is counting. Because such a process could never be completed in a finite amount of time, there can be only potential infinites in the realm of experience and knowledge. Knowledge is limited to those concepts that can either be grasped immediately through a sensory intuition or attained by means of some process of construction or synthesis in the understanding.[123] As long as the objects of knowledge are constructed through human experience, and this is finite, the notion of a completed infinity can occur only as an ideal and never as a possession. At best, metaphysical arguments may reveal the importance of this idea of reason; they will never be able to interpret it as an actual reality.

Kant expresses this general viewpoint when he formulates his definition: "The true transcendental concept of infinitude is this, that the successive synthesis of units required for the enumeration of a quantum can never be completed" (B 460). In the Note he adds, "This quantum therefore contains a quantity (of given units) which is greater than any number — which is the mathematical concept of the infinite."[124] Notice that the world (the totality of

---

122. According to Kant, it is the antinomies "welche mich aus dem dogmatischen Schlummer zuerste aufweckte und zur Kritik der Vernunft selbst hintrieb, um das Skandal des scheinbaren Widerspruchs der Vernunft mit ihr selbst zu heben" (letter to Garve, 21/9/1798; XII, 257-58).

123. An excellent summary can be found in Sebastian Wolf, *Das potentiell Unendliche*, chap. 3 ("Die Kantsche Unendlichkeitsauffassung"), e.g., 155.

124. Kant offers a richer notion of infinity in connection with the forms of appearance, which we examine in the final section of this chapter.

what actually exists) must therefore be finite, if it is the result of a successive synthesis (and assuming that each of its parts is finite). Of course, one could conceive the world as if it were extended "indefinitely far"; and this concept of the size of the world might even pass as "given." Yet we would not thereby actually have thought of the world's extension as infinite, much less proved that the world is given as a whole in the sense of a collective intuition rather than constructed out of parts. All that we can validly say, Kant thinks, is that space is extendable "into infinity" or that a given whole is infinitely dividable (B 550ff.). But this is to say no more than that reason can set no firm limit on the regress that arises in extension or division. Only what is countable is actual, he thinks — at least as far as the constitutive use of reason is concerned.[125]

What is excluded from constitutive use, therefore, is the idea of any (uncountable) whole. Prohibited, for example, are any and all infinite qualities — even if humans always encounter such ideas when they attempt to understand Kant's own limits or to think a whole. Ideas of infinity are limited to a purely regulative function. Notice their fictive status in Wilfred Hinsch's summary, "Although we cannot use measurement to specify the totality of any plurality that is conceived as an infinite quantity, we nevertheless view [the totality] as given in this infinite quantity."[126] For Kant there exists only the mathematical (constructivist) and the transcendental ("as if") use of the notion of infinity, but he gradually (during the years 1762 to 1781) came to exclude the possibility of any metaphysical employment of reason.

The Antinomies

The central argument for the exclusion of real infinites is found in the antinomies, to which we now turn. The antinomies owe their alleged effectiveness more to the problem of infinity than to any other factor.[127] Does the assertion of an actual infinite lead unavoidably, as Kant thinks, to irresolvable paradoxes?

The theme of the first antinomy concerns the question whether the world is spatially and temporally finite or infinite. Kant's argumentative strategy is clear: if he can show that the idea of a world with a temporal beginning cannot be thought without contradiction, and at the same time that the world cannot

125. What would happen, however, if infinite quantities were now to become countable (or at least operationalized), e.g., by means of the set theory discovered by Georg Cantor? Wouldn't Kant's conclusion here have to be changed — or even completely abandoned?

126. Hinsch, "Die Unendlichkeit der Welt in der kritischen Philosophie Kants," *Zeitschrift für philosphische Forschung* 39 (1985): 383-409, quotation 402.

127. It is not possible to provide a complete analysis and critique of the antinomies here. See (among many others) Wolf, *Das potentiell Unendliche*, 165-94.

be conceived at all without such a beginning, then he will have proved that the whole question of ultimate origins is simply inadmissible. In his long analysis of the antinomy of pure reason (B 490-595) Kant develops his thesis that the world with which we have to do does not exist *an sich* — and therefore is neither finite nor infinite *an sich*. The world of our experience is the product of our categories and forms of intuition; above and beyond them no questions can be raised — at least none that have answers. Consequently, ideas of reason such as that of an infinite world must be treated as merely regulative.

The idea of an intrinsic antinomy of reason is brilliant. But does Kant succeed in proving the necessary contradiction of reason with itself?[128] Let's take the first antinomy as our prime example. The thesis — that the world has a beginning in time and limits in space — is supposed to be demonstrated by means of the counterargument that a world without a beginning is unthinkable. Reason can conceive only a finite number of parts within a single whole; yet an infinite world would have infinitely many parts. Note that two presuppositions underlie this argument: first, that infinity can be thought only by means of a completed synthesis of infinitely many parts, instead of through an intuition of the whole in Descartes's sense. Second, as a ground for this first claim, Kant maintains that finite reason is only able to proceed discursively, by means of a process of addition.[129] Both of these presuppositions depend on the earlier parts of the *Critique of Pure Reason*. If we are justified (as I have argued above) in questioning the limits upon which the Kantian theory of knowledge relies, then these two presuppositions — and thus the argument in support of the thesis of the first antinomy — are no longer compelling. In particular, one becomes suspicious of the first antinomy's construal of infinity as an indeterminate quantity produced by means of successive addition.

According to the antithesis, the world has no beginning and no limits in

128. A good overview of the relevant literature can be found in Hinsch, "Die Unendlichkeit der Welt," esp. 390n17. Hinsch refers to, among others, Russell, Bernardete, and Jonathan Bennett. The classical formulation of the criticism in the analytic literature is Bertrand Russell, *Our Knowledge of the External World*, 2nd ed. (Chicago: Open Court, 1929). For an attack on Kant's doctrine of the infinite see Russell, *The Principles of Mathematics*, 2nd ed. (London: Allen and Unwin, 1937), 459. Pamela Huby has written a good (even if not finally successful) critique of Russell's view: "Kant or Cantor? That the Universe, If Real, Must Be Finite in Both Space and Time," *Philosophy* 46 (1971): 121-32.

129. Hinsch ("Die Unendlichkeit der Welt," 389 and note) has shown convincingly that "der Rekurs auf die Diskursivität und damit Endlichkeit des menschlichen Verstandes" is central to the first antinomy. From this point of view, the argument appears as the opposite of the *id quo maius cogitari nequit* of the ontological proof, applied here to the special case of unlimited extendability in space and time. Isn't there a natural development from abandoning the conceivability of the perfection of God to doubting whether infinity is even conceivable?

space (B 455). For if it had one, then there would be "an empty time," when no world existed but time did exist. In this case there could be no specific time, separate from other moments of time, in which the world began to exist, because a truly empty moment of time would possess no attributes that could distinguish it from others, no "distinguishing condition of existence." Therefore the world could not have had a temporal beginning.

Many have found this argument so obscure that they can find no clear meaning in it whatsoever.[130] Perhaps at first blush one is inclined to agree with Kant that the idea of an "empty moment" might contain a contradiction: the final moment before creation, for example, would possess both the characteristic "a temporal moment not differentiated from other empty moments" and the characteristic "the final moment before creation."[131] But the alleged contradiction disappears as soon as one realizes that a temporal moment can possess various types of characteristics.[132] The two characteristics just mentioned do not, it appears upon reflection, exclude one another. Likewise, a moment M, which is t_n temporal units before creation, can be "empty" in the sense that no matter exists at that moment, and yet can be differentiated from other moments by means of the characteristic that it lies precisely t_n temporal units before creation!

It would have been less misleading had Kant utilized an argument drawn from the rationalist tradition: the impossibility of showing that the world had to begin (or end) at a particular point in time leads, by applying the Principle of Sufficient Reason, to the conclusion that the world *could* have no particular starting point and thus has to be actually infinite (cf. B 459). But it is precisely this type of inference that Kant wants to avoid in his critical philosophy. He holds instead that one can no longer presuppose that there is any necessary reason for the emergence of the world. Perhaps Kant could have used a different argument: maintaining that the world began by chance would not be a metaphysical explanation at all, since a metaphysical explanation would have to begin with the necessary emergence of the world at some particular time. Now the basis for this necessity would have to lie either in the moment of emergence itself or in the agency of some necessary being. But both of these possibilities are problematic: it is inexplicable why one among infinitely many "empty" moments should possess the quality of necessarily being the first moment of a

130. Jonathan Bennett claims (in *Kant's Dialectic* [Cambridge: Cambridge Univ. Press, 1974], 159) that he can make no sense of the argument whatsoever.

131. So N. W. Boyce, "A priori Knowledge and Cosmology," *Philosophy* 47 (1972): 69.

132. So Quentin Smith, "Kant and the Beginning of the World," *New Scholasticism* 59 (1985): 339-46.

world (or being the moment that caused it); and exactly the same problem would face a necessary being who would have (ex hypothesi) no sufficient reason (in Leibniz's sense) to create the world at t_n as opposed to t_{n-1}!

Yet even this more traditional attempt to establish Kant's antithesis is inadequate, insofar as it still leaves open at least two responses that would allow one to think the beginning of the world without contradiction. On the one hand, one could admit that the beginning of the world at a particular time is neither necessary nor coincidental, even though the existence of the world itself might remain necessary. On the other, one could discard Leibniz's assumption that God would have to have a sufficient reason for creating the world, substituting instead a radical theory of divine freedom (in chapter 9 we will look at just such a theory).

It appears, therefore, that the idea of the world's having a beginning in time involves no necessary contradiction. Moreover, the contrary position — that the world has an infinite past[133] — represents no insult to reason either. If human reflection is to avoid antinomy at this point, it must indeed distance itself from particular aspects of traditional metaphysics, admitting for instance that the decision among the various metaphysical options is underdetermined. This move opens the way for a genuinely pluralistic metaphysics. It may well be that no single metaphysical response wins a clear victory in the battle between the first antinomy's thesis and antithesis. Yet this outcome means only that a decision about the infinity of the world in space or time will have to rest, at least in part, on empirical research — as has become increasingly the case in this century.[134] Precisely this result, I suggest, is the one that we should embrace.

---

133. A number of arguments against the claim that the world has an infinite past are summarized and effectively dispatched in Quentin Smith, "Infinity and the Past," *Philosophy of Science* 54 (1987): 63-75. For an overview of the relevant literature, esp. the medieval arguments for and against an infinite past, see William Craig, "The Finitude of the Past," *Aletheia* 2 (1981): 235-42. In his "Kant's First Antinomy and the Beginning of the Universe," *Zeitschrift für philosophische Forschung* 33 (1979): 553-67, Craig makes an even stronger claim: "Thus, Kant's antithesis, far from disproving the beginning of the universe, actually provides a dramatic illumination of the nature of the cause of the universe; for if the universe began to exist, and if the universe is caused, then the cause of the universe must be a personal being who freely chooses to create the world" (566-67). Craig's attempt to build a positive philosophical theology out of this argument is less convincing than his careful presentation of contemporary set theory, in which he effectively demonstrates its static nature and its status as merely potential.

134. A good example can be found in the demonstration by Stephen Hawking that the universe could have a beginning in the sense of the Big Bang without it being necessary for us to postulate a first moment or $t = 0$. See Stephen W. Hawking, *A Brief History of Time: From the Big Bang to Black Holes* (New York: Bantam, 1988), and the analysis of his argument by

(Acknowledging the empirical element in formerly "metaphysical" questions does not, by the way, support the mistaken inference that only physical questions remain, or that all questions raised by the hypotheses and theories of physics are answerable by physics alone.)

Whereas the first antinomy begins with a finite whole and asks whether it can be extended infinitely, the second begins with a composite object and asks whether it is indefinitely (infinitely) divisible. In the thesis Kant tries to prove the existence of basic or simple parts by showing that the contrary assumption — namely, that the process of division is infinite — is unthinkable. Infinite divisibility is supposedly excluded by the observation that a finite subject could never complete an infinite process of division. Alongside this explicitly "critical" argument, Kant also employs a more traditional one: a complex object could indeed be infinitely divided in principle; yet even then it would have to consist of finite substances. Since the object is extended, each of its parts would itself have to be extended, that is, have some (even if very small) size. Therefore, no object could in fact be infinitely divided, since then its parts would be infinitely small. In formulating the problem of the division of an existing object in this way, Kant reveals his dependence on Leibniz's treatment of the problem of the continuum (see chapter 4 above).

In the context of the second antinomy's thesis, Kant explicitly rejects the Cartesian distinction between *in infinitum* and *in indefinitum,* calling it "an empty subtlety."[135] Elsewhere he writes that an infinite division could only be conceived at all if the totality were empirically given, as in the case of a physical body; otherwise the regress would be indeterminate. In no case, however, "may the series of conditions be regarded as being given as infinite in the object" (B 541-42). Kant's criticism of the *infinitum* idea is, however, unconvincing. As Geissler has emphasized, "The infinite . . . [Kant] construes as an action, as something empirical — although obviously not an action that could be completed empirically (and much less one that is transcendental or absolute or *an sich*, a totality)."[136] This is exactly correct: Kant's primary presupposition is that the understanding's "synthesis, therefore, if the synthesis be viewed by itself alone, is nothing but the unity of the act" (B 153). Division is indeterminate,

---

Robert J. Russell, "Finite Creation without a Beginning: The Doctrine of Creation in Relation to Big Bang and Quantum Cosmologies," in *Quantum Cosmology and the Laws of Nature: Scientific Perspectives on Divine Action,* ed. Robert J. Russell, Nancey Murphy, and C. J. Isham (Vatican City State: Vatican Observatory Publications, 1993).

135. B 539; but cf. 548.

136. Kurt Geissler, "Kants Antinomien und das Wesen des Unendlichen," *Kant-Studien* 15 (1910): 195-232, quotation 203. As Geissler notes, using Kant's assumptions there can be no distinction between "Beliebigkeit" and "Unendlichkeit" (204).

never infinite, because the series of constructive acts of the understanding must remain incomplete, even in principle.

The view of the infinite as "action without end" of course excludes any type of constitutive metaphysics of the infinite. But must we view it as the only acceptable modern account? I think not. The mathematical grounds for this approach — and they were highly significant for Kant — are no longer compelling in the wake of Georg Cantor's theory of infinite sets. Along with his contemporaries, Kant held that all mathematically acceptable units could be constructed, at least in principle, from simple components (e.g., from the series of integers), and that physics can only make use of real numbers. Contemporary set theory offers, by contrast, a formal framework for introducing infinite quantities as primitives without producing paradoxes. Further, Kant's constructivism, along with his view of space-time as something "unitary and all-encompassing" or as "an infinitely given quantity," reveals a certain inner tension. In the final analysis his understanding of infinity, as Hinsch has shown, cannot be applied to cosmology. For the object of cosmology "is from the start, because of its empirical character, not a quantity that could be construed or produced by the subject. It is therefore unclear why the infinite temporal and spatial extension of *this* object should be excluded only on the basis of its nonconstructability. . . . The assertion that no 'empirical' quantity is infinite cannot be accepted in the same manner as the claim that no number is infinite."[137]

Yet it was this argument, whose cogency we have just called into question, that was the basis for Kant's conclusion that only the concept of the potentially infinite, and not that of the actually infinite, may be utilized within philosophy (B 768). Philosophy should be concerned only with our process of counting or of constructing the world, not with talk of the world itself.[138] Otherwise, Kant thinks, the world would be reified as a thing-in-itself or noumenon. In this sense he writes that questions like that of the infinite "refer to an object which can be found nowhere save in our thoughts, namely, to the absolutely unconditioned totality of the synthesis of appearances" (B 509).

Kant's theory of the infinite thus applies exclusively to our process of

---

137. Hinsch, "Die Unendlichkeit der Welt," 406, 407. I maintain that this view is epistemologically unacceptable; to show this would, however, require a complete critique of Kant's theory of knowledge, only the beginnings of which can be sketched in the present chapter.

138. "Demnach werde ich nichts von dem ganzen Gegenstande der Erfahrung (der Sinnenwelt), sondern nur von der Regel, nach welcher Erfahrung ihrem Gegenstande angemessen, angestellt und fortgesetzt werden soll, sagen können" (B 548). On the theme of the potentially infinite see Wolf, *Das potentielle Unendliche*.

counting. And clearly, there can never be a solution to the second antinomy as long as only counting (i.e., constructing from finite parts) determines the concept of the infinite. For such an approach allows only two operations and the concepts that result from them: the "act of addition" and the act of "division." These two acts can be repeated "infinitely" in the sense of indeterminately long, and through this repeatability "they form a series that has no conclusion."[139] Yet, as Röd notes, "Only if infinite totalities could exist independent of thinking would an actually infinite be possible. Yet totalities are not given (as *Dinge an sich*), but rather emerge by means of a synthesis of phenomena" (ibid.). If we accept Kant's presupposition here, we have already conceded the impossibility of an actually infinite: "The absolute whole of quantity (the universe), . . . along with all questions as to whether it is brought about through finite synthesis or through a synthesis requiring infinite extension, have nothing to do with any possible experience" (B 511). If we appeal solely to a process of conceptual construction that operates by means of successive finite operations alone, we will never be able to formulate the distinctiveness of the infinite in contrast to the merely indeterminate. Thus, I argue, it is necessary to use as one's starting point a concept of the infinite that is not limited to a series of successive finite mental processes — even if the nonempirical origin of this concept forces us to accept significant limitations on its epistemic status and on the inferences that can be drawn from it.

The final two antinomies have a less direct relationship to our theme and will not be further treated here. The third antinomy concerns freedom and necessity. In terms of the theme of infinity the question might be formulated: Must the causal chain be infinite and unbroken, or can freedom, as an interruption of the causal context, be preserved? The fourth antinomy treats the two poles, "A being that is absolutely necessary exists" or "No such being exists." This being, Kant notes, would be an instance of an absolute totality, the personification of the infinite. If a "necessary condition of the absolute totality of the [causal] series" (B 484) cannot be accepted — say, because of the failure of the cosmological proof — then there will be no chance of climbing up from innerworldly objects to an infinite cause. As a result, we would have to speak instead merely of the "contingency of states of the world" (B 485).

In the case of the two first antinomies, at least, Kant believes he has found the main argument for his transcendental philosophy. Actual infinity can never be ascribed to the objects of the world, "because we have to do, in the case of the world itself and also the things in it, not with things in themselves but only

---

139. Röd, "Das Problem des Unendlichen," 501. The next reference in the text is also to this essay.

with mere appearances."[140] How does it then come about that the idea of an infinite is even formed? This occurs on the basis of a "transcendental subreption," by means of which we "ascribe objective reality to an idea that serves merely as a rule."[141] In the second antinomy, for example, the finite whole is the given, and it is grasped in a single intuition. An actual infinite could however never be grasped, because it would have to be constituted either through a sensible intuition or through a successive addition. Insofar as all sensible intuitions are finite, the former is impossible; and because an infinite number can never be constructed in a finite time, so also is the latter.

The Lectures

Kant expresses a similar view in the *Vorlesungen über die Metaphysik*, in which he presents two different definitions for the infinite. In one context it occurs as a concept of the understanding, namely as *infinitum reale*, "that is, [that] in which there are no negations, i.e. no limitations." In the other context Kant is referring to space and time, and thus to empirical objects. Here he allows only "the mathematical infinite, which is formed through the successive addition of one-to-one" (p. 63). The alleged opposition is unmistakable: "In the case of the *infinito reali* I think the *omnitudinem*, and I thus have a determinate concept; but in the case of the *infinito mathematico* I can never think the *omnitudinem collectivam*" (p. 65), because the latter implies (and depends on) the idea of a totality of all appearances.

Precisely here lies the problem: The *ens reale* is infinite, "because this word expresses at the same time *our* inability." Unfortunately, according to Kant, we cannot grasp what relation real infinity has to mathematical infinity or to number. If space and time were attributes of things-in-themselves, "from [their] inconceivability would flow already the impossibility of an infinitely given world" (pp. 65-66). The world *an sich* might *be* infinite, but it could never be *given to (for) us* as infinite. Analogously, Kant concludes that a set that is greater than any number is not impossible, whereas an actually infinite set is in fact impossible (p. 86).

---

140. Wolf, *Das potentielle Unendliche*, 166.

141. B 537-38, 509, 543-44. Cf. the Dissertation of 1770 (II, 412): "Quoniam autem praestigiae intellectus, per subornationem conceptus sensitivi, tanquam notae intellectualis, dici potest (secundum analogiam significatus recepti) *vitium subreptionis*, erit permutatio intellectualium et sensitivorum *vitium subreptionis metaphysicum* (*phaenomenon intellectuatum*, si barbarae voci venia est)."

Pushing against the Limits: The *Critique of Judgment*

The dichotomy that we have been exploring is unsatisfying in several respects. Just like the Kantian opposition between understanding and reason, it allows the two concepts of infinity to stand side by side without mediating between them or including them within a unified theory. Moreover, one wonders whether a concept of the infinite that refers to a totality or whole could have *only* a regulative function in human thought and otherwise play no positive role. It is therefore highly significant to discover that in his later writings, and against his own strictures, Kant attempts again and again to reintroduce holistic intuitions, to conceive the whole. Admittedly, he tries to do so without breaking out of the limitations imposed by the first *Critique*. In one passage, for instance, while discussing the unconditioned and the notion of absolute quantity, he now insists that "we do not know nature as representation [of the transsensible] but can only think it as such" (V, 268).

The treatment of infinity in the *Critique of Judgment* goes beyond the earlier treatments in that it attempts to do justice to the givenness of the concept of the infinite (V, 254). This approach assumes that the actual infinite is more fundamental than the merely potential infinite. Indeed, this change of view is indispensable to Kant's theory of the imagination, which, he holds, has the power to extend itself "into infinity" (V, 253). Nevertheless, he still insists that the infinite must be given a different, a nonconstitutive status, namely that of an idea of reason. Kant treats the concept of reason, which

> for every given magnitude — even for those that can never be entirely apprehended, although (in sensible representation) they are judged as entirely given — requires totality. Reason consequently desires comprehension in *one* intuition, and thus the [joint] *presentation* of all these members of a progressively increasing series. It does not even exempt the infinite (space and past time) from this requirement; it rather renders it unavoidable to think the infinite (in the judgment of common reason) as *entirely given* (according to its totality). (V, 254, §26 [trans. J. H. Bernard])

To think the infinite as a totality is "a capacity of the mind *(Gemüt)*"; it requires that we postulate "a capacity that itself is trans-sensible" (ibid.).

Because Kant has already excluded a direct theoretical comprehension of the infinite, he must locate a different type of capacity; and for this he turns to an examination of the power of judgment. Instead of analyzing the intuition of the infinite itself, Kant gives precedence to the sense of the sublime. The sublime is that which is "absolutely and in every respect (above every analogy) great" (V, 250). For example, we can think of the greatness or fearfulness of God in this manner: "we merely think of the case that we might try to offer resistance to him, and we immediately realize that all resistance would be utterly futile. . . . With regard to every such case, which [humans] can conceive as in itself not impossible, we recognize God as fearsome."[142] Similarly, the "striving to progress into the infinite" or the striving "for absolute totality" (V, 250) has precisely the same structure, since "the infinite is absolutely (and not merely comparatively) large" (V, 254).

Like the two earlier *Critiques,* the third also begins with the sensible world and progresses onward to the idea of an intelligible world and to the notion of God.[143] As in the earlier cases, here it is also reason that "demands totality" and that attempts "to think the infinite as completely (according to its totality) given" (V, 254). The *Critique of Judgment,* however, stretches the limits of what is thinkable somewhat further than the first two *Critiques.* Now for the first time we have to do with a concept that is related to the whole — the concept of *purpose* — which is at the same time thought of as part of the world, that is, of sensible objects themselves. (In the earlier cases it was clear from the beginning that one was dealing with a fiction, such as the notion of infinity in the *Critique of Pure Reason,* or at least with a sharp dichotomy, as in the second *Critique,* with its fundamental opposition between causality in nature and freedom in the human realm.) A purpose, as a cognition of a totality, always pertains to the level of the whole; yet this whole "determines the scientific object in every step of scientific praxis"![144] As a result, "infinity" in the *Critique of Judgment* has a significantly different meaning than in the earlier works. As Wundt concludes, "Viewed within a teleological framework, the intelligible shines forth without mediation from the sensible world. Kant's justification of his original [i.e., precritical] worldview here finds its completion, in that the sensible and the supersensible world are not only set over against one another in opposition, but

---

142. *Kritik der Urteilskraft,* V, 260-61. Schmalenbach notes, "Erhaben ist . . . eine Macht, die mit unsrer eigenen in überhaupt keiner Vergleichbarkeit steht" (quoted in Redmann, *Gott und Welt,* 56n.16). It is interesting that Kant chooses to employ the double negative here: one ascribes to God the attributes that one conceives as *not impossible.*

143. Nevertheless, it remains questionable whether this progression is unambiguous enough that we could conclude with Wundt, "So gipfelt das philosophische Bemühen in dem Ringen um den Gottesbegriff. Die Philosophie führt zur Theologie und endet in ihr" (Max Wundt, *Kant als Metaphysiker: Ein Beitrag zur Geschichte der deutschen Philosophie im 18. Jahrhundert* [Stuttgart: F. Enke, 1924], 372).

144. George di Giovanni, "The Spinozism of Kant: Paragraph 76 of the *Critique of Judgment,*" in Funke, ed., *Akten des 7. Internationalen Kant-Kongresses,* II/2, 21-31, quotation 24.

are related to one another and in their unification are dependent on one another."[145]

There is something fundamentally right about Wundt's attempt to interpret the three *Critiques* as "constantly renewed attempts . . . to advance from the sensible to the supersensible."[146] As it appears, Kant had been able to give the notion of God somewhat more content in the second *Critique* and in *Religion within the Limits* than had been possible in the *Critique of Pure Reason*. The *Critique of Judgment* brings this effort another step further. The key to Kant's progress is his wrestling with the "problem of realization," that is, with the question, Under what conditions can freedom be realized in the world of our senses? Konhardt characterizes the new approach accurately:

> If freedom is to be realized in the "world" of experience, then this world itself, the *mundus sensibilis*, must be structured in such a way that the attempt to realize freedom is not condemned to failure from the outset; put differently, nature must be grasped in such a way that (1) the forming of purposes is possible within it at all, and (2) the highest purpose, that which is demanded by the moral law, can be realized within it.[147]

Of course, in undertaking this project Kant did not mean to characterize the world *an sich*. Nonetheless, this new task demands a type of answer that cannot be limited to pure or practical reason alone. The sublime (and something similar would apply to the beautiful) may be a "feeling in us"; nonetheless, "the power of nature" "excites" this feeling and must therefore be understood as its cause (V, 264).

In his analysis of this phenomenon Kant comes rather close to the structure of the infinite as we explored it at the end of chapter 3 above: "Only under the presupposition of this idea in us and in relation to it are we capable of attaining to the idea of the sublimity of this being, which arouses inner reverence within us not merely through the might that it manifests in nature, but even more through the ability, which is placed within us, to judge it without fear and to think our determination as sublime even with respect to its might" (ibid.). In

---

145. Wundt, *Kant als Metaphysiker*, 373. Wundt builds directly on the results of his analysis of the third *Critique* when he turns in chap. 8 ("Die Transzendentalphilosophie als Metaphysik," 375ff.) to the central thesis of his book.

146. Ibid., 381. By contrast, I find rather less convincing Wundt's claim that "diese Versuche von immer besserem Erfolge gekrönt waren."

147. Klaus Konhardt, *Die Einheit der Vernunft: Zum Verhältnis von theoretischer und praktischer Vernunft in der Philosophie Immanuel Kants* (Königstein/Ts.: Forum Academicum, 1979), 315.

this argument, Kant now defends a notion of the infinite that is placed on the level of the whole. As such, it has little or nothing in common with the level of the quantitative, the finite; it also goes beyond the mathematical infinite as presented above. The infinite whole has a logical — Kant might say: an aesthetic — priority over against its parts; it represents (in a particular sense) a condition of the possibility of the parts. In this new conception, the parts remain finite phenomena: physical power, the extension of the universe, the aggregate of the world order, the feeling of fear, the representation of a very powerful being. At the same time, all of these point unavoidably toward the idea of an infinite and are thus constitutive of that idea, if not actually contained within it.

God and the Infinite in Kant's Late Work

It is certainly not the case that Kant believed he had overcome the skepticism of his critical philosophy in his very latest writings. The *Preisschrift* is perhaps the most ambitious metaphysical writing among his published works.[148] Nonetheless, even there he insists upon a sharp separation among three stages in the history of metaphysics: the ontological ("theoretical-dogmatic"), the skeptical, and the critical or practical-dogmatic — that is, the stage brought about by his own critical philosophy. From the standpoint of the third stage one finally recognizes the limits of reason: "Thus we cannot form any notion whatsoever of an absolutely necessary entity as such," for "it is a mere concept of modality, which involves a relationship to the object not in the sense of [ascertaining] characteristics of a thing, but only by means of linking the representation of the object with the powers of human reason" (XX, 304). Immediately following, Kant reasserts that knowledge of the divine nature is "unattainable" (XX, 305). Thus even in these passages Kant has not (pace Caimi) cast into question the foundations of transcendental philosophy. Nonetheless, now more clearly than before, he is ready to acknowledge the existence of an actual infinite as a meaningful notion, even if it transcends our knowledge. In the same context, for example, he speaks of the "impenetrable determining ground of our will" (ibid.). Numerous texts in the *Reflections* point in the same direction.[149]

---

148. In "Kants Metaphysik: Zu Kants Entwurf einer metaphysica specialis" (in Funke, ed., *Aktes des 7. Internationalen Kant-Kongresses*, 103-26), Mario Caimi argues for the claim that there is a Kantian metaphysics. His primary textual appeal is to this writing.

149. See Refl. 4780 (XVII, 725): "Unendlichkeit ist die absolute unmoglichkeit einer Vollständigen Synthesis (nicht der Vollstandigkeit des obiekts) der composition oder decomposition eines Gegebenen Gegenstandes." Other passages in the *Reflections*, however, begin with the possibility of an actually infinite.

Therefore, even if it is mistaken to speak of Kant's "post-critical" writings or of his return to a pre-critical stance, one must at least grant that he employs some modified ways of speaking — if not actual falling into outright inconsistency with the first *Critique*.[150] Within the Kantian opus, a particularly fascinating place is occupied by the *Opus postumum*. In these writings Kant appears to complete the process of development that we have already traced through the earlier writings. For instance, consider the new emphasis in his treatment of space and time. As he now emphasizes, "in connection with objects of the senses there is only one space and one time (spaces and times refer only to parts of these) and there is only one world" (XXII, 109). The reason for this changed view lies in a new understanding of the part/whole relationship: "with regard to purposes in the doctrine of practical reason, it is necessary to work analytically not from the parts to the whole, but from the idea of the whole to the parts."[151]

Theologically, also, the *Opus postumum* contains some more explicit formulations than the earlier writings. Thus, for example, Kant repeatedly criticizes pantheism and clearly confesses himself to be a theist. God is the first cause and must therefore be understood as a person — even if in a sense not fully analogous to human persons. He also ascribes a metaphysical significance to the world or universe: It is "the All of things as the one whole universe" (XXI, 29). The ideas *God* and *world* share with one another the important characteristic that they are "thought as components in the dividing up of existing be-

150. The term *transcendental* occurs frequently — and not always in observance of the limitations of transcendental philosophy. In the three *Critiques*, for example, one would never encounter the assertion, "Das All der Wesen ist . . . intuitive Erkentnis" (XXI, 140).

151. Ibid., XXI, 32. See elsewhere in vol. XXI: "Der transcendentale idealism ist die Vorstellungsart Begriffe als Elemente der Erkenntnis in ein Ganzes als ein System der Möglichkeit der synthetischen Erkenntnis a priori aus Begriffen zu machen" (15); the transition to physics presupposes "ein formales Ganze möglicher Erfahrung als Einheit" (15); "Gott und die Welt: Das Übersinnliche und das Sinnenwesen im All der Dinge (universum)" (17); "Gott und die Welt als synthetische Einheit der Trans. Philos." (19); and in vol. XXII: "Physic — Metaph — Transsc. Philos., Theologie" (64, to which he adds, "Der transcendentale Idealism ist der Spinozism in dem Inbegriff seiner eigenen Vorstellungen das Object zu setzen"); "Gott und die Welt. Jede ein der Qualität besonderes Ganze . . . Jedes ein Ganzes und beyde zusammen in Verbindung (das All der Objecte und das Subjects)" (ibid.); "Die Grenzbestimmung der Transz. Philos. durch das Maximum ihrer Erkentnis a priori als absoluter Einheit des complexus der bestimmenden Ursachen" (64-65); "Erfahrung ist das Ganze der Reihe des empirischen Bewußtseyns in beständiger Annäherung. Als ein Ganzes ist sie absol. Einheit" (104); "zum Behuf der Möglichkeit der Erfahrung ein Ganzes der Sinnenvorstellungen in Einem System zusammenfassen" (ibid.); "Das All (synthetisch) ist nur Eines: Es ist Eine Welt" (109); polytheism is false, "weil das absolute All nur Eines seyn kann. Man kann nur die Einheit die Vielheit in einen bestimmten Begrif zusammenfassen. Dieses aber geschieht nur durch die Allheit" (111).

ings" (XXI, 10). In an important analysis, Svend Andersen has shown that Kant understands these and similar expressions as transcending the realm of practical reason or morality, so that one cannot do adequate justice to the idea of God within the practical context alone.[152]

In the *Opus postumum* God is conceived as "substance," as "highest being," as *ens summum, summa intelligentia, summum bonum* (e.g., XXI, 11). God stands in "an active relationship to the whole of all objects of sensible representation, so that the division *(Eintheilung)* can be made" (XXI, 13). The observation that God is "the being *(Wesen)* of all beings as their primordial ground *(Urgrund)*" (XXI, 145; cf. 140) plays a particularly important role. Elsewhere he writes that God is to be understood as the being who is "absolutely and completely determining" (*ens omnimodo determinatum;* XXI, 58). It follows from this definition that God possesses the attribute of individuality (cf. XXII, 127-28). Because the other qualities that Kant attributes to God are taken directly from School metaphysics and do not contain anything philosophically novel, we will not explore them further here.[153]

It would have been nice had Kant achieved a systemic presentation of the central metaphysical concepts employed in his final years' writing, demonstrating, for example, to what extent they can be reconciled with his "critical" writings and in what respects they demand that the reader move beyond that perspective. But Kant was no longer up to this task. Instead, one finds in the late writings only fragments of a system and allusions to what Kant thought was indispensable for a critical doctrine of God. It is as if he realized that the three *Critiques* necessitated a new sort of reflection on the old metaphysical questions of God and world. This new program of reflection would have to be extremely complex, because it would need to include not only the relationship between practical and theoretical philosophy, as Kant began to address it in the third *Critique,* but also the transition from the metaphysical principles of natural science to empirical theories about the world. We find outlines and fragments of this program in the *Opus postumum.* Unfortunately, however, Kant's mental powers had already diminished so much that he was no longer able to work out the details of the important new approach that he envisioned. Any progress we are to make on this program will have to derive from later thinkers — or from a rethinking of pre-Kantian philosophers in light of the challenges Kant has posed. Both of these tasks will concern us in the following chapters.

---

152. *Ideal und Singularität,* 249-50.
153. For further details see Adickes, *Kants Opus postumum,* 769ff.

KANT'S CONCEPTS OF "PART AND WHOLE" AND "SPACE AND TIME"

We have seen that a component of Kant's "metaphysical" shift in the *Opus postumum* was his insistence on the priority of the whole over the parts. In this final section we look at a doctrine from his critical philosophy that apparently has the same structure. It is often overlooked that, according to Kant's theory of space and time, all spatial and temporal parts, and thus presumably all sensible objects, are limitations or modifications of a whole. Certainly this example indicates that the notion of the whole plays a much more important role in Kant's writings than he himself acknowledged. Yet, as we have seen, other parts of his work insist on beginning with the parts; complex ideas such as infinity are the products of construction through repeated acts of synthesis. Could it be that Kant was not able consistently to maintain his constructivist project? And wouldn't the holistic side gain in importance if he is wrong (as suggested above) about the sharp distinction between regulative and constitutive ideas and about the limitation to sensible intuitions? Much rides theologically on the outcome.

Three groups of texts in the Kantian opus bear on the theme of part and whole: those of the pre-critical writings in which Kant identifies the whole within a theological context as the highest and (at least in part) as a knowable reality; the texts of the Transcendental Aesthetic, in which space and time are defined with the aid of the notion of the whole; and finally those of the Transcendental Dialectic, in particular the antinomies, in which Kant most clearly stresses the unattainability of the whole. Obviously, the second and third groups belong to the same period of Kant's development; nonetheless, they remain, in my view, irreconcilable.

1. The first phase stands under the influence of the ontotheological tradition (see chapters 2 and 4 above). As the highest being, God also possesses the highest degree of reality. Thus Kant asserts in his essay on optimism that "the absolute perfection of a thing" lies "in the degree of reality" (II, 30-31), and the "greatest degree of reality" is found in God (32). In this hierarchy of perfections and being, the highest good is identified with the *whole,* so that "the whole is the best" (35). Even in the *Critique of Pure Reason* he retains this basic framework. Reason finds itself confronted with the idea of an All of reality, and "all true negations are nothing but limitations" (B 604). This idea is at the same time the idea of an "unconditioned," which must mean an unlimited (hence infinite) "totality," from which "the conditioned" totality or "that which is limited" is derived. Kant's basic principle is clear: "Reason presupposes God as the transcendental ideal for the purpose of deriving from an unconditioned totality

of complete determination the conditioned totality, that is, the totality of the limited" (B 606).

Kant's early doctrine of space and time presupposes this basic conceptual structure. In the Dissertation, for example, time is interpreted as a "quantum continuum"; time as a whole is "in infinitum" and stands above all possible objects of sense.[154] In the same way, space is an infinite continuum out of which the parts are, so to speak, individually cut.[155] Kant makes explicit (if not uncritical) reference to Newton, who also conceived space and time as independent of and prior to all objects. His opponent is Leibniz, who denies such independence. In the critical philosophy, he then seeks to explain this nonempirical nature of space and time by treating them as the forms of all sensible intuition; they are as such "subjectivum et ideale."[156]

Kant's unmistakable accent on the infinite whole is remarkable, even if he later weakens its epistemological status. Heimsoeth speaks of the "pathos of the infinite in the early period" of Kant, which "fully maintains its significance despite the limitations" of the critical philosophy. For Kant retains the view "that we encounter the effects of the infinite primordial being in the infinity of worlds and relations within the world. [The shift in his later thought] is merely that this sensible-intuitive encounter results in a merely symbolic representation, but not in an adequate picture of being."[157] This fact is of some importance; it suggests that we can now develop an overarching framework for reflections on the notion of the infinite, and perhaps also the idea of God — whether one takes the results as knowledge or only as regulating principles.

How might the primacy of the whole in the part/whole relation serve this function? Think, for example, of Kant's well-known dictum, "The starry heavens above me, the moral law within me" (*Critique of Practical Reason*, V, 161).

154. "Pars itaque temporis quaelibet est tempus, et, quae sunt in tempore, simplicia, nempe *momenta,* non sunt partes illius, sed *termini,* quos interiacet tempus" (II, 399); it is a "conceptus verissimus et per omnia possibilia sensuum obiecta in infinitum patens intuitivae repraesentationis condicio" (401).

155. "Quae enim dicis *spatia plura,* non sunt nisi eiusdem immensi spatii partes, certo positu se invicem respicientes" (ibid., 402).

156. (II, 403). Guyer has provided a convincing critique of this view. His analysis shows that "Kant harbored a prejudice against the ultimate reality of relations" (Guyer, *Kant and the Claims of Knowledge,* 351).

157. Heimsoeth, "Metaphysische Motive," quotation 212. The same holds true for time: "Das ganze zeitliche Unendlichkeitspathos der Frühzeit behält insofern seinen vollen inneren Sinn in der praktisch-dogmatischen Metaphysik des Kantischen Idealismus; nur ist das Schwergewicht des Welt- und Daseinsbewußtseins von der Unendlichkeit der kosmischen Entwicklungen übergegangen auf die Unendlichkeit des geistigen Geschehens" (225).

Apparently, the infinity of Spinoza's substance or the infinite worlds of Giordano Bruno have a continuing place even when the infinite has been re-conceived in terms of the synthesizing activity of the rational subject. One of Kant's reasons for moving from a metaphysical to a transcendental theory of infinity appears to have been his anxiety to avoid pantheism and Spinozism. If space is real and forms a mode of the omnipresence of the One, then everything that exists must be a part of it — a conclusion that Kant found inadmissible. Nonetheless, the same primacy and infinity of space is still required even when space is no longer understood as a mode of divine omnipresence but rather as a form of sensibility derived from the subject itself. The same is true of time. The indispensability of the predicate *infinite* was clear even to Feuerbach, insofar as he still found himself compelled, even after his *reductio* of the idea of God, to ascribe infinity to the human species.

2. In the Transcendental Aesthetic the whole of space and time is given priority over the parts. Here Kant realizes that "space is represented as an infinite *given* magnitude" (B 39). The parts of space may be infinitely divided; nonetheless, the priority clearly comes to the whole: "These parts cannot precede the one all-embracing space, as being, as it were, constituents out of which it can be composed." Thus space is "essentially one; the manifold in it, and therefore the general concept of spaces, depends solely on [the introduction of] limitations" (B 39). As Melnick concludes in his detailed study of Kant's doctrine of space and time, "Whatever else, space is a continuum. For Kant this means that it is an extensivity that cannot be represented as a multitude of discrete elements." Nonetheless, "in Kant's mind, it is only the flowing nature of spatial production or construction that can characterize space as a continuum."[158] Thus, even as Kant develops an infinity that is supposed to overcome the metaphysics of the absolute or God in Leibniz and Wolff,[159] he preserves much of what was essential to their conception.

Kant defends a similar position with regard to time: "Different times are

---

158. Arthur Melnick, *Space, Time, and Thought in Kant* (Dordrecht: Kluwer Academic Publishers, 1989), 5. Melnick thus labels as the "backbone" of his interpretation of the mathematical antinomies the fact "that Kant came to reject this very idea of a non-total plurality or collection *of things,* and came rather to restrict non-total (potential) infinity *merely* to rules for proceeding or progressions (making no sense in regard to collections)" (306). One should view Melnick's detailed argument in favor of an early, middle, and late view in the *Critique of Pure Reason* with rather more skepticism. Still, to the extent that the view just quoted is Kant's critical view, it is the object of my criticisms in this section.

159. This appears to be inconsistent, since the whole is supposed to be more than the sum of its parts. Unfortunately, Kant does not allow for any way of speaking of the "something more."

but parts of one and the same time. . . . The infinitude of time signifies nothing more than that every determinate magnitude of time is possible only through limitations of one single time that underlies it" (B 47-48). In these passages Kant comes closest to the absolute concept of space and time developed by Newton and Clarke. The difference is, as Manzke has shown, that Kant transforms Newton's infinite given time "into a *sensorium hominis*," that is, he makes it dependent on the unity of the thinking subjects — indeed, to such an extent that "time itself is conceived as subjectivity."[160]

The question of limits is particularly significant for our present purposes. Kant is prepared to grant a limitlessness in intuition (A 25). He then turns away from limitlessness, however, by focusing instead on the synthesis of the manifold in consciousness (B 202-3). He also draws back from asserting the existence of an unlimited by construing space merely as potential and by denying the existence of an absolute space.[161] In the *Metaphysical Foundations* (IV, 558ff.), Kant distances himself from Newton's doctrine of space. The implication in this later writing is that the passage from the Aesthetic (B 39) can refer only to the possibility of a progression through space. In a similar sense Kant writes even later, "A given *quantum* (in space and time) that is nonetheless *illimitatum* is impossible. Space is infinitely *progressive,* but not *collective.*"[162] Still, Kant saw correctly that he was committed to asserting the existence of a positive infinite: "space itself . . . may be conceived not only as unlimited but must be conceived positively as infinite, since the possibility of an unlimited progression is supposed to be grounded in it."[163] Finally, we know from the *Opus postumum* that spatial representations must be thought as "infinite representations."[164]

Kant's ambiguity about the priority of the whole comes to expression not only in the doctrine of space and time but also in several other areas of his thought. What are we to make of the occasional denials of the priority (or conceivability) of the whole, when other passages so clearly insist on it? For ex-

---

160. Manzke, *Ewigkeit und Zeitlichkeit,* 59. See also his excellent analysis of the Leibniz-Clarke correspondence and of Kant's interpretation of the results (86-98). Kant's critical philosophy ultimately appropriates more of the Leibnizian than the Newton/Clarke position (unfortunately, in my view), since it interprets space and time as dependent on the subject.

161. "Der reine Raum ist blos die potentiale relation und wird vor den Dingen vorgestellt, aber nicht als etwas wirkliches. . . . Der absolute Raum, als vogegen Geschöpfe in wirklichem Verhältnis stehen, ist unmöglich" (Refl. 4512; XVII, 578).

162. Refl. 5890; XVIII, 377.

163. So Hinsch, "Die Unendlichkeit der Welt," 399.

164. XXII, 83.

ample, the various versions of the lectures on logic ascribe a particular significance to the concept of the whole. In the *Logik Philippi* Kant claims, "In any construction of doctrine I must begin with the whole, with the central concept . . . and not with the parts. . . . The plan of the whole must first be sketched out; after that, one can fill it in with the various parts. . . . The ideal or the whole precedes, and only within the whole may the parts be thought" (XXIV, 399). Somewhat later he notes even more clearly, "A *system* is . . . where the idea of the whole comes before the determination of the parts. An *aggregate*, however, is where the knowledge of the parts precedes the concept of the whole."[165] Similarly, one reads in the *Fortschritten* that "all negations must be viewed as derived from the One merely as limitations of the ultimate concept of reality; the same holds for all things, apart from the one exception of their possibility."[166] Finally, in the *Critique of Judgment* (§77) Kant describes a type of understanding that, because of its "intuitive" nature, "proceeds from the synthetic or general *(from the intuition of a whole as such)* to the particular, i.e. from the whole to the parts" (V, 407, my emphasis). The understanding that perceives in the whole "the ground of the possibility of the form" of the parts is an "intellectus archetypus"; it *begins with* the idea of a whole "upon which even the characteristic and mode of operation of the parts" depend (408). An understanding that proceeds in this way is not only thinkable but must necessarily be thought: "According to the characteristics of our human epistemic abilities, it is necessary to seek the highest ground in an originary understanding as the cause of the world" (410).

3. As is well known, for epistemological reasons Kant was not ready to follow this line of thought any further or grant it anything more than regulative significance. The antinomies deny that the concept of the whole can be used without contradiction within philosophy, since in metaphysical cases one lacks the representation of an infinite quantity (B 550-51, 532-33). No theory about the world as a whole may be formulated: "The world is not an unconditioned whole, and does not exist as such a whole, either of infinite or of finite magnitude" (B 533). Kant thinks it is empirically meaningless to speak of the universe as a whole, and he applies this belief as his strategy for overcoming the cosmological antinomies. On what grounds? There can be no representation of the

---

165. *Logik Busolt* (XXIV, 631, my emphasis). See Norbert Hinske, "Die Wissenschaften und ihre Zwecke," in Funke, ed., *Akten des 7. Internationalen Kant-Kongresses,* 1:172-73.

166. XX, 302. The process thus begins with an "Absonderung des Übrigen von einem gewissen Theil des Ganzen, also nur durch Negation." Nevertheless, Kant denies in the same context that this method leads to any knowledge. His interest in the idea of system is confirmed by his emphasis on the architectonic, which he interprets as the "Kunst der Systeme" (B 860).

whole, insofar as the perception of the manifold is not simultaneous but only successive. According to this fundamental principle of Kantian epistemology, the manifold "is grasped as a categorially directed successive synthesis."[167] This means that there cannot be any complete knowledge of an infinite world: "Empirical knowledge must then be conceived as a fundamentally unfinished progression, as an infinite task. This is the foundational concept of Kant's theory of the regulative ideas."[168] Claims for the impossibility of conceiving a whole can be found already in the Dissertation.[169] There, however, Kant was still prepared to admit the possibility of such a conception on the part of the infinite (superhuman) intellect (II, 388). This exception no longer appears in the *Critique of Pure Reason;* now Kant hopes, using his account of the necessary conditions of intuition, to show that a God who conceives the whole is unthinkable (e.g., B 148-49).

What are we to say to the thesis of the inconceivability of the whole? I suggest that more recent empirical developments have made the bulk of Kant's arguments for his view obsolete. Not only is modern physical cosmology now able to formulate and to test theoretical statements concerning the whole universe;[170] relativity theory also presupposes the dependence of local spatiotemporal judgments upon the whole of space-time, as do many versions of quantum field theory. Further, the amplification effects that characterize chaos theory, along with the "nonseparability" of particles that remain somehow bound together despite extreme separations in space and time because of their common source, have led contemporary physicists to connect judgments about

167. Hinsch, "Die Unendlichkeit der Welt," 384.

168. Ibid. Hinsch argues here that "das Ansichsein empirischer Gegenstände durch ihre mögliche Unendlichkeit bestimmt [wird]."

169. "Nam infinitum simultaneum inexhaustam aeternitati materiam praebet, ad successive progrediendum per innumeras eius partes in infinitum, quae tamen series omnibus numeris absoluta actu daretur in infinito simultaneo, ideoque, quae successive addendo nunquam est absolvenda series, tamen *tota* esset dabilis" (II, 393-94). The denial that two things can be simultaneously infinite also lies at the heart of the thesis of the first antinomy (B 456).

170. See, e.g., D. W. Sciama, *Modern Cosmology* (Cambridge: Cambridge Univ. Press, 1971); George Ellis et al., eds., *The Renaissance of General Relativity and Cosmology: A Survey to Celebrate the 65th Birthday of Dennis Sciama* (Cambridge: Cambridge Univ. Press, 1993); John Barrow, *Theories of Everything: The Quest for Ultimate Explanation* (Oxford: Clarendon Press, 1991); W. Stegmüller, "Die Evolution des Kosmos," in Stegmüller, *Hauptströmungen der Gegenwartsphilosophie,* 6th ed. (Stuttgart: A. Kröner, 1979), 2:386ff.; B. Kanitscheider, *Kosmologie: Geschichte und Systematik in philosophischer Perspektive* (Stuttgart: A. Kröner, 1984); and the treatment of these questions in Wolfhart Pannenberg, *Systematic Theology,* trans. Geoffrey Bromiley, 3 vols. (Grand Rapids: Eerdmans, 1991), 2:152ff.

parts of a physical system with the entire context of this system (even when the result looks like action at a distance). The separability of an individual moment from its broader (or broadest) context therefore appears, for empirical reasons, untenable. Kant never quite overcame the atomism of his predecessors.

These empirical developments are of great significance. Advances in physical theory, along with a changed understanding of scientific method itself (i.e., the final overturning of the geometrical-mechanical understanding of science that dominated the late eighteenth century), have reopened the prospect of truly universal theories. If the infinite, as the whole that encompasses all finite parts, should be accessible to reason, instead of being produced by the understanding through a process of gradual construction from parts alone, then a post-Kantian philosophical theory of the infinite would again be possible. Thus my plea for the importance of a mode of reflection that incorporates holistic or "top-down" thinking as a part of the knowledge process.

Interestingly, there are also inner-Kantian reasons for accepting the whole as primary. For one, Kant notes regarding a *regressus in infinitum* — for example, the extension of a line — that it can be extended "possibly to the infinite" (B 542). But when one conceives an infinite line, one first (or at least simultaneously) conceives the infinite space in which it is drawn. This response is reminiscent of Hegel's claim that the infinite, as opposed to the merely indeterminate, is already conceived whenever we speak of its possibility. The problem arises for Kant because he has not separated the infinite in space sharply enough from action: actions alone construct space, and actions are for him like parts, individual, finite, atomistic. An atomism of actions leads just as inevitably to conceptual problems as an atomism of individual points or monads (chapter 4 above).

4. How, then, might the infinite be thought? To overcome the Kantian problems, one would have to speak of the whole as "conceivable in a transempirical sense."[171] One example would be the intuition of an infinite line in the context of a space-time conceived as endless — something ruled out by Kant except as a regulative idea. This intuition might be embedded within something like a Cantorian theory of space-time: the content of the theory would no longer be limited to what is finite, although the mathematical (geometrical, conceptual) framework of the theory, like Cantor's infinite sets, could still be specified in a sufficiently exact and usable sense.[172] But to make use of anything like such theories — in the philosophy of space and time, in meta-

---

171. Geissler, "Kants Antinomien," 212.
172. Perhaps the speculative use of Hilbert spaces in theoretical physics provides a further analog.

physics, or in theology — one must give up the insistence on finite limits and step-by-step construction — an insistence that had its historical roots in an overly limited geometry, a mistaken physics, and the false belief that a mathematics of unequally infinite quantities is impossible.

Next, the assumption of an overarching whole must be given a corresponding ontological status. As Cramer notes, "Real time is the condition of the form 'time.' That which is ontically temporal first makes time as a form of intuition possible."[173] The whole that contains all finite parts could be introduced in a similar fashion, namely as a given. As we already discovered while treating Leibniz's problem of the continuum, a whole cannot be constructed by adding together a large number of parts. If it grows out of pregiven elements, in the fashion of an emergent property, then it is a characteristic that cannot be explained at the level of the individual parts that preceded it. On this view, the newly appearing whole represents the emergence of a new conceptual and ontological level — just as the behavior of a cell or the actions of an organism are not explainable through physical laws alone and mental predicates are something more than complicated biological processes. By contrast, in the case of an infinite whole, it will have to be produced by negating the finite as a whole, and thus transcending it into the realm of the infinite. In both cases, one must change the standpoint to accomplish the transition from the parts to the whole. Geissler calls it the transition "to a higher standpoint of being, above that of the individual sensible object."[174] Kant recognized the necessity of a transition, but the only one he could conceive was the transition from constitutive assertions (knowledge) to regulative ideas (imagined completion).

On the one hand, the status of the whole remains analogous to the three Kantian concepts of freedom, immortality, and God, which, he argues, are foundational for practical reason. On the other, one can scarcely avoid the impression that we here encounter something whose ontological status is not adequately expressed when it is given a regulative interpretation or treated as a transcendental ideal. According to Kant, "through the practical law, which requires the existence of the highest good possible in the world, there is postulated the possibility of those objects of pure speculative reason whose objective reality could not be assured by speculative reason" (V, 134). In this context, at least, Kant is willing to treat God and freedom as "eminent and constitutive" (135). Bound by this limitation, Kant insists again and again in the *Opus postumum* that talk of God is related primarily to "the final purpose that the human being has qua moral" (XX, 305). Nonetheless, his continued appeal to

173. Cramer, *Gottesbeweise*, 122.
174. Cf. Geissler, "Kants Antinomien," 224.

the idea of the whole retains the structure "of a metaphysical ascent toward the transempirical."[175] We may not be able to speak, Kant thinks, "of the theoretical knowledge of the objects of these ideas"; yet we do seem to have encountered the condition "that they have objects *überhaupt*" (V, 136).

I have proposed that space and time are only treated adequately when one has guaranteed a place for and placed adequate emphasis on the category of the whole. We saw above that Kant understands space (and time) in the Aesthetic not as something constructed out of parts but as itself a whole. His reasons for this view are stronger than those on behalf of an atomistic theory of space-time.

What about Kant's case for denying space and time any real status outside the human subject? At some points he even adduces theological reasons for this conclusion,[176] apparently on the assumption that, if space and time were divine attributes rather than human ones, all things in space and time would also be *in* God. But why could this not be? As soon as one questions the need for the absolute separateness of God and world, Kant's theological arguments against placing space and time outside humans, and thus in God, look less convincing. Of course, if God were grasped by means of the forms of space and time, this would tend to lead away from the ontotheological framework that Kant presupposed in the direction of a different theological model. I return to this new model in chapter 9 below. At this point I note only that talk of one infinite extension of space and time casts the sharp separation between God and world into question. The results in the case of time will be a sort of process theology and, for space, the inclusion of the world within God, hence a version of panentheism.[177] Both of these departures from early modern ontotheology stem out

175. Geissler, "Kants Antinomien," 224.

176. E.g., "Die Theologie, [in order that it not contradict itself] sieht sich genothigt, beyde [Raum und Zeit] nur zu der Form unserer Sinlichkeit zu manchen und allen Dingen, die von uns erkannt werden konnen, als Phaenomenen, Noumena, die wir nicht kennen, in Ansehung deren aber das Unbedingte allein stattfindet, unterzulegen. Da nun der Streit zwischen den Principien des Unbedingten in der Synthesis und den Prinzipien des in Raum und Zeit bedingten, mithin die Antinomie der Vernunft, schlechterdings nicht beygelegt werden kan, ohne diesen Unterschied unter den Objecten und ihren Vorstellungen zu machen, so führt die Theologie auf die ästhetische Kritik" (Refl. 6317; XVIII, 626-27).

177. Charles Hansen Toll (*Die erste Antinomie Kants und der Pantheismus,* Kant-Studien Ergänzungsheft 18 [Berlin: 1910]) agrees that Kant's theories of the infinite and of space and time stand close to pantheism. At the same time, he denies that such theories can be brought into consonance with the results of the sciences (p. 46). Ironically, developments in the ten years after Toll wrote already cast his claims into question, and Toll failed to see that panentheism offers a mediating position between theism and pantheism. In chapter 7 I argue that Spinoza provides a means for thinking these two different directions together.

of our consideration of Kant's challenges to theology, and both represent, I believe, theological improvements.

5. In conclusion, we have found that Kant faced a fateful decision right at the beginning of his critical philosophy. On the one hand he could accept a compositional theory of the infinite and similar ideas, according to which they are constructed through successive mental acts. On the other, he could allow for such ideas to function as givens for further reflection. The decision he faced is similar to the choice between the analytic method that Leibniz employed in most parts of his philosophy and the Cartesian theory of the primacy of the infinite. I have made a plea for the latter, repeatedly arguing for the postulation of an infinite space and an infinite time as components of an ontological theory that ascribes primacy to the whole over against the parts. Kant himself gives reasons in the Aesthetic for siding with this view. If it is to be further developed, however, we must abandon an epistemology according to which all knowledge can be traced back only to direct sense impressions and the successive repetition of mental acts.

The result would be a metaphysics of the infinite. Of course, even where it moves beyond the limits of the Kantian critique of knowledge, it could no longer look like classical rationalist metaphysics — even only because of the negative connotations of the *in*finite that we traced in chapter 3. In comparison to rationalism, the positive theoretical conclusions of such a theory will be relatively humble; perhaps it will not be able to move beyond a few minimal attributes and implications of postulating an infinite. Something similar resulted from our study of Descartes and Leibniz, at least after we separated the minimalist theory of the infinite from the ambitious theories of perfection that had been uncritically taken over from the tradition. It is not without significance that we should find the roots of such a theory already within Kant's Aesthetic.

But is it the beginnings of a theology, a doctrine of God, that we are now encountering? This appears to be the view of Wolfhart Pannenberg. If the Aesthetic grants primary to the whole,

> the concept of God should then not have appeared only at the end of the Transcendental Dialectic, as an ideal of pure reason tied to the completeness of the employment of the understanding, but already at the *beginning* of the Transcendental Aesthetic. In this case, the notion of God would be constitutive for reason, which would of course give a completely different character to the Kantian critique of reason as a whole. In particular, it would mean that the position of the critique could no longer be that of a transcendental subjectivity standing on its own. Instead, in the intuition of the Infinite the op-

position between the subject and things-in-themselves would already be bridged over and held together.[178]

Perhaps it is not the idea of God as such that makes its appearance in the Aesthetic, but it is a conceptual development that points strongly in that direction. Be that as it may, what does appear in Kant's doctrine of space and time — namely, the priority of the infinite whole — stands in tension with the official doctrine of infinitude in the *Critique of Pure Reason*. The result urgently demands further reflection, for it just may be the point at which theology's greatest critic in the modern era himself opens the door to sustained theological reflection. Here Pannenberg's conclusion is to be embraced: "We have found reason for viewing our two conclusions — on the one hand, the priority of the infinite whole of space and time over all comprehension of finite entities and relationships; on the other, the so-called transcendental ideal of the *omnitudo realitatis* as the condition of all conceptual determination — as merely different aspects of one and the same theme. If this is correct, then we must grant to philosophical theology a much greater importance in the critique of reason than Kant was willing to ascribe to it" (p. 33).

CONCLUSION

This overview of the notions of perfection and infinity in Kant has underscored his grounds for modifying, and ultimately rejecting, the metaphysics of perfection. It has also revealed sharp contrasts between his notion of infinity, which is constructed by means of repeated mental steps, and the holistic infinite that he rejected. I did not find myself compelled by Kant's arguments to declare the actually infinite unknowable, and I found that Kant himself struggled with inconsistencies as he tried to do away with it.

Kant reached his decisions about perfection and infinity in his pre-critical writings, arguing that the infinite would have to be unknowable and could enter human thought (if at all) only as an idea of reason. One motivation for this view was Kant's determination to fight against all tendencies toward pantheism. If space and time were infinite, and if God was characterized primarily through his infinity, then it would be tempting to interpret space and time as manifestations of the divine infinity, and therefore as internal to God. But, he thought, a world

---

178. Pannenberg, *Metaphysics and the Idea of God*, 31. The next reference in the text is also to this work.

internal to God would become God. As a result, Kant turned away from the infinite God and toward God as the moral lawgiver, characterizing the divine in terms of all-sufficiency *(Erhabenheit)* and excluding every speculative knowledge about its being in itself. I found myself forced to different conclusions, however. Given that the ban on speculation cannot be consistently observed, and given the need to question the concept of all-sufficiency because of its dependence on the now untenable notion of perfection, I found it necessary to judge Kant's attempt to escape from these difficulties a failure. The point can also be put differently: if the finitude of space and time is untenable, and if a purely regulative treatment of metaphysical concepts appears problematic, then a nonfinite and more-than-regulative approach recommends itself — even if the result is a nontraditional model of God such as panentheism. As Manzke has shown, "The insight into the aprioricity of time and into its nature as the essence of all changes in the world" is what led Kant "to move time closer to the status of an attribute of God."[179]

It is now time to return to the question of a post-Kantian metaphysics and theology. In what respects should we condone Kant's critique of metaphysics, and where ought we to question it? I began the chapter with the question of the conditions of human knowledge and later explored the function of the idea of God as a unifying concept. The question led me, as it led Kant, to the debate over whether the antinomies are insoluble. In discussing them I had to acknowledge that they show at least that multiple answers to the basic questions of metaphysics are admissible, depending on one's starting point and argumentative concerns. Classical metaphysics, with its particular striving for absolute unity, is weakened by such pluralistic results, and any speculative theology that one would now write must be modified accordingly. Had I encountered metaphysical conclusions that stood in actual contradiction to one another, then the discipline itself would have been cast into question; but I have disputed that Kant's antinomies express actual contradictions of this sort. It may well be that theories constructed out of intersubjectively testable data by means of finite reproducible steps are more accessible to critical examination — and in this sense have a stronger claim to knowledge — than those that contain holistic concepts such as the infinite or God. But it does not follow that holistic concepts can therefore be dismissed as the product of a "subreption," the illicit extension of reason.

179. Manzke, *Ewigkeit und Zeitlichkeit*, 82; cf. 115, referring to *De Mundi*, Secto IV, Scholion (II, 409-10). Kant conceives of time as the "Medium der die Welt erhaltenden Gegenwart Gottes"; consequently, "nähert sich Kant also sichtbar der Bestimmung der Zeit als reiner Dauer und ihrer 'metaphysischen Beurteilung' als des 'sensorium Dei'" (82). Cf. also Heimsoeth, *Kantstudien*, I, 118; W. Pannenberg, "Theologische Motive im Denken Kants," 899-90.

Clearly, the criticisms sketched at the beginning of this chapter and in the previous section mean that I have distanced myself in certain respects from Kant's own approach, so that the final position can no longer be understood as Kantian in the strict historical sense. Nevertheless, on at least two points the view defended here remains, broadly speaking, Kantian. First, my starting point is a notion of God that presents itself — at least at the outset — as a transcendental ideal and thus, in light of the question of its constitutive employment, more as a *problem* than as a theoretical first principle (hence the title of the book). Whereas pre-Kantian philosophy remained undisturbed that the idea of God also functioned as an ideal of reason (when it realized this at all!), this fact raises for many today, as for Kant, the worry that the God-idea might be a mere limit concept, a projection upward and outward of the human striving for unity. In a word: we today can no longer simply presuppose that a constitutive theory of God is possible — even while it is our hope to move finally beyond Kant's own exclusion of this notion.

Second, we have seen that Kant pushed against his own limits more and more frequently as he progressed through the three *Critiques* and on to the *Opus postumum*. Whether one views the later treatments as repetitions of the basic principles of critical philosophy in more and more subtle form, or as an indirect proof that Kant gradually became aware of the untenability of his own critique of pure reason, depends on how one judges the Kantian project as a whole. I have sought to interpret the later passages as signs of a genuine and novel development, hence not as contradictions but as indications of Kant's ever deepening insight into the limitations of his earlier views. Consequently, I have made a plea for the possibility of a theology today that transcends the context of the merely regulative and the purely practical. If this project proves to be viable, then it may be understood as a further step in the direction of Kant's own development in his later years.

Would the historical Kant have been satisfied with my attempt to move in the end beyond critical philosophy and to establish the possibility of constitutive language about God? Put differently, is the line of development from the *Critique of Pure Reason* to the *Opus postumum* sketched here sufficient to prove that he was actually on the way toward a post-critical metaphysics? Adickes argues in this fashion, claiming on the basis of numerous texts in the *Opus postumum* that "one would do violence [to the texts] if one attempted to construe the terms *God* and *world* in them as mere ideas of reason and not instead as actual realities."[180] By contrast, in the last analysis I would evaluate the his-

---

180. Adickes, *Kants Opus postumum,* 781. Regarding the depth and unquestioned nature of Kant's own belief in God, see 776-77.

torical case somewhat more cautiously. Even if I have been able to establish a clear process of development, one that moves beyond the transcendental ideal of the *Critique of Pure Reason* and the moral-practical context of the *Critique of Practical Reason,* this does not actually prove that the historical Kant would have been ready to follow this line several steps further — much less to its end point, a theistic metaphysics. Whether he ought to have done so is a question that will not be decided through historical studies alone, but only through the success or failure of theistic metaphysics in contemporary thought.[181]

I turn to precisely this task in the next chapter. The question runs: What is the metaphysical interpretation of the limits (or: the difficulties) that we have encountered in our dialogue with Kant? Can we find an appropriate metaphysical expression for them? If so, could it be the finitude of human reason, the finitude of the subject as person? I have stressed the historicity of the conditions within which humans think; thinking by means of them, we are determined by them. Human reason is historical, malleable; it is limited by its own categories, since it cannot know whether they correspond to things-in-themselves. The best metaphysical expression for this fact is finitude. Yet the finite, as we discovered in chapter 2 on Descartes, also carries within it as a seed the idea of an infinite dimension. The important difference from Descartes is that perfection has now fallen by the wayside, allowing the "Kantian possibility" of an unbridgeable dualism between thinking and being, between thought and its ultimate object, to move to the fore. As a consequence of this change, any inferences we might make about the true objects of reflection have become more preliminary, the possibility of a failure of human speculation greater, and the skeptical reservations stronger. It is fascinating to note that precisely this skeptical outcome finds its most powerful expression, once again, in the conceptual pair finite/infinite. In the next chapter we will discover a new use for metaphysical reflection: as an attempt to express human limitedness itself. This result will in turn drive us back to wrestle anew with early modern thought, and in particular with a set of themes that runs from Spinoza to Schelling.

---

181. Can the infinite also be understood as an individual? Dieter Henrich claims that it can: "Auch das Unendliche, das im Denken als Absolutes in Frage steht, hat als Einzelnes gedacht und erfahren werden können. . . . So würde [die Lehre des Buddha] also ihren Ort überhaupt erst an jener Grenze haben, an der ein Geschehen zu denken ist, aus dem sich alle Einzelheit selbst noch bildet und in dem sie vergeht" (Henrich, "Ding an sich," in Rohls und Wenz, eds., *Vernunft des Glaubens,* 92). Henrich adds that one understands "der Verfassung der Welt von einem Ersten her . . . das selbst auch Einzelnes ist." He interprets this as an absolute process, which through no "Gedanken von Einheit . . . entsprochen werden kann."

CHAPTER SIX

On Using Limit Notions:
First Steps after Kant

INTRODUCTION

In the treatment of Leibniz in chapter 4 we encountered insuperable problems with the metaphysics of perfection, the conceptual framework on which most philosophical theology had been based from (at least) Scotus to Kant. Unfortunately, most of the content of early modern theories of God — and as a result much of the content of the systems based on them — was derived from the perfection of God. If, in the central idea of God as infinite perfection that we have been exploring, perfection is demoted, does only divine infinity remain? Wouldn't this entail that there is little left for reason to say about the nature of God? Such is certainly the conclusion drawn by mystics and skeptics from divine infinity: if one can assert only that God is infinite, this perforce implies the failure of anything approximating a theistic metaphysics.

The goal of the present chapter is to show that such a conclusion is overhasty. Stressing the infinity of God does not mean leaving behind all content associated with divinity. We will find an element of the notion of infinity to move a portion of the divine nature beyond all understanding. But ascribing infinity to God also provides, perhaps paradoxically, an important criterion for speaking of the divine nature and hence a start toward theology and a theory of the God/world relation.

Beginning in the next chapter I trace the developing notion of infinity through a series of thinkers running from Spinoza to Schelling. What ties these thinkers together is their adherence to a concept of the infinite that acts as a control and point of orientation for the remainder of their metaphysics. Often the concept of infinity performs its function in a negative sense, for instance by fighting anthropomorphizing tendencies of the type we found again and again to contaminate earlier treatments of the perfection of God. But the metaphysical concept of infinity also works in a positive (constitutive) sense, insofar as it provides some information about that which it posits as qualitatively different from the finite — and hence information as well about what it is to be finite.

This last claim is paradoxical enough that it first requires some defense in this chapter. The defense must address itself specifically to the post-Kantian context, since (as we saw in chapter 5) Kant's arguments are generally taken to rob metaphysical concepts of any content of their own. We will find that the case against Kant is not strong enough to reinstate a full metaphysics of the transcendent, and hence that the epistemic warrant for classical German idealism — the tradition running through the early Fichte and the early Schelling to Hegel — is insufficient. There is, however, at least one response to Kant that acknowledges limits on reason without mandating silence on all metaphysical questions. The framework for this response was developed by Friedrich Schleiermacher in the early nineteenth century, particularly in his theory of knowledge, the *Dialectics*. Suitably reconstructed, his position provides a powerful account of the epistemic status of language about God.

Unfortunately, this account does not appear in so many words in Schleiermacher's texts. The *Dialectics* contains some brilliant insights; but they are useful to us only when retold in light of more recent developments in the theory of knowledge. In particular, I suggest, one must do the opposite of what the German Hegelian, Falk Wagner, has done[1] — not tying the *Dialectics* more firmly to its idealist roots but freeing it from as many of them as one can. Only when one reinterprets the *Dialectics* in light of the plurality of multiple conceptual schemes can it speak convincingly to the context of late-twentieth-century theology.[2] Put briefly, the chapter's thesis is that epistemology requires one to make certain ontological postulations, including the postulation of some sort of transcendent ground. The concepts that one postulates in this fashion turn

1. Falk Wagner, *Schleiermachers Dialektik: Eine kritische Interpretation* (Gütersloh: Gerd Mohn, 1974).

2. In what follows I have chosen to emphasize some portions of the *Dialectics* and have consequently been forced to pass over other themes to which Schleiermacher devoted much space. This applies in particular to the earlier stages of his argument, esp. the sections on thought and willing, power and appearance, idealism vs. realism, freedom and necessity, and world as the unity of nature and spirit. The assumptions underlying these sections are more problematic, and much more conceptual work would be necessary to "redeem" them (if redemption is even possible).

out to have an interesting both/and status: they are both transcendental (i.e., having to do with the conditions that make human reflection possible) and yet also about what is. Human reflection depends on something outside reflection, and we can know something, however limited, about what that something must be if there is to be any knowledge at all.

Central to this task is Schleiermacher's defense of *limit notions (Grenzbegriffe)*. Limits or borders, Schleiermacher realized, are interesting things: insofar as they tell us about the limits of human knowledge, they at the same time reveal to us something of what lies beyond it. "World" and "transcendent ground" are two concepts that express limit cases of knowledge; if Schleiermacher is right, they can also function as criteria for making at least some judgments in Kant's forbidden zone: metaphysics. Limit notions, I suggest, may be the means for saving theology from Kant's first *Critique,* and thus from its demotion to the second.

What emerges, given a reasonable degree of skepticism, is not an interpretation of such theories as literally true, but the possibility of treating them as hypothetical, though still rationally debatable, pictures of the way things may be. Knowers must be concerned with the conditions of the possibility (CPs) of the knowledge that they have or seek; and, if I am right, such CPs include limit notions that can neither be known to be fictions nor simply ontologized as actually existent. The result should be a position that mediates as well today — when the battle lines are drawn between, say, Searle and Plantinga on the one side and Putnam, Rorty, and Derrida on the other — as it did when philosophy was attempting to take its first trembling steps after Kant.

THE CRISIS OF KNOWLEDGE IN METAPHYSICS

As the preceding chapter on Kant has shown, one cannot simply work one's way down from the metaphysical doctrine of infinity, moving in a unbroken line from a theory of the absolute to, say, a philosophy of physics or the foundations of ethics. Human reflection must instead begin from below; our efforts, to the extent that they are metaphysical, move upward toward the highest principle(s). Part of beginning from below is beginning with human knowledge and (for any given discipline) with the question of how we know. Therefore, we must first treat the idea of the infinite in the context of the constitutive conditions of (and the limitations on) human knowledge. This is the lesson from Kant's first *Critique* that our criticisms of his position still leave untouched.

349

The Inevitability of Transcendent Postulates

"All knowing involves reflecting, but not all reflecting is knowing"[3] — so begins the 1814 *Dialectics*. The task of a theory of knowledge, according to Schleiermacher, is to analyze the difference between these two terms. In part this means asking whether the reasons or grounds for one's beliefs are sufficient for them to pass as knowledge, since "Knowing is a truth claim based on objective grounds."[4] But, Schleiermacher reminds his listeners, some of these reasons are also pragmatic; hence we must pay attention to the process, to "intellectual activity" (*geistige Täthigkeit*; cf. J 485) as well as to results. Schleiermacher's awareness that the conditions on knowledge are pragmatic or process-based as well as "formal," along with his stress on intersubjectivity, gives his epistemology a markedly twentieth-century ring right from the outset.[5]

Troubles with Truth

The set of justified true beliefs is the set of what we know. If we could run our existing beliefs through the two qualifiers "justified" and "true" in a machine-like process, the beliefs that satisfy both criteria could then pass as knowledge. Yet there is an obvious disparity between the two conditions; they seem (conceptually) to have little to do with one another. Schleiermacher saw that we require a single theory within which the questions of justification and truth are both assigned their respective places.

It is regarding the question of truth that our puzzlement and conceptual confusion are the greatest. Most philosophers continue to share the traditional

---

3. "Jedes Wissen ist ein Denken, aber nicht jedes Denken ein Wissen" (J 39-40). I use the standard abbreviations for the various editions of the *Dialectics;* all translations are mine.

    J = L. Jonas, ed., *Dialektik,* based on the 1814 MS but containing most of the other MS materials, in Schleiermacher's *Sämtliche Werke* (Berlin: 1834-64), division 3, vol. 4/2 (1839).

    W = Bruno Wei, appendix to "Untersuchungen über Fr. Schleiermachers Dialektik," *Zeitschrift für Philosophie und philosophische Kritik* 73 (1878): 1-43, containing additional MSS.

    H = I. Halpern, ed., *Schleiermachers Dialektik,* based on the 1831 MS (Berlin: Mayer & Müller, 1903).

    O = Rudolf Odebrecht, ed., *Friedrich Schleiermachers Dialektik,* based on the 1822 MS (Leipzig, 1942; repr. Darmstadt: Wissenschaftliche Buchgesellschaft, 1976).

    Tice = Terrence Tice's helpful new translation of the 1811 Notes (*Dialectic, or, The Art of Doing Philosophy* [Atlanta: Scholars Press, 1996]).

4. Tice, 9 note.

5. So also ibid., 59n79.

intuition on the subject: truth is the agreement or correspondence between thought and what is.[6] Yet if we are to employ "true" within the theory of knowledge, we require some criteria for establishing such correspondence claims. This immediately poses what is obviously an ontological question: How is one to interpret the "what is" in this definition of truth, so that one can decide how to verify that a given truth claim has it right? If we lack a theory of "what is," then it is also unclear what we are doing when we move on to spell out theories of justification: justification in terms of what? The answers typically advanced by philosophers are justification in terms of the "commonsense" notion of truth (waving a hand in Tarski's direction), or a theory of multiple (or "internal") truths, each relativized to a language game, linguistic community, or historical epoch. Both of these approaches leave us, of course, with a dichotomy between truths and Truth, in which only the former pole is allowed philosophical employment. The latter pole is usually dismissed with a metaphor: Truth (with a capital *T*) is "logocentric" or presupposes an unattainable, "transcendent" point of view. The result can only be the divorce of justification from the truth question and, ultimately, the banishment of truth.[7] The metaphors that philosophers use to dismiss the latter pole are legion: truth is the God's-eye view, the illusion of the view from nowhere, the confusion that arises when we forget that we always speak out of a language game, the myth of the bourgeoisie, the crutch of the aesthetic priest, the forgetfulness of the Ontological Difference, logocentrism, phallocentrism. . . .

But the skeptics about truth from Marx to Dummett have dismissed this notion too quickly. Perhaps many of the epistemic qualms about it are justified. Yet what is required instead of bald dismissals is an examination of the role that the striving for truth plays in the knowledge endeavor.

Intersubjectivity and Objectivity

Suppose, then, that we think our way into the theory of knowledge from the assumption that the goal is true belief, without losing sight of the pragmatic component just mentioned. Schleiermacher realized correctly that there would then be two major conditions determining the knowledge process. The first condition on knowledge is intersubjectivity: "that thinking is knowing which is nec-

---

6. E.g., Schleiermacher: "The one who thinks something as it is, in his thinking is truth" (J 44).

7. This is equally clear, though in different senses, in Hilary Putnam's expulsion of the "God's-eye view" in *Reason, Truth, and History,* and in Michael Dummett, *Truth and Other Enigmas* (Cambridge: Harvard Univ. Press, 1978); see esp. chap. 1, "Truth."

essarily understood as produced in the same manner by all persons capable of thought."[8] He thus began with the oppositions between reflecting human agents who are attempting to move beyond their differing judgments in order to arrive at the same conclusion.[9] The best and only theory of justification is, in other words, one based on the process of communication.[10]

The knower's task, under this theory, is to comprehend the competing viewpoints of the various participants in intersubjective discussion. But this in turn entails having a single viewpoint from which each can be thought. To "test" this reconciling viewpoint adequately, one must be able to give an account of how one arrived (or could arrive) at it, an account that can survive the scrutiny of other discussants.[11] Think of it as a sort of feedback process. For the account to be rational (intersubjectively checkable), it must envision a process that a group of thinkers could follow, with each one verifying whether his or her original position had been adequately criticized or incorporated in the final position. Not until American pragmatism was an account of intersubjectivity given that did justice to the details of the process. Specifically, I argued in chapter 1 that Peirce's account of the ideal community of inquiry helps to establish the necessary conditions on rational agreement.

Schleiermacher saw that the condition of intersubjectivity provides the best starting point for an account of justification. Nonetheless, as he realized, this condition — achieving consensus in a rational manner — although necessary, is not sufficient for truth. For there is reasoned agreement that is not true (*Überzeugung ohne Wahrheit*, J 44). At this point philosophers generally introduce "formal-semantic" conditions, criteria such as consistency or co-

8. "Dasjenige Denken ist ein Wissen, welches a. vorgestellt wird mit der Nothwendigkeit, daß es von allen denkensfähigen auf dieselbe Weise producirt werde" (J 43).

9. See the MS materials in Jonas's appendices: C (1822), 22; D (1828), 14-15; E (1831), 16-17.

10. So Odebrecht: "Wir als die Redenden sind das zunächst und vordringlich Wirkliche; in der communicatio des Gesprächs erschliesst sich uns unser Menschsein, in dem scheiternden Streit des Dialogs die Wirklichkeit der Transzendenz" (O xxff.). The parallels here with the views of C. S. Peirce, and with latter-day Peirceans (including Habermas's *The Theory of Communicative Action*, trans. Thomas McCarthy, 2 vols. [Boston: Beacon Press, 1984]), are, again, unmistakable.

11. Think of it as a feedback process. For the account to be rational (intersubjectively checkable), it must envision a process that a group of thinkers could follow, with each one verifying whether her or his original position had been adequately criticized or incorporated in the final position. In my view, American pragmatism was the first account of intersubjectivity that did full justice to the details of the process. Specifically, it was Peirce's account of the ideal community of inquiry that first clearly established the necessary conditions on rational agreement.

herence.[12] But such criteria face the same difficulty: as long as truth involves the correspondence between beliefs and states of affairs, it is always possible that a criterion stated in noncorrespondence terms — whether it be coherence, present consensus, or the final convergence of inquiry — would not measure degree of truth but something else instead (such as the degree of coherence or consensus).[13]

At this point one often takes recourse to the notion of idealized criteria, such as ideal consensus or ideal coherence. What about the ideally coherent system of propositions, say the one in which there was mutual implication and which was fully comprehensive, excluding no areas of propositional belief? It is conceivable, however, that such a system might still not be true. The same possibility holds for the ideal community of inquiry: it is logically possible that its conclusions might still be wrong, its best efforts notwithstanding.

But what if we gave the ideal community of inquiry unlimited time? Here a disanalogy with the coherence criterion emerges. There is no way to put a temporal index into the coherence account, since propositions are timeless. But as Schleiermacher saw, temporal indexes fit naturally on the intersubjectivity side: agreement between agents is necessarily achieved over time. For this reason the intuition is stronger that what the ideal epistemic community would arrive at, given unlimited (potentially infinite) time, would be coterminous with truth. (It would at least be indistinguishable from truth for any human agent.) The question now becomes: Does this account, then — truth is that opinion at which the ideal community of inquiry would arrive given a sufficiently lengthy period of inquiry — offer us a sufficient definition of truth?

Schleiermacher realized that pragmatic and intersubjectivity-based criteria can never do it alone. A place must also be preserved for the objectivity condition: truth is the correspondence with states of affairs. Schleiermacher's second condition is the more basic one, since it expresses the sufficient condition for a belief's being true. There is a problem here as well, however: that a belief fulfills the objectivity condition could not even be known unless we had what one might call absolute knowledge. Absolute knowledge requires knowledge of at least three things: of what we know, of what the known object is in itself (apart from being known by us), and of the fact that our knowledge corresponds to (agrees with) its object. Absolute knowledge then becomes a second-order concept, equivalent to knowing that one knows. For, according to the

12. On the latter, see the exposition by Nicholas Rescher in *The Coherence Theory of Truth* (Oxford: Basil Blackwell, 1973).

13. See Rescher's self-correction of his earlier coherence theory of truth in "Truth as Ideal Coherence," *Review of Metaphysics* 38 (1985): 795-806.

common account, we can be said to know if we have justified true belief, that is, if our belief corresponds to the state of affairs that it is about (and if it is justified, which I defined above in terms of the intersubjectivity condition). To know that we know *p* would then mean to be fully justified in our claim to know *p*; and we could be justified in this claim only if we knew all three of the factors in this definition of absolute knowledge.

Now compare the two criteria, intersubjectivity and objectivity. Given the need to know, the pragmatic criterion recommends itself as indispensable. Since human agreement is not sufficient for knowledge, however, Schleiermacher saw that we have to supplement it with the objectivity criterion. The contrast between the two criteria — one epistemically accessible but not sufficient for truth, the other sufficient but not accessible — is basic to the theology of limit notions I wish to defend. As Schleiermacher puts it, where we have (ideal) intersubjective agreement regarding a belief, there can by definition be no further progress, yet the agreement can still be mistaken. By contrast, where there is no agreement regarding a belief, the belief is not recognized or known — though it may well still be true.[14]

Two Types of Postulates

The objectivity criterion entails that we must retain talk of ontology (e.g., of states of affairs, of what really is) within our theory of knowledge. Further, if we wish to follow Schleiermacher and retain the concept of absolute knowledge (in my terms: of knowing that we know), it follows that we will have to posit at least one real object of knowledge that our beliefs grasp or fail to grasp. This talk of the object(s) of knowledge begins as a *postulate*.[15]

The notion of postulates has been widely discussed and employed in recent philosophy.[16] Scientists posit the uniformity of nature and employ simplicity and beauty as regulative ideals; ethicists speak of the value judgments presupposed by a given ethical community; "regulative" theories of truth have

14. "Ist nämlich Uebereinstimmung in irgend einem Denken: so kann darin . . . kein Fortschritt wieter sein, aber sie kann falsch sein. . . . Ist die Uebereinstimmung noch nicht da: so kann in dem Denken doch das wahre sein, es ist nur noch nicht anerkannt" (J 44).

15. "In jedem Denen wird ein gedachtes außer dem Denken gesezt" (J 48).

16. See (to mention just the tip of the iceberg) Peter Bieri and Lorenz Kruger, eds., *Transcendental Arguments and Science: Essays in Epistemology* (Boston: D. Reidel, 1979); Thomas E. Wartenberg, "Order through Reason: Kant's Transcendental Justification of Science," *Kant-Studien* 70 (1979): 409-26; Theodore A. Gracyk, "Kant's Doctrine of Heuristics: An Interpretation of the Ideas of Reason," *Modern Schoolman* 68 (1991): 191-210.

won a following. Unfortunately, both the recent discussion and Kant's original presentation in the first *Critique* underemphasize a crucial distinction that Schleiermacher was careful to draw: the distinction between transcendental and transcendent postulates.[17] According to the transcendental view, we come to make certain postulates as implications of our practice of formulating and defending knowledge claims about the world. A scientist's study of cancer cells employs a particular methodology, which in turn implicitly relies on certain substantive-sounding assumptions such as the unity of nature or the mind-independence of the world. A similar need to make realistic-sounding postulates arises when scientists employ rules or background assumptions (e.g., the assumption that all cellular changes have causes that consist of strings of lower-level physical events). Of course, on the standard ("Kantian") interpretation, one can work with transcendental postulates such as these without construing them in a realist fashion, that is, ascribing qualities to the actual world. Instead, transcendental postulates are at most conditions of the possibility of our realist (scientific or commonsensical) practices and theories, not an extension of those theories. The preceding chapter on Kant demonstrated that the realist/transcendental line cannot, however, simply be drawn between empirical claims on the one hand (which one interprets realistically) and metaphysical claims on the other (all of which Kant took to be merely transcendental). At any rate, a central part of philosophical reflection continues to involve specifying such postulates and exploring their implications.

When Fictions Are Not Enough

Schleiermacher saw, pace Kant, that postulates understood only as transcendental are not sufficient to account for knowledge. Let me reconstruct his case in the form of a dilemma: Scientists, qua scientists, need not ask about the ontological status of the principles they employ, but this question cannot be dodged when one moves into the field of philosophy. What might philosophers say about the ontological status of these principles? On the one hand, if they answer, "They correspond to nothing, really," then they have reduced them to

17. Unfortunately, the two terms come to us so muddied by the tradition that they may be irredeemable. Falk Wagner (*Schleiermachers Dialektik*) argues that Schleiermacher strictly separates between the two terms. Michael Eckert makes the case that Schleiermacher uses the two terms synonymously (*Gott: Glauben und Wissen: Friedrich Schleiermachers Philosophische Theologie,* Schleiermacher-Archiv 3 [Berlin: de Gruyter, 1987], 48). Kant clearly defines them differently in the *Prolegomena* (A 204n) but occasionally runs them together in the first *Critique.* I need argue only that Schleiermacher's position, if it is to be successful, requires a distinction between the two.

pure fictions. Something like this is implied by Henry Allison's interpretation and defense of Kant's transcendental idealism: only empirical statements can meaningfully be given a realist interpretation; hence transcendental claims can only be understood idealistically, as postulates of our epistemic practices but not as really existing things at all.[18] This "necessary fictions" view is, I take it, what some modern theologians mean when they say that God is a regulating principle for ethics or social action. They seem to mean, "We know that there is no God, of course, but employing this idea as a fiction works well to encourage the sorts of values we advocate." The problem with this response is that it works only as long as one does not ask too closely about the status of such a belief in God. For wouldn't theistic belief cease to motivate a person if one began thinking of it as no more than a fiction?

This worry brings us to the other hand: We cannot rule out the possibility — the possibility that I think is central to the strategy of the *Dialectics* — that what is postulated may be more than a fiction. Yet as soon as we formulate this response, we find ourselves faced with a position that makes more than a (strictly) transcendental claim. We have broken the barriers of the transcendental, even if all we say is that there might be something that gives rise to the series of appearances the conditions of whose possibility the *Dialectics* is concerned to discover. Recall that positing a Something that gives rise to appearances *just was* the transcendental move in the first place. Schleiermacher realized, in other words, that the only way to do transcendental philosophy is to do more than transcendental philosophy. This was of course Kant's fatal difficulty: he could not help but speak of things-in-themselves and their causal effect on appearances, even though there was ultimately no way for him to make sense of such talk from within his own transcendental perspective. The dilemma, in short, is that transcendental postulates force one to raise questions that one cannot answer from within that perspective.

Let me put the matter yet another way: The transcendental perspective itself only seems to work given more than a fictional account of its postulates. Only if the object of thought is really outside of thought can it impact consciousness and can consciousness be an image of it. Recall that we turned to the notion of transcendental postulates in order to explain what sort of ideal it is we pursue when, for example, we use the predicate "truth." It turned out that the predicate "truth" posits an object outside of thought to which thought is said to correspond. Yet if we identify the postulate as a fiction from the very beginning, then we are saying that there is no object to which thought corre-

---

18. Henry Allison, *Kant's Transcendental Idealism: An Interpretation and Defense* (New Haven: Yale Univ. Press, 1983).

sponds — which amounts to claiming at the outset that our thought cannot be true![19] Thus it appears that the fictional view of transcendental postulates (e.g., the view of God as a fiction) must be dismissed — or at least that the fiction view is more costly than at first appeared, since it entails the denial of such central predicates as "truth," "knowledge," and "the world as a whole."

Why Postulates Rather Than a Final Theory?

Up to this point my proposal sounds like an invitation to classical metaphysics, or at least to something like German idealism. But it need not be. Here is the difference: as the book's opening lines suggested, I share with many contemporary thinkers a deep skepticism about the lofty metaphysical systems of previous centuries. Perhaps we cannot show that the rationalists' equation, The Real = The Rational, is false — how could one demonstrate this without contradiction? — but we can dismiss it as an ungrounded assumption. That is, there is insufficient reason to accept the claims made by absolute idealists (e.g., by unregenerate Hegelians) to know that thought does correspond to reality — despite their best attempts to prove this correspondence via a completely systematized philosophy. Such philosophers maintain that the concept of, say, Absolute Spirit is fully coherent and dialectically encompasses all lower concepts. Hence, they claim, it is the most rational concept, and thus we have more reason to accept it as real than to accept any other competing concept. So, we are told, our choice is between an absolute skepticism concerning human rationality and the acceptance of a philosophy of the Absolute.

A similar move has been made by a number of well-known analytic philosophers under the title of "Anselmianism" and under the leadership of the Notre Dame Philosophy Department.[20] This influential contemporary movement accepts the rational-real link in one special case: that of a necessary being. Once the latter-day Anselmians have shown (with the help of a reworked ontological argument) that the concept of a perfect being entails its existence, they attempt to deduce from this first principle a number of the divine attributes and to work out the implications for other theological themes such as creation,

19. See J 48ff., 450-51; and Wagner, *Schleiermachers Dialektik,* 61ff.

20. Although the most famous exponent of this line of argument is Alvin Plantinga, the term itself comes from Thomas Morris; see the latter's *Anselmian Explorations: Essays in Philosophical Theology* (Notre Dame: Univ. of Notre Dame Press, 1987); idem, "Perfect Being Theology," *Nous* 21 (1987): 19-30; and idem, ed., *The Concept of God* (Oxford: Oxford Univ. Press, 1987); see also chapter 3 above. I prefer to use "Anselmianism" as a general term to designate a commonality of approach shared by many members of the Society of Christian Philosophers and many publications in *Faith and Philosophy*.

human nature, ethics, and divine action.[21] Both the Hegelians and the "perfect-being theologians" claim to establish the existence of an absolute, a highest principle at which truth and rationality meet — the one group through the dialectic of self-unfolding consciousness, the other through philosophical, "modal," and Christian intuitions plus the ontological argument.

I shall not attempt to refute both Anselm and Hegel in this chapter, for obvious reasons. Here I can only counterpropose that unaided human reason does not possess the first principle from which a complete system of this kind can be derived. Indeed, there is some reason to doubt whether such a completion is even possible. For example, many have argued against Hegel that the attempt to think everything must necessarily fail, that something must lie outside thought for the human thinker. One finds (rather compelling) versions of this argument based variously on Kantian things-in-themselves, on the incompleteness of history, on Gödel-inspired incompleteness theorems, and on the impossibility for a conscious self at time t to know the act of its knowing p at t. They can be further buttressed by more general skeptical arguments familiar to epistemologists, cultural anthropologists, and devotees of deconstruction.[22] If that is not enough, it is sufficient to argue that the epistemic status of an alleged highest principle is fatally ambiguous at present, since there is no general agreement that we possess a universal philosophical system that can encompass the required oppositions. Put differently, if the "completed system" ideal cannot be met at present by any system, and if we have some reason to think that this failure is an inevitable one, then we are more than justified in seeking an approach to metaphysics that treats such ideals as ideals, not as present actualities or necessary fictions.

What then is left if neither an objective metaphysics nor a purely transcendental successor to metaphysics will do the trick? Schleiermacher's answer to this dilemma involves a theory of transcendent postulates.[23] The idea is to do justice to the strongest arguments on both sides of the debate, neither of which can be denied. The postulates that are constitutive of our knowing are to be "resolved" neither realistically (as if we possessed a theory of the Absolute) nor transcendentally (as if we could treat them as mere fictions made by reason). Rather, although transcendent postulates such as world or ground

21. See Thomas V. Morris, ed., *Divine and Human Action: Essays in the Metaphysics of Theism* (Ithaca: Cornell Univ. Press, 1988).

22. For instance, there are some parallels between the notion of limit notions defended here and the work of the early Derrida; the present-yet-deferred structure of the transcendental signified in *Of Grammatology* (Baltimore: Johns Hopkins Univ. Press, 1964) is not fundamentally different from the position that I have been developing.

23. See esp. J 43-44, 48-51, 315, 366-67, 449-50, 484ff.

or God may initially be introduced for transcendental reasons (as conditions of the possibility of knowing), the very arguments that led us to postulate them also require us to entertain the continuing possibility that the postulates are objectively true. When philosophers of science reflect on assumptions that are basic to scientific practice — such as the mind-independence of the world, or the denial of occult causes, or even the conditions of the possibility for knowledge in general — they do so by introducing theories that might also be true of the world. Why should the same logic not extend to the theologian as well?

TOWARD A THEOLOGY OF LIMIT NOTIONS

Defining Limit Notions

The Schleiermacherian approach to knowledge just outlined suggests a new role for the notion of the limits of thought. Admittedly, limit talk was classically held to face an insoluble problem: we acknowledge that there are limits to what humans can know; yet in order to specify and know those limits, one would need already to stand outside them. Hence (it is said) a knower cannot know the limits of his or her own thought.

But this criticism overlooks Schleiermacher's crucial distinction between reflecting (or thinking) and knowing.[24] Surely it is possible to reflect on the areas where human thought seems to break down or is unable to make any further progress, without claiming to know that these are the definitive borders to knowledge and that everything beyond them is forever unknowable to the human mind — clearly a rather difficult claim to substantiate! The project of a theology of limit notions is instead to explore reason's difficulties and areas of embarrassment, without falling into any dogmatic claims about what reason can or cannot ever know.

A Phenomenology of the Limits of Human Reason

I suggest that we think of this part of the *Dialectics* as a phenomenology of the apparent limits of human reason. In an extremely insightful analysis, Schleiermacher shows how limits arise in a variety of areas and come in several differ-

---

24. Again, "All knowing involves reflecting, but not all reflecting is knowing" begins the 1814 *Dialektik* (J 39-40).

ent types.[25] He finds limits, for example, both in the conceptual movement toward unity and in the movement toward diversity. The limit case for the latter would be infinite diversity without any organizing (unifying) principles whatsoever — a concept familiar to the metaphysical tradition through the Greek notion of matter *(hylē)*, the undifferentiated substratum, completely without form, which (Aristotle argued) has to be posited as the "something" that takes on shape or form in any instance of becoming. By contrast, absolute unity would be, obviously, the One (e.g., the *hen* of Plotinus's metaphysics), beyond all contrast or differentiation.

An additional (second-order?) limit arises when one considers the opposition between the unifying and the pluralizing movements of thought itself. Schleiermacher begins with a distinction mentioned in the discussion of truth criteria above: the difference between the agent who thinks and what she or he thinks about or, to paraphrase his labels, between human beliefs and transpersonal judgments or propositions. Different limits emerge when one specifies the end points of ultimate diversity and ultimate unity for each of these two cases. Take first the limit case of multiple beliefs and multiple judgments. Beliefs are most diverse as unorganized (random) predicates entertained by a subject, and would be most unified in an "absolute subject," for whom all aspects of its thought would have a place within the unity of its self-understanding.[26] By contrast, the domain of propositions is regulated (bordered) by the distinction between a possible infinite diversity of judgments (unorganized content) on the one hand and ultimate conceptual unity (pure form or pure being) on the other.[27]

Beliefs have to do with the subject's ideas and her or his perceptions of them, whereas concepts are judgments about truth, about what is the case. The opposition Schleiermacher has in mind therefore boils down in the end to that between two ultimate limit notions. Call them Absolute Subject and Being, or the subjective and the objective; one could also speak of the opposition between a fully coherent belief system and truth or, simply, between epistemology and ontology. And what are the limits to the possible convergence (unity) or difference between these ultimate limits? If Subject and Being were fully reconciled, they would be unified as "absolute being," or as what philosophers have called the Absolute; if they were fully diverse, we will be left with a complete

---

25. It would be interesting to explore the parallels between the following discussion and the (pre-Kantian) theory of limits in, say, Nicholas of Cusa's *De docta ignorantia*.

26. What I am calling "beliefs" are technically "judgments" *(Urteile)*. Also, Schleiermacher says they are unified "as" the absolute subject, not "in" it.

27. Cf. Wagner, *Schleiermachers Dialektik,* 97.

multiplicity of appearances and no knowledge at all. These two possible outcomes represent the limits in the quest to establish a correspondence between thought and reality. Since they must be taken as limits and not as actual metaphysical concepts or outcomes, the two (possible) final end points of the quest for truth are both in fact transcendental ideas, "the transcendental roots of all thought."[28]

I must skip over Schleiermacher's (to me unconvincing) claim that these two limits of thought, in the directions of diversity and of unity, are actually identical[29] — except to note that the unity of opposites is also a central claim in theories of the infinite (e.g., Nicholas of Cusa's argument for the coincidence of opposites at the level of infinity). In the post-Kantian context, transcendental reflection may replace traditional theories about the infinite (summarized in chapter 3 above); yet both types of reflection appear to have the same function: to reveal the limits of thought.

The Highest Opposition

Suffice it to say that this opposition — that between epistemology and ontology, or between thought and being — appears indeed to be the highest thinkable opposition (cf. J 397). With this opposition we appear to reach that proverbial Wittgensteinian point beyond which nothing more can be said. For the natural "next step" would to construct a justified theory that unifies the absolute subject and the absolute unity of being; yet it appears impossible to do so (J 99). Here is why the failure looks inevitable: the Absolute Subject would be a subject that had thought all that is (i.e., all being), and the absolute unity of Being would be that outside of which nothing else could be that could be thought (J 100). But how could we think together Being and Thought? There is no third term outside this opposition in terms of which it could be viewed as a unity. The reconciliation eludes us; indeed, we are not even able to say in principle what it would be for these two things no longer to be different. For one, the reconciliation of thought and what lies outside thought could ipso facto never be contained within thought; hence it does not admit of a theoretical resolution. Moreover, the concepts in this opposition are already so abstract that the contemporary thinker wonders whether any claims made about them — and espe-

---

28. Schleiermacher notes that the postulation *(Sezen)* of an absolute unity or the postulation of an absolute diversity "weder Begriff noch Urtheil ist; aber beides sind die transcendentalen Wurzeln alles Denkens und also auch alles Wissens" (J 92).

29. "Das absolute Sein . . . und die absolute Mannigfaltigkeit des Erscheinens . . . sind wesentlich ein und dasselbe" (O 211; cf. J 93-94, 465-66).

cially claims to have brought them to definitive theoretical unity — are genuinely criticizable. For criticism involves tests such as (1) freedom from contradiction, (2) coherence, and (3) comprehensiveness, or the ability to serve as the basis for other areas of thought. Yet "Being itself" and similar terms are too broad to be contradictory, given their abstractness cannot fail to be coherent, and are by definition comprehensive. If one could compose a list of aspirants to the theoretical reconciliation of Thought and Being, would one really be able to evaluate their competing claims in any meaningful fashion? Reason would, it seems, forever underdetermine the choice.

Hence "the pure thought of Being is nothing else than the schema for the subject."[30] The "highest" metaphysical categories do represent a task for thought. Yet at first blush they appear to tell us merely about our own limits as knowers, about where our thought cannot go — or at least where we lose control of it (cf. philosophy as poetry, as hope, as deconstruction, as mysticism, as silence). What lies at the boundaries of conceptual thought is itself no longer conceptual thought, since at this point one can no longer discern specific (thinkable) characteristics.[31] Such, perhaps unsurprisingly, are the results of the conceptual movement toward a final conceptual reconciliation, a highest principle or absolute One. As Schleiermacher saw, we can say some things about this ultimate step, even if we cannot take the step ourselves. For example, we can specify its content as "what is" (but at such a general level that no specific concept of it can be conceived) as it is thought by an "absolute subject" (by whom nothing more specific could be produced and of whom nothing more could be said); and we can even assert that it would involve some final reconciliation of these two. But clearly these conclusions are so abstract as to be almost purely formal. How is one to derive a theology from such assertions? Can the limits be used to produce any specific (constitutive) theological conclusions?

From Limit Notions to Theology

With the idea of limit notions in place, let us see what can be said about their nature.[32] Schleiermacher's method for taking this step involved a thought experi-

30. "Der reine Gedanke des Seins ist nichts als das Schema zum Subjekt" (J 92). The following pages in J attempt to show that Schleiermacher's view cannot be resolved into either idealism or realism.

31. "Was an der Grenze des Begriffs ist, ist seiner Form nach kein Begriff mehr, weil wir keine Mannigfaltigkeit von Merkmalen davon aufstellen können" (J 99).

32. Schleiermacher himself did not quite get the limits idea right — as Jonas sadly points out in several of his longer footnotes (e.g., to §137 [J 78-81] and to §183 [J 114-16]). In his later

ment: Is it possible to locate a "highest" idea, a highest genus, or most general concept, one that unifies (overcomes) all the oppositions that lie below it? For example, one might chose the idea of a highest power, perhaps something like a unified field theory in physics: that which unifies all existing things and provides a single explanatory principle for all subjects (actors) and objects (what is acted on). But the notion of power still implies something that it acts on, and hence fails the test for the highest synthetic idea. Or perhaps an answer could be found by further exploring the idea of the unity of the real and the ideal, or of being and concept (*Sein* and *Begriff*), as we did in the previous section.

Even following the thought experiment only this far reveals that the notion of a highest idea involves an essential ambiguity: Would such an idea actually allow us to think together all of the elements that fall under it, or would it offer instead an ideal, a task for thought? If the former, it would still be one particular concept within the domain of concepts. Such concepts have the advantage that they can still be given conceptual explications (in principle); their disadvantage is that they could not yet, even in principle, convey the Absolute. For each of them still presupposes a dichotomy between conceptual reflection and that upon which we reflect, whereas the Absolute implies the perfect union of thought and being. So suppose we understand the highest idea instead as expressing a task for thought. If we do so, we must view it in Kantian transcendental terms; it becomes a regulative ideal, a postulated unity that guides human thought without human thought ever actually attaining the ideal. But in this case, it appears, we have defined it from the outset as a fiction, an imagined unity that in fact corresponds to nothing. How can a fiction serve as the ideal for knowledge?

The thought experiment raises, however, a third possibility, which represents perhaps the central contribution of Schleiermacher's theory of knowledge: Couldn't the notion of a highest idea simultaneously serve both functions? Couldn't it be viewed both as a transcendental ideal and as a metaphysical principle? If this is possible, then we could employ and discuss aspirants to this role (concepts such as the absolute, infinity, or God) within theology. Of course, it would be a theology whose status is, at least initially, regulative, since it would consist of concepts that we postulate rather than infer or intuit directly. Yet it would be a theology that aspires to — and in principle could eventually — move toward constitutive statements about God.

---

years, as he came to believe more and more that he could derive the content of a theology from the feeling of absolute dependence alone, he fell further and further in my view from the limits insight. He came closest, I think, in the 1814 edition on which Jonas based his text, and it is these ideas that I have taken as the chief basis for my reconstruction.

Every mediating view is liable to criticism from both sides; this one is no exception. Many readers will see no problem in saying that something may lie outside thought, or that one can formulate notions (such as the highest idea) that elude philosophical analysis. Aren't such notions easily enough explained in terms of transcendental ideals, or the final convergence of inquiry (Peirce), or the unavoidable fiction of the transcendental signified (Derrida), or just as pure projections from what we do know? For these readers the only question is why anyone would have believed humans capable of giving actual (constitutive) accounts of theological ideas in the first place (I return to this objection below). In contrast to this view, Hegelians will object that there is no necessary ambiguity in the notion of a highest concept, if it is in fact the highest.[33] The task is merely to correctly locate the concept that really is the highest, along with the correct (dialectical) method for thinking together all the oppositions that lie below it.

I cannot make the case against all forms of rationalism here. At least, we could perhaps agree, the epistemic status of an alleged highest concept is fatally ambiguous at present, since there is no general agreement on a universal philosophical system that can encompass the required oppositions. Put differently, if the "completed system" ideal cannot be met at present by any system, and if we have some reason to think that this failure is an inevitable one, then we are more than justified in seeking an approach to theology that treats such ideals as ideals, not as present actualities or necessary fictions. Let's call it the Incompleteness Postulate.

The Incompleteness Postulate

This postulate has initially a negative function. It provides grounds for criticizing those philosophical proposals that introduce alleged absolutes too quickly, or those that propose unifying principles that fail to unify on the highest level. Obviously, this means dismissing much of the history of metaphysics and philosophical theology as inadequate. For example, at one point Schleiermacher criticizes Spinoza for not rising above the level of oppositions, because his notion of substance "is nothing more than the idea of a highest power," and hence cannot be the absolute.[34] Yet this postulate is emphatically not a dismissal of the project of theology as such. Correct attention to the ideals of re-

33. Wagner's *Schleiermachers Dialektik* provides an excellent example of this second type of response.

34. He argues that Spinoza's substance "nichts andres ist als jene höchste Kraft" in the 1818 lectures; see Jonas's excerpt following §186 (J 118n). Interestingly, although Schleiermacher calls actual pantheism — "die Gleichsetzung von Gott und Welt" — "irreligiös," he does not put Spinoza in this category (§183).

flection, even if it involves showing how rigorous and rarely met these ideals actually are, should have the effect of supporting efforts to think our way to a higher and more adequate theory of God — unless such efforts are destined from the outset to failure.

The Incompleteness Postulate may also have a positive function, for limit language may actually produce constructive theories of God. Even if competing systematic proposals are underdetermined by concrete evidence (which has been the conclusion of our discussion to this point), we can still judge them to be more or less consistent with the limits. In this respect we have to raise three separate questions, which will guide a theology of limit notions:

1. Does a particular theological proposal make claims that are consistent with the apparent limits (call it the strict consistency test)? For example, is it consistent with the general assumption of a limited reason striving to make clear its own limits?[35]
2. More generally, is the theology in question developed in the general spirit of a limited reason that strives to make clear its own limits (the general coherence test)?
3. If so, would the theology, if true, help to explain accepted items of knowledge and the generally accepted limits on human knowledge? For even if we cannot directly evaluate certain claims about the nature of God, it may be that they can win indirect support by explaining our epistemic condition better than any of the alternatives.

Let us turn now to Schleiermacher's own limit notions in order to see what types of theological ideas are rationally indicated by these three criteria — or, perhaps better, which ones are counterindicated by them.

FUNDAMENTAL LIMIT NOTIONS

The basic argument is now in place: knowers, including theologians, must be concerned with the conditions of the possibility (CPs) of the knowledge that

---

35. The latter can be expressed either as a note of skepticism, or as the transcendental moment, or as the possibility that the truth is ineffable, that "the world" as it is, is forever beyond (our concepts). It is the direction in which Schleiermacher resolved his thought in the *Speeches* and in the 2nd edition of the *Glaubenslehre,* where he stresses the unknowability of God. Especially helpful is Louis Dupré, *The Other Dimension* (New York: Seabury, 1979), chap. 7.

they have or seek; and we now recognize that such CPs can neither be known to be fictions nor simply ontologized as actually existent. According to the theology of limit notions, even if competing theological proposals are underdetermined by direct evidence, we can still judge them to be more or less consistent with the (apparent) limits of reason themselves. It was thus part of Schleiermacher's project in the *Dialectics* to spell out the types of ideas to which his approach leads. (Of course, given the limits here, I will not be able to show, much less prove, that such ideas are literally true.)

World

The first idea to introduce is the notion of *world*. The world is the philosopher's placeholder for complete knowledge; by definition, everything that we know is an element of the world.[36] When we speak of the world, we understand it to encompass the plurality and diversity of all existing things, in their context of interaction and opposition. "Knowing the world" would entail possessing complete, unified explanations of all the forces that account for change and of subjects such as ourselves who are both entities within and knowers of the world. In Schleiermacher's terms, world is the anticipated realization of unity in a de facto plurality.[37] Since it obviously reflects an epistemic ideal not currently satisfied, this notion transcends the knowledge we currently possess (clearly we do not yet know the world in its entirety); it is a future and, in this sense, a transcendent concept. Further, since knowers must assume that there is something that their knowledge is about, we use the notion of world as a condition of the possibility of knowledge or, in Kantian terms, a transcendental or concept. The quest to know the world regulates the practice of science.

The notion of world is also, however, a constitutive notion. If we possess any knowledge now, it is the world of which we possess the knowledge. It is a theory of the world (and of its parts) that science is about. As long as there is anything that we refer to or claim knowledge of, we cannot dismiss the idea of world as purely fictional. Thus "world" gives us at least one concept that is both regulative or transcendent (Schleiermacher's term) and at the same time constitutive, a concept that refers to a (not yet present) whole, parts of which we

36. It stands for the "Totalität des endlichen Seins" (O 299) or the "System der Totalität des Wissens" (Wagner, *Schleiermachers Dialektik*, 215-25): "Jedes reale Wissen muß sich auf ein Element der Welt beziehen" (J 334).

37. Schleiermacher conceives the world "als Vielheit ohne Einheit," as "Raum und Zeit erfüllend," and as "die Totalität der Gegensäze." It is the "Grund unseres Wissens als eines fortschreitenden" (J 162-63).

nonetheless know in the present (if we know anything). World is thus the epistemic goal toward which science is working, its *terminus ad quem.*

What does it mean to speak of the world as the totality of what would be (finally) knowable? Here I prefer Peirce's formulation, which specifies "knowability" in terms of the activities of the ideal community of inquiry over a sufficiently long period of time. By contrast, Schleiermacher appeals to the more psychological idea of the world as the "driving force behind knowledge"; according to him, the "nonidentity" of the world drives the knowledge process, whereas talk of a unitary source of knowledge would lead to quietism.[38] Still, Schleiermacher's treatment correctly expresses the core insight: we are aware of the differences between present appearances and our epistemic goal of a unified body of all knowledge, differences that justify our postulation of (hope for?) an "approximation" of our theories to the physical world they seek to describe.

Indeed, if we take the ideal seriously enough, the term *physical world* in the last sentence is probably too limited. A completed theory of the world would seem ultimately to have to encompass both physics and ethics, if in fact there are any things that are actually good (and not merely good in virtue of our calling them good). All forms of moral realism may well be false; but if moral realism is the case, then "world" includes value predicates as well. Following Schleiermacher, we might then speak of the ideal of a unified body of physical knowledge as one goal, and the ideal of unifying the realms of fact and value as an even more distant limit case. (It is not obvious that the latter goal could be fulfilled even in principle; if it is impossible, it does not share the status of the other limits that I am giving a positive role in human reflection.)

It is not easy, by the way, to preserve the balance between knowledge as ideal and knowledge as actuality. If we say that notions such as "world" or "completed science" are mere fictions, we claim to know that we can have no knowledge — a rather unpromising line of argument. If, on the other hand, we equate presently justified theories with the final outcome of science, we claim to know that there will be no further theory change, also a hard claim to make stick.[39] Asserting that the world could never be known, even after an infinite process of inquiry,[40] would make "world" into a purely formal (transcendental)

---

38. Schleiermacher writes that the world as anticipated realized knowledge is the "Trieb des Wissens" (J 165).

39. Schleiermacher's presentation, though somewhat confused on the subject, tends toward the first error. When he alleges that there must always be a difference between essence and appearance, principle and *principiatum,* he loses the delicate balance between the regulative and constitutive use of "world."

40. The world is transcendental, "sofern nämlich, als sie uns nie und nirgend, auch nicht im unendlichen Prozess der Zusammenfassung aller Erscheinung, kann organisch

notion, invalidating the very epistemic argument that justifies its introduction in the first place. It would amount to saying that science has to be a *progressus in infinitum*, that scientific inquiry pursues a goal that it can never reach.[41] Since neither of these two options is acceptable, I conclude that there is good reason to follow Schleiermacher in construing "world" as a transcendent notion.

Consider the parallels with the notion of being. Since Aristotle, metaphysicians have taken being to stand for the broadest category (or, in Aristotle's case, metacategory), encompassing all that is but viewing it as a unity beyond all distinctions. Yet in reality, of course, we cannot think everything together under the term *being;* what we encounter instead is irreducible diversity. (To deny the actual diversity, Süskind argues, is like cutting off the patient's injured limb in order to restore the health of the whole.) The notion of world is analogous to the notion of being, except that the former does not stress undifferentiated unity over multiplicity and it does place a greater emphasis on the question of knowledge. Perhaps we could say that "world" is being as knowable or known. Both terms nevertheless represent the implied subject matter of the human quest for knowledge, the posited unity that the would-be knower pursues. In Schleiermacher's terms, the idea of the world is the transcendent ground for all thought about nature, that is, for all representational thought *(abbildliches Denken),* including both physical and ethical perspectives, both world order and law. All specific knowledge claims presuppose that we have the idea of a highest unity, but "that we cannot actualize [this idea] either in thought or in deed."[42]

---

gegeben sein, sondern immer nur gedacht" (O 303; cf. J §218). Schleiermacher defends this claim with the observation that the totality of being could never be grasped in a single appearance or experience *(Erscheinung).* But this works better to show the limits of his Kantian dichotomy between the organic and the intellectual than it does to render the notion of world a mere transcendental fiction.

41. The structure of Schleiermacher's thought is ambiguous here. At times it seems to reflect the same structure as Fichte's philosophy of identity, in which striving results out of (and is explained by) difference — except that Fichte's difference between *das absolute Ich* and *das Ich als Idee* here becomes the distinction between God and world (so Wagner, *Schleiermachers Dialektik,* 222; cf. the detailed graph in n. 100). Additional arguments for a Fichtean interpretation of Schleiermacher can be found in G. Wehrung's monographs, e.g., *Die Dialektik Schleiermachers* (Tübingen, 1920). In my judgment, Süskind's case against the Fichte interpretation and for a closer link with Schelling remains the most convincing; see Hermann Süskind, *Der Einfluss Schellings auf die Entwicklung von Schleiermachers System* (Tübingen: 1909; repr. Aalen: Scientia, 1983), esp. 244-64.

42. See H 214-17: all specific claims presuppose "daß wir die Idee der höchsten Einheit weder im Gedanken noch in der Tat vollziehen können" (p. 217). We can accept this claim without granting to self-consciousness the constitutive role that Schleiermacher and many of

Deriving Criteria from Limit Notions

How can limit notions such as "world" function as criteria in theology? Not, I suggest, as the cornerstones of yet another philosophical system that one can then hold up as necessarily true, or at least truer than all its competitors from Plato to Whitehead. Their most obvious role lies in clarifying the epistemic status of theological proposals, reminding theologians that their proposals can neither be determined as fictions in advance nor accepted as simply true in their present form. Beyond the status question, however, a limit notion like "world" also has something to say about the content of theological proposals. For example, it suggests that theories of creation and humanity must be about an object (the natural world) that is taken to exist and to be knowable. If it is to be knowable, it must be relatively constant; we must be able to make statements about it as something that has objective existence, that is, existence on its own above and beyond our own language and belief. Hence the object of all such theories must be like human reason (and the human speaker) without being identical to it. As I construe it, then, the limit concept of "world," even if it is to be both regulative and constitutive, militates against a strong Kantian dualism. On such a view, the thing-in-itself has nothing to do with space and time nor with any of our conceptual categories but must always remain for the human knower an "X," an utter unknown; even to say that it consists of objects (substances) or that it "causes" the perceptions that we have (and that we take to be about the world) is an illicit extension of our categories.[43] Equally, the limit concept of "world" would tell against a strong subjective idealism, according to which the world is wholly the product of minds and their thoughts. The problem with the latter view is the opposite from Kantian dualism: subjective idealism would make the world exactly what we think it to be, thus erasing the very difference on which the possibility of knowledge is based.[44]

Of course, none of this is to claim that Schleiermacher's notion of world fully determines the choice between the alternative theories, only that this limit

---

his interpreters (Halpern, Wagner) ascribe to it. According to these thinkers, *Selbstbewußtsein* can think both Being and its other, and God becomes for them the identity in self-consciousness of both (or better, I think: the awareness of God includes the identity of both).

43. Obviously, this was not always Kant's view; he often spoke of things-in-themselves in substantival terms and attributed to them a causal function via-à-vis our perceptions. Indeed, I take it to be intrinsic to the argument of the *Critique of Pure Reason* that Kant speaks in this way.

44. At first glance, such an argument would seem clearly to tell against contemporary antirealisms such as the "irrealism" of Nelson Goodman, e.g., in Goodman, *Ways of Worldmaking* (Indianapolis: Hackett, 1978).

notion can supply some parameters for evaluating theological proposals. Indeed, that limit notions radically underdetermine the selection of theories is not only to be accepted grudgingly but to be hoped for. Contrary to the claims of the rationalist traditions, it strikes me as highly desirable that empirical (esp. scientific) considerations should play a major role in assessing the credibility and the explanatory power of metaphysical hypotheses.[45] Indeed, since the addition of empirical considerations will still leave the choice underdetermined, one is forced to think in terms of a "pluralistic" metaphysics or theology consisting of various competing models and sometimes subjective choices among them (a very unrationalist picture).

Transcendent Ground

Further analysis reveals that there are actually two types of limit conditions regarding knowledge. Along with the idea of a final unity of knowledge already discussed, there is also the concept of a source of knowledge or a ground of its unity. For reasons that will become clear, I speak of this idea — which, recall, is possibly a mere fiction of thought — as the postulation of an *unconditioned* (e.g., O 241ff.). It is a venerable concept: the source notion played a ubiquitous role in Greek philosophy as the search for an *archē* or originating principle; it is analogous to Aristotle's first principle, which conditions all else without being itself conditioned by them; and it received its "highest" (or most notorious) expression in full-fledged philosophies of the absolute such as Hegel's. Philosophical theories of God from Thomas Aquinas to Plantinga also make use of this sort of grounding principle. Now admittedly, such theories strike some philosophers today as more quaint than convincing. But I suggest that something interesting happens to them when they are reformulated within the limits framework we have been exploring.[46]

When we look at an idea as a limit notion, we do not in the first place ontologize it (we remain neutral on the existence question) but rather focus on the way it functions at the limits of human reflection. Functionally, the concept of a transcendent ground makes its appearance in Schleiermacher's *Dialectics* by analogy with the concept of world and shares the former's both/and struc-

---

45. Jonathan Bennett's commentary on Spinoza, *A Study of Spinoza's Ethics* (Indianapolis: Hackett, 1984), is a masterful example of the use of contemporary science as the framework and the criterion for deciding what sorts of metaphysical proposals make sense today (see chapter 7 below).

46. The following is, as before, a loose reconstruction of Schleiermacher's theory in the *Dialectics*.

ture. In other words, as the postulation of an epistemic ultimate that is not presently known yet is posited in the present, the unconditioned begins as a regulating (or transcendental) notion. Yet if there is any knowledge, then whatever grounds it must be actual; hence (if there is knowledge) the source of knowledge is also presently existing and constitutive of knowledge. Still, since the unconditioned could not itself be an item of knowledge — because it imagines a source of knowledge rather than (as in the case of world) the whole of what is known — it involves the notion of something world-transcendent.[47]

Once again, this criterion underdetermines the selection among a number of alternatives. Clearly, God could function as the ground for the existence of the world, and thus as the condition of the possibility for there being any knowledge. Yet one might also take the existence of finite subjects as an adequate ground for knowledge of the world. A physicist might say, much more skeptically, that whatever existed before the Big Bang is the ultimate ground of what is; only, the physicist would add, nothing can be known about such a prephysical state of affairs, even in principle. Schleiermacher himself makes the attempt to construe the notion of ground in nontranscendent, temporal terms, namely as the difference between our present state of knowledge and an imagined final set of justified true beliefs.[48] Only if one expects that metaphysical debates will have unitary resolutions will this possibility of an irreducible plurality of answers (at least in the present) be cause for alarm.

Despite the similarities, the notion of an unconditioned is definitely not identical to that of the world. While the world is the sum total of the knowable, a (possible) ground of knowledge would not be a member of this set. Where world is a future epistemic goal, its ground is what is always presupposed along the way. Schleiermacher consequently speaks of world as the *terminus ad quem* of the epistemic process, and the ground of knowledge as its *terminus a quo*. Above we defined the world as the totality of what could ultimately be known — say, by a Peircean ideal community of inquiry, given sufficient time. And philosophers have taken the Absolute to stand for the complete unity, without remaining difference, of Thought and Being. The transcendent ground might then be interpreted as the difference between these two; in contemporary terms it becomes the (possible) difference between world (as the set of justified be-

---

47. Schleiermacher writes of "diese Idee von der transzendenten Voraussetzung alles Denkens als allgemeiner Bedingung dafür, daß unser Denken ein Wissen sei" (O 271).

48. Schleiermacher tends to speak of it in psychological terms, as whatever leaves us dissatisfied with agreement, even apparently justified agreement, and keeps us inquiring; in this context he employs the notion of *Wissenwollen* or "wishing to know" (e.g., O 271-72). But I find the difference condition too negative to pass as a ground; and there are dangers with an overly psychological account of ground in terms of "wishing to know."

liefs) and truth. As the ground of all knowledge or as the "totality of the whole," the transcendent ground so defined can serve as a stand-in (in these epistemically leaner times) for what the tradition used to call the Absolute.

Why the Absolute Is Not a Limit Notion

Metaphysicians formerly took the Absolute to stand for the complete unity of thought and being. Why couldn't the above presentation be criticized for not going far enough? Shouldn't world and ground be thought together as the two sides of the Absolute? Doesn't my argument ultimately point in the direction of Hegel?

Philosophers' preoccupation with absolutes has taken many forms: mathematical absolutes (e.g., Cantor's absolute infinite), epistemic absolutes (forms, or the Form of the Forms), cosmological absolutes (the *archē* or ultimate source that motivated Greek philosophers), and the Absolute Itself (along with its religious counterpart, God) that dominated Western philosophy from Philo to Hegel. In each case, philosophers sought for the highest conceivable notion, one that as unconditioned would be above all opposition and all dependence; or they sought a being who possesses all great-making qualities and possesses them to the greatest possible degree (as in the Anselmian perfect-being theology explored in chapter 3).

Given the epistemological conclusions of this and the previous chapters, the fate of the Absolute today looks rather bleak. Haven't serious criticisms been raised by "post-structuralist" thinkers such as Emmanuel Levinas and Jacques Derrida? If even the "upper limits" of concepts and judgments — ideas like the highest concept or the highest subject — no longer fall within the domain of knowledge, then certainly the notion of the all-synthesizing Absolute has even less of a chance.[49] The Absolute, traditionally speaking, was to have been that which is known to be the source and culmination (or unifying instance) of all knowledge. But I have argued that human thought is not in the position to resolve its own most fundamental oppositions, namely, to demonstrate that there is no difference between thought and being. We can speak of states of affairs, and we can spell out our highest epistemic criteria (reasoned agreement of the relevant experts), but we cannot ascertain that the beliefs le-

---

49. "Gehören nämlich schon die 'obern Grenzen' von Begriff und Urteil, der höchste Begriff und das höchste Subjekt, nicht mehr dem Gebiete des Wissens an, so natürlich noch weniger das Absolute" (Paul Häberlin, *Über den Einfluss der spekulativen Gotteslehre auf die Religionslehre bei Schleiermacher* [Zurich: A. Schaufelberger, 1903], 30).

gitimated by our criteria must be true of states of affairs. Yet exactly such a synthesis of thought and being is implied by the notion of the Absolute. A theology of limit notions must therefore distance itself from this notion, which is in its very nature incompatible with the limits explored here.

The net effect of Schleiermacher's thought is thus to turn theology away from the fixation on the Absolute. He was never inclined to jump on the bandwagon of Hegel's philosophy of *Absoluter Geist*,[50] sharing instead Kant's skepticism about the limitations of reason. Nonetheless, in the dust left by the Absolute's demise, his crucial contribution is to reintroduce talk of the unconditioned as a limit concept suggested by the human epistemic situation. If there is something that is unconditioned, it lies beyond the limits on human knowledge, and what is known about it (if anything) is known through reflection on these limits.[51]

The connection between the theory of limits and that which is unconditioned (unlimited) is twofold. On the one side, postulating something that is unconditioned gives one a way of speaking of the contrast between this postulation and the (otherwise) conditioned character of human knowledge.[52] That is, the postulation helps to make sense of our epistemic efforts as conditioned (by various factors) and as conditional (since we do not know, and it seems could never know, whether our best epistemic efforts actually lead to the Way Things Are or merely provide an inaccurate but indistinguishable version of it).[53] Approached from the other side, the apparent limits that we do discover tell us something about what the nature of an unconditioned ground (if such exists) would have to be, if it is both to transcend these epistemic limits and to "condition" or account for them as their source.

The following section may thus be viewed as a thought experiment. I pro-

---

50. Thus Odebrecht's comment, "Dem Rausch des Höhenfluges ins Absolute steht Schleiermacher mit sokratischer Nüchternheit und Ironie gegenüber" (O v).

51. Cf. the powerful statement by Langdon Gilkey: "The ultimate or unconditional element in experience is not so much the seen but the basis of seeing; not what is known as an object so much as the basis of knowing; not an object of value but the ground of valuing; not the thing before us, but the source of things" (*Naming the Whirlwind* [Indianapolis: Bobbs-Merrill, 1969], 43). The parallels with Tillich are clear and will be developed further in chapter 9.

52. If the goal of language is to signify, it gives us a way of speaking of the signified when all we encounter is an apparently endless progression of signifiers (Jacques Derrida, *Of Grammatology*, trans. Gayatri Chakravorty Spivak [Baltimore: John Hopkins Univ. Press, 1976]).

53. This skeptical thesis lies at the core of Putnam's post-1976 position and is now widely accepted. More recently, see Nicholas Rescher, "Conceptual Idealism Revisited," *Review of Metaphysics* 44 (1991): 495-524.

pose we ask how this (possible) transcendent ground of thought should be understood — or better: how it may not be understood if it is to serve its role as epistemic ideal. Which of the concepts available to us, if any, best express this ideal that regulates the entire pursuit of knowledge: the idea of a unity between justified beliefs and actual states of affairs (i.e., between thought and being)? What notion has enough content to convey this structure without claiming to know more than (apparently) can be known?

The Infinite as Limit Notion

The notion of the infinite immediately suggests itself as one of the intuitively most promising options.[54] As we saw in chapter 3, the Cartesian tradition treated the infinite as that which is free of all limits and all constraints — in short, as the unconditioned. For Descartes it was what stands over against the finite and serves as its source, since infinity must be prior to all finite things. Just as the idea of the Absolute can be boiled down to that which is not conditioned by anything else, so the unconditioned can be reformulated using the notion of infinity. Doing so allows one to draw from mathematical theory, from the philosophy of infinite quantities (such as Cantor's transfinite theory), and from theories of contingency. In brief, a concept of the infinite represents a particularly apt way of expressing the ultimate context of limitation for epistemic agents such as ourselves.

Of course, postulating an infinite dimension as a condition of the possibility of human knowledge cannot be construed as an argument for the existence of an infinite being. Infinite beings are problematic entities, since the notion of "a being" implies some sort of limitation — viz. one being as over against other beings (see chap. 8 below). Even less can one immediately equate the concept of infinity with God in the traditional sense: if reflection is stumped by the very notion of an infinite being, we will certainly need further reason to construe it as an actually existing agent of its own.

Hence a theology of limit notions must begin rather more minimally with the notion of a possibly fictitious, possibly actual, infinite dimension. Such a dimension, like the notion of the unconditioned, is the conceptual "other" of the finite, is in some sense be prior to it, and hence can be spoken of as its source. Merely introducing this concept, even if there is a certain necessity

54. Most of what follows is mine; Schleiermacher did not actually develop a theory of the infinite in much detail. One might, however, introduce the concept of infinity as a natural outcome of the epistemology defended in his *Dialectics*. See n. 56 below.

to its postulation, does not of course make for a very robust theology. Still, it is the sort of concept that corresponds to the epistemic need for a transcendent ground that we have discovered, whereas some other proposals — those that deny the existence or possibility of a highest principle in advance — conflict with this need. For instance, it seems that Heraclitus's "all is flux" metaphysics would fail to allow for a final unification of reason, unless (as seems to be the case) he subsumes the flux under some other principle *(logos)* that underlies the flux. Polytheism in most of its guises would also make it impossible to formulate questions of the ground of reason, as would many forms of dualism (e.g., Gnosticism, Zoroastrianism).[55] Conversely, full theories of the Absolute are guilty of ignoring the epistemic limits that emerged in our analysis of reason. By contrast, the postulation of an underlying infinite dimension, even when interpreted in a constructive (not purely fictional) sense, could serve the required epistemic role, providing the framework for making sense of all finite things as finite. It is also consistent with a wide variety of theological proposals, from Philo's view of God through the major medieval theologians and into the modern period. It therefore remains a live option at a time when various other metaphysical positions are cast into question by the epistemological conclusions we have reached.[56]

Indeed, a theory of a (posited) infinite dimension can in fact serve some of the functions that theories of the Absolute once served in the Western metaphysical tradition. Think of it as an epistemically pared-down absolute, lacking some of the more problematic claims formerly made on behalf of metaphysics' highest principle (such as the claim that it is a person or must have all

55. It might seem at first as though Leibniz's monadism would have to be rejected for similar reasons. But this is not true: it is emphatically a hierarchical metaphysics, culminating in a highest monad, God, which serves as the model for all else.

56. I have introduced the concept of infinity as a natural outcome of the epistemology defended in Schleiermacher's *Dialectics*. It is common knowledge that Schleiermacher stressed the infinite as prior to the finite in the *Speeches;* yet to my knowledge no one has demonstrated how convincingly the *Dialectics* works as an after-the-fact justification for the position taken in the *Speeches.*

A Hegelian (or a theologian such as Wolfhart Pannenberg) might object at this point that Schleiermacher should have gone a step further. One can ask what sort of structure reason would have to have if it were going to be able to move from the finite to the infinite, to grasp the infinite, to overcome the difference between thought and being, between the subjective and the objective. And, the objection might continue, such a structure would have to be a dialectical structure such as Hegel offers. Hegel follows the limitations of Kantian dualism to a certain point and then proposes his dialectical conceptual movement as the sort of structure that could overcome all remaining dichotomies, just as (he might add) God is the sort of concept that could be constitutive given the limitations that we have explored.

Anselmian "great-making" properties). Even if it looks rather thin compared to the expansive theories of the Absolute found in traditional metaphysics, a notion of infinity based on the epistemic limits of finite knowers provides a more adequate account of what the source of human reason (or of its success) would have to look like if our occasional epistemic success is to be explainable even in principle. It is also consistent with a wide variety of metaphysical and non-metaphysical proposals, from Plotinus's One through (certain versions of) classical theism to the Absolute Infinite of Cantor's set theory. Since the postulation of an underlying infinite dimension evidences the structure required by an epistemology of limit notions, it remains an attractive starting point for philosophical theologians today.

A classical metaphysician might object at this point that the previous paragraph imposes an arbitrary stopping point that is inconsistent with the nature of metaphysical reflection. If we use a term such as "the infinite," have we not already claimed to know something about it? And if so, must we not also ask what sort of structure or internal dynamic compels human reason to move from the finite to the infinite and to understand itself in the light of these two poles? Here the Hegelian might extol the merits of a dialectical theory of reason. As is well known, Hegel followed Kant's critique of classical metaphysics, and then proposed his dialectical logic as the structure that will eventually overcome all remaining dichotomies, including that between thought and being. The decision is a difficult one: on the one hand, it does seem that an infinite would not be truly infinite if it were "limited" by a finite world that is opposed to it and hence lies "outside" it. (Indeed, this realization will play a crucial role in the constructive position developed in the following chapters.) On the other hand, we have discovered massive reasons to be skeptical about final unifications of thought and being. Once again, reason appears to face requirements that it is able neither to satisfy nor to set aside — in this case, an infinite dimension that must encompass the finite and yet must also be thought as other than or opposed to it. Yet this is precisely the nature of the philosophy of limit notions that I have been advocating: to find itself confronted with lines of thought that point, even propel, one in the direction of a final unification of thought that nonetheless eludes one's grasp.

GOD AS LIMIT NOTION

What then of the central concept of theology, the concept of God? Of course, the introduction of the idea of the infinite as a limit notion helps the theologian

Here is the argument: the movement toward the abstract is an inevitable part of reflection, yet we seem to have no prospect at all of explaining concrete and commonsensical beliefs as entailments of such general categories. Hence we have no reason to think that the explanatory principles of the world as we know it really are to be sought in the most abstract of all categories. It is equally possible that the explanatory grounds (if any) are rather more concrete than the metaphysicians have imagined. Indeed, there is some reason to expect this result, since it is in general more likely that a phenomenon will be explained (i.e., genuinely accounted for) by a principle (an *explanans*) close to it in specificity than by one many orders of magnitude more abstract than it. Of course, more concrete explanatory principles — say, those expressed in scientific terms, or in concrete religious terms, or in aesthetic language — are not deducible from a theory of being or the Absolute; but since it appears that nothing can be deduced from such a theory, this fact should not bother us much. In short, more specific scientific or religious accounts might well be true, and might well provide much more effective explanations of the world and our experience, even though they are expressed in terms considerably more concrete than those of classical metaphysics.

Suppose we call such explanatory principles *metaphysical hypotheses*. The term suggests that they may fulfill many of the functions formerly assigned to metaphysical theories alone, even though they are no longer under the control of metaphysicians but may have their sources elsewhere. It also suggests that, being more concrete, they may be testable in a way that global metaphysical accounts are not. A number of general but not traditionally metaphysical contenders fall within this category: physical cosmologies such as the Big Bang theory; philosophical cosmologies such as those by Teilhard de Chardin or A. N. Whitehead; humanist (or karma-based) theories of cosmic evolution; and of course the various specific beliefs about God stemming from the major world religions, such as the belief in God as personal or as the Father of Jesus Christ.

Toward a Pluralistic Theology

Opting for concreteness in this way will undoubtedly sound dissonant to the philosophical ear. Isn't it paradoxical to reach a skeptical conclusion about traditional metaphysics and then to find that conclusion multiplying rather than constricting the available options? But this consequence should not be surprising. Skeptics assumed that the failure of a certain kind of metaphysical project — the metaphysics of totality — would relieve them of the need to assess proposals about the nature of God; yet this assumption was unjustified. As pluralists in philosophy and religion have effectively argued, skeptical conclusions expand rather than constrict the available options. If the interest in the limits of human reason and language — and in what lies beyond — is as inescapable as I have argued, then the failure of metaphysics qua deductive science can only result in opening the field to other aspirants.

Note that one does not immediately get a full-fledged systematic theology as a payoff from this approach, at least not in its traditional form. But reflection on ultimate explanations and first principles does become again what it used to be: the best account, religious or otherwise, of what reality might be. Religious hypotheses are not fundamentally different from other types of theories; they represent one type of account among many that people have put forward and that philosophy must now consider, even though they are much more concrete than, for example, talk of being qua being. That metaphysicians must as a result become students of religious and scientific theories as well as of the history of metaphysics, dirtying their hands with vocabularies that originally grew out of religious or empirical concerns, may actually enrich the discipline more than it harms it. Given the limitations uncovered above, the only alternative is to conclude that there is an unbreachable gap between our best accounts of reality and the true account, or a necessary gap between human desire and its realization. Such stoicism — for example, the stoicism in the face of the alleged impossibility of ever knowing metaphysical truth that we find in a Nietzsche, Rorty, or Putnam — is not true just because it is stoic (though one may indeed find something stirring about it).

In short, one cannot avoid filling in the category of an Absolute or transcendent ground with particular content. The more concrete hypotheses that one may now introduce need not be deduced from some most general category; one posits them instead with the (criticizable) claim that they are consistent with the apparent limit points of the human quest for knowledge, and hence plausible candidates for expressing the unconditioned ground of the finite world. Recall Schleiermacher's clear criterion: which proposed explanations are consistent with what (apparently) cannot be known and, at the same time, with what would have to be the case if the oppositions of reason were to be overcome in a unifying instance? Since this question underdetermines the answer between the various alternatives, one needs to add additional criteria. One might ask, for instance, which broader hypotheses best explain the full range of the data of human existence, or which are compatible with our scientific, ethical, or religious interests. (That this last criterion is interest-relative is obvious.) These criteria launch a new and fascinating project in the comparative assessment of theological accounts, even while a final reduction to a single alternative can no longer be guaranteed in advance.

What, finally, is the status of a theology of limit notions? Unlike traditional metaphysics, the approach allows for accounts of reality that may be concrete or even narrative in form; many will include elements that are not deduced from ultimate starting points or certain grounds. Does this mean, ontologically, that they are necessarily false? No, they could be true. Do we then have any reason, epistemically, to think that they are? Yes: we can ask whether the accounts are consistent with the limit conditions explored above; we can also test them by the more traditional criteria of internal consistency, coherence, comprehensiveness, and the rest of the criteria well known to epistemologists. Moreover, since the accounts are offered as explanations, one can use many of the standards advanced in recent theories of inference to the best explanation.[60]

Choosing between the Infinite and God

It should now be obvious why I have devoted so much time to limit notions in a book on the problem of God in modern thought. The philosophical theologian introduces theistic language in order to avoid the stultifying abstractions into which traditional metaphysics fell (among other reasons). Theistic language is one type of more concrete answer to the ultimate questions that have preoccupied metaphysicians for millennia. For instance, there are several more concrete ways to think the infinite as limit notion. If we find that it is best thought as a passive principle — say, the undifferentiated One above all distinctions — then the notion of God will be falsified. But if we find that the infinite is best thought as active, as a source of life or creativity (or as itself creative), as mental (say, as *nous noētikos*, thought thinking itself), or as purposive, then the notion of God remains a live option.[61]

---

60. See, e.g., Peter Lipton, *Inference to the Best Explanation* (London: Routledge & Kegan Paul, 1991), and my application of it to theology: "Inference to the Best Explanation," *Zygon* 32 (1997): 377-91. The growth industry of speculation about theories of everything (TOEs) in contemporary physics provides both a remarkable parallel and some further criteria of selection. For example, we can ask which theological hypotheses better explain the universe as we would expect it to be given ourselves (i.e., given agents who can pose the question). See John Barrow, *Theories of Everything* (London: Oxford Univ. Press, 1991).

61. Schleiermacher speaks of the choice between thinking the transcendent ground as "freies Einzelwesen" and as "mechanische Nothwendigkeit," along with the question of whether God and world are thought to be identical, separate but ontologically linked, or radically distinct (J 525).

CONCLUSION

We have followed Schleiermacher through his groundbreaking exploration of the conditions for knowledge. In many ways Schleiermacher remained a Kantian; the epistemic limitations that he discussed militate against the strong knowledge claims that were fundamental to classical metaphysics. Nonetheless, in the aftermath of its demise, he realized that the limits of knowledge themselves provide a fruitful tool for evaluating proposals about the nature of God (and other metaphysical entities). If there is something that is unconditioned, for example, it lies beyond the limits on human knowledge, and what is known about it (if anything) is known through reflection on these limits.

These conclusions, I argued, can give rise to a constructive program of theological reflection. We can ask what proposals about the nature of God are consistent with (and would help us to understand) a transcendent ground of thought, and which proposals would be inconsistent with the existence of this ground and its role in the knowing process. Which concrete accounts of the unconditioned, if any, best express the ideals that regulate the pursuit of knowledge in general: the concept of God? the physical universe? the infinite? Post-Kantian philosophical theology in this guise allows for (partially) criticizable positions without the overly optimistic epistemic claims formerly made on their behalf. It would certainly be an interesting result, for example, to find that the very epistemic worries that are currently leading "postmodern" theologians to turn from metaphysics to neo-pragmatism and deconstruction in fact open new doors for a (pluralistic) reappropriation of the theistic tradition! Precisely this is our task in part III.

At the same time, it is obvious that I have in some ways departed from the *Dialectics* in these last paragraphs. On my account, the richness of theistic language should help one to avoid the stultifying abstractions into which traditional metaphysics fell. The failure of metaphysical deductions frees one to use concrete language about divine intentions and actions. Such language is just as effective in reaching out toward Schleiermacher's (presupposed) final convergence of knowledge and being as are the abstract concepts of metaphysics.

Although Schleiermacher helps one to get to this point, I fear it is of less help now that we are ready actually to do theology — which is perhaps as it ought to be. Schleiermacher's treatment of the idea of God in the *Dialectics* is no longer a serious contender in the contemporary discussion. Some of his relativizing arguments — such as the claim that the outcome of the debate depends in part on whether one's purposes are religious or speculative (e.g., J 526ff.) — deserve further attention. As we move on to the constructive theory in the remaining chapters, however, Schleiermacher offers more of an agenda for reflection than actual solutions. Are God and world to be distinguished as basic correlates?[62] Do the internal problems in Spinoza's notion of *natura naturans* invalidate pantheism as a viable concept (O 238-49, 265)? Is *creatio ex nihilo* required by the limits we have discussed, in order to guarantee that the first principle has the requisite sort of ultimacy; that is, would a principle of ultimate unity rule out a God who faced a preexistent matter (O 268)? What views of humanity would and would not be consistent with the epistemic plight that we have described? With an epistemology and criteria in place, we now have the requisite framework for answering these questions.

Nevertheless, we have found in the *Dialectics* a line of argument that speaks directly to the situation of late-twentieth-century theology. For it remains vital in the present-day context of pluralism and skepticism about definitive theistic proofs or metaphysical theories of God. Moreover, it does justice to the enduring sense that humanity can nonetheless discover "signs of transcendence," pointers or limit notions within the realm of our all-too-human reasoning, which point finally beyond the limits of our comprehension toward its transcendent ground.

62. E.g., J 166, 168, 475, 525ff.; O 302ff.

PART III

TOWARD A THEOLOGY
OF THE INFINITE

CHAPTER SEVEN

The Temptations of Immanence: Spinoza's One and the Birth of Panentheism

We have followed the major strands of modern thought about God from Descartes's infinitely perfect being to Leibniz's Architect of the best of all possible worlds. After Leibniz, however, we ran into the brick wall of Kant's critique of metaphysics. The last two chapters were devoted to the task of understanding how devastating is the possibility raised by Kant — that God-language reveals much about how human reason functions but nothing about whether there is a God or what the divine nature is. We did find a way over the wall, but only at the cost of circumscribing theology's claims, of acknowledging how much God-talk is about the limits of *human* understanding. Yet Kantian skepticism does not have the last word, for we also found that some God-language has to be taken not only regulatively (as describing the limits on what we can know) but also metaphysically — as offering models for thinking the divine nature. It may be a humbled theology that beckons us after six chapters, but it is a viable theology nonetheless.

It may seem strange to begin part III with a movement back in time, to Spinoza, a thinker who preceded both Leibniz and Kant. The reasons to do so are compelling. Spinoza offers a greatly circumscribed view of the divine, a view fully compatible not only with the science of his day but also with the science of our own. His stress on immanence rather than transcendence avoids some of the pitfalls for theology that Kant discovered. Most importantly, Spinoza's approach to the God-question is designed to avoid the reliance on theories of perfection (both medieval and Cartesian) that we have found to be conceptually inadequate.

In this and the following chapters, then, we follow what I believe to be the most productive strand in the tapestry of modern thought about God. We will see how other strands came to and were woven in with Spinoza's initial insight, leading finally to the rich theories of the self-revealing God in the early nineteenth century. But first we must deal with the other conclusion that is often drawn from the Kantian criticisms: the postmodern attack on transcendence, with its claim that God-language should henceforth be given a purely immanent interpretation.

Yovel's Spinoza

In an important two-volume work on *Spinoza and Other Heretics,* Yirmiyahu Yovel has proclaimed the adventures of immanence, the thrills of the denial of transcendence.[1] The book has attracted significant attention.[2] Yovel has not, strictly speaking, provided a history of Spinozism since, as he notes, he is more interested in a particular theme, immanence, with a particular twist. The modern father of immanence, Spinoza,

> rejected both the dualistic transcendence of the Christians and the de-naturized, transcendence-ridden this-worldliness of his fellow Jews. A "Marrano of reason," he shed all historical religions (though not all religous concerns), and offered salvation neither in Christ nor in the Law of Moses, but in his own kind of religion of reason — naturalistic, monistic, and strictly immanent. (p. 169)

Yovel nowhere offers a precise definition of immanence; indeed, I believe his project depends on stretching it well beyond the early modern context. For Yovel writes out of a contemporary context in epistemology, which he labels neo-pragmatism and which we might associate — loosely perhaps but with surprising accuracy — with the name Richard Rorty. It would be only a slight exaggeration to say that the "adventures of immanence" encompass those mod-

1. Virmiyahu Yovel, *Spinoza and Other Heretics,* 2 vols. (Princeton: Princeton Univ. Press, 1989). Unless otherwise noted, references are to vol. 2, *The Adventures of Immanence.* The next reference in the text is also to this work.
2. It was, e.g., the object of an American Philosophical Association (Midwestern) session in April 1991. Expanded forms of the papers appeared in *Inquiry* 35 (1992): Henry Allison, "Spinoza and the Philosophy of Immanence: Reflections in Yovel's *The Adventures of Immanence*" (pp. 55-67); Richard Schacht, "Adventures of Immanence Revisited" (pp. 69-80); and Y. Yovel, "Spinoza and Other Heretics: Reply to Critics" (pp. 81-112).

ern thinkers who turn out to have been (at least under Yovel's interpretation) in some sense or another precursors of postmodernism à la Rorty.

Why then title the book *Spinoza and . . . ?* As one of the great outsiders of the tradition, and as a clear opponent to a God who is separate from and transcendent of the world, Spinoza might appear to represent the perfect starting point, the opening chapter in a narrative of the birth and blossoming of postmodernism from Spinoza to Rorty. This fact explains Yovel's choice of thinkers (Kant, Hegel, Heine, Hess, Feuerbach, Marx, Nietzsche, Freud), many of whom are only tangentially connected to Spinoza — or connected to him more by opposition than by agreement. Whatever the principle of selection, it is bound to be an exciting story, touching as it does on most of the controversial thinkers of the late eighteenth century, the nineteenth century, and spilling over via Freud into the twentieth century. There are some omissions — Lessing, Schopenhauer (almost), and Heidegger — but these presumably provide room for follow-up articles. And the connections make for dramatic reading — linking Kant to Nietzsche, Herder to Marx, Heine to Freud, and all to their ultimate source in Spinoza.

Those of us who are unpersuaded by Yovel's case could, of course, criticize Rortyan neo-pragmatism. (Of course, Rorty has over the years proved rather impervious to frontal assaults — a distinct advantage of being a postphilosopher holding a nonposition.) But I suggest an alternative route instead. Suppose we began by granting Spinoza the role of spokesperson for the philosophy of immanence. After all, he has developed a naturalistic metaphysics of the sort congenial to many of our contemporaries. On his view, if the term *God* is to play any role in philosophy at all, it must be as a tag for (some aspect of) the natural world and not as designating a supernatural, transcendent being. For Spinoza, God exists if and only if the equation *deus siva natura* ("God or Nature") holds. By implication, then, all those who advocate a purely immanent account of divinity — the viewpoint that has traditionally been called *pantheism*[3] — will check in as "Spinozists" for purposes of this discussion.

Are the "adventures of immanence" the correct response to the Kantian problem of God? My thesis will be that Spinoza's own mature doctrine, his thoroughgoing pantheism, is unsuccessful, and that no philosophically adequate form of pantheism has been developed in modern Western philosophy. As we turn to Spinoza's followers (those who qualify as Spinozists according to the definition just given), we will discover that pantheism, when worked out systematically in Western philosophy, has invariably turned into *panentheism*

---

3. See Michael P. Levine, *Pantheism: A Non-Theistic Concept of Deity* (London: Routledge, 1994).

— the view that the world is within God although God is also more than the world. Of course, when this occurs these views cease to be purely immanent and become immanent/transcendent philosophies. The present chapter traces this transformation — which I take to be both inevitable and desirable — in the case of Spinoza and his early followers (and critics) themselves.

How is the theological debate between pantheism, theism (or panentheism), and atheism to be adjudicated? As the methodological reflections in chapter 1 suggested, one must ask which of these systems provides the best overall metaphysical explanation. Naturally, this question can be resolved only by means of a careful analysis of competing explanatory proposals.[4] In particular, this chapter chronicles the fundamental competition between Spinozism and what I call *minimal personalist (panen)theism* or *MPT*. I will argue that the series of criticisms and modifications of Spinoza's original position that we will encounter point gradually toward some variant of MPT as the most viable systematic answer. In subsequent chapters we will observe how the core of a panentheistic metaphysic, still little more than a set of basic intuitions in the later eighteenth century, gradually took sophisticated form during the early years of the nineteenth century. (Volume 2 of this work will offer a systematic defense of panentheism in the contemporary context.)

If I am right about the strengths of MPT, the most urgent contemporary choice is between it and a non- (or post- or anti-) metaphysical position such as Rortyan immanentism. Since I take it that Rorty will be little moved by metaphysical criticisms or alternatives (and perhaps the same holds for Yovel), it is unlikely that this chapter's careful look at the history of Spinozism will be sufficient to sway the Rortyan reader.[5] Still, it is not unreasonable to hope that working through the various criticisms of Spinoza will aid most readers in forming their own rational evaluations of this influential modern thinker.

The Case against Immanence Alone

In this chapter I counterpose to the "adventures" of immanence the thesis of the modern *temptation* of immanence. The seductiveness of this temptation cannot be overestimated. Among its charms are the widespread dissatisfaction

---

4. To spell out and defend this method of analysis would require a paper as long as the present one. See chapter 1 above and Peter Lipton, *Inference to the Best Explanation* (London: Routledge & Kegan Paul, 1991), esp. chap. 3, "The Causal Model."

5. I also provided some epistemological counterarguments to Rorty's position in chapter 1.

with transcendence and the attractiveness of the mystical sense of oneness or interconnection. But immanence will remain no more than a promise or temptation as long as mystical/experiential attractiveness remains a substitute for conceptual adequacy. As an antidote to the temptation I seek to show, first, that no satisfying pantheism has been presented, and second, that panentheism need not be epistemically naive but can be formulated in a manner that takes into account the Kantian worries addressed in the previous two chapters.

The case against Spinozistic immanence cannot be made by vague generalizations about seventeenth- and eighteenth-century philosophy; it requires one to work analytically through the arguments of specific thinkers. In the interests of juxtaposition and setting the context, I begin with a (brief) summary of the contemporary discussion of Spinoza's doctrine of God/Nature, which provides a somewhat clearer picture of the difficulties that Spinoza resuscitators should have faced in their efforts. We turn next to three initial (but significant) critiques from the early years after Spinoza's death. Finally, we proceed to the three major Spinoza reconstructors of the eighteenth century: Lessing, Jacobi, and Mendelssohn.[6] Even when their motives were critical, these thinkers managed to move Spinozism to a higher level of sophistication.

As we will see, Spinoza's philosophy is not adequate in its original form. In particular, Spinoza's philosophy of the one infinite substance with infinite attributes and his inability to derive the finite from the infinite are problematic. This exposition then serves as the backdrop for the question: If Spinoza failed to develop an adequate version of naturalistic pantheism, did his followers fare any better at this task? Was any of them able successfully to modify Spinoza's system in some way — say, by reducing its naturalistic bias, or by relying more heavily on the concept of self-consciousness? If they were, was the result a model of God that is philosophically preferable to personalist theism?

What one discovers, I believe, is that no such model was advanced in the first 110 years after Spinoza's death — that is, prior to German idealism. None of the figures I examine was able to establish the connection between the finite and the infinite without pushing outside the bounds of pantheism, that is, without reintroducing some aspect of transcendence. By contrast, in the following chapters on Fichte and Schelling I find increasingly sophisticated formulations of the "immanence plus transcendence" view of the divine. The net effect, I argue, is to raise panentheism to one of the most (if not *the* most) seri-

---

6. The three receive but passing mention by Yovel; see pp. 63-64. Henry Allison takes him to task for the omission ("Spinoza and the Philosophy of Immanence"), a criticism that Yovel concedes in the symposium and to which he responds in the afterword of *The Adventures of Immanence* (pp. 188ff.).

ous metaphysical options that has emerged out of the first three hundred years of the modern period.

SPINOZA'S *ETHICS*

The Attractiveness of Spinoza

It is not as though Yovel was mistaken to choose Spinozism as a watershed in metaphysical thinking, for there is much here to attract the contemporary philosopher. Spinoza's one substance does provide the unifying perspective required of a metaphysical theory. What is most fundamental in Spinoza's great work, the *Ethics*, is Absolute Substance, which he calls "God or Nature" *(deus siva natura)*. Spinoza defines the one substance as "that which is in itself and is conceived through itself" (E 1, def. 3).[7] He then works to demonstrate in his first fourteen propositions that, given this definition, only one substance can exist. Human individuals, since they are not separate beings, must therefore be modes; humans are the states or "affections" of the one substance, being "in something else and conceived through something else" (E 1, def. 5).

Spinoza contends that his metaphysics provides a place for real (albeit reconceived) human selves, individuated in both body and mind. Now it might seem that, if God is the only substance, human selves could not have separate existence. But selves can still be *modes* of substance: "Particular things are nothing but affections of the attributes of God; that is, modes wherein the attributes of God find expression in a definite and determinate way" (E 1, P25 cor.). This dichotomy is exhaustive: everything is either substance or mode. Substances, or, rather, the one substance, has fully independent existence; it "requires nothing else in order to be thought." This is not true of us: we are clearly contingent, and require other things in order to be understood. So we must in some way be expressions of substance. At best, then, we are distinctions within substance. Moreover, no individual is correctly regarded as the "cause or sufficient reason of any other: the only sufficient cause can be God or Nature."[8]

Against classical theism, then, Spinoza argues that everything is in God (P15). It follows that God is not a transient but the immanent cause of modes

---

7. Parenthetical references, unless otherwise noted, are to Spinoza's *Ethics* (cited as E); I usually follow the translation of Samuel Shirley, *Ethics* (Indianapolis: Hackett, 1982).

8. Richard Mason, "Spinoza on the Causality of Individuals," *Journal of the History of Philosophy* 24 (1986): 197-210, quotation 207.

(P19): God's causes do not pass over to the modes like the motion of billiard balls, but rather God as indwelling cause is *in* his effects.[9] God is the efficient cause also of their essence (P25). Therefore, Spinoza argues, "in the same sense *(eo sensu)* that God is said to be self-caused he must also be said to be the cause of all things" (ibid., scholium, emphasis mine). Hence Spinoza's famous dictum: "particular things are nothing but affections of the attributes of God."

Of course, it is not easy to map contemporary debates about individuals back onto substance theories — Spinoza's or anyone else's. Still, at first blush philosophers and theologians today seem clearly to mean something more by "individual" than a way in which the one substance is expressed (manifested, affected) at a certain place and time. (That the person on the street means something more by "individual" than a mode of substance needs no arguing.) We think of an individual as a part of nature who is really distinct from other individuals; Spinoza speaks of the parts of nature as distinct "not really but only modally" (*modaliter tantum distinguuntur, non autem realiter;* E 1, P15). We think of the individual as more than, while Spinoza makes it only equal to, one of the properties that follow with necessity from the definition of nature or God (P16).

Still, this strange-sounding notion that we are all modes of one substance may have gained in credibility in the contemporary context. Spinozists can ascribe predicates to the modes that do not pertain to God/Nature as a whole. They can freely employ all finite predicates, including the individual striving to persevere *(conatus)*, just as much as Cartesians were able to predicate qualities of things taken as independent substances. Yet the Spinozist does not thereby ascribe to the modes real separate existence; they remain only moments of a single reality. Such a picture is highly compatible with contemporary physics, with its talk of a single universe of energy that takes form, locally, as "objects" (relatively defined).

Moreover, Spinoza's one substance, "God or Nature," is not explanatorily intrusive, so to speak, since individual finite modes are fully explained with reference to other finite modes (and something he calls "infinite modes" — but they can be cashed out as natural laws). The independence of the attributes "thought" and "extension" allows the Spinozist to develop a physics and a purely physicalist psychology at the same time that one uses mental predicates in mental contexts like reasoning or intuiting. Since the two attributes are parallel — both describe features of the one universe-as-a-whole — neither needs to be reduced to the other. And Spinoza's compatibilism (the view that something is free if it is determined to act by itself alone) holds impeccable credentials in contemporary philosophy.

9. *Ethics,* 25.

In a word, Spinoza offers a physicalism that can be made as rigorous as one would like, while at the same time avoiding reductionism and leaving a (circumscribed) place open for metaphysical reflection. His position ascribes a central role to the body in individuating, without suggesting that all things can be reduced to the physical. According to his view, each of us is both mental and physical, Mind and Body, for these are the (known) attributes of the one substance of which we are modes. We are mental not in that we are mental substances (for there can be only one substance); we are mental just to the extent that we think. For Spinoza, to "be" Mind is to have ideas, since these are the product of thought. (There is a serious weakness here, to which we will return momentarily.) But what ideas do we have that individualize us mentally? We have ideas of our own body.

In individuating the self, then, Spinoza thinks that the body must have a priority. Since his argument for defining bodies is crucial for his entire theology, we need to look at it in some detail. In a famous section (following P13 in book 2), Spinoza defines bodies as "individual things" by means of motion and rest (lemma 3 proof). The first isolatable bodies are the *corpa simplicissima*, bodies with a relatively small quantity of motion and rest, which, as Rice correctly notes, need not be taken as basic particles in the sense of atomism.[10] At this first level of modal differentiation, bodies are continuous and homogenous; since no further distinguishing characteristics can be found for them, even in the purely physical terms of motion and rest, all their relations are external and no "internal" change can be recognized.[11]

What happens when we move to complex bodies?

> "When a number of bodies . . . form close contact with one another through the pressure of other bodies upon them, or if they are moving at the same or different rates of speed so as to preserve an unvarying relation of movement among themselves, these bodies are said to be united with one another, and all together to form one body or individual thing *(unum corpus, sive Individuum)*, which is distinguished from other things through this union of bodies." (E 2, P13 def.)

10. Lee C. Rice, "Spinoza on Individuation," in Maurice Mandelbaum and Eugene Freeman, eds., *Spinoza: Essays in Interpretation* (La Salle: Open Court, 1975), 195-214, esp. 200ff.

11. So also Matheron in his detailed treatment of the *corpa simplicissima:* "pour qu'ils possèdent une individualité distincte, il faut, ou bien que l'un d'entre eux se déplace alors que l'autre reste immobile, ou bien qu'ils se meuvent à des vitesses différentes . . . ce sont des individus qui se définissent entièrement par leur rapport externe à autrui" (Alexandre Matheron, *Individu et communauté chez Spinoza* [Paris: Minuit, 1969], 27).

This must mean that these composite bodies have distinct identities; they can come to be individuated and lose their individuality. The complexity of individuation increases again when "several individual things of different natures" are brought together (lemma 7, scholium). A molecule is already such a body, for it is composed of different atoms; a simple organism is composed of a number of molecules; humans are composed of organs, such as the liver; and so forth. The result is a hierarchy of ever more complex bodies composed of subbodies.

From this hierarchy Spinoza draws his famous metaphysical conclusion: "If we thus continue to infinity, we shall readily conceive the whole of Nature as one individual whose parts — that is, all the constituent bodies *(omnia corpora)* — vary in infinite ways without any change in the individual as a whole" (ibid.). Only when viewed from the top of the hierarchy, from the perspective of carrying the progression on "to infinity," is it true to say that there is only one self-existent thing, Nature, and that our identity is in some sense dependent on it. Viewed from lower points in the progression toward unity, there will appear to be many individual things. Thus, in Moreau's defense of Spinoza, the metaphor of the body is the key for combining substantial monism and modal pluralism: "the diversity of singular things . . . is a collection of single modes that are unified as the organs of one body. The universe must be considered as an individual Soul, of which the parts change without its ceasing still to persist in its form as a total Individual."[12]

What then of mind? According to book 2, the mind is the idea of the body: "The object of the idea constituting the human mind is the body . . . and nothing else" (E 2, P13). It is this idea "which constitutes the formal being of the human mind" (P15 proof). The content of this idea is the content of the interactions that the body undergoes. Note that no solipsism is meant here: when "the idea of the body" is adequate, it includes knowledge of the nature of the individual body as well as the natures of the external bodies with which it interacts (P16). We can thus say that knowledge of external bodies is mediated through the experiences of one's own body while not limited to the knowledge of that one body.

The idea of the mind is nothing else than the idea of an idea *(idea Mentis, hoc est, idea ideae;* E 2, P21 scholium), and — Spinozists now argue — this is just what we mean today by "consciousness."[13] These are murky waters upon first im-

---

12. Joseph Moreau, "Spinoza est-il monist?" *Revue de théologie et de philosophie* 115 (1983): 23-35, quotation 26.

13. I assume here, with many commentators, that the *idea ideae* was intended to fulfill a function similar to our concept of consciousness. Of course, as will become clear, there will

mersion (and not only then!). "The idea of an idea" certainly seems too passive to play the role of consciousness or the thinking self.[14] But Spinoza's defenders claim that no conscious center of the self is needed; it is sufficient to have the ascending ideas of ideas of ideas — embedded layers of propositional content — up to the universe as a whole. Indeed, this is what many most like about Spinoza's metaphysics: the naturalistic theory of consciousness. Human mental states are rooted in feeling for Spinoza (cf. E 3, P7-9), and "feeling is rooted in the bodily affections (emotions) of which the mind has only a partial and inadequate knowledge."[15] Self-consciousness is thus nothing more than the degree of the clarity of an individual's ideas. The human mind lacks adequate knowledge of itself: "The idea of the idea of any affection of the human body (Idea ideae cujuscunque affectionis Corporis humani) does not involve adequate knowledge of the human mind" (E 2, P29 and cor.). Awareness will thus necessarily be limited and defective: "We need not be conscious of all the elements that constitute our body: 'we' — 'our' soul-life, 'our' conscious selves — subsist for the most part as a vague feeling of bodily function. . . . An infinite number of the constituents of our 'mind' never for us enter into, or form part of, our soul-life at all."[16] Hence Bennett, for example, suggests that we read Spinoza as providing a "field metaphysic," according to which only space exists and all "bodies" are states or modifications of space in the sense of relativistic physics.[17]

Spinozism as it is being defended today represents in many ways an attractively modern stance. While providing the way to individuate persons by means of bodies, it also grants that bodies are only approximately defined entities, which change through time based on a (only partially stable) collection of atoms and molecules. Because there are constant exchanges of atoms ("simple bodies"), and because bodies only approximately retain their shape, identities

---

be changes if "there is in the mind no volition or affirmation and negation, save that which an idea, inasmuch as it is an idea, involves." Wallace Matson, "Spinoza's Theory of Mind," in Spinoza: Essays in Interpretation, ed. Maurice Mandelbaum and Eugene Freeman (La Salle: Open Court, 1975), 49-60, quotation 60, nicely describes the changes that must be made to the usual notion of self-consciousness when the will is taken away as a separate power and mind becomes "intelligence itself."

14. The criticism goes back to Hegel and his followers — and even earlier, as we will see below. See, e.g., Wolfgang Cramer, Spinozas Philosophie des Absoluten (Frankfurt: Vittorio Klostermann, 1966), 96-108.

15. Rice, "Spinoza on Individuation," 208; see the entire article for further arguments and references on Spinoza's view of the reflexive ideas. The major competing position is Jonathan Bennett, A Study of Spinoza's Ethics (Indianapolis: Hackett, 1984), 186ff., 357ff.

16. Harold H. Joachim, A Study of the Ethics of Spinoza (New York: Russell & Russell, 1901, repr. 1964), 131.

17. Bennett, Study of Spinoza's Ethics, par. 24.

become temporary, relative things; undecidable borderline cases need present no difficulties. Spinozism can give rise to a constructive research program in psychology as well.[18] One need not be exclusively a materialist or identity theorist to hold that psychological states depend on what the brain states are. Finally, Spinoza's naturalized view of God, while providing a metaphysical unification of all that is, does not stand in any tension with the methods or results of the natural sciences in the way that many other theological options do.

Criticisms

These strengths notwithstanding, Yovel is right to insist that Spinozism in its original form is no longer a viable option today. A series of recent treatments have driven home these difficulties, which I summarize under four main headings:

First, the appearance in the *Ethics* of deductive rigor is just that, an appearance; Spinoza's actual argument is not deductively valid. This conclusion comes as no surprise to those who have looked closely at the argumentative steps even in book 1. It is also suggested by the key role of the scholia in the development of Spinoza's position. Careful analyses of the definitions, axioms, and propositions that Spinoza cites make unmistakably clear that, whatever strengths the position has for those who wrestle with the God-question, the system is not a product of necessary inferences from indubitable definitions and axioms. Many individual steps in the argument of the *Ethics* are blatantly invalid.[19]

Second, the crux of Spinoza's argument in book 1 is his position on the relation between the one infinite substance and its infinite number of finite modes. But Spinoza fails to explain successfully the existence of finite modes based on the existence of the one substance. One of the central themes in the recent literature is Spinoza's failure to derive the finite modes from the infinite

18. For a detailed analysis of the parallels with contemporary philosophy of mind, especially the positions of Armstrong and Strawson, see Douglas Odegard, "The Body Identical with the Human Mind: A Problem in Spinoza's Philosophy," in Mandelbaum and Freeman, eds., *Spinoza: Essays in Interpretation,* 61-83.

19. See esp. Bennett's commentary, *Study of Spinoza's Ethics,* and the standard commentaries and collections, e.g., Alan Donagan; *Spinoza* (New York: Harvester-Wheatsheaf, 1988); Richard Kennington, ed., *The Philosophy of Baruch Spinoza* (Washington, D.C.: Catholic Univ. of America Press, 1980); Mandelbaum and Freeman, eds., *Spinoza: Essays in Interpretation;* and more recently the essays in Yovel, ed., *God and Nature: Spinoza's Metaphysics* (Leiden: Brill, 1991).

One.[20] What is required is that he connect the two parts of his position, show-ing how one can move rationally from the one substance to its division into in-finite modes. For it is not at all obvious why a single, simple substance should be modified into an infinite number of finite modes. (Taking them merely as empirical givens cuts against the grain of Spinoza's rationalist project.)[21] If all true predicates are to be predicated, ultimately, of the one substance, on what grounds can one say that there is any real difference between God and things?

How then does Spinoza explain the existence of finite modes or modifica-tions? It seems he cannot. The strength of his proposal lies in the absolute unity of substance and in the sufficiency of the modes for fully (and reciprocally) ex-plaining one another. In this system, the totality of finite determinations is sup-posed to explain any particular object and its behavior; each is this object and not another precisely because of the way it is limited by other finite objects (E 1, P28). Conversely, no finite predicates pertain to the one substance as such: modes may be expressions of the one, but it is not modified by or defined in terms of them. (In fact, it is not limited in any way; as fully positive, it can have no negative determinations.) Hallett has correctly portrayed the limit case of this process. He speaks of each mode as a "microcosm," a locus of relations that reflects the relations below it and is reflected in those above.[22] Under this con-ception, Nature is "an infinite 'web' or 'lattice,'" and finite agents are "the 'nodes' operating so as to form the indivisible integrity of the 'whole'" (p. 158).

Here is Spinoza's great unsolved problem: How are we to understand the derivation of the universe of finite modes from the one simple and eternal sub-stance? None of the qualities of God/Nature — eternality, necessary existence, simplicity — pertains to its modes, which are transitory, contingent, and com-

20. See esp. Joel Friedman, "How the Finite Follows from the Infinite in Spinoza's Metaphysical System," *Synthese* 69/3 (1986): 371-407; Frank Lucash, "On the Finite and Infi-nite in Spinoza," *Southern Journal of Philosophy* 20 (1982): 61-73; Bernard Rousset, "L'etre du fini dans l'infini selon l'Ethique' de Spinoza," *Revue philosophique de la France et de l'étranger* 176 (1986): 223-47; Errol Harris, "Infinity of Attributes and *Idea Ideae*," *Neue Hefte für Philosophie* 12 (1977): 9-20; Alan Donagan, "Spinoza's Dualism," in Kennington, ed., *Philoso-phy of Baruch Spinoza*, 89-102; and the literature cited in Emilia Giancotti, "On the Problem of Infinite Modes," in Yovel, ed., *God and Nature*, 114n.1.

21. Precisely this was the unsolved project that Spinoza inherited from the theistic tra-dition, which had worked to show why and how an infinite God could have created some-thing outside himself (if creating was a contingent choice, not dictated by his nature, why was it not arbitrary? if necessary, why should God be subject to some law "above" himself, and, if he is, how can he be given any credit for what he has created?).

22. H. F. Hallett, *Benedict de Spinoza* (London: Athlone, 1957), cited from the reprint in *Spinoza: A Collection of Critical Essays*, ed. Marjorie Grene (Garden City, N.Y.: Anchor, 1973), 154-60. The next reference in the text is also to this work.

plex.[23] Even if the move from individual modes (taken as extended spatio-temporal moments) to the whole of the physical universe were unproblematic, it is unclear how one should move from modes as thinking individuals to the one substance understood as pure thought, since Spinoza explicitly denies that God/Nature is conscious. I conclude that, viewed rigorously, this system offers the reader *two* realms, the finite and the infinite, which are linked in name alone. As the mind begins to see clearly, it sees *sub specie aeternitatis,* perceiving the connection of all together; it intuits the final unity. At the ultimate limit (but only there), "the distinction between part and whole absconds entirely."[24]

Third, if this is true, Spinoza is faced with a dilemma: either he preserves the monism of the *Ethics,* in which case the source of finite modes and their individuality remains unexplained; or he explicitly acknowledges the de facto independence of the modes (e.g., physical objects in the world), in which case monism is abandoned in all but name. The problem of individuation is ultimately insoluble for Spinozism.[25] It is not surprising that the more one stresses absolute monism, the more difficult it becomes to individuate persons and things adequately. Study of Spinoza's monistic passages reveals exactly this to be the case in his thought.[26] Obviously, Spinoza meant his system to be compatible with physical explanations of objects in the world, rather than dismissing ordinary experience as illusory. But then it becomes unclear what work the One does in accounting for finite things.

Fourth, is Spinoza's conception of the subject adequate? This question has been often raised in the history of Spinozism. Put in its strongest form, the criticism suggests that Spinoza's theory of mind is only a preliminary stage to German idealism, *ein Vorstadium zu Hegel.* As the rest of this chapter shows, I do think Spinoza's theory of the subject is unsatisfactory. To construe mind

23. In an important article Yovel shows that the problem — the unsolved gap — arises already in the move from the one substance to the infinite modes; see his "Infinite Mode and Natural Laws in Spinoza," in Yovel, ed., *God and Nature,* 79-96, e.g., 89.

24. William Sacksteder, "Simple Wholes and Complex Parts: Limiting Principles in Spinoza," *Philosophy and Phenomenological Research* 45 (1985): 393-406, quotation 403.

25. See Amihud Gilead, "Spinoza's *Principium individuationis* and Personal Identity," *International Studies in Philosophy* 15 (1983): 41-57; Mason, "Spinoza on the Causality of Individuals"; Marx W. Wartofsky, "Nature, Number and Individuals: Motive and Method in Spinoza's Philosophy," *Inquiry* 20 (1977): 457-79; Amélie Oksenberg Rorty, "The Two Faces of Spinoza," *Review of Metaphysics* 41 (1987): 299-316; Hermann de Dijn, "The Articulation of Nature, or the Relation God-Modes in Spinoza," *Giornale Critico della Filosofia Italiana* 8 (1977): 337-44.

26. See William Charlton, "Spinoza's Monism," *Philosophical Review* 90/4 (1981): 503-29; Peter Loptson, "Spinozist Monism," *Philosophia* 18 (1988): 19-38; Moreau, "Spinoza est-il moniste?"

merely as "the idea of the body" is too passive; it does not do justice to *thinking* — to mind as activity. Yet to introduce mind as a separate center of activity distinct from body, as I argue is necessary, is to break the bonds of Spinozism.

Mind understood as agency would also raise serious problems for his conception of God/Nature. According to Spinoza, "[God] constitutes the essence of our mind" (E 2, P34 proof); the two are understood as fully parallel. If there is any human consciousness that is not reducible to the reflection of body in the language of ideas, or any activity in God that is not just the idea of physical processes, then there will be a part of God-as-mental that is separate from (or more than) the physical universe. This would transform Spinoza's pantheism into panentheism; it would yield a God who encompassed the world but also transcended it. Most of the rest of this book defends precisely this move.

Yovel takes these (and other) difficulties to be sufficient reason for dismissing Spinozism. Arguing that Hegelianism also fails — an argument I cannot evaluate here — he attempts then to propel the reader on through Marxian materialism to a joyful acceptance of whatever Nietzsche has to offer.[27] But this sort of argument from history — Spinoza and Hegel fail in their projects, therefore philosophical theology as a whole shoud be abandoned — does not stand up to closer examination. (And if Yovel's is not an argument from history, it becomes unclear where the argument for immanence might lie.) For the eighteenth century also witnessed a number of reconstructions of Spinozism aimed at developing a more adequate theology after Spinoza. To the extent that these new positions make progress over Spinoza, the alleged inevitable movement toward Hegel (and, ultimately, Rorty) disappears.

Despite my critical comments on Spinoza, I do not deny the continued attractiveness of his view. Spinoza seemed (and seems) to many to offer the culmination of early modern metaphysics, as well as the perfect fusion of naturalistic physics with the meta-physical quest for a single substance as the ultimate basis for all that exists. Moreover, as the last chapter showed, Spinoza also worked out the logic of the infinite more adequately than any other thinker before him. He saw correctly that the infinite would have to exclude the finite — unless the finite could be understood as existing *within* the infinite. But if we exist "within" God then we are not really separate from the divine; we are in some sense modes of the One. If this is true, then Spinoza (and the religious mystics) would be partially vindicated.

---

27. The distance from Spinoza increases in the epilogue as Yovel dismisses the notion of the universe as *causa sui* (*Spinoza and Other Heretics*, 2:173) and asserts that "there is no *natura naturans* in Spinoza's sense, no infinite substantive unity underlying finite things in the world" (p. 175).

Yovel is right that the importance of Spinoza lies as much in the tradition of thought that was initiated by him (including his highly influential critics) as it does in his writings themselves. Grant for a moment (as I think we should) the validity of Spinoza's attack on Cartesian substance — that is, his demonstration that, given Descartes's theory of substance, there could ultimately be only one substance. Spinoza saw that, in this case, there is no longer a place for a world of independently existing substances, of individual things ontologically separate from God. Descartes's insight — "substance is that which exists in itself and is dependent on nothing else for its existence"[28] — spelled the end for the substance metaphysics that had dominated the Western philosophical tradition; now radical change was called for. Spinoza's solution was to say that all things are aspects of the one, universal substance, which is simultaneously God *and* Nature. This solution would represent the culmination of Western metaphysics — if serious difficulties with pantheism (and the need to conceive God as agent) do not make it incoherent to assert that God *just is* the world. If one rejects Spinoza's monism, it becomes urgent to work out some mediating position.

The quest for this mediating position provides the focus of this chapter. Could God still be conceived as *more than* the world even if the world is also *in* God? This will work only if God has (is) a conscious agency, that is, if God is more than the set of all existing things and includes the awareness of them. But what kind of theology can accomplish this? The reason the Spinozistic tradition deserves our close attention is that it struggled with these issues at a time when other thinkers (especially those in the Leibniz/Wolff school) were still working within the confines of traditional perfect-being theology. The thinkers explored in this and the following chapters recognized the difficulties with that tradition and attempted to find in a modified Spinozism a more adequate replacement.

THREE EARLY CRITICS

Before moving on to the major constructive thinkers of the eighteenth century, let us look at three of Spinoza's earliest critics — those who wanted nothing more than to expose the complete inadequacy (if not outright heresy) of his theology. Spinozism has been unfairly attacked more than any other position in modern thought. But in at least these three cases acute critics exposed serious weaknesses, setting in motion the constructive engagement with Spinoza's thought that was to follow.

28. *Principles,* I, 51.

Bayle

Pierre Bayle may be like many in his insistence that Spinozism is obviously wrong: "it is the most absurd and monstrous hypothesis that can be imagined, and the most contrary to the most evident notions of our mind."[29] Unlike most of his contemporaries, however, he became a serious student of Spinoza in order to make the case against him. Typically, he notes, "few people are suspected of adhering to his doctrine; and among those who are suspected of it, few have studied it; and among the latter, few have understood it, and most of them are discouraged by the difficulties and impenetrable abstractions that attend it" (French p. 418; Eng. p. 217).

What Bayle attacks in this famous article, "Spinoza" — the longest article in the entire thirteen-volume *Dictionnaire* — is no caricature of Spinoza's view. According to Bayle, Spinoza holds "that God, the necessary and most perfect Being, is the cause of all things that exist, but does not differ from them." In section N Bayle then considers six criticisms or "absurdities" of Spinoza's system — many of which, suitably reconstructed, are worthy of serious consideration today. If one leaves out the rhetorical flourishes and Christian question-beggings, one encounters the core of a rather substantial critique.

1. The first criticism has to do with the problem of thinking the unity of Spinoza's thought:

> It is impossible that the universe should be the only substance; for whatever is extended must necessarily consist of parts, and whatever consists of parts must be compounded: and as the parts of extension do not subsist one in another, it necessarily follows that extension in general is not a substance, or that each part of extension is a particular substance, and distinct from all others.

In other words, each extended thing must be its own substance. For Spinoza, extension and God are "one and the same thing." But this must be wrong, Bayle argues; the parts of a whole are distinct, just as each inch in a twelve-inch object is distinct from the others. Moreover, we find real distinctions between things; we can affirm real qualities of some that we cannot affirm of others. Indeed, Spinoza himself acknowledges as much when he grants (in Bayle's words) "that stones and animals are not the same modification of the infinite Being."

---

29. Pierre Bayle, "Spinoza," *Dictionnaire historique et critique de Pierre Bayle,* new ed. (Paris: Desoer Libraire, 1820), 13:416-68. See vol. 5 of *Mr Bayle's Historical and Critical Dictionary: The Second Edition* (London: 1738). The following references in the text are to these works.

What then of Spinoza's "pretended difference" between a real part and a modification? The seductiveness of Spinoza's system lies in the fact that he attempts to have it both ways. For purposes of immanence — or: from the perspective of infinity — modifications do not entail full difference. But for purposes of natural science — that is, from the perspective of finite (or ordinary) language — Spinoza's "extended modes" are supposed to capture all that we ordinarily mean by "part." This claim leads Bayle to raise the serious problem of *inconsistencies within the one substance.* Spinoza's theory requires that all actual states of affairs be predicated of a single substance. But how can this be done without contradiction? Whenever there are inconsistent modifications, Bayle insists, there must be multiple substances. This is certainly how we ordinarily talk; we say, for instance, that the round and the square table in a room must be different things. Can Spinozistic pantheism ultimately do justice to this sense of difference?

2. According to Bayle, not only does extension rob God of his simplicity, it also raises two further problems. First, it "reduces [God] to the condition of matter, the vilest of all beings," that which is immediately next to Nothing. Here orthodoxy begs the question against Spinoza; we can disregard this criticism. More interesting, however, is Bayle's argument that a spatially extended God (a God with a body) falls into contradiction. An immutable being never acquires any new (essential) qualities, whereas a mutable one may acquire and lose modifications. Now matter, generically speaking, undergoes modifications, hence it is essentially mutable stuff, "actually liable to all sorts of alternations and internal changes." Hence "the god of the Spinozists is a Being actually changing, that goes continually through several states internally and really different one from another. It is not therefore the most perfect Being." If Spinoza's god is immutable, Bayle adds, so too are the Roman gods![30]

3. Next comes a worry about the connection of the divine attributes. How are extension and thought combined in one and the same substance? Bayle asks. If they are one identity, then "they are therefore identified among themselves." Clearly Spinoza does not want to deny the distinction among the attributes. But how is the Spinozist to think their difference? This criticism, though rhetorical, is effective: Spinoza derided the doctrine of the Trinity, "and yet, properly speaking, he ascribed as many persons to the divine nature as there are persons upon earth." Thus he held "that the extended substance, though but one and indivisible, is all at once everywhere, cold in one place, hot in another,

---

30. For those of us willing to accept process within the divine, the loss of immutability may actually seem a desirable outcome. But Spinoza's own system does not allow for the one substance itself to change.

melancholy in one place, merry in another, etc." We accept as a basic rule of logic that "Two opposite terms cannot be truly affirmed of the same subject in the same respects, and at the same time"; are not Spinozists guilty of affirming this?

Worse, since attributions are made of substances, all the qualities that we attribute to persons should in Spinoza's system be attributed to God, so that "it is properly God who denies, who wills, who affirms, and consequently all the denominations, resulting from the thoughts of all persons, do properly and physically belong to the substance of God." Yet, again, this makes the law of opposites false: "As a square circle is a contradiction, a substance is so too, when it loves and hates the same object at the same time." Hence "all the variety and antipathy of the thoughts of humankind are made true and consistent at the same time in one and the same most simple and indivisible substance" — in short, "all the minds or thoughts of all persons are in one head."

4. Bayle thinks the problem is worse in the area of morality. In a famous passage he writes,

> for one good thought the infinite Being will have a thousand foolish, extravagant, filthy, and abominable. It will produce in itself all the follies, idle fancies, lewd and unjust practices of humankind . . . ; it will be united to them by the most intimate union that can be conceived; for it is a . . . perfect identity, since the modification is not really distinct from the modified substance. . . . Here is a philosopher, who is pleased to make God himself the agent and patient, the cause and subject of all the crimes and miseries of humankind.

In a passage made famous by Hegel, Bayle concludes that Spinoza holds the absurd position that, since there are only modifications, "human persons are only the modifications of one and the same Being, that consequently God only acts, and that the same individual God, being modified into Turks and Hungarians, wars and battles."

This, perhaps the most picturesque of Bayle's criticisms, is also, I suggest, one of his weakest. Bayle assumes that "modes do nothing; and that substances only act and suffer." Consequently, he infers that the proposition *the Germans have killed ten thousand Turks* really implies *God modified into Germans has killed God modified into ten thousand Turks.*[31] It is not difficult, however, to de-

---

31. This assumption allows Bayle to spin out a litany of absurdities: "God hates himself ; he asks favours of himself, and refuses them to himself; he persecutes himself, kills himself, eats himself, calumniates himself, executes himself, etc." — while remaining all the time in a state of "the most perfect simplicity."

fend the doctrine of modes without making God the sole agent. Modes can be viewed as actual agents, even if they are not taken as, *ultimately,* ontologically real. There is nothing inconsistent, for example, in a physical reductionist speaking of an organism or a person as the agent of an act (eating, reproducing) while still maintaining that the ultimate physical units are subatomic. God may well bear responsibility for occurrences if he has determined all outcomes, but this is not a problem that Spinoza bears alone; any personalist theism that accepts a deterministic doctrine of creation faces exactly the same problem.

5. Bayle's penultimate criticism fails if (4) fails. He points out that atheists as well as theists have always agreed that, if God exists, he possesses happiness or beatitude; even the Stoics, who denied God immortality, attributed unsurpassable happiness to the divine. But Spinoza's God "is subject to death, as to his parts or modalities" — indeed, "he destroys his own modalities." For Spinoza's God "would annihilate himself if he could; . . . he deprives himself of as many things as he can; he hangs himself, he throws himself headlong down a precipice." Unfortunately, in this passage Bayle again employs the assumption that if humans are only a modification, they do nothing. Since we have already seen that this assumption need not be true, this criticism falls for the same reason as the previous one.

6. Finally, Bayle argues, if all thoughts are modes of the infinite being — that is, "realities as necessary to the perfection of the universe as all his speculations" — then how "can [Spinoza] pretend that they want to be rectified?" If nature acts necessarily, then Spinoza's ethical exhortations are needless, for how can a mere mode change God, the whole? Bayle was one of the first to raise the famous charge that Spinozism implies fatalism. We return to this charge below. For now, note that the criticism presupposes a forced choice between libertarianism (which Spinoza rejects) and fatalistic determinism. If, however, compatibilism is an option, then this particular threat is declawed.

Bayle's six criticisms represent the best of the early opposition to Spinoza. Metaphysics and theology were still very closely allied. Thus the critics combined a sense of outrage at the heretical nature of Spinoza's philosophy with the best conceptual criticisms they could muster.[32] The complaints that were moti-

---

32. "Sans doute, il [Bayle] ne faut pas attacher d'importance au ton indigné qu'il prend pour stigmatiser l'impiété du spinozisme, ni aux airs qu'il se donne d'un sant Michel terrassant le dragon. . . . Nul doute que Bayle au fond n'estime très haut Spinoza, pour la beauté de sa morale et la hardiesse de ses interprétations de la religion révélée" (Jean Delvolve, *Religion, critique et philosophie positive chez Pierre Bayle* [Paris: 1906; repr. Geneva: Slatkine, 1970], 260). See also Leszek Kolakowsky, "Pierre Bayle, critique de la métaphysique spinoziste de la Substance," in Paul Dibon, ed., *Pierre Bayle: Le Philosophie de Rotterdam* (Paris: Vrin, 1959), 66-80.

vated only by outrage are no longer of interest to us. But Bayle's *Dictionnaire* article is a step above the rest; it offers serious criticisms — some of which, I suggest, Spinoza's philosophy is not in the position to answer.

What then is the upshot of this first round?[33] As Yovel has suggested, Spinozism stands for the project of immanence, the denial of transcendence. If the project is to succeed, Spinozists will have to address Bayle's criticisms, formulating for example an account of God/Nature that encompasses both good and evil (and contradictions) within itself. This will require a viable theory of how finite modes stem from and are contained within the infinite. If they fail to meet this challenge, if finite things or modes cannot be explained by positing a single overarching substance, then it becomes mere metaphysical hand waving to assert that they are encompassed within the One. Put differently, pantheism will constitute the best explanation only if it can explain the finite.

Horchius

Yovel tells one side of Spinoza's story: the outsider who became a whipping boy for orthodoxy. There is definitely truth in this tale, since Spinozism did come to be equated with atheism and thus with everything that the early eighteenth century found evil. Many early critics dismissed Spinoza with charges that he was heretical, Satanic, and worse.[34] Still, others raised difficulties that did not turn on the authors' preference for orthodox morality or more traditional theologies. Consider, for example, the two central criticisms raised by Heinrich Horch (Horchius) in his 1692 *Investigationes theologicae circa origines rerum ex Deo contra Spinozam,* which poses serious questions about the tenability of Spinozism as a philosophical position.

Horchius first asks about the status and coherence of the divine attributes in Spinoza's theology.[35] Does he predicate qualities of the one substance

---

33. See Ira O. Wade, *The Structure and Form of the French Enlightenment,* 2 vols. (Princeton: Princeton Univ. Press, 1977), 1:78.

34. For a detailed account of the early criticisms see Han-Ding Hong, *Spinoza und die deutsche Philosophie* (Aalen: Scientia, 1989). Other works that trace the massive influence of Spinoza on German philosophy in the eighteenth and early nineteenth century include S. Zac, *Spinoza en Allemagne: Mendelssohn, Lessing et Jacobi* (Paris: 1989).

35. The following criticisms are drawn from Heinrich Horch (Horchius), *Investigationes theologicae circa origines rerum ex Deo contra Spinozam* (1692; Breslauer Stadtbibliothek). I have been especially helped by the excerpts and excellent summary in Franz Erhardt, *Die Philosophie des Spinoza im Lichte der Kritik* (Leipzig: O. R. Reisland, 1908), 480ff.

that are conceptually coherent? Horchius answers in the negative. On the one hand, the various divine attributes in the *Ethics* lack any necessity of their own, since they are only infinite in their own species (rather than absolutely perfect). This means that they do not exist through the necessity of their own nature independent of any cause outside themselves. On the other hand, they must lack any interdependent necessity, since they are supposed to be fully independent of one another. The problem is actually compounded: there is supposed to be an irreducible multiplicity of attributes. But Spinoza defines attributes in the same way as substances in the famous Ninth Letter.[36] Thus, Horchius concludes, either there are multiple substances corresponding to the multiple attributes — which makes extended things separate from thinking things — or Spinoza must posit a single, ultimately simple attribute that expresses everything contained in the nature of God. For example, he might take the route of idealism and say that the attribute of thought has precedence. Of course, this would mean denying that God/Nature is both mental and extended.

Second, according to Horchius the situation is equally bleak for Spinoza's modes. As modes of the divine attributes, flowing with necessity from God, they must share in all the divine perfections (they must "be God"). Hence their imperfections must pertain to God: "For singular things in the infinite mode necessarily exist, since they flow from the necessity of the divine nature; in the finite mode they do not exist necessarily. At the same time they both depend on God, indeed depend necessarily, and do not depend on God but on themselves invincibly and infinitely."[37] Thus, it appears, things are both necessary and nonnecessary (since their essence does not include their existence); they are both eternal and noneternal (since they are in time); and extension is both indivisible (to the extent that it is a simple attribute) and divisible (in order to differentiate the extended modes). Not a happy state of affairs for a rationalist theology!

---

36. "By substance I understand what is in itself and is conceived through itself, i.e. whose concept does not involve the concept of another thing. I understand the same by attribute, except that it is called attribute in relation to the intellect, which attributes such and such a definite nature to substance" (in Edwin Curley, ed. and trans., *The Collected Works of Spinoza*, vol. 1 (Princeton: Princeton Univ. Press, 1985), 195.

37. "Res enim singulares modo facit infinitas et necessario existentes, quippe ex necessitate divinae naturae oriundas; modo finitas et non necessario existentes. Rursus easdem facit dependentes a Deo, imo necessario dependentes, et mox non dependentes a Deo, sed a se invicem tantum, idque in infinitum" (Horchius, 37; cited in Erhardt, *Philosophie des Spinoza*, 481).

Lami

Horchius's criticisms are supplemented by the 1696 *Traités* by Lami, which revolve around two major themes. According to *Traité* I, body and soul must be taken as true substances, not as mere modes. Lami argues that this follows directly from Spinoza's requirement that a substance be comprehended through itself: since body and soul must each be comprehended through themselves and not through the other, they must represent separate substances. Further, multiple attributes should entail multiple substances; hence God may be characterized by the attribute of thought, but not by both thought and body. (His following argument — that the union of body and soul in humans requires us to posit an infinitely wise God as its external cause, and that order in nature requires the same — is no longer convincing. Nor need we pause to consider the lengthy defense of Christian doctrine in *Traité* II.)

In the third *Traité* Lami righly rejects the crucial E 1, P4 ("Two or more distinct things are distinguished from one another, either by a difference in the attributes of the substances or by a difference in their affections"). Instead, things can really be distinguished "without there being any diversity either in their essential perfections or in their accidents."[38] But then the alleged impossibility of one substance bringing forth another is no longer convincing; P7 and P8 in E 1 become suspect, and we no longer need to assert that all things are either attributes or modes of God.

A second important criticism involves the claim that the divine attributes are completely separate. It is false that every attribute can only be understood through itself, for each also includes (as Spinoza himself admits) the idea of substance. But then the attributes cannot be understood without connection to the others; they share the common property of belonging to the same substance, and where they lack this they must belong to different substances (299-30). "A diversity of attributes results in a diversity of substances; in reality, therefore, Spinoza has instead of one substance infinitely many substances."[39]

Like others at the turn of the century, Lami argues that Spinoza is a fatalist and hence an enemy of morality. Denying human uniqueness and leaving no impetus for moral improvement, he "transforms man into a beast, after having transformed God into a machine." Such criticisms need not detain us, but two

---

38. "Sans qu'il y ait aucune diversité, ni dans leurs perfections essentielles, ni dans les accidentelles" (*Traité* III, 269, cf. 310ff.; quoted in Erhardt, *Philosophie des Spinoza*, 483. To my knowledge this work is available only at the library of the University of Leiden).

39. "Verschiedenheit der Attribute ergibt eine Verschiedenheit der Substanzen; in Wirklichkeit hat daher Spinoza statt der einen unendlich viele Substanzen (301ff.)" (Erhardt, *Philosophie des Spinoza*, 484).

final (passing) criticisms should. Lami points out, interestingly, that Spinoza's God cannot be an efficient cause of things. For things can come into existence only by emanating from God or being brought into being with God as their efficient cause. Hence Spinoza's "god is not the cause of anything. . . . One can be assured that nothing exists, that is, no creature, no particular being."[40] Lami also observes that modes are both necessary (as part of God) and not necessary (because their essence does not imply existence). This ambiguity in their status exactly parallels what I have called the root difficulty in Spinoza's system — his failure to derive the finite from the infinite.

It would be false to say that any of these three early critiques decisively falsifies the Spinozistic system or makes the subsequent popularity and influence of Spinoza inexplicable. Still, they do correct the widespread misapprehension that Spinozism encountered nothing but prejudice and misunderstanding until (roughly) Lessing. Serious philosophical difficulties were raised by some of the early critics and were part of the public conversation, helping to justify the turn away from Spinoza. Yovel's tale of the Spinoza tradition thus needs modifying: not (only) an outmoded desire for transcendent certainties but also the inherent flaws in Spinoza's own theology of immanence justified its rejection.

As we will see later, it may be possible to maintain the notion of the whole, the one substance, as a limiting principle, an ideal of transcendental unity.[41] But this will require a rethinking of Spinoza's metaphysics in a Kantian direction that he could never have intended. In order to see whether such a reconstruction of Spinozism may be successful, it is first necessary to examine the series of modifications and refinements that it underwent in the course of the eighteenth century.

SPINOZISM AS CONSTRUCTIVE THEOLOGY: THE "SPINOZA DISPUTE"

We skip over Leibniz, Wolff, and their followers to roughly the year 1760.[42] These "ontotheologians" provide Yovel with his best evidence of anti-Spinoza

---

40. "Son dieu n'est cause de rien; . . . on peut assurer que rien n'existe, c'est-à dire nulle creature, nul être particulier" (345; in Erhardt, *Philosophie des Spinoza*, 484).

41. So William Sacksteder, "Simple Wholes and Complex Parts: Limiting Principles in Spinoza," *Philosophy and Phenomenological Research* 45 (1985): 393-406.

42. In the following I focus on the German discussion. Space allowing, one could, however, make the same argument by tracing the Spinoza reception in France. For an idea of

prejudice, since they show no interest in understanding Spinoza but only in refuting the dangers of his heresies by any means, fair or unfair.[43] Yet it is hardly adequate to determine the role of a thinker on the basis of those who have ignored him; one must look at those who drew explicitly on his work (whether as admirers or opponents). No event was more significant for modern philosophical theology than the famous "Spinoza Dispute" *(Spinozastreit)* between Jacobi and Mendelssohn regarding the alleged Spinozism of the recently deceased Lessing. There is no point in reconstructing in full detail the course of the *Spinozastreit*, as it may be the most discussed dispute in the history of German philosophy.[44] Instead, after the briefest sketch of the historical background, let us concentrate instead on the arguments and positions of the disputants themselves.

---

how the argument would proceed, see Olivier Bloch, ed., *Spinoza au XVIIIᵉ Siècle* (Paris: Méridiens Klincksieck, 1990); Paul Vernière, *Spinoza et la pensée française avant la Révolution*, 2nd ed. (Paris: Presses Universitaires de France, 1982); Ira O. Wade, *The Structure and Form of the French Enlightenment*, vol. 1: *Esprit Philosophique* (Princeton: Princeton Univ. Press, 1977).

I am grateful to Frederick Beiser for criticisms of a version of the following pages that I read at the Central Division American Philosophical Association meetings in May 1994.

43. Wolff makes a particularly interesting study. He treats Spinoza in a chapter of the *Theologia naturalis* entitled "De Paganismo, Manicheismo, Spinozismo et Epicuraeismo" — certainly unpleasant bedfellows in eighteenth-century eyes! But his treatment of this, "the most terrible of the dangerous enemies of the truth" (see the German edition, under "Spinosisterey"), concentrates on the definitions rather than the arguments in the propositions. Even so, he treats them out of order and omits any discussion of the definitions of freedom and eternity, areas in which his own philosophy had been labeled "Spinozistic"!

44. See recently Gérard Vallée, ed., *The Spinoza Conversations between Lessing and Jacobi: Text with Excerpts from the Ensuing Controversy*, trans. G. Vallée, J. B. Lawson, and C. G. Chapple (Lanham: Univ. Press of America, 1988). For details on the chronological development of the dispute see Kurt Christ, *Jacobi und Mendelssohn: Eine Analyse des Spinozastreits* (Würzburg: Königshausen & Neumann, 1988); also cf. Alfred Hebeisen, *Friedrich Heinrich Jacobi: Seine Auseinandersetzung mit Spinoza* (Bern: Paul Haupt, 1960); Hans Hölters, *Der spinozistische Gottesbegriff bei M. Mendelssohn und F. H. Jacobi und der Gottesbegriff Spinozas* (Emsdetten, 1938); and Helmut Thielicke, *Offenbarung, Vernunft und Existenz: Studien zur Religionsphilosophie Lessings* (Gütersloh: Bertelsmann, 1957), e.g., 105-14. It is undoubtedly the personal element of this dispute — passionate, often unfair, in many ways counterproductive to any serious study of Spinoza's texts, but immensely influential — that has attracted such massive attention in the secondary literature, going back all the way to the first years after its publication. From the start (and up to the present) it has remained unclear what morals should be derived from the dispute, with each author listing his own detailed versions of the dispute and its implications. The tradition goes back to Thomas Wizenmann's monograph *Die Resultate der Jacobischen und Mendelssohnschen Philosophie* (Leipzig: G. J. Göschen, 1786; repr. Hildesheim: Gerstenberg, 1984).

The dispute was launched by Jacobi's claim that the recently deceased Lessing had been a closet Spinozist. The gauntlet was cast down in Jacobi's famous sub-rosa letter to Elise Reimarus of July 21, 1783, in which he provides an (allegedly) verbatim account of his conversations with Lessing and of Lessing's enthusiastic embrace of Spinoza's theology.[45] If this account were accurate — and many believed (and believe) that it was — Lessing would have been in complete accord with Spinoza's philosophy, denying belief in the transcendence of God, divine personhood, creation, the ontological preeminence of divine wisdom, final causes, and the liberty of belief of both God and humankind. What makes the whole debate particularly interesting is that we have ample reason to discount Jacobi as a reliable narrator, which makes what Lessing might really have said painfully elusive. But we must pass over the complicated arguments for and against Jacobi's intentions and ultimate reliability.

Stunned by this shocking exposé of his long-time friend and one of the key champions of the German Enlightenment, Mendelssohn decided to present his own account of the precise sense in which Lessing was and was not a Spinozist; he rushed to publish the *Morgenstunden*, before Jacobi could corrupt the public with his version. But Jacobi, not about to let Mendelssohn define the debate in his own terms, proceeded immediately to publish a complete record of his private correspondence with Mendelssohn, complete with (unflattering) embellishments. The published work includes at least three separate accounts of the essence of Spinoza's doctrine, which (despite their critical intent) were immensely important in advancing Spinozistic thought. Deeply upset at what he judged to be an unforgiveable breach of confidence, Mendelssohn realized that if Jacobi's charges were believed it would discredit the entire project of rational theism, insofar as it would imply that the use of reason had in the end finally driven Lessing, the Enlightenment leader, to atheism and fatalism. In the few remaining years before his death, Mendelssohn worked frantically in his correspondence and in his final book, *An die Freunde Lessings,* trying to show that Jacobi's account of Spinoza was deeply flawed and even "incomprehensible."

What is ironic about the whole debate and its significance for our question is that neither was really an advocate of Spinozism. In *An die Freunde Lessings* Mendelssohn says he is sure of the untruth of Spinozism; worse, Jacobi sees Spinozism as the archetype of natural theology and rational metaphysics, which must be supplemented by Christian faith in order to yield orthodox belief. Strict pantheism, the position that no one holds, is everyone's preoccupation and no one's thesis!

Out of this mess of confusions and mutual recriminations, however,

---

45. See Christ, *Jacobi und Mendelssohn,* chap. 5, esp. pp. 76ff.

emerged important new ideas for interpreting Spinoza, for reconstructing Spinozistic theology in a more rigorous and palatable form — and the first positive press Spinoza ever received in the history of modern thought. The whole debate became a crucial ingredient in the thought world out of which German idealism — and later Schleiermacher, the so-called father of modern theology — would soon emerge. This fact gave Spinozism an immense influence on nineteenth-century philosophy and theology. As Yovel writes, Spinoza's name "dominated German philosophy for half a century, next to Kant's philosophy and as a complement to it."[46]

Lessing

When one goes back to Lessing's writings after the confusion of the later *Spinozastreit,* one is struck afresh by his creativity and insight. Lessing is not afraid of heresy (nor of playfulness!); he deeply respects Spinoza's thought and plays openly with all the various possibilities of God's relation to the world. Among pre-Kantian philosophers, none better instantiates the attractive side of Spinozism than Lessing. His religious pluralism, his nondogmatic style of philosophizing, and his creative experimentation with a variety of theological positions are refreshing antidotes to Continental rationalism of the Leibniz and Wolff varieties.[47]

Here is the (alleged) conversation that shocked the German intellectual world: Jacobi: "Then you would indeed be more or less in agreement with

46. Yovel, *Spinoza and Other Heretics,* 2:188.

47. It is the first of these qualities, Lessing's theological pluralism, that Henry Allison admits was the motivation for his *Lessing and the Enlightenment: His Philosophy of Religion and Its Relation to Eighteenth-Century Thought* (Ann Arbor: Univ. of Michigan Press, 1966). The Lessing he defends is the Lessing of "It is not the truth which a man possesses, or believes that he possesses, but the earnest effort which he puts forth to reach the truth, which constitutes the worth of a man. For it is not by the possession, but by the search after truth that he enlarges his power, wherein alone consists his ever-increasing perfection. Possession makes one content, indolent, proud" (G. E. Lessing, *Gesammelte Werke,* 10 vols., ed. Paul Rilla [Berlin, 1956], 8:27). Allison's preference is especially clear in the reading of *Nathan der Weise* that culminates the book. See also Allison, "Lessing's Concept of Revelation as Education," in Harold Pagliaro, ed., *Studies in Eighteenth-Century Culture,* vol. 4 (Madison: Univ. of Wisconsin Press, 1975), 183-93.

When he does metaphysics, Lessing is probably closer in attitude to the typical contemporary Anglo-American philosopher than any other German thinker between Spinoza and Kant. We must thus agree with Allison when, in his major criticism of Yovel's *Spinoza and Other Heretics,* he faults him more strongly for ignoring Lessing than for any other omission.

Spinoza"; Lessing: "If I am to call myself by anybody's name, then I know none better." Hardly conclusive proof. But even if Jacobi completely fabricated the report of his conversation with Lessing, Lessing's important borrowings from Spinoza would still be unmistakable.[48] Indeed, the passages in Lessing's theological/metaphysical writings that are the most intriguing are precisely the ones in which he reflects *sub specie Spinozitatis*. God's unity, he writes in *The Education of the Human Race* §73, "must be a transcendental unity which does not exclude a sort of plurality"; he must have "the most perfect conception of himself, i.e. a conception *which contains everything which is in him*."[49] Could it be, then, that Lessing is the philosopher who completed Spinoza's unfinished task, overcoming the finite/infinite gap and explaining how finite modes derive from the infinite within the whole of nature?

The Theological Position

The passages from *The Education of the Human Race* just cited, when read together with other of Lessing's writings, clearly espouse some form of *panentheism*. For these passages assert both the immanence and transcendence, the unity and diversity, of God, as well as God's creation of a world that is in some sense made out of — and hence somehow remains within — the divine self. Merely to note this both/and is not enough, however; one needs to know the precise view that Lessing held, why he held it, and whether he achieved a position that is superior to the alternatives. It is my thesis, first, that Lessing's view is not fully distinct from classical theism, and certainly not fully Spinozistic; second, that where he makes suggestions that *are* distinct from it, they remain at the level of hints and promissory notes rather than offering a viable theological alternative. Because we can observe in Lessing's writings both what is tempting about Spinoza and why these temptations fail to convince, his work amounts to a particularly good example of what is seductive about theologies of immanence.

48. Allison marshals some of the key evidence in his "Lessing's Spinozistic Exercises," in Ehrhard Bahr et al., *Humanität und Dialog: Lessing und Mendelssohn in neuer Sicht*, Beiheft zum Lessing Yearbook (Detroit: Wayne State Univ. Press, 1982), 223-33. Since Allison makes his case primarily from early letters and fragments, however, one could still argue that Lessing later forsook Spinoza for Leibniz. Even more persuasive is a possibility Allison himself mentions in closing: that Lessing is trying to show Mendelssohn that, on the latter's own premises, "Spinoza emerges as something more than a stepping stone to Leibniz." (The Jacobi conversation is quoted from Vallée, ed., *Spinoza Conversations*, 85.)

49. See §§73-74 of *The Education of the Human Race*, in Henry Chadwick, ed. and trans., *Lessing's Theological Writings* (London: Adam and Charles Black, 1956), italics added.

Lessing may have been dissatisfied with traditional theism, but he could not accept a full pantheism. He speaks of God not as ultimately one and simple; instead, the "Christianity of reason" meant for him *multiplicity within God*. He does advance, after the fashion of the neologians[50] (and later Hegel), several arguments for a trinitarian understanding of God. In his early essay "The Christianity of Reason," in language reminiscent of Leibniz, Lessing writes: "(13) God contemplated his perfections individually, that is, he created beings each one of which has something of his perfections; for, to repeat it once again, every thought is a creation with God. (14) All these beings together are called the World."[51]

Yet clearly a trinitarian account of the divine economy stands closer to orthodox concepts than to Spinoza's single substance with modifications. Thus Jacobi is certainly wrong to call §73 a pantheistic theology of identity *(pantheistische Identitätstheologie)*. Still, Lessing correctly realizes the difficulties for Christian theology. As Leibniz had already noted, there is a very close relation between God's thinking of the best of all worlds and the existence of that world: "There could therefore be an indefinite number of possible worlds were it not that God thinks always of the most perfect, and thus amongst all these thought the most perfect of worlds, *and so made it real*" (ibid., emphasis mine). Clearly, no separate act of will would be required on God's part, for his knowing the best possible overall state of affairs already assures its existence.

This text has given rise to a debate between two very different versions of panentheism, and we must pause for a moment to resolve the debate. Clearly, if merely to think of the world is to "make it real" (and necessarily so), then the world would have to depend ontologically on God. The question has to do with the sense in which panentheists understand creation.[52] At first it appears that Lessing is arguing that to be thought by God is a sufficient condition for existence. We might call such a theology "ontological inflation": to be thought by God is a sufficient condition for existence, and all existence is "within" God. Unfortunately, this sort of theology removes God's ability to think anything as merely possible or to think any counterfactuals at all (e.g., "although the photon was omitted at t_1 it might have be omitted at t_2"). It also threatens to reduce the very meaning of "existence" to "being a divine thought" (and the relationship would have to be necessary, since it could not "just happen" that the denotation of the two terms was the same); but this conflates two terms that there is

50. See the classic study by Karl Aner, *Die Theologie der Lessingzeit* (Halle, 1927).

51. Chadwick, ed. and trans., *Lessing's Theological Writings*, 100. The next reference in the text is also to this work.

52. For more details, see Clayton, *God and Contemporary Science* (Edinburgh: Edinburgh Univ. Press; Grand Rapids: Eerdmans, 1997).

good reason to keep conceptually separate. Finally, such a view would imply either that all God's thoughts exist in a robust way outside him (every thought gives rise to another creation), or that existence means nothing more than being a thought of God.[53]

Preferable, then, is a version of panentheism that retains a logical difference between God's thinking and a thing's existence; they are logically distinct states, even if temporally simultaneous. God could think of something without creating it, for instance, by having the thought of something without willing or intending to create it. Lessing's position, construed in this way, is thus compatible with conceiving (and is theologically more acceptable if we conceive) the world as conceptually distinct from God (even if internal to God), for example, as the set of contingent things that are grounded in the divine necessity. Certainly Lessing's emphatic concern with God's revelation in the world (e.g., with Christ as divine self-revelation) presupposes an ontological distinction that is foreign to Spinozism. Many studies of Lessing on religion note his preoccupation with God's revelation in the historical or positive religions.[54] How can one understand Lessing's concern with Christ as moral teacher without imagining the world as conceptually distinct from God? "Thus Christ came. One will forgive me that I can only view him here as a divinely inspired teacher."[55] And how else can one interpret his concern with progressive human insight into the divine nature and character? "And why should not we too, by means of a religion whose historical truth, if you will, looks dubious, be led in a similar way to closer and better conceptions of the divine Being, of our own nature, of our relation to God, which human reason would never have reached on its own?"[56]

I conclude that the heart of the position is a version of panentheism rather than Spinozistic pantheism, albeit one that relies mainly on aphoristic hints of a more intimate, "internal" relation between God and world than theistic orthodoxy had allowed. Where Lessing speaks of a full unity, it should be interpreted as a final abstraction: God understood as ultimate transcendental One, logically prior to (or in abstraction from) all divine development and cre-

---

53. Yet I see no reason why one would need or wish to use the term *God* in this manner.

54. For Lessing on religion see Gottfried Fittbogen, *Die Religion Lessings*, Palaestra 141 (Leipzig: Mayer und Müller, 1923; repr. New York: Johnson, 1967).

55. "Christus kam also. Man vergönne mir, daß ich ihn hier nur als einen von Gott erleuchteten Lehrer ansehen darf" (Kurt Wölfel, ed., *Lessings Werke*, 3 vols. [Frankfurt: Insel, 1967], 3:241).

56. See K. Lachmann and F. Muncker, eds., *G. E. Lessings Sämtliche Schriften* (Leipzig, 1900), 15:610-11; quoted in Chadwick, *Lessing's Theological Writings*, 95; and Allison, *Lessing and the Enlightenment*, 158.

ation. The ultimate stage in this process of abstraction might well be something like Spinoza's monism, *deus siva natura* — even though Lessing never took it this far. Henry Allison notes correctly that "the unity of God cannot be conceived in the same manner as finite things, that the unity of an infinite being must be a 'transcendental unity, which does not exclude a sort of plurality, which is grounded in divine self-consciousness.'"[57]

The Criticisms

Recall that we are looking for an answer to the problem raised by Spinoza's philosophy: How can the world be thought as essentially linked to God, even as internal to God, without facing the unacceptable consequences of equating the world and God? We found evidence that Lessing (in his more speculative moments) was struggling with the same set of issues. Did he find a solution? There are two major reasons to think that he did not. First, Lessing was unfortunately no more a metaphysician than, say, Nietzsche was. Though his aphorisms are intriguing and suggestive, the intuitions behind them remain undeveloped; he offers no systematic (or even consistent) theology to tie them together.[58] However much Lessing personifies the ideal of religious tolerance, one finds no overarching vision underlying the numerous intriguing hints in his writings. Even his famous allusion to God as the "one and all" *(hen kai pan)* reported by Jacobi is just an offhand comment in a conversation, presumably half in jest, and certainly one incompatible with his own trinitarian speculations elsewhere. Lessing remains important because he was the first major (popular) intellectual to be brought out of the closet as a sincere follower of Spinoza — if only posthumously, unwillingly, and to serve the purposes of the orthodox theologian Jacobi with whom he was presumably in deep disagreement.[59]

---

57. Allison, *Lessing and the Enlightenment,* 157.

58. That Lessing failed to be a systematic thinker, and even had reasons intentionally to eschew this ideal, has long been recognized. See, e.g., Joachim Desch, "Vernünfteln wider die Vernunft: Zu Lessings Begriff eines konsequenten Rationalismus," in Bahr et al., *Humanität und Dialog,* 133-41; and, more strongly, Gerd Hillen, "Lessing — ein Philosoph?" in ibid., 165-73. Isn't Lessing's very interest in religious pluralism a sign that he is not interested in a single theory of religion? I suggest that Lessing was far more concerned with the problem of history and Christianity — whether and how Christian truth could be based on a historical occurrence — than he was with resolving metaphysical disputes.

59. Jacobi's revelation of Lessing's Spinozism was a brilliant rhetorical ploy for refuting Mendelssohn's free-thinking Enlightenment rationalism. On the one hand, if Mendelssohn denied Lessing's Spinozism, it would appear that he did not really know Lessing that well — but his friendship with Lessing was a major component of his attempt to overcome suspicion of his Jewishness and to win acceptance for his rationalist theology. On the other

Second, many of the broader themes of Lessing's philosophy are incompatible with Spinozism. *Nathan the Wise* urges tolerance of the existing positive religions, not the attempt to transcend them into a single religion of reason.[60] *The Education of the Human Race* imagines a historical process of development quite foreign to the timeless mystical process envisioned by Spinoza. Where he does speculate about an absolute unity, Lessing's purpose is not to defend metaphysical monism but rather to suggest a rational demonstration of the dogma of the Trinity, a way to think the Son eternally begotten. Moreover, his insistence on a place for the will within God has no parallel in Spinoza. In the final analysis the oft-cited essay, "The Christianity of Reason," is undoubtedly more Leibnizian (and trinitarian) than Spinozistic, inasmuch as it is controlled by the opening propositions: "The one most perfect Being has from eternity been able to be concerned only with the consideration of what is the most perfect thing. The most perfect thing is himself; and thus from eternity God has only been able to contemplate himself."[61]

Lessing's life project, I suggest, was to think together both immanence and transcendence, both unity and plurality, in God. He continually seeks to avoid the two main mistakes (and the traditional dichotomy) of philosophical theology: on the one side, an anthropomorphic view of God as a perfect individual, a quasi-human person with intellect and will; on the other, a purely negative concept of God as the absolutely undifferentiated infinite, the apophantic One above all distinctions. Lessing's answer in his few speculative passages is a trinitarian panentheism, according to which God is a pure activity that gradually externalizes (from) itself into the world as we know it.[62] His

---

hand, if he affirmed it, he would associate his rationalist program with atheism and heresy — exactly the slurs from which he was trying to free it. Trying to fight this dilemma drove Mendelssohn back to one of the closest studies of Spinoza's writings of any of his contemporaries — and, unfortunately, ever deeper into the trap that Jacobi had set for him. Little wonder theirs became one of the most bitter correspondences of the late eighteenth century.

60. See Sylvain Zac, "Lessing et Spinoza," in Bloch, ed., *Spinoza au XVIIIᵉ Siècle*, 255ff., e.g., "Chez Spinoza la religion philosophique est constituée seulement de vérités nécessaires, démonstrables par la seule raison" (p. 257).

61. Others have noted the relative priority of Leibniz over Spinoza in Lessing's thought; see Fittbogen, *Die Religion Lessings* and Bernd Bothe, *Glauben und Erkennen: Studie zur Religionsphilosophie Lessings* (Meisenheim am Glan: Anton Hain, 1972). One hardly needs a monograph to see this point: the perfection argument, foreign to Spinoza, runs throughout "The Christianity of Reason"; §15 appeals explicitly to the possible worlds argument in its Leibnizian form; §§16-18 presuppose the hierarchy of monads; §20 appeals to a (preestablished) harmony; and §27 uses the principle of the plenum.

62. I draw support for this claim from Hermann Timm's excellent book, *Gott und die Freiheit: Studien zur Religionsphilosophie der Goethezeit*, vol. 1: *Die Spinozarenaissance*

overriding interest is not the one substance but the notion of spirit *(Geist)*. The advantage of this concept, Lessing claims (again anticipating German idealism), is that it overcomes the traditional dichotomy by allowing for a fusion of identity and difference. Since discursive reflection necessarily distinguishes between the various aspects of divine creative activity, whatever view of God one develops cannot limit itself to viewing them merely as "moments of God's consciousness" or "modes of God/Nature." Instead, it is rationally preferable to speak of them as individual things, that is, as parts of a world that is not identical to God.[63] To put it baldly: if God thinks himself, he is already dualistic or trinitarian. If God/Nature were to be one, strictly speaking, it could not even be characterized as spirit — which is perhaps why Spinoza denied God/Nature its own consciousness.

Consequently, what is distinctive in Lessing's doctrine of God is his attempt to think personality into Spinoza's impersonal absoluteness of divine being.[64] Lessing's starting point is perhaps closest to the undifferentiated One of Neoplatonism,[65] to which he adds (e.g., in "The Christianity of Reason") the idea of a threefold divine movement. Or (in Hermann Timm's terms) Lessing combines ontotheology's necessary being with the Christian tradition's immanent Trinity of consciousness; that is, he relies on a notion of God's transcendent unity that does not exclude plurality — a notion clearly more reminiscent of Descartes than of Spinoza.[66] This makes his theology more monarchist than traditional trinitarianism; still, we are concerned here with the minimal conditions of theism, not (yet) with trinitarian orthodoxy. (Perhaps Lessing could respond that the full equality of the trinitarian persons is in some sense anticipatory, awaiting the eschatological completion of history: the role of Spirit is played out in, and thus the Spirit emerges within, the realm of history, through the gradual "education" of the human race.)

(Frankfurt: Vittorio Klostermann, 1974), esp. 121ff. Timm argues that Lessing's "trinitäts-theologischen Pantheismus" interprets God as a "sich selbst zur Allheit bestimmende Tätigkeit."

63. Whether this world is internal or external to God is the basic (and ongoing) debate between panentheism and classical philosophical theism.

64. So also Timm: "Was Lessing am Trinitätsdogma faszinierte, war der Glaube, das individuelle Ichbewußtsein in die impersonale Allgemeinheit des göttlichen Seins hineinnehmen zu können" (*Gott und die Freiheit*, 128).

65. And to this extent Leibnizian; recall the arguments for Leibniz's Neoplatonism in chapter 5.

66. Timm: God's "transzendentaler Einheit, welche eine Art von Mehrheit nicht ausschließt." In *Sämtliche Schriften*, 14:175-76, Lessing argues from perfection to the Trinity: "God thought his perfections separately, that is, he created" (14:178; cf. 13:341, 359).

Evaluation

So do we interpret Lessing as the great mediator, incorporating what is attractive about Spinoza yet tempering it enough to be at least semi-orthodox? It is certainly possible to compile the pithy, often ambiguous statements in Lessing's writing, to play with the provocative allusions, until he reads like a Spinozist, which is one of the reasons that he became the occasion for the *Spinozastreit*. But Lessing was an essayist, an occasionalist; he provides no systematic exposition of his theological position (if he even has "a" position!); and he writes in much more detail on aesthetics and christology than on metaphysics.[67] Exactly what attracts one so much to Spinoza — his unitary vision, his fascination with a single overarching infinite explanation worked out with uncompromising rigor and consistency — is utterly missing in Lessing. In fact, *The Education of the Human Race* is markedly less metaphysical than even Schleiermacher's *Speeches*, which are definitely closer to the spirit of Spinoza. At bottom, Lessing's religious interests are ethical, as one can see in *Nathan the Wise* and summarized perhaps most clearly in the famous words from "Gedanken über die Herrnhutter": "What does it help to believe correctly if one lives unjustly? . . . Can one not make use of his understanding in a better manner than by preoccupation with unresolvable matters?"[68]

With these caveats in mind, my reconstruction of Lessing suggests the following conclusion. It is often claimed (beginning apparently with Jacobi) that one's choice is between Spinozistic pantheism and Kantian skepticism about all metaphysics.[69] But this is a false dilemma. The movement away from Aristote-

---

67. This is also the conclusion of Leonard P. Wessel's important study of Lessing, *G. E. Lessing: A Reinterpretation: A Study in the Problematic Nature of the Enlightenment* (The Hague: Mouton, 1977). Wessel argues that, although Lessing made both monistic and dualistic (transcendent-God) statements, it would be false to interpret him as fitting into either camp: "It is my contention that Lessing's philosophy and theological speculations were never fully consistent. Lessing's thinking was caught on the horns of a cognitive crisis" in Enlightenment thought (p. 235).

68. "Was hilft es, recht zu glauben, wenn man unrecht lebt? . . . Kann man seinen Verstand nicht in etwas Besserm üben als in unerforschlichen Dingen?" (in Wölfel, ed., *Lessings Werke*, 3:243, 245-46).

69. This presupposition underlies (and thus obviates) Thomas McFarland's impressively erudite treatment of the Spinoza tradition and its effect on British Romanticism; see McFarland, *Coleridge and the Pantheist Tradition* (Oxford: Clarendon, 1969), esp. chap. 2. McFarland calls these two approaches "I am" and "it is" philosophies, and cites a 1690 Dutch theologian: "There are two, and only two, systems of philosophy that can be offered: The one posits God as the transcendent cause of things; the other makes God the immanent cause. The former carefully distinguishes and separates God from the world; the latter shamefully

lian substances and Neoplatonic emanations does not immediately entail Spinozism; the questions are immensely more complicated than that. Viewed with a healthy dose of charity, I suggest, Lessing's sketches of a metaphysical position represent a sort of mediating position. If his idea of a spiritual force or power, perfect and self-unfolding, could be developed systematically, it would make better sense of human (personal) finitude than Spinoza's impersonal whole, which is infinitely distinct from its parts at the same time that they are contained within it and share its attributes. Lessing was one of the earliest modern thinkers to define God as *Geist* and then to develop the relationship between the finite and infinite, between world and God, in historical (and moral/ ethical) terms. If (as I think) these moves represent a step in the right direction from Spinoza, one will have to look not to Lessing but to post-Kantian thinkers, to Schelling, Hegel, or Whitehead, for its culmination.

Jacobi

The Position

The core of Jacobi's position emerges in his commentary on §73 of Lessing's *Education of the Human Race,* which according to Jacobi demands a Spinozistic interpretation:

> The God of Spinoza is the pure principle of the reality in everything that is real, the being in everything that exists; it is thoroughly without individuality and absolutely infinite. The unity of this God rests on the identity of what cannot be distinguished and consequently does not exclude a type of plurality. Viewed just through this transcendental unity, however, divinity must absolutely dispense with reality, which can only express itself in particular individuals. The latter reality, together with its concept, therefore depends on the *natura naturata* (the Son from all eternity), just as the former — the possibility, the essence, the substantial side of the infinite, along with its concept — depends on the *natura naturanti* (the Father).[70]

---

confounds God with the universe. . . . The former derives all things from the free harmony of an infinite and omnipotent Mind; the latter from a certain brute and blind necessity of the divine nature or of the universe" (preface to *Christoph Wittichii Anti-Spinoza sive Examen Ethices Benedicti de Spinoza* [Amsterdam, 1690], cited in McFarland, 53-54).

70. "Der Gott des Spinoza ist das lautere Principium der Wirklickheit in allem Wirklichen, des Seyns in allem Daseyn, durchaus ohne Individualität, und schlechterdings unendlich. Die Einheit dieses Gottes beruhet auf der Identität des Nichtzuunterscheidenden,

This is admittedly an intriguing interpretation of Spinoza's doctrine of God, though one not entirely innocent of Kantian anachronism. Jacobi claims that Spinoza's infinite is the absolutely transcendent — and hence purely empty — concept of the unity of all things. Whatever content religion may attempt to add to it, philosophically speaking the One is above all distinctions; anything concrete (indeed, anything at all) that can be said will be said of this or that particular thing within the One. In fact, on this interpretation Spinoza's one substance now becomes a purely formal principle, pure being itself, which would mean that it cannot obtain as an existing entity at all. By contrast, the infinite modes do exist, insofar as they mutually limit and determine one another. Spinoza's verbal/substantive metaphor for expressing this relationship — nature "naturing" and nature "natured" — becomes for Lessing (under Jacobi's new interpretation) a speculative analog to the trinitarian Father and Son.

Suppose it is the case that Lessing's theology depends conceptually on Spinoza; what does that say about its possible truth? Jacobi tries to argue that any theology that borrows from Spinoza becomes ipso facto unacceptable. The argument consists of four steps. First, Spinozism is the inevitable result of Cartesian philosophy taken to its logical conclusion. This insight, which I believe is profoundly correct, played a major role in the "new direction" taken by the German idealists from Kant to Hegel. Second, as the logical end point of Cartesianism, Spinozism is also the inevitable result of rationalism. The latter is certainly a more controversial claim: if Jacobi means "rationalism in the early modern, Cartesian sense," then his claim is tautologically true; if he means rationalism in a sense broad enough to include the later German idealists, then the claim is false, since (as we will see) they clearly moved beyond Spinoza at a number of points. Third, Jacobi maintained that Spinozism is the purest form of pantheism. This thesis, too, shows a deep understanding of Spinoza, whose

---

und schließt folglich eine Art der Mehrheit nicht aus. Bloß in dieser transcendentalen Einheit angesehen, muß die Gottheit aber schlechterdings der Wirklichkeit entbehren, die nur im bestimmten Einzelnen sich ausgedrückt finden kann. Diese, die Worklichkeit, mit ihrem Begriffe, beruhet also auf der Natura naturata (dem Sohne von Ewigkeit); so wie jene, die Möglichkeit, das Wesen, das Substanzielle des Unendlichen, mit seinem Begriffe, auf der Natura naturanti (dem Vater)" (IV/1, 87-88). References to Jacobi's *Werke* (Leipzig: Gerhard Gleischer d. Jüng., 1816) appear parenthetically in the text with volume number and page; "Scholz" refers to the standard compendium edited by Heinrich Scholz, *Die Hauptschriften zum Pantheismusstreit zwischen Jacobi und Mendelssohn* (Berlin: Reuther & Reichard, 1916). Portions of Scholz's collection have been translated into English by Vallée et al., *Spinoza Conversations*.

71. For a rigorous exposition of philosophical pantheism see Michael Levine's excellent book, *Pantheism: A Non-Theistic Concept of Deity* (London: Routledge, 1994). whose

account of the complete unity of God (qua the one substance) and all things is based on rigorous argument and logic rather than on mystical appeals.[71]

Finally, Jacobi argued, pantheism, rightly understood, is equivalent to atheism and fatalism. Add to this last claim the assumption that atheism/fatalism is untenable, and the conclusion is clear: Spinozism — and the whole tradition of rational theology that led to it — should be rejected. It follows, further, that the alternative cannot be any other form of rationalism or another variant of Cartesianism. Hence Jacobi's ultimate position: there must be a radical break between faith and reason, a sacrifice of the intellect, which he frequently calls a "death leap" or *salto mortale*.[72] One leaps into the arms of the waiting God.

Criticisms of Jacobi

There is much in this line of argument for a philosopher to find problematic (not the least of which is the assumption that atheism and fatalism are obviously false). First, though, it is not hard to show that Spinoza is not the arch-rationalist, the inevitable culmination of (pre-Kantian) metaphysics, such that a choice for metaphysics is *eo ipso* a choice for him — or as the battle cry had it, "Kant or Spinoza."[73] For in a number of respects Spinoza fits the rationalist paradigm rather poorly. He may present his conclusions in geometric form, but the argument of the *Ethics* in fact fails to proceed deductively (as analytic treatments such as Jonathan Bennett's have demonstrated and as the crucial role of the scholia also suggests). Spinoza's first concern is to provide an ethics; his metaphysics is constructed with the goal of bolstering the "third kind of knowledge" and the *amor dei intellectus* with which it culminates. Moreover, the highest form of knowledge for Spinoza is not deductive knowledge (*ratio*) but *cognitio intuitiva*, knowledge of the immediate, intuitive sort. The final mystical propositions of book 5 represent an inalienable part of the Spinozistic system

---

72. Jacobi makes clear in a letter to Jacobi Neeb that he derives the term from a dangerous jump called by acrobats the "death leap." Critics had equated the *salto mortales* with "a headlong fall from a rock into an abyss ("einem Kopfunter hinabstürzen von einem Felsen in einen Abgrund"), but Jacobi insists that he means by it a flying above rocks and abyss and landing safely on one's feet on the far side ("einem, von ebenem Boden aus, sich über Felsen und Abgrund Hinwegschwingen und jenseits wieder fest und gesund auf die Füße zu stehen kommen") (letter of 5/30/1817, in Friedrich Roth, ed., *Auserlesener Briefwechsel*, 2 vols. [Leipzig, 1825-27], 2:466, cited in Klaus Hammacher, *Die Philosophie Friedrich Heinrich Jacobis* [Munich: Wilhelm Fink, 1969], 90). On the concept see Hammacher, 70-91.

73. The charge is Jacobi's: "pantheism in its Spinozistic form" is "the most consistent form of rationalism (*die konsequenteste Ausprägung des Rationalismus*)" (cited in Hebeisen, *Jacobi*, 28).

— and, perhaps, their ultimate telos (though this is not an outcome that sits well with contemporary philosophers):[74] "Our mind, insofar as it knows both itself and the body under a form of eternity, necessarily has a knowledge of God, and knows that it is in God and is conceived through God [P30]. . . . God loves himself with an infinite intellectual love [P35]. . . . Blessedness is not the reward of virtue, but virtue itself [P42]."

Finally, the counterarguments already adduced in this chapter reveal that Spinoza's cannot be the consistent outworking of Cartesian metaphysics for the simple reason that it is not a consistent metaphysical position at all. To take a highly problematic and incomplete metaphysical proposal and to equate it with the outcome of metaphysics as such is to get a lot of mileage out of a straw man.

We have seen that it was not exactly Jacobi's task to provide a dispassionate exegesis of Spinoza's texts. During the turbulent last years of the eighteenth century he was the great defender of orthodoxy and a more traditional theology. What Jacobi does provide, however, perhaps more clearly than any before him, is an interesting hypothesis to test. His claim is that the doctrine of God faces a fundamental dichotomy: either classical theism or pantheism. Note that this challenge is a version of a related dichotomy, which alleges that one must choose either a theology of transcendence or a theology of immanence. Recall, for example, that this was Yovel's motivation for revivifying Spinoza, as it might be for many postmodern thinkers: since (it is assumed) we cannot possibly accept classical theism, we should join Spinoza and his followers in "the adventures of immanence" and abandon all appeal to *meta*-physical or transcendent beings. (Jacobi and Yovel would obviously fall on different sides of the dichotomy if it were formulated this way.)

On closer examination, however, it turns outs that Jacobi and Yovel are trying to construct a rather similar dilemma for theology (or philosophy, for that matter). In Jacobi's terms, the choice is either rational knowledge of a single, all-encompassing substance (of which we are, at best, modes) or opting out of the metaphysical task altogether. For Yovel, it is either metaphysics (along with transcendent beings and truths) or Rortyan immanentism (choices that

---

74. Take, e.g., Bennett's disparaging citation of an 1880 Spinoza commentator: Spinoza's "doctrine of the eternity of the mind must remain one of the most brilliant endeavours of speculative philosophy, and it throws a sort of poetical glow over the formality of his exposition. . . . The essence of S.'s thought is already secured for us. . . . M. Renan has expressed it in the perfectly chosen words . . . : *Reason leads Death in triumph, and the work done for Reason is done for eternity*" (Frederick Pollock, *Spinoza, His Life and Philosophy* [London, 1880], 308, cited in Bennett, *Study of Spinoza's Ethics*, 374). Bennett calls Pollock's comments "babbling," though he also expresses his discomfort at making sense of book 5 without losing his respect for Spinoza.

are no longer grounded in Truth or God). There are differences, of course: once free of metaphysics Jacobi turns to belief in a fully personal God, while Yovel revels in the human freedom to create values and truths. Still, from the perspective of the dichotomy *metaphysics or beyond* they are clearly on the same side; the remaining differences need not concern us here (though perhaps it should concern Yovel a bit more to note the vast variety of ways there are to move beyond rationality).

Jacobi argues that, given the four theses sketched above, the only way to rescue theism is the leap of faith. The argument's underlying assumption is that theism can only be defined as belief in the existence of a supernatural personal cause of the world whose nature and creative activity is a mystery: "The natural realm, the universe, can proceed, and has proceeded, from this supernatural being in no other way than supernaturally."[75] This is the point where Jacobi's Kantianism emerges. Jacobi takes Spinoza as the ultimate representative of the ontotheological tradition (which we traced through Descartes and Leibniz in chapters 3 and 4). Spinoza's problems — the (alleged) incompatibility of his thought with any serious belief in God — are the inevitable result of the philosophical starting point: "If the understanding posits an end to the unconditioned series of conditions and names this end 'the beginning' or 'totality,' should this imaginary beginning be called God? What an impoverished anthropomorphism! But this is precisely the trap in which all pantheists are stuck."[76] Contrary to Spinoza, Jacobi insists, there is no rational connection between the finite and infinite; reason can say nothing about how the universe arose, since (exactly as Kant argued) all causal descriptions apply only to the phenomenal realm.[77] A supernatural creation must be an incomprehensible creation.

Challenging Jacobi's Dichotomy: Minimal Personalist Theism

Jacobi has brought us a challenge formulated as a dichotomy: one must either take Kantian skepticism about all metaphysical knowledge, supplemented by a

---

75. "Aus diesem Übernatürlichen kann denn auch das Natürliche, oder das Weltall, nicht anders, als auf eine übernatürliche Weise hervorgehen, und hervorgegangen seyn" (IV/2, 155; Scholz, 276; cf. IV/1, 59; Scholz, 80).

76. "Setzt der Verstand der unbestimmten Reihe von Bedingungen ein Ende, und nennt dieses Ende den Anfang, oder Totalität; soll dieser erdichtete Anfang Gott heißen? Welch ein armseliger Anthropomorphismus! In ihm sind alle unsere Pantheisten befangen" (IV/1, xxxiii, in Hebeisen, *Jacobi*, 32).

77. "Diese Kluft füllt keine Philosophie, und des bedarf, um hinüber zu kommen, einer Brücke — oder Flügel" (I, 248, cited in Hebeisen, *Jacobi*, 32).

faith-choice for Christian theism, or Spinozistic pantheism with its identification of world with God. It is now time to step back from Jacobi and to evaluate whether his dichotomy is successful. The dichotomy is based on three assumptions, each of which is, I believe, highly problematic. Jacobi assumes that Spinozism is the inevitable result of rigorous metaphysical reflection (an assumption criticized above); that Kant's epistemic limitations are justified; and that a fully personal theism, derived from faith, is the only acceptable form of theism. Regarding the second assumption, we found (in chapter 5) that Kant's case for the impossibility of metaphysical knowledge was unconvincing, reflecting finally an indefensible bias in favor of empirical knowledge. Even if Kant were right, it is obvious to the twentieth-century reader (as it was not to Kant's contemporary Jacobi) that Kantianism can ally as readily with the critique of religion as with its defense.

What then of the third assumption? Between Kant and "the adventures of immanence," I suggest, lies what I have called *minimal personalist theism* (MPT).[78] MPT starts from the premise that there is no better option for thinking of a being that is infinitely greater than finite agents than to ascribe to it the highest predicates with which we are acquainted. MPT grants that there are difficulties with drawing analogies between God and human persons, which make it problematic to conceive of God as personal in all the senses in which we speak of human persons. Yet, it continues, since one certainly cannot conceive of God as less than a human person, at least analogs of what we mean by personhood should be attributed to God as well.[79]

Whatever (adapted) personal attributes one ends up ascribing to God following the logic of this argument can be predicated of the divine only in the limited manner defended in chapter 6: as models that must make good on the claim to be the best available explanation. This means that one cannot view the resultant theology as a final result, whether "proved" by rationalist proofs or by a leap of faith (Jacobi's *salto mortale*). Instead, any attributions to God depend

---

78. As I noted above, in using the term *theism* I do not mean to prejudge the question of whether the world is in some sense included within God, though I do mean to exclude pantheism. So by this term one might just as well understand "minimal personalist panentheism."

79. "The universe of our ordinary experience — the world of matter and intellect and value — depends for its existence on a divine reality to which human beings have *direct* access only in exceptional instances. This reality is rightly conceived by us as personal, not because we know that it literally possesses the attributes of human personhood, such as (normally) a single center of will or consciousness, but because we cannot suppose that it is *less* than personal, and we have no name for what is *more* than personal" (Steve Knapp, unpublished correspondence).

crucially on the regulating assumption that one is justified (for the present) in viewing the best explanation of which one is aware *as true* (an argument spelled out more fully in chapter 1).

Note that this outcome is a far cry from Jacobi, who (at least sometimes) insists that God literally bears all the personalist predicates that we ascribe to him, as in his famous pronouncement, "Creating humankind, God theomorphized himself. Humans therefore necessarily anthropomorphize."[80] But surely this is wrong; surely we cannot argue that every nonanthropomorphic view of God is equivalent to atheism, and that we can therefore project the whole set of (relevant) human attributes onto the divine without reservation. Instead, one may take that theory of the infinite being to be true which best makes sense of its relation to humanity and to the finite order as a whole — again, not as literal ascription, but as the best model that reason can derive. As we found in previous chapters, such models are neither necessarily true (so Jacobi, through the leap of faith) nor necessarily fictions (as in Kantianism sans the fideistic addition). Instead, they are taken as true for the present and pending the outcome of inquiry.

Contra Jacobi contra Spinoza

What then do we say of Jacobi's major charge? Was Spinoza really an atheist, insofar as he denied of God such theistic attributes as will, understanding, insight, consciousness, providential care? For Jacobi, if God is to be in relationship with humans at all, God must be fully personal:

> If the relationship of the individual to God is to be understood as the same as any other I-Thou relationship, the God experienced in this way — and this is the major theme of the Spinoza discussions as Jacobi sees it — must also be an individual and personal being. His potential and comparatively infinite superiority notwithstanding, God must be related to humans in homologous conceptual structures as a spiritual being, as his "own, specific, individual reality . . . , personality and life," as spirit, creator, archetype of man.[81]

---

80. "Den Menschen erschaffend theomorphisirte Gott. Nothwendig anthropomorphisirt darum der Mensch" (III, 418).

81. "Ist aber die Beziehung des Individuums zu Gott gleichgeordnet einer jedweden Ich-Du-Beziehung, so muß er, unangesehen potentieller und gradmäßig unendlicher Überlegenheit, dem Menschen in homologen Denkstrukturen als Geistwesen verwandt sein, als 'eine eigene, besondre, individuelle Wirklichkeit [. . .] Persönlichkeit und Leben,' als Geist, Schöpfer, archetypus des Menschen" (Christ, *Jacobi und Mendelssohn*, 164).

One is confronted with a series of either/or's, Jacobi insists: God is interpreted either as substance or as spirit, either as individual being or as transcendental oneness, either as the sum of all mental units/monads or as himself an individual center of consciousness.

But here again the dichotomies are unconvincing and a mediating position is indicated. Jacobi wants to center his doctrine of God on the understanding and will of a divine person. But one cannot speak literally of God as agent since a number of the features of agency as we know it are inapplicable, or at least problematic, in the case of an infinite being or ground.[82] For example, it is natural to speak of intending, planning, and willing in the case of imperfect beings who strive to change themselves and their circumstances. But in God there need not be the distinction between intention and result that is so basic to human action; whatever God conceives he realizes.[83]

Nonetheless, the intelligibility and coherence of the notion of a divine being demand that one not conceive it as less than the sort of agents that we ourselves are. This means that one must ascribe to it (at least) ends and actions that achieve (or aim to achieve) these ends. Since this does not require that God have a will separate from the having and achieving of ends — nor an awareness of wanting these ends to be achieved or waiting for their achievement — one is not rationally compelled to go as far as Jacobi does in personifying God. On the other hand, the argument does mitigate against construing God as a purely impersonal force. Once again, a form of MPT is indicated.

It is more difficult to work out a mediating position in the case of the necessity question. Jacobi criticizes Spinoza for his "blind fatalism," since "a world order whose first ground is an absolute necessity above all choice must result finally in blind necessity."[84] Several of Jacobi's reasons for criticizing Spinoza here are unpersuasive: that a necessary ground of the world would be unworshipable[85] need not make it automatically false; the philosophical arguments may lead to a position that does not preserve religious devotion. Also, if compatibilism is the case, then a necessary order need not falsify all attributions of moral responsibility. Still, it is hard to see how one can maintain that

---

82. Features of human and natural history also raise questions about the hypothesis of God as an agent who frequently intervenes miraculously in the natural order.

83. See Richard Francks, "Omniscience, Omnipotence and Pantheism," *Philosophy* 54 (1979): 395-99; cf. Hebeisen, *Jacobi*, 42.

84. "Weil eine Welteinrichtung, deren erster Grund absolute und wahllose Notwendigkeit ist, auf blinde Notwendigkeit hinaus gehe" (quoted in Hebeisen *Jacobi*, 35, who incorrectly cites III, 527).

85. "Wozu also einen Gott ehren und anbeten, der, was er tut, durchaus mußte" (Hebeisen, *Jacobi*, 35, incorrectly citing III, 527).

the world is both the necessary consequence of (or part of) its infinite ground and a free creation of a personal agent. (We come back to the freedom question in chapter 9.)

At least this much is clear: Jacobi unnecessarily sharpens the contrasts in such a manner that no mediation could be found. He thinks that human freedom has to be guaranteed by grounding it in a fully personal God who is free in the same robust sense in which (he thinks) humans are free. Since such a being has no place in Spinoza's system, Spinoza could not have preserved full libertarian freedom; and that, Jacobi maintains, proves that one cannot derive freedom from the metaphysical perspective alone, but only from an actual spiritual experience of the self and its creator.[86] But is this correct? If freedom is an intrinsic part of some systematic theological position — either in the compatibilist sense of Spinoza or in the sense of the Hegelian dialectic — then Jacobi's leap beyond all systematic reflection is, again, unnecessary. Jacobi simply assumes that the only viable notion of freedom is one involving both will and the process of self-constitution understood in the manner of German idealism, in which all other aspects of reality were conceived on the basis of the structure of self-consciousness.[87] In fact, freedom for Spinoza and Leibniz is something very different from what it became in Fichte and Schelling; it *just is* the expression of necessity. We return to the relative strengths of the Spinozist notion in the final chapters.

Strengths of Jacobi's View

Despite the difficulties, at a number of points Jacobi's Spinoza interpretation and critique represent an important advance in modern thought about God:

1. Jacobi correctly shared with Spinoza (and with Descartes) the recognition of the primacy of the whole — the one substance or infinite being — over the finite parts.[88] Of course, differences remain as to whether the infinite is in any sense itself dependent on the parts. Jacobi reduced the Spinozistic position to *Ohne Welt kein Gott* ("without the world, no God") and the theist's to *Ohne*

---

86. "Die eigene geistige Selbsterfahrung" (IV/1, 161.1).

87. See Hammacher, *Philosophie Jacobis*, 73ff.

88. "[Der] Inbegriff ist keine ungereimte Zusammensetzung endlicher Dinge, die ein Unendliches ausmachen, sondern, der strengsten Deutung nach, ein Ganzes, dessen Teile nur in und nach ihm gedacht werden können" (IV/1, 176). Interestingly, Jacobi cites *Kritik der reinen Vernunft* A25/B39 here, where Kant argues that individual spaces and times are *Einschränkungen* of the presupposed infinite and homogenous forms of intuition. In his discussion of the parallels, Hong notes correctly, "Das Unendliche ist eine Einheit des Endlichen, während das Endliche durch Beschränkung des Unendlichen entsteht" (*Spinoza und die deutsche Philosophie*, 73-74).

Gott keine Welt ("without God, no world").[89] Still, there is a common recognition that parts (e.g., finite beings), once they exist, will be ontologically dependent on the infinite. The open question involves their origin, then, not their nature. Jacobi wanted their creation to be absolutely free and unconstrained, whereas Spinoza insisted that the infinite modes, indeed "all things," follow from God with the same necessity that it follows from the nature of a triangle that it has 180° (E 1, P17S, Curley 1:426).

2. Jacobi thus saw that there was no philosophical way to attack Spinoza's notion of a single overarching substance, given that each individual thing within it is determined not by the whole but only through its relations with other things. As we saw at the opening of this section, he even granted the conceptual necessity of postulating a transcendental principle of unity above the multiplicity of existing things. Yet he also realized that connecting God-talk even to a transcendental principle of unity is not the same as establishing theism as the (metaphysical) best explanation of our experience and the world around us. A successful theology must work out an adequate theory of the nature of this unifying principle — a philosophically sophisticated systematic theology. Jacobi helped to demonstrate that Spinoza had failed in his attempt to provide such a theory, though he wrongly concluded that the project must therefore be impossible in principle.

3. In the process of spelling out his disagreement Jacobi was able to locate two of the major shortcomings in Spinoza's view. First, he demonstrated that Spinoza was unable to derive his finite modes from the infinite, explaining them only in terms of each other. He showed, second, that the author of the *Ethics* was consequently incapable of specifying the real individuality of things but could only specify their logical difference from one another. In this respect, Jacobi — and the idealist tradition that emerged during his lifetime — was able to demonstrate that Spinoza had to be supplemented by some sort of conceptual framework that could successfully preserve a place for the individual as a mental center of activity. With this insight, Jacobi brilliantly set the stage for the fusion of Spinoza and idealism that was to occur just after the turn of the century. Note, for example, Jacobi's concept of the person: "The unity of self-consciousness constitutes personhood, and each entity that has a consciousness of its identity — of itself as a continuing, self-existent, and self-knowing I — is a person."[90] Jacobi may

---

89. Jacobi, III, 419.

90. "Einheit des Selbsbewußtseyns macht die Persönlichkeit aus, und ein jedes Wesen, welches das Bewußtseyn seiner Identität hat: eines bleibenden, in sich seyenden und von sich wissenden Ich, ist eine Person" (IV/2, 76-77). The parallels with Kant's transcendental unity of apperception are unmistakable.

have been mistaken to read this structure directly onto God: "we must . . . necessarily ascribe to the highest intelligence also the highest degree of personality, which is the perfection of self-existence and self-knowledge."[91] But his insight remains a necessary condition for any adequate theological account of God's relation to finite human agents.

Conclusion

So much for the strengths and weaknesses of Jacobi's anti-Spinozistic personal theism. Ironically, the result of his work was exactly the opposite of what he had hoped. The more he pointed out the flaws in Spinoza's philosophy, the more thinkers like Mendelssohn, Goethe, and Herder — and later (with modifications) Fichte, Schelling, and Hegel — sought with ever increasing subtlety to develop a form of pantheism (or, better, panentheism) able to avoid them. As Yovel points out, "Ironically, however, the polemics . . . had the opposite effect. Instead of staining rationalism with the disdain attached to 'Spinozism,' they helped rehabilitate Spinoza and turn him into a cultural hero. For over half a century . . . Spinoza stood at the center" of German philosophy.[92]

Lessing had first pointed in the direction of a refined version of Spinoza's pantheism, a panentheism according to which God contained the world but was in a sense more than the world. I have argued that Jacobi is right in his criticism of Lessing's metaphysics as speculative theology. Early Spinozism, both in its original form in the *Ethics* and in Lessing's metaphysical aphorisms, fails to stand up to careful scrutiny. Should one therefore conclude that this failure spells the end for Spinozism as a constructive contribution to theology? Or could a still more refined reformulation of Spinozism, a more subtle philosophical theology, solve the problems that, as Jacobi correctly showed, Lessing had failed to solve?

Mendelssohn

Once again we begin with an irony: Mendelssohn, the great apologist for Lessing-the-Spinozist, was not an advocate of Spinoza's pantheism at all. He may have been one of the greatest defenders of philosophical theism in the late

---

91. "Wir müssen . . . nothwendig der höchsten Intelligenz auch den höchsten Grad der Persönlichkeit, das ist die Vollkommenheit des Insich Seyns und von sich Wissens, zuerkennen" (IV/2, 77).

92. Yovel, *Spinoza and Other Heretics,* 2:191.

eighteenth century, and he does take Spinoza with extreme seriousness as a philosopher, providing no less than three major summaries of Spinoza's philosophy in his *Morgenstunden*. But his interests in Spinoza are more those of a historian of ideas and an apologist for Lessing and for rational theology (the two tasks being to him virtually equivalent).

I will not attempt to settle the disputed question of the subjective grounds for Mendelssohn's preoccupation with Spinoza. They presumably included an interest in defending Judaism and its great philosophers, a more general concern with correcting the historical record regarding Spinoza, and a certain fascination with Spinoza's religious (mystical) temperament. Objectively, Mendelssohn's major works are of importance to us because of their contribution to the influence of Spinoza on the development of eighteenth-century philosophical theology. Philopon's conclusion in Mendelssohn's second *Gespräch* perhaps states his own goal in the matter most clearly: "I understand [your defense of Spinoza] fully, and now see all the more how much we owe to Spinoza's mistakes. It was only a small step from him to the truth."[93]

Nonetheless, although he represents a major step forward in the transformation of Spinoza's pantheism, Mendelssohn does not manage to offer a fully developed panentheistic alternative to it. First, as I will show, for conceptual as well as political reasons Mendelssohn carefully (and correctly) distances himself from the major tenets of the Spinozistic position. Where he does defend Spinoza, it never amounts to an actual acceptance of Spinozism as a system. When all is said and done, Mendelssohn's basic contribution is to show that Spinoza's position is no worse than Leibniz's (or, sometimes, that it is indistinguishable from Leibniz's). Most importantly, though, we find in his reinterpretations of Spinozism the seeds of a new position, one that will come to full expression in the philosophies of Fichte and Schelling.

The "Leibnizian Defense" of Spinoza

In his four *Gespräche*, published in 1755, Mendelssohn works to show the compatibility, even identity, of Spinoza's philosophy with that of Leibniz. The first *Gespräch* argues that Spinoza's position contains something like Leibniz's preestablished harmony, and the second demonstrates that both these thinkers

---

93. "Ich begreife dieses alles sehr wohl, und sehe nunmehr, wie viel wir Spinoza's Irrthume zu verdanken haben. Es war nur ein kleiner Schritt von ihm zur Wahrheit." See Moritz Brasch, ed., *Moses Mendelssohn's Schriften zur Metaphysik und Ethik sowie zur Religionsphilosophie*, 2 vols. (Leipzig: Leopold Voss, 1880), 1:19. Further references to Mendelssohn's *Schriften* are preceded by "Mend."

maintain that the world is in some sense internal to God.[94] Mendelssohn's strategy is understandable, of course, in an age when (Wolff's) Leibniz amounted to philosophical orthodoxy and Spinozism to heresy. But since I assume that most present readers take the doctrine of preestablished harmony to be more of an embarrassment than a boon, this line of argument holds little apologetic value to the contemporary Spinozist.

Nevertheless, one difficulty raised by these arguments must be addressed as part of my defense of minimal personalist theism. Mendelssohn first suggests that any adequate theism must understand the world as internal to God, whether or not it also posits a world outside God. This assumption is not too revolutionary; it has been held in more limited forms by a number of theists, as in Thomas Aquinas's doctrine that the forms of all existing things have real existence as thoughts in the mind of God. Mendelssohn then argues that for the theist there can be no distinction between things existing in the mind of God and their "real" existence: to exist in the former sense *just is* to exist in the latter. If this were correct, it would mean that the idea of God's externalizing the world outside himself (i.e., creating a world above and beyond the divine thought of the world) is meaningless, which would imply that Spinoza is right to construe things as merely modes within God. Or, more moderately, it would at least imply that, given God, the existence of the world is necessary, and hence that there can be no free creation by God. It does not seem that either Spinoza or Leibniz has the resources to counter this challenge to the (even minimally) theistic doctrine of creation; we return to it below.

In a word, then, even if Mendelssohn's argument is successful, it gives us at best Leibniz. But we found reasons enough in chapter 4 to view Leibniz's philosophical theology as unacceptable. Thus, once again, whatever temptations of immanence Spinoza offered us, Mendelssohn has so far not managed to make Spinoza more attractive.

"Refined" Spinozism

Of course, ultimately Mendelssohn does not want the reader to accept the *Ethics* as it stands, any more than Yovel wishes to defend the actual Spinoza the metaphysician. The whole thirteenth lecture of the *Morgenstunden* is an attack on Spinoza's pantheism, which Mendelssohn paints as utterly untenable because of its necessitarianism, its inadequate account of the source of motion, and its denial that God is a thinking subject. What Mendelssohn wishes to bring to the defense of his friend, the alleged pantheist Lessing, is a new, "re-

---

94. See Mend. 1:5-13 and 14-20, respectively.

fined" version of Spinozism,[95] one that, he thinks, incorporates the strengths of both Spinoza and Leibniz while being preferable to both.

What one finds in these passages, albeit in nascent form, are the first interesting sketches of a truly panentheistic theology. The world is taken to be internal to God, for reasons that Mendelssohn has learned from Spinoza; yet as conscious agent, God is also more than this world. For example, in the fourteenth lecture Mendelssohn construes the one divine substance not only as the source of what is true but also of what is good (Mend. 1:403). What this means is that "[we] have attributed to the divine, just as much as the theist does, the highest perfection."[96] Thus Mendelssohn, in contrast to Spinoza, has ascribed to God consciousness, intentionality, and agency, for God must be capable of representing to himself *(sich vorstellen)* all finite things, together with their moral qualities, beauty, and order, and of giving preference to the best and most perfect series of things.[97]

Of course, there is also much to criticize here. Mendelssohn has incorporated exactly the features of Leibniz's philosophy that we found (in chapter 4 above) to be most problematic. For example, he seems to imagine an unbroken hierarchy of perfections stemming from an *ens perfectissimum,* a move that reads onto the "levels of reality" an absolute scale of perfection. If Spinozism were to be more than a slogan today, one would have to begin not with the hierarchy of perfection but instead with the ontological side, that is, with a demonstration of why a world internal to the one substance is philosophically preferable to a world external to God.

Mendelssohn does at one point offer an interesting version of such an argument, one directly relevant to our search for a panentheistic Spinozism that might be a serious competitor to theism. An omniscient God, he notes rightly, must have full and adequate knowledge of all things that exist; in fact, his ideas must so perfectly correspond to their ideata that the two are rationally indistinguishable. What then is gained, he asks, by positing an external world and, more importantly, how would we know that the world that appears to exist really exists external to God? Could not our ideas of objects all have been planted in our minds by a divine agent? Now in at least one case, it seems, we know something is distinct from God: ourselves. We know ourselves to be limited consciousnesses, limited rational agents. Presumably not all the divine ideas

---

95. Mendelssohn speaks here of a "geläuterte Spinozismus" or, elsewhere, of a "verfeinerte Pantheismus" (Mend. 1:421).

96. "Da wir also . . . der Gottheit, eben sowohl als der Theist, die allerhöchste Vollkommenheit zuschreiben" (ibid., 403-4).

97. "Und dass er vermöge seiner allerhöchsten Billigungskraft der besten und vollkommensten Reihe der Dinger den Vorzug gegeben habe" (ibid., 404).

have this self-reflexive property of knowing themselves, but at least some of them do — namely agents like us who are conscious of themselves as limited. God could know that humans, if any exist, are finite (or that the idea of us, prior to actualization, is finite), but of course he would not thereby think *himself* to be limited. Since we know ourselves actually to be limited, we must be ontologically distinct from God. Thus it cannot be the case that all things are merely modes of the one substance.

Consequently, the Spinozist's radical immanentism — everything we perceive, and even we ourselves, could be merely modes of the one God-or-Nature — is counterindicated wherever we encounter conscious agents like ourselves who know their own finitude. God could never truly think that he is finite; only really existing finite agents could think themselves to be so. Mendelssohn assumes, incidentally, that this is the only way to overcome the claim that all things are modes of (and thus identical with) God. His own conclusion is that this argument is not sufficient to decide the question between classical philosophical theism and panentheism (the doctrine that there are multiple substances, although all that exists is part of, is "contained in," God). For, he maintains, the argument does not provide sufficient criteria for distinguishing between them:

> [For both theist and panentheist,] I, a human, a thought of the divine, will never cease to be a divine thought . . . hence [the two positions] are distinguished only by a subtlety that could never make a practical difference . . . : whether God let this idea of the best group of contingent things shine out, roll out, stream out — or with what picture should I compare it? (since this subtlety cannot be described other than with pictures); whether he let the light shine away from him like lightning or only illumine within? Whether it remained a spring or whether the spring flowed out in a stream? . . . Fundamentally, it is a misinterpretation of the metaphors that transforms God too pictorially into the world or places the world too pictorially within God.[98]

98. "Ich Mensch, Gedanke der Gottheit, werde nie aufhören, ein Gedanke der Gottheit zu bleiben . . . so unterscheidet sich ferner diese Schule von unserm Systeme bloss in einer Subtilität, die niemals praktisch werden kann . . . ob Gott diesen Gedanken des besten Zusammenhanges zufälliger Dinge hat ausstrahlen, ausfliessen, ausströmen, oder mit welchem Bilde soll ich es vergleichen? (denn diese Subtilität lässt sich kaum anders, als durch Bilder beschreiben) ob er das Licht hat von sich wegblitzen, oder nur innerlich leuchten lassen? Ob es bloss Quelle geblieben, oder ob die Quelle sich in einen Strom ergossen habe? . . . im Grunde ist es Missdeutung derselben Metapher, die bald Gott zu bildlich in die Welt, bald die Welt zu bildlich in Gott versetzt" (Mend. 1:412).

Recall that theists (including those in the Cartesian tradition) already deny that the world has full ontological independence, acknowledging that it remains ontologically dependent on God and that its existence at every moment of time is explainable only by God's continued sustaining act.[99] Mendelssohn thinks that there is no clear conceptual difference between theism, with its dependent world, and panentheism, which allows for conscious agents within God. For him it boils down to a combat between competing images; which picture one chooses is a matter of aesthetics rather than argument.

I think he is mistaken. Through this whole process of revision one sees a new panentheistic theology gradually emerging that is distinct both from traditional theism and from strict Spinozistic pantheism. What is true is that there were still serious inadequacies in Mendelssohn's own formulation of "refined pantheism"; it would be another couple of decades before the conceptual resources were present to resolve them. For example, Mendelssohn's philosophy of perfection is utterly foreign to Spinozism. Spinoza places the one substance above all moral predicates, such that it is literally meaningless to call it either good or bad. One cannot simply add consciousness and the quality of moral perfection to Spinoza's one substance without altering his understanding of things and persons as internal modes of the one whole. A similar point applies, second, to Mendelssohn's doctrine of divine consciousness: it is impossible to see how consciousness can be ascribed to something that is not limited in any way.

Finally, Mendelssohn's argument notwithstanding, it does make sense to ask whether something really exists outside God. Whether or not we know what "picture" to use in describing the matter, it certainly represents a philosophical (and presumably personal!) difference whether a conscious agent understands her- or himself to be inside or outside God, to be substantially identical with an infinite substance or substantially separate from (even if dependent on) it. Mendelssohn could be said to be cashing in an ambiguity that goes all the way back to Descartes's *Principles* (I, 51), where the Frenchman defined *substance* both as what is absolutely independent (in which case, "strictly speaking," there is only one substance) and as something having relative independence (which amounts to the "commonsense" view of substance). It is tempting to view Mendelssohn's refined pan(en)theism as a natural theological expression of the Cartesian both/and: there really are finite conscious substances, although they remain within the one substance. But to systematize an ambiguity is not yet to resolve it. To think both sides of the God/world relation, identity and differ-

99. For one reasonable account of this view, see Colin Gunton, *The Triune Creator: A Historical and Systematic Study,* Edinburgh Studies in Constructive Theology 3 (Edinburgh: Univ. of Edinburgh Press; Grand Rapids: Eerdmans, 1998).

ence, will require a dialectical mode of thinking not available to either Spinoza or Mendelssohn. We return to this task in the coming chapters.

In conclusion, Mendelssohn contributes most to the development of Spinozism in post-Kantian philosophy by separating Spinozism from materialism, perhaps for the first time, and bringing his thought closer to the concerns of the idealists.[100] Arguably, this was *the* crucial transformation that made Spinoza palatable to Goethe and the German romantics, as well as to the central figures of German idealism. If there is space within the divine for separate conscious centers of activity, then one cannot dismiss Spinozism as fundamentally materialist and fatalist. Further, as the last quotation suggests, refined Spinozism is compatible with the emanation doctrine of Neoplatonism.[101] By reintroducing divine intellect and perfection into a quasi-Spinozistic framework, Mendelssohn achieved virtually everything theism offered — yet without the philosophical difficulties of an ex nihilo creation outside God. As Mendelssohn quotes from Lessing, "Representing, willing, and creating are all one for God. Thus [since God thinks his perfections from all eternity] one can say that everything that God represents to himself he also creates."[102]

Mendelssohn's Retreat from Spinoza to Leibniz

Ultimately, however, Mendelssohn found himself compelled to supplement his Spinozism with a large dose of Leibniz. The difficulties we have already traced in the latter's philosophical theology make it unnecessary to treat the Leibnizian dimensions of Mendelssohn's argument in equal detail. It is already clear from earlier chapters that Mendelssohn's introduction of the perfection concept and levels of reality into Spinozism would have to take the predictable form: a rational theology centered on the ontological argument. As Kurt Christ notes at the conclusion of his treatment of Mendelssohn, "The essence of Men-

---

100. This comes out most clearly in the fifteenth lecture of the *Morgenstunden*.

101. We found in earlier chapters that this doctrine ran throughout (if on the margins of) the history of Western theism, leaving not insignificant traces in Descartes and Leibniz; the fusion of the anti-emanationist Spinoza with emanationism thus represents an interesting philosophical development. Mendelssohn draws explicit parallels with *Emanationssysteme* in 1:423. For an (only partially successful) case for Spinoza's Neoplatonism see Paul Oskar Kristeller, "Stoic and Neoplatonic Sources of Spinoza's *Ethics*," *History of European Ideas* 5/1 (1984): 1-15.

102. "Vorstellen, Wollen und Schaffen ist bei Gott eins. Man kann also sagen, alles was sich Gott vorstellt, alles das schafft er auch" (Mend. 1:421, from Lessing's *Christenthum der Vernunft*, §3).

delssohn's *Morgenstunden* [his most mature work] lies in the attempt to provide a renewed buttressing for the ontological argument."[103]

In the last lectures of the *Morgenstunden,* Mendelssohn turns his panentheistic argument — that there are conscious centers of activity within the one substance — into a "new" theistic proof, a variation on the "synthetic" ontological proof of Descartes's Fifth Meditation. To achieve this end he must reintroduce and defend all the major categories of the ontotheological tradition in its Leibnizian/Wolffian form. Thanks to these passages, rather than being known for his modifications of Spinozism, Mendelssohn has gone down in history as one of the last great representatives of Leibnizianism.[104] The irony of this outcome is twofold. On the one hand, in his last major work Mendelssohn failed to preserve what was really distinctive about Spinoza's philosophy, just as in his early work (the *Gespräche*) he had argued for the virtual equivalence of Leibniz's and Spinoza's metaphysics without adequately distinguishing them. On the other hand, he also completely failed to appreciate the significance of the challenge posed by the publication of Kant's *Critique of Pure Reason* in 1781, some four years before the publication of the *Morgenstunden.*[105]

The above treatment of Mendelssohn provides yet more evidence against Yovel's supposedly historical case for an eighteenth-century metaphysics of immanence. Mendelssohn was perhaps the only figure in the famous Spinoza Dispute who might have been in a position to offer a fully immanence-based alternative to traditional theology. Yet what most interested him was a synthesis of traditional theism and Spinozistic immanence, not a replacement of the one by the other. If there is to be any successful pre-Hegelian (pre-Rortyan?) philosophy of immanence, we will have to find it in the nineteenth century, for no philosopher in the first 110 years after Spinoza's death has provided us with one.

---

103. "In dem Versuch der erneuten Befestigung des ontologischen Gottesbeweises liegt demnach die Essenz der *Morgenstunden* Mendelssohns" (Christ, *Jacobi und Mendelssohn,* 162).

104. Dieter Henrich is thus exactly right when, in his classic *Der ontologische Gottesbeweis: Sein Problem und seine Geschichte in der Neuzeit* (Tübingen: Mohr [Siebeck], 1960), he concludes his section on "die Schule von Leibniz" with Mendelssohn: "Mendelssohn ist der letzte, der zur Theorie des ontologischen Gottesbeweises, wenn auch nur zur Methode der Darstellung, eigene Beiträge geliefert hat" (pp. 68-73, quotation 72).

105. In fact, Mendelssohn had not even read the *Critique* by that time. He admits that his knowledge of Kant's "existence is not a predicate" — which he criticizes in the *Morgenstunden* — was only second- or third-hand, stemming "nur aus unzulänglichen Berichten [seiner] Freunde oder aus gelehrten Anseigen" (see lecture 17; quoted in Christ, *Jacobi und Mendelssohn,* 161).

CONCLUSION

My case is now complete. I began with the agreement among contemporary philosophers that Spinoza himself was unable successfully to derive the finite from the infinite and thereby to achieve a monistic metaphysics. He suggested, correctly, that the infinite can be "modified" according to infinite modes and that finite things can be defined by a process of mutual limitation through other finite things. Still, this fails to explain how the infinite would come to be modified in finite ways or to take finite form — precisely the explanatory task that Spinoza would have to resolve were he to provide a philosophical alternative to theism.

I then turned to the tradition of Spinoza's critics and advocates, to see whether a successful theology of immanence could be obtained through modifications of Spinoza's system. Consideration of three early critics falsified Yovel's reconstruction of the early years as one long series of unjustified opposition. Serious and philosophically insightful criticisms of the *Ethics* were in fact raised, even though it would be false to pretend that they removed Spinoza from serious contention.

What of the famous *Spinozastreit?* Its origins in Lessing's thought (spoken and written) are intriguing, but Lessing can by no stretch of the imagination serve as the originator of a revised Spinozistic doctrine of God. His often contradictory (if inevitably intriguing) aphorisms begged for a more systematic presentation, which they began to receive in the correspondence of others only months after his death. Jacobi and Mendelssohn, the two most significant thinkers between Lessing and Kant, did develop genuinely new theological positions — the former a fideist version of traditional theism that reflected the influence of both Spinoza and Kant, and the latter an intriguing "refinement" of Spinoza that preserved the immanence of all things within God without identifying world and God in a pantheistic sense.

One does not want to be unfair to the advocates of a full-on philosophy of immanence. We have found some intriguing phrases, some intimations of immanence. But none of these thinkers formulated a real philosophy of immanence; none achieved an updating of Spinozism that dispensed entirely with transcendent claims. All three thinkers found it necessary, for instance, to distinguish God as agent or spirit from finite things, leaving behind the strict equation *deus siva natura*. Lessing saw the need for complexity and for dialectical development within God; Jacobi pointed the way toward a Kantian transcendental reading of Spinoza; and Mendelssohn showed why the world must be thought as both within God and yet not as identical with God. Yovel may be right that the quest for a philosophy of immanence is adventuresome. Yet, at least until the period after Hegel's death, it remains a poetic seduction (or a Rortyan conversation?), falling short of coherent systematic expression.

What then do we conclude? Some form of minimal personalist theism (or panentheism) may still emerge as philosophically viable, even if it leaves this discussion and enters the next saddled with several specific unresolved difficulties. Pantheism, by contrast, is faced with apparently insurmountable problems. It may still be true that the mystical yearning for immanence, or for the absolutely transcendent One (the two, interestingly, may turn out to be equivalent), finds its quintessential expression in Spinoza's philosophy. But his actual position and arguments have not provided the philosophical grounding for this intuition that can stand up to critical examination. Nor, apparently, is it to be found in any of those, so far, who followed after Spinoza and used his name.

CHAPTER EIGHT

EXCURSUS
Limits of Divine Personhood: Fichte and the Atheism Dispute

> Let us begin with the recognition, which is made in all the main religious traditions, that the ultimate divine reality is infinite and as such transcends the grasp of the human mind. God, to use our christian term, is infinite. He is not a thing, a part of the universe, existing alongside other things; nor is he a being falling under a certain kind. And therefore he cannot be defined or encompassed by human thought. We cannot draw boundaries round his nature and say that he is this and no more.[1]

Since the dawn of Western philosophy, the attribute of infinity has been used to express the unknowability of God. If God is infinite — or so the argument goes — then he cannot be limited in any fashion whatsoever. Among other things, this means that he cannot be limited by *any distinction;* he is not "this" in opposition to "that," since there is simply nothing that is excluded from his essence. Unfortunately, there can be human knowledge only where at least some distinctions are present. Hence God must be absolutely unknowable.

There is no modern thinker whose work brings home the problem of the infinity of God as powerfully as Fichte. Somehow he saw more clearly than his contemporaries how deep are the conceptual difficulties raised by the idea of an infinite God. In the context of the famous "atheism dispute" *(Atheismusstreit)*

---

1. John Hick, *God and the Universe of Faiths* (London: Macmillan, 1973), 139.

Fichte showed exactly where the notion of a personal God is cast into question by a sufficiently radical understanding of the divine infinity. Indeed, he was a bit too successful: his sharp formulations made him notorious overnight and led ultimately to the loss of his teaching position at Jena, a great personal tragedy. Fichte himself could not bear the purely negative implications of his early argument from infinity, and therein lies the second main reason for his continuing importance today: late in life, seeking to avoid his own negative conclusions, Fichte altered his starting point and attempted to develop a positive theory of God. Both aspects of his thought — the skeptical critique and the positive approach — remain crucial for philosophical theology today. Fichte brought the integration of Spinozism and German idealism that we followed in the previous three chapters to a new high point; in so doing he set the stage for a more sophisticated theory of divine personhood.

It cannot be our task within the framework of a short excursus to reconstruct the entire development of Fichte's subjective idealism or to chronicle the various versions of his system as they appear in the progressive editions of his *Science of Logic* (*Wissenschaftslehre*, or WL). Instead of taking the usual approach, I concentrate on presenting and interpreting his later work. It is of course useful to know the genesis of Fichte's subjective idealism, but more useful for the theme of this book is an examination of how he later *transformed* his earlier position and sought to get beyond it. The story of the later Fichte is the story of replacing the ego as ultimate principle with the notion of the absolute or God. Understanding the story allows one to grasp the strengths and weaknesses of philosophical theologies based on the idea of the absolute. What might "absolute knowledge" be: attainable or not, is it even thinkable? As we will see, this question forces one to grapple with how the nature of an object and the knowing of that object are unified, and thus — as in chapter 6 above — how questions of knowledge *may* lead ultimately to a religious metaphysics or theology.

This particular story requires that we begin with Fichte's acknowledgment of a supersensible reality in the key transition years 1799 and 1800, since supersensible reality formed the basis of the position developed in his later work (analogous to the role played by absolute being in Schelling's later writings). In particular, we must concentrate on the arguments that led Fichte to the conclusion that understanding God as an infinite being is incompatible with the belief in a personal God.

FICHTE AND SPINOZA

As will also emerge in the study of Schelling in the next chapter, a major theme of Fichte's philosophy involved the task of thinking together Kant and Spinoza. Recall that Spinoza's quest was to conceive an absolute substance that was not limited by any other. The idea of such a substance required that all individuals be viewed as mere modifications of it. Even in his early years, Fichte realized that one would never manage to conceive God by beginning with a concept like substance whose proper application was to the input of the senses. Substance metaphysics could only mean falling back into a "dogmatism" in the (negative) Kantian sense of the word.[2]

Despite Fichte's criticisms of the concept of substance, he did not completely leave behind the basic concern of pre-Kantian metaphysics — and there is good reason to think that one *cannot* do so. Pannenberg notes correctly that Fichte "returned, in fact, to the metaphysics of the 17th century, insofar as he renewed his relationship with Spinoza. In this manner, Fichte prepared the way for a deepening and extending of the link between Kant's critical philosophy and Spinozism in the work of Schelling and Hegel."[3] On the one hand, we discern Fichte's distance from Spinoza in the fact that his methodological approach was actually much closer to that of Descartes. Beginning with the ego, he discovered an idea — the idea of infinite — that he believed preceded the ego and was thus constitutive for the very idea of the ego. On the other hand, Fichte remained much closer to Spinoza in his theory of the ego, and especially in his manner of treating the question of the absolute. Recall that Descartes conceived the infinite as a divine person who created a world that was different from him and yet remained dependent on him. Fichte, by contrast, agreed with Spinoza's criticism of ontotheology and his rejection of a world separate from God. Fichte's importance for theology thus lies in his updating Spinoza's theory of God in light of the new resources brought by German idealism, especially with regard to the God-world relation.

As is well known, Fichte did not begin his philosophy with the one substance but rather with the dynamics of the self-developing ego. According to Fichte, the ego is the active principle that forms the foundation for any adequate

2. I, 426. Page references in the chapter refer to J. H. Fichte, ed., *Johann Gottlieb Fichtes sämmtliche Werke* (Berlin, 1845-46). References preceded by "NW" are to J. H. Fichte, ed., *Johann Gottlieb Fichtes nachgelassene Werke* (Bonn, 1834-35).

3. See Wolfhart Pannenberg, "Fichte und die Metaphysik des Unendlichen. Dieter Henrich zum 65. Geburtstag," *Zeitschrift für philosophische Forschung* 46 (1992): 348-62, quotation 357. This article and ongoing discussions of its argument with Professor Pannenberg have significantly influenced the approach to Fichte taken in this chapter.

theory of knowledge; it offers the best explanation for the phenomena we observe in the world. But — echoing the question raised by contemporary neuroscience — is there also a transcendent dimension to human selfhood? Is it possible to think the ego or self, understood as a pure principle of activity or pure intelligence, also as something that exists beyond the limitations of the empirical world? Following Kant, the early Fichte took the transcendent ego to be unthinkable. Spinoza's "highest unity" appears only in a critical guise in his *Science of Logic*: not as something that actually exists, but rather as something that *should* be brought into existence by us but *cannot* be. "I note that when one moves beyond the *I am*, one necessarily comes to Spinozism; I also note that there are only two completely consistent systems: the *critical* system, which acknowledges this limitation, and the *Spinozistic* system, which rises above that limit."[4]

In what sense, then, does the ego exist? It could, for example, exist before every other principle, so that every possible distinction would only be a distinction within its own being. In this case, the ego would indeed be truly infinite, but it would also be unthinkable: every distinction would have to be thought as *within it,* whereas it would not exist as distinct from any other. Or, conversely, the ego could exist in the context of a dynamic relation to an Other, an approach that Fichte explored in the *Science of Logic* of 1794. Here one is not concerned with an infinite ego but rather with a finite ego, which one comes to know through the techniques of empirical science.[5] On this view, although one may still possess the idea of an infinite ego, such an idea is only the product of the human ability "to posit something, something absolutely limitless *(etwas schlechthin)*" (I, 93), which links it to what Fichte calls "the first absolutely unlimited foundational sentence" (I, 91ff.). The only ego that we can conceive is the ego that is finite insofar as it is limited by an Other, "for the consciousness of individuality is necessarily accompanied by another consciousness, that of a Thou, and it is only possible under this condition" (I, 476). Fichte uses the title "Spinozism" for the continuing temptation to think the metaphysical first principle as lying beyond all relationships whatsoever. Interestingly, Fichte seems to have "fallen" to precisely this temptation in his own later philosophical theology — as perhaps the subject matter itself requires.

---

4. I, 101. Cf. the excellent presentation by Reinhard Lauth, "Spinoza vu par Fichte," *Archives de Philosophie* 41 (1978): 27-48.

5. "Darum müssen alle Urtheile, deren logisches Subject das einschränkbare oder bestimmbare Ich, oder etwas das Ich bestimmendes ist, durch etwas höheres beschränkt oder bestimmt seyn: aber alle Urtheile, deren logisches Subject das absolut-unbestimmbare Ich ist, können durch nichts höheres bestimmt werden, weil das absolute Ich durch nichts höheres bestimmt wird; sondern sie sind schlechtlin durch sich selbst begründet und bestimmt" (I, 119).

Fichte first introduces in his ethical writings *(Sittenlehre)* the concept of the absolute that characterizes his entire later philosophy. One encounters it in the context of the activity of the ego: "The only absolute, on which all consciousness and all being is grounded, is pure activity. . . . The active ego can only be grasped as a unifying subject and object, that is, as the ego, or as the power to work upon something outside myself. . . . The only actually true thing is my self-activity" (IV, 12). If this is true of each ego, then in one sense, as Fichte himself saw, it must be true that "everyone is God." Although many aspects of Fichte's position after 1800 evidence a change of view, the fundamental balance between the individual-empirical ego and the absolute remains unaffected.

In order to draw attention to the parallels with the doctrine of panentheism that I am developing here (chaps. 7–9), I will treat the position of the earlier Fichte under the title of "idealistic panentheism" and that of the later Fichte under the title of the "mystical or metaphysical panentheism." In both cases Fichte places great emphasis on the individual. Not only is the individual given a central place in his thought insofar as it is not subordinated to any power outside of itself, but Fichte even seems to understand it as an ultimate instance: "Everyone becomes God *(Jeder Wird Gott)*, as far as he or she may be it, that is, consistent with preserving the freedom of all individuals" (IV, 256). At the same time, Fichte understands the individual to be the expression of a phenomenon which transcends the individual himself: "The complete abolition of the individual and the fusing of him into the absolutely pure form of reason or into God is certainly the final goal of finite reason; this abolition is, however, not possible at any time" (IV, 151). In the final analysis, there is only the One: "One exists, and outside of this One nothing. Everything else is nothing: this sentence remains eternally and unchangeably true. The concept of the absolute is preserved as this is understood in every true system" (NW II, 331). What makes Fichte's position panentheistic is that it combines the irreducible existence of individuals with the overarching unity of all things supplied by the One.

Despite the fact that this focus on the absolute One is inspired by Spinoza and remains indebted to his philosophy, Fichte breaks sharply from the approach of his predecessor in several central passages. Again and again, he repeats his criticisms of Spinoza's "dead substance," which he says is "being without thought." In the *Science of Logic* of 1804, he writes that his system breaks "from Spinoza's system and its claims to provide an absolute unity, since it is unable to build any bridges to the level of plurality, and since, when Spinoza begins with plurality, he is not able to make the transition to unity" (NW II, 116). Spinoza "killed . . . his absolute or his God" (NW II, 147), because he conceived it as being without life, whereas Fichte wishes to begin with the absolute as absolute being. For him, substance does not precede thought or the subject, as if it were characterized only by its infinite nature and thus remained incomprehensible. Throughout his work Fichte ascribed to the subject or active principle (whether ego or absolute One) a priority over the world that arises out of its activity.

This starting point implies, however, that whatever might transcend the finite subject will be unknowable. Consequently — and this is what led to the scandal — *the highest unity could not be thought as an individual,* or indeed in any way whatsoever: "The One which is separated, which thus serves as the foundation for all consciousness, and as a result of which the subjective and the objective [component] in consciousness are immediately posited as one, is absolute; it = X. It thus cannot come to consciousness as a simple thing in any fashion" (IV, 5). It was this conclusion that led to the charge of atheism: the infinite, whether conceived as substance or in some other fashion, must remain unknowable, and thus cannot be known as an individual or as personal. In the passage just quoted, the infinite appears as absolute activity; later, in the "Appellation," it appears as the necessity that beings of reason "remain absolute and completely free, dependent on themselves and independent of everything that is not, in itself, reason" (V, 205). Finally, the infinite appears in the later philosophy as the unknowability of the "absolute ground," which can only be understood in a quasimetaphorical sense as "Life" or "Light."

Fichte posed theology with a painful dilemma: either one begins with the finite empirical ego and the concrete parts of sensible experience, or one begins with the absolute. Both options rule out any knowledge of the source of the ego or of the finite realm as a whole. Beginning with the finite ego leads to agnosticism because an absolute ego would transcend the development of the ego as presented in the *Science of Logic;* beginning with the absolute leads to agnosticism because subjective idealism could no longer explain the process by which the ego, its own core principle, comes to be. This dilemma is reminiscent of the problem of the continuum (chap. 4 above): either one begins with the individual parts, whose combination can never result in the whole *qua* whole, or one begins with the whole, with the result that the parts remain mere fictions or imagined endpoints.[6] Thus Baumann comments about the attempt that Fichte undertook in the *Science of Logic* of 1804 to mediate between Kant and Spinoza, "While Kant only perceived the Absolute on the horizon of the actually sensible

---

6. Fichte thus writes to Dr. Scheu: "daß Spinoza das *hen* verliere, wenn er zum *pan* komme, und das *pan,* wenn er das *hen* habe, weil er den Uebergangs-, Wende- und realen Identitätspunkt zwischen beiden nicht anzugeben vermöge" (quoted from Johann Loewe, *Die Philosophie Fichte's nach dem Gesammtergebnisse ihrer Entwickelung und in ihrem Verhältnisse zu Kant und Spinoza* [Stuttgart, 1862], 254). The logic of the part-whole debate is summarized in chapter 5 above.

and the actually supersensible, without placing himself into the standpoint of the Absolute and deriving from it its own actuality, Spinoza, who began with the Absolute, was not able to achieve the transition to disjunction or appearance. . . . Kant saw value in appearances (experience and morality) both in themselves and in light of the Absolute, but did not however derive them from the absolute. Spinoza's thought is absorbed in the absolute, and [as a result] does not discover any possibility of proving the necessity of appearance, finitude, and consciousness."[7] Had Fichte seen himself compelled to make a decision, there is no doubt that, at least after his decisive turn away from (or better: beyond) Kantian idealism, he would have erred in the latter direction, choosing an approach that placed the whole before the parts.

It may well be that Fichte himself was not able to overcome the tension between Kant and Spinoza that he himself often emphasized.[8] Still, his struggles with this dilemma provide a clear picture of the severity of the problem that theologians face. Let me put it bluntly: *after Fichte it can no longer be presupposed that the traditional philosophical/theological doctrine of an infinite personal God represents a defensible conceptual position.* (Of course, that there are difficulties with the idea of an infinite personal God does not prove that no solution can ever be found.) His work brought home that thinking God requires thinking about the whole, the all *(pan)*, the totality of what exists, *including God.* Classical philosophical theism had conceived the ultimate principle of reality as infinite, and as personal, but it had not managed to actually think these two qualities together. We also owe to Fichte some first indications of the route that one might take in order to get to an answer to this crucial theological problem. From his earliest work to his final writings, Fichte continued to emphasize that an acceptable answer would have to meet at least three minimal conditions. It would have to do justice to the insights of German idealism over against earlier metaphysics (subject over substance), and particularly to Kant's critique of knowledge; it would have to think the absolute or the whole as prior to its parts; and it would have to understand the resulting relation between independent existence and dependence (or participation in) the whole in a dialectical fashion.

7. Peter Baumanns, *J. G. Fichte: Kritische Gesamtdarstellung seiner Philosophie* (Freiburg: K. Alber, 1990), 256-57.

8. The weaknesses in subjective idealism that are often used to defend this conclusion cannot be summarized here. A particularly helpful presentation is available in Martial Gueroult, *L'évolution et la structure de la Doctrine de la Science chez Fichte* (Paris: Société d'édition Les Belles lettres, 1930), 2:80ff. Gueroult shows how and why the attempt made by Fichte in the *Science of Logic* of 1801 to mediate between Spinozistic realism and Kantian subjectivism was unsuccessful.

These three parameters for theology represent the starting point for pan-entheism. Note that "panentheism" here may be taken either as a particular constructive position in theology or as shorthand for a set of formal require-ments on theologizing in general. Its strengths and weaknesses as a concrete theological position are a matter of ongoing debate, and there have been some encouraging results.[9] But panentheism remains interesting as an expression of the formal requirements on theology even if one is skeptical (for whatever rea-sons) about constructive theology. One may believe, skeptically, that "God" can be used only as a regulative idea — or that the best we can do is to express the conditions that a successful theology would have to meet (even though none can) — and still agree on these requirements. The continuing service of Fichte's panentheism is to have clearly expressed the formal conditions on the relation-ship between the whole and its individual parts within which *any* adequate the-ism must work.

THE ATHEISM DISPUTE

The early essays of Fichte that we have been considering reach their climax in the writings of the famous Atheism Dispute *(Atheismusstreit),* to which we now turn. At their most radical moments, the early essays had identified God with the moral order itself. Thus Fichte wrote in "On the Ground of Our Belief in a Divine Government of the World" (1798): "This living and efficacious moral order is itself God; we need no other God and cannot conceive any other. There is no basis in reason to move outside of the moral world-order or to assume the existence of a special being as its source on the basis of some inference from what is 'grounded' to its 'Ground'" (V, 186). This quotation might give rise to the impression that the only thing that stands above the ego is a rigid moral or-der or a moral principle, and yet instead of a static order Fichte conceives "an active ordering *(Ordo ordinans)*" (V, 382). The Atheism Dispute gradually makes clear that Fichte had come to these conclusions as a result of recognizing the need to give precedence to the infinite over the finite. For the "active order-ing" could only be attributed to "something that exists and is active in itself

---

9. I have defended a panentheistic theology in *God and Contemporary Science* (Grand Rapids: Eerdmans, 1998); "The Case for Christian Panentheism," *Dialog* 37 (1998): 201-8; "The Panentheistic Turn in Christian Theology," *Dialog* 38 (1999): 289-93 (responding to four critics); and "On the Value of the Panentheistic Analogy: A Response to Willem Drees," *Zygon* 35 (2000), in press.

(Für sich)," in other words, to a principle of pure activity. This activity is not to be understood as "a world soul understood in a substantival sense, but rather as an entity that exists in itself" — albeit in the sense of transcendental philosophy (V, 368). Not unlike what we found in chapter 6 above, Fichte here pushes up against the limits of the transcendental approach and, I believe, has already begun to leave it behind. He wishes to describe something that exceeds his own abilities at comprehension, "and the ability *of all finite being*." A genuinely "moral or intelligible context" must posit "the moral order not within finite moral beings themselves, but outside of them; it thus assumes without doubt something outside or beyond these entities" (V, 392).

Fichte hopes to show that belief in God is dependent on the concept of fulfilling one's duty and not the other way around. Only in the course of defending his moral understanding of religion does Fichte discover an additional argument, one that — together with the difficulties that he had already discovered in the *Science of Logic* — finally lifted his thoughts beyond the horizon of morality itself. His new (or newly understood) argument — the one that launched the Atheism Dispute — is meant to show that "the concept of God, understood as a particular substance, is impossible and self-contradictory" (V, 188). Fichte's overall argument for this conclusion turned on at least three main arguments. I have already mentioned the first one: "The concept of God cannot by any means be specified by means of existential propositions, but only through the predicates of activity" (V, 371). The notion of substance is too passive to serve as the foundation for the primary definition of God. Even worse, "substance" means "necessarily an entity which exists in a sensible fashion, in space and time" (V, 216) — and hence, a being that would contradict the essential nature of the infinite.

A second argument anticipates Feuerbach's "projection" criticism of religion; although Fichte later repudiated this argument, it was to have a strong impact on nineteenth-century thought. When humans "speak of the various relations of that [moral] order to themselves and to their action, when they speak with others of this order and summarize and fix it by means of a concept of an existing Being, which they perhaps call God, this is the result of the finitude of their understanding. . . . Whoever, however, asks for a concept of the being of God that is in any way developed without relation to our moral nature and is taken to be even in the least degree independent of it, this person has never known God and is alienated from the life which comes from God" (V, 208-9). In this passage Fichte expresses the dilemma once again: to ascribe to God some sort of content above the sphere of morality is unjustified, but to develop a theory of God on the basis of morality only makes visible the limits of our own finitude. For "every belief in something divine which contains more than the concept of the moral order is to that extent a poetic composition and superstition; this belief may be harmless, and yet it is always unworthy of a reasoning being as well as highly suspicious" (V, 394-95). If human knowledge has its limits at the point of the individual and her ethical consciousness or feelings, everything *trans*-individual must be viewed as merely metaphorical. (The same applies if knowledge is limited to what can be empirically studied.) In this case, the concept of that which is above the individual can at best serve as a moral exhortation; at worst, it draws attention away from one's moral obligations. Unfortunately, all talk of metaphysical substances falls in this latter category.

Finally, Fichte is concerned to show that God simply cannot be understood as an ego, insofar as an infinite ego would not allow for any Other that would stand over against it:

> because in God that which is reflected would have to be all in one and one in all, and that which reflects would likewise have to be all in one and one in all. Thus, that which is reflected and reflecting in and through God — consciousness itself and the object of consciousness — would not be able to be distinguished. The self-consciousness of God would remain unexplained on this view; indeed, it will remain eternally unexplainable and incomprehensible for *all* finite reason, that is, for all reason that remains bound to the law according to which whatever is reflected upon is understood by drawing distinctions. (I, 275)

With this third argument, the critique of the metaphysics of substance in Western thought, which one can trace as far back as the Hellenistic philosophers, reaches its high point. Not only does substance appear as an unknown "X" that cannot itself possess any qualities; according to Fichte it must also be understood as a postulate that is unknowable in its very essence if Kant's critique of knowledge is correct. Further, any substance that is not understood as Spirit (e.g., Spinoza's) must in some sense be material; it is a "material thing" (V, 262), "an entity that has a sensible existence in space and time."[10] Of course, substance conceived in this manner would stand in complete contradiction to the pure activity that formed the core of Fichte's philosophy — as it would contradict most forms of theism. Worse, such a concept of divine substance would tend to work against the moral activity that is fundamental to religion instead of supporting it. Fichte thus believes that he possesses a positive reason for re-

10. V, 216. Fichte also expresses this position in the *Science of Logic* of 1804: "Ich sage: So viel aus allen Philosophien bis auf Kant klar hervorgeht, wurde das Absolute gesetzt in das Sein, in das todte Ding, als Ding; das Ding sollte sein das Ansich" (NW II, 95).

jecting every substantial theory of God: "Build within yourself an attitude that is in accord with obligation, and you will know God" (V, 210). Later, Fichte summarizes his position with a quote from Jacobi: "One comes to dwell within God by means of a God-like life" (V, 232).

Such a theology will have to be understood as practical and moral instead of theoretical; it will be at home not in abstract reason but rather at the level of feeling. According to Fichte, this position also means turning away from a God who could be proven through sensory experience: "To me, God is merely and exclusively the regent of the supersensible world" (220). Similarly, "our philosophy denies the existence of a sensible God and of one who serves the appetite; still, the supersensible God is on this view All in All; he is the one who alone is, and we other rational spirits all live and move only in him" (223-24). We will look at Fichte's turn from the sensible realm further below; at this point it is sufficient to note his insistence on the close affinity between the concepts of the sensible and the finite. Defending the idea of a supersensible God, as Western theism has, thus means asserting the existence of a God who is truly infinite.

Throughout the course of the Atheism Dispute, then, Fichte advocated a form of moral panentheism. His point of departure remained the sense of obligation and the limits imposed by transcendental philosophy. Nonetheless, this sense of obligation, however individual, was also transcendent with regard to its absolutely binding status — indeed, transcendent in the only sense acceptable for thinkers who work within a strictly post-Kantian framework. Thus, as Chifu notes, "God is the idea of a principle that remains immanent within individuals, and yet at the same time stands over against all individuals in its totality."[11]

FICHTE'S LATER PHILOSOPHY

Fichte's later philosophy has often been interpreted as a form of monism in opposition to the dualism of Cartesian thought or the trinitarian structure of Christian theology. Thus, Dominik Schmidig lists eighteen interpreters who construe Fichte's doctrine of God as monistic or pantheistic.[12] But is monism

---

11. Cf. C. Chifu, *Die Entwicklung des Gottesbegriffs bei J. G. Fichte* (Weida i. Th., 1913), 25. Chifu denies that Fichte's philosophy, even at this point, can actually be made consistent with basic principles of an idealist theory of knowledge.

12. See R. D. Dominico Schmidig, "Gott und Welt," in *Fichtes Anweisung zum seligen Leben* (Wald, 1966), 13. Cf. Pannenberg, 359.

really the correct term for characterizing this view? Or does Fichte not rather make a fundamental break with monistic thought? How, we must ask, does he construe the relation between the absolute and the finite? Admittedly, Fichte greatly emphasizes the priority of the one absolute after 1800, a reorientation that makes his thought appear increasingly as a version of the philosophy of unity. In the later writings the individual ego is clearly presented as part of something larger: "The real appearance appears as a manifold of a unity of egos which is given in its self-intuition."[13] Still, however much Fichte's later thought was molded by the motif of unity, he never abandoned the individual. Until the end of his life the freedom of the individual subject and the transcendence of God — two doctrines that presuppose and supplement one another — remain unquestioned core assumptions of his theology.

The Problem

Even before 1800 (and ever since then in the secondary literature) Fichte's theory has been confronted with the problem of the beginning. If the ego exists only in and through its opposition to the Other, then how can the concept of the ego explain its own primordial origin? Either one must treat the ego as something given, as a primitive — perhaps by holding that it always existed so that no account of its genesis is possible — or it is necessary to supplement one's account with another principle outside of the ego in order to explain the ego's origin in another way.

Basically, the latter route was the direction that Fichte took after 1800. If God cannot be understood as the highest Ego or greatest subject — and the problems discussed above in conjunction with the concept of an infinite person clearly show why the divine cannot be comprehended in this manner — then God must be understood to represent something that stands beyond the ego. But for finite reason, according to Fichte, whatever is not ego is ultimately a product of the activity of (some) ego or subject. Thus finite reason cannot grasp the divine. If God cannot be understood by reason, then the divine can only be understood by faith or feeling. In his anthropological work *Die Bestimmung des Menschen* (1800), Fichte begins to move in this direction. The

---

13. Fichte, *Die Thatsachen des Bewußtseins* (1813), NW I, 551. Metaphorically, this would mean that the existence of things in this world has become a picture of the appearing God; things in the world have only pictorial being as parts of the picture, but do not exist in the pre-Kantian ontological sense. Of course, it hardly needs to be said that this theory of pictures (*Bildtheorie*) is an extremely speculative one.

will, at least in the supersensible world, becomes the "principle for a whole se-ries of spiritual consequences." This result suggests a new inference: "according to the former perspective, whereby the will is understood as pure act, it stands completely under my control. That this becomes the case, and becomes it as first principle, does not depend on me but rather on a law under which I myself stand: the law of nature in the sensible world, and a supersensible law in the supersensible world" (II, 297). Now "every sensible life within the finite realm points toward a higher life, into which the will leads one almost through itself alone" (II, 289). As a living principle, this higher life is also infinite will, creator of the world, parent of all finite individuals.

This radical shift from Fichte's earlier writings reflects once again the pri-ority of the infinite over the finite, a theme that has occupied us since examin-ing the work of Descartes at the dawn of modern thought (chap. 2 above). In-stead of the primacy of the ego, which Fichte emphasized in the earlier editions of the *Science of Logic,* he now affirms a priority of the whole above the parts: "I am only a link in the chain of it [sc. the spiritual order], and I can no more judge concerning the Whole than an individual tone within the song could judge concerning the harmony of the whole. . . . Thus, I exist in connection with the One that exists and participate in its being" (II, 299).[14] The history of Fichte's intellectual development is the history of the increasing content and importance that he attributes to the principle of the whole — a shift that he makes (or at least attempts to make) without negating reason, but rather by considering the very limits of reason that he had explored, following Kant, in his earlier epistemological writings.

Fichte can reach his goal only in one manner: by introducing a *trans*-ra-tional ability, the faculty of intellectual intuition, which he believes is capable, at least in part, of grasping the content of this highest principle. Fichte learned through his study of Spinoza that an unlimited extension of the finite could never reach the infinite. Thus, he wrote already in *Die Bestimmung des Menschen:* "what I grasp becomes finite solely by means of my grasping it; and this [result] can never be transformed into the infinite even if I increase it and raise it endlessly. You [God] are different from the finite not only in degree but also in type" (II, 304). Only turning away from philosophy and turning toward

---

14. Compare this view to that taken by Walter Schulz, *Der Gott der neuzeitlichen Metaphysik* (Pfüllingen: G. Neske, 1959), 49: "Einmal muß sich der Mensch freigeben für das Seiende im Ganzen, das heißt er darf nicht bei diesem und jenem bestimmten Seienden stehenbleiben und Halt suchen, er muß vielmehr das, was das Seiende im Ganzen ist, zu erfahren suchen. *Wie* dieses geschehen kann, sagt die zweite Grundmöglichkeit: der Mensch muß sich loslassen ins Nichts, das heißt [nach Heidegger] 'freiwerden von den Götzen, die jeder hat und zu denen er sich wegzuschleichen pflegt.'"

religious feeling — that is, only by means of holistic thought — could the infinite ever be grasped.[15]

Fichte's Later Thought as a Model for Theology

The shift from Fichte's earlier subjective idealism that we have been discussing can be understood as more or less drastic. Some commentators interpret it as a total break; thus Horneffer writes: "Now, in place of a restless striving towards an ideal that is never reached, one finds a unification with eternal being in intuition and in life."[16] I have tried to show, however, that important continuities bind the earlier and the late conceptions. Clearly, Fichte felt that he could work at a new level after 1800. He now explicitly advanced a concept of God, which became important for all aspects of his philosophy: for the theory of the ego and of knowledge, for his speculative philosophy, and not least for his ethical theory, which he based on the ideas of an infinite and highest Good, God and immortality. Increasingly, religion, and with it metaphysics, moved into the center of Fichte's philosophy. He no longer presented his theory as a philosophy of the ego, but now in a completely new fashion: "Metaphysics, and by that I mean the supersensible, is the element of religion. From the beginning of the world up to the present day, religion, in whatever form it may have appeared, has been metaphysics; and whoever despises and makes fun of metaphysics — or, to use the Latin, everything a priori — either does not know what he is looking for, or he is despising or making fun of religion" (VII, 241). Of course, Fichte uses the term "metaphysics" not in a primarily epistemological or ontological but rather in an ethical and voluntaristic sense.[17] What kind of metaphysics or theology does he then have in mind, and why does he believe that it represents the final consequence of his newly reconceived science of logic?

Fichte maintains that the absolute as such is never present in our consciousness; instead, it *precedes* every thought. Absolute knowing has to possess the knowledge of its own process of origination, and for this the existence of a true absolute must be presupposed. This highest principle Fichte labels Abso-

15. For details, see Jürgen Stolzenberg, *Fichtes Begriff der intellektuellen Anschauung. Die Entwicklung in den Wissenschaftslehren von 1793/94 bis 1801/02* (Stuttgart: Klett-Cotta, 1986).

16. See Martha Horneffer, *Die Identitätslehre Fichtes in den Jahren 1801-1806 in ihren Beziehungen zu der Philosophie Schellings* (Leipzig: F. Meiner, 1925), 44.

17. See Ernst Gelpcke, *Fichte und die Gedankenwelt des Sturm und Drang. Eine ideengeschichtliche Untersuchung zur Ergründung der Wurzeln des deutschen Idealismus* (Leipzig, 1928), 233.

lute Being, "independent of knowing, and ground of all reflection."[18] Admittedly, such a line of argumentation distances itself from the earlier project of a science of logic: "The unity can certainly not lie in what we see and comprehend as the science of logic, for this is merely an objective thing; it must instead live and move in that which we ourselves, internally, are."[19] The very idea of "Absolute Being" implies a No, a negation of all finite insight and of all concepts. The Light lives completely through itself: "But 'completely through itself' also means independent from all insight, and absolutely negating the possibility of all insight" (150). All abstract predicates, "with the preeminent predicate at the very top, that of absolute substance, involve only negative characteristics; they are in themselves dead and nothing. The living reality is 'the tombstone of the concept'" (150-51), for "insight . . . is thoroughly destroyed in [by?] the living Light" (163). Note that Fichte now views this result as the inescapable implication of his own starting point: subjective idealism or the philosophy of the subject. This can only mean that he has in mind the possibility of a synthesis of transcendental philosophy with an (admittedly revised) metaphysics — exactly the same synthesis we have been working toward since the first chapter.[20]

Despite a number of essential differences, the similarities of Fichte's approach with that of the later Schelling — similarities that have been emphasized again and again since Hegel's day — are particularly interesting.[21] For both thinkers the absolute is "the principle of organic unity, the principle of unity and diversity simultaneously. And yet it stands above the opposition between subjective and objective; the two come together into one in the Absolute, even though the division remains preserved in it, at least as a potential."[22] The two thinkers differ, among other things, in that Fichte maintains and Schelling

18. See Lucie Albers, *Der Gottesbegriff bei Fichte* (Breslau, 1915), 30.

19. *Science of Logic*, 1804; NW II, 133. The following references in the text are to this work.

20. Cf. I, 496. Fichte now seeks to ground transcendental philosophy upon (a type of) metaphysics, since the latter serves as the only real philosophy.

21. See, e.g., Georg Wilhelm Friedrich Hegel, *Differenz des Fichte'schen und Schelling'schen Systems der Philosophie*, Philosophische Bibliothek, vol. 62a (Hamburg: Felix Meiner, 1962); Jakob Friedrich Fries, *Fichte's und Schelling's neueste Lehren von Gott und der Welt* (Heidelberg, 1807); Jakob Barion, *Die intellektuelle Anschauung bei J. G. Fichte und Schelling und ihre religionsphilosophische Bedeutung* (Würzburg: C. J. Becker, 1929); Salomon Gewurz, *Studien zur Entwicklungsgeschichte der Schelling'schen Philosophie unter besonderer Berücksichtigung seiner Beziehungen zu Fichte* (n.l., 1909); George Joseph Seidel, *Activity and Ground: Fichte, Schelling, and Hegel* (Hildesheim and New York: G. Olms, 1976). Important texts for this debate are found in Walter Schulz, ed., *Briefwechsel Fichte-Schelling* (Frankfurt: Suhrkamp, 1968). See also chapter 9 below.

22. Albers, *Der Gottesbegriff bei Fichte*, 31.

denies that God can be known in his actual nature. Fichte argues that God's nature is in itself differentiated, since we ourselves *are* this Life, whereas Schelling is more skeptical about knowing the divine nature because God's freedom sets unsurpassable limits for any knowledge of God's nature.[23]

Of course, a number of reservations can be raised about various of the late "systematic" assertions that Fichte makes. Must not a philosophy that speaks of absolute negation fall back into the realm of metaphors and symbols alone? How compelling a philosophical proof can be given for the claim that what is negated *must be* understood as "Light" or "Life"? Why, for example, should the unity of being and thought be construed as "Light" and not rather as a coincidence of opposites *(coincidentia oppositorum)* as in the theology of Nicholas of Cusa (chap. 3 above)? Fichte understands knowing as a "picture" of God, and he takes science to be the purest expression of the absolute.[24] But why should we interpret this formulation as a "scientific" and not rather as an "apophatic" answer? It may well be, as we will see in the next chapter, that God may not be understood as *less than* that which he has produced: humanity. But is *this* insight enough to determine the content of a systematic-speculative philosophy?

The Synthesis

Already in *Die Bestimmung des Menschen,* Fichte emphasizes that the will is to become the new unifying category: "reason active in itself is will. The law of the supersensible world must therefore be a will."[25] As a result, Fichte must concern himself with the question, "How is the will of an incomprehensible entity to be comprehended?" He answers that the practical sphere, and not pure specula-

---

23. On Schelling's critique of Fichte, see his *Sämmtliche Werke,* VII, 1-126, e.g., 7-8. Unfortunately, we lack sufficient space to offer a detailed comparative analysis of the two thinkers.

24. NW II, 127. Somewhat later he identifies "ein Wissen schlechthin" with "reinem Licht" (II, 233) und links *Licht* und *Vernunft:* "Hier [sc. im Fall des nach aller Abstraktion Übrigbleibenden] haben wir es reines Licht, oder Vernunft genannt" (ibid.).

25. II, 297. Cf. 303-4: "Erhabener lebendiger Wille, den kein Name nennt, und kein Begriff umfasst, wohl darf ich mein Gemüth zu dir erheben; denn du und ich sind nicht getrennt. Deine Stimme ertönt in mir, die meinige tönt in dir wieder; und alle meine Gedanken, wenn sie nur wahr und gut sind, sind in dir gedacht. — In dir, dem Unbegreiflichen, werde ich mir selbst, und wird mir die Welt vollkommen begreiflich, alle Räthsel meines Daseyns werden gelöst, und die vollendetste Harmonie entsteht in meinem Geiste."

tion alone, must now provide the foundation for specifying the nature of God. Moreover, he argues, dependence on this sort of practical intuition is the true definition of faith. Hence faith, like life, comes to serve as the fundamental epistemic quality of the religious realm.

In chapter 3 we were forced to conclude that, even if appeals to immediate intuition are unavoidable, they cannot provide a sufficient justification for theological claims to knowledge. Unfortunately, it appears that in his late philosophy Fichte made precisely this claim for the faculty of intuition. On the basis of an allegedly indubitable *internal* consciousness of the principle of life, he claims *external* or philosophical certainty for his own systematic inferences — at the same time that he insists that the truths he refers to are actually inexpressible. I find this particular combination of ineffability and formulation, of the philosophical and the metaphilosophical, scarcely convincing, and will thus pass quickly over it. Instead of pausing to consider, and to refute, the epistemic faculty of intuition that supposedly guarantees Fichte's results, let us consider instead the *theological content* that Fichte developed in his later years.

Fichte's late theology grows out of his attempt, after the Atheism Dispute, to find an adequate solution to the fundamental problem of idealism: the problem of how to distinguish between thinker and absolute thought. After 1801, in the context of his new version of the *Science of Logic,* he began to look for the solution by using the tools of theism rather than (as in his early work) by appealing first to the concepts of faith and praxis. "Knowing, as something absolute and bound to its primordiality, must therefore be characterized as the One, . . . as Being itself, which is unchangeable, eternal, non-interchangeable, and self-identical. Or it could be [characterized] as God, if one can think of him as having an awareness of knowing and a being related to that knowing" (II, 61). At first Fichte was not quite willing to make the theological move to its full extent, since he still attributed the specifically theological attributes to knowing itself. But as the years went by, the more Fichte's presentation of the qualities of absolute knowing came to approximate the classical idea of God, the greater became the cleft between his emerging theology and the idealistic argumentative structure of the *Science of Logic* in its early editions. And yet Fichte never returned to metaphysics in the pre-Kantian, pre-idealist sense — the metaphysics of a Thomas Aquinas, Descartes, or Spinoza. This is the point of the stress on knowing in the previous quotation: to understand God as substance is to conceive the divine in terms of "dead being"; only a position that starts with divine activity and willing, and with a connection between the knowing and what is known, can do justice to the divine nature.

How should thinker and thought be thought together? What or who could know an object and at the same time overcome the very difference between knowing and being known? According to Fichte, the difference could be overcome only at the level of absolute knowing: "Now everyone, if he only reflects a little, can have immediate awareness that absolutely all being presupposes a thinking or consciousness, and therefore that mere being is only one half to a second [half], namely, to the thinking of that being; [mere being] is only one member of a more fundamental disjunction that lies above it. . . . Absolute unity can thus no more be located in being than it can in some consciousness that stands over against being. Rather, absolute unity is located in . . . the principle that we have discovered: the principle of the absolute unity and indivisibility of the two." This principle is what "we wish to call pure knowing" (NW II, 95-96). The reader discovers in this central text what von Hofe calls the "enduring subjectivism" of Fichte's approach: "enduring subjectivism, for this absolute unity that stands *above* all thinking is at the same time only our thinking and is in it. And if we try to think it in itself, independent of thinking, we find ourselves thinking precisely the same thing."[26]

Theology as the Theory of the Absolute

Again, I wish to set aside Fichte's epistemology, since the difficulties with an alleged intellectual intuition are already clear enough. Still, even without intellectual intuition the theologian still finds herself confronted with the task of conceiving a divine reality that is actually able to bring together thinking and being (cf. chap. 6 above). How is one to think this reality? Hegel at least attempted to find an answer to this question that would be theoretically ("logically") as well as historically *("realphilosophisch")* adequate. Fichte, by contrast, did not attempt to write a systematic theory of God, not even in his great later work, *The Science of Logic* of 1804. He does make use of a whole range of metaphors, at first speaking of "feeling," later of "pure knowing" or "pure light" or "life," and in the end of "appearance," "revelation," "expression of the absolute," and "love." None of these metaphors, however, functions analogously to the concept of the dialectic in Hegel; none answers the question of how one is to think unity in difference. The appeal to religion is also not adequate in and of itself.[27] Ad-

26. Joh. von Hofe, *J. G. Fichtes religiöse Mystik nach ihren Ursprüngen untersucht* (Bern, 1904), 54.
27. "Erhebe dich nur in den Standpunct der Religion, und alle Hüllen schwinden; die Welt vergehet dir mit ihrem todten Princip, und die Gottheit selbst tritt wieder in dich ein, in ihrer ersten und ursprünglichen Form, als Leben, als dein eigenes Leben, das du leben sollst und leben wird" (V, 471). The philosophical problems of the absolute are certainly more difficult than Fichte assumes here.

mittedly, Fichte now corrects for the excesses of his earlier subjective idealism. But now he opens himself to the charge that he has altogether eliminated the concept of the subject, which had dominated the early phase of his thought, in order to find an appropriate place for God: "As long as a person desires to be anything at all in himself, God does not come to him, for no human can become God. As soon as he destroys himself — purely, totally, and down to the roots — only God remains, and becomes All in All. A human cannot produce a God, but he can destroy himself as the true negation, with the result that he then sinks into God" (V, 518).

What, then, is the basic conceptual structure that underlies Fichte's later theology, once he has shown that the idea of God as an infinite subject is untenable?[28] I have argued that he advances a form of panentheism, according to which all finite subjects are understood as part of the divine All — distinct parts of a whole that nonetheless transcends them. On the one hand, one might criticize this interpretation by pointing to some of the later texts that seem to presuppose an absolute monism or pantheism. For example, one reads in the *Anweisungen:* "Being is thoroughly simple, not manifold; there are not several beings, but only the one Being. . . . Only the one Being *is,* and there simply *is* nothing else that would not be Being but would lie above Being" (V, 404-5). Or even more clearly: "In the love [that I have described] Being and existence, God and humanity, are one, completely fused and run together" (V, 540). It is hard to avoid the suspicion that some kind of monism or henoism underlies passages such as these.[29]

Against this interpretation, on the other hand, stand the two dominant themes of Fichte's later writings: the transcendence of God and the freedom of the finite, self-conscious individual. God "pours forth . . . his essence out of himself; he lets it stand truly independently and free . . . existence grasps hold of

---

28. We will have to pass over the question of the epistemic status of this view — e.g., the question whether Fichte's concept of picture *(Bild)* is capable of bringing together his language about God and being in a manner that remains consistent with the Kantian limits on knowledge. Cf. Peter Reisinger, *Idealismus als Bildtheorie* (Stuttgart: Klett-Cotta, 1979). The defenders of Fichte's *Bildtheorie* often assume that Hegel has solved the problem of an absolute beginning; they thus find in Fichte's later writings anticipations of the Hegelian solutions, and the anticipation is then taken as a sort of confirmation of Fichte's work.

29. See, e.g., Wilhelm Lütterfelds, "Fichtes Konzept absoluter Einheit (1804) — ein performativer Selbstwiderspruch?" *Fichte-Studien* 6 (1994): 401-22, e.g., 402: "Und diese absolute Einheit sieht F. bekanntlich in jenem 'Sein' erreicht, das eine in sich geschlossene, einzigartige, lebendige Einheit darstellt, die in sich, durch sich und von sich existiert, die sich selber konstruiert, die letztlich auch identisch mit dem Wir und Ich ist und die die einzig angemessene Form des Absoluten–Gottes–darstellt."

itself with its own independent power" (V, 455). Fichte clearly rejects absolute unity: "Even when it falls together with the One, our basic form cannot disappear. Even when we come together with it, it does not become our ownmost being, but it [or he] stands before us as something that is foreign and that dwells outside of us, something that we can only give ourselves to and attach to an inner love . . . even after the return to and unification with him, the world does not disappear to us" (V, 461).

In these texts one discerns once again the structure of panentheism.[30] The inseparability of God and the world does not mean that the one disappears into the other or vice versa. Thus Gelpcke correctly notes: "Fichte's divinity is like Herder's; it is eminent and lives in the world. Nonetheless Fichte avoids the danger, again like Herder, of allowing God to be subsumed into the world. Thus there remains a final remnant of transcendence. The position links eminence and transcendence, pantheism and theism, yielding a type of religious worldview that is nothing other than panentheism — a view that Christian Frederich Krause, who was the first to construct this distinction from pantheism, has called the All-in-God doctrine."[31] The position could also be called "ethical pantheism": it is neither naturalistic pantheism in Spinoza's sense nor a variant of Kantian ethical theism, but rather a synthesis of the two. Being in itself may have to be labeled unknowable and the concept of an infinite personal Being may be self-contradictory, so that God cannot be conceived as one particular substance (V, 188). Still, one can say rather more about the God-world relation: "Ex-istence [sc. Dasein]/God in his energies is both identical with and yet ineffably distinct from Being/God in his essence (that is, we are compelled to make statements that suggest both monism and dualism). . . . The world is created by the energies (that is, we may locate here some analog of Fichte's claim that 'Consciousness [= Ex-istence] is the creator of the world')."[32]

---

30. I must emphasize once again that we are dealing here with a conceptual structure but not with a metaphysical position in the pre-Kantian sense. Fichte's text is to be understood as a protest against a dogmatic ontologizing, but it is not a rejection of the structure of panentheism: "Einige, die der W.-L. viel Ehre anzuthun und Löbliches nachzusagen glauben mit Sätzen solcher Art: wir sind in Gott, haben unser Leben in ihm, und dergl.; möchten sich erst umthun, in welchem Sinne etwa, und unter welcher Beschränkung man dies auch in der W. L. sagen könne. — Dieser Meinung müßte Kant gewesen sein, wenn er ins Reine gekommen wäre" (NW II, 331). In previous chapters I have already questioned whether Kant's limitations are necessary, and whether they can be consistently maintained. Note also the structural relations with Neoplatonism.

31. See Gelpcke, *Fichte und die Gedankenwelt des Sturm und Drang*, 228.

32. Cf. Anthony N. Perovich, Jr., "Fichte and the Typology of Mysticism," in Daniel Breazeale und Tom Rockmore, eds., *Fichte: Historical Contexts/Contemporary Controversies*

This is a fascinating position and one that remains significant for philosophical theology today. At some points the ego threatens to disappear in forgottenness; other passages give rise to the impression that God is being reduced to the ego.[33] Fichte gives a convincing reason for this sort of vacillation, even if it is questionable whether he himself possessed the conceptual means for overcoming it. In the passages in which this vacillation comes to clearest expression, Fichte often appeals to the "fact that" without giving sufficient attention to the question of "how." For example, he writes that "our love for him" is merely "his own love of himself," with the result alluded to above: "In this love, Being and existence, God and humanity, are one, completely fused and run together" (I, 540).[34]

Despite these weaknesses, Fichte has probably grasped *the fundamental metaphysical problem for theology after Kant,* as he also grasped the problem of an infinite being, with more acuity than any other thinker in the modern period. I quote in full one of numerous texts that convey this insight:

> Just as this faith disappears through the highest act of freedom and in its completion, the ego it has become falls into the pure divine existence. Speaking strictly, one cannot even say that the affect, the love, and the will of this divine being belong to it, for there simply are no longer two, but only one, no longer two wills, but only one, and this one will is All in All. As long

---

(Atlantic Highlands, N.J.: Humanities Press, 1994), 138. Perovich emphasizes the both/and structure of this view in such a fashion that it appears as a clear contradiction. He reads the passages where Fichte conceives a dialectical relationship between God and the individual empirical ego merely as the assertion of opposites. For this reason he attributed to Fichte an exclusively negative theology, whereas Fichte himself maintains that both poles can be asserted without contradiction. Cf. Akira Omine, "Intellektuelle Anschauung und Mystik," *Fichte-Studien* 3 (1991): 184-203.

33. In this manner Russell Warren Stine (*The Doctrine of God in the Philosophy of Fichte* [Philadelphia, 1945], 68-69) writes, "If one who has been attending the lectures which Fichte called *Die Anweisung zum Seligen Leben* asks, 'What then is God', he will be ready for F's prompt answer: 'The moral man is God.' The inward essential nature of God Himself, as it is absolutely, in itself and through itself, immediately, purely, and without any intervening medium, without being modified, veiled or obscured by any form which is contained in the personality of the Ego, and which is on that account, obstructive and limiting, but broken only by the indestructible form of infinity is seen in the man of good will, the moral man." And yet even Stine is compelled to add, "He who is inspired by God will reveal to us the very Nature of God's Being."

34. Cf. 543: "Das lebendige Leben ist die Liebe, und hat und besitzt, als Liebe, das Geliebte, umfasst und durchdrungen, verschmolzen und verflossen mit ihm: ewig die Eine und dieselbe Liebe."

as man desires to be anything at all, God does not come to him, for no person can become God. But as soon as he destroys himself completely, wholly, and right to the roots, only God remains, and is All in All. A person cannot produce God, but he can destroy himself as the actual negation, with the result that he then sinks into God." (I, 518)

This text is in accordance with the earlier passages we have looked at and beautifully summarizes the entire later thrust of Fichte's thought. God remains the life and the activity; he must be thought and can only be thought as an active principle, as one who acts. This means that Fichte's position represents a form of the "theology of action." We have already noticed his claim that religion is the driving force behind the ethical life. Now he takes a more extreme step: the assertion of an absolute ego leads to the belief that every individual is made in the image of God, and thus to a belief in all of humanity. In such an approach the old rational or theoretical construal of metaphysics is subordinated to the immediate feeling of love. When one allows the religious dimension to add concrete content to the speculative concept of the ego, as Fichte does, the relation between the ego and the absolute is redefined. This relation now takes its final form in his thought: "In so far as man is love . . . , and in so far as, in particular, he is the love of God, he remains always and eternally the One, the True, the Unchanging, just as God himself is, and he remains God himself. This is not a mere metaphor, but is the literal truth, just as John has said: Whoever remains in love, he remains in God, and God in him" (V, 543).

Fichte and the Critique of Theism as Projection

The development of Fichte's thought — from the early ethical and idealist writings through the combative essays of the Atheism Dispute and on to his later philosophy — is of more than merely historical interest. In my view, this conceptual development provides the basis for an answer to the critique that all theism is a mere human projection. This famous critique of religion may have moved into the center of cultural awareness with Feuerbach's treatment of religion, but it already represented a fundamental theme in Fichte's intellectual career. In particular, the worry about projection played a decisive role in his movement away from his early equation of religion and morality[35] to the *Science of Logic* of 1804.

35. This equation can be clearly seen, e.g., in the "Appellation": "Dass der Mensch . . . auf den Glauben an diese Ordnung einer moralischen Welt . . . sich stütze, jede seiner

Even in the later writings, morality remains the human means of access — and perhaps our only access — to religion. On this view, the notion of God provides the key for understanding the moral order, even though it cannot serve as the foundation for a metaphysical theology. One can see Fichte's opposition to metaphysical theology most clearly in his stress on the notion of *activity*, as Gelpcke correctly sees: "'Nothing is besides God, and God is nothing besides Life,' we read in one of Fichte's sonnets. . . . This quote conveys two things: first, that God is the highest principle and the only absolute; and second, that God can only be thought as the Word become action, that he is completely acting, completely making, indeed, completely Creator, and the Creator of the world."[36] And yet one notices that the metaphysical dimension of theology has not been eliminated, since it continues to be crucial to theology to maintain that God cannot be equated with the world as a whole.

How then should the difference between God and world be understood? The question represents a dilemma for post-Kantian theology because the answer, however important it may be, transcends the realm of moral activity. It is hard to miss the parallels between Fichte's appeal to the distinction *ordo ordinans vs. ordo ordinatus* in order to answer the question and Spinoza's appeal to *natura naturans vs. natura naturata*.[37] Recall that Spinoza did not introduce *natura naturans* ("nature naturing") as a being above the world but rather as equivalent to the totality of actions within the world. In contrast to Spinoza's pantheism, Fichte as a panentheist retains the moment of transcendence. His concern instead is to deny that God must be introduced as a cosmic Orderer who stands above and beyond the world order: "To conceive God as a specific being means to reduce him down to the level of empirical senses and limitation. For all specific beings are finite beings."[38] Fichte's own position demands that the existence of an absolute be presupposed — an absolute which is in the world and yet at the same time remains transcendent in a specific sense. In the final analysis, it is this paradigm of the God-world relation that represents Fichte's most valuable contribution to theology.

The later Fichte achieved a subtle combination of two factors that are es-

---

Pflichten betrachte als eine Verfügung jener Ordnung, jede Folge derselben für gut, d. i. für seligmachend halte, und freudig sich ihre unterwerfe, ist absolut nothwendig und das wesentliche der Religion. Dass er die verschiedenen Beziehungen jener Ordnung auf sich und sein Handeln . . . in dem Begriffe eines existirenden Wesens zusammenfasse und fixire, das er vielleicht Gott nennt, ist die Folge der Endlichkeit seines Verstandes" (V, 208).

36. Gelpcke, *Fichte und die Gedankenwelt des Sturm und Drang*, 226.

37. See, e.g., Fichte's so-called Privatschreiben of 1800 in V, 382.

38. See Heinrich Rickert, *Fichtes Atheismusstreit und die Kantische Philosophie. Eine Säkularbetrachtung* (Berlin, 1899), 19.

sential for theology today: the need for some form of metaphysical or philosophical speculation, and the awareness of sharp epistemic limits. When these two factors are combined, a view like Fichte's can help defend against the tendency to anthropomorphize God. All human attributes, including the attribute of personality itself, are excluded from his idea of God. Only one attribute remains unaffected in Fichte's later work: the primacy of infinity over the finite. In order to answer the projection critique, theologians must recognize the failure of Fichte's early attempt — and all similar attempts — to ground theology in the insights or wishes or self-development of the human subject, and instead move to a philosophically minimal view such as Fichte's later position. Every thinker who interprets the human species as infinite (in Feuerbach's sense) ignores Fichte's careful arguments against an infinite ego, since he showed that an ego must be understood as finite and as set over against an Other.

Fichte was compelled to the famous shift in his theology by the inability of a completely speculative system to explain how the finite ego could arise through and out of itself. *The mere existence of a finite self-consciousness requires the postulation of an absolute dimension or instance.* Of course, the status of such a postulate is not yet decided in this formulation. It might be merely a regulative idea of thought; it might involve traditional metaphysical claims to existence, as in claims for the existence of God; it might involve a concept that is known within and transformed by the religious dimension or religious experience; or it might involve a whole series of other options that lie between these. Since multiple options exist, one cannot simply presuppose that Fichte's language of God be taken in the sense of pre-Kantian theology — even though traditional theological terms appear within it. Above all else, Fichte was concerned with the search for an adequate concept of God and with its relationship to the concept of the ego or subject. However one finally interprets the epistemic status of the idea of God, it is clear that in Fichte's system it lies far from the anthropomorphic representations that Feuerbach and his school have attacked.[39] Fichte's postulation of God is motivated by the finitude of the human subject and not by the presupposition that the infinite must be very similar to us. To this extent, his intellectual development provides a sort of anticipatory answer to the later projection critique of religion with its campaign against every kind of thought of a transhuman infinite being.

---

39. See Van Harvey, *Feuerbach and the Interpretation of Religion* (Cambridge: Cambridge University Press, 1995).

CONCLUSION

It would of course require a much more detailed examination of Fichte's work in order to fully flesh out the line of argument that we have begun to trace in this excursus. Still, the significance of Fichte's starting point should have become clear. We have found reason in particular to question Feuerbach's thesis of the infinity of the human species. Such positions require that the infinite or the absolute subject arise out of the empirical subject and be understood as its consequence. Against such accounts, the steps of Fichte's development offer a strong argument for the impossibility of carrying out such a reductionistic program in theology. In the early years of the nineteenth century, Fichte correctly saw that "the infinite as Absolute Being precedes the ego's knowing of itself."[40] Fichte thus plays an essential role in grasping the conflict between the personality of God and the notion of a Highest or absolute. He thus points us once again to the centrality of limit concepts for post-Kantian theology.

The question that remains is how the idea of the infinite can best be given conceptual expression. Obviously a natural theology based on absolute foundations is no longer a viable option. Other possibilities, such as the dependence on a self-developing history (Hegel, Dilthey), would require a volume of their own to work out. We have, however, found sufficient reason to be skeptical about Fichte's appeal to mystical experience in order to ground assertions about God and world. Can the concept of a self-manifestation of the absolute be given more content without compelling one into the necessity claims of Hegel's dialectic? Is there an approach to theology that grants more room for speculation without neglecting the empirical limits on knowledge and without subordinating God and the absolute to some law of necessity? In the final chapter, we will turn to a different option, and perhaps the most promising one to emerge out of the Kantian crisis: the metaphysics of freedom developed by Schelling.

40. See Pannenberg, "Fichte und die Metaphysik des Unendlichen," 360.

CHAPTER 9

Beyond the "God Beyond God": Schelling's Theology of Freedom

TILLICH'S DEBT TO SCHELLING

It is helpful to begin a treatment of Schelling's concept of God by considering first the position of his most influential twentieth-century disciple, Paul Tillich. Tillich's brand of theism has been widely hailed as avoiding many of the conceptual difficulties haunting more traditional positions and approaches within philosophical theology. Tillich's theology is also intriguing because of its combination of Kantian skepticism and (what he calls) "positive theology." By tracing the foundations of Tillich's thought in the philosophy of Schelling, we will gain an initial sense of the enduring strength of Schelling's metaphysics of freedom.[1]

To most readers, Tillich's position is probably better known than Schelling's: "God" is the symbol for God,[2] for whatever is finally a matter of ultimate concern. God is not a person, yet neither can the divine be less than a person; it must be *überpersönlich*.[3] In place of God Tillich puts the God above

1. Equally important is the contrast of Schelling with Hegel, which justifies my claim that Schelling represents the most adequate German idealist from the standpoint of theistic metaphysics. Since this argument cannot be made without a detailed interpretation and critique of Hegel's own position, however, I have delayed this important task for an eventual second volume.

2. Tillich, *Gesammelte Werke*, 14 vols. (Stuttgart, 1959ff.), 8:143.

3. Tillich, *Systematische Theologie*, 3 vols. (Stuttgart: Evangelisches Verlagswerk, 1956, 1958, 1966), 2:18; translated as *Systematic Theology* (abbreviated *ST*), 3 vols. (Chicago: Univ.

God, *den Gott über dem Gott des Theismus,* who is Being-itself or the Ground of Being.[4] Being-itself is above even the contrast between finite and infinite. Elsewhere, Tillich tries to give the term *infinity* some constitutive content by giving it the meaning of "unlimited self-transcendence" (*ST* 191). He then restates the Kantian categories (space, time, causality, substance) in terms of this primary distinction. Ultimately, "'God' is the answer to the question implied in man's finitude" (*ST* 211). "God above God" is an important part of Tillich's attempt to go beyond traditional theism and to find a way of formulating Christian theism adequate to its object (and to the human knower). Of course, the phrase itself is not Tillich's most frequently used or most central term. But as commentators have shown, it plays a by no means peripheral role in his thought.[5]

Theologians have acknowledged that Tillich drew heavily on the later Schelling in constructing his theology.[6] But Tillich's goal was to be more than an interpreter. He reread Schelling based on three assumptions about post-Cartesian philosophy, only the first two of which, I suggest, we should accept. First, against traditional theologians Tillich assumed that modern attempts to develop a nonanthropocentric notion of the perfection of God have all failed (think of the "perfect-being theology" of present-day Anselmians discussed in previous chapters, or of the "ontotheology" that we have traced from Descartes to Leibniz). Second, Tillich held (with Descartes) that our experience of ourselves as finite justifies us in postulating an infinite dimension, a dimension that precedes and grounds traditional language about God. Third, but more problematically, Tillich maintained with Kant that language about the infinite could be introduced only as regulative or limit language: "infinity is a directing concept, not a constituting concept. It directs the mind to experience its own unlimited potentialities, but it does not establish the existence of an infinite be-

---

of Chicago Press, 1951, 1957, 1963), 2:12 ("suprapersonal"). When not otherwise noted, references are to vol. 1.

4. Paul Tillich, *The Courage To Be* (New Haven: Yale Univ. Press, 1952), 186ff.; *Gesammelte Werke,* 1:369; 11:137-39; D. Mackenzie Brown, ed., *Ultimate Concern: Tillich in Dialogue* (New York: Harper & Row, 1965), 51.

5. See in particular the excellent presentation by Martin Repp, *Die Transzendierung des Theismus in der Religionsphilosophie Paul Tillichs* (Frankfurt: Peter Lang, 1986).

6. Tillich's interest in the later Schelling goes back to his first publications, *Die religionsgeschichtliche Konstruktion in Schellings positiver Philosophie, ihre Voraussetzungen und Prinzipien* (Breslau: H. Fleischmann, 1910), translated by Victor Nuovo as *The Construction of the History of Religion in Schelling's Positive Philosophy: Its Presuppositions and Principles* (Lewisburg: Bucknell Univ. Press, 1974); and *Mystik und Schuldbewusstsein in Schellings philosophischer Entwicklung* (Halle: C. Bertelsmann, 1912), translated by Victor Nuovo as *Mysticism and Guilt-Consciousness in Schelling's Philosophical Development* (Lewisburg: Bucknell Univ. Press, 1974).

ing" (*ST* 190). Given the results of the Kant critique above (see esp. chapter 6), we must reject this dichotomy between regulative and constitutive, treating theistic language instead as having both dimensions, as being both metaphysical and existential.

Doing Philosophical Theology

Regarding the epistemology or methodology of philosophical theology, let me briefly review the conclusions that have emerged out of the earlier chapters. The great break for philosophical theology — and it continues to be the great divide — can be expressed by the opposition "Kant versus Hegel." Hegel undoubtedly made an advance over earlier rationalists when he proclaimed *Sein als Subjekt*, "being as subject." But like them (and perhaps even more strongly) he held that reality was fully knowable, that there are no limits to what human reason can attain. Kant is, by contrast, the great advocate of a philosophy of limits — the limits on what reason can know of God. The standpoint from which I defend a modified form of Schelling's later philosophy seeks to retain the strengths of Hegel's metaphysics of the self-unfolding subject while preserving the Kantian insistence that not all is (or can be) known, that no place would remain for freedom if everything were deducible from theoretical reason. I presuppose that some such synthesis of Hegel and Kant is both necessary and possible.

We have also found that claims fully to grasp the end of history before the end of history, or for finite agents fully to express the infinite, involve a contradiction; they entail that we know something for which the means are not and could not now be available. I call this impossible claim to knowledge *the Hegelian fallacy.*[7] It is my contention in this chapter that Schelling's approach is correctly balanced between the need to do theology and the need to acknowledge the limits on theological knowledge — indeed, markedly better balanced than Tillich's (supposed) appropriation of Schelling.

An Aside on Tillich's Mistakes

But why move backward from Tillich to his mentor Schelling? One word must be said first about the difficulty with Tillich's position — although the more important goal remains to show directly the superiority of Schelling's doctrine of God on the questions of the God/world relationship and on human freedom.

7. Again, anticipating arguments to be spelled out more fully in volume 2.

Many have argued that Tillich's doctrine of God is not ultimately successful in making the transition from negative to positive theology; it remains pre-
dominantly a *via negativa*. In his works philosophical concepts of God are summarized and then either lumped together under the heading "dialectic" or used
to show the limits of reason. When Christian language is introduced, it wins its
positive theological function at the cost of becoming purely symbolic. Yet religious or theological language is offered in response to philosophical or metaphysical questions, giving the impression that the questions are actually being
answered. Not infrequently, the result is a confusion of the two levels, the philosophical and the existential/symbolic, with appeals to the latter cutting short
those lines of philosophical reflection that one does find in Tillich's writings.
(Where the confusion is not Tillich's it belongs to his commentators.) This is
the negative side in Tillich's existentialism: it rests on the denial that constructive reflection on the nature of God is possible. The "premetaphysical" can too
easily become the antimetaphysical.

The root of this problem is a mistaken theory of theological language.
Tillich wants his statements about God to be understood as symbolic. But since
not only theological language but all language is symbolic, the symbolic function is not sufficient to separate theological from other language — language's
symbolic function, being universal, divides through and cancels out. Tillich
thought he could use symbolism as a principle of demarcation because he was
writing against the backdrop of naively realist theories of language; it was after
all the heyday of logical positivism. Today, however, the symbolic nature of all
language is better understood, and even relatively traditional theists are happy
to call themselves "*critical* realists."[8] Consequently, Tillich's insights into the
symbolic functions of theological language no longer justify leaving behind debates about the strengths and weaknesses of particular metaphors for God and
particular conceptual construals of the nature of the divine. It could be that
models of God can be evaluated only on the basis of their usefulness to us (or to
a particular group of us).[9] But if these views go too far — and here I can only
repeat my disagreement with the claim that there are no nonrelative criteria of
adequacy for religious language — then in every case of theological evaluation
we will be doing what Tillich thought was so radical about his approach: evaluating competing conceptual notions of God to see which is the most adequate.

8. See J. C. Polkinghorne, *The Way the World Is* (Grand Rapids: Eerdmans, 1984); Ar-
thur R. Peacocke, *Intimations of Reality: Critical Realism in Science and Religion* (Notre Dame:
Univ. of Notre Dame Press, 1984); Wentzel van Huyssteen, *Theology and the Justification of
Faith: Constructing Theories in Systematic Theology* (Grand Rapids: Eerdmans, 1989).

9. See, e.g., the works of Sallie McFague, *Metaphorical Theology* and *Models of God*,
discussed in chapter 1 above.

If this is correct, there will be no ultimate difference between the supposedly regulative concept "God above God" and the actual constitutive categories of a theory of God. Consequently, our task will be to move beyond the "what God is not" debate, and thus beyond negative theology, in order to reflect on the adequacy and inadequacy of specific types of language about the divine — if only in the guise of a theology of limit notions (see chapter 6).

One final word: many theologians today are, if anything, more ready than in Tillich's day to give up on theories, to satisfy themselves with the existential courage to be, or with moral rectitude, or with the politically correct thing to do. Such responses are important, but they ought to be entailments of a philosophical theology, not substitutes for one. Recall Tillich's exhortation: "Since the breakdown of the great synthesis between Christianity and the modern mind as attempted by Schleiermacher, Hegel, and nineteenth-century liberalism, an attitude of weariness has grasped the minds of people who are unable to accept one or the other alternative [sc. biblical religion or ontology]. They are too disappointed to try another synthesis after so many have failed. But there is no choice for us. We must try again!"[10] Perhaps, ironically, the exhortation should be applied equally to Tillich's own doctrine of God.

SCHELLING'S THEORY OF GOD

What follows is not a historical survey of Schelling's position and its development but rather an analytic reconstruction of certain insights from his work that, I argue, are central to addressing the problem of God in modern thought. No attempt will be made to demonstrate where and why other aspects of Schelling's opus are mistaken. In particular, the difficulties with his early objective idealism and with his later philosophy of mythology and revelation — difficulties often emphasized in the secondary literature — can unfortunately not be presented in full, even though the failures of Schelling's other approaches help to justify my emphasis on his middle period. Instead of historiography, the primary goal is to make constructive theological use of the most important insights in light of this book's project, stopping to look at the errors only where they are instructive for present purposes.

10. Tillich, *Biblical Religion and the Search for Ultimate Reality* (Chicago: Univ. of Chicago Press, 1955), 57.

The Demise of Early Modern Theism

It has been the thesis of this book that Schelling's early modern predecessors formulated the problem of God with remarkable clarity; their problems remain our problems. We have traced the collapse of the early modern view of God, the God of infinite perfection, which had dominated Western thought from the medieval period through Descartes and on to Leibniz and Wolff. As eighteenth-century theists confronted the challenges posed by Spinoza's monism, the difficulties facing traditional theism became increasingly clear. Descartes's theory of substance, they realized, depended on a crucial ambiguity: on the one hand, strictly speaking, there could be only one substance, one thing that depended on nothing outside itself (viz. God); on the other hand, natural science and common sense require a world of separate, interacting substances.[11] As we saw, Spinoza claimed that the ambiguity could be resolved and an adequate theory of God developed only if things in the world — and indeed the world as a whole — were no longer conceived as separate and independent from God. There is only *deus siva natura* — "God or Nature" — and every individual thing or person is a mode of the one whole, understood under the attribute of either thought or extension.

The reemergence of the Spinoza tradition in the 1780s and '90s brought the Spinozistic challenge home to Jewish and Christian theism. In examining the "Spinoza Dispute" between Jacobi and Mendelssohn in chapter 7, we found that no adequate theory of God can countenance a final opposition between God and the world, for a God to whom the world was truly "other" would not be an infinite God but would be limited by the world. In the previous chapter a new difficulty emerged out of the *Atheismusstreit* surrounding Fichte: God could not be both infinite and personal, it seemed, for a person or individual is defined in contrast to other individuals or to some background context, whereas an infinite being could not be so defined. As Schelling summarized the problem, "To ascribe to God consciousness and personality means to make him into a finite being; for consciousness — and its higher stage, personality — are tied to limitation and finitude" (8:73; 4:449).[12] Only universal qualities, it ap-

11. Descartes, *Principles* I, 51.

12. Unless otherwise indicated, citations refer to *Friedrich Wilhelm Joseph von Schellings sämmtliche Werke*, 14 vols. in two divisions, ed. K. F. A. Schelling (Stuttgart and Augsburg: J. G. Cotta'scher, 1856-61). I indicate the four volumes of the 2nd division as vols. 11-14, respectively. Where a second reference is included, it is to the parallel passage in *Schellings Werke, Nach der Original Ausgabe in neuer Anordnung*, 6 vols. and 6 supplementary vols., ed. Manfred Schröter (Munich: C. H. Beck und R. Oldenbourg, 1927-59). Page refer-

peared, could pertain to God as absolutely infinite. Either the quality must be rethought (e.g., God does not have personhood but is the ground of personhood), or some aspect of God must be distinguished from the divine infinity — or, as we shall see, perhaps both routes, taken together, can contribute to a solution to this urgent problem.

Beyond Spinozism

The Spinoza Dispute and the Atheism Dispute, combined with Kant's attack on metaphysics and the worry that theological language is a human projection, spelled the end of the early modern theory of God as an infinitely perfect being. Indeed, these four skeptical worries remain the major hurdles for philosophical theology to overcome today. All that was left, it appeared at first blush, was Spinoza: the one infinite substance, of which every "thing" that exists is a mode. Yet, as we saw, Spinoza still conceived this God-as-nature statically, as an object, lacking the internal dynamism of a true subject. My thesis has been that the German idealists provided the required correction, and that somewhere between Mendelssohn's Spinozism and Hegel's absolute idealism the optimal balance was reached — specifically, I shall now argue, in the later writings of Schelling.

There is no question of the strong influence of Spinoza on Schelling;[13] indeed, it justifies the present interpretation of Schelling as the synthesizer of the Spinoza tradition with transcendental idealism. Because of the many parallels that we will discover, it is important to note their differences, at least in passing.

---

ences to English translations are not given, since they invariably include marginal numbers keyed to the German critical edition.

English translations include: from vol. 1 of the Cotta edition, *The Unconditional in Human Knowledge: Four Early Essays (1794-1796)*, trans. Fritz Marti (Lewisburg: Bucknell Univ. Press, 1980); from vol. 3, *System of Transcendental Idealism*, trans. Peter Heath (Charlottesville: Univ. Press of Virginia, 1978); from vol. 4, *Bruno, or On the Natural and the Divine Principle of Things*, trans. Michael G. Vater (Albany: SUNY Press, 1984); from vol. 7, *Schelling: Of Human Freedom*, trans. James Gutmann (Chicago: Open Court, 1936); from vol. 8, *The Ages of the World*, trans. Frederick de Wolfe Bolman Jr. (New York: AMS Press, 1942, repr. 1967). A translation from the *Mythology* is currently underway at the New School for Social Research.

13. Schelling speaks of him as "the sole son and heir of true science throughout the entire modern period" (8:340), in whom are "scattered the seeds of higher developments" (10:40). Spinozism represents "realism in its most sublime and perfect shape" (4:110). For some more recent accounts of Spinoza's influence see Manfred Walther, ed., *Spinoza und der Deutsche Idealismus* (Würzburg: Königshausen und Neumann, 1991), esp. the essays by Ehrhardt and Dietzsch.

First and most important, Schelling construed infinite substance *as subject*. This idealist insight contrasts sharply with the *Ethics*, which "determined the absolute as an absolute *object*" (1:242n.). Schelling's goal was to escape from Spinoza's "pure realism" (and from Fichte's "pure idealism"), in order to conceive God as genuinely personal.

As a direct consequence of this move, Schelling maintained that he had succeeded in avoiding determinism and fatalism, the "system of necessity" into which Spinoza had fallen.[14] This break with Spinoza explains, in part, the 1809 shift in which Schelling made the concept of *freedom* central to his metaphysical system. The human agent is able to act freely, even in light of knowledge of the absolute, as long as freedom is defined as action in accordance with one's nature or essence (7:384). The key, Schelling realized, is an adequate theory of subjectivity of the sort that Spinoza failed to achieve. The view of the subject that Schelling shared with the other idealists allowed him to contrast internal (subjective) necessity with external (empirical) necessity. Lacking an adequate theory of the subject, Spinoza was unable to draw this distinction. Theologically, Schelling's richer theory of subjectivity also allowed him to construe the world's creation as a free act — as long as he could show that the absolute is pervasively subject and is determined by its nature alone. For the same reason, as he tried to show in *The Ages of the World* (8:269ff.), universal history can also be understood as an open process of genuine or novel development.

Schelling could thus claim that he had been able to overcome the limitations of both Kant and Spinoza, correcting the shortfalls of each using the resources of the other. Indeed, one could even interpret Schelling's project in this middle period as the appropriation of Spinoza in the context of post-Kantian philosophy. The previous chapters of this book have sought to show that this task remains a central one for philosophical theology if it is to meet the challenge raised by modern thought. (The need to reappropriate Spinoza in a post-Kantian context also explains treating the Kantian challenge prior to presenting the Spinoza tradition.) To be satisfied with the Kantian limits would mean, for example, assigning the concept of God a merely regulative role (it tells more about reason's striving for unity than about any metaphysical entity) — and then, perhaps, jumping across the great divide into the field

---

14. 10:47. Schelling writes, "Spinoza calls God *causa sui*, but in the narrower sense that he *is* by the mere necessity of his nature, therefore *only is* without being able to be retained as ability to be (as *causa*); the cause has vanished completely in the operation and stands simply as *substance*" (10:35). Spinoza's God is *das Seiende* but not *das Sein* (11:372). "Had [Spinoza] posited the living substance instead of the dead, blind one, then that dualism of attributes would have offered a means of actually comprehending the finiteness of things" (10:44).

of ethics, where language about God becomes tied to the language of moral obligations.

To be dissatisfied with the Kantian limits requires a new mode of reflection on the divine. We took a first step in that direction with the theology of limit notions (chapter 6). Recall that this involved a form of reflection that is informed by the limits on human knowledge yet at the same time also derives some theological insight from those limits themselves. In the present chapter we take a further step of reconstruction. For if Schelling is right, it should be possible to build genuine divine — and human — agency and freedom into the structure of metaphysical explanations. The cost of acknowledging the dimension of freedom, we will find, is a limitation on the full knowability of God, creation, revelation, and so on. The task for the philosophical theologian, then, is to show how one can accept this limitation without falling back again into the complete agnosticism about God that Kantian dualism entails.

God as Infinite

For a start, then, let's follow the Spinozists' lead and begin with the finite/infinite distinction, which (I have argued) must now be the starting point for any philosophical theory of God. God is infinite; or, one can say — as long as one resists the Hegelian claim to full knowability — God is the ultimate ground of all that is and all that can be thought. This is the idealist insight that every adequate theism must preserve: "Initially we presuppose nothing but a final [or infinite] ground for the reality of all knowledge. . . . The final ground of all reality is a Something that is only conceivable through itself, i.e., through its being; it is thought only as existing, in short: it is that in which the principle of being and the principle of thought coincide" (1:163; 1:87).

Schelling's early transcendental idealism (and arguably his philosophy as a whole) was dominated by the notion of the infinite as prior to and constitutive of the finite. Following Spinoza's lead, he wished to think the infinite as rigorously as possible — neither dependent on the finite nor conceived only partially (as he put it), as in those varieties of "limited theism" that posit a source of the world without viewing it as absolutely infinite and hence as strongly discontinuous with the finite. Again following Spinoza, Schelling argued (already in the mid-1790s) that when the logic of the infinite is correctly understood it becomes clear that the finite cannot exist fully separate from the infinite but must in some sense be contained within it.

Idealism added a new dimension to these Spinozistic insights, however. The idealist thinkers began with the epistemic problem: How could an absolute be known (if it were to be knowable)? Not by means of something outside it, for then it would not be absolute. This is why Schelling insisted on the faculty of intellectual intuition (or later *Ekstase*) as the means for getting inside the closed circle of the absolute.[15] The results of intellectual intuitions would have the status of border or limit notions *(Grenzbegriffe);* each limit notion would represent an anticipation *(Vorgriff)* of what a fully worked out theory of God would involve, were such a theory possible for human knowers at all.

This formulation is significant because it reveals the analogy between the metaphysics of the infinite and the epistemology of limit notions. On this view knowers are relativized by an object of knowledge that cannot be fully grasped, just as finite human agents are relativized by (i.e., shown to be contingent on) an infinite ground. Once one sees this connection, one wonders, in retrospect, whether the notion of the infinite should not have required the relativizing of human knowers all along. Why did philosophical theologians think they could develop a theory of the infinite God without granting a corresponding limitation on what finite knowers could achieve? Why did they not see that their theories were as likely to reflect their own perspectives as finite and limited as they were to reflect the world and God "as they really are"? Analogously, accepting an epistemology of limit notions (or a related position) causes one not to look for a theology of the absolute unfolding itself with rational necessity — for why should such limits on knowledge arise in that case? — but rather for a theology of the (at least partially) unknowable God.

The element of unknowability could have several sources: perhaps human rationality intrinsically falls short of knowing the divine, or perhaps God's actions are fundamentally free and thus cannot be derived from rationality alone (or both). If the former is true, that is simply the end of the story (and of the aspirations of metaphysics). But consider, as Schelling did, the implications of the second possibility. A freely acting God could also not be fully known by finite human knowers through their reason alone; such a God would have to make himself known within the human agent: "Not I know, but the All knows in me; not *we* have reason, but reason has us; not the empirical subject knows, but the absolutely general *(das schlechthin Allgemeine)* knows."[16] From this perspective one can see what Spinoza did and did not grasp. Spinoza saw correctly that understanding God as infinite requires that God be the *hen kai pan,* the one and all, thereby including all things and knowers within the One *(deus siva*

15. On his doctrine of intellectual intuition see Margarete Adam, *Die intellektuelle Anschauung bei Schelling in ihrem Verhältnis zur Methode der Intuition bei Bergson* (Patschkau/Schlesien: Carl Buchal, 1926).

16. See Walter Kasper, *Das Absolute in der Geschichte: Philosophie und Theologie der Geschichte in der Spätphilosophie Schellings* (Mainz: Matthias-Grünewald, 1965), 53, paraphrasing 4:140, 7:149, and 7:148, respectively.

natura). But Spinoza did not go far enough. His God of pure extension and pure thought remained an entity (albeit an all-embracing one) conceived by us as thinkers. Spinoza could *say* that this One, *natura naturans,* included the active principle of thought, but in fact he left the human knowing of it, and even its own knowing of itself, outside it. Yet, if divinity is absolute, it must also incorporate within itself the process of its being thought, since an absolute could not be correctly conceived by something outside it. Hence the absolute, insofar as it must contain its own thinking, is adequately conceived only as *absolute and all-encompassing subject.*

The Connection of World and God

Thus the basic starting point for modern theistic metaphysics — the understanding of God as infinite — points unmistakably to a particular ontological position: the world cannot be fully separate or different from God. "Since [this knowledge of the infinite] encompasses the intuitions of the individual as well as the thought of the general, it encompasses the unity of the general and specific, of thought and being, of infinite and finite. The infinite *knowledge* of the absolute is at the same time the *being* of the absolute. With this we reach absolute idealism."[17] Of course, theologians have long granted that there must be a relation of continual dependence between the creation and its creator. But the preceding quotation entails more than that: the world is encompassed within God. *Participation* then becomes a crucial concept for thinking the infinite/finite relation, as it had been in the Neoplatonic tradition. As we saw in chapter 3, if the world really participates in God, there is no place for a final ontological separation of the participating beings from their participated source.

For Spinoza and Schelling, God is the All; there is no "space" outside God (if one wishes to speak in spatial terms); hence the world is within God, as are we.[18] Yet theism requires that the world not be identical with God. Here we reach perhaps the most difficult question: How is one to specify the world's difference from God? Theologians have not always seen that this is the crucial issue: not how the world can be connected to its infinite source, but rather how things in the world are to be individuated given such a source.

We have found that the logic of the infinite is inescapable: the absolute can only differentiate itself into self and other, infinite and finite, God and world. The reason an adequate theism remains inescapably dialectical is that

17. Kasper, ibid., 53, quoting 4:240, 4:325, 4:247 (emphasis mine).
18. Pace Wolfhart Pannenberg, *Systematic Theology,* trans. Geoffrey Bromiley, 3 vols. (Grand Rapids: Eerdmans, 1991-98), 1:356-57.

what results must both be not-God (as finite) and God. Given that there can be nothing outside the infinite, whatever becomes remains in some sense still part of the infinite. How then is one to separate God and creatures?

The answer lies in the understanding of God as the *ground* of being. We are the beings that stem from this ground. As we will see, Schelling presents a number of ways to think of this process of creation, the issuing of the world from its ground in the divine. No single way of expressing the contrast between God and world needs to be selected; a number of the proposals complement one another.[19] For instance, (1) one can speak of God as Being-itself (as *Sein* or as Schelling's *Seinheit*). Beings are entities that, as existing, participate in that being. The very notion is dialectical, as Schelling saw: an existing person *(ein Seiendes)* is different from "Being-itself," and in this sense can be said to exist independently; yet one *is* only because of one's relation to the ground of being. In this sense it is false to say that one is finally independent from God. Or (2) one can (and must) distinguish between God's necessary being and the contingency of all created beings. Or (3) one can distinguish between what is essential about God and the nonessential characteristics of historical human individuals. (4) Other ways of expressing the same difference include the distinctions between what is implicit and explicit, what is hidden and manifest, and what is potential and actual. (We return to these below.) Even though metaphysics may underdetermine the choice between them, the Ground/Consequent relation remains fundamental for thinking the relationship of finite beings to their infinite source.

God as Ground and as Personal

The trouble for traditional theism is that a similar dilemma seems also to apply to God. Is God the highest being (in some still-to-be-specified sense) or the ground of being? Philosophical theologians have long struggled to show how an entity can be at the same time an individual being and Being-itself. On the one hand, a ground of being lacks the attributes for being personal, for example, being in relationship to something outside itself (there is nothing outside itself!). On the other, *a* being is per se finite, since only in contrast to something else is it *this* being. Yet the notion of God is supposed to encompass both of these concepts; God is supposed to be *the infinite being.*

19. Tillich likewise explicitly grants that the various terms he uses "all mean the same": infinite, unconditional, ultimate, as in Kierkegaard's "infinite passion," Kant's "unconditional imperative," and every person's "ultimate concern"; see *Ultimate Concern: Tillich in Dialogue,* 49-50.

The result appears inescapable: as long as one wishes to incorporate both notions, one has to advocate a dipolar concept of God. Divinity must include the ground of being as well as the highest personal being. They cannot be posited as separate: the ground of being (for Schelling, *Sein*) cannot exclude the highest being *(das höchste Seiende)*, nor could a being be God without including the ground of being within itself. The two must be conceived as combined, yet they cannot be identical. Let us first find a way to express the distinction, and then gradually work our way to an adequate conception of their connection.

As already noted, Tillich, borrowing from Schelling, found himself forced to posit a "God above God," which functioned as the ground of being, the ground of personhood, and so on. For his part, Schelling started with the distinction among theism, pantheism, and monotheism. *Theism* (in the narrow sense) is the view that sets God up in opposition to the world. Since it conceives God not as truly infinite but rather as (too) closely analogous to human agents, its God is in effect a divinization of the human subject; it thus becomes vulnerable to Feuerbach's criticism that theistic language projects human attributes onto the divine. *Pantheism* in its strict sense is Spinozism: there is only the All, and everything that exists is contained within it. Unfortunately, pantheism can understand this All only as object rather than as subject, since there is no Other in relation to which it could emerge as subject. The most adequate position is what Schelling calls "true theism" or later (in his philosophy of mythology) "monotheism"; it is the view that I am here labeling *panentheism*. True theism incorporates the pantheist principle, the principle that "outside of God there is no other God."[20] Any ultimate dualism would conflict with this principle; thus God is, strictly speaking, the only one, and all nondivine being is and remains dependent on God's causality.[21] Thus it will have to follow that the true finite is included within (or participates in, or stands in a part/whole relation to) the infinite.[22]

How is this God to be understood? We might say that Schelling accepted Spinoza's thinking on the absolute (at least as interpreted by Jacobi) as far as it went, taking this to be the first pole of God, God in his aseity. In the early works, where the positive connection to Spinoza is the strongest, one finds the fullest treatment of the theory of the absolute. But from early on Schelling also reads Spinoza though the lenses of the freedom problem: he is worried that the very success of the Spinozistic system seems to eliminate any place for an absolute subject. A free God would have to be freely self-unfolding, and hence in-

---

20. Schelling, 12:13; 6:269.
21. Kasper, *Das Absolute*, 195.
22. See the excellent presentation in Jaganath das Choudhury, *Das Unendlichkeitsproblem in Schellings Philosophe* (Berlin: A. Collignon, 1926).

volved in a process of becoming. (One is thus tempted to present Schelling's "Kehre" around 1805 as analogous to Hartshorne's movement away from the God of perfection to a process notion of God.) By the time of the *Essay on Freedom (Freiheitsschrift)*, Schelling has reconceived Spinoza's God so that it becomes God's free unfolding of himself into a world. In this process the framework remains panentheist because of Schelling's insistence that there are individual substances within the one divine substance. They are "inseparable but distinguishable" (7:358), or, put differently, they have "derivative absoluteness" (7:347). The distinguishability of the individual substances stems from our finitude, that is, from the contingency of all that exists.

Methodologically, this mid-course correction of Spinoza turned Schelling in the direction of romanticism and mysticism, earning him the title "the philosopher of German romanticism."[23] On the one hand one finds (as in Spinoza) a thoroughgoing naturalism; on the other, the subject/object identity that characterizes idealism led him to speak of God in vitalistic and teleological terms. Substance became a living force, manifested by all of nature. By moving from Spinoza's mechanism to an organic philosophy, Schelling was able to view mind and body as "different degrees of organization and development of living force."[24] The pantheistic side remains: "everything that exists, insofar as it exists, is God" (*alles, was ist, ist, insofern es ist, Gott*, 6:157). But now the teleology is expressed through a panentheistic correction: "By 'the absolute' Schelling understood that which stands above everything that exists, the ideal as well as the real world, encompassing and including all within itself."[25]

We will return to the question of creation, but we can already draw a first contrast between this view and theories of the emanation of the world. The doctrine of emanation, or of modes within the one divine substance, is mistaken in its fatalism, its belief that everything that occurs happens by necessity;

23. On the interaction with romanticism see, classically, Horst Fuhrmans, *Schellings Philosophie der Weltalter. Schellings Philosophie in den Jahren 1806-1821: Zum Problem des Schellingschen Theismus* (Düsseldorf: L. Schwann, 1954), 75-151, e.g., esp. 79. On the interaction with German mysticism see Robert F. Brown, *The Late Philosophy of Schelling: The Influence of Boehme on the Works of 1809-1815* (Lewisburg: Bucknell Univ. Press, 1977); and Thomas Franklin O'Meara, O.P., *Romantic Idealism and Roman Catholicism: Schelling and the Theologians* (Notre Dame: Univ. of Notre Dame Press, 1982), esp. 78ff.

24. Frederick Beiser, "Introduction: Hegel and the Problem of Metaphysics," in Beiser, ed., *The Cambridge Companion to Hegel* (Cambridge: Cambridge Univ. Press, 1993), 1-24, quotation 6.

25. "Unter dem Absoluten versteht Schelling das, was alles Wirkliche, die ideale wie die reale Welt, übergreift, umgreift und in sich befaßt" (Wilhelm Weischedel, *Der Gott der Philosophen*, 2 vols. [Darmstadt: Wissenschaftliche Buchgesellschaft, 1971], 1:252).

it also incorrectly maintains that the world emanates from the One in a mechanistic manner, that is, apart from the agency of a subject. Where it is correct is in maintaining that whatever things are created are not fully separate from their ultimate source. Whatever emerges from the ground will be conceptually distinct from its source; it will be an existing thing (or a set of them) rather than the ground itself. Yet, in contrast to doctrines of the emanation of the world from God, the source or beginning for this process of the world's emergence is a free decision by the ground, which is therefore better understood as subject than as object. It thus becomes a ground that objectifies itself in the process of creation through free subjective choice. This is the view to which I must now give fuller expression.

CHANGE IN GOD

Divine Self-Manifestation

How then are we to think this free, self-conscious ground? How, in particular, can God-as-absolutely-infinite be thought together with God understood as *a* being who is in relationship with and affected by the world? It appears to make little sense to speak of the ground (or the "God above God") itself entering into relationship with something outside itself or being changed by something, whereas a personal God cannot be conceived otherwise than in relation to something else. What do these conclusions say for the relation between ground and God?

Let's start with the personal aspect of God. Schelling specifies it as the self-manifestation of the Godhead *(die Gottheit)*. Consider Schelling's notion of God as "Being revealing itself" (7:394). The notion is already dipolar, implying both a something (Being-itself) that is being revealed and an aspect that does the revealing. As the gerund implies, there must then be a process of revealing. Finally, awareness of the revelation implies a process of becoming aware of what was being revealed. In Schelling's terms, "being is only aware of itself in becoming," for "in actualization, there is necessarily a becoming" (7:403). The process of actualization requires a goal; hence, we can say, God's final goal is "complete actualization" (7:404).

On the one hand, if there is now something finite "within" God that did not always exist, then God must be in a sense different from before; and if this finite dimension is in a state of becoming, then God also is becoming. On the other hand, the "other" side of God — the absolute in its limitlessness, or as the

481

ground of being — remains always self-identical. This pair of terms (ground, and result or "consequent") best expresses the two sides of divinity: the sameness and difference, God's position "above" creation and God's intimate involvement with it. It would be interesting to pursue the parallels and implications of this conclusion for the doctrine of the Trinity in its "immanent" and "economic" forms.[26] Suffice it to say that the ground/consequent structure is congenial to trinitarian reflection, even though it does not directly entail it. (As is well known, Schelling was not alone among the idealists in emphasizing the trinitarian outworkings of his philosophical theism.)

God is the ground of being for finite beings; can God also be the ground of change in such a way that he incorporates the resulting changes, or will all change be external to God as in certain strands of traditional theism? Clearly, the change that finite beings undergo must in the end be grounded in God. To deny this would be to leave change a metaphysical surd, ungrounded and unexplained, a process version of the Greeks' prime matter that just always was. Also, recall that the finite cannot be fully separate from its infinite ground. If becoming is not just illusory (as some metaphysicians have held) but real, then one must also locate *its* ground in God and God must participate in becoming as well. Indeed, becoming must ultimately be understood as a dimension of God.

Schelling is among those who make self-manifestation central to the doctrine of God. Must this imply a temporal process? Where the self-manifestation takes place within the finite and to finite agents, yes. From the standpoint of the finite recipient, the process of divine self-manifestation will appear as change over time, since it must involve the communication of information that was not present at some previous time. But does this mean, more strongly, that God must always have been in process, that, for instance, there must have been a time when the personal God did not exist at all — or that God does not yet fully exist even now? Not necessarily; as Horst Fuhrmans argues in his Schelling monograph (note 24 above), the "development" that we posit within God may take place prior to the creation of the world; it may be a logical development rather than a temporal one. After 1812, Schelling argues that "God constitutes his own complete being in an eternal, 'pre-temporal' process"; as Brown adds, "time and temporal process are taken up into the larger context of the eternal process which is God."[27]

26. See Clayton, "Pluralism, Idealism, Romanticism: New Resources for a Trinity in Process," along with the other essays in *Trinity in Process: A Relational Theology of God*, ed. Joseph A. Bracken and Marjorie Suchocki (New York: Continuum, 1997).

27. Brown, *Late Philosophy of Schelling*, 145n.86.

DUALITY IN GOD

To recap: we began our reflection with God's infinity or unlimitedness. If the being of God is absolutely undifferentiated, how can it explain (or ground) change and development? This is possible only if there is complexity or plurality within God's being. Anything that changes over time is not absolutely infinite and undifferentiated. Indeed, the more God's internal life is like the world's finitude and change, the more credible are claims that these phenomena are grounded in the divine; conversely, the more we stress God's pure actuality (with Aristotle or the Scholastics), or the more God is identified with the absolute, the harder it is to find in God the ground of becoming.

As is well known, Schelling's theism is dualistic; his is a bipolar God, with abstract predicates like being and aseity prior to the historical process, and a personality — including life, striving, and suffering — that emerges through the historical process.[28] This both/and position may be a troubling one for traditional theists. Still, I suggest, there are more and less adequate ways to think the two sides of the divine. The least adequate ways, for traditional theism anyway, are the ones that marginalize or eliminate all God's essential properties in order to make room for a divine becoming in history. Such approaches hold that God in himself is essentially incomplete or that God does not yet exist prior to his becoming in history. Hoping to prove the necessity of God's becoming in the world, they make God ontologically dependent on the world, such that if there were no world there would be no God. One can easily see the irony: seeking to escape the Scholastic God who is propelled only by his own necessity, they end up finally with a God who needs the world in order to become whole — which makes the world's creation, once again, a necessary consequence of God's antecedent nature: because of who God is, God could not exist unless he created a world with which to be in relation.

It is equally problematic, however, to meet this challenge by dividing God into two equal principles, as Schelling did at some points. The *Essay on Freedom* clearly subdivides God into two parts and two wills: "the will of love" and "the will of the basis," with the result that God "has in him a *nature* which though it belongs to God himself, is, nonetheless, different from him" (7:375). The "basis" is also referred to as "the irrational principle" (7:374), "the will of the deep," and "the dark ground" (7:381). Both wills exist in God and both are, allegedly, necessary for the development of self-conscious love. The alleged necessity is twofold, the first sense apparently surviving from Schelling's early idealist period: no self, no self-conscious action, is possible unless there is a division that

28. Kasper, *Das Absolute,* 194; see esp. Schelling's *Essay on Freedom* (1809).

can subsequently be unified. The second sense stems from a related but different principle: "every nature can be revealed only in its opposite" (7:373). This dictates an important part of Schelling's cosmology:

> For as in the beginning of creation, which was nothing other than the birth of light, the dark principle had to be there as its basis so that light could be raised out of it (as the actual out of the merely potential); so there must be another basis for the birth of spirit, and hence a second principle of darkness, which must be as much higher than the former as the spirit is higher than light. This principle is precisely the spirit of evil. (7:377)

As das Choudhury notes, "The primordial ground [in God] divides itself into these two essences, which he now describes as real and ideal, and later as darkness and light, ego-centeredness and love, necessity and freedom."[29] This approach leaves God fundamentally divided in the manner of Gnostic or Zoroastrian thought. (Unfortunately, Tillich made significant use of exactly this facet of Schelling's thought.)

But this sort of ontological dualism, which is traceable back to Jakob Boehme, represents precisely the side of Schelling's metaphysics that has least well survived the test of time.[30] It is a novelistic projection onto God, a confusion of romantic cosmogony and theogony with idealistic arguments for a necessary dialectical progression in history — exactly the sort of arguments that have become increasingly suspect after Hegel. Theological reasons also militate against the dualism of equal principles, since it makes God also evil, albeit (allegedly) in a necessary manner. Further, the dualism makes creation necessary, at least to the extent that it places the (inevitable) Other outside God rather than inside God, as I am attempting to do. Finally, there are also philosophical objections. Talk of the dark and light principles ontologizes values, presupposing something like the old "ontology of perfection" that we encountered in Descartes and Leibniz, though now with a (dualistic) twist: instead of "whatever exists must be perfect" one finds the claim that the per-

29. Das Choudhury, *Das Unendlichkeitsproblem*, 53.

30. It remains unconvincing even in those passages where Schelling attempts to nuance it and lighten its impact. For instance, he later adds, the dark principle is not in itself evil: "if evil consists in strife between the two principles, then the good can only consist in their complete accord" (7:392). Elsewhere, he hints that "basis" in "the will of the basis" might merely mean ground (7:406). It would of course strengthen Schelling's position if it could be shown that his use of Boehmian dualism was merely incidental; but the treatments by Brown and others make clear that Schelling took the idea of a primordial battle between Good and Evil with utmost seriousness.

fect must emerge at the end of the cosmic struggle between good and evil, an equally problematic claim. Finally, this ontological dualism posits not just multiplicity within God but incompatible principles, making it rationally impossible to conceive the divine unity. Indeed, from the standpoint of the theory of agency it is difficult to see how a being with two distinct wills could ever be a single self or entity.

Reacting against such an unmediated dualism, the philosophical mind seeks inevitably to resolve it by reintroducing monism at a higher level. Schelling attempted to do so in 1809 with the notion of an *Ungrund* in God that preceded the dualism (7:406ff.). (Arguably, Tillich did the same thing with his "God above God," and some rereadings of Whitehead do the same to Creativity.) Thinkers who make such moves relativize the cosmic struggle — or the struggle within God — by positing a unity-above-all-differentiation, even above being or good or personhood. Their solution is one response to a genuine dilemma: if the One is not more ultimate than the struggle of the two principles, it does not truly transcend the two poles, so that it is hard to see why one should even speak of the existence of an ultimate One above them. If, on the other hand, the ultimate One is more real than the struggle of principles at some level beneath it, then the struggle itself threatens to become unreal. The position then devolves into a form of Neoplatonism, in which a posited One, the true highest principle and the source of all else, gives rise to levels (emanations) that are less and less real. With this danger in mind, Tillich's positive comments on the Neoplatonic Pseudo-Dionysius are revealing: "God is beyond even the highest names which theology has given to him. . . . He is supradivinity, beyond God, if we speak of God as a divine being."[31]

To choose Neoplatonism in this way is to side ultimately with negative theology; it is to say that no theological language is finally true. Even the term "the God above God" may illicitly import more content than one is entitled to; all Schelling or Tillich should really have said is "the One above all distinctions." Tillich, for example, refused to assert that God was infinite, since he took even the predicate *infinity* — the divine attribute that is the most free from anthropomorphic projection — to be merely a regulative fiction, a concept that directs the human mind to "its own unlimited potentialities."[32] This move is again reminiscent of Plotinus, whose adherence to the *via negativa* was so strict that he also refused to predicate infinity (unboundedness) of the One (see

31. Tillich, *A History of Christian Thought*, ed. Carl E. Braaten (New York: Harper & Row, 1968), 192. See the excellent discussion by Adrian Thatcher in *The Ontology of Paul Tillich* (Oxford: Oxford Univ. Press, 1978), 84-86.

32. *ST* 1:190, emphasis mine.

chap. 3 above). If one gives to Neoplatonism the final word (or rather the final silence!), no positive metaphysic whatsoever can follow.[33]

Now admittedly there is no quick way to dismiss these two possibilities: the replacement of all positive language about God by negative theology, and the complete reduction of all theological language (of either type) to statements about humanity. The unconditional, the ultimate, the infinite — all can be taken as merely expressing this or that feature of the human (i.e., the finite) condition. But advocating either of the two options means leaving behind theistic metaphysics, turning over the metaphysical court to the opposing teams, whatever they may be (materialism, physicalism, pantheism). If one of them is true, a constructive theory of God becomes an oxymoron: either the Neoplatonists do theology, which is perforce negative theology, or they perform existential analysis à la Heidegger's *Being and Time*, which is no longer theology. To achieve constructive results,[34] it must be possible to say something more or less adequate about the nature of the divine. A theology of the infinite of the sort advanced in this book — which uses as its point of departure one of the most minimal starting points for positive metaphysics to be found in the Western tradition — must (and can) reflect more than human existential drives and projections.

Apophatic theology, like the reduction of theistic language to anthropology, is not the final word in philosophical theology, though it might be if efforts toward a theistic metaphysics fail. It may be that neither a full dualism nor a full monism is philosophically or theologically acceptable. But their inadequacy should turn our attention to potential mediating positions such as dipolar theism. The resolution emerges, I have suggested, when one returns to the distinction that underlay Schelling's occasionally misguided dualism. As Schelling observes in introducing his discussion, "the general basis of this doctrine . . . lies in the distinction between existence and that which is the ground of existence" (7:373). It is this distinction that we need to hold onto, while letting the others fall.

---

33. Indeed, if even an apparently pure philosophical notion like infinity pertains only to human potentialities, what now becomes of Tillich's more specific (anthropomorphic) language about the Trinity, the Spirit, or God's self-revelation in Christ?

34. Again, Tillich is no exception here: he wished for constructive philosophical or theological conclusions, and claimed in the opening of vol. 2 of his *Systematic Theology* that he had achieved them.

INFINITY, POTENTIALITY, AND THE GOODNESS OF CREATION

Creation as God's Self-Manifestation

The position that Schelling developed in *Ages of the World* (*Die Weltalter*, 1815), albeit anticipated also in earlier works, construes the infinite God as containing "potencies" *(Potenzen)* for development. Of course, from the concept of the infinite alone one could not conclude that it has the potential to become something else. But we do not have the infinite alone; we also have a world. Thus we know that God as infinite must have contained the potential for giving rise to a world. Indeed, there is no contradiction in speaking of the infinite containing potentials that are manifested at some point in human history. Admittedly, an infinitely perfect, fully actualized being could not have such potential for development; it would have to be already everything it could possibly be, that is, fully actual, at every moment. But perfect-being metaphysics faces insurmountable problems, as we have seen in earlier chapters. Bereft of the perfection notion, at least as the cornerstone of philosophical theology, the idea of God as infinite allows one to speak instead of potencies that gradually come to be expressed in the course of history.[35]

It follows that the basic mode of change, at least in a theological view of the world, is the movement from potential to actual. The advantage of this conceptuality, as Aristotle already saw, is that it allows for real development without essential change. When a potential quality of x becomes an actual quality, the existing x is something different than it was before, yet since x was always x potentially, we need not say that there has been a change in x's essential nature.[36] God was always the (potentially) self-manifesting God, and hence the creator God, even though there was a phase (metaphorically, a time) when God was not manifest in anything outside himself. The advantage of this framework is that it allows us to say that the questions of how divinity can be (in itself) and how it can become manifest are two different ways of formulating the same question (cf. 8:255-56). Nonetheless, there remains a real difference (probably

---

35. In what follows I skip over the details of Schelling's three *Potenzen*, the understanding of which he vastly altered in his various publications. See Kasper, *Das Absolute;* and Brown, *Late Philosophy of Schelling,* for detailed examinations of the doctrine(s), and esp. Klaus Hemmerle, *Gott und das Denken nach Schellings Spätphilosophie* (Freiburg: Herder, 1968), 156-228.

36. A number of passages in *Ages* are strongly reminiscent of Aristotle, e.g., 8:242-43, in which earlier potencies serve as "material and substratum" for higher ones. I will not stop to review Aristotle's position or to demonstrate the parallels fully.

stronger than Aristotle's metaphysics grants) between the not-yet-manifest and the now-manifest, between the "time" before and after there was a world. There may be a natural movement to the next potency, as Schelling thinks (8:275), and nature may (indeed must) be spoken of as a potentiality vis-à-vis the godhead (8:280-81), which may (but not must!) eventually develop into something godlike; still, God is only *actually* conscious, and thus actually the being whom he has become, when the actual process of creation and the subsequent development of the universe to which he is related have taken place (cf. 8:262).

The parameters of Schelling's theology enable us to specify how change is different in God and in the world. The world emerges out of its infinite ground; although it never attains an existence outside or completely separate from this ground, it has a different nature than its source (viz. a finite one). It is also true that God-as-personal emerges from the infinite divine ground; as a being involved in actual relations with the world, God undergoes real change and development through those relations (e.g., as the world changes God enters into and is affected by new relations). Yet unlike the creation, which is finite, God's nature is essentially the same as the infinite ground — at any rate, as similar as an individual being can be in manifesting that which is without any limit whatsoever. Since God's nature is eternally the same, we need not say that God was born at some moment or will someday cease to exist. In the case of a divine being there is no generation or corruption; God's dependence on his nature as infinite ground is a logical rather than temporal dependence. Thus we cannot say, Schelling insists, that there was a time when God did not exist or that in some sense he does not yet exist. By contrast, God's relations with the world must be other than logical if they are to be real relations with finite beings; hence, again, there must be real development in God.

Creation, on this view, is the process of transition from potentially manifest to actually manifest or existing. The cause of creation is whatever is responsible for the transition — however exactly one conceives the causal process itself (and there are reasons, including natural scientific ones, to think that our knowledge of the causal process will be severely limited, e.g., we have no other experience of *creatio ex nihilo*). It is thus not surprising that Schelling would come to speak of the world as a "manifestation" of God. This position is consistent with our earlier discovery that the world cannot be fully separate from its infinite source, and hence with the panentheism defended above. It is also required by the logic of the absolute: things could only be distinguished from an absolute by being derived from it, not by being ultimately different from it. Indeed, even traditional theism with its insistence on the world's ontological dependence on God (as in the doctrine of conservation or *creatio continuo*) in fact implies a similar view of creation.

Beyond this basic framework there are multiple theological models of creation that one can employ. Here pluralism again makes its appearance: apart from more specific purposes and assumptions — provided, perhaps, by the backdrop of Jewish or Christian theology, or by some set of philosophical assumptions, or by a particular natural scientific cosmology — the choice between the models will be underdetermined. Schelling, for instance, speaks variously of an *explicatio Dei*, a movement from *Deus implicitus* to *Deus explicitus* (8:81), and of a self-limiting of God, whereby the *ens illimitatissimum* "limits himself from within, renders himself, to a certain degree, finite (as an object) for himself" (8:212). All of these models presuppose a making manifest, a self-revealing, of God. Schelling does argue that God can ultimately become manifest only in something that is similar to him; specifically, in beings who, like him, are free.[37] This insight, which theologians have expressed as the *imago dei* or the divine nature in humanity *(die Gottebenbildlichkeit)*, plays an important role in Schelling's later efforts to develop a theory of personhood and human freedom.

The Moral Status of Creation

To allow division within the infinite as I have done, to include within it the potential to be manifested as finite or limited being, does come closer to acknowledging an ontological — and axiological — dualism in God than most of the theological tradition has been willing to do. Critics — referring to Schelling's famous claims about the No or the Nonbeing or the evil in God — have called this the "dark" side of Schelling's thought, a side that Tillich (notoriously) drew on in his theology as well. Must we say, with Schelling, that humans are the result of a fall *(Abfall)* from God, that "the transition from the absolute (God or being itself) to reality is a fall"?[38] Such a moral dualism unfortunately may well imply a negative moral judgment concerning the status of creation. Is it consistent for theologians to assert that creation is evil? Certainly this view with its overtones of Gnosticism raises serious problems, since it appears to be incompatible with both Judaism and Christianity. If the world is a "fall" from God, how can one say it is better (or even good) for God to have created a world at all?

Now one could respond that the Godhead itself contains both an evil and a good principle, and hence that the morally ambivalent status of creation (and

---

37. Das Choudhury, *Das Unendlichkeitsproblem*, 52.

38. Ingeborg C. Henel, *Philosophie und Theologie im Werk Paul Tillichs* (Stuttgart: Evangelisches Verlagswerk, 1981), 26. Of course, the observation applies equally to Tillich and to Schelling.

of human agents) exactly reflects the nature of the divine ground. But we have already examined the considerable difficulties with this position. Or, moving in the opposite direction, one could complain that Schelling unnecessarily ascribes to evil a real ontological status, assuming that it actually exists in the way that good exists. Wouldn't it be easier to develop a theological account of God and evil if evil were construed differently, say, as pure negation? Yet the problem does not disappear even under the Augustinian view, according to which evil is a privation (the privation of good) and hence has an ontological status inferior to and dependent on the existence of good. Since we have found reason to reject the belief of classical philosophical theism that creation is "outside" God, we cannot say that evil exists "in" the world but not "in" God; if it is in one, it is in both. Here Schelling's is the braver metaphysics: if evil really exists, it seems one must say that creation is partially evil in its very being or nature, not just to the extent that it is "deficient in being." And this fact would have consequences for construing the nature of God as well.

I suggest taking a different tack. To the extent that the created world exists at all, it must partake in the nature of God, who is Being-itself. Suppose that we allow this fact to take the lead in thinking about the God/world relation, rather than treating evil as an ontological principle that has to be included in one's account of things that exist. I suggest, then (against Schelling), that we should avoid speaking of the initial act of creation as involving evil, either in the sense of a deficiency of being or because it issues forth from an evil principle. Creation would then not be construed as a fall. Schelling's thought shows the "cost" of this response, if one is to be consistent: no valuation of the act of creation — as it were, from a standpoint prior to God's choice to create — can be given. "Whether to create" was not a moral (axiological) question with which God was faced prior to the existence of the world. Nor, as we have seen, is creation a rationally necessary consequence of the divine nature. It is a brute fact, a free decision of the divine will. It can be reconstructed, that is, correlated with God's nature *post factum,* but never deduced from the eternal nature of God *ab initio* (whether that nature is wholly good or a dualistic combination of good and evil principles).

Of course, given creatures, obligations toward God (or of God toward them) do arise; we can therefore now construct tentative accounts of divine purposes and values. Moreover, it is possible, given the fact of creation, to imagine various accounts of why it was good for God to create (e.g., because the world is to reflect the glory of God, or because a world of creatures freely responding to God is better than no such world). But if we do not place a moral value on the decision to create as such — except from our standpoint as finite created beings, and hence subsequent to the divine decision to create — then we do not need to posit two different moral sides (or potencies) in God, and the initial creation does not become a moral question. Consequently, it is not necessary to introduce preexisting good and evil into God in order to explain evil or to make the act of creation "good," and we can avoid speaking of a dark and a light principle or a moral division within God.[39] Indeed, if perfect-being theologies fail (as I have argued), we could not deduce the moral status of a possible world from God's eternal nature anyway — at least not a priori and in abstraction from the empirical facts about the world that has resulted.

The fundamental tenets of Schelling's doctrine of God, then — the concept of a unity that overarches difference or multiplicity, and the freedom of God's creative act — should be separated from its mythological components. We do not have to call freedom the dark side or the abyss or the fall from God, we do not have to speak of an evil principle within God, and we do not have to call God's freedom evil.[40] But the "cost" of making the existence of the world depend on a morally neutral decision is that we cannot speak, a priori, of the inherent goodness of the initial act of creation. The world has an element of finitude (or even nonbeing) that is not present in the Godhead itself; yet the metaphysician or theologian cannot (and need not) conclude that this finitude is, as such, evil. We can still say, with Schelling, that God creates because he freely wills "to lift the nonbeing within his essence to being" (13:310). That is, even without a morally good and bad principle, God can contain the potentialities that later become manifest as contingency or nonbeing. (Indeed, if the source of contingency or nonbeing does not lie within God, then its arising could not be explained.)[41] Still, to contain such potentialities is not a flaw or moral shortcoming and need not be expressed in morally dualistic terms.

Is Creation Irrational?

The (modified) Schellingian theory of creation just presented presupposes neither the idealist (e.g., Hegelian) claim that the real must finally be rational nor the anti-idealist claim that it must finally be irrational. The former claim I have criticized in chapter 6 above, arguing that we do not have access to the information necessary for showing that human knowledge claims do genuinely correspond to the nature of what is. When Schelling began to rethink philosophical theology from the standpoint of freedom prior to 1809, he left behind the ideal-

---

39. Cf. Brown, *Late Philosophy of Schelling,* 129.

40. Sometimes it appears that Tillich has emphasized this dark side even more than Schelling did. No wonder he says that God is no more than a symbol of God: the problems of asserting the actual existence of such a being appear to be insurmountable!

41. See also *ST* 2:8.

ist assumption that the real (the nature of God and creation) can ultimately be reconstructed in rationalist terms. Yet rather than suspending belief in the claims of rationalism, Schelling moved to the opposite position, viz. that the real must ultimately be *ir*rational.

His argument begins with the claim that God's actions are fundamentally irrational, since they cannot be understood or coherently reconstructed in human terms. Hence one must say that what God has created is also not ultimately rational. But God's actions must be an expression of God's nature, so the divine nature, too, must be at odds with human rationality. There are many ways to develop such an argument; in Schelling's case several of them evidence close parallels to the Hegelian attempt to defend (or at least the Hegelian presupposition of) the rationality of what is. The first way, for example, ontologizes the irrationality, positing an irrational principle within God. Whenever a theist does this, and like Schelling also posits as metaphysically basic both a good and an evil principle, the irrational and evil principles almost invariably line up, being jointly opposed to the rational and good principle. The resulting position, which is also Schelling's, is to my mind triply suspect: it unnecessarily divides God into multiple sets of competing principles (criticized above); it creates parallel scales of goodness and rationality (and, often, of being) and then attempts to establish one-to-one parallels between them, raising again all the difficulties we found with Leibniz's scale of perfection/rationality; and it subsumes God's creation of the world under a framework of necessity — now not the necessity of self-revelation or divine triumph, but rather the necessity of a creation that mirrors the intradivine battle between these two sets of principles.[42]

Are theists caught, then, between Hegelian arguments for the necessary rationality of the world and dualistic arguments for its irrationality? Clearly they are, it seems, if they try to demonstrate that any world God creates must necessarily be fundamentally good, or rational, or evidence a dialectical battle

42. The problems are worse. For a theist there are only two places where the principle of evil or irrationality can be introduced: either within the nature of the Godhead itself (as in Boehme's dualism), or as a necessary entailment of the act of creation (or of the emanation of a world from the absolute). Under the latter view, one holds in effect that evil is a consequence of the transition from the infinite to the finite, which I have earlier argued to be a confusion of the concepts of infinity and perfection.

Unfortunately, arguments for some cosmic struggle between two competing principles — including some in Schelling's writings — inevitably descend to the level of philosophy qua universal myth. Authors begin by developing a theogony or a cosmogony, describing the birth of the principle of evil (within God or in creation) and its subsequent development in human history. It is hard to see why one should agree with the authors that such stories represent either good empirical (historical) explanations or any sort of philosophical necessity.

between the principles of good and evil, reason and unreason. But there is a second way, also present with more or less clarity in Schelling's later writings, that may avoid this dilemma. We can posit that God's decision to create, and the decision of what *sort* of world to create, is essentially free and unconstrained. As Fuhrmans established in his classic treatment of the later Schelling, Schelling's thought consistently includes both the standpoint of negative theology — a fundamental limitation on the possibility of theistic metaphysics — and subsequent positive speculation concerning God and creation.[43] The starting point for Schelling's positive theology is the absolute freedom of God, which entails that no natural theology can deduce a priori that there must be a world or what its nature must be. The existence of the world is on this view (almost) as much of a brute given for the theist as for the physicist.

The objection arises immediately: If one begins with a divine decision that transcends all human reason, why should this not leave one with an utterly unknowable world and with the impossibility of any knowledge of God, as in the more skeptical versions of late medieval nominalism? First, the failure of a purely rationalist theology does not entail the failure of all philosophical theology. As Fuhrmans shows in detail, Schelling's stress on divine freedom is consistent with an epistemic ascent to (or toward) God, an ascent that relies on certain features within this world that may indicate (without proving) a divine source. Further, given the existence of the world and its history, one can offer a variety of theological accounts of its guiding principles, of the possible divine purposes within it, and of the future states to which this divine direction might lead. Some of these accounts are more coherent, adequate to scientific knowledge, and consistent with human experience in the world than others. A free act of creation thus does not rule out constructive work in philosophical theology subsequent to the act of creation any more than it rules out constructive work in physics, even though it does rule out such endeavors *ab initio*.[43]

Nonetheless, a metaphysics of divine freedom does have at least one liability when consistently conceived. Schelling was right to turn in his later years to "positive philosophy," understood as a reconstruction of the possible divine intentions in creation and in subsequent physical and intellectual history. But he was wrong to think that such accounts could be developed with rational necessity, as if, barring only the freedom of God's initial creative act, everything else could be deduced with the inevitability of a Hegelian philosophy of history

---

43. Horst Fuhrmans, *Schellings letzte Philosophie: Die negative und positive Philosophie im Einsatz des Spätidealismus* (Berlin: Junker und Dünnhaupt, 1940). For an account of part of Fuhrmans's argument, see Lewis Ford, "The Controversy between Schelling and Jacobi," *Journal of the History of Philosophy* 3 (1965): 75-89.

and nature. Any explanations developed in the aftermath of a radically free decision of God must claim for themselves a different, lesser status, for all that follows that decision will be affected by "the freedom of God with regard to his own existence" (10:22). In particular, I suggest, the sort of theology that follows must be, at best, *hypothetical* — both in the sense that it puts forward hypotheses for testing and in the sense of Kant's hypothetical reasoning: it will *begin* with regulative assumptions based on limit notions.

In retrospect, much of this book's argument turns on this shift from the necessary and a priori to the hypothetical, pluralistic, and historically contingent. For example, in accord with the hypothetical modes of reasoning now dominant in epistemology and the philosophy of science, I construed even the claim that the world is rational as a viable hypothesis on which to base specific research programs and further research. It may be a claim that we can no more know to be false than we can at present know to be true. Still, it is an assumption that it makes sense for us to make — either as a gamble that our scientific endeavors (for example) are not doomed to failure, or as a necessary regulative assumption that is entailed by any and all attempts at pursuing truth. Likewise, it has been my thesis that the idea of God has a status similar to the assumption of the rationality of the world. Proofs of both ideas are destined to failure, and, ironically, for similar reasons: one can find no grounds to prove first principles such as these, since all supporting arguments have to assume them. At the same time, both ideas do represent reasonable hypotheses for further reflection. Indeed, the two ideas might be even more intimately related; there may be certain relations of mutual entailment or exclusion between them. Some have argued, for example, that if there is no God there is no reason to assume that the world will be rationally accessible to us.[44] Arguments of this form are not, of course, direct arguments for the existence of God, for it could be true that the world is not ultimately rational. Yet the links between the rationality of the world and theistic belief do contribute to the power — the coherence and potential explanatory value — of philosophical theology.

The results of this section also help to make clear the interpretive strategy taken in this chapter. I have not dealt in detail with Schelling's accounts of the birth of the world or the principle of evil; there are simply insufficient reasons for viewing these as credible theories. Yet I have sought to incorporate the un-

---

44. Alvin Plantinga has given a precise formulation of this argument in an unpublished paper, forthcoming in his Gifford Lectures. A briefer version of the argument appears in the final chapter of his two-volume *Warrant and Proper Function* (New York: Oxford Univ. Press, 1992). The best-known counterargument is that evolutionary principles make it likely that any conscious species will have to enjoy a match between its inner reasoning processes and its environment if it is to be biologically successful.

derlying principles that form the foundation for Schelling's efforts at a concrete philosophy of mythology. I believe that this interpretive strategy has a further advantage: it more fully conveys the continuity of Schelling's thought through its various periods. For instance, the theories of the *Essay on Freedom* and of the *Ages of the World,* when treated in this way, turn out to have much more in common than one might think with Schelling's early attempts to express the relationship between the absolute and the human subject. Admittedly, the reservations raised above do not allow me to endorse the conclusions of Schelling's late philosophy of mythology, since writing a "positive philosophy" in this sense requires too close a link between a priori metaphysical considerations and the actual course of history. But the *approach* is right: the increased emphasis on philosophical theology as mythology is close to narrative theology,[45] and the focus on the world as it actually develops would encourage a fruitful interaction between theology and the natural and social sciences.

TOWARD A THEISTIC METAPHYSICS OF FREEDOM

The Two Poles of God

In responding to the central challenges of modern theology we have been led to posit two poles within the divine. Using the framework of ground and consequent, I have suggested a theology that understands divinity both as the infinite ground of being and as personal being (God as personal or as tripersonal). We saw that these two aspects could not be construed as lying on an equal level, lest our metaphysic fall into a dualism of good and bad. We then looked at the world as a process of God's self-manifestation, using the concept of a "potency" in God (e.g., the potential to create an other or finite world) which might later become actual. In a similar manner, we shall now see, the personal side of divinity — God as *a* being — can be construed as a becoming actual of what was always potential in the divine nature (infinite being).

This view should not be allowed to suggest that in the process of self-manifestation God is suddenly born as "a being" — as if at some time there was only the ground and then later a free personal being emerged, or as if absolute infinity somehow spawned a limited God or Demiurge. God may become internally more complex (more complex as a subject) by becoming manifest in creation and in

---

45. See Hans Frei, *The Eclipse of Biblical Narrative: A Study in Eighteenth and Nineteenth Century Hermeneutics* (New Haven: Yale Univ. Press, 1974).

human history. But as I argued above, the divine itself, and thus the bipolar relationship between God as ground and consequent, must have been present from the beginning. The infinite includes its finite manifestation, but it does not make sense, Schelling insists rightly, to hold that at one time there was no God but only an infinite ground and then later God came into existence.

Thus the notion of a One or unitary principle is not utterly discarded. It is not as though there was once One and then later Two; rather, God always existed in the complexity of ground and consequent. The present conception is thus not opposed to the various metaphysics of unity, such as those in the Neoplatonic tradition, for it acknowledges the important philosophical impetus toward resolving all oppositions within an overarching unity. Schelling's correction to monism turns on the insight that the final goal must not be thought as an absolute unity, excluding all duality; this is why he posits, from the beginning, division within God. Similarly, the pluralism that I have advocated attempts to think of divinity using multiple principles. In either case, one should be skeptical of a priori philosophical arguments that attempt to prove that there must be precisely two principles, or just three, or more.[46] In some contexts it makes sense to speak in binary oppositions, as Whitehead does: "it is as true to say that God is permanent and the World fluent, as that the World is permanent and God is fluent. It is as true to say that God is one and the World many, as that the World is one and God many. . . . It is as true to say that God creates the World, as that the World creates God."[47] In other contexts we are better served by tertiary concepts: body, soul, spirit; self, other, consciousness; Father, Son, Spirit. I admit to some skepticism about threes, since they are often bound up with (unconvincing) necessity-based arguments that all oppositions must be overcome through some transcending (aufhebenden) principle. At any rate, given the history of debate on this topic, and in part as a corrective to the monist and the trinitarian excesses of much philosophical theology, I have particularly stressed Schelling's use of twofold distinctions.

Among these distinctions the ground/consequent relationship must be placed in the foreground. The centrality of this pair of categories stems from the need to speak of God both as "a" being and as the absolute that, as such, cannot be a being — an insight that we have traced forward from the birth of modern philosophical theology in Descartes. In this century, Heidegger has become the most famous defender of this insight, however inadequate were his

46. For a similar argument, see Arthur Peacocke's *Theology for a Scientific Age* (Minneapolis: Fortress, 1993).

47. Alfred North Whitehead, *Process and Reality: An Essay in Cosmology* (Cambridge: Cambridge Univ. Press, 1929), 410.

own halting attempts to overcome the problem of the ontological difference. "The onto-theological constitution of metaphysics stems from the prevalence of that difference which keeps Being as the ground, and beings as what is grounded and what gives account, apart from and related to each other."[48] Without the conceptual pair "ground/grounded" there is no theistic metaphysics; and unless theism includes not only the ultimate ground but also a divine being who stands in relation to other beings, there is no God. One might retain an impersonal absolute, the so-called God above God, which grounds all that is. But one cannot think God without the personal, lest God become an empty absolute, lower than — because lacking qualities found in — finite subjects. Ironically, this would produce an absolute that is unable to include human agents (being impersonal) yet must (being absolute). Herein lies the importance of Schelling's insight: one must speak of the absolute as containing the potential to know the world, and hence the potential to know itself in (as) response to the world; in other words, one must speak of the absolute as potentially personal. This potential becomes actual in the process of God's interaction with the world.

How could this be? How could an absolute have the potential to be personal? The answer is that, faced with the dilemma of calling it free or determined, we have found reason to label it free, and freedom requires personalist rather than impersonalist categories. We say that God creates freely, but not that God is self-creating, since he must always have been. At bottom, volition better characterizes the absolute than blind force or necessity. An absolute might not have given rise to a world but did, and the result has not been random. What stems from the individual, yet is neither necessary nor random, is willed. But how could the ground of being be said to have a will, since wills are ascribed only to self-conscious agents? I find only one answer: it could not. These various strands of modern metaphysics, taken together, justify the affirmation both of an absolute ground of being and of the categories of freedom, will, and person. There appears to be only one adequate solution: the attribute of will is ascribed to that part of the infinite ground which is eternal freedom, eternal potential to decide and to respond. The personal side of God, as Schelling argues at length in *Ages of the World*, depends on a nature that is within and yet not identical with the personal — in short, on the divine

---

48. See Martin Heidegger, *Identität und Differenz* (Pfüllingen, 1957), 63: "Sein als Grund und Seiendes als gegründetbegründendes" (Eng. trans. Martin Heidegger, *Identity and Difference*, trans. Joan Stambaugh [New York: Harper & Row, 1969], 71). Jean-Luc Marion's discussion of God and the ontological difference is extremely insightful, even if, again, his project of a *Dieu sans l'être* is unsuccessful; see his *God without Being: Hors-texte*, trans. Thomas Carlson (Chicago: Univ. of Chicago Press, 1991).

ground. On this view, then, God becomes the creative response to his own ground, and in this sense, its consequence. Once again we find ourselves pointed toward the minimal personalist theism that we first encountered in previous chapters.

Divine Freedom

If Schelling's construal of the task is correct, as I think, freedom becomes the major problem for philosophical theology. The more we might explain who God is and how and why God created, and the better our theories might get, the more the divine freedom would elude us. One limit case is randomness, of course: the view that there is absolutely no rhyme or reason to what proceeds from God.[49] Consistently construed, this limit case entails pure mystery — and the failure of the philosophical project in which Schelling and others are engaged. The other limit case, again, is Hegel: the world issued forth from God with necessity, and with necessity it will lead to the fullness of *Absoluter Geist*.

Schelling's attempt is to find a middle ground between these two poles. The ground of being is pure essence; it specifies God's nature without determining future divine actions in relation with others. The transition from this essential nature to a created realm of existing beings cannot be a logical or rational step, a requirement of the System (as in Hegel) or of the nature of God. Even to say that God's nature as love requires God to create is to remove the freedom that an adequate theory of God must preserve. Rather, Schelling insists,

> God created beings outside himself not because of a blind necessity of his nature but with the greatest freedom. More precisely, on the basis of mere divine necessity, since it applies only to his own existence, there would be no creatures. Therefore, through freedom God overcomes the necessity of his nature in the creation; freedom is placed above necessity, not necessity above freedom.[50]

49. A position often associated with Søren Kierkegaard, e.g., in *Fear and Trembling* or *Concluding Unscientific Postscript*. But is it not already a conceptual determination — and hence a limitation and an explanation, an understanding — to construe God as infinite subjectivity?

50. Schelling, 8:210. Cf. the famous passage from the *Essay on Freedom*: the division between the parts of God exists so that the two "should become one through love; that is, it divides itself only that there may be life and love and personal existence. For there is love neither in indifference nor where antitheses are combined which require the combination in order to be; but rather . . . this is the secret of love, that it unites such beings as could each exist

Nothing in the infinite as such would require a world; the existence of the world cannot be inferred from the infinite as an inevitable correlate of its existence. Thus the necessity criticism is not difficult to avoid. Note that avoiding it still leaves, at first blush, two options instead of one: the creation of the world could be a free act — an intentional product of God's will or agency — or it could be a chance event, an unexplained (and inexplicable) chance by-product of a nonpersonal infinite (à la Spinoza), without a source in volition.

But remember that we left Spinoza's absolute behind because of the need for knowledge of an absolute to coincide with the being of that absolute. When we encountered the basic choice between the subjective and objective ways of construing God in the course of the Spinoza Dispute (chap. 7), the limitations on understanding God as an object, as Spinoza ultimately did, became amply clear. Spinoza's unity is "only the dead unity of mere *Being*, to which the processes of life and development (which grow out of antithesis) remain entirely foreign."[51] Rejecting Spinozism suggests turning to the model of God as a self-unfolding subject. It is not necessary to move all the way to a controlling theory of self-consciousness, according to which the subject necessarily externalizes itself into an other and then synthesizes self and other; indeed, to do so is again to subordinate the self to a structure of necessity and thus to lose freedom as its distinguishing feature. Hence the mediating conclusion: If God possesses the attribute of thought, as Spinoza insists, then God must ultimately be construed primarily as subject and not merely as object.

Incidentally, note that God's freedom does not have to be construed as full libertarian freedom; one can remain neutral between compatibilist and noncompatibilist accounts of freedom. The argument does, however, require that we construe it as the freedom of a subject rather than as the chance motions of an object (as in quantum physics). Beyond that, the argument says only that we must attribute mental spontaneity to God, the power of self-motivated thought. It could still be that the content of this thought will turn out to be determined by the nature of the being in question (in Schelling's terms: by the Ground). In this case, God would have compatibilist but not libertarian freedom.

Schelling's focus on freedom also follows from a consideration of what will be required if self-revelation is to be possible:

---

in itself, and nonetheless neither is nor can be without the other. Therefore, as duality comes to be in the groundless, there also comes to be love, which combines the existent (ideal) with the basis of existence" (7:408).

51. Brown, *Late Philosophy of Schelling*, 248, citing Schelling, 8:340.

Now a free being is free in the sense that it does not have to reveal itself. To reveal itself is to act, and all acting is a self-revelation. In order to be a free being, it must be free either to remain with its mere ability [to act], or to make the transition to action. If this transition were made with necessity, [God] would not be what he really is, namely free. (8:306)

Beyond this point, however, we must depart from the unconvincing idealist logic of the early Schelling. It is not that a philosophy of self-consciousness *requires* an affirmative and a negating moment within God, and hence that the infinite God *had* to create a finite world or that an all-good being had to "fall" into an evil state. Rather, it is that if an ultimate principle is to be (adequately) thought at all, it must be thought out of the unity of the finite and infinite: "Until our doctrine acknowledges such a power in God, or until it grasps the absolute identity of the infinite and finite" (8:74), there is no place to speak of the personality of God. Schelling's insight is to see that freedom provides the best means for thinking through the relationship of infinite and finite. "Freedom," he argues in *Ages*, "is the affirmative concept of unconditioned eternity" (8:235). We must now consider the structure, and then the content, of the theological position that reflects this starting point.

For Schelling the infinite or unconditioned was understood as nonbeing, as irrational will.[52] This might be correct in the sense that the unconditioned cannot be limited from the start by the specific connotations of objective being or substance ontology, and in the sense that the unconditioned is better interpreted as subject (or potential subject) than as object in the Spinozistic sense.[53] And "irrational will" might suggest that the subsequent developments cannot be grasped as necessary steps according to some transcendent dialectic.

Yet, beyond these more minimal insights, Schelling falls into the same sort of difficulty that Hegel had, albeit on the other side. Where Hegel remained bound by necessity, Schelling is unable to rise above the irrationality of his starting principle. As Bolman saw, "The problem of positive knowledge for Schelling was how to make the indefinable definable, the unutterable utterable. When he proceeds to ascribe freedom to this indefinable object, he merely ex-

---

52. 8:220-21; cf. the excellent summary in Paul Tillich, *Die religionsgeschichtliche Konstruktion in Schellings positiver Philosophie, ihre Voraussetzungen und Prinzipien* (Breslau, 1910), 17-18.

53. Thus Schelling's phrase "das absolute ich." Usually he refuses to speak of it as an *actual* subject: the absolute is neither subject nor object, knower or known. Among many supporting passages see Schelling's "Fragment einer Abhandlung zur Strukturtheorie des Absoluten," published by Barbara Loer in *Das Absolute und die Wirklichkeit in Schellings Philosophie* (Berlin: de Gruyter, 1974), 32.

presses the conviction [typical of claims to] positive knowledge that that object may come to be defined."[54] In order to avoid the difficulties inherent in making God into the irrational principle, we would do better to remain agnostic on this question. Although God is better understood as will than as object, it is better to assert neither that the divine nature or Ground is irrational nor that God's development proceeds according to an inexorable internal logic.[55]

THE PERSONALITY OF GOD
AND THE LIMITS OF PHILOSOPHY

Divine Personality

If, as Schelling suggests, freedom is the highest principle in God, *it* is what is unlimited (or infinite) in God. Hence the will is crucial, since the concept of will connotes actions not dictated by the nature or properties of an entity. Now we associate will exclusively with persons. Personality, therefore, is the final step in our reflection on God as infinite. The final corollary of the move from (Spinozistic) infinite object to subject, in addition to freedom, is the personality of God — in however a minimal or attenuated sense.

Schelling argues that "personality consists . . . in the connection of an autonomous being with a basis which is independent of it, in such a way namely that these two completely interpenetrate one another and are but one being" (7:394-95). He claims that it follows that God is the highest personality. But this will only work, he realizes, if one avoids both pure realism (Spinoza) and pure idealism (Fichte), that is, if one says neither that the whole is beyond subjectivity (for this would imply that subjectivity is only an illusion) or that all *just is* subject. The most attractive alternative to these two extremes is panentheism, since "God's personality can only be based upon the nexus between him and nature" (7:395).

Schelling's own way of making the argument is to view the divine will in two parts, incorporating Spinoza's realism as the divine "will of the basis" and

54. Cf. the Bolman translation of *Ages of the World*, 124n.

55. One could, however, imagine the following gamble: if the ultimate principle, and hence the ultimate nature of reality, is irrational, then we can have no justified knowledge of reality anyway. So if we wish to pursue knowledge of what is, we must assume that it is (to some degree) knowable; we will therefore treat it as such. This does not mean, of course, that we know it to be such, just that our project presupposes it, and perhaps someday we will know which assumption was right.

Fichte's idealism as the will of love (7:397). With its intricate detail and host of questionable assumptions introduced as alleged necessities of personal development, the position remains unconvincing, and I will not pause to give it a full exposition here.[56] Instead, let's remain with the basic idea of the position: there can be freedom in God — or, what amounts to the same thing, God can be conceived as person — only if panentheism is the case. For there are good reasons to follow Schelling in espousing his central principle: "All existence must be conditioned in order that it may be actual, that is, personal, existence. God's existence, too, could not be personal if it were not conditioned, except that he has the conditioning factor *within* himself and not outside himself" (7:399). Division, he adds, is the condition of God's own existence qua personal (7:403).

Thus there are two clear conditions that the doctrine of God must satisfy: (1) God as our infinite source cannot be less than we are; God must at least have abilities comparable to ours, even though, as greater, they will be different; and (2) there must be a free decision to create. But freedom is the quality of a being with a certain degree of self-awareness and with the attribute of will. Because God must be conceived as a subject with this degree of self-awareness and will, we speak of God not as "it" but as person.

Schelling did justice to the personhood of God only in his later philosophy. Earlier (e.g., in the *Bruno*) his thought was dominated by his fascination with the undifferentiated One in which all distinctions, even the finite/infinite distinction, are resolved. Only later — after he had worked through the stages we have covered here — did he see that the specificity of personhood language could properly apply to God.

But personhood is bought with a price. If creation is the result of a free creation by a personal being, then no theory will be able to proceed forward step by step from the structures of possibility that we have been exploring to deduce the world as we know it. Metaphysics, as the study of what must have been the case to give rise to the world as it actually is, will have to give way to empirical science, the a posteriori exploration of what actually is. Nor should it be otherwise: the most embarrassing moments for both philosophy and science occurred when philosophers like Descartes and Hegel (esp. in the latter's philosophy of nature) attempted to deduce philosophically what only empirical experimentation could establish.

56. For an exposition of Schelling's position see Brown, *Late Philosophy of Schelling*, 133-40, and the works cited therein. The union of principles required for divine life cannot be within the actual being of God as existent, Schelling argues, but only in the distinction between the ground and the existence; and the dynamics of this process cannot be spelled out with necessity. The concept of "primal ground" (7:406) should thus be retained, along with that of the "groundless" (7:407).

This contrast has been nicely formulated by Schelling in his distinction between negative and positive philosophy. According to Brown, the main idea behind the distinction is that "actual existence or real being cannot simply be inferred from the structures of thought itself."[57] Since contingent (finite) being is the product of God's will and not a necessary by-product of his nature, one cannot conceptually derive finite being from God's being. Philosophical theology can show the preferability of a free God over, for instance, a (Spinozistic) blind force of nature. But having done this, it too must turn to the record of the development of the world and humankind for actual empirical guidance. Thus Schelling shifted in his final years to a philosophy of "mythology," examining the history of religion as the record of revelation in human history. Likewise, the theologian has to turn, finally, from philosophical theology to the history of religions, to potential sources of revelation such as religious experience, and to the systematization of the resultant beliefs.[58] I would even suggest that something like the doctrine of the Trinity belongs within this sort of "positive" examination, functioning not as an a priori condition of the possibility of any revelation at all but as the most adequate expression of the nature of God, at least as revealed in the Christian tradition. (What reasons there are, if any, to think that the Christian tradition is the most adequate record of divine revelation is clearly not part of our project here.)[59] That beliefs of this sort are not grounded in metaphysical deductions does not bar them from having any rational content or intersubjective justification. They now become religious hypotheses, concrete proposals regarding what God's will may be in human (and world) history and what the outcome of the process of revelation might be.

We can now, at the conclusion rather than the beginning of this section, consider the connection between Schelling's theory of personhood and his philosophy of spirit *(Geist)*. A strong case has been made that the theory of *Geist* is the overarching framework that ties together the various stages of Schelling's career. The same general understanding of *Geist* shines through the various stages of his intellectual development: transcendentalism, objective idealism, and positive philosophy.[60] Many of the German commentators select only the

---

57. Brown, *Late Philosophy of Schelling*, 249: "Concepts can represent either the possible structures of real being, or an a posteriori analysis of real being. But concepts cannot account for the actual existence of being."

58. See Wolfhart Pannenberg, "The Reality of God and of the Gods in the Experience of the Religions," in his *Systematic Theology*, vol. 1, chap. 3; cf. pp. 378-81 above.

59. See Pannenberg, *Systematic Theology*, vol. 1, chaps. 4–5.

60. See H. Beckers, *Schellings Geistesentwicklung in ihrem inneren Zusammenhang* (1875); Erna Stamm, *Der Begriff des Geistes bei Schelling* (Wesermünde-Lehe/Göttingen: Franz Rehbock, 1930), e.g., 6.

first period as philosophically significant; others, like Erna Stamm, search for a necessary progression through Schelling's three stages of affirmation, negation, and reaffirmation/synthesis. I think both approaches stand in need of correction. The middle period (objective idealism), I have argued, is closest to correct because it best does justice to the logic of the infinite incorporating the finite within itself. Yet, as Stamm shows, it is not as though Schelling succeeds at this synthesis by obscuring the distinction between spirit and nature; instead, as we have seen, he develops an evolutionary theory of spirit as emerging from a source that is better comprehended as spirit than as pure object.

Divine Agency

Arguably, the question of divine agency is one of the least well-articulated challenges facing theism today. To avoid deism, theists must say that God can be, and is, active in the world subsequent to creation. Yet there are serious problems with maintaining that God continues to intervene directly into the natural order. For example, it would seem to threaten the integrity of this order, disrupting the regularity and predictability of the natural world that is necessary for free and reasonable human action. It also threatens to make a mockery of scientific method, since if there were regular miraculous divine interventions one could never know whether a given natural occurrence even had a natural cause. Finally, divine interventions seem to break the law of the conservation of energy — unless God could act by introducing information into the natural order without any influx of energy.[61]

On the one hand, if the finite and infinite are defined as incompatible, as having nothing to do with one another, then clearly an infinite being could not act within a finite creation. But in that case neither could the absolute have a personal side, nor be a being (much less a personal one), nor be related to any finite thing or person. In short, there could be no God as the Western traditions have understood this being. On the other hand, surely one cannot define the finite and infinite as identical.

The dilemma cannot be easily solved, but panentheism does seem to soften it in comparison to classical philosophical theism. Refusing the separation of

---

61. The suggestion has been made by John Polkinghorne in *Science and Providence: God's Interaction with the World* (Boston: New Science Library, 1989), chap. 2, 18-35, and is made in Arthur Peacocke's *Theology for a Scientific Age*. I have pursued noninterventionist models of divine action in *God and Contemporary Science* (Edinburgh: Edinburgh Univ. Press; Grand Rapids: Eerdmans, 1997).

world and God does bring the two closer and thus minimizes the difficulties with divine action.[62] The action is now not "into" a realm that is "outside" God; it is easier to speak of God's causal action when that action takes place within God. For panentheists, divine agency is a matter of causal sequences that are internal to God, just as, on the ordinary view of human will and action, minds have the capacity to act on bodies to bring about particular goals. Yet, in another sense, God remains different from the world — indeed, absolutely different, since he has an infinite nature whereas the world's is finite. The greater the difference between God and world — be it spatial, essential, or temporal vs. atemporal — the more difficult it is to develop a coherent theory of divine action.

I can see only one possible answer to this dilemma: a dialectic between the infinity and the finiteness of God. We have already discovered a dialectical relation between the absolute as ground and the personal God as consequent. A similar relationship of difference-in-sameness characterized God's relation to the world, understood neither as external to God (for what could be external to infinity?) nor as identical to God (since the essential features of the absolute such as eternality and necessary existence certainly cannot be predicated of us as finite individuals). The same paradigm provides the framework for understanding divine agency — not surprisingly, since the causality question is always a subset of the ontology question. In one sense, all interactions within the world include a divine cause as a component, since the world remains a part of its infinite source. In another sense, insofar as God is also different from the world, those "lures"[63] that stem from God-as-transcendent represent an influx from something that is also distinguished from the world. Of course, if divine influence were not limited in frequency and scope, humans would lose all ability to distinguish the natural order from its divine source; thus the influence must remain somewhat isolated and limited in scope.

It is clear that, given the resources of panentheism, a theory of divine agency no longer confronts the problem of absolute differentness. Further, the position sketched here, which links God as a being to the world and yet also to the infinity of God's nature, does offer possibilities for reconciliation that are not open to more traditional positions. I pursue the details of this position in a separate work.[64]

---

62. I have developed this argument in more detail in "In Defense of Christian Panentheism," *Dialog* 37 (1998): 201-8. Four critiques of this defense of panentheism and my response to these critiques appeared in *Dialog* 38 (summer 1999).

63. See Lewis Ford, *The Lure of God: A Biblical Background for Process Theism* (Philadelphia: Fortress, 1978).

64. See Clayton, *God and Contemporary Science*, esp. chapter 8.

CONCLUSION

We began this chapter with Schelling's most famous disciple in twentieth-century theology, Paul Tillich, moving backward from his "God above God" to Schelling's much more sophisticated theory of God as infinite ground and God as personal subject. I believe I have shown that there is no reason to treat this philosophical theology as merely mystical or negative theology, and no reason to follow Tillich in reducing it to its existential implications. For Tillich, perhaps, there were rhetorical reasons to do so. Tillich wrote from an apologetic interest, hoping to rekindle theological appetite in readers who were dissatisfied with theism but who still recognized areas of ultimate concern. "The God above God" thus had for him a negative function, as an attack on inadequate notions of God found in classical philosophical theism that are artificially abstracted from the world. Yet, we found, the insight into the two poles of God can also be given a positive expression of the sort that we discovered in Schelling's theology of freedom and in panentheism. Rhetoric aside, one who presents a more adequate theory of God is still a theist; one corrects previous, flawed views rather than becoming a meta-theist or something of this sort. It is just that the most defensible understanding of theism is one that moves beyond the dichotomy between God and world.[65]

I have therefore suggested a correction of theological method away from the use of theistic language as merely fictitious and more in the direction of criticizable systematic proposals. The oppositions that fuel theological debates should lead not to a "premetaphysical" (and therefore symbolic) theory of divine reality expressed in terms of human existential reality, but to a theory of God that is both regulative and constitutive. Indeed, only this sort of theory would constitute a true correlation of metaphysical reflection with "the question implied in man's finitude" (Tillich).

In what terms would the details of this proposal be worked out? In his later years Schelling called it the philosophy of mythology. More recent philosophy of language suggests a different route: construing theological proposals as hypotheses to be tested on the basis of their conceptual (and sometimes empirical) adequacy and their ability to make sense of present human experi-

---

65. Indeed, Tillich admits as much in his *Systematics:* "In this respect God is neither alongside things nor even 'above' them; he is nearer to them than they are to themselves. He is their creative ground, here and now, always and everywhere" (*ST* 2:7; cf. *Systematische Theologie,* 2:13: "Damit ist Gott weder 'neben' noch 'über' dem Seienden, er ist jedem Seienden näher als dieses sich selbst. Er ist sein schöpferischer Grund, hier und jetzt, immer und überall").

ence.[66] By these means one can perhaps move far beyond the minimal onto-logical and metaphysical conditions for philosophical theology defended in this book. The more concrete theories we attain — detailed theories of divine agency or of God's trinitarian life, say — may not play the same sort of foun-dational philosophical role as does the idea of God as ground and conse-quent, yet this does not make them mere fictions or mere symbols used to convey only human existential truths. Even as metaphors or models, they may still serve as hypotheses that are plausibly true — and they may also fail to do so.[67] In sum, Schelling did not make a category mistake when he distin-guished between his groundwork in metaphysics and biblical language about God. But we should not give up on the possibility of a rational evaluation of constructive theological proposals such as his.

Remember that the epistemic limits that we encountered above them-selves stemmed from a conceptual argument, namely the argument for a pan-entheism based on the concept of freedom. Under this view, the divine life is not the result of a necessary development *(Entäußerung)* of some a priori struc-ture into an existing world, as in Hegel's philosophy; rather, only a pure act of freedom can accomplish the transition from the infinite nature of the divine to reality.[68] Consequently, no system of thought could know or predict the self-revelation of God a priori (or at least could not know if it had). Reason's job — as "positive philosophy" — is only to recognize what has already come to be through the pure freedom of divine decision. Even if one understood God only as the triune structure or *potentia universalis*, Schelling realized, one would al-ready have "presupposed [God to have] a relationship to the world, and indeed, with one that would be essential to him."[69] In this case God's transcendence would remain unthought. Instead, Schelling suggested, God is "subject in the truest sense of the word," "that which is absolutely prior" (see 13:159). Where Hegel offers a necessary externalization, a dialectical unity of being and thought, Schelling lays greater stress on the negative moment: reason "sets" be-

---

66. See Philip Clayton, *Explanation from Physics to Theology: An Essay in Rationality and Religion* (New Haven: Yale Univ. Press, 1989), chaps. 5–6.

67. Recent philosophy of science has moved in this direction. The shift, and its impli-cations for theology, are clearly spelled out in Ian G. Barbour, *Myths, Models and Paradigms: A Comparative Study in Science and Religion* (New York: Harper & Row, 1974). For a detailed account of the evaluation of theological statements as metaphors, see Janet Martin Soskice, *Metaphor and Religious Language* (New York: Oxford Univ. Press, 1985).

68. This is the main theme of Heidegger's masterful treatment of Schelling's *Essay on Freedom* (n. 48 above).

69. He would be "mit einer Beziehung auf die Welt und zwar mit einer ihm wesentlichen gesetzt" (11:293).

ing "as an absolute *outside-of-itself*" (13:163). In Pöltner's words, "Being that cannot be predicted or conceived in advance appears as blind facticity, as *factum brutum,* because it is determined by reason in a *purely negative* fashion, as its other."[70]

Schelling saw correctly that reason must be in some sense *verlassen,* left behind: "The great, final and fundamental crisis lies in the fact that God, the one who is found at the end, has been ejected from the Idea, and thus that the 'science of reason' itself is thereby rejected or left behind."[71] Here, finally, is Schelling's exhortation to constructive philosophical theology: to grant that the metaphysical project is unavoidable; to take on the rigorous demands of this sort of reflection; to hold one's results, however tentatively, as true; and at the same time to acknowledge that the object after which one is searching partially recedes beyond even one's most perceptive conceptual grasp. One cannot help but notice that in this final point, Schelling is again true to his Spinozistic heritage — this time to the Spinoza of the closing pages of the *Ethics:*

> Insofar as our Mind knows itself and the Body under a species of eternity, it necessarily has knowledge of God, and knows that it is in God and is conceived through God. . . . The Mind's intellectual Love of God is part of the infinite Love by which God loves himself.[72]

---

70. Pöltner, "Der Gottesbegriff beim späten Schelling," 109, my emphasis: Gott ist "das wahrhafte Subjekt," "das absolute Prius" (13:159). Reason "setzt" das Sein "als ein absolutes Außer-sich" (13:163); in Pöltner's words, "Das unvordenkliche Sein erscheint als blinde Faktizität, als factum brutum, weil es von der Vernunft *bloß negativ* als deren Anderes bestimmt wird."

71. "Die große, letzte und eigentliche Krisis besteht nun darin, daß Gott, das zuletzt Gefundene, aus der Idee ausgestoßen, die Vernunftwissenschaft selbst damit verlassen (verworfen) wird" ("Darstellung der reinrationalen Philosophie," 11:566). There are a number of parallels to the later Fichte that might be explored. Fichte writes of God's appearance, "Die Erscheinung ist darum schlechthin ein *Freies:* durch und an Gott, ein bloßes, reines Vermögen, zu erscheinen und sichtbar zu machen *so Sich wie Gott.* Dieses ist ihr [der Seele] *ideales* Sein durch Gott" (Johann Gottlieb Fichte, *Fichtes Werke,* 11 vols. [Berlin: W. de Gruyter, 1971], 10:383). At the end of his comparison of the two thinkers, Buchheim writes of Schelling, "Selbstsein ist Verhältnis nicht als Reflexion, sondern als Oeffnung-zu" (Thomas Buchheim, "Die reine Abscheidung Gottes: Eine Vergleichbarkeit im Grundgedanken von Fichtes und Schellings Spätphilosophie," *Zeitschrift für philosophische Forschung* 42 [1988]: 95-106, quotation 106).

72. Spinoza, *Ethics,* trans. Curley, book 5, P30, P36.

Index